UNIVERSITY LIBRARY
UW-STEVENS POINT

W9-BHE-264

MANAGERIAL ACCOUNTING

MANAGERIAL ACCOUNTING

Second Edition

RONALD M. COPELAND
University of South Carolina

PAUL E. DASCHER
Drexel University

John Wiley & Sons
Santa Barbara   New York   Chichester   Brisbane   Toronto
A Wiley/Hamilton Publication

Copyright © 1978 by John Wiley & Sons, Inc.
All rights reserved. Published simultaneously in Canada.

No part of this book may be reproduced by any means,
nor transmitted, nor translated into a machine language
without the written permission of the publisher.

Library of Congress Cataloging in Publication Data:

Copeland, Ronald M
  Managerial accounting.

  "A Wiley/Hamilton publication."
  Includes bibliographies and index.
1. Managerial accounting.   2. Cost accounting.
I. Dascher, Paul E., joint author.   II. Title.
HF5635.C762   1978   658.1'5   77-20266
ISBN 0-471-17171-9

ISBN 0-471-17171-9
Printed in the United States of America
10 9 8 7 6 5 4 3 2 1

HF
5635
.C762
1978

ABOUT THE AUTHORS

Ronald M. Copeland is the Business Partnership Foundation Fellow and Professor of Accounting at the University of South Carolina. He received a B.B.A. degree from the University of Massachusetts, an M.S. degree from The Pennsylvania State University, and a Ph.D. from Michigan State University. He has been a member of the faculties of Elizabethtown College, The Pennsylvania State University, and Michigan State University. Professor Copeland has coauthored two books, *Financial Statements: Problems from Current Practice*, and *Advanced Accounting*, and has contributed a chapter to the *Accountants' Handbook*. In addition, he has written many articles for leading academic and professional journals, and is an active member of several academic and professional organizations. His current research interest is in the development of new techniques for applying managerial accounting to nonprofit organizations.

Paul E. Dascher received B.S., M.S., and Ph.D. degrees from The Pennsylvania State University. Currently he is Dean of the College of Business and Administration of Drexel University. He has taught on the accounting faculties of Virginia Polytechnic Institute, The Pennsylvania State University and Drexel University. He has written many articles that have appeared in leading academic and professional journals. Professor Dascher has served as President of the Philadelphia Chapter of the National Association of Accountants, Vice President of Administrators of Accounting Programs Group, American Accounting Association, and Vice President of Community Accountants, in addition to other professional duties. He has served on the editorial board of *The Accounting Review* and was the founder and original director of the Intercollegiate Clearing House for Computer Programs.

329679

PREFACE

Managerial accountants process information to support four major objectives of many profit and nonprofit organizations: (1) planning for routine and non-routine operations, (2) determining the status of current operations, (3) exercising control by establishing conformity between goals and actions, and (4) making decisions. This book considers accounting in relation to all four objectives. Although these functions are inherently related, we discuss them separately for pedagogical purposes. Our goal is to introduce students to managerial accounting in a logical, sequential manner that will not overwhelm them on first exposure. Overall integration is provided mainly in the last three sections of the book and in some of the more comprehensive problems at the end of each chapter.

An introductory course in financial accounting is not a prerequisite to this text, although many students may have had this background. This text provides ample material for a one-semester or a two-quarter managerial accounting course, especially if the formal assignments presented in each chapter are supplemented with outside readings, cases, or individual projects. Since managerial accounting now covers a wide range of topics, the material was especially selected to show this diversity. The topics we have emphasized are designed to challenge students, to spur their curiosity, and to motivate them to apply their knowledge. In particular, we have attempted to provide students with a broad coverage of concepts, analyses, and procedures as a basis for comprehending the uses and limitations of data supplied by typical managerial accounting information systems. To do this, we have developed normative, nondogmatic descriptions of managerial accounting systems as well as the information provided for planning, processing, and control purposes.

This second edition retains the basic theme of the first edition. The structure and sequence of selected topics have been reorganized, however, in response to suggestions from some instructors who used the first edition. New sections, chapters and appendices have been added to clarify topics that continue to be of professional interest.

This edition is divided into six sections. The first section introduces students to the role of managerial accounting in the typical organization and then describes the relationship between accounting and managerial functions. The objectives of managerial accounting systems are set within a framework of organizational goals and constraints. Much of this material was condensed from the first two chapters of the first edition.

The second section includes three chapters on planning for routine operations. Changes from the first edition include the introduction of additional examples to illustrate key points, clarifications of the text to eliminate ambiguities, and an expansion of the discussion on pro-forma financial statements. The discussion of planning for safety stocks and economic order quantities has been expanded into a new Chapter 17 and is included in the new Section Five, which deals with decision making. The discussion of using calculus to solve curvilinear breakeven problems has been eliminated from the text and shifted to the Instructor's Manual.

The five chapters in Section Three are directed toward information processing and deal with topics typically classified as cost accounting. The topics of transfer pricing and service department cost allocation have been combined into a new chapter, while the discussions of by-products and direct costing have been sharpened.

Section Four consists of four chapters on control. This edition includes an expanded discussion of the use of ratio analysis for internal control evaluations and introduces the subject of residual income. Our chapter on managerial control in nonprofit organizations remains intact in this edition.

The new Section Five was created in response to users' suggestions that decision-making topics be more concentrated. This section contains two chapters from the previous edition on capital budgeting and network analysis, as well as two new chapters dealing with incremental analysis and inventory management. As in the first edition, the last section contains a chapter that relates behavioral literature to managerial accounting.

Each chapter is preceeded by a set of learning objectives that indicate what the student can be expected to accomplish after absorbing the material. The Glossary has been shifted to the back of the book to accommodate those instructors who choose to reorder the sequence of chapters for their classes. A list of current suggested readings appears at the end of each chapter.

The end of chapter assignment material in this second edition has been expanded and reorganized. More than forty percent of the questions, exercises, and problems are new. Questions are designed to focus on concepts, definitions, and descriptions. We have substantially increased the number of short data-manipulation exercises that require students to apply concepts in a straightforward manner. Problems are based on the textual material but present reasonably complex analytical or discussion situations. All of these assignment materials have been class tested to insure their reliability and relevance. At least three homework problems correspond to each chapter objective. These assignments vary in difficulty and offer a range of integrated exercises requiring students to demonstrate skills in data manipulation, verbalization, and conceptualization. Problems that refer to a chapter's appendix, such as journal entries, are indicated by a dagger (†); problems that extend coverage beyond the discussion in the chapter are indicated by an asterisk (*). CPA and CMA examination questions are explicitly identified. Many of the CPA and CMA problems have been modified to simplify the requirements or to eliminate issues that are not pertinent to the chapter discussion.

The chapters may be assigned in sequence, or they may be reordered to reflect the inclination of the instructor, the objectives of the course, or the background of the students. Each of the major sections represents a semi-autonomous module that is not dependent on the preceding sections, as long as the instructor provides some frame of reference. Students who have just completed a procedurally oriented financial accounting course may begin the book with Section Three.

If time does not permit coverage of all eighteen chapters in the second edition, Chapters 7, 8, 9, 13, 16, 17, or 18 may be excluded without affecting the integrity of the book's organization, though students would be given only a cursory exposure to some of the topics. Instructors who wish to relate budgeting more directly to control may wish to cover Chapters 2, 3, 4, 10, 11, and 12 in that order. Many other variations are logical. Our experiences in class testing this book and the reactions of many users of the first edition suggest that the present sequence will accomplish our original purposes.

Supplementary learning materials are available to aid students who use the second edition. A *Study Guide to Accompany Managerial Accounting* has been prepared by Professor Richard Schroeder of the University of Kentucky. The *Study Guide* highlights key issues raised in the text and provides students with self-testing questions (and solutions) so that they may monitor their learning progress. Professor Schroeder also has prepared two *Practice Sets* which develop all of the problem areas — planning, information processing, control and decision making — in a comprehensive business setting.

The *Instructor's Manual* contains extensive teaching notes for each chapter and a set of simple demonstration problems for class use. Transparency masters are provided. Full solutions to all questions, exercises, and problems are provided along with discussions of common mistakes made by students. Also, a *Comprehensive Examination Set* is available which provides the instructor with more than 200 class-proven, standardized test questions keyed to the chapter coverage of the book.

We are indebted to many people for their ideas and assistance. The following professors made constructive comments on earlier drafts of the manuscript:

Floyd Beams (Virginia Polytechnic Institute and State University)
Edgar Bitting (Elizabethtown College)
Joe Boyd (University of Illinois)
Vince Brenner (Louisiana State University)
John Cerepak (Fairleigh Dickinson University)
Jess Dillard (Ohio State University)
Art Francia (University of Houston)
Joe Ford (Drexel University)
Robert Hines (California State University at Humboldt)
Wayne Hudgens (Virginia Commonwealth University)
Phil Jones (University of Richmond)
Henry Longfield (Indiana State University at Terre Haute)

Mo Onsi (Syracuse University)
David Reeder (University of Evansville)
Hal Reneau (Arizona State University)
Michael Scanlan (University of Missouri)
Richard Schroeder (University of Kentucky)
Robert Strawser (Texas A&M University)
T. Vaughn (Grand Valley State College)

Special thanks are due Floyd Beams for his participation in editing material on control in nonprofit organizations for Chapter 13. In addition, we appreciate the helpful suggestions received from colleagues at the University of South Carolina and Drexel University. We also wish to acknowledge the support of Jim Kane and Herb Raynes, both of whom provided an administrative climate conducive to creating this book. An extra measure of thanks is due the staff of Wiley/Hamilton for their help.

Many students read the manuscript and worked the problems to ensure that they were readable and as free as possible from error. Our students also contributed ideas and materials that helped in revising manuscript chapters and preparing new problems. Appreciation also goes to the American Institute of Certified Public Accountants, the National Association of Accountants, and the American Accounting Association for their generous permission to quote from their copyrighted publications. Material from the Uniform CPA Examination, copyright © by the American Institute of Certified Public Accountants, Inc., is adapted with permission. Material from the CMA Examination, copyright © by the Institute of Management Accounting, is adapted with permission. Although we have not cited authors whose original contributions are so widely felt that they are now an integral part of managerial accounting, needless to say, we owe them our thanks. Finally, we welcome comments from the users of this book.

Ronald M. Copeland
Paul E. Dascher

CONTENTS

SECTION ONE

SECTION TWO

CHAPTER 3

Budgeted Financial Statements, Cost Behavior, and Flexible Budgets   69

CHAPTER 4

Cost-Volume-Profit Analysis   115

SECTION THREE

CHAPTER 5

Product Costing —The Job-Order Alternative   155

CHAPTER 6

Product Costing—The Process Alternative   189

CHAPTER 7

Service Department Costs and Transfer Prices   223

CHAPTER 8

Joint and By-Product Costing   255

CHAPTER 15

Capital Budgeting: Search for Long-Run Alternatives 479

CHAPTER 16

Additional Complexities of Project Planning 511

CHAPTER 17

Accounting Data for Inventory Management 549

ONE

Scope of Managerial Accounting

Managerial accounting is concerned with all aspects of reporting financial information to those people within the organization who are responsible for planning, ascertaining the status of operations, controlling the behavior of subordinates, or making decisions. Section one of this text describes the environment in which managerial accounting functions.

CHAPTER 1

Scope of Managerial Accounting

Objectives

After studying this chapter, you should be able to do the following:

Describe the steps in a reporting system and the interrelationships within the system.

Portray the accountant's role in the managerial process.

Determine where managerial accountants gather source data and to whom they issue final reports.

Contrast managerial accounting with other classes of accounting.

Identify the major purposes of managerial accounting.

Describe the common criteria for evaluating the effectiveness of managerial accounting reports and relate these criteria to methods for improving the reports.

To operate a complex organization efficiently, top management needs detailed information about its operations. Think for a moment about the range of information the managers of General Motors might need in the course of one day, such as, for example, the tons of steel to be purchased, the hours of labor needed to keep the assembly line going, and the number and models of cars to be shipped to dealers. Nonprofit organizations such as the U.S. Department of Health, Education, and Welfare also need data about the inputs and outputs of their organizations. Inputs consist of people, materials, and facilities. Outputs consist of the goods or services distributed by the organizations.

How do managers acquire the information they need about their organization's inputs and outputs? Often managers' offices are located far from the buildings or departments where the organization manufactures its products or performs its services. They cannot form their judgments on the basis of on-the-spot observations of their organization's far flung operations, which may be conducted in separate buildings, cities, states, or even nations.

Lower-level managers devote most of their attention to the department or division for which they are responsible, but they too need information about their role in the entire organization's operations. Managers on many levels must rely on detailed information that comes to them in the form of reports on activities. Those reports that contain information specified in financial terms often originate in an **accounting system**. (Terms printed in boldface type are defined in the Glossary at the end of the book.)

REPORTING SYSTEM WITH FEEDBACK

The relationships among activities, accounting reports, and the management process are illustrated in Exhibit 1–1.

Activity and reports   Exhibit 1–1 portrays a **reporting model** like those found in many organizations. The reporting process starts with an operating activity, one that has an economic impact on the organization, such as acquiring material, using labor, or delivering goods or services as outputs. Most large organizations have formal procedures for producing source documents at the point where economic events occur. For example, sales slips and cash register tapes report sales activity; time cards record use of employee labor; and delivery invoices indicate receipt of raw materials. Copies of these original source documents are sent to the accounting department. Accountants observe these documents rather than the actual events, record the data they present, classify and interpret them, and summarize them in a report to the appropriate managers. Usually, the accounting system completes its data-collection activity by preparing a summary of organizational activity for management.

Analyzing summaries   Managers use the reports sent to them by the account-

EXHIBIT 1–1   ACCOUNTING REPORTS AND THE MANAGEMENT PROCESS

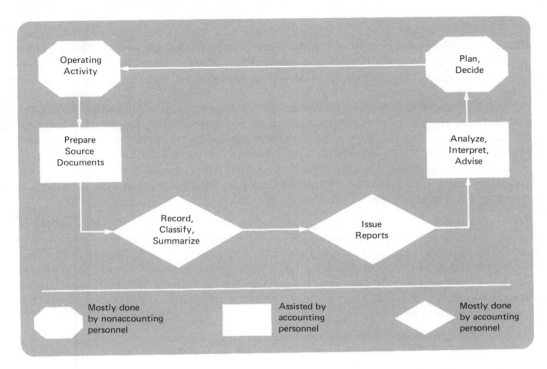

ing department in various ways. Reported information can be used for scorekeeping, attention directing, and problem solving.[1] It can be used to answer such questions as "How well am I doing?" "What is the problem?" and "What is the answer to the problem?" Reported information may also affect the manager's expectations of future events.[2] That is, when reported information enables a manager to calculate the probability that a given event will occur, he is better able to predict the expected rewards from alternative decisions. In addition, reported information is useful to inform, instruct, and motivate the receivers of the report.[3] It tells report readers what has happened (is happening, or is about to happen), what to do about it, how to do it, and why it should be done. Reported information can also help clarify the manager's view of the organization or his

[1]H. A. Simon, H. Guetzkow, G. Kozmetsky, and G. Tyndall, *Centralization and Decentralization in Organizing the Controllers' Department* (New York: Controllership Foundation, 1954), pp. 2–3.

[2]J. Marshak, "Economic Theory of Information," Working Paper No. 118, Western Management Science Institute (University of California, Los Angeles, May 1967).

[3]R. L. Ackoff, "Towards a Behavioral Theory of Communication," *Management Science* (1957–58), pp. 218–234.

conception of the forces operating in a given situation.[4] Furthermore, information can improve the effectiveness of the manager's actions and help to refresh his memory.

Management   Managers of complex organizations have many functions. They plan, organize, coordinate, and make decisions. They inform their subordinates of the tasks expected of them, measure their work or output, and try to motivate them to achieve organizational goals.

Decisions may be relatively simple, such as evaluating an employee's productivity, or they may be complex, taking into consideration a myriad of factors. For many decisions, formal decision models can be constructed. A *model* is a set of plans or rules that is a facsimile of a process. The model can be used as a guide or it may be imitated by the decision maker. Decision-making models often simplify and abstract a situation, providing a framework within which the manager can organize his data and analyze them.

Feedback   After a decision has been made and implemented, management looks to the accounting system for information about the effectiveness and efficiency of that decision. If the new accounting information indicates that the goal of that decision is not being achieved, the manager will need to alter the decision or some policy or factor that pertains to it. Thus, the feedback process helps managers to understand events more clearly, correct their models, and refresh their memories. For example:

Foreman Smith was told to produce 570 units of a product by the following week, and he needed to determine the amount of raw material required to start production. Three weeks earlier, he started 200 lbs. of material to reach a targeted 200 units, but he could produce only 190 units with that amount of material. Two weeks earlier, Smith had started 400 lbs. of material to reach his expected production level of 400 units, but he could produce only 380 units. Last week, Smith met his production quota of 114 units when he started 130 lbs; in fact, Smith ended up with 10 lbs. of surplus material. If Smith starts 600 lbs. of material next week, he should be able to meet his 570 unit quota exactly. Feedback should indicate that one pound of material produced only .95 units, or conversely, 1.05263 lbs. produced one unit.

THE ROLE OF ACCOUNTANTS IN THE MANAGERIAL PROCESS

Managerial accountants and accounting reports provide managers with information specifically designed to clarify the situation under consideration. Managers usually set goals, recognize, evaluate, and ultimately choose between alternative courses of action, and follow up or control actions needed to imple-

[4]T. J. Mock, "Concepts of Information Value and Accounting," *The Accounting Review* (October 1971), pp. 765–778.

ment them. Accounting information may be useful to the manager in performing each of these activities.

The accountant, on the other hand, is primarily concerned with gathering, organizing, and presenting information about alternative courses of action to managers. Management is thus made more efficient when information specialists—managerial accountants—provide it with accurate and complete information on which to base their decisions.

The relationships between the activities of management and those of managerial accountants are illustrated in Exhibit 1–2. The left column lists typical activities of management, and the right column lists the corresponding activities typically performed by managerial accountants. The activities listed in Exhibit 1–2 dovetail with those illustrated in Exhibit 1–1. Accountants are directly responsible for recording, classifying, and interpreting source data on basic activities; they clarify potential misunderstandings by helping managers interpret the reports; and they advise managers about the consequences of alternative decisions.

EXHIBIT 1–2　ACTIVITIES OF MANAGERS AND MANAGERIAL ACCOUNTANTS

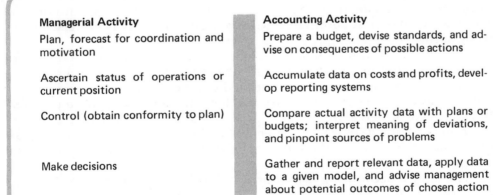

Managerial Activity	Accounting Activity
Plan, forecast for coordination and motivation	Prepare a budget, devise standards, and advise on consequences of possible actions
Ascertain status of operations or current position	Accumulate data on costs and profits, develop reporting systems
Control (obtain conformity to plan)	Compare actual activity data with plans or budgets; interpret meaning of deviations, and pinpoint sources of problems
Make decisions	Gather and report relevant data, apply data to a given model, and advise management about potential outcomes of chosen action

LOCATION OF THE ACCOUNTING FUNCTION

Where in the typical organization do managerial accountants gather the data for their reports? They must gather information on activities in all parts of the organization; thus all departments are potential subjects of the managerial accountant's attention.

Most manufacturing concerns recognize each major business function as a separate area of responsibility, and structure their organizations accordingly. Each rectangle in the organization chart in Exhibit 1–3 represents a separate function in the organization. The overall management function is the responsibility of the board of directors and the president of the corporation. At the next level, responsibility is separated for finance, manufacturing, and sales, the three major subfunctions of the firm.

The managers of the three major subfunctions are directly responsible to higher management for their operations and performance; that is, they serve in a *line relationship* to top management. The vice-president in charge of sales is directly responsible for maintaining and increasing sales activities; the vice-president in charge of manufacturing is responsible for maintaining production at levels established or projected by top management.

Staff relationships, on the other hand, exist when one department serves in an advisory capacity and provides services to other departments only when it is requested to. On most organizational charts, staff relationships are presented in a horizontal relationship to the line functions that they service, whereas line functions are represented by vertical connectors between subordinates and their immediate supervisors. Line and staff relationships are portrayed by solid and broken connectors, respectively, in Exhibit 1–3. Although the distinction between line and staff may be hazy, it is generally agreed that line authority is exerted downward over subordinates, whereas staff authority is exercised laterally or upward.

Managerial accountants perform a staff function by providing line managers and other staff managers with specialized information. Accordingly, the accounting function in Exhibit 1–3 is related to other functions by broken-line connectors. Accountants provide advice and help in planning operations, determining actual costs, developing controls, and making special decisions. After the information is collected, reports are prepared and distributed both to the line or staff functions from whom information was gathered and to the manager who requested it.

The typical accounting department is headed by a **controller**. Accountants generally assume responsibility for systems and procedures, cost accounting, taxes, internal auditing, general accounting, and special reports and studies. Cost accounting is generally subdivided into budgeting, cost records, and cost analyses; general accounting is subdivided into billing, payroll, property accounting, general ledgers, accounts receivable, and accounts payable. The term *managerial accounting* usually is applied to internal budgeting, cost control, and decision-making; it excludes financial accounting, auditing, and tax accounting.

The immediate supervisor of the controller is generally an officer in the finance division, often the vice-president in charge of finance. To summarize, the

EXHIBIT 1-3 TYPICAL ORGANIZATIONAL CHART

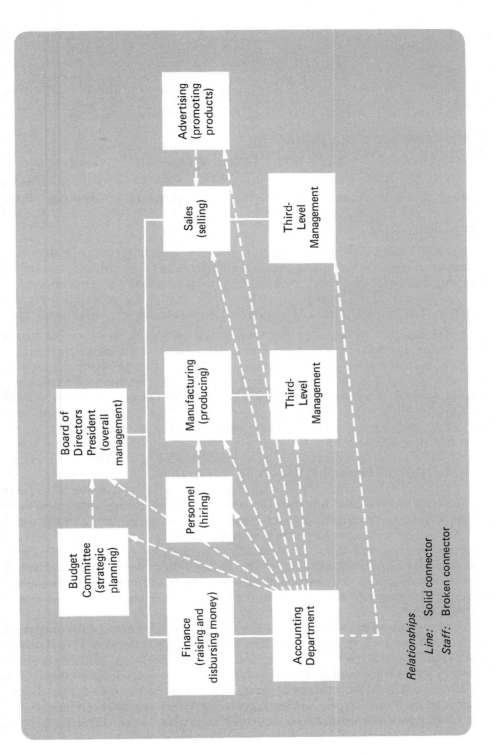

controller and his accountants are directly responsible to the vice-president of finance, but they also act in a staff capacity to the rest of the organization.

RELATIONSHIP BETWEEN MANAGERIAL AND OTHER CLASSES OF ACCOUNTING

Accounting is commonly subdivided into the following classes: **tax accounting**, **financial accounting**, **auditing**, and **managerial accounting**. Managerial accounting both differs from, and has elements in common with, the other forms of accounting.

Differences The differences between managerial and other forms of accounting are shown in Exhibit 1–4. This exhibit compares tax accounting, financial accounting, auditing, and managerial accounting in terms of: (1) underlying authority, (2) purpose of the report, (3) method of gathering data, (4) time period covered by the report, (5) form of final report, and (6) receivers of the final report.

Tax accounting The basis of the federal tax system is the Internal Revenue Code. Income tax law is applicable to all income earners, although the Code does exempt some individuals and organizations. More than 90 million income tax returns of individuals, corporations, and other entities are filed with the Internal Revenue Service every year. In addition to the 1,950 pages of the Internal Revenue Code, there are thousands of pages of official Regulations, and thousands of Revenue Rulings, Tax Court cases and appeal decisions, and Federal Court tax decisions. (Regulations and Rulings are detailed applications of the Code to specific situations.) Tax accounting is applicable also to state taxes as well as to excise taxes, estate taxes, gift taxes, and many others.

Although the primary purpose of taxation is to raise revenue to finance governmental operations, federal tax policy has nonrevenue objectives as well. Tax law is designed to promote price stability, economic growth and full employment, economic development, the redistribution of national wealth, and other objectives. Income tax law is continually changing to accommodate shifts in national policy or in business conditions. In relation to individuals, tax accounting is concerned primarily with determining tax liability and then minimizing that liability. Taxes can be minimized through the taxpayer's judicious selection of tax options.

Every taxpayer is responsible for maintaining records of his income and expenses. These records may be informal, such as a collection of check stubs, invoices, or calendar pages denoting travel plans, meetings, and engagements. Taxpayers with larger tax liabilities usually must keep more formal records. Such records, both formal and informal, are often prepared in the normal course of business to facilitate the exchange of goods and services between parties.

Taxpayers periodically review their records to select information to include on their tax returns. Accountants may prepare worksheets to facilitate the

EXHIBIT 1–4 COMPARISON OF TYPES OF ACCOUNTING

	Tax Accounting	Financial Accounting	Auditing	Managerial Accounting
Underlying Authority	Internal Revenue Code	Generally Accepted Accounting Principles	Generally Accepted Auditing Standards and Generally Accepted Accounting Principles	Economic decision theory, CASB Standards
Purpose	To determine tax liability	To record, classify, summarize, and interpret transaction data; issue financial statements	To express opinions on fairness, consistency, and conformity	To facilitate planning, cost accumulation, control, and decision-making
Data Collection Method	After the fact worksheet based on financial records	Concurrent recording in journals, ledgers	After the fact worksheet based on records and on new evidence gathered in the audit	Future, concurrent, and past determinations, as required.
Time Period of the Report	Annual, quarterly (past period)	Annual, quarterly, possibly monthly (past period)	Annual, two-year comparison (past period)	Any time period, as required (past-future)
Form of Report	Federal forms 1040, 1120	Balance sheet, income statement, funds flow statement	Auditor's opinion	Budgets, cost reports, performance reports, special analyses
Receiver of the Report	Top management, Internal Revenue Service	Top management, public	Top management, public	Top management

transfer of data from records to tax returns. Tax returns must be filed annually; supplemental returns may be filed quarterly. Different types of taxpayers use different forms to file returns. Form 1040 is the primary form for individuals, and Form 1120 is the primary form for corporations.

Many taxpayers make out their own tax returns. Some, however, have a "tax specialist" prepare their returns. Although anyone can claim to be a tax specialist, the true specialist usually has a background in accounting or law. Each return is submitted to the Internal Revenue Service, where it is checked for mathematical accuracy and legal conformity by a carefully programmed computer. Some returns are individually reviewed by one of the 61,000 employees of the IRS. Thus, only a select group of people ever see the return: the taxpayer (or top management for corporate taxpayers), the tax specialist who acted in the taxpayer's behalf, and possibly an employee of the Internal Revenue Service.

Financial accounting   Financial accounting is the process of identifying, measuring, and communicating selected economic information about the activities of a particular entity to interested parties. The type of economic information measured, the entity concerned, and the group reported to are all more or less defined by a traditional set of Generally Accepted Accounting Principles, or **GAAP**. Modern accounting practices and GAAP slowly evolved from fifteenth-century Italian bookkeeping practices. No single set of GAAP is universally acknowledged, but financial accounting practices in the United States are fairly well specified in the pronouncements of the Securities and Exchange Commission (**SEC**), the American Institute of Certified Public Accountants (**AICPA**), and the Financial Accounting Standards Board (**FASB**). Public accounting disclosure requirements are specified by the SEC, and accounting principles have been articulated by the AICPA and FASB.

The Securities and Exchange Commission is a federal regulatory body created in the 1930s to oversee all activities related to the public securities markets, including the financial reporting practices of companies traded on the stock exchanges. The SEC designed its own forms and specifically stated what data should be reported on them. In addition, the SEC also requires that each business under its jurisdiction issue periodic reports to its security holders, that these reports be examined by a certified public accountant, and that he express an opinion about those reports. In other words, the SEC delegated to CPAs effective control of the financial reporting practices of publicly owned concerns. Three-fourths of the more than 120,000 CPAs licensed to practice in the United States, are members of the American Institute of Certified Public Accountants (AICPA), which has promulgated a code of professional ethics and summarized generally accepted accounting principles. The AICPA has affected the financial accounting practices of all businesses in which there is a large public interest.

Thus, financial accounting follows a relatively uniform procedure throughout the United States: an accountant who transfers from one company to another usually has little difficulty adapting to the new accounting environment.

Within an organization, accountants examine the source documents resulting from the acquisition or use of productive inputs and the sale or distribution of goods and services. Information about these events is recorded chronologically in books of original entry, called *journals*, and then transcribed into books of secondary entry, called *ledgers*. The information that is listed chronologically in journals is regrouped in a "like kind" listing in the ledger, that is, all data concerned with one unit of information are grouped in one *account*, or listing. Using a ledger, an accountant can determine the balance in each account when preparing reports.

Financial accounting data are of interest both to parties within the organization and to parties outside it. Internally, financial accounting data help managers to identify those who owe them money (as well as how much and when it is due), those to whom they owe money, the quantity and value of inventories (or other resources) on hand, and the rate of sales or purchase activity. All business activity that can be reduced to dollars is subject to measurement by financial accounting. Financial accounting reports are distributed to the appropriate executives within the organization. This "inside" information is not made available, however, to a host of "outside" parties who are interested in the affairs of the organization. This group includes the stockholders, potential stockholders, creditors, financial analysts, competitors, and employees.

Three types of summaries of financial accounting data are distributed to the public yearly, however, and in some cases, semiannually or quarterly.

The first type of financial statement, an **income statement**, summarizes revenue activity for the period, reporting the dollar values received from the distribution of goods and services. It also lists the costs of such inputs as labor, materials, and facilities used during the period. The difference between the revenues received and the costs incurred is called *income*. A **balance sheet** reports the financial position of the company at the end of the accounting period, detailing an adjusted historical cost of all resources available for future use. It also summarizes creditor and owner claims against the resources. A statement of changes in financial position, commonly called a **funds flow statement**, lists the sources and applications of funds received or expended during the period. Funds flow activity occurs as a result of normal operations, buying or selling property other than merchandise, borrowing or repaying long-term debts, issuing additional capital stock to owners, or paying dividends,

Auditing   Auditing is a process of obtaining evidence regarding the assertions made in financial statements and determining their conformity to established criteria. Conformity to generally accepted accounting principles is one such criterion. After examining financial statements, the auditor expresses an opinion about them. This expression of an auditor's opinion is called **attestation**. Attestation is a statement of opinion, based on convincing evidence, by an independent, authoritative person, concerning the degree of correspondence between accounting information in the financial statements and established criteria.

Most audits are conducted in accordance with **generally accepted auditing standards**, which have been codified by the American Institute of Certified Public Accountants. These standards require that the auditor possess specific personal characteristics, behave ethically, and follow prescribed auditing practices. Yearly audits by certified public accountants must be conducted on the accounting records of all companies that report to the Securities and Exchange Commission. Many companies also assign a group of their own employees to perform an internal audit of company accounting activities.

Auditing involves an after-the-fact investigation of the accounting process. Auditors engage in three types of activities: they question, they observe activities, and they take actions. Auditors question top executives of the company being investigated, inquiring about changes in operations made during the year, which might bear on the financial statements. Next, they observe the workings of the client's accounting system to ascertain whether all events that should be recorded are being recorded and all events that should be excluded are being excluded. Auditors also make tests of the accounting records, such as counting inventories, contacting creditors and debtors, or submitting to the accounting system a "test deck" of fictitious transactions containing errors to see if the system will detect the errors.

After an auditor completes his investigation, he issues an opinion, which is ordinarily published along with the financial statements. If the auditor is satisfied with his client's financial statements, his opinion follows a standard format of two paragraphs. The first paragraph lists the scope of the audit engagement (what the auditor did), and the second paragraph expresses his opinion. The opinion reports that the financial statements are "fairly presented, in conformity with generally accepted accounting principles, applied on a consistent basis." Of necessity, this opinion covers accounting practices for a period of two or more years (to meet the "consistency" criterion). This opinion has a limited technical meaning; it does not mean that the financial statements are suitable for any and all uses. A longer copy of the opinion, describing specific observations made by the auditor, is forwarded to the top management of the client.

Managerial accounting   Managerial accounting is an information-processing system designed to help managers plan, accumulate data, control operations, and make decisions. Different sets of information may be prepared for each of these purposes. Managerial accounting includes both routine and special analyses. Most firms have accounting systems that gather product cost information and control information on a routine basis, but **planning** and nonroutine decision data must be gathered by special analysis.

Planning includes selecting objectives, together with the means for attaining them. All organizations, both business and nonbusiness, have particular objectives or goals, and some may be accomplished without planning. Most firms, however, adopt formal plans before trying to achieve their objectives. A formal plan of action, expressed in figures, is called a **budget**.

Managerial accounting provides methods for accumulating data (**cost accumulation**) on actual experience. Most business firms and many nonprofit organizations have accounting systems designed to record, classify, interpret, and report on actual business operations. Often, the system assigns manufacturing or operating costs to specific jobs or to specific processes in proportion to the amount of productive inputs associated with those jobs or processes. This *scorekeeping* process enables managers to evaluate the financial performance of their organization.

Control is the process of obtaining conformity to plans through actions and evaluations. The role of managerial accountants in the control process is in identifying *controllable* costs, that is, those which may be directly regulated at a given level of managerial authority, in either the short or the long run. Information on controllable costs, often called feedback, is distributed to the executives responsible for the activity that generates the costs. A system of control includes all measures and methods designed to promote efficiency, encourage adherence to managerial plans and policies, and safeguard the organization's assets. The control function applies to executives working in nonprofit organizations as well as to businessmen. Good managerial accounting systems submit controllable cost data to the appropriate managers.

Reports issued by managerial accountants do not follow a standardized form. They may be long or short, horizontal or vertical. The content of these reports is not standardized either; for example, budgets contain expected future data, whereas inventory lists contain actual historical costs, that is, costs incurred in the past. The time frame considered in managerial accounting may relate to past, present, or future events. Furthermore, the period of concern may span a single day or several years, as, for example, in daily cash budgets or in ten-year capital projections. Although managerial accounting reports may be available at any level within the organization, they are rarely released to parties external to the organization.

No single institution is recognized as the official source of managerial accounting principles. The **Cost Accounting Standards Board** (**CASB**) has been authorized by federal law to establish accounting standards applicable to defense contractors funded under federal contract. Most of the standards issued by the CASB concern cost determination, i.e., which accounting methods must be used and which elements of costs will be recognized when determining reimbursements for work done under federal contract. A second organization, the National Association of Accountants (**NAA**), a voluntary association of managerial accountants, publishes a monthly periodical and a series of research reports devoted to managerial accounting topics. NAA pronouncements on managerial accounting practice tend to summarize current practice; they have no official sanction.

Similarities Frequently, the different classes of accounting use the same source documents. For example, the source document that identifies a dollar value of inventory for financial accounting may serve as evidence in the auditing process, produce a valuation figure in the tax return, and help the managerial accountant determine the relative profitability of different product lines.

In the same fashion, one accountant may perform several of the different functions of accounting. For example, the financial accountant may collect and classify information used on the tax return, or he may make reconciliation statements that will be relied on by the auditor or by the managerial accountant. In addition, the final reports for all forms of accounting may go to the same groups, such as, for example, top management.

Finally, all classes of accounting are interrelated. Taxes affect financial accounting, auditing, and managerial control and decision-making policies. Each class of accounting affects the other classes of accounting.

CRITERIA FOR EVALUATING
ACCOUNTING REPORTS

The usefulness of any accounting report is determined jointly by the content of the report and the user's skill in interpreting it. One of the managerial accountant's staff duties is to help managers understand the meaning and proper use of the accounting report he submits to them.

The American Accounting Association, a national organization of educators and practitioners, has attempted to set guidelines to help accountants prepare better reports. They have established four criteria for evaluating accounting reports: **relevance**, **quantifiability**, **verifiability**, and **freedom from bias**. Others have listed such criteria as timeliness, clarity, and conciseness.

Relevance The concept of *relevance* has been defined as follows:

> For information to meet the standard of relevance, it must bear upon or be usefully associated with the action it is designed to facilitate or the result it is desired to produce. This requires that either the information or the act of communicating it exert influence . . . on the designated actions.[5]

Relevance is the most important criterion for accounting information. Accounting information is relevant only if it has the capacity to influence the manager's decisions or his decision-making processes. Relevance is a subjective concept, however, one that may differ among managers using different decision-making processes.

Quantifiability Quantifiability is defined as "the association of a number with

---

[5]*A Statement of Basic Accounting Theory* (Evanston, Ill.: American Accounting Association, 1966), p. 9.

a transaction or an activity where the numbers assigned obey prescribed arithmetic laws or procedures."[6] Quantifiability provides a means for comparing alternative objectives, actions, or events. Furthermore, different types of objects or events can be combined according to their quantifiable attributes. For example, two different combinations of the labor, material, and overhead inputs required to produce a given output can be evaluated in relation to their respective dollar values.

Most business decisions have both quantitative and **qualitative** consequences. *Quantitative consequences are those that can be reduced to a number*, such as a dollar and cents figure. *Consequences that are not subject to precise or direct measurement are said to be qualitative.*

Verifiability Verifiability is "that attribute [of a report] . . . which allows qualified individuals working independently of one another to develop essentially similar measures or conclusions from an examination of the same evidence, data, or records."[7] This criterion assures the data user that each report is reproducible, given the same underlying set of events, and independent of the accountant who originally prepared it. Verifiability can be achieved only if rules for measuring and combining values of events or objects are well understood and applied consistently. Using verifiable data and systems permits more than one accountant to work on a project at the same time. The output of each accountant can be checked (audited) for accuracy, consistency, and conformity to external rules, and accounting work already completed can guide future work.

Freedom from bias Accounting information should be presented without bias; for example, benefits or an appearance of "better" performance should not be ascribed to one group at the expense of another. If accounting data falsely imply that one executive or function always performs "better" than another, management may very well make incorrect policy decisions in regard to allocation of resources or rewarding executives. As another example, the output or performance of employees should be accounted for by a process that reflects their true efficiency, not one that assigns favorable ratings to inefficient workers.

Timeliness If managers are expected to use accounting information in planning, product costing, or decision-making, they must receive the information when they need it. Timeliness may require that some reports be prepared on a prearranged schedule, and others whenever they are needed.

Clarity All reports should be clear and understandable, both in form and in content. Like items should be grouped, and unlike items should be segregated. The form of the report should separate and highlight important items. The report should be neat, legible, and grammatically correct.

---

[6]*A Statement of Basic Accounting Theory*, pp. 11–12.
[7]*A Statement of Basic Accounting Theory*, p. 10.

Conciseness   Clarity and conciseness are closely linked. A concise report is brief and to the point. The report should be complete and include all information that is vital, but none that is unnecessary. Concise reports enable a busy manager to obtain the information he needs quickly, without having to read through unnecessary material.

SUMMARY

Accounting is a formal system for identifying, measuring, and reporting economic information about a particular entity to a particular group. Subclasses of accounting include auditing, financial accounting, managerial accounting, and tax accounting, all of which are interrelated. The subclasses of accounting each have unique elements as well as common characteristics. Managerial accounting is concerned with identifying, measuring, and communicating information to internal management for planning, information processing, control, and decision-making purposes. The managerial accountant acts in an advisory capacity, gathering data throughout the organization for inclusion in his reports, which may be produced on a routine basis or may require special studies. Managerial accounting reports may be evaluated in terms of: relevance, quantifiability, verifiability, freedom from bias, timeliness, clarity, and conciseness. Like many technical fields, managerial accounting employs a vocabulary of specialized terms: the first time a specialized term is used in this text, it appears in boldface type. The Glossary at the end of the book defines all words appearing in boldface.

SUGGESTED READINGS

Hayes, David. "The Contingency Theory of Managerial Accounting." *The Accounting Review*, January 1977.

Hill, L. W. "The Growth of the Corporate Finance Function." *Financial Executive*, July 1976.

MacLean, Donald. "The Controller: Who Is He?" *Managerial Planning*, January/February 1976.

Mock, T. J. "Concepts of Information Value and Accounting." *Accounting Review*, October 1971.

"Report of the Committee on Courses in Managerial Accounting, 1971." *Accounting Review*, Supplement to Volume XLVII (1972).

"Report of the Committee on Internal Measurement and Reporting, 1972." *Accounting Review*, Supplement to Volume XLVIII (1973).

QUESTIONS[a]

1-1 "Decision makers require quantitative information to make optimal decisions." List reasons why this statement might be true.

1-2 The decision-making process described in this chapter is sometimes referred to as an *open* system, that is, one which external information can enter. At what points in the process can external information enter?

1-3 What are two contributions that the managerial accountant makes to a typical organization's decision-making process?

1-4 Differentiate between line and staff authority. Which type of authority does the controller have?

1-5 The data-collection method of the managerial accountant is similar to which other two functional areas of accounting?

1-6 Describe the role of accountants in the management process.

1-7 What are three purposes of managerial accounting? Which of these functions is the least defined by tradition? Why?

1-8 An auditor's opinion lends credibility to financial statements, but internal reports do not require an auditor's certificate. Does this imply that internal reports are less credible than external financial statements? Discuss.

1-9 Michael Johnson, the sales manager of Computation, Inc., is discussing with the president, Thomas Sampsene, the pricing of a new product soon to be placed on the market:

> Tom, we have to set the price on our new calculator before the end of the day so that we can order the sales brochures.
> I thought that question was settled at the weekly executive meeting yesterday, Mike. According to the cost figures prepared by our new accountant, yesterday's decision seems perfectly reasonable.
> But what does an accountant know about trying to sell a product against stiff competition?
> Well, Mike, why don't you write out your objections and present them at next week's meeting?

What problem do you observe in this organization?

1-10 In the following examples, identify the problem that may exist in either the accountant's role, the decision-making process, or the purposes of the managerial accounting system.

> (A) The logistics department manager schedules truck departures on the basis of information he receives from the production department

---

[a]Questions, exercises, and problems that extend coverage beyond the discussion in the chapter are indicated by an asterisk *.

manager, whom he has known for 12 years. The shipping clerk is complaining because backlogs have built up.

(B) The sales projection committee meets on the last working day of each month to update the monthly projected sales quota for the next 12-month period. The sales figures employed at this meeting are furnished by the assistant vice-president of sales. The accounting department's monthly performance reports are issued on the 10th of the following month.

(C) The Kord Tire Company has a flexible pricing structure. The sales department uses the production cost sheets as prepared by individual machine operators to price each order. The accounting department manager has argued that the pricing policy does not include charges for administrative expenses. The sales manager says that he is using last year's figures to approximate the administrative and sales expenses.

(D) John Thompson, a lathe operator for the Twilight Lamp Company, has complained to his line foreman that the performance standards set by the accounting department are too stringent. Furthermore, John asks, "How does that accountant know what it's like to work down here on the production line? He never leaves his plush office." The line foreman agrees with John but says that he has no control over upper management.

1–11   The managerial accountant studies real activities and tries to translate them into data that can be reported to the managers who are concerned with the activities. What activities would an accountant be concerned with in a typical manufacturing operation? On which attribute of the activity does the accountant report, for example, height, weight, depth, and so on?

1–12   How does management process the information contained in accounting reports? That is, what questions may be asked?

1–13   List some activities that managers might plan for on a routine basis. List some activities that require nonroutine planning.

1–14   What is a decision model?

1–15   Can a decision model, which is abstract, help managers make decisions about real situations? How?

1–16   Define *feedback*. In addition to helping managers improve their view of the real world, how can feedback improve the managerial process?

1–17   Both the managerial accountant and the manager are involved in the decision-making process. How do their roles differ?

1–18   Does management or the managerial accountant set the goals and objectives of the organization? Does management or the managerial accountant determine the means by which the chosen goals and objectives will be achieved?

Does management or the managerial accountant determine what information should be reported, when it should be reported, and how it should be reported?

1-19 When management wishes to plan or forecast to achieve organizational coordination or motivation, what action does the managerial accountant take?

1-20 How can a managerial accountant help management ascertain the status of current operations or the organization's financial position?

1-21 The managerial accountant may compare data on actual activities with plans or budgets so that management will be better able to engage in what type of activity?

1-22 The managerial accountant may gather and report relevant data and/or apply data to a given decision model to help management take what type of action?

1-23 Where in the typical organization would the managerial accountant gather source data to prepare the reports he issues?

1-24 To whom in the typical organization would the managerial accountant issue reports?

1-25 List some differences between managerial accounting and financial accounting; between managerial accounting and auditing; between managerial accounting and tax accounting.

1-26 List some similarities between managerial accounting and other forms of accounting.

EXERCISES

1-27 In the column on the right are four classes of accounting; on the left are terms associated with each class. Match each term with the number of the class to which it corresponds most closely.

Accounting Terms	*Classes of Accounting*
a. AICPA ____	1. Financial accounting
b. Attestation ____	2. Tax accounting
c. Balance sheet ____	3. Auditing
d. Budget ____	4. Managerial accounting
e. Control ____	
f. Cost accumulation ____	
g. Decision making ____	
h. Feedback ____	
i. Funds flow statement ____	
j. Income statement ____	
k. Planning ____	
l. SEC ____	

1–28 Which of the accounting terms listed in question 1–27 are primarily associated with managerial accounting? Define each of the managerial accounting terms.

*1–29 The functions of the controller in various companies in the automobile industry are similar. The role of division and plant controllers is different in two major companies, however. In Company A, division managers are usually engineering-oriented and have general, overall authority, and the division controller reports directly to the division manager. All reports from the division to central management are signed by, and come from, the division manager. Plant managers who report to division managers exercise parallel authority and also employ parallel relations with plant controllers. In Company B, a system of dual control exists—the division controller gives staff assistance to the division manager but reports directly to the company controller. At the plant level, the same situation exists, that is, staff assistance to the plant manager but direct reporting to the division controller.

(A) Under Company A's approach to reporting, what problems in human relations might arise?

(B) Under Company B's approach to reporting, what problems in human relations might arise?

(C) Which approach do you prefer? Why?

(D) If the plant manager and the plant controller disagree about reporting certain costs in Company A, what action could the controller take? In Company B, what could the controller do? What do you think would actually happen?

1–30 One of the first steps in management control is to produce an organizational chart. Producing an accurate chart may be difficult if job performance does not conform to the sphere of activity implied by the job title. Strong employees tend to view their jobs and spheres of activity broadly, whereas others view their jobs narrowly.

For the following problem, assume that each job is exactly what its title implies. Identify any title that might be ambiguous. Next, draw an organizational chart using the same job titles.

(A) Controller
(B) President
(C) Head Designer
(D) Vice-President of Manufacturing
(E) Vice-President of Personnel
(F) Manager of Accounting
(G) Manager of Salary Personnel
(H) Manager of Hourly Personnel
(I) Vice-President of Sales

(J) Manager of Budgeting
(K) Manager of General Accounting
(L) Production Superintendent
(M) Sales Manager
(N) Assembly Line Foreman
(O) Maintenance Foreman
(P) Production Control Foreman

1–31 Accounting reports and the management process have been depicted graphically in the text. Title the various boxes presented below and answer the following questions about the flow.

(A) What are the activities in boxes U, V, W, Y, and Z?

(B) How can activity be altered or controlled in a system that has activity as the first step?

(C) Is managerial accounting simply a form of scorekeeping? Explain what managerial accountants hope to do.

(D) Where does the managerial accountant fit into the picture below?

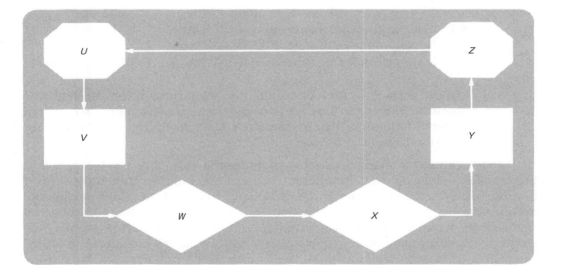

*1–32 The controller of the Evens Company, a large manufacturer of camping equipment, takes his job of cost control very seriously. In order to remain impartial, he does not associate with other members of the management group. He also strongly encourages his subordinates to associate only with other members of the accounting group or with people outside the Evens Company. The controller has stated that *respect* is the one word he would select to represent the accounting function.

(A) Is *respect* the most important concept for which an accounting department should be known? In the Evens Company, what term is probably the most frequently used by other departments to describe accounting?

(B) What problems are likely to result from the controller's policy of separatism?

(C) Is the function of controller that of an impartial observer?

1–33   The Wayco Company has suffered a terrible year. Sales dropped 40%, costs increased 5%, income went from a profit of $1,500,000 to a $5,000,000 loss, and the president's wife told him her brother wanted to enter the business. The company was listed on the New York Stock Exchange and wished to remain there. When asked for cost-reduction ideas, the production manager recommended reducing the accounting costs. The accounting department has four major cost segments: financial accounting, tax reporting, the auditor's bill, and managerial accounting. The controller determined that no excess cost could be cut from any of these segments without the loss of that function.

(A) If the production manager is right, which accounting function could be eliminated by this company? Why?

(B) What arguments could be used for keeping all the accounting functions at operating strength?

(C) Which accounting function would be the hardest to defend? Why?

(D) In periods of financial difficulty, would the accounting department be one of the first areas to contract? In actual practice, which other functions or departments are more likely candidates for contraction than accounting?

1–34   A small company producing parts for the automobile industry is taking a hard look at its staff functions to determine whether they have "grown beyond their worth." The standard functions of financial, tax, and managerial accounting are performed by three men. The reason for having a managerial segment seems hazy. As the president states, "I handle any control problems. If someone needs a push, I know it before the accountants tell me. All the accounting people do is confirm that I push the right one."

(A) If the president is right, should the managerial segment be abolished?

(B) What could be done to improve the existing control function?

(C) If the president believes control is the only function of managerial accounting, what could be done to expand his viewpoint?

(D) Do you think the president worked his way up to his position through the financial side of the business? Is the president's background of any importance in ascertaining possible problems between the financial side of the business and top management? Explain.

1–35   Eight uses of managerial accounting information are listed in the column on the right, and twelve questions appear in the column on the left. Match the number of the use to the letter of the question that best describes what a manager might ask while performing his job. Any of the eight numbers may be used more than once, and any situation may describe more than one use.

a. What is the last day that I can order more raw material and still get it on time to meet the production schedule? _____

b. Why should I produce the amount requested? _____

c. What is the problem? _____

d. What is the likelihood that costs of labor will increase? _____

e. Will costs really behave relative to volume as I have them predicted in my budget? _____

f. How should I do the next task? _____

g. How well am I doing on this job? _____

h. What did I do the last time this type of event occurred?

_____

i. Which type of input is being used excessively and incurring excessive costs? _____

j. How much labor cost was incurred by Department 1 on Wednesday? _____

k. What is the likelihood that production volume can be maintained at the current rate? _____

l. Is revenue really a function of unit price and volume? _____

1. Direct attention
2. Change expectations of future events
3. Clarify view of real world
4. Instruct
5. Motivate
6. Solve problems, choose among alternatives
7. Reinforce memory
8. Inform, keep score

1–36   Below are two lists: a numbered list of criteria for evaluating an accounting report and a lettered list of hypothetical situations. Match the number of the criterion that is being violated with the letter of the situation that describes the effect of the violation.

a. Tempco has just installed a real-time computer system with high-speed output capability, which allows immediate printout of all information in the computer's memory. When the production manager requested some information on the activity in Department 1, the computer department provided him with a "dump" of all data on Department 1, amounting to 56 pages.   _____

b. Customers of Westco started complaining about the quality of the products they purchased. Westco's production manager requested some detailed information on quality control from the accounting department, but all he received was a report of the costs for each input, the quantities of each input used, the budgeted costs and quantities that were planned for use, and the deviations of actual cost and quantity from the budget.   _____

c. Johnson, an elderly accountant at Eastco, was asked to prepare a forecast of the expected costs of producing a new product. Johnson retired before he could complete the project, and Jones was assigned to the task. Jones examined some of Johnson's preliminary figures and worksheets, but could not figure out how the numbers had been derived.   _____

d. Arnold, sales manager for Blink, Inc., wondered what would happen to profits if he modified the prices of the company's five products, undertook a major advertising campaign, and switched the company's advertising from magazine ads to television spots. The accounting department could supply

1. Relevance
2. Quantifiability
3. Verifiability
4. Freedom from bias
5. Timeliness
6. Clarity
7. Conciseness

Arnold with income statements and balance sheets for past periods only. ____

e. Boyle did everything in his power to run his machining department efficiently, and when his boss told him to cut down on scrap, he made sure that his men tried to waste fewer materials. Boyle knew that his department was cutting down on scrap, because every day the pile of floor sweepings was growing smaller. Yet, the accounting report indicated that Boyle's department was actually increasing the amount of scrap it produced. ____

f. Donne requested that the accounting department provide him with a report of which items were in stock, which items were currently in production, and which items were out of stock. The report he received listed items by account number and reported balances in dollars. The report contained three columns that did not bear any headings, so Donne was unsure of their meaning. ____

g. As purchasing agent, Smith frequently had to make speedy decisions, especially when "bargain" purchases became available. If Smith didn't move fast enough, the agent for some other company would buy the items offered to Smith. On Monday morning, Smith learned of a bargain sale of Widgets, and he requested that the accounting department report on the number of Widgets currently in stock and the expected demand for them in the near future. The accounting department replied on Wednesday, but by then, the bargain Widgets had been sold to a competitor. ____

1. Relevance
2. Quantifiability
3. Verifiability
4. Freedom from bias
5. Timeliness
6. Clarity
7. Conciseness

TWO

Budgeting for Short-Term Operations

Budgeted Financial Statements, Cost Behavior, and Flexible Budgets

Cost-Volume-Profit Analysis

The next three chapters describe the planning activities of business organizations and focus on the managerial accountant's role in this process. The methods, techniques, and procedures of managerial planning will be explored in detail.

CHAPTER 2

Budgeting for Short-Term Operations

Objectives

After studying this chapter, you should be able to do the following:

Define budgeting *and describe the budgeting process.*

Describe the interrelationships among those who prepare budgets, the budget form, and those who use budgets—where the data come from, how they are presented, and to whom they are distributed.

Prepare operating budgets *and* financial budgets *from a given set of case data.*

Discuss some of the human limitations inherent in the budgeting process.

Managerial accounting is conducted within the limits imposed by a framework of organizational goals, constraints, and evaluation processes.

ORGANIZATIONAL GOALS

All organizations, even the largest, have limited resources, and these limited resources impose limits on the number and range of goals that the organization can hope to attain. The limits on available manpower, capital, plant facilities, or raw materials available to an organization compel it to select certain activities for its operations and to exclude others. An organization employs only the number of workers and the amount of capital and raw materials it needs to produce a given quantity of goods, provide a certain range of services, or accomplish the goals it has set itself. Common organizational goals include maximizing profits or achieving a satisfactory level of performance (profit **satisficing**), achieving continual growth or ensuring the survival of the organization, avoiding risk in making investments, and performing a social service by providing goods and services desired by others.

ORGANIZATIONAL CONSTRAINTS

Scarcity of resources imposes restraints on an organization. A firm may lack financial or operating (physical) resources, talented managers, technological ability, skilled employees, or other elements essential to efficient or profitable operation.

Further constraints are imposed on organizations by laws regulating their activities. For example, the Sherman Antitrust Act may prevent a company from acquiring other firms or from engaging in certain lines of business. The Robinson-Patman Act may prevent a company from lowering its prices for a special customer. The price and wage control acts of the 1940s, 1950s, and 1970s prevent businessmen from raising prices or wages beyond specified limits. Business transactions with foreign countries are constrained by import and export licensing requirements; governmental agencies may undertake only the tasks prescribed by the legislation that created them. These legal constraints often affect operating plans or decisions or the organization's data-collection system. For example, federal income tax law requires employers to withhold a part of their employees' pay and to establish an accounting system to accumulate information on such withholdings.

RELATIONSHIP OF GOALS AND CONSTRAINTS TO ACCOUNTING

Managerial accounting is an information system that supplies management with relevant information for planning, cost determination, control, and decision-making. It records, classifies, and reports quantifiable (numerically describable) data. It helps to specify the organization's goals or the means for obtaining those goals, to indicate the probable or actual effects of specific constraints, and provides a basis for evaluating the organization's performance. In addition, the managerial accountant may help managers analyze this information.

Managerial goals are the focus of all organizational activity. These goals are formulated into policy and translated into decisions and/or actions. But each goal, policy, decision, or action is limited by the numerous constraints imposed on the firm. *Managerial accounting reports provide executives with the information they need to attain the organization's goals, given its constraints.*

PURPOSES OF BUDGETING

One of top management's planning functions is searching for short-run alternatives. Without short-range planning, businesses, hospitals, and governmental units would be unable to produce goods or provide services on a basis flexible enough to meet day-to-day demands. Day-to-day planning requires selecting one set from among all alternative objectives and implementing procedures. Thus, short-run budgeting can become quite complex. Daily operations demand answers to questions, such as "How many units should we produce today?" or "How many doctors should be on call today?" or "To which customers should our salesmen devote their attention today?"

Most managers have formalized the planning process. *A formal plan expressing a course of action in quantitative terms is called a* **budget**. The purposes of budgets and budgeting are:

1. To state expectations in formal terms so that most of the underlying assumptions may be identified.

2. To communicate with or inform others about the goals and methods selected by top management so that all managers will understand and support the budget.

3. To coordinate all factors of production so that subordinates can achieve the common objective.

4. To establish expectations as a framework for judging performance so that employees may know what is expected of them, be motivated to accomplish the budgeted objectives, and ultimately be judged according to budgeted criteria.

EXPLICIT STATEMENT OF EXPECTATIONS

The primary goal of most managers is to provide the best quality or quantity of goods or services at the least cost. At the same time, they may pursue other more personal goals: survival, profit, personal power, prestige, or empire-building.

All long-run goals must be pursued in successive, short-run steps, and budgeting helps bring and keep short-run steps in line with those goals. Before a budget is prepared, managers must formulate targets of expected performance. These targets help them direct their operations, identify problems, help motivate lower-level employees, and clarify the relationship between current activities and future policies. More important, the assumptions underlying any goal or the means for attaining it must be stated explicitly. For example, a projected sales level of $1 million implies certain assumptions about prices and quantities of product to be sold. This explicit statement of assumptions is one of the most important contributions that budgeting makes to management.

The short-run policies adopted by management must be modified whenever the assumptions underlying them change. Economic, social, or business conditions may change, supply or demand may fluctuate, competitors may leave the market, consumer taste may change, or technological innovation may occur. For example, increased competition may compel a firm to lower its prices and increase its sales volume in an effort to attain the level of revenue stipulated in a budget. Budgets help managers adjust their operations and plans to unexpected changes by providing a framework or measure against which to evaluate the consequences of the change.

COMMUNICATION

Budgeting is designed to give employees explicit information in regard to the level of performance expected of them. Simply making a broad formal statement of an organization's goals and the means for attaining those goals does not automatically ensure that henceforth the firm's activities will be directed toward meeting those goals. Managers have to understand the budget first. Through the budget, top management communicates its expectations to lower-level employees, so that all members of the firm may understand the goals and coordinate their efforts to attain them.

COORDINATION

If an organization is to attain its long-run goals, the operations of all its departments must mesh. Labor, material, facilities — all factors of production — must be coordinated. Raw material purchases must be coordinated with production schedules. Production schedules, in turn, must be based both on employees' capabilities and plant or machinery capacities. Thus, budgets compel managers to examine the relationships between their own operations and those of other departments, and in the process, to identify potential bottlenecks or weaknesses.

The first draft of a budget often fails to produce a perfect meshing of results. For example, it may call for the acquisition of raw materials in amounts or at times that make a smooth flow of production in the manufacturing departments impossible. Such imbalances must be corrected before the budget is set in final form. Everyone affected by the imbalance should be consulted when the budget is revised. To reconcile the purchasing-manufacturing imbalance, raw materials might be purchased in larger quantities, purchase orders could be submitted more frequently, or the production schedule might be lengthened.

A good budget gives managers enough flexibility to accommodate their plans and operations to unexpected situations. For example, consider an original purchasing budget which called for acquisition of 9,000 tons of raw material per month, while the production budget called for the manufacture of 90,000 finished units. An increase in production to 100,000 units would require an increase in the purchasing schedule as well. The budget should be flexible enough to permit these increases.

EXPECTATIONS AS A FRAMEWORK
FOR JUDGING PERFORMANCE

After a budget has been drafted, revised, and set in final form, it must be sent to employees. The budget informs employees of the level of performance expected of them, and it is hoped, motivates them to accomplish the goals set forth in the budget.

One of the manager's tasks is judging the performance of his subordinates. Many criteria can be used to measure employee performance. Current performance is usually measured against some standard such as past performance, performance of other workers doing the same task, some independently derived goal, or the level of output indicated in the budget. Budgets can serve as a useful yardstick in judging performance, because they define goals, the means of implementing the goals, and the level of employee performance required to attain the goals.

THE BUDGETING PROCEDURE

Preparing a budget demands the joint efforts of all executives involved with setting goals and devising the policies and activating the procedures needed to implement the goals. Most often, the responsibility for preparing and distributing the budget is delegated to a budget committee.

The budget committee   In many organizations, the budget committee is frequently composed of members who represent the sales, production, and finance functions. The controller or chief financial officer is often responsible for organizing and administering the budget program. He ensures that all necessary budget estimates are received by the committee and revised in the light of any additional information obtained by the committee.

In some organizations the budgeting procedure includes participation of employees and administrators at all levels of operations. Opinions and estimates are sought from individual salesmen, production foremen, and credit officers. This type of budgeting is called *participative budgeting*. Many authorities believe that participative budgeting fosters cohesiveness and strengthens motivation among employees. Nonetheless, in many organizations, budgeting executives establish goals and determine means for accomplishing them without consulting lower-level employees.

Flow of budget information   After the committee has agreed on general policies and actions, the controller prepares a draft of the budget for the committee's approval. When the committee has approved the budget, the controller distributes copies of it to the managers. The interrelationships between the budget committee and the operating divisions of the firm are illustrated in Exhibit 2–1. Data estimates or forecasts flow up from the divisions to the budget committee, and finished budgets flow out from it.

For example, one flow of data might originate in the sales division when individual salesmen notify their territorial sales managers of their expectations for sales in their territory. The sales manager may modify these estimates on the basis of his knowledge of the salesman's ability or judgment, and his own knowledge of historical trends, projected advertising campaigns, or potential changes in sales compensation. Then he sends the revised estimates up to the division manager, who once again adjusts them in light of his understanding of prospects for the industry, the economy, or conditions within the company itself. The division manager then sends the revised estimates up to the budget committee, who gives them careful consideration in view of future pricing policies, produc-

EXHIBIT 2–1 INTERRELATIONSHIPS IN BUDGET CONSTRUCTION

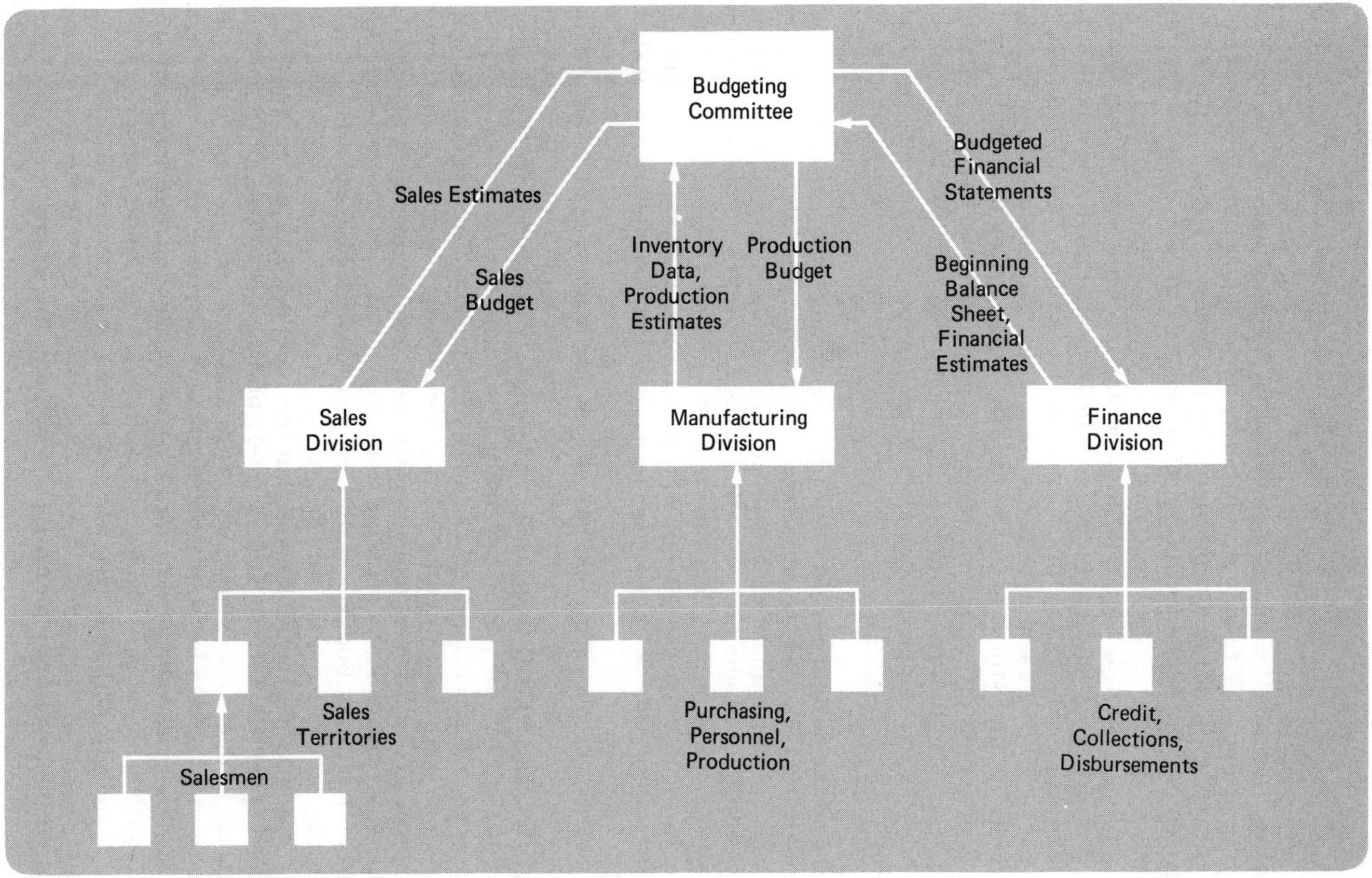

tion capacities, profit expectations, and other internal and external constraints. The estimates may be revised yet further by use of sophisticated techniques such as trend analysis or cycle projections, or by action of top executives or their budget committee representatives, all of whom can take part in the revision process.

After careful deliberation and, perhaps, several preliminary drafts, the budget committee prepares a series of schedules that are distributed downward throughout the sales organization. Abstracted versions of sales projections are sent out to executives representing production, purchasing, finance, and administration. After studying the budget, these executives turn to the lower-level managers in their divisions for further information to send back up to the budget committee. The budget committee then may prepare additional budgets or schedules for transmission back down the chain of command, as shown in Exhibit 2–1.

Detail and the budget period   The policies formulated by top management may be set forth in a broad, brief statement, but the schedules used in operating divisions must be much more detailed. For example, an executive could set a policy calling for production of 10,000 units of output in a one-sentence memo. Operating managers need carefully detailed schedules covering the number and type of workers, the necessary flow of raw materials, and availability of machines, supplies, and facilities in order to accomplish the goal spelled out in that one-sentence memo.

The time period of a budget as well as the amount of detail in a budget varies with the level of the organization to which it applies. The top executive who established the 10,000-unit production policy is concerned with a budget that covers the entire time period necessary to produce the 10,000 units. Operating budgets, on the other hand, cover a very short period of time. Foremen schedule the work of their departments on a day-to-day basis, or, at most, on a week-to-week basis. They have to make certain that enough workers, materials, and machines are available to maintain continuous production every day. The time period and detail of budgets at different organizational levels are illustrated in Exhibit 2–2.

Budgets may be so detailed that the time, place, and amount of required input are specified. At the other extreme, a budget may call only for a specific level of output. Budgets may span periods ranging from one day to a year or longer. Some capital budgets for plant and equipment purchases may cover a period as long as ten years. *The usual planning period for top management in most organizations is one year, broken down into quarters or months.*

Typically, different levels of management are concerned with different types of tasks, as illustrated in Exhibit 2–2. Top management is responsible primarily for **strategic planning**, or setting the organization's objectives. Second-level (or divisional) management is concerned with **tactical planning**

**EXHIBIT 2–2 TIMING, DETAIL, AND FUNCTION OF BUDGETS
AT DIFFERENT ORGANIZATIONAL LEVELS**

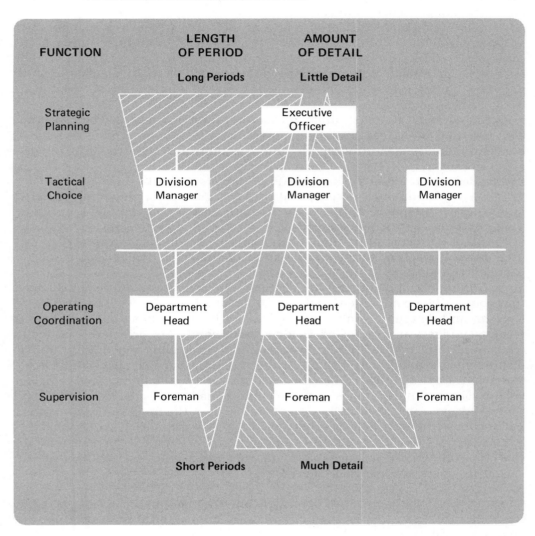

(what means should be used to achieve the goals). Third-level (departmental) management is concerned with operating decisions, particularly coordinating labor, materials, and facilities to achieve the organization's goals. The last level of management (foremen) is responsible for supervision of production activities.

Budgeting practices vary widely. A comprehensive system of budgeting or **master budget** consists of at least three types of budgets: **operating budgets**,

financial budgets, and **special-decision budgets**. Most medium-sized or large companies prepare budgets for some of their operations, but many do not prepare truly comprehensive budgets.

Operating budgets deal with primary activities of the organization, such as sales, production, purchasing, and labor scheduling. *Financial budgets* are concerned with expected cash receipts or disbursements, financial position, and results of operations. Sub-budgets produced under financial budgets include: cash receipts budgets, cash disbursement budgets, administrative expenditure budgets, budgeted balance sheets, income statements, and statements of sources and applications of funds. *Special-decision budgets* may be concerned with inventory levels, capital budgets, graphic presentations of budgets, such as break-even analysis, control reports, and feasibility studies. Operating budgets are discussed in this chapter. Financial budgets are described in Chapter 3, and special-decision budgets are discussed in Chapters 4 and 14 through 17.

Many companies prepare individual segments of the comprehensive budget for certain purposes but do not prepare a master budget that coordinates them. Although segmented budgeting is feasible, its major weakness is the lack of coordination between the individual budgets. A principal advantage of comprehensive budgeting is the coordination of the individual division and departmental budgets.

Exhibit 2–3 illustrates the relationships among the different schedules that constitute a comprehensive budgeting plan. The sales forecast directly relates to, and determines, amounts appearing in the production budget, cash receipts budget, and budgeted **income statement**. The production schedule contributes inputs to the labor, material, and purchasing schedules, the cash disbursements budget, as well as to the budgeted balance sheet and income statement. Capital budgets affect the cash disbursements budget and budgeted balance sheet. Similarly, most other schedules may be affected by or may affect these budgets. After all other budgets are prepared, the budgeted balance sheet and income statement may be constructed. They are produced last because they rely on figures derived from other budgets and schedules. For example, the expected-ending cash balance uses data from the beginning cash balance, the cash disbursements, and the cash receipts.

An example   The construction of budgets and the relationships among separate schedules are illustrated by the following projections and facts concerning the Acme Corporation.

The Acme Corporation has a planning horizon of three months, January, February, and March. Acme manufactures and retails two products in three sales territories. Ordinarily, sales increase as the year progresses. Thus, the materials, labor, and other expenses needed for production increase with each passing month, but cash collections do not keep pace with them because some sales are made on credit. Acme meets this cash shortage by short-term borrowing from banks.

EXHIBIT 2–3   MASTER BUDGET INTERRELATIONSHIPS

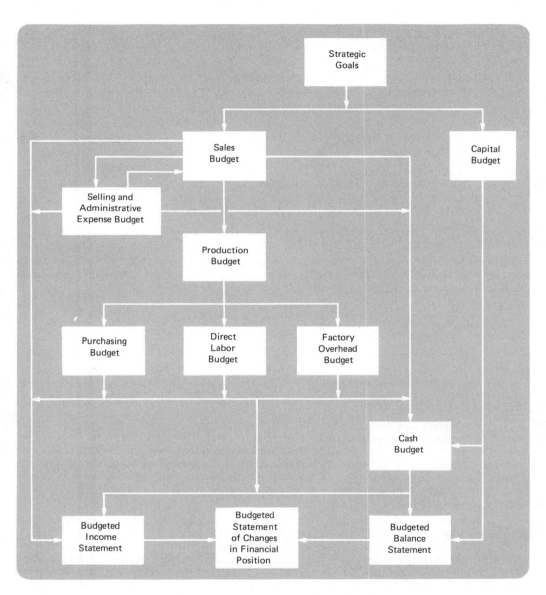

Data about the assets and liabilities for the period just ended are obtained from the December 31, 19X1 balance sheet. Assets represent the inputs available to Acme at the start of the current planning period, and liabilities represent its obligations at that time. As of December 31, 19X1, Acme had:

Assets		
Cash	$	4,000
Accounts receivable		5,000
(from December sales)		
Raw materials		5,250
Finished product X[1]		1,920
(480 units at $4.00)		
Finished product Y		6,000
(1200 units at $5.00)		
Plant and equipment		100,000
(less depreciation)	−	20,000
Total assets		$102,170
Liabilities		
Accounts payable	$	4,100
(December purchases)		
Dividends payable		1,000
(due Jan. 5, 19X2)		
Total liabilities	$	5,100

Sales for the past December were $10,000. Monthly unit sales are forecast as illustrated below. Territories 1, 2, and 3, respectively, produce 10%, 20%, and 70% of Product X sales and 50%, 30%, and 20% of Product Y sales. Product X sells for $5 per unit, Product Y is priced at $7.

Units	Jan.	Feb.	Mar.	Apr.
X	600	700	800	900
Y	1500	1600	1700	1800

Fifty percent of all sales are made for cash. The credit sales are collected in the following month. The accounts receivable in January represent the credit sales made in December (50% of $10,000).

Both Products X and Y are made with one common material, which costs $.50 per pound. X requires 2 lbs. of material per unit, and Y requires 4 lbs. Labor receives $3 per hour. One unit of either X or Y can be produced in one hour. Inventories of X, Y, and raw materials available at the beginning of January are described above. At the end of any month, Acme wishes to maintain a basic finished-goods inventory equal to 80% of the next month's sales and a raw material inventory equal to 150% of the amount used for current production.

Purchase terms available to Acme are net, 30 days, and all purchases are paid for the month after they are made. Accounts payable on January 1 represent purchases made in December. Salaries and wages are paid during the month they are earned. Sales commissions are 5% of sales and are paid during the month earned. A production machine costing $500 is on order. It will be delivered and paid for during February. Acme wishes to maintain a minimum cash balance of $4,000 at the end of each month. Money may be borrowed or repaid in multiples of $1,000. Interest on loans is 6% per year. Loans are

[1]Acme values finished-goods inventory at the cost of direct labor and material, a form of "direct costing" discussed in Section Three of this book.

initiated on the first day of the month and repaid on the last day of a month. Interest on loans of 6% per year, is paid when principal is repaid.

Other monthly expenses are as follows:

Salaries	$500	paid as incurred
Rent	$200	paid as incurred
Depreciation	$600	
Miscellaneous	1% of sales	paid as incurred

OPERATING BUDGETS

Operating budgets are concerned primarily with specified physical activities. For example, the sales budget is distributed to the sales division, the production budget to the production division, and the purchasing budget to the purchasing division. All production budgets contain information on the timing of expected events as well as on the amounts of inputs or outputs required.

Because the sales function is the focal point of all business activity, the sales budget is of prime importance. After sales activity has been budgeted in terms of units or dollars of various products to be sold, production schedules can be prepared. Like the sales budget, the production schedule is presented in terms of units. It must consider existing quantities in inventory and the level of ending inventory desired at the end of the period. The production budget may consist of several schedules, one for each major type of production input, that is, one for direct labor, direct materials, and collateral activity. Given the production schedules for materials, a purchasing budget of raw materials can be prepared. Here again, a separate purchasing schedule could be prepared for each type of raw material.

Each type of budget would be prepared in several versions and distributed to every executive responsible for the activity discussed in the budget. Each version would cover a period corresponding to the receiver's needs, and would contain enough detail for him to accomplish his task.

Sales budget   The sales budget for Acme Corporation might look exactly like the raw sales projection data, or these data might be combined, as shown in Exhibit 2–4. One copy of the budget would be distributed to the territory sales managers and their superior to serve as a communication, coordination, and motivational device.

Production budget   Production forecasts are based on sales estimates. The desired level of sales of each product is combined with information about the beginning level and desired level of ending inventories. The units of budgeted production may be calculated as follows: Units to be produced = planned sales + desired ending inventory balance − beginning inventory balance, as shown in

EXHIBIT 2–4   ACME CORPORATION SALES BUDGET

Month/Product	Units	Price	Revenue	Territory 1	Territory 2	Territory 3
January						
Product X	600	$5	$ 3,000	$ 300	$ 600	$ 2,100
Product Y	1,500	$7	$10,500	$ 5,250	$ 3,150	$ 2,100
Total			$13,500	$ 5,550	$ 3,750	$ 4,200
February						
Product X	700	$5	$ 3,500	$ 350	$ 700	$ 2,450
Product Y	1,600	$7	$11,200	$ 5,600	$ 3,360	$ 2,240
Total			$14,700	$ 5,950	$ 4,060	$ 4,690
March						
Product X	800	$5	$ 4,000	$ 400	$ 800	$ 2,800
Product Y	1,700	$7	$11,900	$ 5,950	$ 3,570	$ 2,380
Total			$15,900	$ 6,350	$ 4,370	$ 5,180
First Quarter Total			$44,100	$17,850	$12,180	$14,070
April						
Product X	900	$5	$ 4,500	$ 450	$ 900	$ 3,150
Product Y	1,800	$7	$12,600	$ 6,300	$ 3,780	$ 2,520
Total			$17,100	$ 6,750	$ 4,680	$ 5,670

SOURCE: Information in the problem.

Exhibit 2–5. This budget format includes an entry for Total Production Needs. Most manufacturing organizations produce units of output both for immediate sale and for future sale. Units currently produced for future sale are identified in the budget as Desired Ending Inventory, i.e., unsold units remaining on hand at the end of the period. Total production needs can be satisfied both by using units out of beginning inventory and by using new units from current production.

The Acme production budget also highlights two common relationships. First, notice that the desired ending inventory balance for one period and the beginning inventory balance for the next period are equal. The amount remaining at the end of one period is the amount available at the start of the next period. A second relationship links the desired balance of ending inventory with next period's expected sales. For example, a department store would wish to maintain a large inventory balance of toys at the end of November so that December could open with the same large balance in anticipation of large sales during December. In contrast, the department store would desire a small ending balance of toys at the end of December in anticipation of reduced toy sales during January. For Acme, **expected** sales of Product X during January and February are 600 and 700

EXHIBIT 2-5   ACME CORPORATION PRODUCTION BUDGET

	Jan.	Feb.	Mar	Apr.
X Units for Sale[A]	600	700	800	900
+ Desired Ending Inventory[B]	560	640	720	
Total Production Needs	1,160	1,340	1,520	
− Beginning Inventory	480[C]	560	640	
X To Be Produced	680	780	880	
Y Units for Sale[A]	1,500	1,600	1,700	1,800
+ Desired Ending Inventory[B]	1,280	1,360	1,440	
Total Production Needs	2,780	2,960	3,140	
− Beginning Inventory	1,200[C]	1,280	1,360	
Y To Be Produced	1,580	1,680	1,780	

SOURCES: [A] Exhibit 2-4.
  [B] 80% of next month's sales.
  [C] Information in the problem.

units, respectively. Desired ending inventory for January is established at 80% of sales for February: .8 × 700 = 560. These 560 units of Product X remaining at the end of January will be available at the start of February, i.e, beginning inventory is linked to the ending balance of the preceding month. Another way of stating this second relationship is that the *beginning* inventory balance is linked with the *current* period's sales activity, e.g., the 560 units on hand at the beginning of February represent 80% of February's expected sales.

Purchasing budget   Once the budgeted production level has been determined, a material usage and purchasing budget can be constructed. Here again, material usage depends on the level of production activity as well as on beginning and desired ending inventory levels. The purchase amount may be calculated as follows: Purchases = planned usage + desired ending material inventory − beginning inventory balances. Both the purchasing budget (Exhibit 2-6) and the production budget are calculated in the same way.

The Acme purchasing budget highlights three common relationships. First, notice the link between the production budget and the purchasing budget. The number of units to be produced is transferred from the production budget to the purchasing budget, since the need to maintain a supply of material on hand

EXHIBIT 2-6   ACME CORPORATION PURCHASING BUDGET

	Jan.	Feb.	Mar.
Units of X to be Produced[A]	680	780	880
Pounds Per Unit[B]	2	2	2
Material Pounds for X	1,360	1,560	1,760
Units of Y to be Produced[A]	1,580	1,680	1,780
Pounds Per Unit[B]	4	4	4
Material Pounds for Y	6,320	6,720	7,120
TOTAL POUNDS FOR PRODUCTION	7,680	8,280	8,880
+ Desired Ending Balance[C]	11,520	12,420	13,320
Total Material Needs	19,200	20,700	22,200
− Beginning Inventory	10,500	11,520	12,420
Amount to be Purchased	8,700	9,180	9,780
Amount to be Purchased	8,700	9,180	9,780
Cost Per Pound[B]	$ .50	$ .50	$ .50
Cost of Purchases	$ 4,350	$ 4,590	$ 4,890

SOURCES: [A] Exhibit 2-5.
          [B] Information in the problem.
          [C] 150% of current month total production pounds.

for production requirements is one reason for purchasing raw material. For example, the 680 units of Product X to be produced in January can be translated into 1,360 pounds of material needed for production during the month. Second, the balance remaining at the end of one month is available at the beginning of the following month: the 11,520 pounds of material remaining in inventory at the end of January is available for use in February. Third, the desired ending balance in inventory is linked to the amount used for current production. Acme maintains an ending balance equal to 150% of total pounds for current production: in January, the balance of 11,520 pounds is determined at 150% of 7,680 pounds. Need for such large ending balances hinges upon many factors such as the reliability of suppliers, the length of time between placing an order and receiving delivery, and the steadiness of the production process. (Further discussion about the size of inventory balances appears in Chapter 17.) Unlike Acme,

EXHIBIT 2–7 ACME CORPORATION LABOR SCHEDULE

	Jan.	Feb.	Mar.
Units X to Be Produced[A]	680	780	880
+ Units Y to Be Produced[A]	1,580	1,680	1,780
Total Units	2,260	2,460	2,660
Total Hours at 1 Hour per Unit[B]	2,260	2,460	2,660
Total Cost at $3 per Hour[B]	$6,780	$7,380	$7,980

SOURCES: [A]Exhibit 2–5.
[B]Information in the problem.

some producers link the desired ending balance for one month to the production needs for the following month.

Labor schedule   A direct labor schedule also may be prepared from data contained in the production budget. The direct labor hours to be incurred depend on the number of units to be produced and the amount of labor required per unit, as shown in Exhibit 2–7.

FINANCIAL BUDGETS

All the data contained in the operating budgets can be translated into dollar amounts for representation in financial budgets. The budgeted sales activity can be converted into estimated revenues. Cost of production may be calculated in separate schedules, one for materials, another for labor. Purchase costs can be calculated by multiplying the raw material needs by the estimated costs of obtaining those materials.

Expenditures budgets   Management allocates specific amounts to certain service functions within the organization, and these amounts set a limit on the activities they can undertake. For example, many manufacturing firms have research and development departments. Research and development activities can be conducted on any scale the company is willing to finance. The scope of advertising, promotion, and other internal services is outlined in like manner. In each case, management sets the maximum amount it is willing to spend on the particular functions.

The maximum amount allocated to each service department is often set forth in a schedule called an expenditures budget. An expenditures budget for

EXHIBIT 2–8   ACME CORPORATION ADVERTISING BUDGET

	Jan.	Feb.	Mar.
Total Expenditure Allowed	$135	$147	$159
Radio	$ 50	$ 27	—0—
Newspaper	85	—0—	—0—
Magazine	—0—	120	$159
Total Allocation	$135	$147	$159

Acme's advertising department is illustrated in Exhibit 2–8. The total amount to be spent on advertising would be determined by top-level management, but the total advertising expenditure would be allocated to different media by the advertising department. The Acme advertising budget reflects a total cost of $135 for the month of January.

Cash collections schedule   Exhibit 2–9 illustrates a summarized cash collections schedule for Acme Corporation. The total sales amounts are obtained directly from the sales budget. This total is broken down into credit sales and cash sales: for Acme, credit sales amounted to 50% of total sales. Collections on account are added to cash sales to determine total cash collections. The $5,000

EXHIBIT 2–9   ACME CORPORATION CASH COLLECTIONS SCHEDULE

	Jan.	Feb.	Mar.
Total Sales[A]	$13,500	$14,700	$15,900
— Credit Sales (50%)[B]	6,750	7,350	7,950
Cash Sales	$ 6,750	$ 7,350	$ 7,950
+ Collections on Account[B]	5,000[C]	6,750	7,350
Cash Collections	$11,750	$14,100	$15,300

SOURCES: [A] Exhibit 2-4.
[B] 50% of all sales are for credit, and these amounts are collected during the month following sale.
[C] Information contained in the problem.

EXHIBIT 2–10   ACME CORPORATION CASH DISBURSEMENTS SCHEDULE

	Jan.	Feb.	Mar.
Raw Material Purchases	$ 4,100[A]	$ 4,350[B]	$ 4,590[B]
Salaries [A]	500	500	500
Wages (labor)[C]	6,780	7,380	7,980
Sales Commission (.5%)[D]	675	735	795
Rent[A]	200	200	200
Miscellaneous (advertising)[E]	135	147	159
Purchase of Machine[A]		500	
Dividends[A]	1,000		
Total Disbursements	$13,390	$13,812	$14,224

SOURCES: [A]Information in the problem.
        [B]Exhibit 2-6.
        [C]Exhibit 2-7.
        [D]Exhibit 2-4.
        [E]Exhibit 2-8.

collected on account in January relates to the credit sales in December: credit sales in one month are linked to cash collections in the following month.

Cash disbursements schedule   A cash disbursements schedule for Acme Corporation is illustrated in Exhibit 2–10. The line labeled "raw material purchases" really represents the payment of accounts payable, since there is a one-month lag between making purchases and paying for them. The $4,100 listed for January represents purchases made in December. Information about salaries, rent, cost of the machine acquired in February, and dividends are specified on pages 42–43. Sales commissions are .5% of sales, as determined in the sales budget. Wages and advertising are determined on their separate schedules. Total disbursements represent the sum of the monthly expenditures for each item.

Cash budget   Exhibit 2–11 illustrates a cash budget for Acme Corporation. The $4,000 beginning balance for January represents the ending balance for December; this relationship between beginning and ending cash balances applies every month in Acme's cash budget. Information on cash collections and disbursements is obtained from separate schedules listing details on these topics. The desired ending balance of cash reflects management's policy of maintaining a sufficient balance to ensure liquidity. Deficiencies of cash needs over the amount available will be borrowed (as in January), and excess cash will be used to repay loans (as in March). Interest is paid upon the repayment of principal.

EXHIBIT 2–11   ACME CORPORATION CASH BUDGET

	Jan.	Feb.	Mar.
Beginning Balance	$ 4,000[A]	$ 4,360	$ 4,684
+ Cash Collections[B]	11,750	14,100	15,300
Cash Available	$15,750	$18,460	$19,948
– Cash Disbursements[C]	13,390	13,812	14,224
Balance	$ 2,360	$ 4,648	$ 5,724
Desired Ending Cash Balance[A]	$ 4,000	$ 4,000	$ 4,000
Borrowing (repayments)	$ 2,000	–0–	$ (1,000)
Interest[D]		–0–	(15)
Cash Balance, Ending	$ 4,360	$ 4,648	$ 4,709

SOURCES: [A] Information in the problem.
          [B] Exhibit 2-9.
          [C] Exhibit 2-10.
          [D] $1,000 at 6% per year for three months. Another $15 is accrued but unpaid.

Budgeted financial statements   Last of all, budgeted financial statements, such as an income statement and balance sheet, may be prepared. The budgeted income statement consists of estimated revenues from the sales budget, selling costs from the expenditures budget, cost of goods sold from the production budget, and administrative expenses from the expenditures budgets. This information produces a budgeted profit figure.

Data for a budgeted balance sheet come from the cash budget, the production budget, the sales budget, and the expenditures budget, for cash, inventory, accounts receivable, and plant or equipment, respectively. Data on liabilities also come from the cash budget. On the basis of this information, combined with data from last year's balance sheet, a balance sheet can be prepared. Budgeted income statements and balance sheets are illustrated in Chapter 3.

SPECIAL-DECISION BUDGETS

Operating and financial budgets are usually prepared on a routine basis. Special-decision budgets, on the other hand, are nonroutine forecasts dealing with such things as investment decisions, graphic presentations, control reports, and feasibility studies. Special budgets on inventory levels, capital expenditures, break-even analysis, and others are discussed in following chapters.

HUMAN ASPECTS OF BUDGETING

Budgets are prepared to help managers communicate goals to employees, to coordinate their activities, motivate them to accomplish the goals, and evaluate their performance. The budget itself is simply a tool used by management. If budgeting is abused, however, **dysfunctional consequences** may affect the whole organization.

The importance of human behavior in budgeting cannot be overemphasized. For example, consider a manager who demands that his budgeted goals be attained although underlying conditions have changed or employees are incapable of producing at the desired level. In such a case, a successful manager modifies his goals, even though they may deviate from the budget as a result. Similarly, if the budget calls for performance that is beyond the capabilities of a given department, the executive should not make unreasonable demands on his employees, or he may be faced with slow-downs, high absenteeism, sabotage, or high employee turnover.

Consider a case in which a department head thinks that a budget infringes on his authority by limiting his ability to incur costs, schedule labor, or reroute material handling. This department head may supply misinformation to the budget committee when it requests data and then ignore the modified budgets that are sent to him. The department head may further disrupt the budgeting process by permitting unproductive delays or slack time in the operation of his department. Here the budgeting process fails.

Budgeting succeeds only when employees are sympathetic to its aims, cooperative in working to attain those aims, and conscientious in their performance. If budgets are properly understood, they can do much to help management advance its objectives.

SUMMARY

A budget is a quantitative expression of a plan, which lists future objectives and the means for attaining those objectives. Objectives may relate to activities, such as purchasing, selling, producing, or disbursing, or they may relate to positions, such as desired ending balance of inventory, cash, or debt-equity positions. Budgets serve several purposes: they communicate budgeted goals to lower-level employees, coordinate their activities, motivate them to strive to attain the goals, and provide a yardstick against which to measure the performance of those employees.

Budgets always cover some period in the future. The length of the budget period depends on the activity being budgeted. For example, cash budgets may be prepared on a day-to-day basis, work schedules on a weekly basis, sales forecasts on a monthly basis, desired debt-equity position on a yearly basis, and budgets for capital acquisitions over a span of several years.

The foundation for budgeting is the expected level of goods to be distributed or services to be performed. Production, purchasing, labor scheduling, and cost incurrence all depend on the rate of output activity that is expected. The information upon which budgets are based is obtained from all levels of the organization and combined by the budget committee. Unit sales information is derived from the sales division, production information from the manufacturing division, and finance information from the finance division. The data are combined in terms of physical units first and are then translated into dollars. In many firms, comprehensive budgeting plans involve schedules for sales, production, purchasing, cash receipts, cash disbursements, and budgeted financial statements. After budgets are reviewed, revised, and completed, they are usually distributed back down through the organization to the people responsible for attaining the budgeted goals. Many specialized accounting terms are associated with the budgeting process: the Glossary at the end of the text provides definitions for each term printed in boldface type.

SUGGESTED READINGS

Foran, Michael. "Relating the Budget Process to the Organization and Its Members." *Managerial Planning*, May/June, 1976.

Fox, Harold. "A Budget Format with Operational Relevance." *Managerial Planning*, January/February, 1976.

Martin, Donald. "Planning and the Corporate Philosophy." *Managerial Planning*, September/October, 1976.

Nelson, W. G. "The Use of the Economic Forecasting Staff." *Financial Executive*, September 1976.

QUESTIONS[a]

2–1   Define the word *budget*.

2–2   List three purposes of budgets and explain why each is important.

2–3   Which key executives should be included on the budgeting committee? Why?

[a]Questions, exercises, and problems that extend coverage beyond the discussion in the chapter are indicated by an asterisk *.

2–4 Which of the budgeting committee members has the responsibility of actually drawing up the budget? Why?

2–5 Budget detail decreases as one climbs the organizational ladder. Why?

2–6 Alco Company maintains a finished-goods inventory equal to 130% of next month's expected sales. The 30% excess provides a margin of safety in case actual sales exceed expected sales. The budgeted sales for January, February, and March are 30,000, 20,000, and 30,000 units, respectively. How many units should Alco produce during the month of February?

2–7 The expected production for June and July are, 200 units and 150 units, respectively. Managerial policy states that ending inventory of raw materials should be equal to 20% of the amount needed for next month's production. One unit of product requires two pounds of raw material. How many pounds of raw material should be purchased during June?

2–8 Bell Company makes 60% of its sales for cash and the remainder on account. It is expected that 75% of charge sales will be collected in the month following the sale, 20% in the second following month, and that 5% will be uncollectible. Sales for May and June were $200,000 and $300,000, respectively. Budgeted sales for July are $100,000. How much are the budgeted cash receipts for July?

2–9 Canco Company has an inventory of 30,000 units on hand, and the budget calls for an ending balance of 25,000 units on hand at the end of the month. The budget calls for Canco to produce 75,000 units during the month. How many units must Canco sell to meet its budget?

2–10 Dell Company has 80,000 units on hand but expects to sell 100,000 during the coming month. Dell's budget calls for it to have 95,000 units on hand at the end of the coming month. How many units must Dell produce?

2–11 Eazy Company has a budget that sets expected sales at 170,000 units, expected production at 165,000 units, and an expected ending inventory at 70,000 units. How many units are in beginning inventory?

EXERCISES

2–12 Below are data on three independent cases. Substitute a number for each letter to complete a production budget.

	Case 1	Case 2	Case 3
Beginning finished-goods inventory	7	4	6
Ending finished-goods inventory	5	b	4
Units to be produced	14	15	c
Units to be sold	a	9	13

2–13   The supervisor of the material handling department had to develop a labor schedule for the month of June. Each handler can move 2,000 pounds (or 1 ton) of raw material per hour, 40 hours per week, 4 weeks per month. One finished unit requires ½ a ton of raw material (1 ton per 2 finished units), and the company expects to sell 75,000 finished units during June. Beginning and desired ending balances of finished goods and raw materials are as follows:

	Beginning Balance	Ending Balance
Finished goods (units)	15,000	10,000
Raw materials (tons)	1,000	1,200

How many material handlers must be scheduled to transport the raw materials purchased during June?

2–14   Copen Company expects to sell 2,000 units in June and 4,000 in July. At the end of May, Copen has 500 units on hand, since its policy is to maintain ending finished-goods inventories at ¼ expected next-month activity. Raw materials on May 30 amount to 5,000 pounds; the desired level on June 30 is 3,000 pounds. Eight pounds are required to make one finished unit. How many pounds of raw materials should Copen buy in June? How many finished units does Copen expect to make in June?

2–15   The Zel Company, a wholesaler, budgeted the following sales for June, July, and August:

	June 19X1	July 19X1	August 19X1
Sales on account	$1,500,000	$1,600,000	$1,700,000
Cash sales	200,000	210,000	220,000
Total sales	$1,700,000	$1,810,000	$1,920,000

All merchandise is marked up to sell at its invoice cost plus 25%. Merchandise inventories at the beginning of each month are at 30% of that month's projected cost of goods sold.

(A)   What is the cost of goods sold for the month of June 19X1 expected to be?

(B)   What are merchandise purchases for July 19X1 expected to be?

(AICPA adapted)

2–16   The Acme Company started the month of June with 10,000 units in its inventory. Each unit costs $3. During the month of June, Acme expects to sell 50,000 units at $5 each. Acme would like to have 8,000 units in inventory at the end of June, both to ensure adequate stock on hand and to facilitate sales in July. Inventory costs are expected to be constant during June, and all purchases made in June will be paid for during July. What dollar amount will Acme have to pay during July for June's purchases?

2–17 Popup Company plans to sell 11,000 widgets in January. Each widget is made with three pounds of material that costs $5 per pound. Twenty percent of purchases made in any month are paid for during that month and the remaining 80% are paid during the following month. Popup plans to start February with the following balances on hand: 3,000 widgets and 10,000 pounds material. Popup's balance sheet for the year just ended reflects the following balances: 4,000 widgets; 8,000 pounds of raw material; $82,000 accounts payable. During January, how many units will be produced? How many pounds of raw material will be purchased? How much cash will be paid out during January?

2–18 Flybi Company plans to sell 11,000 widgets in January at an average price of $10 per unit. In recent months, 80% of sales have been collected during the month of sale, and the remaining 20% have been collected the following month. Labor and other operating expenses, which are expected to be $40,000 for the month, are paid as incurred. Depreciation amounts to $6,000 per month. Raw materials purchases during January are expected to cost $60,000; half of them will be paid for in February. Flybi's balance sheet for the year just ended reflects the following balances: Cash, $13,000; Accounts Receivable, $15,000; and Accounts Payable, $25,000. If Flybi doesn't borrow or lend during January, what will the balances be in the Cash account, the Accounts Receivable account, and the Accounts Payable account at the end of the month?

2–19 (A) Arrange the following budgets in the order in which they would most likely be prepared.

(1) Special-decision budget
(2) Cash budget
(3) Production budget
(4) Sales budget
(5) Raw materials purchasing budget
(6) Expenditures budget

(B) Using the following data, prepare a raw materials purchasing budget.

	Units
Predicted Sales	10,000
Units of Raw Materials Required for One Unit of Finished Goods	6
Current Finished-goods Inventory	2,500
Desired Finished-goods Inventory	4,000
Current Raw Materials Inventory	23,000
Desired Ending Raw Materials Inventory	29,000

2–20 (A) On December 31, 19X3, the Orion Co. had a cash balance of

$7,000, accounts receivable of $30,000, and accounts payable of $40,000. The company expects to sell $50,000 worth of goods for $70,000 in January. One-half of all sales are collected during the month of sale and the other half the following month. All purchases are made on account and paid for during the following month. Inventory levels are to remain constant during January. Other expenses and dividends are expected to equal $60,000 during January. If Orion desires to maintain a cash balance of $5,000, what amount must it borrow?

(B) The Orion Co. produces and sells one product at $10 per unit. The company expects to sell 9,500 units during the year. Beginning inventories consisted of 1,000 units, and the desired ending inventory is 1,500 units. Two pounds of raw material are needed to produce one finished unit. At the beginning of the year, 4,000 lbs. were on hand, and the desired ending balance is budgeted for 1,000 lbs. How many pounds of raw material should be purchased to meet all of the budgeted objectives?

2–21   The Prentice Mill Company produces its budget in September or early October for a budget year that starts January 1. This year, the purchasing department failed to submit a budget, because, the purchasing agent stated, the department was too busy purchasing material for the next year's production to draw up a budget.

(A) What is wrong with this budget system?

(B) What should be done with the time constraints of budgeting?

(C) Are the purchasing department and the budget department working at cross-purposes? Discuss.

(D) What purpose does the Prentice Mill Company budget serve?

2–22   Howard Tull is the superintendent of the stamping plant. He called the accounting office as soon as he heard that the company had received a large order for steel stampings, because he knew that added labor and additional machinery and materials would have to be rented or purchased to fill the order. Howard was upset because he knew that this increase in labor and material would make it impossible to meet this year's budget.

(A) What should the accounting department tell Howard?

(B) If the labor budget were tied to production units, would Howard's labor problem be relieved?

(C) Would a drastic decrease in production make Howard happy? If labor is directly related to production, shouldn't the budget reflect this relationship? Discuss.

2–23   The Strom Brewing Company based its yearly budget on the formulas developed by Ed Bush. Only Ed knew how they worked, and he took all year to develop next year's budget. When Ed died, the new budget director found that Ed's formulas were nothing more than last year's actual costs rounded to even thousands and augmented by any additional data about future volumes or prices that Ed could glean during the year.

(A) Why had this type of budget worked in the past?

(B) Because last year was a poor year for Strom Brewing, the plant manager decided to post the monthly budget figures as an incentive to the employees this year. Would Ed's budget work well this year? What type of budget base would work best for this year?

(C) Would a budget based on maximum capacity serve management best for control purposes? For incentive purposes? For any purpose?

2-24   The Northwest regional sales manager, Hap Loman, was strongly opposed to budgeting. Said he, "I'm wasting a whole day estimating next year's sales figures for the budgeting department. Then during the year, I'll spend most of my time explaining differences in these figures to these same people. If they don't like my figures, why do they ask me for them? Why don't they do it themselves, and then they can call each other up all year?"

(A) Why do accountants rely on sales managers to forecast sales? Can accountants forecast sales as accurately as sales managers?

(B) What alternatives to estimates by sales managers are available? What are the problems with these methods?

(C) Since sales figures are so hard to estimate, why not take cost figures and add the expected profit in order to "back into" expected sales?

2-25   The Box Company has made certain estimates for next year. These estimates are necessary for establishing the comprehensive budget. The estimates are as follows:

Sales
Territory 1: 200 units Product A, 300 units Product B
Territory 2: 400 units Product A, 300 units Product B
Price per unit: Product A, $10, Product B, $15

Material
Product A, 21 lbs. of sand; Product B, 10 lbs. of sand

Inventories
Finished Goods to increase by 80 units of Product A and 40 units of Product B. Raw Materials to remain the same as last year.

(A) Who establishes the figures for the sales by territory? Who establishes the unit price? Material weight per unit of product? Unit cost of materials?

(B) Do these figures depend on the sales estimates? Explain.

(C) Where do the estimated inventory figures come from?

(D) Which of the estimates above would be the most crucial? Why?

(E) How much sand should be purchased?

2–26 Figures for the financial budgets are arrived at by manipulating operating budgets.

(A) From which budget does the raw materials inventory figure come? Who is responsible for its accuracy?

(B) From which budget does the finished-goods inventory come? Who is responsible for its accuracy?

(C) From which budget does the cash figure come? Who is responsible for its accuracy?

PROBLEMS

2–27 The cash receipts budget reacts drastically to minor changes in various accounts. For the following items decide (1) whether the net of cash receipts over disbursements went up, went down, or stayed the same, and (2) whether this change would normally cause a drastic change in the cash receipts balance.

(A) The average accounts receivable went from 30 days to 45.

(B) Total sales increased by 5%, but sales on account increased by 10% over last month.

(C) The accounts payable average went from 20 days to 40 days.

(D) Stock dividends were given in a ratio of 1 share for each 10 already held.

(E) Wages had been paid one week after the work period ended, but now will be paid at the end of the work period.

(F) A $5,000 machine was purchased for cash.

(G) Hourly wages increased by 2%.

2–28 Tomlinson Retail seeks your assistance in developing cash and other budget information for May, June, and July 19X3. At April 30, 19X3, the company had cash of $5,500, accounts receivable of $437,000, inventories of $309,400, and accounts payable of $133,055.

The budget is to be based on the following assumptions:

Sales

1. Each month's sales are billed on the last day of the month.
2. Customers are allowed a 3% discount if payment is made within ten days after the billing date. Receivables are booked gross.
3. Sixty percent of the billings are collected within the discount period, 25% are collected by the end of the month, 9% are collected by the end of the second month, and 6% prove uncollectible.

Purchases
1. Fifty-four percent of all purchases of material and selling, general, and administrative expenses are paid in the month purchased and the remainder in the following month.
2. Each month's units of ending inventory are equal to 130% of the next month's units of sales.
3. The cost of each unit of inventory is $20.
4. Selling, general, and administrative expenses of which $2,000 is depreciation, are equal to 15% of the current month's sales.

Actual and projected sales are as follows:

19X3	Dollars	Units
March	$354,000	11,800
April	363,000	12,100
May	357,000	11,900
June	342,000	11,400
July	360,000	12,000
August	366,000	12,200

(A) How much are budgeted cash disbursements during the month of June 19X3?

(B) How much are budgeted cash collections during the month of May 19X3?

(C) What is the budgeted number of units of inventory to be purchased during July 19X3?

(AICPA adapted)

2–29 The Ajax Company has a planning horizon of three months, January through March. Ajax manufactures and sells three products in two sales territories. The following is a forecast of monthly unit sales.

Territory 1 and 2, respectively, account for 20% and 80% of Product X, 60% and 40% of Product Y, and 70% and 30% of Product Z. Products X, Y, and Z, respectively, sell for $6, $7, and $8. Forty percent of all sales are made for cash; all credit sales are collected during the following month. All three products are made with one common material that costs $1 per pound. Products X, Y, and Z, respectively, require 1, 2, and 2 pounds of material per unit. Labor costing $4 per hour produces output at the following rates: 2X per hour, 4Y per hour, and 6Z per hour. At the end of any month, Ajax wishes to maintain a basic finished-goods inventory equal to 70% of next month's sales, and a raw material inventory equal to 120% of the current month's production needs. Ajax pays for one quarter of its purchases during the current month and pays the balance during the following month. Salaries, wages, rent, and research and development costs are paid as incurred. Sales commissions are 5% of sales, and research and development costs are 2% of sales. Salaries amount to $600 per month, and rent is $400 per month. Monthly depreciation is $1,000, and Ajax plans on buying a machine for $4,000 at the end of March. Ajax wishes to maintain cash balance of $5,000 at the end of each month. Money can be borrowed at 6% interest in multiples of $1,000, and all loans must be outstanding for a minimum of 30 days.

Presented below are two schedules, the first a sales forecast and the second a balance sheet for the year just ended, 19X0.

Ajax Company Sales Forecast, 19X1 (in units)

Products	January	February	March	April
X	500	500	500	500
Y	600	700	800	900
Z	900	500	300	100

Ajax Company Balance Sheet, 19X0

Cash			$ 5,100
Accounts Receivable (from Dec. sales)			8,600
Inventories (direct labor and materials):			
Raw Materials	(4,320 lbs. @ $1)	$ 4,320	
Product X	(350 @ $3.00)	1,050	
Product Y	(420 @ $3.00)	1,260	
Product Z	(630 @ $2.67)	1,680	8,310
Plant and Equipment		$150,000	
Accumulated Depreciation		30,000	120,000
Total			$142,010
Accounts Payable (Dec. purchases)			$ 2,700
Loan Payable			5,000
Interest Payable			100
Owners' Equity			134,210
Total			$142,010

Prepare a master budget consisting of a sales forecast, production budget, purchasing budget, labor schedule, and a cash budget.

*2–30   The usual planning period in many organizations is one year, broken down by quarters or months. *Continuous budgets* maintain a twelve-month forecast by continually adding a month or a quarter in the future, as the month or quarter just ended is dropped. Thus, it would be possible in continuous budgets to schedule activity for the next week on a day-to-day basis, activity for the following three weeks on a week-to-week basis, the following two months on a month-to-month basis, and the following three quarters on a quarter-to-quarter basis. As each week passes, a continuous budget can be updated by dropping the week that is just completed, scheduling activity for the forthcoming fourth week, and adjusting the remaining monthly and quarterly periods in the budget. That is, continuous budgeting requires a constant rethinking about the forthcoming twelve months.

The Cope Corporation has a three-month planning horizon, and it maintains a continuous purchasing budget. Cope wishes to have an ending inventory balance equal to 150% of the current month's production needs. The current inventory of ten tons of material is just sufficient to produce the current month's production of 100,000 units. Production is expected to grow at a rate of 10% per month for the next two months and shrink by 20% per month thereafter.

(A) Prepare a purchasing budget for the first three months.

(B) At the end of the first month, the actual ending inventory equalled 17 tons, rather than the amount originally planned. The deviation was caused by a one-time efficiency spurt that is not expected to continue. Prepare a revised three-month budget for periods 2, 3, and 4.

2–31 Many criteria can be used to measure employees' performance. Current performance can be measured relative to past performance, performance of other workers doing the same type of tasks, some independently derived goal, or the level of output indicated in the budget.

Assume that you are a production manager who is responsible for the performance of four foremen. You are given a summary report of the output (in units) for each foreman's department for three years, as shown below. Data for each year consist of a forecast made by management at the beginning of the year and the actual results for the year.

| | 19X1 | | 19X2 | | 19X3 | |
Department	Forecast	Actual	Forecast	Actual	Forecast	Actual
1	6,000	5,000	7,000	6,000	8,000	7,000
2	5,000	6,000	6,000	6,000	7,000	6,000
3	8,000	9,000	1,000	1,000	9,000	8,000
4	7,000	9,000	4,000	6,000	1,000	3,000

Which department best fulfills the following descriptions?

(A) Worst in its direction of trend of actual production
(B) Best in its rate of change in production
(C) Best in the absolute size of production at the end of 19X3
(D) Worst in its stability of production
(E) Best in meeting the forecast
(F) Worst in meeting the forecast
(G) Better than other departments—the "best"
(H) Worse than other departments

2–32 Arment Co. has sales in the range of $25 to $30 million. It has one manufacturing plant and employs 700 people, including 15 national account salesmen and 80 traveling sales representatives. The home office and plant are in Philadelphia, and the product is distributed east of the Mississippi River. The product is a line of pumps and related fittings used at construction sites, in homes, and in processing plants. The company has total assets equal to 80% of sales. Its capitalization is: accruals and current liabilities, 30%; long-term debt, 15%; and shareholders' equity, 55%. In the last two years, sales have increased 7% each year, and income after taxes has amounted to 5% of sales.

(A) Decisions by top management on a number of important topics are the basis for the annual profit plan. What are these topics and why are they important?

(B) What specific procedures will be followed each year in developing the annual profit plan?

(CMA adapted)

2–33   The Dilly Company marks up all merchandise at 25% of gross purchase price. All purchases are made on account with terms of 1/10, net/60. Purchase discounts, which are recorded as miscellaneous income, are always taken. Normally, 60% of each month's purchases are paid for during the month of purchase, and the other 40% are paid during the first 10 days of the first month after purchase. Inventories of merchandise at the end of each month are kept at 30% of the next month's projected cost of goods sold.

Terms for sales on account are 2/10, net/30. Cash sales are not subject to discount. Fifty percent of each month's sales on account are collected during the month of sale, 45% are collected in the succeeding month, and the remainder are usually uncollectible. Seventy percent of the collections in the month of sale are subject to discount, and 10% of the collections in the succeeding month are subject to discount.

Projected sales data for selected months are shown below. Using this information, answer the following questions about the Dilly Company.

	Sales on Account—Gross	Cash Sales
December	$1,900,000	$400,000
January	1,500,000	250,000
February	1,700,000	350,000
March	1,600,000	300,000

(A) How much are projected gross purchases for January?

(B) How much is projected inventory at the end of December?

(C) How much are projected payments to suppliers during February?

(D) What is the amount of projected sales discounts to be taken by customers making remittances during February?

(E) How much are projected total collections from customers during February?

(AICPA adapted)

*2-34 The administrator of Wright Hospital has presented you with a number of service projects for the year ending June 30, 19X2. Estimated room requirements for inpatients by type of service are:

Type of Patient	Total Patients Expected	Average Number of Days in Hospital		Percent of Regular Patients Selecting Types of Service		
		Regular	Medicare	Private	Semi-Private	Ward
Medical	2,100	7	17	10%	60%	30%
Surgical	2,400	10	15	15	75	10

Ten percent of the patients served by the hospital are expected to be Medicare patients, and all of them are expected to select semi-private rooms. Both the number and proportion of Medicare patients have increased over the past five years. Daily rentals per patient are: $40 for a private room, $35 for a semi-private room, and $25 for a ward.

Operating room charges are based on man-minutes (number of minutes the operating room is in use multipled by number of personnel assisting in the operation). The per man-minute charges are $.13 for inpatients and $.22 for outpatients. Studies for the current year show that operations on inpatients are divided as follows:

Type of Operation	Percentage of Operations	Average Number of Minutes per Operation	Average Number of Personnel Required
A	40%	30	4
B	35	45	5
C	15	90	6
D	10	120	8
	100%		

The same proportion of inpatient operations is expected for the next fiscal year, and 180 outpatients are expected to use the operating room. Outpatient operations average 20 minutes and require the assistance of three persons.

Prepare schedules showing the computation of:

(A) The number of patient days (number of patients multiplied by average stay in hospital) expected by type of patients and service.

(B) The total number of man-minutes expected for operating room services for inpatients and outpatients. For inpatients, show the breakdown of total operating room man-minutes by type of operation.

(C) Expected gross revenue from routine services.

(D) Expected gross revenue from operating room services.

(AICPA adapted)

2–35   A severe illness kept John Johnson, managing partner of a large CPA firm, away from the office for more than four months in late 19X1. Numerous problems arose during his absence, mainly because other personnel were unfamiliar with many aspects of the practice.

After Johnson returned to work, a plan was developed to provide for delegation of administrative authority and responsibility and for standardization of procedures.

The goals of the plan included (1) income objectives, (2) standardized billing procedures (with enough flexibility to permit adjustments by the partners), and (3) assignment schedules to eliminate overtime and to allow for nonchargeable time, such as vacations and illness. The firm plans a 52-week year with five-day, 40-hour weeks.

Continued growth of the firm has required hiring of additional personnel. The current complement, including approved salaries for the fiscal year ending June 30, 19X3, is as follows:

	Annual Salary
Partners	
John B. Johnson, CPA	$24,000
Walter L. Smith, CPA	18,000
Professional Staff	
Supervisor:	
Harold S. Vickers, CPA	17,500
Senior Accountant	
Duane Lowe, CPA	12,500
Assistants	
James M. Kennedy	10,500
Viola O. Quinn	10,500
Secretaries	
Mary Lyons	7,800
Johnnie L. Hammond	6,864
Livia A. Garcia	6,864

The partners have set an annual income target (after partner's salaries) of at least $55,000. The budget for fiscal year 19X3 is 700 hours of chargeable time at $45 per hour for Johnson, and 1,100 hours at $40 per hour for Smith. Johnson and Smith are to devote all other available time, except as specified below, to administration. The billing rates for all other employees including secretaries are to be set at a level sufficient to recover their salaries plus the following overhead items: fringe benefits of $15,230, other operating expenses of $49,380, and a contribution of $20,500 to target income.

The partners agree that salary levels are fair bases for allocating overhead in setting billing rates, with the exception that salary costs of the secretaries' nonchargeable time are to be added to overhead to arrive at total overhead to be allocated. Thus, the billing rate for each secretary will be based upon the salary costs of her chargeable time plus her share of the total overhead. No portion of total overhead is to be allocated to partners' salaries.

The following information is available for nonchargeable time:

1. Because of his recent illness, Johnson expects to be away an additional week. Smith expects no loss of time from illness. All other employees are to be allowed one day off for illness each month (12 days each).

2. Allowable vacations are as follows:

1 month	Johnson
	Smith
3 weeks	Vickers
	Lyons
2 weeks	All other employees

3. The firm observes seven holidays annually. If the holiday falls on a weekend, the office is closed the preceding Friday or the following Monday.

4. Kennedy and Quinn each should be allotted three days to sit for the November 19X2 CPA examination.

5. Hours are budgeted for other miscellaneous activities of the personnel as follows:

	Johnson	Smith	Vickers	Lowe	Kennedy	Quinn	Lyons	Hammond	Garcia
Firm Projects		100	40	40	40		200		
Professional Development	80	80	56	40	40	50	24	16	24
Professional Meetings	184	120	40	40	16	16	24	8	8
Firm Meetings	48	48	48	24	24	24	48	8	8
Community Activities	80	40	40	24	16	16	12		
Office Time (other than firm administration)	—	—	84	72	—	—	1,000	716	808
Total Other Miscellaneous	392	388	308	240	136	106	1,308	748	848

6. Unassigned time should be budgeted for Lowe, Kennedy, and Quinn as 8, 38, and 78 hours, respectively.

(A) Prepare a time allocation budget for Johnson, Smith, and each employee ending with budgeted chargeable time for the year ending June 30, 19X3.

(B) Independently of your solution to part (A), and assuming the following data is to budgeted chargeable hours, prepare a schedule computing billing rates by employee for the year ending June 30, 19X3. The schedule should show the proper allocation of appropriate expenses and target income contribution to salaries applicable to chargeable time in accordance with the objective established by the partners. (Round allocation calculations to one decimal place. Round billing rate calculations to the nearest dollar.)

	Budgeted Chargeable Hours
Vickers	1,600
Lowe	1,650
Kennedy	1,550
Quinn	1,450
Lyons	500
Hammond	1,150
Garcia	1,200

(AICPA adapted)

*2-36   Over the past several years, the Programme Corporation had difficulty estimating its cash flows. Programme's controller would like to develop a means by which he can forecast the firm's monthly operating cash flows. The following data were gathered to facilitate the development of such a forecast.

1. Sales have been increasing, and are expected to continue to increase, at .5% each month.
2. 30% of each month's sales are for cash; the other 70% are on open account.
3. Of the credit sales, 80% are collected during the month following the sale, and the remaining 20% are collected during the second month after the sale. There are no bad debts.
4. Gross margin on sales averages 25%.
5. Programme purchases enough inventory each month to cover the following month's sales.
6. All inventory purchases are paid for during the month of purchase at a 2% cash discount.
7. Monthly expenses are: Payroll—$1,500; Rent—$400; Depreciation—$120; Other cash expenses—1% of that month's sales. There are no accruals.
8. Ignore the effects of corporate income taxes, dividends, and equipment acquisitions.

Using the data above, develop a mathematical model the controller can use for his calculations. Your model should be capable of calculating the monthly operating cash inflows and outflows for any specified month.

(CMA adapted)

2–37 Modern Products Corporation, a manufacturer of molded plastic containers, determined in October 19X8 that it needed cash to continue operations. The Corporation began negotiating for a one-month bank loan of $100,000 which would be discounted at 6 per cent per annum on November 1. In considering the loan the bank requested a cash budget for the month of November.

The following information is available:

1. Sales were budgeted at 120,000 units per month in October 19X8, December 19X8, and January 19X9 and at 90,000 units in November 19X8.

    The selling price is $2 per unit. Sales are billed on the 15th and last day of each month on terms of 2/10 net/30. Past experience indicates that sales are even throughout the month, and that 50 per cent of the customers pay the billed amount within the discount period. The remainder pay at the end of 30 days, except for bad debts, which average ½ per cent of gross sales. On its income statement the Corporation deducts from sales the estimated amounts for cash discounts on sales and losses on bad debts.

2. The inventory of finished goods on October 1 was 24,000 units. The finished goods inventory at the end of each month is to be maintained at 20 per cent of sales anticipated for the following month. There is no work in process.

3. The inventory of raw materials on October 1 was 22,800 pounds. At the end of each month the raw materials inventory is to be maintained at not less than 40 per cent of production requirements for the following month. Materials are purchased as needed in minimum quantities of 25,000 pounds per shipment. Raw material purchases of each month are paid in the next succeeding month on terms of net 30 days.

4. All salaries and wages are paid on the 15th and the last day of each month for the period ending on the date of payment.

5. All manufacturing overhead and selling and administrative expenses are paid on the 10th of the month following the month in which they were incurred. Selling expenses are 10 per cent of gross sales. Administrative expenses, which include depreciation of $500 per month on office furniture and fixtures, total $33,000 per month.

6. The cost of a molded plastic container, based on "normal" production of 100,000 units per month, is as follows:

Materials—½ pound	$ .50
Labor	.40
Variable overhead	.20
Fixed Overhead	.10
Total	$1.20

Fixed overhead includes depreciation on factory equipment of $4,000 per month.

7. The cash balance on November 1 is expected to be $10,000.

Assuming that the bank loan is granted, prepare the following for Modern Products Corporation. (Do not consider income taxes.)

(A) Schedules computing inventory budgets by months for

1. Finished-goods production in units for October, November, and December.

2. Raw material purchases in pounds for October and November.

(B) A cash forecast for the month of November showing the opening balance, receipts (itemized by dates of collection), disbursements, and balance at end of month.

(AICPA adapted)

CHAPTER 3

Budgeted Financial Statements, Cost Behavior, and Flexible Budgets

Objectives

After studying this chapter, you should be able to do the following:

Construct budgeted income statements *and* budgeted balance sheets *with data obtained from other budget schedules.*

Define flexible budgets *and contrast them with* static *or* fixed *budgets.*

Identify the behavior of fixed *and* variable costs, *given changes in volume.*

Contrast the two types of fixed costs, committed *and* discretionary. *Identify which type of cost can be modified to reflect changes in short-run managerial policy.*

Separate a mixed cost *into its component fixed and variable elements.*

Describe how flexible budgets *may be modified to incorporate management's expectations.*

BUDGETED FINANCIAL STATEMENTS

Companies preparing comprehensive budgets ordinarily compile a budgeted income statement and a budgeted balance sheet. These budgeted financial statements are constructed from data found in the operating, financial, and capital budgets, and, hence, are prepared last. The technical terms for *budgeted* financial statements is *pro forma*, i.e., pro forma income statement and pro forma balance sheet.

A simple example will illustrate the interrelationships between budgets. The Johnson Corporation's beginning of the year balance sheet reflects the following balances:

Cash	$ 10,000		Accounts Payable	$ 24,000
Accounts receivable	50,000		Loans Payable	-0-
Inventory	20,000		Owners' Equity	141,000
Investments	85,000			
Total	$165,000		Total	$165,000

Expected sales for the next month are 10,000 units at $9 each. Typically, 40% of current sales are for cash, and 60% are collected during the following month, in accordance with the 30-day terms allowed credit customers. Inventory can be purchased for $4 per unit, payable within 20 days. The desired ending inventory balance is set at 4,000 units. Typically, 30% of the purchases are for cash, and 70% are paid during the following month. Johnson's cash policy specifies a desired minimum ending balance of $10,000; any deficiencies are made up by borrowing under existing lines of credit. Rental payments of $30,000 for the building and fixtures are made on the last day of the month. Additional investments are to be purchased for $35,000 during the current month.

The sales budget, purchasing budget, and cash budget for Johnson Corporation for one month are presented in Exhibit 3–1. Key amounts that appear on more than one schedule are indexed by letter. For example, the $90,000 (labeled a) from the sales budget also appears on the cash receipts schedule, and the $36,000 (labeled d) from the purchasing budget also appears on the cash disbursements schedule.

A budgeted income statement can be constructed from the information contained in Exhibit 3–1. A budgeted income statement for the Johnson Corporation would combine expected sales data from the sales budget with expense data from the purchasing budget and cash disbursements schedule, as shown in Exhibit 3–2. To produce a budgeted income statement for a more realistic (and complex) example, additional data about deferral, accrual, and other noncash events would be required. A budgeted balance sheet also reflects many dollar amounts derived from the preceding schedules. Note that the Owners' equity

EXHIBIT 3–1   JOHNSON CORPORATION BUDGETS FOR CURRENT MONTH

	Dollars	Key
Sales Budget: 10,000 units @ $9	$90,000	a
Purchasing Budget (at cost):		
Expected sales 10,000 units @ $4	$40,000	b
+ Desired ending inventory 4,000 units @ $4	16,000	c
Total needs 14,000 units @ $4	$56,000	
− Beginning inventory	20,000	*
Amount to be purchased	$36,000	d
Cash Receipts Schedule:		
Expected sales	$90,000	a
− Credit sales (60% of $90,000)	54,000	e
Cash sales	$36,000	
+ Collection of accounts receivable	50,000	*
Total cash receipts	$86,000	f
Cash Disbursements Schedule:		
Budgeted purchases	$36,000	d
− Credit purchases (70% of $36,000)	25,200	g
Cash purchases	$10,800	h
+ Payments of accounts payable	24,000	*
+ Rent payment	30,000	i
+ Acquisition of investment	35,000	j
Total cash disbursements	$99,800	k
Cash Budget:		
Beginning cash balance	$10,000	*
+ Receipts	86,000	f
Total cash available	$96,000	
− Disbursements	99,800	k
Net deficiency	$ (3,800)	
− Desired ending balance	10,000	l
Amount to borrow	$13,800	m

SOURCE: *Data from beginning balance sheet.

EXHIBIT 3–2   BUDGETED FINANCIAL STATEMENTS FOR JOHNSON CORPORATION

Budget Income Statement

Expected Sales Revenue		$90,000	a
Cost of goods sold	$40,000		b
Rent expense	30,000		i
− Total Expense		70,000	
Expected net income		$20,000	n

Budget Balance Sheet

Cash		$10,000	l	Accounts payable		$25,200	g
Accounts receivable		54,000	e	Loans payable		13,800	m
Inventory		16,000	c	Owner's equity	$141,000		*
Investments	$85,000		*	+ Expected profit	20,000		n
+ Acquisition	35,000		j				
		120,000				161,000	
Total		$200,000		Total		$200,000	

SOURCES: Letter references relate to Exhibit 3-1; * data from beginning balance sheet.

balance in Exhibit 3–2 reflects the expected income derived from the budgeted income statement.

STATIC AND FLEXIBLE BUDGETS

The comprehensive budgeting plans we have discussed thus far have all been directed toward attainment of one specific level of sales activity. Budgets for one fixed level of activity are called **fixed** or **static** budgets; they pertain to business activity in a predictable environment. Many businesses, however, cannot accurately predict their future activities because the conditions under which they operate can fluctuate sharply from one period to the next. For such businesses, static budgets are of little use.

A **flexible budget**, on the other hand, estimates costs at several levels of activity. Flexible budgeting assumes that costs of labor, material, or facilities used in production vary in accordance with changes in the volume of activity. A flexible budget is useful for control purposes, as well as for planning, in an uncertain environment. Planning is discussed in this chapter. (Control aspects of flexible budgets are discussed in Section Four.) An alternate approach to dealing with uncertainty in budgets involves recognizing probabilistic estimates, a subject discussed in Appendix B of this chapter.

RELATIONSHIP OF COSTS TO VOLUME

Flexible and fixed budgets are constructed in exactly the same manner, but flexible budgets project costs and other business operations at several different levels of productive activity. The accuracy of a flexible budget depends on identifying the relationship between costs and the volume of production. Three different types of cost behavior are identified with changes in volume: (1) **fixed costs**, (2) **variable costs**, and (3) **mixed costs**.

MEASURES OF VOLUME (ACTIVITY)

The term **volume**, which is frequently used in discussing budgets or budgeting, is related to another term, **capacity**. Capacity constitutes the fixed amount of plant, equipment, or personnel that an organization has committed to its operations. *Volume* is the usage of capacity. Both terms refer to measures of goals or target points that are the focus of budgets. Many measures of volume are used in budgeting, such as units of production or output, man hours of labor expended, pounds or feet of material committed to production, machine hours worked, and dollar costs of each of these inputs.

A measure of volume is of prime importance in budgeting, because some costs fluctuate as a direct result of changes in volume. Although many factors cause costs to vary, managers focus attention on volume—they attempt to create the largest volume possible from an existing capacity. If the relationship between changes in costs and changes in volume is known, then preparing a budget for any level of activity is a relatively easy task.

But, which of all the measures of volume should be considered in preparing budgets? Budget committees frequently select the activity or factor that *causes* costs to vary. For example, the factor that causes labor costs to vary is the number of hours worked; the factor that causes material costs to increase is the quantity of material consumed, and so on. Furthermore, the measure of activity must be related to something that management can control, such as the number of hours worked, the quantity of materials consumed, or the number of machine hours operated. If the basis of the budget is not controllable by management, then the budgeted variable costs also will be uncontrollable.

In addition, the activity chosen as a unit of measure should be one that is not greatly affected by factors other than volume. For example, if the base can be either direct material quantities or direct material costs, the quantities would be a more useful indicator for volume than the costs, because costs may be affected by fluctuations in physical quantities *and* price fluctuations. Using material quantities, labor hours, machine hours, or other physical measures eliminates the influence of price fluctuations on these inputs.

FIXED COSTS

Fixed costs are associated with inputs that do not fluctuate in response to changes in the total activity or output of the firm. [1] Fixed costs remain at the same level whether activity increases or decreases. Included under this classification are such items as depreciation, property insurance, real estate taxes, executive salaries, rent, and lease payments. Since these costs are fixed (or nonvariable), any increase in volume means that the costs will be allocated to a greater number of units; that is, more units will absorb a fixed amount of costs. In other words, fixed costs per unit become progressively smaller as production increases. Exhibit 3–3 illustrates the relationship between volume and both total fixed costs and fixed cost per unit. Whereas fixed costs remain constant at $100,000 in total, cost per unit at 10,000 units of volume is only half as high as it is at 5,000 units of volume.

The vertical axis of Exhibit 3–3, Part A, represents total costs: greater dollar costs are shown higher on the axis. The horizontal axis represents volume of activity. Fixed costs are shown as a line parallel to the volume axis. As volume

---

[1]"Nonvariable," is a more appropriate name for these costs, but "fixed" is more traditional.

EXHIBIT 3-3 FIXED COST AND FIXED COST PER UNIT

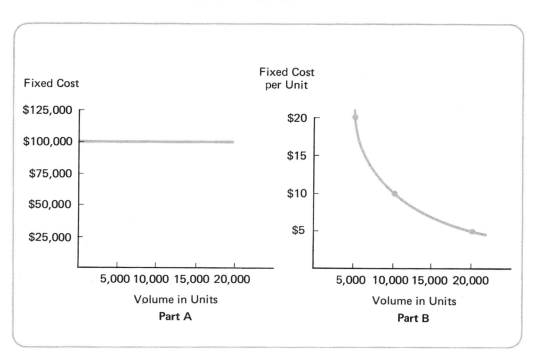

increases (moves toward the right), the dollar value of fixed costs remains at the same height on the vertical axis.

The vertical axis of Exhibit 3–3, Part B, represents cost per unit: greater unit cost is shown higher on the axis. The horizontal axis represents volume. As volume increases (moves toward the right), the dollar value of fixed cost per unit decreases.

Although fixed costs will not change in total over a wide range of volume, often called the *relevant range*, they will fluctuate beyond that range. For example, a firm that regularly operates at activity levels between 50,000 and 100,000 man hours per month may maintain given fixed costs within that range of activity. But, a prolonged strike will cause fixed costs to be reduced if executives or employees are laid off. Similarly, because an expansion of activity beyond 100,000 hours will require the hiring of additional supervisors and the leasing of more plant and equipment, additional fixed costs will result from these new inputs. Furthermore, fixed costs must be analyzed in relation to a given period of time. All costs can be made to vary over the long run. For example, property taxes can be considered fixed in relation to volume during any one year, even though they are expected to increase over time.

Committed fixed costs that provide capacity   Fixed costs that arise from the acquisition of capacity-producing assets such as plant or equipment are frequently called **committed fixed costs**. Such assets provide capacity for long periods of time, and a portion of the original acquisition cost is allocated to each year of their usefulness. As companies continue to automate their production processes, their fixed costs increase because of increased expenditures on plant and equipment. Property taxes, insurance, salaries of key personnel, and depreciation on plant or equipment are additional examples of committed fixed costs. These committed fixed costs cannot be reduced substantially without impairing the organization's capacity to continue operations at the present level. Although plant and equipment may be sold or managers fired, in order to achieve short-run cost reductions, committed fixed costs are rarely reduced in this fashion.

Discretionary fixed costs   Another type of cost that is independent of volume is **discretionary fixed costs**, sometimes known as *managed* or *programmed* costs. These costs result from management decisions to undertake such activities as research and development, training programs, consulting, advertising, and sales promotion. Such costs are incurred, or, conceivably, reduced, at the discretion of management.

At the start of the budget period, top executives decide on the size of discretionary costs that may be incurred. For example, they may decide on a $10 million research and development program. The engineers and scientists in the research and development department are unlikely to spend more than that amount, or, for that matter, much less than that amount. Although discretionary fixed costs can be changed from one period to the next, the activities associated with the fixed costs probably will not have any substantial effect on the firm's level of production during the current budget period. For example, even a technological breakthrough that could shorten production time appreciably would have no effect until it was properly tested, installed, and checked, a process that would most likely extend into some future budget period, at which time, volume of production might be definitely affected.

PLANNING FOR FIXED COSTS

Each of the two types of fixed costs, committed and discretionary, has a different implication for the budgetary process. Because committed fixed costs are of a long-run nature, the budget committee can learn much about the expected size of future committed fixed costs by examining past committed fixed costs. For example, knowing how large executive compensation was last year and what changes have occurred in compensation policies during the current year will enable budget makers to project executive compensation for the coming year.

Discretionary fixed costs may be budgeted also, but without making a historical evaluation. Discretionary costs are generally related to appropriations budgets, the size of which is determined by executive policy. Therefore, budgeting for discretionary fixed costs depends on inquiries made of the policy-making executives. For example, the budgeter would ask the chief sales executive what the desired level of advertising should be for the coming year.

VARIABLE COSTS

Costs that fluctuate in direct proportion to production activity, sales activity, or some other measure of volume are called variable costs. Raw materials, labor costs, and supplies are examples of variable costs. These productive inputs should increase in proportion to increases in volume because they can be used in the exact quantities needed. Exhibit 3–4 illustrates the relationship between variable costs and volume. As volume doubles from 5,000 units to

EXHIBIT 3–4   VARIABLE COST

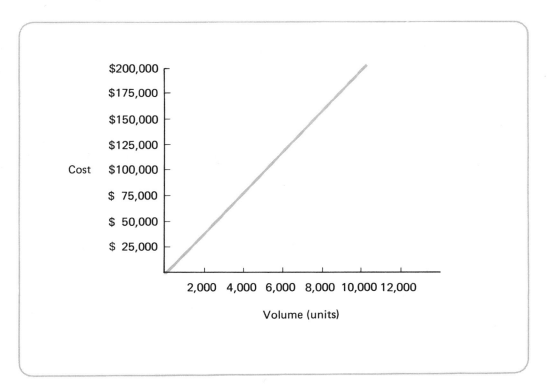

10,000 units, costs double from $100,000 to $200,000. Note that per-unit variable cost is constant at $20 per unit.

Variable costs appear in Exhibit 3–4 as a diagonal line penetrating the junction of both axes. At the junction, both the dollar amount of costs and production volume equal zero. Given some level of activity, say, one unit toward the right on the volume axis, costs increase. The costs associated with producing two units of output are twice as high as the costs associated with the first unit of output. In other words, costs are proportionate to volume, and every additional unit of volume will produce a corresponding increase in costs.

PLANNING FOR VARIABLE COSTS

The level of variable costs at any volume can be estimated easily if the relationship between costs and volume is known. Once costs that vary with volume have been identified, the planner may be able to extrapolate them. However, he must modify the historic cost-volume relationship in the light of any new information that may affect the future size of variable costs. For example, if labor rates go up, the budgeter should assume that costs will rise next year, simply as a result of the increase in labor rates (assuming, of course, that workers' productivity has not changed).

MIXED COSTS

Mixed costs are composed of both fixed and variable elements. The fixed part of mixed costs often represents a cost of capacity, whereas the variable element is influenced by changes in activity. For example, business telephone costs frequently involve both a fixed and a variable element. The fixed charge is a cost of capacity, a basic cost for telephone service, whereas the variable charge is a measure of actual use of the service. Costs associated with a delivery truck illustrate mixed behavior also: every year, fixed costs for insurance, taxes, registration, and garaging are incurred, whereas variable costs for tires, gas, oil, and repairs depend on the miles driven. Although the miles driven by a delivery truck may not be directly proportional to sales dollars or production activity during the year, they are likely to be closely related.

Additional examples of mixed costs include salaries of foremen, supervisors, accountants, buyers, typists, clerks, janitors, employees' insurance, pension plans, and other wage-related costs. Nonwage mixed costs would include maintenance of buildings and grounds, power, water, gas, telephone, office machine rentals, fuel, supplies, and so on.

BUDGETING MIXED COSTS

Before mixed costs can be budgeted, they must be broken down into their fixed and variable segments. Once this is done, the budgeter can devise a formula expressing the amount of fixed costs and the rate at which total variable costs change in proportion to total changes in production volume. That is, the fixed costs remain constant regardless of activity, but the variable portion is assumed to change in direct proportion to increases in labor hours, labor costs, machine hours, materials costs, or materials quantities.

Two techniques are useful in separating the fixed and variable elements in mixed costs: (1) the historical cost approach and (2) the analytical approach.

The historical approach   The historical approach deals primarily with past cost data. For example, assume that data on direct labor hours and factory clerical expenses (as shown in Exhibit 3–5) are available. An obvious relationship exists between direct labor inputs and clerical inputs: extra clerical effort is required to account for the extra workers and/or extra output produced by the input of more direct labor. The tabulation indicates that factory clerical expenses never fall below a certain amount regardless of the changes in direct labor hours. By rearranging the data with the lowest number of hours first, the relationship between activity and costs is better reflected (see Part B of Exhibit 3–5). These past costs may be arranged in the form of a scatter chart or graph, as in Part C of Exhibit 3–5. The vertical axis indicates the dollar value of mixed costs; the horizontal axis measures volume.

The two-point method. The tabulation indicates that for every 100-hour increase in direct labor hours there is a corresponding $5 increase in clerical costs, or $.05 per direct labor hour (DLH). One way to derive this figure is to segregate the fixed and variable elements by calculating the relationship between the high and low figure for both production and expenses. That is, the variable rate is determined by dividing the dollar change in mixed costs by the physical change in volume or, in our example,

$$\frac{\$1{,}250 - \$950}{15{,}000 - 9{,}000} = \frac{\$300}{6{,}000} = \$.05/\text{DLH}$$

The fixed overhead component of mixed costs is equal to the total mixed costs at a given volume less the variable component at that volume. For our example, fixed costs at 15,000 hours are:

$$\$1{,}250 - (\$.05 \times 15{,}000) = \$1{,}250 - \$750 = \$500$$

The example contains fixed costs that are truly fixed and variable costs that vary directly with changes in volume, a situation that seldom occurs in practice. Since actual cost behavior rarely matches the theoretical pattern exactly, the two-point method for establishing cost behavior may be misleading.

EXHIBIT 3-5   FACTORY CLERICAL COST

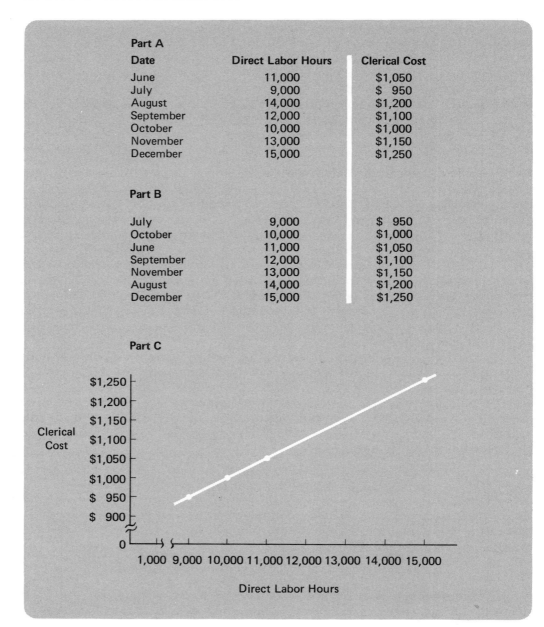

Part A

Date	Direct Labor Hours	Clerical Cost
June	11,000	$1,050
July	9,000	$ 950
August	14,000	$1,200
September	12,000	$1,100
October	10,000	$1,000
November	13,000	$1,150
December	15,000	$1,250

Part B

	Direct Labor Hours	Clerical Cost
July	9,000	$ 950
October	10,000	$1,000
June	11,000	$1,050
September	12,000	$1,100
November	13,000	$1,150
August	14,000	$1,200
December	15,000	$1,250

Part C

The two-point method produces useful cost estimates only when each of the two points is representative of the underlying cost-volume relationship.

To continue the example, the cost estimates obtained from the two-point method could then be used to prepare a budget. Budget estimates for three potential volumes are presented below:

Volume (DLH)	8,500	12,500	15,500
Variable cost			
(at $.05 per DLH)	$ 425	$ 625	$ 775
Fixed cost	500	500	500
Budgeted total cost	$ 925	$ 1,125	$ 1,275

The budgeted variable cost is estimated by multiplying the expected volume by five cents per direct labor hour. Fixed cost is estimated to remain unchanged at $500. (Note, however, that both variable and fixed-cost estimates must be modified if certain changes are definitely expected, e.g., a 10% increase in rent.) Total budgeted cost is the sum of the fixed and variable components.

The graphic method. An alternate technique for analyzing semivariable or mixed costs uses a statistical analysis of the cost-volume relationships for all relevant historical data. First, the cost-volume relationships of historical data can be plotted on a scatter graph, as shown in Part A of Exhibit 3–6. Each dot on the chart represents an expense for a particular month. For example, the dot labeled "June" represents the telephone expenses ($230) for the month of June, when 6,000 units were produced. The x-axis (horizontal) shows a volume of production units and the y-axis (vertical) shows the dollar amount of expense.[2]

The mixed costs represented by dots or points may be divided into their fixed and variable components by fitting a line, labeled *AB* (in Part B of Exhibit 3–6), to the data in an attempt to derive the average relationship between costs and volume. Fixed costs are represented on the vertical axis at point *A*, where the average-cost line intersects the vertical axis. The second line, *AC*, drawn parallel to the base line from the point of intersection on the y-axis, represents the fixed costs. This graphical representation of cost-volume relationship between telephone expense and production units can be used for budgeting purposes. Once an expected volume for the budget period has been selected, the corresponding cost can be read from the graph. For example, if volume in January is expected to reach 4,500 units, expected telephone expense would be budgeted at $300.

Just how accurate will cost estimates based on the graphic method be? An answer depends upon how representative the *AB* line is: if it is not representative of the underlying cost-volume relationship, then the cost estimates will not

[2]Note that volume in this example is measured in units or physical output, whereas volume was measured in hours of input in the previous example. Alternate measures of volume were discussed under the heading "Measures of Volume" in this chapter.

EXHIBIT 3–6   TELEPHONE EXPENSE

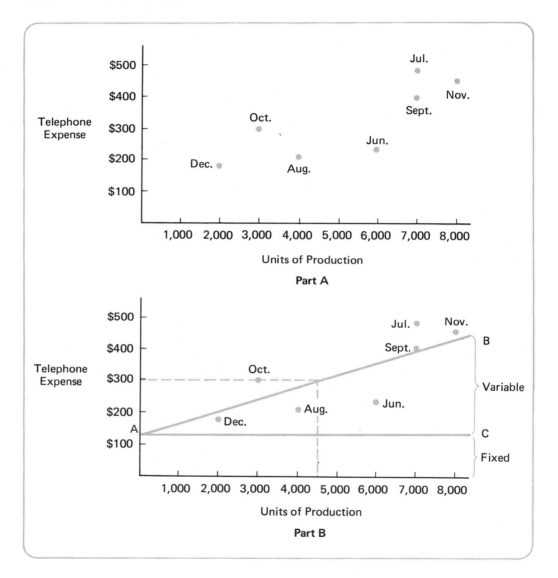

Part A

Part B

be very accurate. However, if the observed data points lie very close to the line, the estimates can be quite accurate. Ideally, there should be as many dots above the average cost line as there are below. Another way of stating this is that the total vertical distance to the average-cost line from the dots above the line should be equal to the total vertical distance from the dots below the line to the average-cost line.

Different criteria may be used to define the average cost-volume relationship. One common technique is the **method of least squares** (one form of regression analysis). Under the method of least squares, a straight line is fitted to the data according to the formula:

$$y = a + bx$$

where a is fixed cost and b is the rate of variability. The least-squares method fits a line to the data in a way that minimizes the total squared vertical deviation from the dots to the line. Thus, points farther away from the average point (line) are weighted more heavily than points nearer the line. Appendix A to this chapter discusses the least-squares method in more detail.

In summary, then, the historical approach to determining the fixed and variable portions of mixed costs relies on examining the historic relationship between costs and volume and applying it to future projections.

The analytical approach In most accounting systems, individual accounts are created to collect information about each unique type of cost incurred by the organization. Natural names such as *Wages-assembler*, *Lubricants*, or *Depreciation-lathe* are usually assigned to each account, and similar types of accounts are grouped by organizational unit or function, e.g., Department No. 4, maintenance. The recording of data in each account is initiated when a clerk in the accounting department receives a source document that was created as cost was incurred in the normal course of business. Thus, numbers recorded in the accounts reflect the dollar values associated with inputs or outputs of the production process.

An analyst familiar with cost accounting procedures and terminology would be able to estimate the change in cost expected from a given change in volume for the majority of accounts. An examination of the historical records would indicate the level of costs incurred and the level of volume achieved in each past period. In projecting future costs, the analyst would first determine whether budgeted volume was expected to be larger or smaller than the current volume. Starting with the cost data for the most recent period, the analyst would then project a cost estimate for each account for the budget period. Some costs such as wages for labor working directly in the production processes would be expected to increase when budgeted volume increased: other costs such as salaries for managers would not be expected to vary with volume. In the same fashion, materials directly used in production would be expected to increase with increases in volume while supplies used on grounds maintenance would not increase.

A flexible budget could be prepared on the basis of analyzing each account. The budget manager would estimate the cost of each item (account) for levels of operation above and below the anticipated level: for example, 10%, 20% and 30% above and below the anticipated level. Thus, the flexible budget would detail costs at seven operating levels ranging from 70% to 130% of the antici- pated level.

The analytical approach to developing budgets that consider relation- ships between costs and volume stimulated the development of **zero-based budgets**. A zero-based budget requires each budgeting unit to justify all costs each year, rather than just the year-to-year cost change, as is traditionally done. Zero-based budgeting thus allows new programs to compete on an equal footing with old programs. Like most budgets, zero-based budgets begin with objectives, but then priorities are established and resources are realigned to reflect these priorities. Because of this realignment of resources in accordance with current priorities, an analysis of historical cost-volume relationships is less meaningful for zero-based budgeting than for traditional budgeting.

SETTING UP THE FLEXIBLE BUDGET

We have already examined the information necessary for preparing a flex- ible budget. Any increase or decrease in business activity must be reflected in the comprehensive plan. Every expense in every department is scrutinized to deter- mine its fixed, variable, and mixed elements. A budget is first prepared at the expected level of activity, say, 100% of capacity. Additional columns are added to the budget for costs above and below 100%. At 90% capacity, the fixed costs may remain unchanged but the variable costs will decline. At 110% of capacity, the fixed costs still may remain unchanged but the variable costs will increase. Exhibits 3–7 and 3–8 provide examples of flexible budgets for a machining department and a maintenance department.

The budgeting procedure requires that costs of all inputs be estimated over the budgetary period. Costs are a function of both the per-unit price paid for factors of production and the quantities of those factors that will be used in the production process. Very frequently, planning managers will have predetermined targets for both prices and quantities of inputs needed to produce a single unit of output. These predetermined targets are combined to produce the costs dis- closed in the budget. In Exhibits 3–7 and 3–8, management made an estimate of the prices and quantities of each input for the particular volume of operations called for by the tactical plan. The cost-volume behavior of each input also was identified, and then budgets for other levels of volume were developed. For exam- ple, the variable costs at 8,000 hours of production in Exhibit 3–7 are 80% of the costs at 10,000 hours. At the same time, committed fixed costs are set at one magnitude and there they remain. Mixed costs are separated into fixed and variable elements and recomputed for each budgeted volume. Discretionary costs

EXHIBIT 3–7   FLEXIBLE BUDGET—MACHINING DEPARTMENT

Volume, Machine Hours	25	30	35	40	45
Variable Costs:					
Helpers	$ 250	$ 300	$ 350	$ 400	$ 450
Supplies	125	150	175	200	225
Discretionary Fixed Costs:					
Training	400	450	450	450	500
Tools	100	100	100	150	150
Committed Fixed Costs:					
Depreciation	600	600	600	600	600
Rent	500	500	500	500	500
Total	$ 1,975	$ 2,100	$ 2,175	$ 2,300	$ 2,425

are established by management agreement. The budgeting procedure for preparing Exhibit 3–8 was similar to the one just described.

EXHIBIT 3–8   FLEXIBLE BUDGET—MAINTENANCE DEPARTMENT

Volume Labor Hours	8,000	9,000	10,000	11,000	12,000
Variable Costs:	$	$	$	$	$
Direct Labor	12,000	13,500	15,000	16,500	18,000
Direct Materials	4,800	5,400	6,000	6,600	7,200
Lubricants	1,600	1,800	2,000	2,200	2,400
Mixed Costs:					
Indirect Labor	4,600	4,800	5,000	5,200	5,400
Maintenance	2,800	2,900	3,000	3,100	3,200
Other Supplies	5,000	5,500	6,000	6,500	7,000
Discretionary Fixed Costs:					
Training Costs	3,000	4,000	4,000	4,000	5,000
Experimental Methods	7,000	8,000	8,000	8,000	9,000
Committed Fixed Costs:					
Depreciation	10,000	10,000	10,000	10,000	10,000
Rent, Lease Cost	7,000	7,000	7,000	7,000	7,000
Total Machining	$57,800	$62,900	$66,000	$69,100	$74,200

MODIFIED FLEXIBLE BUDGETS

The major weakness of the static budgets discussed in Chapter 2 is their inability to indicate the potential variability of various estimates used in building the budget. The amount for each item in the budget was subjectively estimated. Furthermore, static budgets do not indicate the range within which one could confidently expect costs to fall. Although flexible budgets do present estimates of costs at different volume levels, they do not explicitly consider the relative **probability** that any particular volume or cost will be achieved.

A flexible budget may be modified to contain columns for the most likely estimate, an optimistic estimate, and a pessimistic estimate. For example, a machining department prepares a flexible budget, as illustrated in Exhibit 3–7. Note that fixed costs are classified as either discretionary or committed costs. Discretionary costs can be modified in the short run, but little change can be introduced in committed costs.

The information from this type of budget can be reformulated into a **modified flexible budget**, as shown in Exhibit 3–9. This exhibit clearly indicates the range of costs and revenues that management expects under the most and least favorable circumstances, in addition to the results of the most likely events.

Although this modified flexible budget contains more information than traditional flexible budgets, it still does not consider explicitly the relative probability that any particular level of revenue or cost will be achieved. For example, the probabilities of accurately estimating committed fixed costs are much higher than are those for accurately estimating variable costs, since there is much more uncertainty associated with variable costs. Flexible budgets that introduce the individual probabilities that any line item will occur are called **probabilistic budgets**. They are discussed in greater detail in Appendix B to this chapter.

SUMMARY

Flexible budgets consider several levels of activity, as opposed to the one level considered by static or fixed budgets. To produce flexible budgets, the relationship between costs and volume must be understood: fixed costs remain unchanged with changes in volume, whereas variable costs change proportionately with volume. Fixed costs are either discretionary (subject to year-to-year changes at management's discretion) or committed (unchanging, related to past capital acquisitions). Mixed costs are composed of fixed and variable elements, and can be separated by manipulation of historical data or analysis of future expectations. Probabilistic budgets explicitly consider the likelihood that a future event will occur.

EXHIBIT 3-9   MODIFIED FLEXIBLE BUDGET—MACHINING DEPARTMENT

	Pessimistic	Most Likely	Optimistic
Volume, Labor Hours	8,500	10,000	11,700
Variable Costs:	$	$	$
Direct Labor	12,750	15,000	17,550
Direct Materials	5,100	6,000	7,020
Lubricants	1,700	2,000	2,340
Mixed Costs:			
Indirect Labor	4,700	5,000	6,850
Maintenance	2,850	3,000	3,170
Other Supplies	5,250	6,000	5,340
Discretionary Fixed Costs:			
Training Costs	3,500	4,000	4,500
Experimental Methods	7,500	8,000	8,500
Committed Fixed Costs:			
Depreciation	10,000	10,000	10,000
Rent, Lease Cost	7,000	7,000	7,000
Total Matching	$60,350	$66,000	$72,270

APPENDIX A: LEAST-SQUARES METHOD
FOR FITTING A STRAIGHT LINE

Cost behavior can be illustrated graphically, as shown in Exhibit 3–10. The vertical axis of this graph represents total input costs, ranging from zero to $8. The horizontal axis represents output volume, ranging from zero to 6. (Single digit numbers are used here to make computations easier to follow and do not reflect realistic costs.) At the junction of the two axes, the dollar amount of costs and the production volume both equal zero. Greater amounts of input costs are required to produce greater quantities of output volume, as is true of most production processes.

If costs (measured on the vertical axis) are designated y, and volume (on the horizontal axis) x, then any straight line depicting the relationship between costs and volume is described by the general formula $y = a + bx$, where a and b are both constants. To describe a specific straight line, numerical values for a

EXHIBIT 3–10   GRAPHIC PRESENTATION OF A STRAIGHT LINE

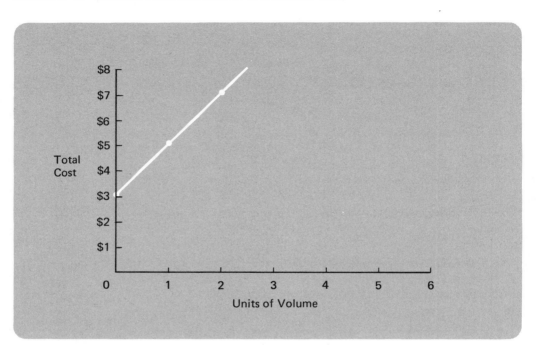

and b must be specified. The line shown in Exhibit 3–10 can be described as $y = 3 + 2x$. That is, when volume equals zero, the cost y is equal to $3, but as volume increases by 1 unit, costs will increase by $2 and will total $5.

The least-squares method of fitting a straight line to a group of data points is based on this formula for a straight line. The least-squares technique measures the vertical distance from any point to the line. For example, assume that the output units of volume and the corresponding input costs for a particular department for six weeks are as shown in columns 2 and 3 of Exhibit 3–11. Here again, we shall label the costs y and the volumes x. For convenience, the square of each value of x (volume) is placed in the fourth column, while the fifth column shows a product of each x times the coresponding y (cost). The values in each column are then totaled and the symbol Σ is used to denote the totals.

The constants a and b in the equation for a straight line can be determined by solving the following two simultaneous equations:

$$1. \quad na + b(\Sigma\, x) = \Sigma\, y$$
$$2. \quad a(\Sigma\, x) + b(\Sigma\, x^2) = \Sigma\, xy$$

n is the number of observations (that is, the number of x, y pairs). For our data,

EXHIBIT 3–11   LEAST-SQUARES CALCULATION OF A STRAIGHT LINE

(1) Period	(2) Units of Volume X	(3) Costs Y	(4) X^2	(5) XY
1	2	$ 6.50	4	13
2	1	$ 5.00	1	5
3	3	$ 8.00	9	24
4	2	$ 7.50	4	15
5	0	$ 3.00	0	0
6	3	$10.00	9	30
Σ	11	40.00	27	87

$\Sigma \dot{x} = 11$, $\Sigma y = 40$, $\Sigma x^2 = 27$, $\Sigma xy = 87$, and $n = 6$. The simultaneous equations given above can be restated as follows, simply by substituting values obtained from Exhibit 3–12:

$$1. \quad 6a + 11b = 40$$
$$2. \quad 11a + 27b = 87$$

Solutions to simultaneous equations may be determined by restating the original equations so that either the a or b terms are of equal value, and then subtracting one equation from the second. For example, the a term of both equations can be converted in the number 33: multiply the first equation by 5.5 and the second by 3. The restated equations become:

$$1'. \quad 33a + 60.5b = 220$$
$$\underline{2'. \quad 33a + 81.0b = 261}$$
$$20.5b = 41$$

Subtracting Equation 1' from Equation 2' produces $20.5b = 41$, and after dividing, $b = 2$. Substituting b in our first equation, we have $6a + 22 = 40$, or $a = 3$.

Therefore, the least-squares equation for the line described by the data of Exhibit 3–11 is $y = 3 + 2x$. That is, when volume is zero, costs are $3, and for each unit of production beyond zero, costs will increase by $2.

The results of this least-squares regression can be used to estimate total costs for any volume within the relevant range. For example, the expected costs associated with a production volume of 5 units of output is $y = \$3 + (\$2 \times 5) = \$13$.

The least-squares method has advantages over other estimation methods described in the text, in that measures of confidence to be placed in the cost estimates can also be determined. Least-squares regressions ordinarily are determined with the aid of a computer, and many packaged programs available on the market routinely present one measure of the "goodness of fit," as well as measures of "variance" for each term (used to assess confidence), in addition to estimates for the fixed costs and the variable costs. However, extended discussion of the least-squares method is beyond the scope of this text.

APPENDIX B: PROBABILISTIC BUDGETS—ANOTHER APPROACH TO UNCERTAINTY

A probabilistic budget explicity recognizes uncertainty by stating each line item as a range of values. *Probability* is a useful measure of the likelihood that an event will occur, and is represented by a decimal ranging between 0 and 1. A zero probability indicates that an event will not occur, whereas a probability of 1 indicates that the event will definitely occur. A .1 probability indicates that the event will occur only 1 out of 10 times, and a .9 probability indicates that the event is likely to occur 9 out of 10 times. Experienced executives have insights that should enable them to make probability estimates for events under their supervision. Other probabilities can be obtained through simulation analysis and other advanced estimation techniques.

To prepare a probabilistic budget, probability estimates must be made for every volume of activity and every manufacturing cost considered feasible by the firm. For example, consider the following problems and solutions:

1. Management estimates three values for expected future revenue: $2,000,000, $2,500,000 and $2,800,000. Probabilities of realizing these three values are 0.3, 0.6, and 0.1, respectively, determined on the basis of experience. What is the expected value of future revenue? *Solution:* $2,380,000, determined as the sum of the products of respective probabilities and likely values, i.e.,

$$\$2,000,000 \times 0.3 = \$\ \ 600,000$$
$$\$2,500,000 \times 0.6 = \$1,500,000$$
$$\$2,800,000 \times \underline{0.1} = \underline{\$\ \ 280,000}$$
$$\text{Expected} \qquad 1.0 \quad \underline{\$2,380,000}$$

2. Three variable-cost estimates are $600,000, $700,000 and $800,000, and the associated probabilities are 0.7, 0.2, and 0.1, respectively. What is the expected future value of variable cost? *Solution:* $640,000, representing the sum of $420,000 + $140,000 + $80,000.

3. The likelihood of three estimates of fixed cost are 0.1 for $200,000, 0.4 for $300,000, and 0.5 for $400,000. What is the expected future value of fixed cost? *Solution:* $340,000, determined as follows — (0.1 × $200,000) + (0.4 × $300,000) + (0.5 × $400,000).

The expected value in each of the three cases came nearest to the one estimate having the highest probability; which makes sense because the high probability indicates a high likelihood of occurrence.

Probabilities can be assigned to each of the events that comprise a budget schedule. For example, a manufacturing company sells its product for $10 per unit. Expected volume and accompanying probabilities are estimated at 80,000 units (0.3), 100,000 (0.5), and 110,000 (0.2). Variable manufacturing cost can take on values of $5.10 per unit (0.2), $5.00 per unit (0.6), and $4.80 per unit (0.2). Variable marketing costs are $0.50 per unit, and fixed costs include $280,000 committed costs. Discretionary fixed costs are estimated to be $45,000, $70,000, and $80,000 at volume of 80,000, 100,000 and 110,000 units respectively. The income tax rate is 50%.[3] The possible outcomes for these data are illustrated in Exhibit 3–12. The diagram in the exhibit is called a *tree diagram*, because the branches are added at each junction. Probabilities at the two junctions are labeled p and q, respectively, so that specific probabilities can be referred to without ambiguity.

The sum of the probabilities at each branch level must equal 1. For example, the probabilities, labeled p (column 1), associated with the branch at sales volume are .2, .5, and .3, from the bottom to top; these add up to 1. The probabilities labeled q at the second branch (column 2) are, respectively, .2, .6, and .2, for each of the three sub-branches; and the sum of the probabilities of the sub-branches at each branch equals 1. This means that *one* level of sales definitely will be achieved. Similarly, one level of variable costs *must* occur.

Probability distributions for sales volume and variable costs in this case were artificially created. In real situations, the probabilities (p's and q's) assigned to each level would be estimated at the midpoint of ranges likely to occur. For

[3]This discussion is adopted from W. Ferrara and J. Hayya, "Towards Probabilistic Profit Budgets," *Management Accounting* (October 1970).

EXHIBIT 3-12 TREE DIAGRAM OF BASIC PROBLEM INCLUDING EXPECTED VALUES

(1) Volume (price = $10)	(2) Variable Manufacturing Cost	(3) Variable Marketing Cost	(4) Discretionary Costs	(5) Committed Costs	(6) Net Income after Tax—50% (NIAT)	(7) Joint* Probability (JP)	(8) Combination	(9) JP X NIAT
80,000 p = .3	$5.10 q = .2	$0.50	45,000	$280,000	$13,500	0.06	1	$ 810
	$5.00 q = .6	$0.50	$45,000	$280,000	$17,500	0.18	2	3,150
	$4.80 q = .2	$0.50	$45,000	$280,000	$25,000	0.06	3	1,530
100,000 p = .5	$5.10 q = .2	$0.50	$70,000	$280,000	$45,000	0.10	4	4,500
	$5.00 q = .6	$0.50	$70,000	$280,000	$50,000	0.30	5	15,000
	$4.80 q = .2	$0.50	$70,000	$280,000	$60,000	0.10	6	6,000
110,000 p = .2	$5.10 q = .2	$0.50	$80,000	$280,000	$62,000	0.04	7	2,480
	$5.00 q = .6	$0.50	$80,000	$280,000	$67,500	0.12	8	8,100
	$4.80 q = .2	$0.50	$80,000	$280,000	$78,500	0.04	9	3,140

Expected Value of Net Income after Tax $44,710

*Joint probabilities are calculated by multiplying the probabilities on the path (the succession of branches) moving toward each outcome.

SOURCE: Adopted from W. Ferrara and J. Hayya, "Towards Probabilistic Profit Budgets," *Management Accounting* (October 1970).

each of the nine combinations, variable marketing costs (column 3), discretionary costs (column 4), and committed costs (column 5) are assumed known with certainty, that is, they are not probabilistic. The nine combinations (column 8) in Exhibit 3–12 consider the three probabilistic sales estimates to be independent of the three probabilistic variable manufacturing cost estimates. A joint probability (column 7) is calculated for each combination by multiplying the probabilities on the path, moving from left to right; for example, joint probability of .06 for combination 1 is derived by multiplying the .3 probability for sales volume times the .2 probability for variable manufacturing costs. The outcome of each combination is shown in column 9. This last column represents the expected net income after tax. For example, the $810 of combination 1 represents the joint probability that an 80,000 sales volume and a $5.10 variable manufacturing cost will occur, multiplied by the net income that would result if these two events did occur. The expected value of net income after tax for the whole network shown in the tree diagram amounts to $44,710.

Budgets and probability tree analysis   Exhibit 3–13 presents the mean or expected value of every item for the nine (combinations) income statements. Note that the variable manufacturing costs vary directly with volume and the variable marketing costs and discretionary fixed costs change in steps (a characteristic of mixed costs). The joint probabilities that each combination will occur are shown under the net income row, and are used to calculate the expected profit of each combination. Exhibit 3–13 is actually a flexible budget containing additional information about the likelihood that a combination will occur.

But some activity is certain to occur. What is the expected value of the sales and cost activity? Exhibit 3–14 presents the expected value or mean of every item in the income statement, where the mean is the sum of the products resulting from the multiplication of the values of each combination and the joint probabilities assigned to each value. In mathematical symbols, the expected value is:

$$\Sigma x_1 p(x_1)$$

where x_1 are values of each combination, and $p(x_1)$ are the joint probabilities assigned to each x_1.

In addition, column 2 of Exhibit 3–14 displays a 100% probability range for the budget items. This range considers all nine combinations from Exhibit 3–13 and represents the "certain" limits of all budgeted income statement values. For example, the low values in the range for the first four line items, Sales through Contribution Margin, are $800,000, $384,000, $40,000, and $352,000: these amounts come from Exhibit 3–13, columns 1, 3, 1, and 1, respectively. Note that the low Contribution Margin is not derived by subtracting the low Variable Costs from Sales. That is, each value in the 100% range column represents the most extreme amount from among all nine alternatives rather than the

EXHIBIT 3–13 CALCULATION OF EXPECTED VALUES FOR ALL INCOME STATEMENT ITEMS

Combination	(1)	(2)	(3)	(4)	(5)	(6)	(7)	(8)	(9)
Sales	$800	$800	$800	$1,000	$1,000	$1,000	$1,100	$1,100	$1,100
Variable Costs:									
Manufacturing	408	400	384	510	500	480	561	550	528
Marketing	40	40	40	50	50	50	55	55	55
Contribution Margin	$352	$360	$376	$440	$450	$470	$484	$495	$517
Discretionary Costs:									
Manufacturing	10	10	10	20	20	20	30	30	30
Marketing	10	10	10	10	10	10	10	10	10
Administrative	25	25	25	40	40	40	40	40	40
Short-Run Margin	$307	$315	$331	$370	$380	$400	$404	$415	$437
Committed Costs	280	280	280	280	280	280	280	280	280
Net Income before Tax	$27	$35	$51	$90	$100	$120	$124	$135	$157
Tax–50%	13.5	17.5	25.5	45	50	60	62	67.5	78.5
Unconditional Net Income after Tax	$13.5	$17.5	$25.5	$45	$50	$60	$62	$67.5	$78.5
Joint Probability	.06	.18	.06	.10	.30	.10	.04	.12	.04
Expected Profit (dollars)	$810	$3,150	$1,530	$4,500	$15,000	$6,000	$2,480	$8,100	$3,140

SOURCE: Adopted from W. Ferrara and J. Hayya, "Towards Probabilistic Profit Budgets," *Management Accounting* (October 1970).

EXHIBIT 3–14   PROFIT BUDGET

	(1) Expected Value	(2) 100% Range		(3) 90% Range	
Sales	$960,000	$800,000 — $1,100,000		$800,000 — $1,100,000	
Variable Costs:					
Manufacturing	478,080	384,000 —	561,000	400,000 —	561,000
Marketing	48,000	40,000 —	55,000	40,000 —	55,000
Contribution Margin	$433,920	352,000 —	517,000	360,000 —	495,000
Discretionary Fixed Costs:					
Manufacturing	19,000	10,000 —	30,000	10,000 —	30,000
Marketing	10,000	10,000		10,000	
Administrative	35,500	25,000 —	40,000	25,000 —	40,000
Short-Run Margin	$369,420	307,000 —	437,000	315,000 —	415,000
Committed Fixed Costs:					
Manufacturing	180,000	180,000		180,000	
Marketing	40,000	40,000		40,000	
Administrative	60,000	60,000		60,000	
Net Income before Tax	$ 89,420	27,000 —	157,000	35,000 —	135,000
Tax — 50%	44,710	13,500 —	78,500	17,500 —	67,500
Net Income after Tax	$ 44,710	13,500 —	78,500	17,500 —	67,500

SOURCE: Adopted from W. Ferrara and J. Hayya, "Towards Probabilistic Profit Budgets,"
Management Accounting (October 1970).

result of adding or subtracting previous numbers within this one exhibit. Costs that are not probabilistic, such as the $10,000 Discretionary Marketing Cost, are shown as one dollar value, that is, they are known with certainty.

The range between the high and low extremes can be shortened, if management is willing to be less than certain about expected outcomes. For example, if management is willing to be 90% certain about the expected outcome, columns 1 and 9 of Exhibit 3–13 can be ignored when building a 90% range budget. That is, the 90% range excludes those alternatives having only a 10% likelihood of occurring (those farthest from the expected value). Combinations 1 and 9 had joint probabilities of .06 and .04, respectively, and their deletion produces a 90% interval that is slightly off center. For example, the Net Income After Tax would range between $17,500 and $67,500 with 90% confidence (columns 2 and 8, Exhibit 3–13). A 60% range would include only alternatives 3, 4, 5, 6, and 7;

combinations 1, 2, 8, and 9 would be excluded. These probability ranges aid the planning function by focusing on the potential variability of budgeted items that may occur. An additional modification that might improve the probability budget would consider continuous distributions rather than the discrete alternatives considered in our example.

SUGGESTED READINGS

Ferrara, W., and J. Hayya. "Towards Probabilistic Profit Budgets," *Management Accounting*, October 1970.

Koehler, R. W., and C. A. Neyhart. "Difficulties in Flexible Budgeting." *Managerial Planning*, May/June, 1972.

Pekar, Peter. "A Topology for Identifying Risk." *Managerial Planning*, September/October, 1976, pp. 13–17.

Wu, F. H. "Incremental Budgeting: A Decision Model." *Management Accounting*, May 1976.

QUESTIONS[a]

3–1   What is a flexible budget? How does a flexible budget differ from a static or fixed budget? Does a flexible budget offer any advantages over a fixed budget in situations where the expected level of activity is unknown, or at least uncertain?

3–2   The underlying principle of flexible budgets is that inputs used in production have a known relationship to the volume of business accomplished. In general, what type of relationship must exist between level of inputs, costs, and volume in order to produce flexible budgets?

3–3   Define the three terms *fixed cost*, *variable cost*, and *mixed cost*. Give examples of each. Describe the planning implications of each type of cost.

3–4   What is the relationship between fixed costs and volume of production activity?

3–5   What is the relevant range? How does this relate to fixed costs?

3–6   Fixed costs can be divided into two classes, committed and discretionary. Define and give examples of each. What are the implications of such classification for short-term budgeting?

[a]Questions, exercises, and problems that relate to subjects discussed in an appendix are indicated by a dagger.

3–7   Describe the detailed procedures followed in setting up a flexible budget for a hypothetical machining department of a manufacturing plant.

3–8   Determine the fixed and variable elements of a mixed cost that was $30,000 when production equalled 39,000 units and $20,000 when production was 19,000 units.

3–9   How can analysis of each item of a budget be used to separate the mixed costs into their fixed and variable elements? Who in the organization or what types of talents are required to make such a determination?

3–10   Definine *capacity* and *volume*. How is each measured? What is the relationship of these terms to the budgetary process?

†3–11   Probability is a useful measure of the likelihood that an event will occur. On what type of scale is probability usually measured? What numerical value indicates that the event is expected to occur with certainty? What value indicates that the event is not likely to occur?

†3–12   A probabilistic tree diagram is a graphic presentation of the sequential listings of all possible outcomes of a given event, with probabilities assigned to each outcome. Why is the sum of the probabilities associated with all the branches at any one junction equal to 1.0? What is the meaning of the joint probability, which is calculated by multiplying the probabilities along any path (the succession of branches) moving toward each outcome?

EXERCISES

3–13   It is important to understand the functional relationships among elements in a standard budget schedule. From your knowledge of standard budget formats, determine the missing numbers in A through C, below.

(A) Revenue $100,000; Net profit $60,000; Other expenses $25,000: Cost of Goods Sold $? .

(B) Total Assets $315,000; Total Liabilities $200,000; Owners' Equity $? .

(C) Beginning cash balance $5,000; Disbursements $45,000; Receipts $42,000; Desired ending balance $6,000; Amount to borrow $? .

3–14   Below are the 19X3 Cash Budget and Budgeted Income Statement, the 19X2 Actual Balance Sheet, and the 19X3 Budgeted Balance Sheet for Hylo Corp. Determine the dollar value of each of the missing (lettered) accounts. (Hint: Do them in alphabetical order.)

Budgeted Income Statement	Revenues	$600
	Expenditures	A
	Depreciation	200
	Net Profit	$100

Budget Cash Schedules	Cash Receipts		Cash Payments	
	Revenues	$ B	Pay Dividends	$150
	Issue Stock	C	Repay Notes	700
	Sell Bonds	600	Expenditures	D
	Sell Land	1,000		
	Total	$2,200	Total	$ E

Budgeted Balance Sheet		19X2	19X3		19X2	19X3
	Cash	$1,000	$ G	Current		
	Land	5,000	H	Liabilities	$3,000	$3,000
	Other			Bonds		
	assets			Payable	I	1,600
	(net)	800	600	Notes		
	Investments	F	1,000	Payable	900	K
		$7,800	$7,650	Stock	2,200	2,200
				Retained		
				Earnings	J	L
					$7,800	$7,650

†*3–15   Do you think that management would be able to make three types of projections: a most likely estimate, a pessimistic estimate, and an optimistic estimate for any given recurring activity (such as sales levels for a particular product)?

†*3–16   The least-squares method for fitting a straight line to a group of data is one method for separating a mixed cost into its fixed and variable components. The straight line represents an "average" relationship between dollar costs and volume. Under the least-squares method, is the vertical distance from any one point to the average line given equal weight to the vertical distance of any other point from the line, or are some vertical distances weighted more heavily than others?

3–17   The sales manager of the Howe Tube Company always felt uneasy at budget time. Each year the budget committee requested a sales forecast. "Just give us a figure," they would say, "and we will leave you alone." But then they would try to make him meet the figure if it was higher than last year's, or the president of the company would chide him if the figure was too low. The system seemed to keep him constantly "in hot water."

(A)   Which factors determine whether this company should use a flexible or a static budget?

(B) Would a flexible budget solve all the problems that the sales manager sees?

(C) If the sales department produced a flexible budget based on probabilistic estimates, would the purchasing department have to do the same?

(D) Will a flexible budget increase or decrease the accuracy of the budget figures?

(E) Do you think the problems faced by the sales manager are faced only by the Howe Tube Company?

3–18 The Jones Company has a flexible budget for which the sales manager supplies sales figures. His most conservative figure is 500,000 units, and his most likely figure is 550,000, but it is possible that Jones will sell 625,000 units. The president of Jones says, "If you are going to generate three different budgets, why not produce two more? Give me one for 575,000 units and one for 600,000 units." The product sells for $.50 and has fixed costs of $60,000. Variable costs are 17% of sales dollars, and mixed costs are $30,000 plus 10% of sales. The income tax is 40% of net income before taxes.

(A) What is the flexible budget for each of these volumes?

(B) Is it reasonable to assume that the fixed costs will remain fixed in the volume range of 500,000 units to 625,000 units?

(C) Why would the president request that volumes other than the most likely volume be used?

3–19 Acme Co. is a merchandising concern which buys inventory in large quantities for $20 per unit and resells it to its customers for $30 per unit. Acme buys its inventory on account (terms 30 days) and sells it for cash. Acme's inventory policy requires that the end of the month inventory balance equal 50% of anticipated sales for the next month. Operating expenses typically equal 10% of sales revenues.

Acme ends the month of May with the following balances: Cash $50,000; Inventory $180,000; Accounts payable $100,000. Acme expects to sell 18,000 units in June and 20,000 in July.

Prepare a budgeted income statement and a budgeted balance sheet to reflect expected activity for June.

3–20 A June 1 balance sheet for the Mobley Corporation reflects the following balances:

Cash	$ 15,000	Accounts Payable	$ 30,000
Accounts receivable	45,000	Loans Payable	10,000
Inventory	35,000	Owners' Equity	115,000
Investments	60,000		
Total	$155,000	Total	$155,000

Expected sales for June are 11,000 units at $8 each. Credit sales terms allow customers 30 days in which to pay: typically 30% of the current sales are for cash and the remaining 70% is collected during the following month. The desired ending inventory balance is established at 5,000 units. Inventory can be purchased for $4 per unit, payable within 45 days. Typically, 40% of the purchases are for cash, and the remaining 60% is paid during the following month. Mobley's cash policy specifies a desired minimum ending balance of $10,000: deficiencies will be borrowed under existing lines of credit and any excess will be used to reduce outstanding loans payable. Rental payments of $12,000 for the building and fixtures are made on the last day of the month. Additional invest-ments are to be purchased for $16,000 during June.

Prepare a budgeted income statement for June, and a June 30 budgeted balance sheet.

†3–21   Appendix A presents a discussion of the least-squares regression method for estimating the fixed and variable elements of mixed costs. Below are cost and volume data for two independent cases.

Case 1					Case 2			
Volume X	Costs Y$	X^2	XY		Volume X	Costs Y$	X^2	XY
0	1	0	0		1	2	1	2
1	4	1	4		2	9	4	18
3	8	9	24		4	12	16	48
4	9	16	36		5	14	25	70
Σ 8	22	26	64		Σ 12	37	46	138

(A) Using the two-point method, determine the fixed and variable components of cost for each case.

(B) Using the least-squares method, determine the fixed and variable components of cost for each case, i.e., substitute data for each case in the formula:

$$na + b(\Sigma\ x) = \Sigma\ y$$
$$a(\Sigma\ x) + b(\Sigma\ x_1) = \Sigma\ xy$$

(C) Describe the conditions under which the two methods would produce substantially similar results.

†3–22   Probabilistic budgets require estimates of the likelihood (probability) that each event in the budget will occur. Determine the expected value of a budget event for each of the three independent cases below.

(A) Although future revenue may be of any magnitude, management estimates three likely values at $1,000,000, $1,500,000, and $2,000,000, each having respective probabilities of 0.3, 0.6, and 0.1.

(B) Three variable cost estimates are $700,000, $800,000, and $900,000, and the associated probabilities are 0.2, 0.3, and 0.5.

(C) The likelihood of three estimates for fixed costs are: 0.4 at $150,000, 0.3 at $200,000, and 0.3 at $300,000.

3–23 When Copen Co. produced at a volume of 100,000 units, it incurred mixed cost of $100,000, and when 120,000 units were produced, mixed cost equaled $101,000.

(A) How much are fixed costs?

(B) How much is variable cost per unit?

(C) If volume dropped to 90,000 units, what amount would be expected for mixed costs?

(D) How can you tell which of the following methods will produce the "best" separation of mixed cost into fixed and variable parts: two-point method, visual plot, least-squares, account analysis?

3–24 The travel expenses and other related data for the sales force of Acme are listed below.

Week	Travel	No. of calls	No. of miles	No. of customers
1	500	50	1,800	125
2	300	30	900	215
3	800	80	1,600	140
4	300	30	5,600	115
5	500	50	1,000	225
6	300	30	300	115
7	800	80	1,800	140
8	900	90	1,900	145
9	700	70	1,600	135

(A) Which measure—calls, miles, or customers—provides the best basis for estimating travel expense?

(B) Estimate travel expense for 60 calls, using the basis you selected in part A.

PROBLEMS

†3–25 Labor hours and production costs for the last four months of 19X9, which you believe are representative for the year, were as follows:

Month	Labor Hours	Total Production Costs
September	2,500	$ 20,000
October	3,500	25,000
November	4,500	30,000
December	3,500	25,000
	14,000	$100,000

(A) Express the equation(s) required for applying the least-squares method of computation of fixed and variable production costs.

(B) Would the cost function derived by the least-squares method be linear, parabolic, or quadratic?

(C) If you use the least-squares method of computation, approximately how much is the fixed monthly production cost?

(D) If you use the least-squares method of computation, how much is the variable production cost per labor hour?

(E) Estimate total production costs at the 4,000 labor-hour level.

(AICPA adapted)

*3-26 The Cox Company, which manufactures a single product, operated at 80% of normal capacity in 19X5. Early in 19X6, Cox receives an order for a substantial number of units at 30% off the regular $7.00 sales price. The controller wants to accept the order because the additional units can be produced without expanding the Company's practical capacity.

    (A) Differentiate among
        1. Theoretical capacity,
        2. Practical capacity,
        3. Normal capacity,
        4. Expected capacity.

(B) Using your understanding of the relationship between costs and volume, explain why reduced prices might be justified for the additional units.

(AICPA adapted)

3-27 The cost of telephones is a mixed cost in most cases. A technique referred to as "the historical approach" can be used to determine budget costs. The following production units are listed along with the telephone costs that relate to recent periods.

	Production Units	Telephone Costs
January	20,000	$15,500
February	21,000	15,950
March	17,000	13,900
April	19,000	14,900
May	23,000	16,400
June	25,000	17,000

(A) Produce a scatter chart (graph) with the vertical axis measuring costs and the horizontal axis measuring production units.

(B) Is the fact that the points aren't exactly linear a problem to budgeting management? Could it be?

(C) What should the budgeted telephone expense be at production of 18,000 units? At 22,000 units?

(D) How far up and how far down the horizontal axis could the cost estimate be valid? 30,000 units? 1,000 units?

†3–28 A profit budget is prepared for next year as follows.

	Pessimistic	Most Likely	Optimistic
Sales ($8 per unit)	$800	$1,000	$1,200
Variable Costs	400	375	300
Marginal Contribution	$400	625	$ 900
Fixed Costs	200	200	200
Net Income before Taxes	$200	$ 425	$ 700
Tax (40%)	80	170	280
Net Income	$120	$ 255	$ 420

Management ascribes the following probabilities to these estimates.

	Pessimistic	Most Likely	Optimistic
Sales	.2	.5	.3
Variable Costs	.3	.5	.2

Using this information, answer the following questions.

(A) What is the joint probability of getting net income after taxes of $120?

(B) What is the joint probability of getting net income after taxes of $420?

(C) What is the probability of getting sales of $1,200?

(D) What is the total probability of having net income after taxes equal $180?

(E) What is the expected value of net income after taxes?

3–29 Costs may be classified in several ways: some are normally fixed; others are variable or mixed. Some fixed costs are classified for planning purposes as committed costs, and others as discretionary.

(A) What determines whether a cost is classified as fixed, variable, or mixed?

(B) What determines whether a fixed cost is committed or discretionary?

(C) All costs can be variable, depending on the volume or type of company. Specify whether each cost from the following list is normally fixed, variable, or mixed, and, for fixed costs, whether it is discretionary or committed.

a. Plant depreciation
b. Advertising expense
c. Indirect labor
d. Superintendent's salary
e. Foreman's salary
f. Electricity and heat
g. President's salary
h. Rent
i. Research and development

†3–30 Probabilities can be assigned to each of the events that comprise a budget schedule. For example, a manufacturing company sells its product for $10 per unit. Expected volume and accompanying probabilities are estimated at 80,000 units (0.3), 100,000 (0.5), and 110,000 (0.2). Variable cost per unit will be either $5 (0.6) or $6 (0.4). Fixed costs are estimated at $300,000 (0.7) or $400,000 (0.3).

(A) Prepare a tree diagram of all possible outcomes. Determine the net profit, joint probability, and expected value for each outcome.

(B) Prepare an income statement that reflects the expected values for revenue, variable cost, fixed cost, and net profit.

(C) If the lowest net profit outcome and the highest net profit outcome are eliminated, what will the joint probability of the remaining outcomes be?

3–31 Joe Smith, an apprentice managerial accountant, prepared a first draft of the budgeted financial statements and brought his work to his supervisor. The supervisor questioned several figures and asked for the source of each line item balance. After Smith prepared the schedules shown below, the supervisor found several questionable items. List four line items that reflect questionable sources of data input. Smith's statements follow:

Line	Pro Forma Income Statement lines (sources in parentheses)
a.	Sales Revenue (sales budgets)
b.	Interest income from Investment in Bonds (cash budget, balance sheet)
c.	Labor expense (labor schedules)
d.	Material expense (production budget)
e.	Research & Development (expenditures budget)
f.	Advertising expense (sales budget)
g.	Sales Commissions (sales budget)
h.	Income taxes (balance sheet)
i.	Net profit (difference between items, above)
	Pro Forma Balance Sheet
j.	Cash (cash budget)
k.	Accounts receivable (sales budget, cash budget)

l.   Inventories (purchasing budget)

m.   Other assets (beginning balance sheet, special projects budget)

n.   Wages payable (expenditures budget, cash budget)

o.   Accounts payable (purchasing budget, cash budget)

p.   Taxes payable (income statement, cash budget)

q.   Other liabilities (income statement, special projects budget)

r.   Owners' equity (beginning balance sheet, income statement, cash budget)

3-32   (A) During the first week in August, Direct Labor costs were $66,000 and production equaled 100,000 units. During the second week in August, Direct Labor costs were $61,000 and production equaled 75,000 units. During the third week, the budget calls for production of 80,000 units. At this level, estimated costs are what amount?

(B) Smith Co. has a flexible budget that calls for total cost of $110,000 when volume hits 200,000 units and cost of $125,000 at a volume of 250,000 units. When volume reaches 210,000 units, estimated total costs will be what amount?

3-33   Below is a master budget for one department of Hylo Co., along with the actual results achieved during the month. Top management doesn't know how to interpret the variances, since the actual level of operations was much larger than the budgeted volume. (U stands for "unfavorable.")

	Budget	Actual	Variance
Units produced	10,000	12,000	2,000
Labor	$ 1,000	$ 1,100	$ 100U
Material	2,000	2,500	500U
Variable overhead	3,000	3,500	500U
Fixed overhead	4,000	4,200	200U
	$10,000	$11,300	$1,300

(A) If a flexible budget had been prepared, which inputs would evidence a *favorable* variance?

(B) If a flexible budget had been prepared, which inputs would have evidenced an *unfavorable* variance?

(C) Why might the flexible budget for fixed overhead cost be some amount other than $4,000?

3-34   Department A, one of 15 departments in the plant, is involved in the production of all of the six products manufactured. The department is highly mechanized, and, as a result, its output is measured in direct machine hours. Flexible budgets are utilized throughout the factory in planning and controlling costs, but this problem is concerned only with flexible budgets in Department A.

The following data covering a time span of approximately six months were taken from the various budgets, accounting records, and performance reports (only representative items and amounts are utilized here):

On March 15, 19X1, the following flexible budget was approved for the department; it will be used throughout the 19X2 fiscal year which begins July 1, 19X1. This flexible budget was developed through the cooperative efforts of the department manager, his supervisor and certain staff members from the budget department.

19X2 Flexible Budget—Department A

Controllable Costs	Fixed Amount Per Month	Variable Rate Per Direct Machine Hour
Employee salaries	$ 9,000	
Wages	18,000	$.07
Materials		.09
Other costs	6,000	.03
	$33,000	$.19

On May 5, 19X1, the annual sales plan and the production budget were completed. In order to continue preparation of the annual profit plan (which was detailed by month), the production budget was translated to planned activity for each of the factory departments. The planned activity for Department A was:

	For the 12 months ending June 30, 19X2				
	Year	July	Aug.	Sept.	Etc.
Planned output in direct machine hours	325,000	22,000	25,000	29,000	249,000

On August 31, 19X1, the manager of Department A was informed that his planned output for September had been increased to 34,000 direct machine hours. He expressed some doubt as to whether this volume could be attained.

At the end of September 19X1, the accounting records provided the following actual data for the month for the department:

Actual output in direct machine hours	33,000
Actual controllable costs incurred:	
Employee salaries	$ 9,300
Wages	20,500
Materials	2,850
Other costs	7,510
	$40,160

(A) What activity base is utilized as a measure of volume in the budget for this department? How should one determine the range of the activity base to which the variable rates per direct machine hour are relevant? Explain.

(B) The two-point method was utilized in developing this flexible budget. Using wage costs as an example, illustrate and explain how this method would be applied in determining the fixed and variable components of wage costs for this department. Assume that the two-point budget values for wages are $19,400 at 20,000 direct machine hours and $20,100 at 30,000 direct machine hours.

(C) Explain and illustrate how the flexible budget should be utilized:
1. In budgeting costs when the annual sales plan and production budget are completed (about May 5, 19X1 or shortly thereafter).
2. In budgeting a cost revision based upon a revised production budget (about August 31, 19X1 or shortly thereafter).
3. In preparing a cost performance report for September 19X1.

(AICPA adapted)

†3–35 Bill Majors, budget director for Zinos Co., felt that the static budget traditionally used did not indicate the potential variability of the estimates used in building the budget. Bill polled the other members of the budget committee and found that they, too, were concerned about the static budgeting procedure. Furthermore, they felt confident that they could identify the probability that each type of cost or revenue was likely to occur. Revenues were estimated to reach the $1 million level with a probability of .3; $900,000 with a probability of .5; and $800,000 with a probability of .2. Variable costs were expected to equal 70% of revenue with a likelihood of .8, or 75% of revenue with a likelihood of .2. Fixed costs were estimated at two values, $100,000 or $60,000, with corresponding probabilities of .4 and .6. Bill asks you, as his subordinate, to determine the expected level of profits by constructing a probabilistic budget.

3–36 After reading an article you recommended on cost behavior, your client asks you to explain the following excerpts from it:

1. "*Fixed costs* are variable per unit of output and *variable costs* are fixed per unit of output (though in the long run all costs are variable)."
2. "*Depreciation* may be either a fixed cost or a variable cost, depending on the method used to compute it."

For each excerpt:

(A) Define the italicized terms. Give examples where appropriate.
(B) Explain the meaning of the excerpt to your client.

(AICPA adapted)

3-37   Identify the graph that best illustrates the cost volume relationship for each factory cost or expense element listed below.

The vertical axes of the graphs represent *total* dollars of expense and the horizontal axes represent production. In each case, the zero point is at the intersection of the two axes. The graphs may be used more than once.

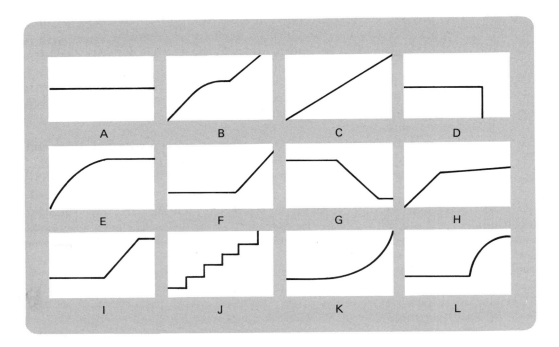

(A)   Depreciation of equipment, where the amount of depreciation charged is computed by the machine-hours method.

(B)   Electricity bill—a flat fixed charge, plus a variable cost after a certain number of kilowatt hours is used.

(C)   City water bill, which is computed as follows:

First 1,000,000 gallons or less	$1,000 flat fee
Next 10,000 gallons	.003 per gallon used
Next 10,000 gallons	.006 per gallon used
Next 10,000 gallons	.009 per gallon used
(and so on)	

(D)   Cost of lubricant for machines, where cost per unit decreases with each pound of lubricant used (for example, if one pound is used, the cost is $10.00; if two pounds are used, the cost is $19.98; if three pounds are used, the cost is $29.94; with a minimum cost per pound of $9.25).

(E) Depreciation of equipment, where the amount is computed by the straight-line method. When the depreciation rate was estabilished it was anticipated that the obsolescence factor would be greater than the wear and tear factor.

(F) Rent on a factory building donated by the city, where the agreement calls for a fixed fee payment unless 200,000 man-hours are worked, in which case no rent need be paid.

(G) Salaries of repairmen, where one repairman is needed for every 1,000 hours of machine hours or less (that is, 1,000 hours or less requires one repairman, 1,001 to 2,000 hours requires two repairmen, etc.).

(H) Federal unemployment compensation taxes for the year, where labor force is constant throughout year (average annual salary is $6,000 per worker).

(I) Cost of raw material used.

(J) Rent on a factory building donated by county, where agreement calls for rent of $100,000 less $1 for each direct labor hour worked in excess of 200,000 hours, but minimum rent of $20,000 must be paid.

(AICPA adapted)

†3-38 The Ramon Co. manufactures a wide range of products at several different plant locations. Its Franklin Plant, which manufactures electrical components, has been experiencing some difficulties with fluctuating monthly overhead costs. The fluctuations have made it difficult to estimate the level of overhead that will be incurred for any one month.

Management wants to be able to estimate overhead costs accurately in order to plan its operation and financial needs better. A trade association publication to which Ramon Co. subscribes indicates that, for companies manufacturing electrical components, overhead tends to vary with direct labor hours.

One member of the accounting staff has proposed that the cost behavior pattern of the overhead costs be determined. Then overhead costs could be predicted from the budgeted direct labor hours.

Another member of the accounting staff suggested that a good starting place for determining the cost behavior pattern of overhead costs would be an analysis of historical data. The historical cost behavior pattern would provide a basis for estimating future overhead costs. The methods proposed for determining the cost behavior pattern included the two-point method, the scattergraph method, simple linear regression, multiple regression, and exponential smoothing. Ramon Co. decided to employ the two-point method, the scattergraph method, and simple linear regression. Data on direct labor hours and the respective overhead costs incurred were collected for the past two years. The raw data and the scattergraph prepared from the data are presented below.

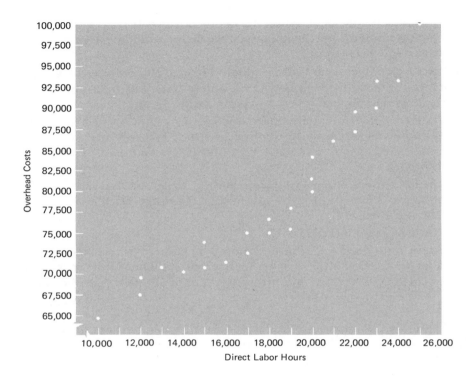

Using linear regression, the constant term a of the regression equation $Y = a + bx$ was found to be 39,859, and the slope, b, was found to be 2.1549.

19X3	Direct Labor Hours	Overhead Costs	19X4	Direct Labor Hours	Overhead Costs
January	20,000	$84,000	January	21,000	$86,000
February	25,000	99,000	February	24,000	93,000
March	22,000	89,500	March	23,000	93,000
April	23,000	90,000	April	22,000	87,000
May	20,000	81,500	May	20,000	80,000
June	19,000	75,500	June	18,000	76,500
July	14,000	70,500	July	12,000	67,500
August	10,000	64,500	August	13,000	71,000
September	12,000	69,000	September	15,000	73,500
October	17,000	75,000	October	17,000	72,500
November	16,000	71,500	November	15,000	71,000
December	19,000	78,000	December	18,000	75,000

(A) Using the two-point method, determine the cost behavior pattern of the overhead costs for the Franklin Plant.

(B) Using the results of the regression analysis, calculate the estimate of overhead costs for 22,500 direct labor hours.

(C) Which of the three proposed methods (two-point, scattergraph, linear regression) should Ramon Co. employ to determine the historical cost behavior pattern of Franklin Plant's overhead costs? Explain your answer completely, indicating the reasons why the other methods should not be used.

(CMA adapted)

3-39 (This problem presents a continuation of facts presented earlier in 2-35.)

The managing partner of Johnson & Smith, Certified Public Accountants, requested your help in preparing the budget for 19X3.

The goals of the plan included (1) income objectives, (2) standardized billing procedures (with flexibility for adjustments by the partners), and (3) assignment schedules to eliminate overtime and to allow for nonchargeable time, such as vacations and illness. The firm plans a 52-week year with five-day, forty-hour weeks.

The partners have set an annual income target (after partners' salaries) of at least $55,000. The budget for fiscal year 19X3 is 700 hours of chargeable time at $45 per hour for Johnson, and 1,100 hours at $40 per hour for Smith. Johnson and Smith are to devote all other available time, except as specified below, to administration. The billing rates for all other employees including secretaries are to be set at a level to recover their salaries plus the following overhead items: fringe benefits of $15,230, other operating expenses of $49,380, and a contribution of $20,500 to target income.

	Annual Salary
Partners	
John B. Johnson, CPA	$24,000
Walter L. Smith, CPA	18,000
Professional Staff	
Supervisor:	
Harold S. Vickers, CPA	17,500
Senior Accountant	
Duane Lowe, CPA	12,500
Assistants	
James M. Kennedy	10,500
Viola O. Quinn	10,500
Secretaries	
Mary Lyons	7,800
Johnnie L. Hammond	6,864
Livia A. Garcia	6,864

The partners agree that salary levels are fair bases for allocating overhead in setting billing rates, with the exception that salary costs of the secretaries' nonchargeable time are to be added to overhead to arrive at total overhead to be allocated. Thus, the billing rate for each secretary will be based upon the salary costs of her chargeable time plus her share of the total overhead. No portion of total overhead is to be allocated to partners' salaries.

The following information is available for nonchargeable time:

1. Because of his recent illness, Johnson expects to be away an additional week. Smith expects no loss of time from illness. All other employees are to be allowed one illness day per month (12 days each).

2. Allowable vacations are as follows:

1 month	Johnson
	Smith
3 weeks	Vickers
	Lyons
2 weeks	All other employees

3. The firm observes seven holidays annually. If the holiday falls on a weekend, the office is closed the preceding Friday or the following Monday.

4. Kennedy and Quinn should each be allotted three days to sit for the November 19X2 CPA examination.

5. Hours are budgeted for other miscellaneous activities of the personnel as follows:

	Johnson	Smith	Vickers	Lowe	Kennedy	Quinn	Lyons	Hammond	Garcia
Firm Projects		100	40	40	40		200		
Professional Development	80	80	56	40	40	50	24	16	24
Professional Meetings	184	120	40	40	16	16	24	8	8
Firm Meetings	48	48	48	24	24	24	48	8	8
Community Activities	80	40	40	24	16	16	12		
Office Time (other than firm administration)	—	—	84	72	—	—	1,000	716	808
Total Other Miscellaneous	392	388	308	240	136	106	1,308	748	848

6. Unassigned time should be budgeted for Lowe, Kennedy, and Quinn as 8, 38, and 78 hours, respectively.

7. Budgeted chargeable hours and billing rates are as follows:

	Budgeted Chargeable Hours	Budgeted Hourly Billing Rate
Johnson	700	$45
Smith	1,100	40
Vickers	1,600	32
Lowe	1,650	25
Kennedy	1,550	15
Quinn	1,450	17
Lyons	500	5
Hammond	1,150	7
Garcia	1,200	7

Prepare a condensed statement of budgeted income for the year ending June 30, 19X3.

(AICPA adapted)

CHAPTER 4

Cost-Volume-Profit Analysis

Objectives

After studying this chapter, you should be able to do the following:

Define cost-volume-profit analysis *and discuss its relationship to budgeted income statements.*

Identify the elements of a cost-volume-profit chart and indicate how the interrelation of the elements would be affected by a change in price, in variable costs, in fixed costs, or in volume.

Calculate a breakeven point *or a desired profit volume, using an income-statement equation technique, called the* unit contribution margin approach.

Calculate a breakeven point or a desired dollar profit volume, using the contribution margin ratio approach.

List the assumptions underlying cost-volume-profit analysis.

Special-analysis budgets are prepared most often on a nonroutine basis. These budgets may consist of graphic presentations, control reports, feasibility studies, or evaluations of alternative decisions. One type of special budget, cost-volume-profit analysis, is discussed in this chapter.

COST-VOLUME-PROFIT ANALYSIS

The *budgeted income statement* was introduced in Chapter 3. Profit budgets are important to strategic planners because they provide a basis for analyzing prices or cost structures and the effects of changes in volume on profits. **Cost-volume-profit analysis** *is a planning tool that considers the inherent relationships among prices, cost structure, volume, and profits.* Cost-volume-profit analysis, or CVP, answers such questions as:

1. Given existing prices and cost structure, what volume of operations is needed to earn a profit of *x* dollars?

2. If prices are cut by *x* percent, how much of an increase in volume is needed to maintain the previous level of profits?

3. If variable costs are to be cut by the acquisition of some automating machinery (hence, an increase in fixed cost), how large a cut is required to provide a profit of *z* dollars, assuming the existing level of operations continues in the future?

4. If variable costs increase by *x* percent, what happens to profits, assuming that volume will increase by *z* percent?

CVP is based on a model of an income statement in which profit represents the algebraic difference between total revenue and total costs. Total costs are divided into fixed and variable components in the typical CVP analysis, as illustrated in the following summarized income statement:

Revenue	$100,000
− Variable Costs	60,000
Contribution Margin	$ 40,000
− Fixed Costs	25,000
Net Profit	$ 15,000

Contribution margin *is the difference between revenue and variable costs*, and represents the amount available first for meeting fixed costs and then for contributing toward profit. As previously discussed, both the revenue and the variable costs vary directly with volume. Assuming that the volume associated with this income statement is 40,000 units, the average price charged for each unit is $2.50 while the variable costs are $1.50 per unit. Fixed costs do not vary with changes in volume.

A GRAPHIC APPROACH TO CVP ANALYSIS

The contribution-margin income statement may be illustrated in a graph, as in Exhibit 4–1. In both parts of Exhibit 4–1, volume is shown on the horizontal axis, and dollars of revenue or costs are measured on the vertical axis. Volume may be shown as units of sales, sales dollars, or some other measure of output activity. In Part A of Exhibit 4–1, variable costs are added to fixed costs (to produce total costs), and revenues are super-imposed on both. (CVP relationships are traditionally described in this manner.) Part B shows a slight variation—a total-cost line produced by adding fixed costs to variable costs. This variation illustrates the contribution margin for all levels of volume, indicated by the shaded area. Although the total-cost lines and revenue lines are identical on both graphs, the traditional form (Part A) does not portray the contribution margin.

EXHIBIT 4–1   GRAPHIC ILLUSTRATION OF CVP ANALYSIS

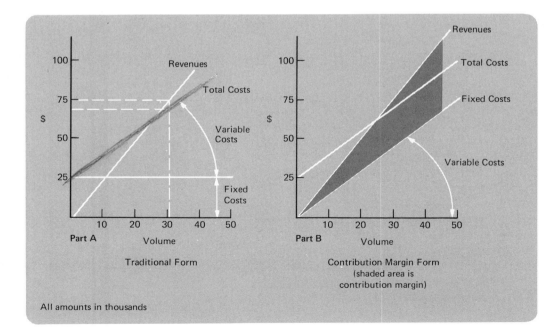

Part A — Traditional Form

Part B — Contribution Margin Form (shaded area is contribution margin)

All amounts in thousands

The graphic presentation of CVP relationships is simply a continuous profit plan. In contrast, a budgeted income statement represents the values at only one level of volume; that is, it is equivalent to a vertical line drawn at the stated level of volume. Thus, CVP charts allow the strategic planner to view all the relationships among cost, volume, and profit at once for all levels of volume. For example, if a manager wished to determine the financial consequences of selling 30,000 units, he could read the values directly off the CVP graph in Exhibit 4–1. At 30,000 volume, fixed cost is $25,000, variable costs extend from $25,000 to $70,000, and revenue is $75,000. More accurate readings at other volumes require an enlarged graph with refined scales.

When the graphic approach to CVP analysis is used, the effects of changes in any of the variables are readily illuminated. For example, profits are indicated as the shaded area on the CVP chart (Part A of Exhibit 4–2). *The point at which*

EXHIBIT 4–2   GRAPHIC ANALYSIS—DROP IN PRICE

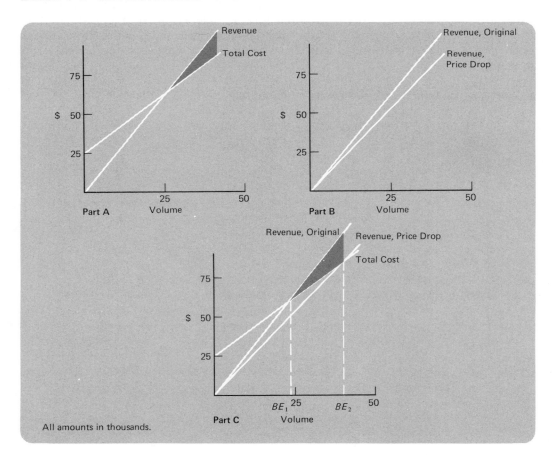

total costs are exactly equal to total revenues is generally called the **breakeven point**. Profits accrue above the breakeven point; losses are incurred below this point. The breakeven point may be described as being a certain distance along either axis; that is, it can be measured by the revenue or volume levels where profits are zero. Breakeven occurs in Part A of Exhibit 4–2 at 25,000 units and $62,500: at this point, revenues of $62,500 exactly equal the sum of fixed and variable costs ($25,000 + $1.50 × 25,000). For any level of volume above the breakeven point, profits can be measured by the vertical distance between the total costs and the total revenues lines.

A drop in price is indicated on a graph by a downward rotation of the revenue line, as shown in Part B of Exhibit 4–2. For any level of volume, the new revenue line is equal to the lower price multiplied by the number of units sold. As volume increases (moves toward the right), the difference between the old revenue line and the new revenue line becomes greater, as indicated by the triangular shaded wedge in Part C. The original breakeven point is labeled BE_1; the breakeven after the price drop is labeled BE_2; that is, reducing prices decreases the unit contribution margin. Therefore a much larger volume will be needed just to reach the former point of profits.

Similarly, an increase in per-unit variable cost is indicated by rotating the variable-cost line upward, which rotates the total-cost line as well, as shown in Part A of Exhibit 4–3. The CVP effect of increasing per-unit variable costs is shown as the shaded area in Part B. Here again, the original breakeven is indicated as BE_1 and the subsequent breakeven is BE_2. Increasing the variable costs from $1.50 to $1.80 extends the breakeven volume from 25,000 units to approximately 36,000 units.

EXHIBIT 4–3 GRAPHIC ANALYSIS—INCREASE IN VARIABLE COST

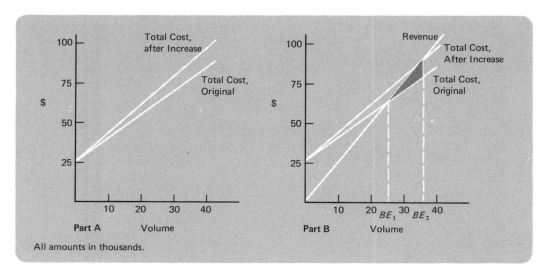

Reducing fixed costs lowers the total-cost line (parallel to the old line) (Parts A, B, and C of Exhibit 4-4). The increase in profit resulting from a drop in fixed costs is represented by the shaded area of Part C. Note that profits are affected by the same amount as fixed costs are. A $10,000 decrease in fixed costs will produce a $10,000 profit at the original breakeven volume of 25,000 units. Here again, the original and subsequent breakeven points are clearly marked. Breakeven volume drops from 25,000 units to 15,000 units.

A graphic presentation is valuable to managers who wish to examine the consequences of alternative courses of action. Cost-volume-profit analysis is an excellent tool, especially if the planner desires only a rough approximation of the effects of changing values for costs, volumes, or profits. CVP charts must be drawn to scale, however, when planners desire exact information.

For example, consider a case in which the price of a product equals $5 per unit, the variable cost equals $4.25 per unit, and the fixed costs equal $30,000.

EXHIBIT 4-4   GRAPHIC ANALYSIS—REDUCING FIXED COST

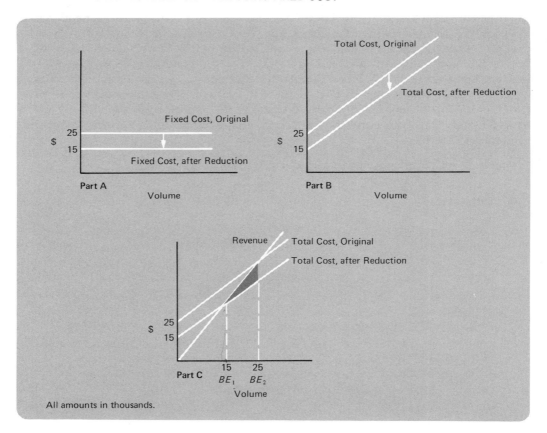

All amounts in thousands.

The breakeven point can be calculated graphically, as shown in Exhibit 4–5. Reading from the horizontal axis, the breakeven point equals 40,000 units. From the vertical axis, it occurs when total revenues and total costs equal $200,000. Note also, in Exhibit 4–5, that the shaded area above the breakeven point represents profits that would occur at any volume of activity, whereas the shaded area below breakeven represents the amount of losses incurred. A strategic planner could see immediately that the loss at 10,000 units of sales volume would be about $25,000 (exactly $22,500), whereas the profit at 50,000 units of volume would be about $10,000 (exactly $7,500).

EXHIBIT 4–5   COST-VOLUME-PROFIT CHART

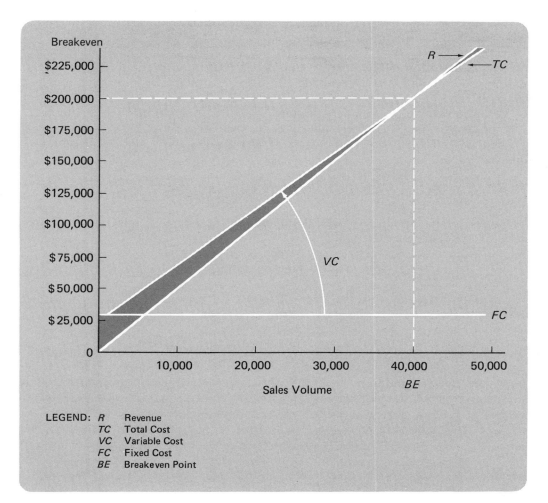

LEGEND: R   Revenue
        TC Total Cost
        VC Variable Cost
        FC Fixed Cost
        BE Breakeven Point

CVP ANALYSIS—UNIT
CONTRIBUTION MARGIN APPROACH

Any particular CVP point can be calculated in units of volume by using an income-statement equation technique called the **unit contribution margin** approach. The unit contribution margin is the difference between the per-unit price and variable costs per unit. The expected profits from operations can be determined by subtracting the fixed costs from the product of the unit contribution margin multiplied by number of units sold.

Albegraic manipulation of the cost-volume-profit variables results in the following relationship:[1]

> Number of units sold equals the sum of fixed costs plus profits divided by the unit contribution margin.

This representation of the cost-volume-profit relationship enables the strategic planner to calculate the effects on the other variables of changing any one variable.

For example, reconsider the case illustrated in Exhibit 4–5, in which the price per unit was $5, the variable costs per unit were $4.25, and the fixed cost was $30,000. The breakeven point is at 40,000 units of volume, calculated as follows:

$$40,000 = \$30,000 \div (\$5 - \$4.25)$$

To translate the breakeven point into dollars, simply multiply the breakeven units by the price per unit,

$$40,000 \times \$5 = \$200,000$$

To calculate expected profits at a volume of 50,000 units, simply plug the known values into the equation and solve for the unknown value.

$$50,000 = (30,000 + \text{Profit}) \div (\$5 - \$4.25)$$
$$\text{Profit} = \$7,500$$

In the same fashion, a 25,000-unit breakeven volume is associated with a $2.50 price, a $1.50 variable cost, and a $25,000 fixed cost, as illustrated in Exhibit 4–1. That is, breakeven volume is determined as follows:

$$25,000 = \$25,000 \div (\$2.50 - \$1.50)$$

---

[1]Add fixed costs to both sides of the equation and then divide both sides of the equation by the unit contribution margin.

CVP ANALYSIS—CONTRIBUTION MARGIN RATIO APPROACH

One reason that the unit contribution margin approach produced a breakeven point expressed in units was that both the numerator and the denominator of the fraction (fixed costs divided by the contribution margin per unit) are expressed in dollars. Dividing dollars by dollars produces a nondollar result. If the denominator is stated in nondollar terms, then the results will be in dollars.

One way to produce a breakeven point in dollar terms is to begin by expressing the contribution margin as a percent of sales price;[2] that is, divide the contribution margin per unit by the price. The result is called a contribution margin ratio. The contribution margin ratio expresses the portion of each sales dollar that contributes first toward meeting fixed costs and, once fixed costs are fully covered, contributes toward producing profits. Breakeven calculated with a contribution margin ratio is expressed in dollars.

Breakeven dollars equal fixed costs divided by the contribution margin ratio. For example, the contribution margin ratio for the previous case is determined by dividing the $5 price into the difference between the price and the $4.25 variable cost per unit: $.75/$5 = .15. Breakeven dollar volume is determined by dividing the $30,000 fixed costs by the contribution margin ratio, $30,000/.15 = $200,000. To translate this breakeven point into unit volume, simply divide the breakeven dollars by the price per unit,

$$\$200,000 \div \$5 = 40,000$$

Mathematical solutions to cost-volume-profit analysis at points other than breakeven treat profits in the same fashion as fixed costs. As you remember, the contribution margin represents the amount per unit sold that contributes first toward fixed costs and then toward the desired level of profit. In other words, a desired level of profit is similar to a fixed cost, for planning purposes. For mathematical solutions to CVP problems having a stated level of desired profits, simply add the desired profit to fixed costs. The unit contribution margin formula then becomes $(NP + FC) \div CM = $ CVP units, where NP represents profits, FC fixed costs, and CM contribution margin per unit. The contribution margin ratio formula becomes: CVP dollars = $(NP + FC) \div CMR$, where NP represents profits, FC fixed costs, and CMR the contribution margin ratio. Remember, the contribution margin ratio is determined by dividing the unit contribution margin by the price per unit.

For example, reconsider the previous case, but now add a desired profit level of $7,500 (as before, price, variable cost per unit and fixed costs are $5,

[2]More technically, as a decimal expression.

$4.25, and $30,000, respectively). The dollar volume needed to achieve a $7,500 profit is determined as follows:

$$(\$30,000 + \$7,500) \div (\$5 - \$4.25)/\$5 = \$37,500/.15 = \$250,000$$

To translate this dollar CVP volume into unit volume, simply divide the CVP dollars by the price per unit:

$$\$250,000 \div \$5 = 50,000$$

Multi-product CVP analysis   The contribution margin ratio approach can be used to calculate the breakeven for the firm as a whole. Assume that a firm sells many products at many different prices and that variable costs differ for each product. In such a case, the contribution margin is determined by subtracting from total revenue all of the variable costs for the whole firm.. Total revenue is then divided into the contribution margin: since revenue is larger than the contribution margin, the result is a decimal smaller than 1.0. The contribution margin ratio in this form can provide the breakeven point for firms selling a mix of goods at varying prices. For example, consider a firm having total revenues of $2,000,000, fixed costs of $300,000, variable costs of $1,500,000, and profit of $200,000. The contribution margin is $500,000 (i.e., $2,000,000 − $1,500,000), and the contribution margin ratio is .25 (i.e., $500,000 ÷ $2,000,000). When the contribution margin ratio approach is applied, the breakeven point equals $300,000 ÷ .25 = $1,200,000.

Use of this form of multi-product CVP analysis depends on two assumptions: (1) that the contribution margin ratios for all products are identical or (2) that the proportion of sales by each product is known and stable. If both assumptions do not hold, then a change in volume will occur at the same time as the firm's total contribution margin ratio changes, and projections from a CVP analysis will be misleading. Although adjustments to multi-product CVP analysis can be made, discussion of these points extends beyond the scope of this book. Interested readers are directed to any standard advanced cost accounting textbook.

Where these assumptions can reasonably be made, the multi-product contribution margin ratio formula becomes: CVP dollars = $(NP + FC) \div CMR$, where NP, FC, and CMR represent profit, fixed cost, and contribution margin ratio, respectively. As a second example, consider a multi-product firm that has fixed costs equal to $10,000,000 and specifies a minimum desired profit of $2,000,000 as part of its budget objectives. Prices for the firm's products are established at 300% of variable costs, so variable costs are known to be one-third of the price. The contribution margin ratio, rounded, is .67 (i.e., 100% − 1/3 = 2/3). A dollar CVP volume that will achieve the desired profit level is determined as follows:

$$(\$10,000,000 + \$2,000,000) \div 2/3 = \$18,000,000$$

A budgeted income statement that reflects these cost-volume-profit relationships appears as follows:

Revenue	$18,000,000
Variable Costs (1/3)	6,000,000
Contribution Margin	$12,000,000
Fixed Costs	10,000,000
Net Profit	$ 2,000,000

CVP solutions for other unknown variables CVP analysis is usually employed to determine the value of either unit or dollar volume measures. CVP analysis also can be used to examine the consequences of changes in any of the following variables: price or revenue, variable cost per unit or total variable cost, fixed cost, net profit, or any combination of these variables. For example, consider the following independent cases.

1. What is the minimum price that can be charged if desired profit is set at $100,000, fixed cost is $400,000, variable cost per unit is $8, and volume is 200,000 units? *Solution:* the traditional unit contribution margin CVP point for this problem takes the following form:

$$(\$100,000 + \$400,000) \div (P - \$8) = 200,000$$

This equation can be transformed, as follows:

$$(\$100,000 + \$400,000) \div 200,000 = (P - \$8),$$
$$(\$500,000) \div 200,000 = \$2.50 = (P - \$8)$$
$$P = \$10.50$$

2. How much will the variable cost per unit be if the price is $8 per unit, fixed costs are $40,000, desired profit is $10,000, and volume is 10,000 units? *Solution:* a contribution margin of $50,000 is required ($40,000 + $10,000) of the 10,000 units, or $5 per unit. The price, less the per unit contribution margin, will equal the variable cost per unit, or $8 − $5 = $3.

3. What amount of fixed costs can be incurred if profits of $30,000 are desired when revenue is expected to equal $500,000 and the contribution margin ratio is 70%? *Solution:* the contribution margin is 70% of $500,000, or $350,000. Subtracting desired profits from the contribution margin produces the estimated fixed costs: $350,000 − $30,000 = $320,000.

GRAPHING CONTRIBUTION MARGIN
RATIO CVP ANALYSIS

A CVP graph like those illustrated earlier could not be prepared for a firm that sells many different products at many different prices, because no one price or variable cost per unit would be representative enough. Nonetheless, the contribution margin ratio approach does provide a mechanism for graphing CVP relationships in which volume is measured in terms of sales revenue. For example, consider the cost-volume-profit relationships expressed in the following income statement:

	Dollars	Percent
Revenue	$100,000	100%
Variable Costs	60,000	60%
Contribution Margin	$ 40,000	40%
Fixed Costs	25,000	
Net Profit	$ 15,000	

A cost-volume-profit graph for this income statement is presented in Exhibit 4–6. Both the horizontal and vertical axes are scaled in terms of dollars. Since a dollar of revenue on the vertical axis is equal to a dollar of volume on the

EXHIBIT 4–6   CONTRIBUTION MARGIN RATIO CVP GRAPH

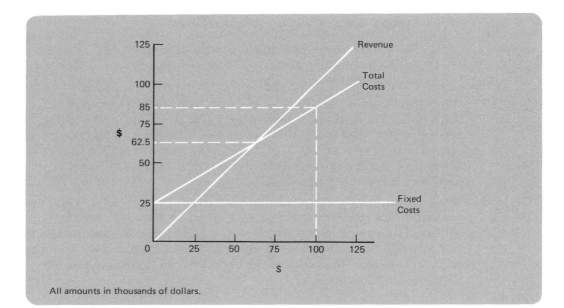

All amounts in thousands of dollars.

horizontal axis, the revenue line passes through the origin and slopes upward at a 45-degree angle. The fixed costs line is drawn as in previous exhibits, parallel to the horizontal axis at $25,000. The total cost line is determined with reference to two points, fixed costs at zero volume and total costs at a volume equal to the revenue; that is, the total costs line starts at $25,000 (at zero volume) and slopes upward to pass through the $85,000 point (at $100,000 volume).

Like all CVP graphs, Exhibit 4–6 can be used to highlight important aspects of cost-volume-profit relationships. Note the breakeven point at $62,500, an amount that can be verified by dividing the fixed costs by the contribution margin ratio ($25,000 ÷ .40 = $62,500). The graph can be used to determine the consequences of changing any of the basic elements: for example, a $25,000 net profit is derived at volume of $125,000 ($50,000 ÷ .40 = $125,000). A reduction of fixed costs will produce a corresponding increase in profit (decrease in loss) at all levels of volume.

COST-VOLUME-PROFIT ASSUMPTIONS

Three assumptions underlie the CVP analysis discussed up to this point: **relevant range**, accounting reliability, and *ceteris paribus* (all other things constant). These assumptions limit the generality and usefulness of cost-volume-profit analysis. Analysts aware of these assumptions may counter their limiting potential, however, by adjusting data inputs in compensating amounts. Unless these assumptions are recognized, serious errors may result from conclusions based on a misleading analysis.

Relevant range The *relevant range* is that band of volume over which fixed costs are truly fixed and variable costs fluctuate in direct proportion to volume. In reality, fixed and variable costs may not behave in the manner described earlier in this chapter.

For example, consider the elements included in fixed costs: depreciation on plant and equipment, salaries of general managers, property taxes, rent or lease expenses on plant and equipment. If the volume of activity fell to zero, some costs could be eliminated or reduced. Supervisors could be dismissed, leased property returned to the lessor, and property taxes abated. On the other hand, if the volume of activity increased sufficiently, additional fixed costs would be incurred as a result of the need for additional supervision, more leased or rented facilities, depreciation on newly acquired plant or equipment, and additional taxes. In other words, fixed costs are fixed only over some particular range of activity, and a more accurate graphic representation of fixed costs would be illustrated in steps, as shown in Exhibit 4–7.

The different levels of steps may simply reflect the magnitude of scales used for the graph. For example, assume that each laborer can produce 1,000

EXHIBIT 4-7   FIXED COST AND THE RELEVANT RANGE

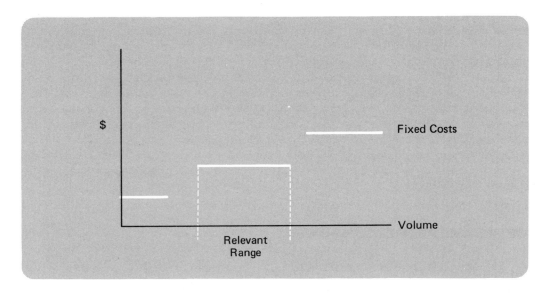

units per month and that a foreman is needed to supervise every five laborers. Foremen are paid $1,000 per month. A graph of foremen supervision costs, with the vertical axis scaled in $1,000 increments and the horizontal scale in 1,000-unit increments, produces a step costs picture. Next, think about supervision costs of General Motors Corp., whose monthly production can vary by tens of thousands of automobiles (note: sales for GM are about 80,000 units per *week*). Consider changing the scales from 1,000 to 10,000. Next, consider changing the scales to 1,000,000. The fixed cost of supervision at low volume turns into step costs at medium volume and into variable costs at high volume.

Variable costs do not always vary in proportion to output. When volume of operations is very low, relatively few laborers are required. As volume of operations increases, more workers will be needed, a production line may be set up, and workers may begin to specialize in a particular task. With further increases in volume, more laborers will have to be trained and more supervisors hired to oversee their work. Furthermore, existing labor may be asked to work overtime or may be put on second shifts, which would result in additional costs.

In any event, efficiency will probably fall off after a point because of inexperience, poor training, limited physical resources, or poor supervision. Variable costs, which may not change by equal amounts for every unit of production, will probably appear as shown in Exhibit 4-8. The first part of the curve, labeled "1," represents efficiencies introduced through specialization: an economic term for this type of cost is "returns to scale." The second part of the curve, labeled "2,"

EXHIBIT 4-8   VARIABLE COST AND CHANGES IN EFFICIENCY

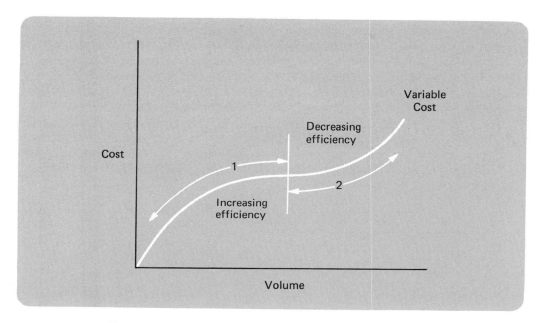

represents inefficiencies resulting from limited resources—this type of cost behavior is termed, "diminishing returns." In range 1, each additional unit costs less to produce, whereas in range 2, each additional unit costs more to produce. Although costs vary with volume, they do not vary proportionately; that is, the cost of any one unit is not necessarily equal to that of all other units.

Adding fixed costs to variable costs produces a total-cost line, as shown in Part A of Exhibit 4-9. Revenues in real situations are not always proportional to sales. We originally assumed that revenue was calculated as price per unit multiplied by the number of units sold, and that price was constant over all levels of activity. In reality, prices in some industries must drop to induce purchases of more goods after a point. A given volume of sales can be attained at a given price, but additional sales can be made only at lower prices. This form of revenue line is shown in Part B of Exhibit 4-9.

Part C of Exhibit 4-9 depicts the cost-volume-profit relationships in a more realistic fashion. Note that there are two breakeven points. The first occurs when revenues overtake costs, and the second occurs as costs overtake revenues. For planning purposes, accountants rarely consider the total range of activity indicated on the horizontal axis, rather, they examine fluctuating cost behavior within a limited range, the *relevant range*. Within the relevant range, accountants can assume that fixed costs are fixed and that variable costs vary equally per unit, as shown in Exhibit 4-10.

EXHIBIT 4–9   TOTAL COST, REVENUE, AND BREAKEVEN

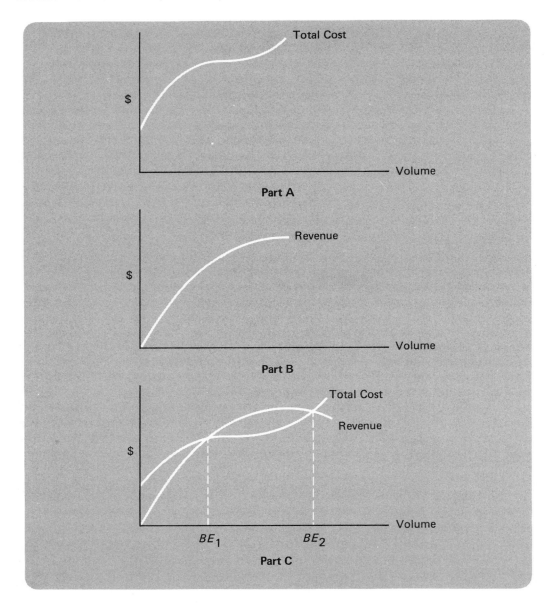

Accounting reliability   The CVP analysis described above assumes that accountants know which costs are fixed and which are variable and that they can ascertain the relationship of costs to various volumes of production. Often, in real situations, fixed and variable costs can be neither counted nor separated.

EXHIBIT 4–10   RELEVANT RANGE

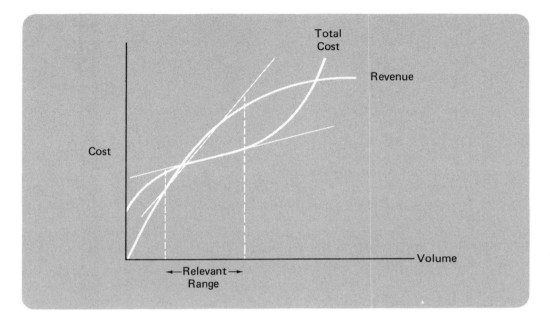

For example, consider mixed costs (discussed in Chapter 3) consisting of fixed and variable elements that may not be separable.

Or, consider direct labor, which is often classified as variable. Labor costs do not usually vary directly with volume. When low volume is required, labor will slow down to accomplish the task. A full day's work (pay) may be given to a laborer even though his task can be accomplished in less than a full day. On the other hand, as volume of activity increases, the laborer can accommodate the increased production demands without costing the firm additional labor expense.

Some costs, such as depreciation, cannot be determined exactly. There are many methods of calculating depreciation, and each produces a different annual charge. Which of the many depreciation charges is the "correct" one is a question quietly disregarded by most practicing accountants.

Ceteris paribus (all other things constant)   We have assumed that all variables other than the particular one under consideration have remained constant throughout the CVP analysis—that is, production efficiency, product mix, costs, prices, and inventory levels do not change during the planning period. Remember, however, that all planning relates to future activities that may be either more or less efficient; equipment breakdowns or "break-ins" may decrease or increase efficiency.

Breakeven analysis for firms selling more than one product is calculated with the contribution margin ratio based on total revenues. For example, a firm that manufactures three products at different costs and sells them for different prices must use the contribution margin ratio form of CVP analysis. If revenue were $1,000,000 and variable costs were $800,000, the contribution margin ratio would be 20%. Use of this ratio assumes a constant service mix, that is, the relative proportions of products produced and sold will be the same in the future as they have been in the past. Furthermore, future prices of outputs, costs of inputs and technology for production are assumed to be unchanging.

Inventory levels are assumed constant because the costs associated with the breakeven volume of activity generally relate to production activity. Revenues, on the other hand, are related to sales activity. The only time production and sales activities coincide is when inventories neither increase from excess production nor decrease from additional sales.

Every cost-volume-profit analysis must be interpreted according to these three underlying assumptions and their corresponding limitations. The user of cost-volume-profit analysis benefits most by understanding the relationships among all factors he has considered. He must realize also that business is dynamic, and that planning for future periods requires constant reexamination of the basic cost-volume-profit assumptions.

EXTENSIONS TO COST-VOLUME-PROFIT ANALYSIS

The previous section discussed two major limitations of conventional cost-volume-profit analysis: (1) straight-line functions were used to portray cost and revenue behavior, and (2) point estimates were used to represent prices, variable rates, and fixed costs. These assumptions do not conform to reality, but these shortcomings may be surmounted. If costs and revenues do not behave in a strict linear fashion (as described above), and if the real curvilinear function is known, then calculus can be used to determine the breakeven points or the level of production necessary to achieve a desired level of profit. Similarly, if the manager does not know the future price, variable rates, or fixed costs exactly, but he can estimate the likelihood that they will fall within certain ranges, then he may employ probabilistic methods for calculating expected breakeven points. Probabilistic CVP analysis is described in Appendix A.

SUMMARY

In this chapter, we discussed special-analysis budgeting for cost-volume-profit relationships and presented graphic and mathematical representations of the effects on profit of changes in fixed costs, variable costs, prices, or the number of units sold. The assumptions of conventional CVP analysis were discussed also. Modifications, such as probabilistic estimates, are introduced in the following appendix to this chapter.

APPENDIX A: PROBABILISTIC ESTIMATES FOR CVP ANALYSIS

An alternate method for considering nonlinear cost-volume-profit relationships caused by uncertainty regarding future activity is to introduce probabilistic estimates that explicitly consider the likelihood that a future event will occur. Probabilistic estimates combine flexible budget data with the joint probabilities at each level of expected volume. They can be used in breakeven analysis just as they were used in flexible budgeting (as discussed in Chapter 3, Appendix B).

For example, consider the situation illustrated in Exhibit 4–11. The decision tree portrays dollar values and probabilities of achieving those dollar values for two alternative prices, three variable cost rates, and two fixed cost amounts. The price is expected to be either $10 or $9 per unit, but there is a much greater likelihood that it will be $10, that is, a probability of .9. The variable costs will be $6, $7, or $8, with corresponding probabilities of .8, .1, and .1, which indicates that the $6 variable rate is the one most likely to occur. Fixed costs will be $50,000 or $40,000, with corresponding probabilities of .7 and .3.

Note again that the probabilities at each branch add up vertically to 1.0, which indicates that the event will occur with certainty; that is, there will be a price, a variable rate, and a fixed cost. For each of the 12 combinations, a breakeven is calculated. For example, the breakeven for combination 1 is calculated by dividing the fixed cost of $50,000 by a $4 contribution margin ($10 less $6), producing a breakeven of 12,500 units. The 10,000-unit breakeven for combination 2 is calculated by dividing $40,000 by $4. For combinations 3 and 4, the contribution margin is reduced to $3; and for combinations 5 and 6, the contribution margin is further reduced to $2. All of the breakeven values listed in column E of Exhibit 4–11 have been calculated by the unit contribution-margin approach.

A joint probability (column F) is calculated for each combination by multiplying the probabilities on the path, moving from left to right; for example, the joint probability of .504 for combination 1 is derived by multiplying the .9 probability for sales price, times the .8 probability for variable costs, times the .7 probability for fixed costs. The joint probability for combination 12 is the product of .1 probability of sales price, times the .1 probability of variable costs, times the .3 probability for fixed costs, and equals .003. These joint probabilities indicate the likelihood that a particular combination will occur. The size of joint probabilities for combination 1 and combination 2 implies that these events are the most likely to occur.

The outcome for each combination is shown in column G. This last column represents the amount that any one combination will contribute in the determination of the expected breakeven point. Each value in this column is calculated by multiplying the appropriate breakeven value of column E by the corresponding joint probability of column F. For example, the column G value for combination 1 of 6,300 is determined by multiplying the 12,500 breakeven value

EXHIBIT 4–11   TREE DIAGRAM, COST-VOLUME-PROFIT RELATIONSHIPS

A Price	B Variable Rate	C Fixed Costs	D Combi- nation	E Break-Even	F Joint Probability	G EXF
		$50,000	1	12,500	.504	6,300
		$p = .7$				
		$40,000	2	10,000	.216	2,160
	$6	$p = .3$				
	$p = .8$	$50,000	3	16,667	.063	1,050
$10	$7	$p = .7$				
$p = .9$	$p = .1$					
	$8	$40,000	4	13,333	.027	360
	$p = .1$	$p = .3$				
		$50,000	5	25,000	.063	1,575
		$p = .7$				
		$40,000	6	20,000	.027	540
		$p = .3$				
		$50,000	7	16,667	.056	933
		$p = .7$				
		$40,000	8	13,333	.024	320
		$p = .3$				
	$6	$50,000	9	25,000	.007	175
	$p = .8$					
		$p = .7$				
$9	$7					
$p = .1$	$p = .1$					
	$8	$40,000	10	20,000	.003	60
	$p = .1$	$p = .3$				
		$50,000	11	50,000	.007	350
		$p = .7$				
		$40,000	12	40,000	.003	120
		$p = .3$				

Expected Breakeven Units   13,943

by the joint probability of .504. When all of the values listed in column G are added, the expected breakeven value for the whole network shown in the tree diagram is determined to be 13,943 units. That is, a breakeven value of 13,943 units is most likely to occur, after considering two prices, three variable rates, two levels of fixed costs, and all corresponding probabilities.

More sophisticated techniques of probabilistic cost-volume-profit analysis consider a continuous range of probabilities associated with each of the variables contained in any problem. However, discussion of these techniques is beyond the scope of our book.

SUGGESTED READINGS

Anthony, T., and H. Watson. "Probabilistic Breakeven Analysis," *Managerial Planning*, November/December, 1976.

Goggans, T. "Break-Even Analysis with Curvilinear Functions." *The Accounting Review*, October 1965.

Liaw, M. "The Effect of Change Variation on Revenue and Cost Estimations for Breakeven Analysis." *The Accounting Review*, October 1976.

QUESTIONS

4-1   A cost-volume-profit chart, as illustrated below, is a useful technique for showing relationships between costs, volume, and profits.

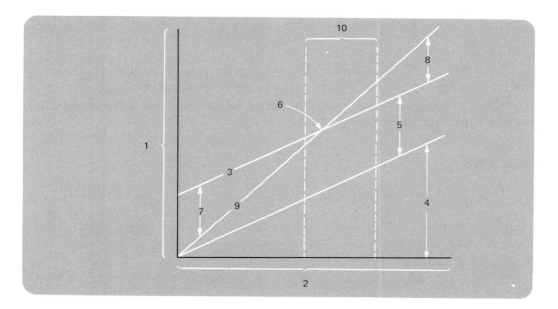

(A) Identify the numbered components of the breakeven chart.

(B) Discuss the significance of the concept of the "relevant range" to breakeven analyses.

(AICPA adapted)

4–2   Fill in the missing words to complete the following sentence: Breakeven is that volume of operations where _____ exactly _____ total revenue.

What is the relationship between breakeven analysis and cost-volume-profit analysis?

4–3   Fill in the blanks to complete the following sentence: Breakeven is a method of analysis that considers cost-_____ relationships useful for _____ and control.

What types of questions can be answered by using a cost-profit-volume analysis?

4–4   Copin Co. has drawn a strategic budget for 19X6 that calls for the following: expected profits, $150,000; fixed cost, $250,000; price $6 per unit; variable cost, $4 per unit.

How much *revenue* must Copin generate to reach its goal?

4–5   Identify the correct choice in the following sentences:

(A) At production volume above the relevant range, fixed costs will be (higher/lower) than in the range.

(B) At values above the relevant range, variable costs (will/will not) vary in direct proportion to volume.

4–6   What are some of the assumptions underlying cost-volume-profit analysis?

4–7   Can fixed costs increase over time?

4–8   Why is the unit contribution-margin approach to cost-volume-profit analysis not appropriate for use by multi-product companies?

4–9   Will the breakeven point increase or decrease for a firm that automates its production facilities?

EXERCISES

†4–10   Determine the expected profits for the following assumed facts:

	Probabilities		
	.3	.5	.2
Revenue	$1,000,000	$900,000	$800,000
Variable Cost	800,000	600,000	500,000
Fixed Cost	100,000	100,000	50,000

4–11   The Acme Co. sells a single product for $20 per unit. The Company's cost structure is composed of $100,000 fixed costs and variable costs of $15 per unit. Acme will have to generate how much revenue in order to earn a desired profit of $20,000?

If fixed costs are reduced $10,000, by how much will profits increase (losses decrease)?

If variable costs decrease, what will happen to the volume of profits at any level of production?

4–12   Bilo Co. has a budget that reports the following:

Revenue	$2,000,000
Variable costs	1,500,000
Fixed cost	300,000
Expected profit	$ 200,000

At what volume of revenue does Bilo just break even? How much revenue must Bilo generate to earn profits of $400,000?

4–13   (A) Dice Co. has drawn a budget that calls for the following: expected profits, $250,000; fixed cost, $300,000; and a contribution margin ratio of 20% (i.e., variable costs are 80% of revenue). How much revenue must Dice generate to reach its goal?

(B) The Emac Co. sells a single product for $300 per unit. The Company's cost structure is composed of $540,000 fixed costs and variable costs equal to 90% of revenue. How many units must Emac sell to earn a profit of $10,000?

4–14   (A) The Filup Co. sells a single product for $90 per unit. Fixed costs are $160,000, and variable costs equal 80% of revenue. If fixed costs increase by $80,000, Filup will have to increase sales by how many dollars just to earn profits equal to those it earned before the cost increase?

(B) Gala Co. has drawn a budget that calls for the following: expected profits, $150,000; fixed cost, $200,000; and a contribution margin ratio of 40% (i.e., variable costs are 60% of the revenue). How much revenue must Gala generate to reach its goal?

4–15   (A) Hyup Co. produces a unit with a variable cost of $6 each and sells them at a price of $8 each. Hyup breaks even when it sells $800,000 worth of units. Hyup's fixed costs are what amount? When Hyup sells $900,000, how much profit will it earn?

†(B) Inco's budget calls for the following: expected profits, $40,000; fixed cost, $50,000; variable cost $3 per unit. The price Inco charges will depend upon the price set by its competition: there is a 60% chance that competitors will

set a price of $4 and a 40% chance that the price will be $9. If Inco had to aim for one amount, how many *units* should Inco expect to sell in order to reach its goal?

4-16   In a recent period Zero Company had the following experience:

Sales (10,000 units @ $200)			$2,000,000
	Fixed	Variable	
Costs:			
Labor	$ —	$ 200,000	
Materials	—	400,000	
Factory overhead	160,000	600,000	
Administrative expenses	180,000	80,000	
Other expenses	200,000	120,000	
Total costs	$540,000	$1,400,000	1,940,000
Net Income			$ 60,000

Each item below is independent.

(A) Calculate the breakeven point for Zero in terms of units and sales dollars. Show your calculations.

(B) What sales volume would be required to generate a net income of $96,000? Show your calculations.

(C) What is the breakeven point if management makes a decision that increases fixed costs by $18,000? Show your calculations.

(AICPA adapted)

4-17   The Dooley Co. manufactures two products, baubles and trinkets. The following are projections for the coming year.

	Baubles		Trinkets		
	Units	Amount	Units	Amount	Totals
Sales	10,000	$10,000	7,500	$10,000	$20,000
Costs:					
Fixed		2,000		5,600	7,600
Variable		6,000		3,000	9,000
		8,000		8,600	16,600
Income before taxes		$ 2,000		$ 1,400	$ 3,400

(A) Assuming that the facilities are not jointly used, determine the breakeven output in units for baubles.

(B) Determine the breakeven volume in dollars for trinkets.

*(C) If baubles and trinkets become one-to-one complements and

there are no changes in the Dooley Co.'s cost function, the breakeven volume in units would be what amount?

*(D) Given the assumption in part C above, determine the composite contribution margin ratio.

(AICPA adapted)

4–18 The following data relate to a year's budgeted activity for Patsy Corporation, a single-product company:

	Units
Beginning inventory	30,000
Production	120,000
Available	150,000
Sales	120,000
Ending inventory	30,000
	Per Unit
Selling price	$ 5.00
Variable manufacturing costs	$ 1.00
Variable selling costs	$ 2.00
Fixed Manufacturing Costs	$25,000
Fixed Selling Costs	$65,000

Total fixed costs remain unchanged within the relevant range of 25,000 units to total capacity of 160,000 units.

(A) Determine the projected annual breakeven sales in units for Patsy Corporation.

(B) Determine the net profit of Patsy Corp., assuming that volume reaches the budgeted level.

(C) Assuming that volume reaches the budgeted level, consider the following changes: selling price increases by 20%; variable manufacturing costs increase by 10%; variable selling costs remain the same; and total fixed costs increase to $104,400. How many units must now be sold to generate a profit equal to 10% of the contribution margin?

(D) A special order is received to purchase 10,000 units to be used in an unrelated market. Given the original data, what price per unit should be charged on this order to increase Patsy Corporation's net income by $5,000?

(AICPA adapted)

4–19 Mr. Calderone started a pizza restaurant in 19X0. For this purpose he rented a building for $400 per month. Two ladies were hired to work full time at the restaurant, and six college boys were hired to work 30 hours per week delivering pizza. An outside accountant was hired for tax and bookkeeping purposes.

For this service, Mr. Calderone pays $300 per month. The necessary restaurant equipment and delivery cars were purchased with cash. Mr. Calderone has noticed that expenses for utilities and supplies have been fairly constant.

Mr. Calderone increased his business between 19X0 and 19X3. Profits have more than doubled since 19X0. Mr. Calderone does not understand why his profits have increased faster than his volume.

A projected Income Statement for 19X4 prepared by the accountant is shown below:

Calderone Company
PROJECTED INCOME STATEMENT
For the Year Ended December 31, 19X4

Sales (38,000 pizzas @ $2.50)		$95,000
Cost of food sold	$28,500	
Wages & fringe benefits of restaurant help	8,150	
Wages & fringe benefits of delivery boys	17,300	
Rent	4,800	
Accounting services	3,600	
Depreciation of delivery equipment	5,000	
Depreciation of restaurant equipment	3,000	
Utilities	2,325	
Supplies (soap, floor wax, etc.)	1,200	73,875
Net income before taxes		$21,125
Income taxes (30% of Net Income)		6,338
Net income		$14,787

(A) What is the breakeven point in number of pizzas that must be sold?

(B) Revenue is at what dollar level at the breakeven point?

(C) Mr. Calderone would like an after-tax net income of $20,000. What volume must be reached in number of pizzas in order to obtain the desired income?

(D) Briefly explain to Mr. Calderone why his profits have increased at a faster rate than his sales.

(E) Briefly explain to Mr. Calderone why his cash flow for 19X4 will exceed his profits.

(CMA adapted)

4–20 The president of Beth Corporation, which manufactures tape decks and sells them to producers of sound reproduction systems, anticipates a 10% wage increase for the manufacturing employees on January 1 of next year (variable labor). He expects no other changes in costs. Overhead will not change as a result of the wage increase. The president has asked you to assist him in developing the information he needs to formulate a reasonable product strategy for next year.

You are satisfied by regression analysis that volume is the primary factor affecting costs. You have separated the semivariable costs into their fixed and variable segments by means of the least-squares criterion. You also observe that the beginning and ending inventories are never materially different.

Below are the current-year data assembled for your analysis:

Current selling price per unit	$ 80.00
Variable cost per unit:	
Material	$ 30.00
Labor	12.00
Overhead	6.00
Total	$ 48.00
Annual volume of sales	5,000 units
Fixed costs	$51,000

Provide the following information for the president using cost-volume-profit analysis:

(A) What increase in the selling price is necessary to cover the 10% wage increase and still maintain the current breakeven point (in terms of units)?

(B) How many tape decks must be sold to maintain the current net income if the sales price remains at $80.00 and the 10% wage increase goes into effect?

(C) The president believes that an additional $190,000 of machinery (to be depreciated at 10% annually) will increase present capacity (5,300 units) by 30%. If all tape decks produced can be sold at the present price and the wage increase goes into effect, how would the estimated net income before capacity is increased compare with the estimated net income after capacity is increased? Prepare computations of estimated net income before and after the expansion.

(AICPA adapted)

4–21 The Peters Company converts steel from ingots to sheets. Most of its expenses are fixed, and only a fraction are variable. Those costs that do fit the mixed category have been broken into their fixed and variable segments. The estimates for next year include sales of $2,000,000, fixed costs of $800,000, and variable costs of 40% of every sales dollar. The tax bracket for the Peters Company is 50%.

(A) Graph the breakeven point before taxes from the information given.

(B) Add the tax computation to the breakeven chart.

(C) What does the area between the costs after tax and the sales line represent?

(D) What are the assumptions underlying cost-volume-profit analysis? Since these assumptions may not be met in any given situation, are the results of CVP analysis totally useless to management?

(E) Can cost-volume-profit analysis be calculated for firms selling more than one product? If so, what type of measuring unit is shown on the volume (horizontal axis) scale?

(F) Since costs and revenues do not behave strictly in a linear fashion, do techniques exist that make it possible to calculate a breakeven point for situations in which the mathematical description of cost and revenue functions is known? In such situations, will it be possible to calculate the volume at which profits will be maximized?

4–22   The president of the Midway Company has estimated that he will need profits of $50,000 this year to satisfy the stockholders, and he asks you for a volume that will attain his goal. He intends to use this information to motivate and direct the sales manager. He gives you the following information:

Unit Selling Price	$50.00
Variable Cost per Unit	$35.00
Fixed Costs per Unit	$ 1.00
(based on 9,000 units)	
Plant Capacity	12,000 units

(A) Compute the volume needed to achieve the $50,000-profit goal.

(B) Graph the cost-volume-profit relationship.

(C) Which cost seems higher than normal? Would a sales or a manufacturing company be more likely to have this type of cost structure?

(D) If the 9,000-unit production last year was the highest that sales had ever been, is it likely that the stockholders will be satisfied?

(E) Do variable costs always vary directly with volume? Give an example of a variable cost that may increase at an increasing rate as volume increases. Give an example of a variable cost that may increase at a decreasing rate as volume increases.

PROBLEMS

4–23   The following are examples of cost-volume-profit graphs for three separate companies. Analyze each graph and answer the following questions about them. All measurements are in hundreds of thousands.

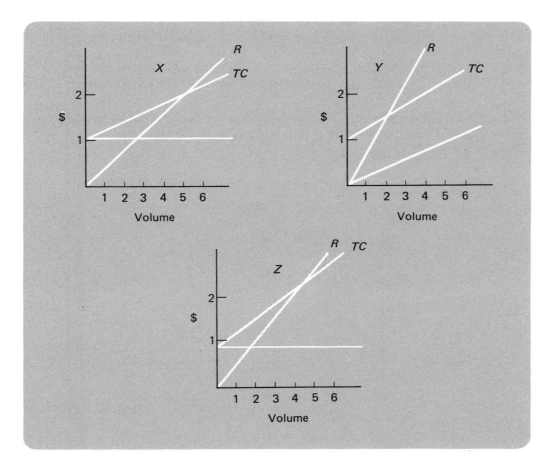

(A) Are the fixed costs in Company X considerably more than in Company Y? Explain.

(B) Are the breakeven units smaller for Company Y than Company Z? Explain.

(C) If volume is at the 400,000 level, will Company X produce more profit than Company Z at the same volume level? Explain.

4–24 The managers of Hickey Company prepare a cost-volume-profit analysis to understand better their goals and budgeting. Certain figures had to be estimated: sales were forecast at $5,000,000, fixed costs at $1,000,000, and variable costs at $3,000,000.

(A) Who would supply the estimates needed for the analysis?

(B) Compute the breakeven point by using the estimated figures given above.

(C) Graph the cost-volume-profit relationship.

(D) If variable costs increased by 20%, what will the breakeven point be?

(E) The president sets a profit of at least $45,000 as the company's goal. Calculate the production volume and the total revenue at this volume.

4–25 The illustration shows the cost-volume-profit graph of a company contemplating two separate pricing policies. Analyze the graph and answer the following questions.

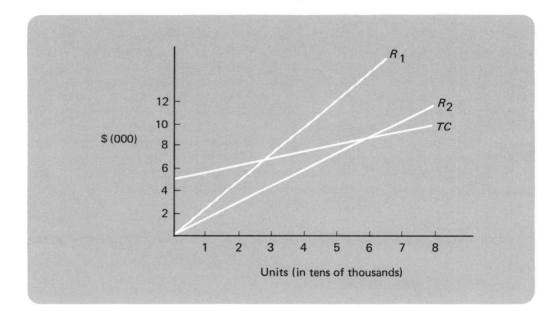

(A) Which pricing policy, R_1 or R_2, represents the lower price? Which will have the lower breakeven point?

(B) Which pricing policy, R_1 or R_2, will produce the most profit at 50,000 units of production? Why?

(C) What considerations other than breakeven must be considered in selecting a unit price? If breakeven were the only consideration, what price would produce the smaller (lower) point?

4–26 The following graph represents one company that has two different total cost lines. Analyze the graph and answer the following questions.

(A) Which of the two cost lines has the higher fixed cost? Which has the more variable cost per unit?

(B) At the production level of 20,000, which cost profile will lose more money? Why?

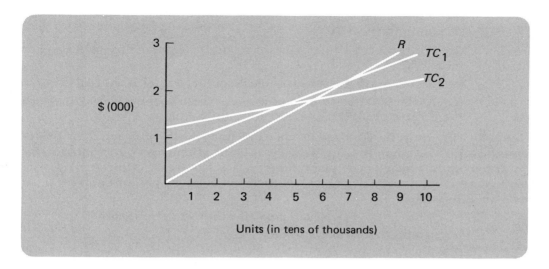

(C) What is the breakeven point (approximately) to total cost TC_1 and total cost TC_2?

(D) Would businesses operating near breakeven prefer TC_1 over TC_2? Explain. Would businesses operating well above the breakeven prefer TC_1 over TC_2? Which total-cost line would be preferred by businesses operating below the breakeven point?

4-27   The graph below represents one company that has two different total-cost lines. Analyze the graph and answer the questions below.

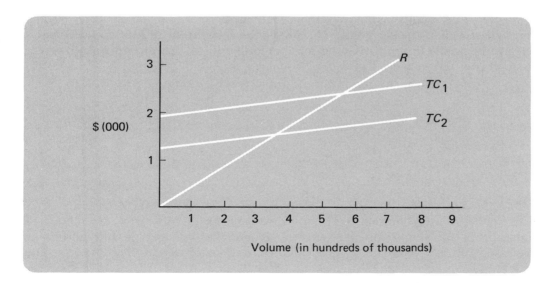

(A) What is the approximate breakeven point in units for total cost TC_1 and total cost TC_2?

(B) Which of the two cost profiles has the greater variable costs per unit?

(C) Which of the two cost profiles has the greater fixed costs?

(D) At the 500,000-unit volume level, which cost profile will produce the greater profit? At the 900,000-unit volume?

4-28   The Green Company, a producer of small parts, has each of its plants compute a breakeven point. The West Penn Plant produces a part that sells for $5. At maximum capacity the plant can produce 1,000,000 of these parts. The cost manager estimates that the total variable costs are $4 per unit and the fixed costs are $200,000.

(A) What is the breakeven point for the West Penn Plant?

(B) Graph the breakeven point.

(C) If variable costs go up by $.50, what is the breakeven point? Will the plant be able to continue production?

(D) If the president of Green requests a profit of $50,000, how many units must be produced? Will the West Penn Plant be able to produce this many units? What would be the total revenue needed to provide the $50,000 profit?

(E) We usually assume that the price, variable costs per unit, fixed costs, and/or level of production are known with certainty. If these amounts are not known with certainty, but you do know probabilities expressing the likelihood that certain amounts will occur, can a probabilistic breakeven point be calculated? If so, describe the process.

4-29   The Blanks Company can select from several alternative sales volumes and prices to achieve set goals. The president estimated various costs for each sales price and volume, thus producing a contribution-margin figure. However, some of the figures were lost.

(A) Using the remaining figures, try to reconstruct the lost figures.

Sales Volume	Sales Price	Variable Expenses	Fixed Expenses	Before-Tax Income	Contribution Margin
10,000	$ 5.00	_____	$15,000	_____	50%
9,000	$ 6.00	_____	_____	6,400	40%
8,000	$ 7.00	$29,700	_____	9,300	____
6,000	$10.00	$30,000	$20,000	_____	____

†*4-30   The Robert R. Baker Company has a product that sells for a price ranging between $15 and $20. The sales manager thinks the price should be $15 but expects that the president, Robert R. Baker, Sr., will overrule him and make the price $20. He assigns a 60 to 40 chance to the adoption of the $20 price. The

variable rate could be $12 or $10 per unit, and the cost department thinks the $12 figure more likely by 75 to 25. They also estimate fixed costs at $100,000, with a probability of 60%; $120,000, with a 30% probability; and $150,000 at 10% probability.

(A) Calculate the total expected breakeven volume for this situation. Remember, $20 has a 60% chance of being the established price this year.

(B) If you are 100% sure that fixed costs will be $120,000, what is the total expected breakeven point?

(C) If you knew with certainty that the variable cost would be $12 and the price $20, how many units would have to be sold to produce a profit of $10,000?

(D) How would an employee of Baker Company derive estimates for the likelihood that an event will occur?

*4-31 The Beams Bottle Works produces glass containers that are used in the packaged foods industry. The containers are generally sold in large lots to a limited number of customers. Competition in the bottle business has been somewhat sporadic in the past and, consequently, Beams has had several periods of widely fluctuating profits. This profit situation disturbed top management and was difficult to explain to the stockholders of the firm.

Therefore, management has decided to investigate the cost-volume-profit relationships that exist relative to its glass containers. You, as a managerial accountant, have been called in to help on this project.

Management has selected two time periods from the past, which they feel are representative of a "normal" situation for the firm. The following information, relating to these two periods, was taken from the accounting records:

	Period 1	Period 2
Volume (units produced and sold)	10,000	15,000
Sales Revenue	$120,000	$180,000
Manufacturing Costs (includes material, labor, and overhead)	70,000	85,000
Gross Margin	$ 50,000	$ 95,000
Selling Expense (consists only of sales commissions)	10,000	15,000
Administrative Expense (includes salaries and supplies)	30,000	35,000
Net Income before Taxes	$ 10,000	$ 45,000

(A) What is the breakeven point in units? What is the breakeven point in sales dollars?

(B) What is the effect on the breakeven point of an increase in the unit selling price of 10% combined with a 20% increase in the sales commissions?

(C) Referring back to the original data, if management feels that 7,000 units is a feasible and attainable breakeven point, what must variable manufacturing costs be on a per-unit basis to achieve this goal?

(D) Referring again to the original data, if management wants to earn a profit of at least $20,000, what is the highest that fixed costs can be if the breakeven point is no more than 10,000 units?

4–32   R. A. Ro and Company, makers of high-quality handmade pipes, has experienced a steady growth in sales for the past five years. Increased competition, however, has led Mr. Ro, the president, to believe that an aggressive advertising campaign will be necessary next year to maintain the Company's present growth.

To get ready for next year's advertising campaign, the Company's accountant has prepared the following data for the current year, 19X4 for Mr. Ro:

Cost Schedule	
Variable Costs:	
Labor	$ 8.00/pipe
Materials	3.25/pipe
Variable Overhead	2.50/pipe
	$13.75/pipe
Fixed Costs:	
Manufacturing	$ 25,000
Selling	40,000
Administrative	70,000
Total Fixed Costs	$135,000
Selling Price per Pipe	$ 25.00
Expected Sales, 19X4 (20,000 units)	$500,000
Tax Rate	40%

Mr. Ro has set the sales target for 19X5 at a level of $550,000 (or 22,000 pipes).

(A) What is the projected after-tax net income for 19X4?

(B) What is the breakeven point in units for 19X4?

(C) Mr. Ro believes that, all other costs remaining constant, an additional selling expense of $11,250 for advertising in 19X5 will be necessary to attain the sales target. What will be the after-tax net income for 19X5 if the additional $11,250 is spent?

(D) What will be the breakeven point in dollar sales for 19X5 if the additional $11,250 is spent for advertising?

(E) If the additional $11,250 is spent for advertising in 19X5, what is the required sales level in dollars to equal 19X4's after-tax net income?

(F) At a sales level of 22,000 units, what is the maximum amount that can be spent on advertising if an after-tax net income of $60,000 is desired?

(CMA adapted)

4-33 Your employer leased manufacturing facilities for production of a new product. The following data have been made available to you:

Estimated Annual Sales	24,000 Units	
Estimated Costs:	*Amount*	*Per Unit*
Material	$ 96,000	$4.00
Labor	14,400	.60
Overhead	24,000	1.00
Administrative Expense	28,800	1.20
Total	$163,200	$6.80

Selling expenses are expected to be 15% of sales, and profit is to amount to $1.02 per unit.

(A) Compute the selling price per unit.

(B) Project a profit and loss statement for the year.

(C) Compute a breakeven point expressed in dollars and in units assuming that overhead and administrative expenses are fixed but that other costs are fully variable.

(AICPA adapted)

4-34 The officers of Bradshaw Company are reviewing the profitability of the Company's four products and the potential effect of several proposals for varying the product mix. An excerpt from the income statement and other data follows:

	Totals	Product P	Product Q	Product R	Product S
Sales	$62,600	$10,000	$18,000	$12,600	$22,000
Cost of Goods Sold	44,274	4,750	7,056	13,968	18,500
Gross Profit	$18,326	$ 5,250	$10,944	$(1,368)	$ 3,500
Operating Expenses	12,012	1,990	2,976	2,826	4,220
Income before Income Taxes	$ 6,314	$ 3,260	$ 7,968	$(4,194)	$ (720)
Units Sold		1,000	1,200	1,800	2,000
Sales Price per Unit		$ 10.00	$ 15.00	$ 7.00	$ 11.00
Variable Cost of Goods Sold per Unit		$ 2.50	$ 3.00	$ 6.50	$ 6.00
Variable Operating Expenses per Unit		$ 1.17	$ 1.25	$ 1.00	$ 1.20

Each of the following proposals is to be considered independently of the others. Consider only the product changes stated in each proposal; the activity of other products remains stable. Ignore income taxes.

(A) Determine the effect on income, assuming that product R is discontinued.

(B) If product R is discontinued and the consequent loss of customers causes sales of product Q to decrease by 200 units, how will income be affected?

(C) How will income be affected if the price of R is increased to $8, but this increased price causes sales volume to decrease by 300 units?

(D) The plant in which R is produced can be utilized to produce a new product, T. The total variable costs and expenses per unit of T are $8.05, and 1,600 units can be sold at $9.50 each. If T is introduced and R is discontinued, how will income be affected?

(E) Part of the plant in which P is produced can easily be adapted to the production of S, but changes in quantities may make changes in sales prices advisable. If production of P is reduced to 500 units (to be sold at $12 each), and production of S is increased to 2,500 units (to be sold at $10.50 each), how will income be affected?

(F) Production of P can be doubled by adding a second shift, but higher wages will have to be paid, which will increase variable cost of goods sold to $3.50 for each of the additional units. If the 1,000 additional units of P can be sold at $10 each, by what amount will income increase?

(AICPA adapted)

4-35 Whenever a company sells more than one type of product or charges different prices for its products, the unit contribution margin approach to cost-volume-profit analysis is not feasible, because "price" and "units of volume" lose their meaning. The contribution margin ratio approach to CVP is feasible for such companies. Under this approach, the contribution margin is stated as a percentage of the revenue (i.e., the difference between revenue and variable cost divided by the revenue). The Contribution Margin Ratio is then divided into fixed cost plus desired profit. Calculate the missing data in each of the following independent cases:

	Case A	Case B	Case C	Case D
Revenue	$100,000	$200,000	$300,000	$?
Variable Cost	80,000	120,000	?	210,000
Fixed Cost	15,000	?	25,000	35,000
Original Desired Profit	?	30,000	35,000	55,000
Contribution Margin Ratio	?	?	?	?
Breakeven Revenue	?	?	?	?
CVP Revenue at $20,000 Profit	?	?	?	?

†4–36 (A) Smith thought he would be able to sell his product at $10/unit with a .8 probability or at $9/unit with a .2 probability. Variable costs are $7/unit, and fixed costs are $20,000. What is Smith's expected breakeven volume, in terms of units?

(B) Jones thought he could sell his product for $100,000 with a .7 probability or for $120,000 with a .3 probability. Variable costs are 60% of revenues. Fixed cost will be $30,000 with a .8 probability or $40,000 with a .2 probability. What is Jones' expected breakeven volume, in terms of revenue dollars?

4–37 Breakeven analysis is just a special case of cost-profit-volume analysis in which desired profit is set equal to zero. Determine the missing data in each of the following independent cases:

	Case A	Case B	Case C	Case D	Case E
Price	$ 10.00	$ 9.00	$ 8.00	$ 7.00	$?
Variable Cost	$ 8.00	$ 6.00	$ 6.00	$?	$ 7.00
Fixed Cost	$20,000	$30,000	$?	$20,000	$20,000
Desired Profit	$10,000	?	$10,000	$10,000	$10,000
Units of Volume	?	40,000	20,000	15,000	30,000

4–38 Use the contribution margin ratio approach to cost-volume-profit analysis and calculate (a) the contribution margin ratio, (b) the breakeven revenue, and (c) the CVP revenue in each of the following independent cases:

	Case A	Case B	Case C	Case D
Price	$ 10	$ 20	$ 30	$ 40
Variable Cost	$ 9	$ 14	$ 18	$ 32
Fixed Cost	$30,000	$90,000	$60,000	$40,000
Desired Profit	$10,000	$10,000	$20,000	$30,000

4–39 Carey Company sold 100,000 units of its product at $20 per unit. Variable costs are $14 per unit (manufacturing costs of $11 and selling costs of $3). Fixed costs, which are incurred uniformly throughout the year, amount to $792,000 (manufacturing costs of $500,000 and selling costs of $292,000). There are no beginning or ending inventories.

(A) Determine the breakeven point in terms of dollars and units.

(B) How many units must be sold to earn before-income-tax income of $60,000?

(C) How many units must be sold to earn $90,000 income after taxes, assuming that the tax rate is 40% of income?

(D) If labor costs are 50% of variable costs and 20% of fixed costs, a 10% increase in wages and salaries would increase the number of units required to break even by how many units?

(AICPA adapted)

THREE

*Product Costing—
The Job-Order Alternative*

*Product Costing—
The Process Alternative*

*Service Department
Costs and Transfer Prices*

*Joint and
By-Product Costing*

*Direct Costing Reports
for Decision Analysis*

*Decision makers within an organization also have
access to large quantities of potentially useful
data. The managerial accountant, as an
information specialist, is responsible for
accumulating this data and preparing it for use.
The process of accumulation and preparation
includes observing, collecting, recording,
classifying, and summarizing data about the
activities and events that affect the firm. Once the
accounting system has processed the
information and organized it into a clear and
precise form, the reports are presented to the
decision makers who have requested the data.
The next five chapters discuss procedures,
techniques, and methods used by the
managerial accountant to process information.*

CHAPTER 5

Product Costing— The Job-Order Alternative

Objectives

After studying this chapter, you should be able to do the following:

Specify the purposes of product cost accumulation.

Discuss two modes of manufacturing and determine the sources and types of cost information for each.

Apply typical job-order costing *procedures to account for the direct labor, direct material, and factory overhead for a given set of case data.*

Describe the Cost of Goods Sold statement.

Many users of accounting information consider product costing the essential function of managerial accounting. Manufacturing organizations generally employ one of two approaches to accumulating product cost information: **job-order costing** or **process costing**. To understand the output of each system, one must understand the techniques, procedures, and terminology associated with them. Managerial accountants must be able to identify manufacturing situations in which either job-order costing or process costing is applicable, and must be able to interpret each system's output. This chapter is concerned primarily with job-order costing; the following chapter explores process costing in detail.

THE PURPOSES OF COST ACCUMULATION

Product cost information directly determines the value of units produced and sold, as shown on a manufacturer's income statement and balance sheet. Cost of goods sold and ending inventories include cumulative cost inputs for the period. Managers use historical product cost information to determine which products or product lines are most profitable, and, thus, which product lines to expand or contract, or whether to modify prices or distribution policies for certain products. Historical costs are useful also in measuring the performance of supervisory personnel and ensuring that actual expenditures are kept as close as possible to the budget. Using historical costs for pricing, product-line decisions, and control is discussed in detail in the following chapters.

THE MANUFACTURING PROCESS

The manufacturing process of any firm includes all tasks required to combine a set of productive elements into some finished product. There are many ways to classify the costs typically associated with manufacturing activity. Essentially, the classification of costs is based on the productive elements themselves, which include *materials*, *labor*, and *overhead*.

Materials and labor are directly combined into the finished product. Therefore, the costs associated with materials and labor are directly traceable to the units of finished product. The term, **directly traceable costs**, implies that there is an observable causal relationship between input and output, that is, as people work, one can see progress in production. The combined costs of direct labor and direct materials are called **prime costs** because of their direct correspondence to productive inputs and outputs.

Other cost elements that are necessary for production are not associated directly with the finished product. For example, a machine may service many output units before it eventually reaches an unproductive state. It is virtually impossible for the cost accountant[1] to determine how much depreciation should be charged to a particular unit of output. Production costs that cannot be directly traced to the finished product are called *overhead*, and are treated as **indirect costs** of production.

The manufacturing process is an assembly system geared to combine materials, labor, and overhead into some desired output. As these three elements enter the process, they are assumed to combine physically, or attach. The basic cost accumulation system is designed to parallel the physical flows of these inputs into the production process. As inputs are physically added to production, their associated costs are assumed to accumulate and flow into the cost of the finished output.

As an example, consider the following:

A company manufactures custom-made rocking chairs for a select clientele. The chairs are generally made from sketches supplied by the customers, and each chair is different. Because most of the orders call for either cherry or oak, the company keeps a supply of these woods in its inventory.

The production process begins when an experienced craftsman in the factory receives a customer's sketch and starts to determine how to construct the chair. At this point, labor has entered the process. Next, the appropriate wood is requested from the warehouse and delivered to the craftsman. At the time of delivery, materials also have entered the production process. The materials and labor will become physically combined as the craftsman completes his product. To this point, the items identified have been directly traceable to the physical output of the process — the rocking chair. After the cost accountant monitors the costs associated with the craftsman's time and the value of the wood, he can assign a cost to the rocking chair.

What about other, less obvious, elements of production? The chair was assembled in a factory building. Obviously, some of the value of this structure has expired during the production of the chair. How much of this cost should be assigned to one unit of output? The glue that was used in constructing the chair, was taken from a large container at a central location. Unused glue was returned to the container. Again, there is an accounting problem: How much of the cost of refilling the central glue container should be assigned to each rocking chair?

Building depreciation and glue expense both represent overhead in this example. Because of the difficulty of determining a relationship with a given unit of output, glue may also be included in this category, but for a different reason. The accountant could monitor the actual amount of glue used and determine its cost, but, such an undertaking would be costly and of little value, since the cost of glue will not be significant in relation to the cost of other elements of produc-

---

[1]*Cost accounting* is a subfield of managerial accounting primarily concerned with information processing.

tion. The total overhead cost, however, will be significant and worth assigning to products.

As materials and labor are added to the production of the chair, corresponding dollar equivalents are assigned to each product by the managerial accountants. Periodically, certain amounts of overhead are indirectly assigned to the product to become part of the total cost accumulation. Thus, when the rocking chair is physically complete, so is its cost history.

TYPES OF MANUFACTURING PROCESSES

Most manufacturing activity can be described as either **discrete** or **continuous**. A discrete manufacturing process treats each unit or order (batch) separately. Different orders require different amounts of skill, attention, and effort to produce. Building construction, for example, generally uses discrete production processes. In the previous example, the rocking chair factory operated as a discrete production process. The orders were differentiated by each customer's request, and each chair represented a unique output. The craftsman's tasks and the other productive inputs varied from order to order.

A continuous manufacturing process is geared to produce many identical units, each requiring the same amount of skill, attention, and effort. Products flow continuously through the manufacturing process. Chemical producers require this type of production process. Although the custom-made chair factory does not use continuous production, it could modify its operation to mass-produce large quantities of the same style of rocking chair on an assembly line.

Different product costing methods are appropriate for each of these production situations. A discrete process is generally characterized by a *job-order costing* system, whereas a continuous process usually employs a *process costing* system.

SELECTING AN ACCOUNTING SYSTEM

Accountants consider several factors in selecting a cost system, including the *amount of precision* required and the *cost of collecting* the information. The greater the detail or precision required, the higher the costs of the accounting system. The cost accountant (the preparer of the information) and the decision maker (the user of the information) must establish some acceptable balance between cost and precision in constructing a system for collecting product cost data.

A discrete production process generally results in a limited number of unique or differentiated output units. Organizations using such a manufacturing process can benefit from the precision of an independent cost determination for each output unit. Job-order costing data are used primarily to obtain feedback information for pricing decisions and to determine product profitability.

In contrast, the continuous process manufactures many similar units of output. Accountants assume that similar units should bear equal amounts of the production costs for a period. This assumption seems justified after considering the expense of collecting individual cost data for quantities of similar units of output. A process costing system is much more practical in this case. Process cost accounting data are used primarily for control evaluations and to determine product costs.

JOB-ORDER COSTING

A job-order costing system accumulates production costs by *customer order*. Individual customer orders frequently call for a differentiated, or unique, product output and they are processed as separate jobs.

Customer orders and *job orders refer to output units* in industries that produce specialized, or made-to-order, outputs. Industries that commonly use job-order costing systems include: building construction, printing, machinery production, shipbuilding, and furniture manufacturing. In each of these production situations *both the amount and the type of input vary*, as does the type or amount of output, depending on the particular job being processed.

The job-order accounting system is designed to supply management with two types of information. First, the *cost of a particular job* is determined. Product cost information can also help management decide whether similar orders should be accepted in the future and what price should be quoted on them. Second, information about *cost effectiveness* can be accumulated and reported. This provides management with a means of determinining how closely actual job costs conform to budgeted costs.

PROCEDURES OF THE SYSTEM

The basic job-order accounting procedures are not complex, but they are detailed and follow a logical sequence of tasks. The primary task is to accumulate the three elements of product cost—materials, labor, and overhead—by individual factory jobs. The major effort is to trace specific cost elements to the specific job being processed. The data collection process records all economic events that occur in the production process. These data are refined, condensed, and summarized in the accounting process to supply the necessary information to the decision makers.

Prime costs The combination of direct material costs and direct labor costs is frequently called *prime costs*. Processing information about prime costs is an important and reasonably straightforward task for the accountant, since prime costs represent a significant and measurable part of the product cost. Through informal observation, accountants can determine the amount of material and labor that is directly incorporated into a particular product. Then, following the principle of "costs attach," they can assign the related costs to the product.

Formal procedures have been established to govern these observations, however. There are three reasons why such procedures should be followed. First, some cost elements might escape notice if a formal procedure did not compel attention to each observation. Second, formal procedures introduce efficiency by "batch-processing" the recording of similar observations. Third, under formal procedures all similar observations are classified and recorded consistently. Thus, the use of formal procedures can insure that accounting reports provide a clear picture of past activities and current positions.

Cost accounting traces the flow of materials and labor from the time they enter the firm until they leave it as a finished product. The costs associated with these elements can then be traced or "attached" to the appropriate output. Prime costing procedures are entirely objective because input costs are directly traced to the product output. Indirect costs, however, pose some problems for the managerial accountant.

Indirect overhead costs   Overhead costs are associated with elements of material, labor, and other inputs that will not be directly traced to specific units of output. This indirect association results because: (1) inputs into the production process are unobservable, or (2) the dollar amount of input present in one unit of output is too small to assign conveniently to each unit. For example, some of the value of the factory building expires during production, but it is impossible to measure objectively how much of this cost is related to a specific unit of output. In other situations, certain elements, such as the oil used to lubricate a machine are present in such small quantities that measurement is not economically feasible. Since these indirect costs cannot be assigned directly to individual units of output, the "costs attach" procedure assigns them on indirect bases.

Total overhead costs can be a significant production expense. Ideally, the managerial accountant would like to allocate these costs to output units on the basis of some measure of volume. For example, if overhead is to be assigned on the basis of units produced, the amount charged to any particular unit could be calculated as follows:

$$\text{Overhead per Unit} = \frac{\text{Total Overhead Costs}}{\text{Total Number of Units Produced}}$$

Unfortunately, overhead cannot be assigned so easily. Specific elements of overhead cost include manufacturing rent, depreciation, property taxes, insurance, supplies, electricity, gas, oil, water, and salary (wages) for supervisors, janitors, and other manufacturing personnel that do not work directly with output units. Most of these costs are remotely related to actual production tasks, and no clear relationship between them and output units is determinable. Overhead accounting attempts to average these costs so that units produced during one part of the year will bear identical costs to similar units produced at other times. This averaging is accomplished by basing the overhead calculation on an *estimate of expected yearly overhead costs*.

In the same fashion, the number of units produced is not so easily determinable. Each job or customer order could call for unique products that should bear different overhead assignments. A more equitable assignment of overhead to jobs is accomplished by substituting for output units some other measure of volume. Common measures of volume used in overhead assignments include direct labor hours, direct labor dollars, direct material quantities, direct material dollars, or some other measure common to all output, such as machine hours. That is, overhead accounting is based upon the *estimate of an expected volume measure*.

Accounting for overhead thus becomes a four-step process. First, an *applied overhead rate* is determined by dividing the estimated yearly overhead cost by the estimated yearly volume measure. Second, the actual volume associated with each job is measured, and is multiplied by the applied overhead rate to determine the overhead cost assigned to a particular job. Third, actual overhead costs are recorded in the accounting records. Fourth, an end-of-the-year adjustment is made to the accounting records to reconcile any differences between the actual overhead incurred during the year and the sum of overhead applied to individual jobs during the year. Further discussion of these four steps appears in the following paragraph.

Applied overhead assignment   Overhead accounting procedures are best illustrated with reference to an example. Consider the following information about the Edwards Manufacturing Company, a custom boat builder. When the current budget was prepared, total expected overhead was estimated at $68,000, and expected direct labor hour volume was estimated at 20,000 hours. These two budgeted numbers were used to determine the applied overhead rate of $3.40 per direct labor hour for the current year (i.e., $68,000/20,000 = $3.40). During the year, accumulated actual costs for depreciation, gas, oil, rent, indirect labor, and supplies amounted to $73,000. Three boats were under construction during the year; the actual hours of direct labor incurred on each was 6,000, 7,000, and 8,000. Multiplying the applied overhead rate by the actual hours determines the applied overhead charged to the individual jobs (boats), $20,400, $23,800, and $27,200. All three boats were sold, and the accumulated costs ($71,400 applied overhead, in addition to direct labor and materials) were transferred to the Cost of Goods Sold account. Before preparing an income statement, the accountant for Edwards would determine that overhead had been underapplied (actual overhead was larger than applied overhead), and he would adjust the Cost of Goods Sold account by increasing it $1,600. After the adjustment, the Applied Overhead component of Cost of Goods Sold was equal to the Actual Overhead incurred during the year.

SUPPORTING DOCUMENTS

The supporting documents form the basis of the entire cost accounting process. Although the number and type of these documents vary from one manufacturing situation to another, several documents are in general use: **stores requisitions**, **work tickets**, **overhead vouchers**, and **job-order cost sheets**.

Stores requisitions   Raw materials and preassembled parts usually are held in storage before they are placed into production. An authorization is required to initiate a transfer of materials from the storeroom to the shop. This authorization is commonly called a stores requisition. A sample stores requisition is shown in Exhibit 5–1.

The processing department formally requests materials from the inventory stock center (stores) by completing a stores requisition. In Exhibit 5–1, 1,000 lbs. of sheet steel were requested by Department B for work on Job No. W103. Appropriate authorization and receipt of the material are noted on the

EXHIBIT 5–1   STORES REQUISITION

WIZZARD PRODUCTS, INC.
Stores Requisition

Job Order No. W 103   Date 8 - 17 - X4

Department B   Requisition No. 15796

Description	Quantity	Unit Price	Total
Steel Sheet	1,000 lbs.	$4.20	$4,200
Totals	1,000 lbs		$4,200

Received by: _____

Date: 8-17-X4

Signed: Albert Jacobs

Authorized by:

Signed: Fritz Kaupp.

form before the internal transaction is completed. Mr. Kaupp authorized the requisition, and Albert Jacobs received the steel on 8/17/X4.

The stores requisition supports the transfer of raw materials to the production processes. Use of a formal requisition process helps prevent unauthorized releases of the inventory. The stores requisitions show when raw materials were released from the inventory, to which department they were released, and for which job they were intended to be used.

Clock cards Clock cards or time cards may be used to record the actual time worked by employees paid an hourly wage. Employees "punch in" or record their arrival time and "punch out" to record their departure at the end of the day or the shift. These cards are the basis for payroll computations and subsequently can provide supporting evidence for the amount of direct labor expense charged to each department. The cards fail to show, however, that an employee may work on several different jobs for varying amounts of time during a particular day.

Work tickets The time spent on each job and the resulting charges are important factors in determining product cost. Therefore, a record of the time worked on specific jobs must be kept on *work tickets* or *labor summaries*. A work ticket is illustrated in Exhibit 5–2.

EXHIBIT 5–2   WORK TICKET

WIZZARD PRODUCTS, INC.
Work Ticket

Job Order No. W 103   Date 8-17 X4

Department B

Employee No. WP 74   Stop Time   10.30
Operation Welding   Start Time   9.00
                            Total Time   1.30
                            Rate   #7.50
                            Amount   #11.25

Each employee is generally responsible for completing a work ticket each time he performs a task relating to a specific job. Alternately, the foreman of each department may record the specific work assignments of his employees on a labor summary. The information contained in the work ticket or labor summary is used in the product cost calculation. The work ticket shown in Exhibit 5–2 (also for Job No. W103) indicates that $11.25 of welding was applied to the job.

Overhead voucher The third element of product cost—factory overhead—is assigned to job orders generally by using a *predetermined rate*. The rate is established on the basis of estimated cost and volume levels. Periodically, the predetermined overhead charges are added to the product costs in proportion to the observed volume. The amount of the assigned overhead charge is documented in an *overhead voucher*. Exhibit 5–3 shows an overhead voucher indicating that

EXHIBIT 5–3 OVERHEAD VOUCHER

WIZZARD PRODUCTS, INC.
Overhead Voucher

Voucher No. V 807-89   Date 8-19-X4

Department B

Distribution

Debit: Job Nos.		Credit:	
W101	$1,000.00		$
W102	500.00		
W103	275.00		

Account:
Work-in-Process Inventory
$1,775.00

Account:
Overhead Applied $1,775.00

$275 of overhead was assigned to Job No. W103. The voucher formalizes management's decision concerning the allocation of overhead among departments and factory jobs.

In some work situations, no overhead voucher is issued. Rather, the applied overhead rate is common knowledge and overhead is applied at the same time the base information is recorded. For example, if overhead is applied on the basis of direct labor hours, application of overhead to the job may be coincidental with the application of labor costs.

Job-order cost sheet A record of all costs assigned to a particular job is kept on a *job-order cost sheet* (see Exhibit 5–4). The job-order cost sheet summarizes all the traceable costs associated with producing a job, regardless of the type of job or the department in which the costs were incurred. Job No. W103 was completed on 8/24/X4 after incurring $11,275 of costs in two departments. This job cost sheet shows the managers of Wizzard Products, Inc., exactly where costs were incurred, what they were incurred for, when they were incurred, and who authorized them.

The flow of documents parallels the physical flow of production in job shop manufacturing organizations, as illustrated in Exhibit 5–5. Customer orders are initiated in the sales office. No official accounting recognition is given to the customer order, i.e., receiving an order is not recognized as an accounting event. One copy of the order is sent to the manufacturing department, and pertinent information is copied onto the description part of a job-order cost sheet. As material, labor, and overhead are expended on production of the job, stores requisitions, work tickets, and overhead vouchers are prepared and attached to the job cost sheet. While the job is located in the manufacturing departments, the dollar amounts summarized on the job cost sheets supply details to support the valuation of work-in-process inventory. When the job is completed, it is physically transferred to a storeroom or loading dock. The job-order cost sheet accompanies the job. By then, its columns have been totaled, and the sum of all job cost sheets for jobs in the storeroom represents the valuation of finished-goods inventory. Once a job is delivered to the customer, the cost sheet is stamped "delivered" and filed for future reference: the sum of dollar amounts on the "delivered" cost sheets represents the cost of goods sold.

The form of the job-order cost sheet varies in accordance with the degree of formality required. In some cases, it may be a printed envelope or folder that, in addition to providing a data summary for the factory job, can store the supporting documents.

These supporting documents provide the flow of data into the product costing process. Management may require additional help from the managerial accountant to use these data. For example, the accountant might be called on to condense or to organize the data into a more useful form. The summary section of a job cost sheet indicates per-job profitability. This information can be routed

EXHIBIT 5–4   JOB-ORDER COST SHEET

WIZZARD PRODUCTS, INC.
Job-Order Cost Sheet

Job Order No. _W 103_

Date Started _8 - 1 - X 4_

Date Completed _8 - 21 - x 4_

Date	Department A	Department B	Total
Direct Materials			
8 - 1 - x 4 8 - 10 - x 4 8 - 17 - x 4	$ 3,000.00 1,000.00	$ 4,200.00	
Totals	$ 4,000.00	$ 4,200.00	$8,200.00
Direct Labor			
8 - 4 - x 4 8 - 11 - x 4 8 - 18 - x 4 8 - 24 - x 4	$ 500.00 500.00	$ 750.00 250.00	
Totals	$ 1,000.00	$ 1,000.00	$2,000.00
Factory Overhead			
8 - 14 - x 4 8 - 19 - x 4	$ 800.00	$ 275.00	
Totals	$ 800.00	$ 275.00	$1,075.00
Summary	$ 5,800.00	$ 5,475.00	$11,275.00

	Department A	Department B	Total
Selling Price			$ 19,285.00
Costs:			
Direct Materials	$ 4,000.00	$ 4,200.00	8,200.00
Direct Labor	1,000.00	1,000.00	2,000.00
Factory Overhead	800.00	275.00	1,075.00
			$ 11,275.00
Gross Profit			$ 8,010.00

EXHIBIT 5–5 THE FLOW OF DOCUMENTS IN A JOB-ORDER COST SYSTEM

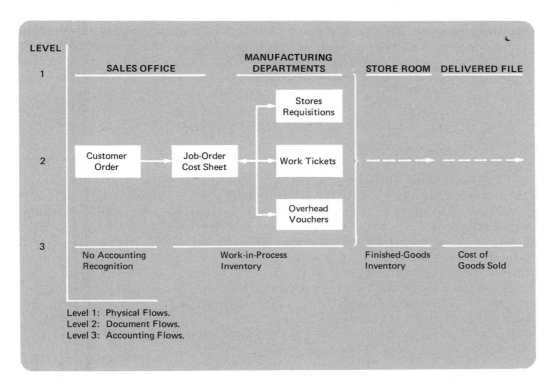

Level 1: Physical Flows.
Level 2: Document Flows.
Level 3: Accounting Flows.

to the appropriate individuals in the sales and production departments so that they may evaluate the feasibility of accepting similar jobs. Typical journal entries illustrating this process are shown in the Appendix to this chapter.

COST OF PRODUCTION

The discussion up to this point has emphasized job-order costing in relation to identifying costs associated with particular factory jobs or customer orders. However, a cost summary of the entire manufacturing process can provide top management with information that is useful for strategic planning and control decisions. Moreover, calculating the total cost of production is a necessary part of determining the overall profitability of the enterprise. As materials, labor, and overhead enter the production process, they are included in the firm's work-in-process (or manufacturing) inventory. This inventory is reduced as manufacturing operations are completed and products are transferred to the finished-goods inventory. Costs assigned to the products in the finished-goods inventory are used to calculate the cost of goods sold, which is directly tied to net income.

Inventory change   During any period, the size of work-in-process inventories may remain unchanged, decrease, or increase, as shown in the cases below.

Work-in-Process Inventory	Case 1	Case 2	Case 3
Beginning Inventory	$ 100	$ 100	$ 100
Plus: Additions to Production	1,000	1,000	1,000
Available for Manufacturing	1,100	1,100	1,100
Less: Ending Inventory	100	150	50
Cost of Goods Manufactured	$1,000	$ 950	$1,050

In each case, the same approach was used to determine manufacturing cost transfers. The beginning inventory reflects costs associated with partially completed units of output remaining in production at the end of the preceding period. Current costs of materials, labor, and overhead added to production during the current period are combined with the beginning inventory to determine the maximum value that must be assigned to completed production and to the ending work-in-process inventory. The ending work-in-process inventory reflects the costs associated with the products that were not completed during the period. The difference between the cost of goods available for manufacturing and the ending inventory is called the *costs of goods manufactured*; this is associated with the units of product output that were completed during the period and transferred to the finished-goods inventory.

In Case 1, the beginning and ending inventories are equal. Thus, the cost of goods manufactured is equal to the current costs added to production. In Case 2, the ending work-in-process inventory is greater than the beginning inventory. This indicates that the work-in-process inventory increased in value and that some of the current costs are included in the ending inventory. The costs assigned to the finished goods are less than the current costs. In Case 3, some of the costs associated with the beginning work-in-process inventory have been released into the finished-goods inventory, along with the current costs. This is reflected in the change in the work-in-process inventory.

The value of transfers to the finished-goods inventory may be found algebraically:

$$\text{Cost of Goods Manufactured} = \text{Current Costs} \\ + \text{Beginning Inventory Value} \\ - \text{Ending Inventory Value}$$

Calculation of the cost of goods manufactured is often formalized into a statement by managerial accountants. The cost-of-goods-manufactured statement summarizes flows of materials, labor, and overhead during a period and calculates the value of transfers to the finished-goods inventory.

Cost-of-goods-sold statement Accountants normally prepare a cost-of-goods-sold statement as part of determining the income for their organization. The statement forms a basis for reconciling changes in the firm's balance sheet with the periodic income statement. A Cost-of-Goods-Sold Statement for Wizzard Products, Inc., is illustrated in Exhibit 5–6. Most of the data contained on the statement are obtained from the Finished-Goods Inventory Control account, as described in the Appendix to this chapter. That is, the Finished-Goods Inventory account would combine the beginning balance with additions received from work-in-process to produce the total costs of goods available for sale. Of this total, some products remain on hand at the end of the period, and the rest have been delivered to customers. The pre-adjustment Cost of Goods Sold can also be determined by adding up the dollar value of all Job-Order Cost Sheets that have

EXHIBIT 5–6   COST-OF-GOODS-SOLD STATEMENT

WIZZARD PRODUCTS, INC.

Cost-of-Goods-Sold

Statement for Year Ended December 31, 19X4

Finished Goods Inventory Beginning Balance 1/1/X4	$175,000
Cost of Goods Manufactured	511,000
Adjustment for Under Applied Overhead	23,000
Total Costs Available for Sale	$709,000
Finished Goods Inventory Ending Balance 12/31/X4	152,000
Cost of Goods Sold	$557,000

been stamped "delivered" during the current period. The adjustment for under-applied overhead was determined by the accountant, who compared the actual overhead incurred during the period with the sum of overhead applied to individual jobs during the period. Although all of the difference between actual and applied overhead is assigned to Cost of Goods Sold in the Wizzard Products, Inc., case, other manufacturing companies allocate the difference among the three accounts, Work-in-Process Inventory, Finished-Goods Inventory, and Cost of Goods Sold.

SUMMARY

A job-order cost accounting system consists of those procedures designed to account for all the production costs incurred by a manufacturing concern and then assign them to particular factory jobs or customer orders. The system gives decision makers useful information about product costs so that they may make pricing decisions, evaluate efficiency, and prepare financial reports. Job-order costing also helps planners identify profitable jobs or types of products and estimate costs of similar jobs. (The technique is also used frequently in government contract accounting.)

The main disadvantage of job-order costing is its expense. For example, if 50 men are employed in one department, and each works on 25 different jobs, 1,250 entires are necessary to record their efforts. For this reason, job-order costing is generally used to account for output of unique products having high costs.

APPENDIX: RECORDING
JOB-ORDER DATA

The files of accumulated stores requisitions, clock cards, work tickets, and job-order cost sheets can support the principal accounting records of the firm's manufacturing activity; these records might even replace some of the special accounting journals as a place of original data entry.

The summary process   The type and amount of production material and effort required for each order processed in a job shop varies because each job is essentially unique. Therefore, a summary of cost information by factory job or customer order, as well as a summary of cost data by production department, can help management make future scheduling, production, and pricing decisions. Financial reporting (to parties outside the firm) also requires data on the total cost of the manufacturing process. The various forms and cost sheets discussed in the chapter are the means by which the data for these summaries are collected.

Traditional accounting systems are designed to process data according to different classifications. Accounts are a method of summarizing data: for example, the account titled "Accounts Receivable" summarizes all the short-term debts owed to the firm as a result of its sales. To report more detail, this account could be subdivided into individual customers: for example, "Accounts Receivable—John Smith," and "Accounts Receivable—Walter Jones." Each of these *subsidiary accounts* would summarize the debt activity of a particular customer. The total balance of these subsidiary accounts should equal the balance of the entire "Accounts Receivable" account—referred to as a *control account*, since it may be supported by subsidiary records and, conversely, can provide a validity check of the total balances of the subsidiary accounts.

Certain general ledger accounts can be used as control accounts to consolidate, or summarize, the activities shown in detail in the subsidiary ledgers. Thus, information relating to the total manufacturing effort is taken from the general ledger, but subsidiary ledger accounts can provide summaries by job, department, or operation.

The traditional flow of activity in the general ledger account is presented in Exhibit 5–7. This illustration traces the flow of production through the organization, from the point of original entry into the firm (materials and labor) to the point of eventual exit (cost of goods sold). Control accounts are supported by detailed information in subsidiary ledgers. Figures in Exhibit 5–7 are derived from the following example.

The flow of data through the accounts—an example Johnson Products, Inc., is a small manufacturing firm that uses a job-order cost accounting system. Customer orders normally are processed in one production department. Overhead costs have been estimated by management, on the basis of prior experience, to be 50% of the total charge for direct labor. All entries will be shown as they would appear in the firm's general journal. The student may relate this to the specific form and content of supporting documents, as discussed earlier in this chapter.

ACQUISITION OF RAW MATERIALS		
Materials Control	10,300	
Accounts Payable		7,200
Cash		3,100

A. (To record the purchase of materials on account and for cash.)

The firm has added raw materials to its inventory. Some of these materials will be used directly in the production processes; others will enter the processes indirectly through overhead operations. Examples of overhead include factory and maintenance supplies. The general account, "Materials Control," is supported by subsidiary accounts that specify the items in inventory.

EXHIBIT 5-7 FLOW OF DATA TO THE ACCOUNTS

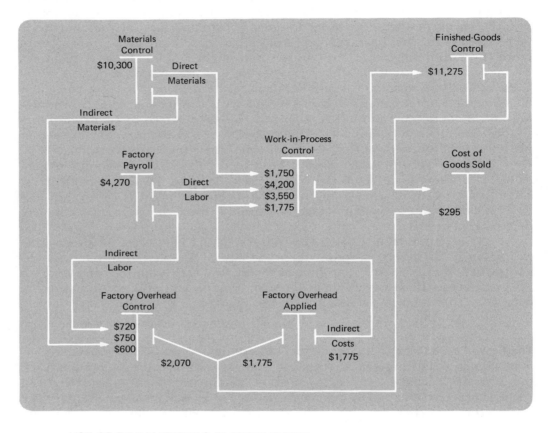

USE OF RAW MATERIALS IN PRODUCTION

Work-in-Process Control	4,200	
Materials Control		4,200

B. (To record the transfer of raw materials to the production departments.)

Again, control accounts provide a general summary of the activity. Work-in-process control reflects a beginning balance of $1,750. The transfer of raw materials is shown in detail by the stores requisition (see Exhibit 5-1), which also serves the basic control function of documenting authorization to release inventory from storage.

USE OF RAW MATERIALS IN PRODUCTION — INDIRECTLY

Factory Overhead Control	750	
Materials Control		750

C. (To record the transfer of raw materials to an overhead operation.)

Materials not directly associated with the product have been issued from the inventory. These materials will enter the production process indirectly. In this case, the cost could be for supplies used in overhauling a machine. Therefore, the charge should be made to the overhead control account, since the expense of repairing a machine cannot be traced directly to any particular output.

ACQUISITION OF LABOR

Factory Payroll	4,270	
Cash		4,270

D. (To record the payment, in cash, of the weekly payroll.)

The payroll account shows the acquisition of labor skills and efforts. The account, "Factory Payroll," summarizes labor for the entire manufacturing process. Some of the labor resources will be used directly in production, whereas others will be grouped in the overhead account, because they are used indirectly.

USE OF LABOR IN PRODUCTION

Work-in-Process Control	3,550	
Factory Payroll		3,550

E. (To record the usage of direct labor in the production process.)

The usage of labor for production would be supported by work tickets (see Exhibit 5–2), which are completed after each task. Tasks that contributed directly to the production of the product are valued and summarized in this entry, which increases the cost base of the work-in-process products.

USE OF LABOR IN PRODUCTION—INDIRECTLY

Factory Overhead Control	720	
Factory Payroll		720

F. (To record the usage of labor in an overhead operation.)

Some labor, for example, employee time spent on maintenance operations, will not be used directly in the production process. The cost of this input is summarized in the Overhead Control account for subsequent distribution among the production departments and factory jobs. Data for this entry would come from the work tickets also.

ASSIGNMENT OF OVERHEAD

Work-in-Process Control	1,775	
Factory Overhead Applied		1,775

G. (To record the application of overhead at the predetermined rate.)

The application of overhead to production is documented by the overhead voucher (see Exhibit 5–3). A predetermined rate of 50% of the cost of direct labor is the basis for this charge. Recognize that overhead is *applied*, in this case, on the basis of an estimate of the actual expenditures that the firm will make during the year.

ACQUISITION OF OVERHEAD		
Factory Overhead Control	600	
Taxes Payable		100
Accumulated Depreciation		200
Cash		300
H. (To record incurrence of actual overhead.)		

Some additional factory overhead costs have been incurred and recorded in the "Factory Overhead Control" account. Source documents and subsidiary accounts would support this entry.

COMPLETION OF MANUFACTURING		
Finished Goods Control	11,275	
Work-in-Process Control		11,275
I. (To record the completion of a customer job and its transfer to the finished-goods inventory.)		

On completion of a job, the product is physically transferred from the factory to the finished-goods inventory to await shipment. The job-order cost sheet (see Exhibit 5–4) summarizes the costs associated with this job.

CLOSING OVERHEAD ACCOUNTS		
Cost of Goods Sold	295	
Factory Overhead Applied	1,775	
Factory Overhead Control		2,070
J. (To close the Overhead Applied and Control accounts.)		

To this point, the "Factory Overhead Control" account contained the actual overhead charges incurred during the period. The "Factory Overhead Applied" account contained the estimated charges made against the factory jobs. If the two do not match, as in this case, the difference must be reconciled. One might charge the $295 difference directly to Cost of Goods Sold, as was done in the preceding journal entry. This method assigns none of the unapplied overhead to the units still in inventory; all is assigned to the units sold.

A sounder approach to reconciling overhead is to prorate the $295 unapplied overhead to Cost of Goods Sold and to Inventory, on the basis of the cost of goods assigned to each account. If no goods have been sold (all are in inventory), the total $295 is charged to Inventory. If half the goods have been sold, the $295 is split, and one-half is assigned to Inventory, and the remainder is charged to Cost of Goods Sold.

SUGGESTED READINGS

Benninger, L. J. "Accounting Theory and Cost Accounting." *The Accounting Review*, July 1965.

Berquist, Richard. "Direct Labor v. Machine Hour Costing." *Management Accounting*, May 1971.

QUESTIONS

5–1   List four uses that managers can make of product cost information. What are the prime costs of manufacturing and why are they so named? Prime costs are direct costs, whereas overhead costs are _____ costs.

5–2   Costs that *cannot* be directly traced (related) to a product (for example, building depreciation) are classified as overhead. Does it follow, then, that all costs that *can* be directly traced (related) to a product are not overhead?

5–3   Indicate whether each of the following businesses would use a *job-order costing system* (associated with discrete processes) or a *process costing system* (associated with continuous processes):

      (A) A house-painting firm
      (B) A shipbuilding company
      (C) A toy manufacturer
      (D) A gasoline filling station
      (E) A custom home builder
      (F) A book publisher
      (G) A salt producer
      (H) An automobile manufacturer
      (I)   An architectural firm

5–4   Accounting systems provide formal procedures for the recognition of direct costs. List three reasons why formal procedures are employed.

5–5   A company assigns overhead to factory jobs on the basis of direct labor hours. The budget specifies 48,000 direct labor hours and factory overhead costs of $96,000. Budgeted direct labor costs are $120,000.

      (A) Determine the overhead cost per direct labor hour.

      (B) If Job No. 1132 required 2,000 direct labor hours to complete, how much of the overhead cost will be allocated to this job?

      (C) Suppose the company changes its allocation base from direct labor hours to direct labor costs. If an hourly rate of $3 is paid to the employees who work on Job No. 1132, how much of the overhead cost will be allocated to Job No. 1132?

5–6   Give two reasons why actual and applied overhead can differ.

5–7 Describe the information reported in the following documents and present two uses made of the information by managerial accountants:

(A) Stores requisitions
(B) Clock cards
(C) Work tickets
(D) Overhead vouchers
(E) Job-order cost sheets

5–8 Substitute the missing words, phrases, or numbers for each letter in each independent case.

Case 1		Case 2	Case 3
Work-in-Process Inventory			
__A__ Inventory	$ 200	$ H	$ 400
__B__ : Additions to __C__	1,000	2,000	J
Available for __D__	1,200	2,600	K
Less: __E__ Inventory	300	300	500
F G	$ 900	$ I	$ 600

5–9 A manufacturing firm had a beginning work-in-process inventory valued at $12,000. At the end of the month, the work-in-process inventory was $14,000. During the period, prime cost of $97,000 and overhead of $32,000 were added to the production process. Determine the cost of goods manufactured for the month.

EXERCISES

5–10 (A) Make the appropriate journal entry to record each of the following events relating to the Bright Idea Lamp Company.

June 1 —Purchased raw materials on account. The invoice price was $17,400.

June 10—The factory payroll of $4,210 was paid in cash. A foreman estimated that 20% of the payroll related to overhead tasks.

June 16—$6,230 of material was released directly into production. Also, $2,910 of material was used in an overhead operation.

June 17—Overhead, which is assigned at a rate of 10% of direct labor cost, was allocated to production.

(B) Refer again to part A. What source or supporting documents would you look for to document the events that occurred on each date?

5–11 Overhead costs arise because: (1) costs cannot be physically *traced* to factory jobs, or (2) costs can be traced but the *expense* of monitoring them is prohibitive. For each of the following manufacturing costs indicate: (1) if it is traceable or not traceable and (2) if it is traceable, whether it is justifiable in terms of cost. Use the terms *traceable* or *not traceable* and *justifiable* or *not justifiable* as your answer.

(A) Direct materials

(B) Maintenance on the factory building

(C) Packing tape used in wrapping the product

(D) Electricity used for lighting the factory

(E) Electricity used to operate power tools

(F) A foreman's salary

(G) The corporate president's salary

(H) The salary of a craftsman working in the factory

(I) The time that a craftsman spends between factory jobs on a coffee break

(J) The salary of a managerial accountant working in the factory

5-12 The Felt Co., a job order shop, traditionally determines prices for its products on the basis of costs: price on any one job is set at 150% of cost. At the end of the year, an analysis of all job-order cost sheets canceled with the "Delivered" stamp and placed in the Cost of Goods Sold Drawer produced the following totals: Direct labor, $100,000; Direct material $200,000; Applied overhead $100,000. An analysis of the Actual Overhead Accounts produced a total of $80,000. After the accountant makes all necessary adjustments, how much gross profit will Felt Co. report?

5-13 ToolCo expected to incur the following costs during 19X4: labor costs, $2,000,000, and overhead costs, $1,000,000. ToolCo uses a job-order cost system and assigns overhead to jobs on the basis of direct labor costs. Job No. 101 required 110 pounds of material at $2 per pound, 560 hours of labor at $10 per hour, and a regular application of overhead. By the end of 19X4, ToolCo had incurred $2,100,000 of labor costs and only $700,000 for overhead.

(A) Determine the total cost of Job No. 101.

(B) Specify the amounts for Actual Overhead, Applied Overhead, and Over/Under Applied Overhead.

(C) Will the Over/Under Applied Overhead adjustment to Cost of Goods Sold increase or decrease Cost of Goods Sold?

5-14 The Muffin Company assigns overhead to job cost sheets on the basis of $3 per direct labor hour worked. Job No. 101 incurred $1,220 material costs and labor costs of $5 per hour at 200 hours, or $1,000. Job No. 101 sold for $4,000. During the year, total labor hours incurred amounted to 10,000, and total actual overhead amounted to $39,500.

(A) How much profit was earned on Job 101?

(B) At the end of the year, Applied Overhead was over/under applied by what amount?

(C) If all production for the year had been delivered to customers, Muffin should have disposed of the Over/Under Applied Overhead by adjusting which account(s)?

5-15 A clerk in a job shop was told to verify that all source documents were accounted for. He thereupon unstapled all documents from the job cost sheets, placed the work tickets and material requisitions in descending numerical order, and promptly lost the cost sheets. The clerk did know, however, that overhead was applied at the rate of $2 for every $1 of direct labor cost. The clerk produced the following summary report on his verification task:

Material Requisition				Work Tickets		
Number	Amount	Job		Number	Amount	Job
mr455	$230	#104		wt 56	$90	#105
mr456	$130	#105		wt 57	$20	#104
mr457	$100	#105		wt 58	$70	#106
mr458	$200	#103		wt 59	$60	#104
mr459	$170	#103		wt 60	$40	#103
mr460	$110	#104		wt 61	$50	#106
mr461	$100	#106		wt 62	$10	#103

At the end of the month, Job No. 105 is still in the shop, Jobs No. 103 and No. 104 are in the finished-goods storeroom, and Job No. 106 has been delivered to the customer.

Determine the end of period balances for work-in-process inventory, finished-goods inventory, and cost of goods sold.

5-16 Wilson Mfg. Co. applied (assigned) $100,000 of overhead to Departments 1 and 2 during January. Actual overhead for the period amounted to $90,000. All goods produced during January were sold on the last day of the month.

(A) Is overhead overapplied or underapplied?

(B) What is to be done with the $10,000 over/underapplied overhead?

5-17 Data for the Hopwell Corporation are presented below. Substitute the missing number for each letter in the following independent cases.

	Case 1	Case 2	Case 3
Estimated yearly overhead cost	$10,000	$20,000	$40,000
Estimated yearly volume (labor hours)	40,000	10,000	C
Labor hours on Job No. 111	200	B	100
Overhead assigned (applied) to Job No. 111	$ A	$ 800	$ 500

5-18 The following inventory data relate to the Shober Corporation.

	Inventories	
	Ending	Beginning
Finished Goods	$95,000	$110,000
Work in Process	80,000	70,000
Raw Materials	95,000	90,000

In addition, the following information is known.

Cost of Goods Available for sale	$684,000
Total Manufacturing Costs to Account For	654,000
Applied Factory Overhead	167,000
Direct Materials Used	193,000
Underapplied Overhead	10,000
Indirect Materials Used	-0-

Determine the following amounts:

(A) Direct materials purchased during the year.
(B) Direct labor costs incurred during the period.
(C) The cost of goods sold during the period.

(AICPA adapted)

5-19 The Theft Brothers Steel Mill is engaged in specialty steel processing and milling. On Job Order No. 207, the following costs and statistics have been maintained, in addition to comparable data for the entire milling operation.

	Job Order No. 207	Estimated Information, Total Factory
Machine Hours	80	800
Direct Labor	$500	$3,500
Materials Used	$700	$7,700
Direct Labor Hours	50	400
Overhead		$4,000

(A) Using this information, calculate the various overhead rates on different predetermined bases.

1. Labor cost base
2. Labor hours base
3. Machine hours base

(B) Calculate the total cost of Job No. 207 that results from the use of each of the three overhead rates.

5-20 During the current year, production costs for the Wilson Job Shop included $50,000 labor, $40,000 material, and $60,000 applied overhead, for a total of $150,000. All production was sold, so Cost of Sales (before adjustments) equaled $150,000. Actual overhead amounted to $70,000, however.

(A) If the overhead rate reflected actual costs perfectly, how much would Cost of Sales have been?

(B) After the adjustment is made for underapplied overhead, how much will Cost of Sales be?

(C) If Sales Revenue was $200,000 and Gross Profit was determined to be $50,000 before adjustment for underapplied overhead, how will the adjustment affect income?

5–21   The assignment of overhead to particular jobs involves three separate components: (1) calculating overhead rates, (2) assigning overhead to specific jobs, and (3) reconciling differences between actual and applied overhead. The first two of these components are the subject of each of the following four independent cases. For each case, determine the missing numbers for each of the letters A through H.

	Case 1	Case 2	Case 3	Case 4
Estimated overhead cost	$10,000	$20,000	$40,000	G
Estimated labor hours	1,000	40,000	E	10,000
Predetermined overhead rate	A	C	$ 2/hr.	$ 3/hr.
Labor hours on Job No. 101	50	D	300	50
Overhead assigned to No. 101	B	$ 100	F	H

5–22   Whenever actual overhead differs from applied overhead, the accountant must reconcile the differences at the end of the period. Below are six independent cases. First, determine the missing numbers for each of the letters A through F. Next, answer the question: "What will happen to the reported income when the over/underapplied overhead is assigned to Cost of Goods Sold?" Use the words "increase" or "decrease" in responding to this question.

	Case 1	Case 2	Case 3	Case 4	Case 5	Case 6
Actual Overhead	$300,000	$300,000	$300,000	$200,000	$ E	$ F
Applied Overhead	290,000	B	C	210,000	300,000	300,000
Over/underapplied overhead	A	(10,000)	10,000	D	(10,000)	10,000
I—increase/ D—decrease income	?	?	?	?	?	?

5–23   The cost-of-goods-manufactured calculation follows a known relationship. In each of the following four independent cases, determine the missing numbers for each of the letters A through G.

	Case 1	Case 2	Case 3	Case 4
Cost in beginning inventory	$1,000	$ C	$2,000	$2,000
Costs added to production	8,000	6,000	E	9,000
Costs available for manufacturing	$9,000	$9,000	D	F
Cost in ending inventory	2,000	B	1,000	G
Cost of goods manufactured	$ A	$7,000	$8,000	$6,000

PROBLEMS

5-24   The Johnson Company custom-builds boats. When the current budget was prepared, total expected overhead was estimated at $88,000, and expected labor hour volume was estimated at 40,000 hours. These two budgeted numbers were used to determine the applied overhead rate for the current year. During the year, accumulated actual costs for depreciation, gas, oil, rent, indirect labor, and supplies amounted to $83,000. Three boats were under construction during the year, and the actual hours of direct labor incurred on each were 16,000, 12,000, and 14,000. The applied overhead rate is multiplied by the actual hours to determine the applied overhead to be charged to the individual jobs (boats).

All three boats were sold, and the accumulated costs (applied overhead, in addition to direct labor and material) were transferred to the account, Cost of Goods Sold. Before preparing an income statement, the accountant for Johnson determines the over/underapplied overhead and he adjusts the Cost of Goods Sold account. After the adjustment, the Applied overhead component of Cost of Goods Sold equals the Actual overhead incurred during the year.

(A)   Determine the applied overhead rate.

(B)   Determine the amount of applied overhead assigned to each of the three boats.

(C)   Assuming that cost of goods sold was $200,000 before the over/underapplied overhead adjustment, determine its balance after the adjustment.

5-25   The Phast Buck Sales Company applies overhead to production orders on the basis of direct labor hours in Department 1 and on the basis of machine hours in Department 2. The total budgeted labor hours in Department 1 are 40,000; total expected overhead is $100,000. Department 2 has 60,000 machine hours available for the year and total expected overhead to be applied of $90,000.

(A)   What are the predetermined overhead rates to be used by Phast Buck Sales Company in Department 1 and in Department 2?

(B)   Assuming that the Company pays a labor rate of $3 per hour, what is the per-unit overhead cost of the following job order?

	Department 1	Department 2	Total
Materials Used	$4,000	$12,000	$16,000
Labor Costs	$1,350	$ 600	$ 1,950
Machine Hours	100	900	1,000
Units Produced			1,500

(C)   Actual overhead costs during the year were $102,500 in Department 1 and $88,000 in Department 2. Actual volume exactly equaled budgeted volume. How much over- or underapplied overhead was incurred in each department?

(D) How does the managerial accountant typically dispose of the over- or underapplied overhead in part C above?

5–26   The Burro Excavating Company uses a job-order costing system to account for its customer orders. At the beginning of the current year, the Company had an inventory of raw materials valued at $102,000. Total purchases of materials (mostly shoring timbers) during the year totaled $56,000. During the year, $6,000 of materials and $10,000 of labor were used to construct an executive swimming pool at the main office of Burro Excavating. It was estimated that the pool would last for ten years and would provide a valuable service to the Company by enabling the executives to stay in shape.

During the year, total direct labor costs were $415,000. Materials valued at $14,000 were used in overhead operations during the year. Maintenance employees were paid $39,000, and the executives' salaries, including bonuses, were $142,000. Miscellaneous overhead expenses totaled $73,000. The year-end inventory revealed that the raw materials inventory was $84,000. At the beginning of the year, two jobs were in process: Job Order No. 916, which had costs of $47,000, and Job Order No. 917, which had a total cost of $87,000. During the year, Job Orders No. 917, 918, and 919 were completed, leaving Job Order No. 916 in process at year's end, with $93,000 of associated costs.

Using the information above, construct a cost-of-goods-manufactured statement for the Burro Excavating Company. Of what use is this statement to the Company?

5–27   The Wayco Company has received an order to build some large concrete ducks for a contractor, who wants to place them in the lake of a housing development so that boat owners have a place to anchor in the lake to fish. The order should take two months to complete. During the first month, $600 worth of material and $700 worth of labor are used. During the next month, $800 in material and $900 in labor are used. The factory overhead rate is 100% of direct labor and it is applied whenever direct labor is used.

(A)   What cost accounting system should be used by the Wayco Company? Briefly explain why.

(B)   What amount should appear in the total column of the cost sheet at the end of the first month?

(C)   What amount should appear in the total column of the cost sheet at the end of the second month? Prepare a facsimile cost sheet for the second month.

(D)   If the other type of cost accounting system were used, what would be the amount in the total column at the end of the second month?

5–28   The Hawley Manufacturing Company, which custom-builds boats, is currently processing two major orders for which it is using job-order costing. Job

Order No. 100 is assigned to the first boat and Job Order No. 101 to the second boat. The following transactions occurred during the first month of production on these orders:

1. Wood and metal fittings were purchased for $4,000 and $5,000, respectively.
2. $1,000 of metal fittings were issued to Job Order No. 100 and $2,500 of metal fittings to Job Order No. 101.
3. The total payroll was $4,000, incurred as follows: Job Order No. 100, $2,000; Job Order No. 101, $1,000; overhead, $600; and selling expense, $400.
4. Sail cloth was purchased for $3,000. All sail cloth was requisitioned for Job Order No. 100 except $500 worth, which was kept in the inventory for future use.
5. Issued $500 of wood to Job Order No. 100 and $600 of metal fittings to Job Order No. 101.
6. Various additional indirect factory costs amounted to $5,000.
7. Overhead is allocated to both Job Order Nos. 100 and 101 at the predetermined rate of 100% of direct labor expense.
8. Job Order No. 100 is finished and delivered to the customer.

(A) Prepare job-order cost sheets for Job Order Nos. 100 and 101.

(B) What are the balances in the raw materials and finished-goods inventories? What is the cost of goods sold?

(C) Identify the source documents that underlie each item recorded on a job-order cost sheet.

(D) Could a process-cost accounting system be used by Hawley? What advantages would be gained and what advantages would be lost by converting to such an accounting system?

†(E) Prepare journal entries to explain Transactions 1–8.

5–29 The Schrader Company builds modular houses. Three models are currently being built: Job-order Nos. 251, 252, and 253. The following information relates to these job orders:

	Job No. 251	Job No. 252	Job No. 253
Materials Requisitioned	$4,500	$3,200	$3,500
Units Completed (as part of the order)	10	8	7
Labor Hours	1,000	900	750

The company pays the workers $10.00 an hour and assigns overhead on the basis of direct labor hours. The Schrader Company expects to have a labor payroll of $500,000 this year and $1,000,000 in overhead.

Using this information, calculate the following:

(A) The total cost of each job order

(B) The per-unit cost of each job order

(C) The per-unit selling price of each job order, if the Company intends to set a price equal to 200% of cost

†5–30 Part of the managerial accounting reporting system for Permanent Design, Inc., is diagramed below.

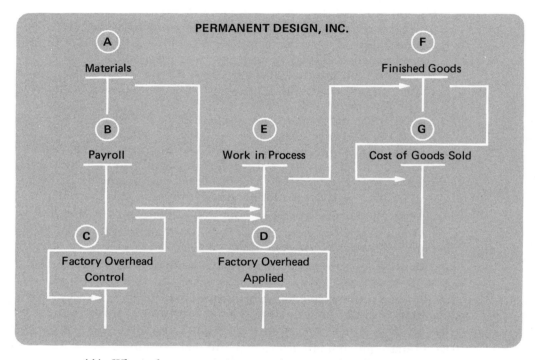

(A) What documentation authorizes the flow from A to E? What documentation authorizes the flow from B to E? From D to E?

(B) Why is factory overhead (C) handled differently from payroll or material? What happens when factory overhead applied is different from factory overhead control?

(C) What documentation authorizes the flow from E to F? From F to G? Which individual could authorize these flows?

(D) Could there ever be a transfer from A to C? Explain why or why not. Could there ever be a transfer from A to D? Explain why or why not.

(E) Manufacturing companies usually have three inventories. What are they called? Why are three inventories needed? Why isn't payroll considered an inventory (or is it)?

5–31   The Stor Moore Company manufactures custom-made cabinets on order for a select clientele. Since the underlying production processes are uniform (although each customer order is unique), manufacturing operations are organized into departments. A job-order cost accounting system is used by the firm to collect product cost information. One job-order cost sheet is as follows:

STOR MOORE COMPANY
Job Order Cost Sheet

Job Order No.   152
Date Started   9/7/X4
Date Completed   12/15/X4

Date	Dept. A	Dept. B	Dept. C	Total
Direct Materials				
9/1/X4	2,407.50	1,504.50	705.40	$ 4,617.40
10/1/X4	1,600.20	1,210.00	501.50	3,311.70
Totals	4,007.70	2,714.50	1,206.90	7,929.10
Direct Labor				
9/30/X4	500.42			500.42
10/28/X4	700.50	500.50		1,201.00
11/30/X4	800.00	1,142.00	1,500.42	3,442.42
Totals	2,000.92	1,642.50	1,500.42	5,143.84
Factory Overhead				
9/30/X4	1,000.84			1,000.84
10/28/X4	1,401.00	1,001.00		2,402.00
11/30/X4	1,600.00	2,284.00	3,000.84	6,884.84
Totals	4,001.84	3,285.00	3,000.84	10,287.68

Summary

	Dept. A	Dept. B	Dept. C	Total
Selling Price				$25,000.00
Cost:				
Direct Materials	$ 4,007.70	$2,714.50	$1,206.90	$ 7,929.10
Direct Labor	2,000.92	1,642.50	1,500.42	5,143.84
Factory Overhead	4,001.84	3,285.00	3,000.84	10,287.68
	$10,010.46	$7,642.00	$5,708.16	$23,360.62
Gross Profit				$ 1,639.38

(A) Which of the departments in the Stor Moore Company has the highest direct labor cost? Which department has the largest amount of prime cost?

(B) How can direct material be requisitioned for Department C on 9/1/X4, when no direct labor was reported on that date? Doesn't it take some labor to transport material?

(C) What overhead rate and base were used to assign overhead costs to factory orders? Can this procedure cause problems in projecting future costs? What happens when the firm's accountant attempts to match costs to the time periods in which they were incurred?

(D) What documentation supports the direct material figures entered on the job-order cost sheet? What documentation supports the direct labor figures entered on the job-order cost sheet? The overhead figures?

(E) Is $25,000 a good selling price for this product? Why or why not?

5–32   You are employed by an engineering consulting firm. Your job is to estimate the total cost of operations per chargeable man-hour, for each member of the professional staff, in order that suitable billing rates may be established.

Your estimates of the hours for which the professional staff will be paid, their annual salaries, and the proportions of their working hours that will not be directly chargeable to any specific client follow:

Employee	Total Hours	Annual Salary	Percentage of Time Devoted to Firm Overhead
Able	1,200	$ 2,400	40%
Briscol	2,400	12,000	10%
Case	2,000	8,000	20%
Dider	800	10,000	40%
Emel	2,400	7,200	5%

Other costs of operating this firm, including clerical wages, have averaged about $39,100 per year for the last three years.

(A) Prepare schedules computing the following:
  1. Total overhead cost.
  2. Total employees' salaries directly billable to clients.
  3. An estimate of the total cost of operations per chargeable man-hour of each member of the professional staff, assuming that total overhead is to be allocated on the basis of total billable professional salaries.

(B) Without regard to the effect on total overhead and assuming that no factor except those noted changes, state whether each of the following unrelated situations will result in

(1) Overabsorption
(2) Estimated (standard) absorption
(3) Underabsorption

of overhead and state the reason for this result:

1. Able spends 50 per cent of his time in overhead functions.
2. Briscol works 100 hours less than expected during the year and his salary is reduced accordingly.
3. Case works 100 hours more than expected during the year and his salary is increased accordingly.
4. Dider works 200 hours more than expected during the year and his annual salary is unchanged.
5. Emel receives a salary increase but his billing rate is not changed.

(AICPA adapted)

5-33   The Haag Company custom-makes components for computers. When manufacturing an order, the Company makes extra components principally to replace defective ones that customers may return within a one-year guaranty period, although orders for more of exactly the same component are received occasionally. The number of extras produced is the sum of (1) the estimated number of normal replacements, (2) an allowance for possible abnormal replacements (since the incremental cost of production is very low in comparison with the cost of reworking), and (3) the estimated number that can be sold after the first order. All product costs are closed to cost of goods sold when the first order is shipped, and hence the extras on hand are not assigned a value in the accounts.

(A) The Haag Company classifies components to be shipped to customers as finished-goods inventory.
   1. Explain the meaning of the term "finished-goods inventory."
   2. Discuss the propriety of classifying the extra components as finished-goods inventory.

(B) Assume that the Haag Company wants to classify all extra components as inventory. Discuss the propriety of carrying the extras at
   1. No or nominal cost.
   2. Full cost.

(AICPA adapted)

†*5-34   The D. Hayes Cramer Company manufactures Product C, whose cost per unit is $1 of material, $2 of labor, and $3 of overhead. During the month of May, 1,000 units of Product C were spoiled. These spoiled units could be sold for $.60 each.

The accountant said that the entry to be made for these 1,000 lost or spoiled units could be one of the following four:

Entry No. 1
    Spoiled Goods $ 600
        Work in Process—Materials $ 100
        Work in Process—Labor   200
        Work in Process—Overhead   300
Entry No. 2
    Spoiled Goods $ 600
    Manufacturing Expenses   5,400
        Work in Process—Materials $1,000
        Work in Process—Labor   2,000
        Work in Process—Overhead   3,000
Entry No. 3
    Spoiled Goods $ 600
    Loss on Spoiled Goods   5,400
        Work in Process—Materials $1,000
         Work in Process—Labor   2,000
        Work in Process—Overhead   3,000
Entry No. 4
    Spoiled Goods $ 600
    Receivable   5,400
        Work in Process—Materials $1,000
         Work in Process—Labor   2,000
        Work in Process—Overhead   3,000

Indicate the circumstances under which each of the four proposed solutions would be appropriate.

(AICPA adapted)

CHAPTER 6

Product Costing — The Process Alternative

Objectives

After studying this chapter, you should be able to do the following:

Distinguish continuous manufacturing from job shop operations.

List the basic steps that support the process costing procedure.

Describe the documents used to record data in process costing systems, and identify potential problems associated with determining physical quantity flows, dollar accumulations, and cost per unit calculations.

Calculate equivalent units of partially completed production.

Contrast FIFO (first-in, first-out) and weighted-average cost flow assumptions, and explain the differences that appear in cost of ending inventories calculated under each method.

Determining product cost is essential to decision making in manufacturing firms. Chapter 5 explored one method of collecting product cost data—job-order costing. In many situations, however, job-order costing is neither practical nor economically feasible. This chapter deals with a second, more efficient cost collection system—**process costing**.

SELECTING A PRODUCT COSTING METHOD

Many factors determine the appropriateness of a particular product costing method for a given manufacturing situation. These factors include: (1) the *types of decisions* to be made, (2) the *cost and benefits* of alternate methods of data collection, and (3) the *nature of the production process*.

Decision-making   Managerial accountants select a product costing method that is relevant to the type of managerial decision that they have to make.

Cost information is perhaps the prime basis upon which pricing and product-line decisions will be made. These decisions are among the most important made in a company. But no universal ready-made formula exists which may be used to indicate just what costs should be used and how they should be calculated. For each [type of] decision the question must be asked, "What costs and what method of allocation are relevant to this decision?" and the information collected will depend upon the answer to this question.[1]

Relevance to decision-making, therefore, is one criterion for selecting a product costing method. Job-order costing primarily provides feedback information about the profitability of specific orders so that sales management can make intelligent pricing decisions. In contrast, process costing provides data for measuring the efficiency and effectiveness of production managers.

Cost and benefits   Relevance, however, is not the only criterion. There is a *cost associated with the information-collecting process* of a firm; more time and effort are required to collect and process detailed information than to process general information. Similarly, *benefits* accruing to the firm from the decision-making process depend on the "rightness" of the decision. Information, which reduces uncertainty, can be valued as a factor in the benefits derived from a "better" decision.

The cost of collecting data should not exceed the expected benefits from these data. For example, a cannery could collect cost data on a per-can basis, but the procedure would be extremely costly and time consuming. Furthermore, it is questionable whether this data would improve the quality of decisions made by managers of the cannery, since the output units (canned foods, in this case) are

[1]*Management Services Technical Study No. 8* (New York: American Institute of Certified Public Accountants, 1963), p. 13.

not differentiated on a per-can basis. In such a case, cost would definitely exceed benefit.

Production processes   The nature of a firm's production process can influence decisions about product costing. Continuous manufacturing does not differentiate production output by customer order; managerial decisions focus on the process involved in production, rather than on the individual order.

Process costing assigns the total manufacturing cost incurred to all output units. Once this assignment is made, costs remain associated with the units of product. This permits costs to follow the flow of units through the firm, from the production processes to the finished-product inventory and eventually to the point of sale. Generally, process costing methods are used in industries that produce large quantities of similar units of output through a continuous production process—for example, chemical plants, petroleum refineries, steel mills, coal mining, and automobile manufacturers. Manufacturers using process costing are those that produce: (1) a single product, such as cement, beer, ice, or sugar; (2) a variety of products using the same production facilities, for example, bricks, tiles, and other ceramic products; and (3) a variety of products using a separate plant for each product. The characteristics of process-costing industries are high output volume and standard (or identical) production processes.

CONTINUOUS MANUFACTURING

Certain characteristics distinguish continuous manufacturing from individual, job-order, discrete processing.

1. *Output demand.* Production is initiated by anticipated market demand rather than in response to individual customer orders, and output is intended for finished-goods inventory.

2. *Unit homogeneity.* Individual units of output are homogeneous, that is, each unit is fabricated with the same amounts of inputs, skill, attention, and effort, as every other unit.

3. *Continuous production line.* Mass production with task specialization under standard operating procedures characterizes the production process.

4. *Departmental cost centers.* The continuous production process is organized into nonoverlapping work stations or departments, each of which is directed by one specific manager. Operating and financial information are collected for each department.

The characteristics that distinguish continuous production line manufacturing from discrete job-order manufacturing also provide a basis for process costing procedures.

An example A food-processing company operates a canning factory. The facility is located in an agricultural region and is designed to process large quantities of fresh vegetables through its preserving and canning operations.

The two basic phases of the factory's operations are preparation and canning. The first phase, preparation, consists of cleaning and sorting the produce. This phase is mainly a manual task that requires a large number of people working at a conveyor belt. The canning operation is totally mechanized and functions with little human intervention, except for a few operators assigned to the equipment.

When the process begins, the accountant starts to monitor and accumulate the total cost of production. He focuses on three components of this cost — *materials*, *labor*, and *overhead*, and collects information on these costs for each production operation.

Initially, the cost of the fresh produce is treated as the raw material cost and is accumulated into the total. The cost of the plant's labor force is also added in. The cost of the empty cans can be treated as a material cost also and added to the total. The indirect, or overhead, costs can arise from machinery repairs and maintenance and depreciation. Again, these costs are added to the total cost without any attempt to trace or relate them to a particular output unit.

When the canning operation is completed, the accountant determines the number of cans produced and then calculates an average cost per can. This process costing system is appropriate in this situation for several reasons. For example, once the processing is started, it is impossible to determine which vegetables were destined for which can. Even if such a determination could be made, it is doubtful whether management could use the information.

The cost of the product can be used to determine prices and efficiency. For either purpose, an average cost per can will suffice. Since prices will be quoted on the basis of a number of cans, it is reasonable to consider costs on a per-can level. The reduction of total cost to a per-can basis is a matter of convenience; some decisions will still be based on the costs of the process in total.

BASIC PROCESS COSTING PROCEDURES

Process costing assigns an *average* amount of the actual production costs incurred during a period of time. The technique of cost determination involves four distinct steps.

1. Determining the total cost of production for each department.
2. Determining the total number of units produced in each department.
3. Calculating the average cost per unit of output.

4. Dividing the total departmental cost of production into two parts: assigning some cost to the units that have been transferred to other departments and the remainder to the units that remain in the department at the end of the period.

An example   Auto chassis pass through the fender welding department of an assembly line on a continuous conveyor belt. Physical counts of chassis are taken in the morning as the line is about to start up (beginning inventory), as the chassis are transferred out of the fender welding department to the next department, and at the end of the day (ending inventory). During one accounting period, total costs of $98,000 were incurred; no units were in beginning inventory; 800 units were transferred to the next department, and 200 completed units remained at the end of the period. The per-unit cost is determined by dividing the $98,000 cost by the 1,000 units: cost per unit is $98. The $98,000 cost can be assigned to ending inventory and to the next department, as follows:

Transferred cost: 800 units @ $98	$78,400
Inventory cost: 200 units @ $98	19,600
Total processing costs accounted for	$98,000

The underlying assumption in process costing is that similar units should bear equal amounts of the production costs for a period. Physical units or other measures of production output (1,000 units in the example) are divided into the accumulated production cost ($98,000 in the example above) to determine per-unit cost. Process costing is a *full-cost* procedure, since all of the accumulated costs are accounted for in the per-unit charges.

An assumption is made that *input costs attach (or become physically associated) with the output units in a uniform manner.* This assumption implies that all units receive equal amounts of attention, skill, and effort. Thus, in continuous manufacturing, the *actual production costs can be expressed as an average cost per unit*, rather than *individual costs traced to the output units.* Tracing individual costs to individual units would be either physically impossible or economically unjustified.

COST ACCUMULATION

Process costing requires that the costs of direct materials, direct labor, and factory overhead all be considered in determining total production costs. These three elements of input enter the process, combine (or interact) to produce outputs which, in turn, are transferred to other departments. In process costing systems, the managerial accountant monitors inputs into the process over time.

For example, he can document flows from the raw materials inventory over a specified period of time. Given a continuous flow in the manufacturing process, individual requisitions by job lot are not needed. Labor inputs, too, can be determined over time, and overhead charges can be added periodically.

Material cost Materials acquired by the firm in anticipation of production are held in the *raw materials inventory*. The release of materials from inventory and their transfer to production, may be documented by a *memorandum*. The memorandum serves the same purposes as a materials requisition, but contrasts with job-order systems because: (1) materials are drawn periodically rather than as needed, (2) specific inputs always go to particular processing departments, and (3) standard uniform lot sizes are shipped. Requisitions are issued for other types of material transfers. Periodically, raw materials inventory levels are reconciled with the stock transfers to production. An example of a stock flow memorandum or **material transfer sheet** is shown in Exhibit 6-1. The

EXHIBIT 6-1   MATERIAL TRANSFER SHEET

HAWKE COMPANY
Material Transfer Sheet

Process Main   Date 8-16-X4

Description	Quantity	Unit Price	Total
Liquid hng.	1,000 lbs	$7.15	$7,150.00
Totals	1,000 lbs		$7,150.00

Prepared by:
Signed: E. C. Hawke

memorandum indicates that 1,000 pounds of material, costing $7,150, were transferred to the main process of Hawke Company on 8/16/X4. A similar material transfer sheet would accompany any goods transferred out of the main process into secondary processes.

The information taken from this material transfer sheet is used to increase the cost of the *work-in-process inventory*. No attempt is made at this point to determine a per-unit cost.

Labor cost   Generally, a continuous manufacturing process is structured around the performance of repetitive, specialized tasks by the labor force. Costs are not traced to jobs but to a particular process or department: labor costs are collected by department instead of by job. The accountant requires information about the employees' total wages and labor assignments. A *clock card* or individual time record provides this information about workers paid on an hourly basis. A clock card is presented in Exhibit 6–2. This record shows that Fred Raquet worked 40 hours during one week in August in the main process department of Hawke Company.[2]

Clock cards provide detailed support for the amount of labor cost added to the work-in-process inventory. Note that these clock cards are simpler than the ones used in job-order systems, since employees are engaged in specialized labor in one department. The clock cards are used also as a basis for payroll computations. Other payroll information provides cost data about salaried employees.

Overhead cost   The third element of the process cost, factory overhead, is generally assigned to the work-in-process inventory on the basis of a predetermined rate. This rate reflects a managerial decision about the amount of indirect costs — depreciation, maintenance, and so forth — that were involved in generating output. The amount of this charge is documented by an *overhead voucher* (see Exhibit 6–3). The main process department of Hawke Company was charged $2,486 as its share of overhead for one week in August. It is not obvious from the overhead voucher how the charge was derived, that is, how large the predetermined overhead rate is and on what base it is applied. Common bases for applying overhead are total labor dollars, total labor hours, or total machine hours. Again, the overhead cost will be charged to the work-in-process inventory account, increasing the accumulated cost balance.

Departmental cost sheet   A **departmental cost sheet** is a summary of the labor, materials, and overhead assigned to a particular department during a given period. In this regard, the departmental cost sheet is similar to a job-order

[2]Clock cards or time cards frequently do not include dollar data. Pay rates and gross earnings data are usually determined with reference to the payroll department records. In Exhibit 6–2, space was provided on the time record to facilitate payroll computations. These computations were completed after the initial recording of labor hours worked.

EXHIBIT 6-2　TIME RECORD

HAWKE COMPANY
Individual Time Record

Name _Fred Raquet_　　　　　　Period: _____

Job Class _Production. 2_　　　Starting _8-10-X4_

Process _Main_　　　　　　　　Ending _8-17-X4_

Date	Time In	Time Out		Total
8-10-x4	8.00	4.00		8 —
8-11-x4	9.00	5.00		8 —
8-12-x4	8.00	4.00		8 —
8-13-x4	8.00	4.00		8 —
8-14-x4	8.30	4.30		8 —
		Total		40
		Pay Rate		$3.15
		Gross Earnings		$126.00

cost sheet, discussed in Chapter 5. A departmental cost sheet can be conceived of as a check-in register placed at the entrance of the department, on which all productive inputs must be recorded before entering the department. In reality, amounts are posted to the departmental cost sheet periodically from the material transfer sheets, clock cards, and overhead vouchers. Departmental cost sheets accumulate the costs incurred in a particular process during a specified period

EXHIBIT 6–3   OVERHEAD VOUCHER

HAWKE COMPANY
Overhead Voucher

Voucher No. V.H · 103   Date   8 - 17 - X4

Process   Main

Debit: Work-in-Process Inventory $ 2,486	Credit: Overhead Applied $ 2,486

and are used to determine the average cost of each unit produced, and hence, amount of cost that should be assigned to other departments along with the units of production.

Exhibit 6–4 shows a departmental cost sheet for the main process of Hawke Company for the month of August. The liquid lug material cost and the 8/17 overhead charge were taken directly from the documents illustrated in Exhibits 6–1 and 6–3. "Class 2 labor" represents Fred Raquet's four weeks of work (Exhibit 6–2). The other costs would be supported by similar source documents. Note that the main process receives inputs that are the outputs of two other departments, subassemblies 1 and 2. Similarly, the output of the main process will be the input for another process.

The Hawke Company Main Process Departmental Cost Sheet shown in Exhibit 6–4 is oversimplified. Realistic departmental cost sheets would reflect many more line-items of information, i.e., accounts. The exhibit implies that there were no beginning inventories or ending inventories, since no data are reported about them. Cost sheets ordinarily reflect both beginning and ending costs classified under input headings for materials, labor, and overhead.

Multiple processes   Manufacturing operations often consist of several related processes. *Subsidiary accounts* can be used to accumulate the costs of each process. Elements of materials, labor, and overhead are traced to separate accounts for each process. The information contained in the subsidiary accounts is summarized and reported in the more general *work-in-process inventory control*

EXHIBIT 6–4   DEPARTMENTAL COST SHEET

HAWKE COMPANY
Departmental Cost Sheet

Process Main   **Month** August

Materials	Costs
Liquid Lug	$ 7,150
Coloring	1,000
Transfers In	
From Subassembly 1	$ 3,000
From Subassembly 2	5,000
Labor	
Class 1	$ 1,126
Class 2	504
Overhead	
8/17	$ 2,486
8/30	2,000
Total Costs	**$22,266**
Total Units Processed	2,000 Gallons
Cost per Unit	$11.133

account. For a more detailed discussion of the entries normally used in process cost-accounting systems, see the appendix to this chapter.

We have discussed procedures that enable the managerial accountant to determine and accumulate costs of production. He must also determine the number of units produced during the period before he can make a per-unit cost assignment.

DETERMINING QUANTITY

In some production situations, determining the number of units produced is simply a matter of monitoring the production line. For example, if 10,000 cans of produce are processed in a cannery at a total cost of $500, the cost per unit is $500/10,000 or $.05. Normally, though, per-unit costs may not be calculated so easily.

In many production situations, the manufacturing process operates continuously throughout several time periods. Any particular period may start with some partially completed units already in process and may end with other units partially completed. But partially completed units in the beginning and ending inventories have not received an equal share of attention, skill, and effort of production; because they are not equal to the finished units, they must be accounted for differently.

Equivalent units **Equivalent units** is a concept introduced by accountants to overcome problems of accounting for partially completed units. Since each element of production (materials, labor, and overhead) is represented in each unit of output, partially completed units are presumed to bear a pro rata share. If 500 units are 50% complete, these units are treated as being *equivalent* to 250 units that are 100% complete. Thus, accountants derive a single production figure for the period, expressed in *equivalent units*. This approach is a practical method for determining the total number of units produced during the current period.

Consider the following examples of equivalent-unit calculations.

Example 1. Assume that the following data have been determined:

	Units
Beginning Inventory—40% Complete	9,000
Transferred Out during Period	77,000
Ending Inventory—20% Complete	10,000

The beginning and ending inventory levels are determined by physical count. The units started in, or entering, this department and those transferred out can be counted as they enter, are started, or are transferred out. All continuous processes have some measure of physical quantity, such as pounds, gallons, inches, cans, and so on, and the quantity measures can change from process to process. The percentage of completion can be determined by the relative proportion of standard inputs already combined in the process.

Accountants must determine the number of equivalent units completed during the period. The number of units transferred out relates to fully completed units. Since some work was needed to complete the beginning inventory, and some work has been done on the ending inventory, the equivalent units of production will equal the transferred units only if the beginning inventory level is equal to the ending inventory. The equivalency concept holds that two half-completed units are equal to one completed unit. The equivalent units of production for our example are calculated as follows:

Units Transferred — 100% Complete	77,000
+ Ending Inventory—20% of 10,000	2,000
Total Production Results	79,000
− Beginning Inventory—40% of 9,000	3,600
Total Equivalent Units Produced This Period	75,400

Example 2. Consider the following data:

Units Transferred Out	90,000
Ending Inventory—30% Complete	4,000
Beginning Inventory—25% Complete	12,000

The equivalent production for the period can be calculated as follows:

Units Transferred Out—100% Complete	90,000
+ Ending Inventory—30% of 4,000	1,200
Total Production Results	91,200
− Beginning Inventory—25% of 12,000	3,000
Equivalent Units Produced This Period	88,200

The input elements, labor, materials, and overhead, do not necessarily enter the production process at the same rate. Usually, some material must be available before workers can start applying their skills. Overhead may be assigned to production at the end of the period, or it may be assumed to accrue to production at the same rate as does labor.[3] Whenever the input elements accrue to production at different rates, the process costing procedure requires that physical counts be kept for each input. Once cost and quantity information are collected for each input element, separate equivalent production may be calculated for each.

Incomplete data   As discussed above, data on units transferred, beginning, and ending inventories, and the percentage completion are all required before the equivalent production can be calculated. But at times not all of these data are

---

[3]Whenever overhead is applied as a percentage of labor costs, it becomes feasible to combine the two inputs to simplify future calculations. Combinations of labor and overhead costs are called *conversion costs.*

provided. Instead, a new piece of information may be given; the quantity of units transferred into the department during the period.

To determine the missing data, first imagine a production line as an endless conveyor belt. Each day begins with some units already on the line remaining from the previous day's production. Once the line starts, more units are transferred in, some units are transferred out, and some remain on the line at the end of the day. That is,

beginning units + transfers in − transfers out = ending units

Once you know any three of the four elements in the production line relationship, you can determine the fourth element. For example, if you knew that the beginning inventory consisted of 2,000 units, and 6,000 units were transferred in while 5,000 were transferred out, you could determine that the ending inventory must consist of 3,000 units.

COST CALCULATIONS

When production costs change from period to period, cost assignment becomes more difficult. This problem arises when inventory levels change between periods. There are two commonly used methods for tracing the beginning inventory costs: **first-in, first-out (FIFO)** and **weighted average.**

FIFO   The first-in, first-out method segments production and costs by period. Identical units produced at different times are assigned different costs. All of the production costs are divided on the basis of equivalent units and proportionally assigned to: (1) the cost base of the beginning inventory (the FIFO flow assumes that these units will be completed first), (2) the cost of units started and finished during the period, and (3) the cost base of the ending inventory.

The units started and completed during the period are assigned the average per-unit charge for this period's operations. Units started last period and completed this period (beginning inventory) are assigned a current period charge corresponding to the percentage of processing done this period. This cost is added to the cost assigned to these units last period to determine the final per-unit cost. Units started but not completed are assigned an amount proportional to their stage of completion, and will represent the value of ending inventory.

For example, consider the following illustration:

Beginning Inventory Costs	$ 4,000
Processing Costs for the Current Period	225,000
Total Processing Costs To Account For	$229,000

	Full Units	Equivalent Units
Ending Inventory—30% Complete	10,000	3,000
Units Transferred Out—100% Complete	74,000	74,000
Beginning Inventory—50% Complete	4,000	(2,000)
Current Equivalent Units of Production		75,000

Cost per equivalent unit produced this period:

Processing Costs for the Current Period	$225,000
Divided by Equivalent Production for Period	75,000
Cost per Current Equivalent Unit	$ 3.00

Allocation of $229,000 total costs:

1. First 4,000 units completed consisting of beginning work-in-process inventory:		
Original Cost (4,000 units 50% completed)		$ 4,000
Current Equivalent Production—2,000 @ $3		6,000
Cost of First 4,000 Units		$ 10,000
2. Cost of next 70,000 units transferred:		
70,000 Units @ $3		210,000
Total Cost of 74,000 Units Transferred		$220,000
3. Cost of ending inventory:		
(10,000 units 30% completed) @ $3		9,000
Total Processing Costs Accounted For		$229,000

The FIFO technique produces different costs for units completed during the same period. The units in the beginning inventory are treated as separate and distinct from units started and completed during the period.[4] To some degree this approach approximates a job-order cost system, in that different costs are assigned to different batches (or customer orders).

Weighted average Costs per unit calculated under the weighted-average method are determined by dividing total processing costs by total equivalent units. Total processing costs include both beginning inventory costs and current processing costs. Total equivalent units include equivalent units from the beginning inventory as well as those produced during the current period. Thus, the weighted-average method combines costs from the past and the current periods.

---

[4]The 2,000 equivalent units in the beginning inventory (50% of 4,000) are associated with $4,000 beginning inventory cost. Thus, the cost per unit in the beginning inventory is $2. Costs have risen from $2 per unit to $3 per unit during the current production period.

Consider again the previous FIFO example. Processing costs will consist of the beginning inventory costs plus processing costs incurred during the current period.

Beginning Inventory Costs	$ 4,000
Processing Costs for the Current Period	225,000
Total Processing Costs to Account For	$229,000

The units will consist of the equivalent units in the beginning inventory plus the current-period equivalent production.

Equivalent Beginning Inventory Units	2,000
Current Period Equivalent Production	75,000
Total Equivalent Production Units	77,000

Thus, the average unit cost will be $229,000/77,000 = \$2.974^*$ per unit (* = rounded). This cost will be assigned to *all* of the units completed during the period and to the cost base of the ending inventory.

1. Cost of 74,000 units transferred	
74,000 @ $2.974*	$220,078*
2. Cost of ending inventory	
3,000 equivalent units (i.e., 10,000	
units 30% complete) @ $2.794*	8,922*
Total Processing Costs Accounted For	$229,000

The main advantage of the weighted-average method is that identical units completed during the one period all bear the same unit cost. Units completed during different periods can bear different costs, however. At the present time, the weighted-average method is more widely used in industry than is the FIFO method.

JOB-ORDER AND PROCESS COSTING—A PERSPECTIVE

Many similarities exist between job-order costing systems and process costing systems. Each system provides a means of assigning production costs to units of output. Once this assignment is made, the costs remain associated with the units of product. As the units are transferred from one department to another, the accounting system transfers costs from one account to another (for example, from Department 1 to Department 2 or from Work-In-Process Inventory to Finished-Goods Inventory).

Most of the differences between job-order and process costing relate to differences in the underlying production process: low-volume production of specialized orders versus continuous production of similar units. The major conceptual difference between the two relates to the use made of the cost data. Job-order cost data are used primarily to determine product profitability as an aid to future pricing decisions. Process costing data, on the other hand, provide insights into departmental efficiency and effectiveness (as will be discussed further in Section Four of this book); that is, the foreman in each department may be asked to explain period-to-period differences in the per-unit costs incurred within his department.

SUMMARY

Labor, material, and overhead costs are collected as incurred for each production department in a continuous manufacturing process. The departmental cost sheet will reflect the costs associated with units in beginning inventory, as well as additional costs incurred during the current production period. Counts are made of the physical flow of production units through each department. These counts compensate for partially completed units by employing a concept called equivalent units of production. Cost per unit calculated under the FIFO assumption is obtained by dividing current processing costs by current equivalent production units. Cost per unit calculated under the weighted-average method is obtained by dividing the total beginning and current processing costs by the total beginning and current equivalent units. The derived cost-per-unit amount is used to allocate the total production costs between costs of ending inventory and costs transferred to other departments.

APPENDIX: RECORDING PROCESS
COSTING DATA

Continuous production processes can take on many configurations within a manufacturing firm. Most common is a sequential arrangement, such as the technique used by the food processor in operating the cannery, as illustrated in this chapter. Exhibit 6–5 demonstrates how the ledger accounts would be set up for this traditional flow of activity. Three classes of inventory accounts are kept for manufacturing concerns: raw materials, work in process, and finished goods.

A single-process firm has a much simpler flow of accounting information. The basic transfers are materials, labor, and overhead to the work-in-process

EXHIBIT 6–5   SEQUENTIAL PROCESSING OF DATA TO THE ACCOUNTS

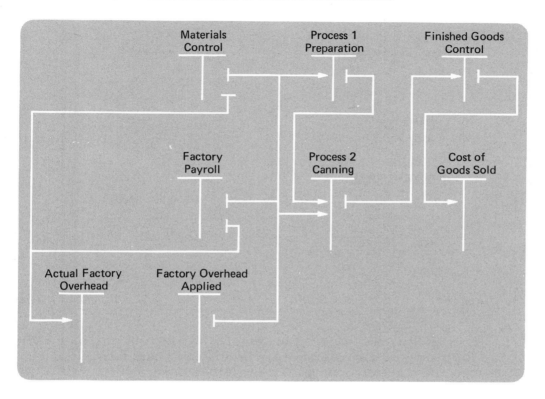

inventory and total processing cost (eventually) to the finished-goods inventory. The methods for recording these activities are described below.

An example   The Hawke Company is a small manufacturing firm using two continuous production processes and a process costing system. Production is initiated in response to market demand. On the basis of prior experience, management estimates overhead costs to be 40% of the total charge for direct labor. Exhibits 6–5 and 6–6 illustrate entries in the general journal of the firm, reflecting the relevant account transfers, keyed to the letters of each transaction.

ACQUISITION OF MATERIALS

Materials Control	9,200	
Accounts Payable		6,000
Cash		3,200

A. (To record the purchase of raw materials for processing.)

EXHIBIT 6-6   PROCESS ACCOUNTING FOR HAWKE COMPANY

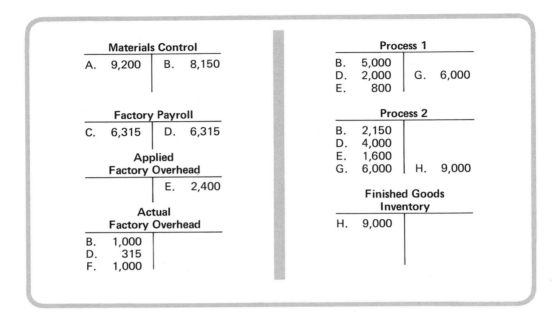

Materials have been acquired and added to inventory. Using *control* in the account title implies that it summarizes several subsidiary accounts. A subsidiary account is kept for each type of material used in production.

USE OF MATERIALS		
Process 1	5,000	
Process 2	2,150	
Actual Overhead	1,000	
Materials Control		8,150

B. (To record the transfer of raw materials to the production process.)

Control accounts for each process summarize material transfers to production. Since materials enter production continuously, this entry represents inputs observed over time. Transactions are supported by material transfer sheets (see Exhibit 6–1). Materials or supplies that cannot be assigned to either process are charged to actual overhead.

ACQUISITION OF LABOR		
Factory Payroll	6,315	
Cash		6,315

C. (To record the payment of the weekly payroll.)

Labor is also combined continuously and charged to each process. Labor such as maintenance, which cannot be assigned to either process, is assigned to actual overhead.

USE OF LABOR		
Process 1	2,000	
Process 2	4,000	
Actual Overhead	315	
Factory Payroll		6,315

D. (To record the use of labor in the production processes.)

The clock cards used by employees paid an hourly wage can document the weekly payroll (see Exhibit 6–2). The accountant uses this same information, either from the clock cards or from a summary memorandum prepared by the payroll department, to charge the cost of labor to each production process.

ASSIGNMENT OF OVERHEAD		
Process 1	800	
Process 2	1,600	
Factory Overhead Applied		2,400

E. (To record the application of factory overhead at the predetermined rate.)

The overhead voucher (see Exhibit 6–3) provides supporting documentation for applying factory overhead to the production process.

INCURRENCE OF ACTUAL OVERHEAD		
Actual Overhead	1,000	
Taxes Payable		100
Accumulated Depreciation		600
Prepaid Insurance		300

F. (To record the incurrence of actual overhead.)

A control account, Actual Factory Overhead, is used to record actual overhead charges for the period. Another $1,000 has been incurred for taxes, insurance, and depreciation. At the end of the period, any differences (reflecting under- or overapplication of overhead) between the applied and the actual control account balances will be transferred either to the income account or to the inventory and income accounts. The procedure is similar to that used for job-order costing data described in Chapter 5.

TRANSFERS FROM PROCESS 1 TO PROCESS 2		
Process 2	6,000	
Process 1		6,000

G. (To record the interdepartmental transfer of $6,000 work in process.)

At the end of the period, the total cost incurred in Department 1 will be determined (from the departmental cost sheet) and the equivalent units of production will be calculated. Total costs will be divided between ending work in process and cost of goods transferred out.

TRANSFERS FROM PROCESS 2 TO FINISHED-GOODS INVENTORY		
Finished-Goods Inventory	9,000	
Process 2		9,000
H. (To record the interdepartmental transfer of $9,000 completed production.)		

At the end of the period, the costs and equivalent production will be calculated in Department 2. Finished products are transferred from production Department 2 to the storeroom, and a parallel transfer of costs will be reflected in the accounting records.

SUGGESTED READINGS

Chatfield, Michael. "The Origins of Cost Accounting." *Management Accounting*, June 1971.

Sharp, Harold. "Control and Management of Indirect Expenses." *Management Accounting*, February 1973.

Witt, Wallace. "Work Measurement of Indirect Labor." *Management Accounting*, November 1971.

QUESTIONS

6–1   Why must the managerial accountant use the concept of equivalent units?

6–2   Why should the accountant consider the cost of collecting data? Should the managerial accountant always select a product costing method that minimizes this cost?

6–3   What is the difference between a departmental cost sheet and a job-order cost sheet? What are the similarities between these two documents?

6–4   What differences in information needs exist between a firm using continuous manufacturing processes and one using discrete manufacturing processes?

6–5   Which of the following firms will generally use job-order costing and which will generally use process costing methods for collecting product cost information? Use the terms "job order" or "process" as your answer.

(A) A distillery

(B) A manufacturer of large airplanes

(C) A pencil manufacturer

(D) A bridge-building firm

(E) A chemical company

(F) An aluminum rolling mill

(G) A custom catering service

(H) A fertilizer factory

6-6   One characteristic of continuous manufacturing is that production is based on anticipated market demand, not on individual customer orders. Would a firm that produces solely on the basis of individual customer orders have occasion to use process costing instead of job-order costing? Why or why not?

6-7   The four basic documents used in process cost-accounting systems are: a material transfer sheet, a clock card, an overhead voucher, and a departmental cost sheet. In each of the cases listed below, indicate which document would be the source of the information. If information would appear on more than one document, identify all those on which it would appear. If data would not appear on any of the four basic documents, use the term "none."

(A) Number of units processed during a period

(B) The pay rate of an employee

(C) The standard price per unit of raw material transferred to production

(D) Periodic overhead charge for a particular process

(E) Raw material purchases

(F) The total manufacturing cost during a given period for a two-process firm

(G) The amount of material periodically transferred into production

(H) Payroll data for hourly employees

6-8   Identify the similarities and the differences between job-order cost accounting and process cost accounting.

6-9   One approach to product costing would be for the managerial accountant to observe each element of cost as it enters into production, and to observe each unit as it is completed. Such an approach is not feasible, however, because of the cost and the demands it would place on the accountant's time. Without actually watching, how does the accountant insure that his information is correct? Is it important that product cost information be correct? Why or why not?

6-10   Identify and briefly explain the distinctive features of continuous manufacturing. Contrast these aspects of continuous manufacturing with those of discrete manufacturing.

6–11   How is overhead normally applied in a process cost-accounting system? Will applied overhead generally differ from actual overhead costs incurred by a firm? Is this always the case? Explain why or why not.

EXERCISES

6–12   Calculate the equivalent units of production in each of the following situations.

		Units
(A)	Beginning Inventory—20% Complete	10,000
	Ending Inventory—20% Complete	10,000
	Started During the Period	80,000
(B)	Transferred Out During the Period	72,000
	Beginning Inventory—50% Complete	22,000
	Started During the Period	60,000
	Ending Inventory—30% Complete	?
(C)	Ending Inventory—25% Complete	28,000
	Transferred Out During the Period	52,000
	Started During the Period	68,000
	Beginning Inventory—40% Complete	?
(D)	Beginning Inventory—10% Complete	12,000
	Ending Inventory—80% Complete	15,000
	Transferred Out During the Period	50,000

6–13   Records of Department No. 1 indicate that beginning inventory had a balance of 20,000 units, ending inventory had a balance of 25,000 units, and 100,000 units were transferred in during the production period. How many units were transferred out?

6–14   During the current production period, Department No. 3 transferred in 50,000 units and transferred out 56,000 units. If the beginning inventory consisted of 27,000 units, how many units were in the ending inventory?

6–15   Department No. 3 transferred in 106,000 units and transferred out only 98,000 during the production period. If ending inventory consisted of 27,000 units, how many units were in the beginning inventory?

6–16   The Fender Welding Department of an automobile assembly plant reported $60,000 for 20,000 equivalent units in the beginning inventory. Costs added during the current production period were $160,000 for 40,000 equivalent units of production. Ending inventory consisted of 10,000 equivalent units, and 50,000 units were transferred out. Using the first-in, first-out method, determine the cost of units transferred and the cost of ending inventory.

6–17   Using the weighted-average method, recalculate the cost of units transferred and the cost of ending inventory of the data in the preceding problem.

6–18   Calculate the equivalent current units of production from the following data: beginning inventory consisted of 20,000 units 30% complete, 90,000 units were transferred out, and ending inventory consisted of 10,000 units 20% complete.

6–19   If Department No. 6 started the period with 30,000 units 10% complete and finished with 40,000 units 20% complete, what was the current equivalent production, assuming that 100,000 units were transferred out?

6–20   The beginning inventory of Department No. 9 consisted of $5,100 for 1,000 equivalent units of production. During the period, $40,000 was incurred to produce 10,000 current equivalent units of production. Ending inventory consisted of 3,000 equivalent units, and 8,000 units were transferred out. Using the weighted-average method, determine the cost of units transferred and the cost of ending inventory.

6–21   Using the FIFO method, recalculate the cost of units transferred and the cost of ending inventory for the preceding problem.

6–22   In this chapter, a canning factory was used as an example of a continuous manufacturing process that used process cost-accounting techniques. Would all canneries use process cost accounting? Does it follow, then, that all continuous manufacturing operations would use process costing? Why or why not?

PROBLEMS

†6–23   A cost-accounting reporting system is diagramed on page 212. The normal process is for the productive output to flow from Process 1 through Process 2 and Process 3 before it is completed.

(A) Which document authorizes the flow from A to D?

(B) Which document supports the flow from B to E and B to F?

(C) How is the value of work-in-process inventory determined at the end of the period?

(D) What documentation authorizes the flow from G to F?

(E) Is overhead applied to the units of output uniformly during production?

(F) When does raw material enter the process?

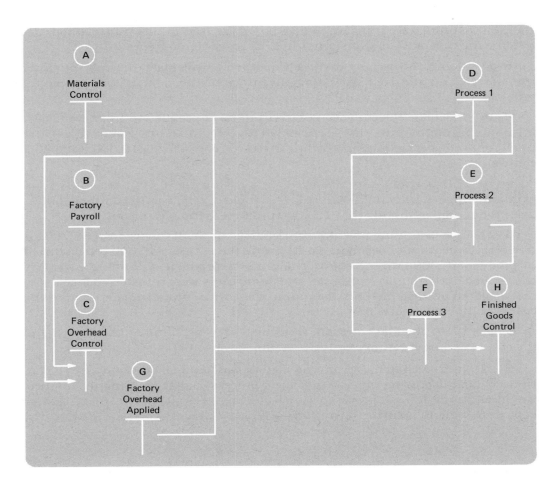

(G) What documentation is required for the flow from F to H?

(H) What happens to accounts C and G at the end of the period?

*6–24 Several managers of the Sharpe Contrast Company are involved in a dispute over product costing. The firm uses continuous manufacturing techniques to produce a standard product output. Consequently, the accounting department employs a process costing system to accumulate product cost information. The cost calculation technique is the main point in dispute. Because production costs have varied considerably from period to period in the past, the sales manager wants the accounting department to use the weighted-average technique. He contends that, "I must be able to predict costs if I am going to set reasonable prices. Only weighted average will give me this information. If the

FIFO technique is used, there is so much cost variability that I have to change prices continually, and this is costing us sales."

This point of view is countered by the production manager of the company, who argues that, "To use weighted average will destroy the effectiveness of the production department. Production cost fluctuations are beyond our control. The FIFO technique associates costs more closely with time periods than does the weighted-average technique. It isn't fair to carry these production costs over on us as weighted-average does."

How would you, as a managerial accountant for the Sharpe Contrast Company, solve this dispute?

6–25   The Johnson Corporation transacted the following business during the month of June 19X4.

1. Materials were purchased for $30,000.
2. Direct labor costs of $25,000 were incurred.
3. The total monthly cost of manufacturing overhead amounted to $18,000.
4. Selling expense totaled $3,000.
5. General expense totaled $5,000.
6. Miscellaneous bills totaled $81,000.
7. Revenue from sales of products for June equaled $80,000.
8. Materials of $27,000 were requisitioned for production.
9. The total cost of completed production orders reached $64,000.
10. Cost of products sold totaled $60,000.

The Johnson Corporation applies factory overhead at a rate of 80% of direct labor cost. The overhead is applied when direct labor enters the production process.

Using this information, answer the following questions about the Johnson Corporation.

(A) How much overhead was applied to production during the month of June?

(B) If the cost of products sold totaled $60,000 (10), but the cost of finished production was $64,000 (9), why was there a $4,000 difference? What happened to this difference in the firm's accounting records?

(C) If materials of $30,000 (1) were purchased, but only $27,000 were used (8), what happened to the other $3,000? Where is this difference recorded in the accounting records?

(D) Why isn't the cost of production of $64,000 (9) equal to the sum of the $25,000 labor (2), $27,000 materials (8), and $18,000 overhead (3)?

6–26   Costs within a process costing system are transferred from one department to the next. Your company has three departments. Costs incurred directly by each department are called "directly traceable costs," and are determined by using the FIFO Method. None of the three departments has beginning inventories. Determine the missing data (indicated by a question mark) for each department.

	Dept. No. 1	Dept. No. 2	Dept. No. 3
Directly traceable costs	$100,000	$200,000	$150,000
Transfer in costs	-0-	?	$245,000
Transfer out costs	?	$245,000	$345,000
Ending inventory	$ 10,000	$ 45,000	?

6–27 An auto assembly production line flows chassis through a fender welding department on an endless conveyor belt. Physical counts of chassis are taken in the morning as the line is about to start up (beginning inventory), as the chassis are transferred out of this department to the next department, and at the end of the day (ending inventory). Four fenders are welded to each chassis. A chassis with only one fender welded at the end of the day is considered to be ¼ complete in terms of fender welding. The fender welding department accounts for the flow of chassis in terms of equivalent units of completed chassis.

Costs in beginning inventory	$ 34,000
Costs added this period	$120,000
Incomplete units in ending inventory, ½ completed	40,000
Incomplete units in beginning inventory, ¼ completed	40,000
Units transferred out	50,000
Equivalent units produced this week	60,000

(A) Determine the cost of ending inventory and the cost of units transferred out under the FIFO cost flow assumption.

(B) Determine the cost of ending inventory and the cost of units transferred out under the weighted-average cost-flow assumption.

6–28 The Jorcano Manufacturing Company uses a process-cost system to account for the costs of its only product, Product D. Production begins in the Fabrication Department, where units of raw material are molded into various connecting parts. After fabrication is complete, the units are transferred to the Assembly Department. No material is added in the Assembly Department. After assembly is complete, the units are transferred to the Packaging Department, where packing material is placed around the units. After the units are ready for shipping, they are sent to the Shipping Area.

At year end, June 30, 19X3, the following inventory of Product D is on hand:

—No unused raw material or packing material.

—Fabrication Department: 300 units, 1/3 complete as to raw material and 1/2 complete as to direct labor.

—Assembly Department: 1,000 units, 2/5 complete as to direct labor.

—Packaging Department: 100 units, 3/4 complete as to packing material and 1/4 complete as to direct labor.

—Shipping Area: 400 units.

(A) How many equivalent units of raw material and equivalent units of direct labor are in the Fabrication Department inventory on June 30?

(B) How many equivalent units of raw material and equivalent units of direct labor are in the Assembly Department inventory on June 30?

(C) How many equivalent units of raw material, equivalent units of direct labor, and equivalent units of packing material are in the Packing Department inventory on June 30?

(D) How many equivalent units of raw material, equivalent units of direct labor, and equivalent units of packing material are in the Shipping Area inventory on June 30?

(AICPA adapted)

6-29 The Incredible Gadget Corp. manufactures a single product. Its operations are a continuing process carried on in two departments—the *Machining Department* and the *Assembly and Finishing Department.* Materials are added to the product in each department without increasing the number of units produced.

In the month of May 19X6, the records showed that 75,000 units were put in production in the Machining Department. Of these units, 60,000 were completed and transferred to Assembly and Finishing, and 15,000 were left in the process with all materials applied but with only ⅓ of the required labor and overhead.

In the Assembly and Finishing Department, 50,000 units were completed and transferred to the finished stock room during the month. Ten thousand units were in process on May 31. All required materials had been applied to the 10,000 units and ⅔ of the labor and overhead.

There was no work in process in either department at the first of the month.

Cost records showed the following charges during the month:

	Materials	Labor	Overhead
Machining Department	$120,000	$ 87,100	$39,000
Assembly and Finishing Department	41,650	101,700	56,810

(A) Prepare in good form a statement showing the unit cost for the month.

(B) Prepare a schedule showing the details of the ending work-in-process inventory in each department.

(AICPA adapted)

6–30   A certain manufacturing process requires that 50% of the necessary raw materials be added to production when the output units are started and that the rest of the materials be added when the units of output are 45% complete. Conversion costs (that is, the cost of direct labor and variable overhead) are incurred evenly throughout the entire manufacturing process.

For each of the independent situations listed below, determine the equivalent units completed of both materials and conversion. Assume that this information will be used in a cost calculation employing the FIFO method.

		Units
(A)	Beginning Inventory	10,000 (50% complete)
	Ending Inventory	6,000 (40% complete)
	Units Transferred Out	40,000
(B)	Beginning Inventory	5,000 (10% complete)
	Ending Inventory	7,500 (30% complete)
	Units Started in Production	60,000
(C)	Units Started in Production	50,000
	Units Transferred Out	60,000
	Beginning Inventory	? (40% complete)
	Ending Inventory	10,000 (75% complete)

6–31   The Morey Company has completed its first year of operations. There were no partially finished goods in the assembly department at the beginning of the year, but there are partially finished goods at the close of the first year. Three materials are used in the assembly process: steel to start the process and to be tumbled, bronze that is added halfway through the process, and a clear, protective paint applied as the last step in assembly. Labor and overhead are applied evenly throughout the assembly process. The Morey Company started 100,000 units and completed 80,000 of them by the end of the year. Exactly $400,000 worth of steel, $200,000 worth of bronze, and $10,000 worth of clear paint were used. The overhead was applied proportionally with labor, and combined labor and overhead costs amounted to $800,000.

(A) If the work in process is one-fourth finished at the end of the year, what cost is transferred to the finished-goods inventory? What amount is still associated with the work-in-process inventory?

(B) If the work-in-process inventory is three-fourths finished, what cost is transferred to the finished-goods inventory? What amount is still associated with the in-process inventory?

(C) In part (A) above, are all the units not finished located at exactly one-fourth of the production cycle? Who made the estimate that work in process was one-fourth completed? How was this estimate made?

6–32 The Puck Company uses a single manufacturing process to produce hockey pucks. The process is highly mechanized and the costs stem primarily from materials. Since Puck has an exclusive contract to produce pucks for the National Hockey League for the next five years and foresees no developing competition, they have adopted the process cost method of cost accumulation. The vulcanizing department incurred $34,500 of production costs during the month of November. Rubber costing $25,000 was introduced to the process at the start. Labor and overhead totaling $9,500 were incurred evenly throughout the production cycle. Fifty-thousand units were started in production and 5,000 are still in production at the end of the month. Work-in-process is half completed for labor and overhead, 100% complete for material.

(A) What is the unit cost of goods transferred to the finished-goods inventory if the FIFO method of cost assignment is used?

(B) Would there be a difference in unit cost if the weighted-average method were used? Why or why not?

(C) What is the dollar amount in the finished-goods inventory under the FIFO method?

(D) What is the dollar amount in the work-in-process inventory under the FIFO method?

6–33 The Ball Company has an odd accounting system. Certain data are readily available, while other, seemingly more important, data are missing. The data available from the accounting system are as follows:

1. The inventory values for raw materials, work in process, and finished goods at the beginning of the year were $25,000, $40,000, and $15,000, respectively.
2. Raw materials purchased during the year totaled $110,000.
3. The factory payroll for the year amounted to $90,000; 60% of this amount was for direct labor and 40% for indirect labor.
4. The overhead rate was based on last year's ratio of direct labor to overhead charges. Last year, direct labor was $100,000, and overhead charges were $150,000.
5. Depreciation charges for the current year are $15,000.
6. The invoices for actual overhead, other than those individually listed elsewhere, totaled $20,000.
7. Materials requisitioned totaled $80,000, of which $15,000 was for overhead.
8. Completed units had accumulated costs of $100,000.
9. Units sold had accumulated costs of $80,000.

Using this information, calculate the following data for the Ball Company.

(A) Actual overhead costs for the year

(B) The rate used to apply overhead to the manufacturing operations during the year

(C) Overhead applied to manufacturing operations during the year

(D) Cost of the ending raw materials inventory

(E) Cost of the work-in-process ending inventory

(F) Cost of the finished-goods ending inventory

(G) Difference between actual and applied overhead during the year

6–34   The Scotch Review Company makes large decorator bottles in a single glass-blowing process. The beginning work-in-process inventory included 25,000 bottles, completed as to the glass, but only half complete as to labor and overhead. The value of the material input was $91,000, direct labor was $52,000, and overhead was assigned at a rate of 75% of direct labor dollars. During the year, 200,000 bottles were completed, and 20,000 bottles were still in process at the end of the year. The ending inventory for material was complete, but labor and overhead were only ¾ complete. The following costs were charged to the production department during the year: material, $900,000; labor, $250,000; and overhead, $187,500.

(A) Using the FIFO method, calculate the unit cost of goods transferred to finished-goods inventory.

(B) Using the weighted-average method, calculate the unit cost of goods transferred to finished-goods inventory.

(C) If there is a difference between (A) and (B) above, what accounts for the difference?

(D) What are the dollar amounts of the ending work-in-process inventory under both methods?

6–35   Ballinger Paper Products manufactures a high-quality paper box. The Box Department applies two separate operations—cutting and folding. The paper is first cut and trimmed to the dimensions of a box form by one machine group. One square foot of paper is equivalent to four box forms. The trimmings from this process have no scrap value. Box forms are then creased and folded (i.e., completed) by a second machine group. Any partially processed boxes in the department are cut box forms that are ready for creasing and folding. These partly processed boxes are considered 50% complete as to labor and overhead. The Materials Department maintains an inventory of paper in sufficient quantities to permit continuous processing, and transfers to the Box Department are made as needed. Immediately after folding, all good boxes are transferred to the Finished-Goods Department.

During June 19X1 the Materials Department purchased 1,210,000 square feet of unprocessed paper for $244,000. Conversion costs (direct labor and overhead) for the month were $226,000. Ballinger applies the weighted-average cost method to all inventories. Inventory data for June are given below.

| | | June 30 19X1 | June 1, 19X1 | |
Inventory	Physical Unit	Units on Hand	Units on Hand	Cost
Materials Department:				
paper	square feet	200,000	390,000	$76,000
Box Department:				
boxes cut, not folded	number	300,000	800,000	$55,000*
Finished-Goods Department:				
completed boxes on hand	number	50,000	250,000	$18,000

*Materials	$35,000
Conversion cost	20,000
	$55,000

Prepare the following for the month of June 19X1:

(A) A report of cost of paper used for the Materials Department.

(B) A schedule showing the physical flow of units (including beginning and ending inventories) in the Materials Department, in the Box Department, and in the Finished-Goods Department.

(C) A schedule showing the computation of equivalent units produced for materials and conversion costs in the Box Department.

(D) A schedule showing the computation of unit costs for the Box Department.

(E) A report of inventory valuation and cost of completed units for the Box Department.

(F) A schedule showing the computation of unit costs for the Finished-Goods Department.

(G) A report of inventory valuation and cost of units sold for the Finished-Goods Department.

(AICPA adapted)

6–36 Crews Company produces a chemical agent for commercial use. The Company accounts for production in two cost centers: (1) Cooking and (2) Mix-Pack. In the first cost center, liquid substances are combined in large cookers and boiled; the boiling causes a normal decrease in volume from evaporation. After the "batch" is cooked, it is transferred to Mix-Pack, the second cost center. A quantity of alcohol is added equal to the liquid measure of the "batch," which then is mixed and bottled in one-gallon containers.

Material is added at the beginning of production in each cost center and labor is added equally during production in each cost center. Overhead is applied on the basis of 80% of labor cost.

The following information is available for the month of October 19X7:

Cost Information	Cooking	Mix-Pack
Work in process, October 1, 19X7		
Materials	$ 990	$ 120
Labor	100	60
Prior department cost		426
Month of October		
Materials	39,600	15,276
Labor	10,050	16,000

Inventory and production records show that Cooking had 1,000 gallons 40% processed on October 1 and 800 gallons 50% processed on October 31; Mix-Pack had 600 gallons 50% processed on October 1, and 1,000 gallons 30% processed on October 31.

Production reports for October show that Cooking started 50,000 gallons into production and completed and transferred 40,200 gallons to Mix-Pack, and Mix-Pack completed and transferred 80,000 one-gallon containers of the finished product to the distribution warehouse.

(A) Prepare in good form quantity reports for the Cooking cost center and for the Mix-Pack cost center.

(B) Prepare in good form a production cost report for each of the two cost centers which computes total cost and cost per unit for each element of cost in inventories and October production. Total cost and cost per unit for transfers should also be computed using the FIFO cost-flow assumption.

(AICPA adapted)

6–37 Zeus Company has two production departments (Fabricating and Finishing). In the Fabricating Department, polyplast is prepared from miracle mix and bypro. In the Finishing Department, each unit of polyplast is converted into six tetraplexes and three uniplexes.

The fabricating and finishing departments use process cost-accounting systems. Actual production costs, including overhead, are allocated monthly.

Raw materials inventory and work-in-process are priced on a FIFO basis.

The following data were taken from the Fabricating Department's records for December 19X1:

Quantities (units of polyplast):	
In process, December 1	3,000
Started in process during month	25,000
Total units to be accounted for	28,000

Transferred to Finishing Department	22,000
In process, December 31	6,000
Total units accounted for	28,000
Cost of work-in-process, December 1:	
Materials	$ 13,000
Labor	17,500
Overhead	21,500
	$ 52,000
Direct labor costs, December	$154,000
Department overhead, December	$198,000

Polyplast work-in-process at the beginning and end of the month was partially completed as follows:

	Materials	Labor and Overhead
December 1	66⅔%	50%
December 31	100 %	75%

The following data were taken from raw materials inventory records for December:

	Miracle Mix		Bypro	
	Quantity	Amount	Quantity	Amount
Balance, December 1	62,000	$62,000	265,000	$18,550
Purchases:				
December 12	39,500	49,375		
December 20	28,500	34,200		
Fabricating Department usage	83,200		50,000	

(A) Compute the equivalent number of units of polyplast, with separate calculations for materials and conversion cost (direct labor plus overhead), manufactured during December.

(B) Compute the following items to be included in the Fabricating Department's production report for December 19X1, with separate calculations for materials, direct labor, and overhead. Prepare supporting schedules.

1. Total costs to be accounted for.
2. Unit costs for equivalent units manufactured.
3. Transfers to Finishing Department during December and work-in-process at December 31. Reconcile your answer to part (B) 1.

(AICPA adapted)

CHAPTER 7

Service Department Costs and Transfer Prices

Objectives

*After studying this
chapter, you should be
able to do the following:*

Identify the purposes for collecting service department costs, and describe methods for collecting these costs.

Assign service department costs to other departments by using the following methods: regular overhead, direct allocation, and step-down allocation.

Discuss transfer price procedures for assigning costs and allocating profit between departments or divisions of a firm. Contrast cost-based transfers with cost-plus-profit transfers and market-based transfers.

Describe acts of suboptimization *that may result from the use of transfer price techniques.*

All manufacturing departments can be classified as **service departments** or as **operating departments**. If the sole responsibility of a department is to provide service to other departments within the organization, it can be classified as a *service department*. Service departments such as personnel and accounting render specialized assistance to other service departments, as well as to *operating departments* that are directly involved in the production process. In conventional accounting systems, service department costs are allocated to the operating departments as charges for the benefits received by the operating departments from the service departments. This chapter discusses methods for collecting service department costs and reassigning them to operating departments.

COLLECTING SERVICE DEPARTMENT COSTS

The functions of service departments include, among others, accounting, purchasing, materials handling, inspection, and maintenance.

The cost-accounting function within a service department is similar to that in an operating department. Costs are classified as departmental labor, departmental material, overhead incurred within the department, and assigned overhead. As used here, the word "departmental" implies that the use of labor, material, and other costs can be traced directly to the department. In service departments, as in operating departments, source documents reflect the acquisition of most cost inputs: one copy of each document is collected within the department as cost inputs are received. Stores requisitions authorize the withdrawal of materials and supplies from the storeroom. Time-clock cards record hours of labor worked. Overhead vouchers or less formal communications evidence the reallocation of overhead costs from other sources to the service departments.[1] Data from all source documents are transcribed on departmental cost sheets, which are periodically totaled and distributed to higher-level management.

Purposes for collecting service department costs   The four purposes for collecting service departments cost data are identical to those for collecting operating department costs: they serve as a basis for planning, information processing, control, and decision making.

Planning for most service departments has to take both capacity and volume considerations into account. Service departments usually require a given amount of fixed plant, equipment, and personnel to maintain their capacity to provide services. For example, a company-run cafeteria requires ovens, racks,

---

[1]Some manufacturing organizations choose to allocate no overhead to service departments, since service department costs themselves can be considered as overhead costs.

furniture, power, and a supervisor (chef) just to be able to provide food services for company employees. The accounting department and the purchasing department both require furniture, telephones, office machines, and supervisors to be prepared to offer services. Other costs of service departments are directly related to the volume of operations they are expected to maintain. Food costs for the cafeteria and bookkeeper (labor) costs for the accounting department represent examples of variable service department costs. In service departments, as in operating departments, historical cost data are useful for identifying cost-volume relationships in preparing or supporting cost budgets.

The information-processing function in a service department includes collection of data used in determining payrolls, measuring costs of services being provided, making control evaluations, and in decision-making. The supervisor of the service department can use cost information in the day-to-day operation of his department.

Control is the process of obtaining conformity between goals and actions. The budget for each service department specifies the departments' financial goals, and systematic accounting for department operations provides data on actual costs. Responsibility accounting reports, which compare actual and budgeted costs, are the basis for control evaluations.

Knowledge of service department costs is vital if sound decisions are to be made in the service department. For example, cost-volume relationships must be known before a decision can be made to expand or contract the level of services provided by a department. Cost information collected in the service department might dictate the elimination of the department itself and its substitution by outside suppliers of similar services.

ASSIGNING COSTS TO OTHER DEPARTMENTS

Service department costs fall under the general classification of overhead. In many ways, these costs are similar to the indirect labor and indirect materials costs that are incurred in operating departments; that is, service department costs are incurred to facilitate normal production activity but they are not easily associated with output units. Service department costs must be allocated to the operating departments if the full costs of production are to be borne by the productive outputs flowing through the operating departments. Although all costs may not be allocated objectively, an allocated cost still provides useful information. A "good estimate" can provide management with sufficient information to make an informed decision, and product costs derived through an allocation process are often the only reasonable estimates available. On the other hand, product costs derived from an arbitrary allocation can be confusing or, still worse, downright misleading.

When allocating service department costs to other departments, accountants strive to attain *reasonable* results. Several techniques are employed to achieve reasonable allocations. These techniques rely on traceable secondary measures that can be related to the cost under consideration. For example, although personnel department costs may not be traced directly to specific operating departments, they may be reasonably assigned in proportion to the direct labor hours (or costs) incurred in each department. Thus, personnel department costs can be passed on through the operating departments to the products that are manufactured. A product that requires 40% of the total direct labor effort will be assigned 40% of the personnel department cost. Such an approach to allocation can provide useful information to the degree that the cost and the secondary measure are functionally related.

At times, costs of service facilities are allocated on the basis of *usage*. With this approach, the total cost of a facility is distributed among departments according to each department's actual usage of the facility. For example, if two departments used a service facility for a total of 100 hours, the first department using 20 hours and the second department using 80 hours, the cost of the facility would be divided 20% to 80% between the departments. Facility usage is a reasonable allocation of benefit received by the departments. However, the approach does not consider a "fair" service charge. All costs are allocated, even if the same services are available from external agencies at substantially lower costs.

Another approach to allocation is based on the *ability to pay*. This technique divides a cost among departments in proportion to their sales revenues. The assumption is that a department earning more revenue can absorb more costs. This approach allocates costs subjectively and, as a result, its usefulness is limited. For example, under this approach, high sales performance would be penalized with a high proportionate share of allocated costs. When operating departments do not generate revenues, the ability-to-pay criterion might imply that service department costs should be allocated to operating departments on the basis of their relative traceable costs: operating departments that incur 60% of the total traceable costs would be assigned 60% of service department costs.

Service department costs treated as general overhead   Probably the simplest method of allocating service department costs to output units is to treat them as part of Actual Overhead. Under this method, an estimate of expected total overhead (including service department costs) would be made at the beginning of the year. This dollar estimate would be divided by total expected volume for the year, and the results would be the applied overhead rate. During the year, the applied overhead rate would be multiplied by the actual volume to determine the amount of applied overhead to charge to operating departments; that is, service department costs would be charged to operating departments as direct labor (hours or dollars) is accumulated. End-of-period adjustments for under/over applied overhead would reconcile differences between Actual Overhead and Applied Overhead.

The major weakness of this method is that the resulting allocations may not accurately reflect use of service department benefits. Assume, for example, that the Personnel Department expends most of its effort on hiring the few skilled employees for Department No. 1 and spends little effort on hiring the many unskilled workers for Department No. 2. If overhead is applied on the basis of direct labor hours (or costs), most of the Personnel Department costs will be charged to Department No. 2, instead of to Department No. 1, which received far more service and should bear a larger portion of the costs. While all allocations of costs are somewhat arbitrary, the allocation of service department costs to operating departments as part of general overhead should be considered very cautiously.

Direct allocation   Services department costs can be allocated directly to operating departments when related measures of volume are known. First, the managerial accountant identifies a measure of volume that is related to service department activities. For example, relative number of employees in each operating department might serve as a good base for allocating cafeteria costs. Relative square footage in each operating department might serve as a base for allocating heating costs. Relative number of service calls might provide a base for allocating maintenance costs. Other common bases and related service departments are listed in Exhibit 7–1. Next, the managerial accountant combines the base figures of all operating departments to determine the total base. Finally, the service department cost is allocated to each operating department in proportion to its relative contribution to the total base.

EXHIBIT 7–1   SERVICE DEPARTMENT COST ALLOCATION BASES

Service Department	Allocation Bases
cafeteria	number of employees
maintenance	services calls, machine hours
personnel	direct labor hours, number of employees, direct labor cost
cost accounting	number of source documents
inspection	hours spent in department
purchasing	direct material costs
materials handling	direct material quantities or cost

An example   The Evans Manufacturing Company has three operating departments and two service departments, one a cafeteria and the other a maintenance department. Management has decided that the relative number of employees and the relative number of service calls are representative bases for allocating cafeteria costs and maintenance department costs to the operating departments. The production managers wish to allocate service department costs before the end of the year (i.e., before the amount of such costs is known). Therefore, estimates of the expected service department costs for the year are prepared and used for reassignment purposes. Expected cost and volume data for Evans are as follows:

| | Operating Departments | | | Service Departments | |
	1	2	3	Cafeteria	Maintenance
Number of Employees	20	30	40	2	10
Number of Service calls	100	80	20		
Estimated Costs				$18,000	$70,000

Department 1 is highly automated; Departments 2 and 3 are labor intensive.

The $18,000 estimated cafeteria costs would be allocated on the basis of 90 men working in the three operating departments, in the following proportions: 20/90, 30/90, and 40/90, respectively. Allocated yearly cafeteria costs are $4,000, $6,000, and $8,000, and these costs would be prorated to each reporting period. Thus, if monthly reports were prepared, Department 1 would reflect a cafeteria cost of $333.33 (i.e, $4,000 ÷ 12 = $333.33.).

The $70,000 maintenance department costs would be allocated on the basis of relative service calls, as follows: 100/200, 80/200, and 20/200. Allocated yearly costs are $35,000, $28,000, and $7,000, and these costs would be prorated to each reporting period. In practice, service calls might be "billed" to the operating departments at $350 per call (i.e., $70,000 ÷ 200 = $350).

The direct allocation method would distribute the $88,000 total estimated service department costs ($18,000 + $70,000) to Departments 1, 2, and 3 in the amounts of $39,000, $34,000, and $15,000, respectively. An end-of-the-year adjustment would reconcile any differences between the estimated costs and the actual costs by assigning any residual to the general Over/Under Applied Overhead account.

Step-down allocation   In the previous example, none of the cafeteria costs were allocated to the maintenance department. While this omission created a simpler allocation situation, it may not have been realistic. For example, the ten maintenance men provide most service to Department 1. If cafeteria costs had been charged to maintenance, then the reallocation would have loaded more of these costs onto Department 1. If the maintenance men are counted as part of the base, the cafeteria allocation base becomes 100, and the relative proportions for Departments 1, 2, 3, and Maintenance become 20/100, 30/100, 40/100, and 10/

100. The yearly allocated cafeteria costs become $3,600, $5,400, $7,200, and $1,800, respectively. This allocation boosts the total maintenance costs from $70,000 to $71,800, an amount which will be reallocated as follows: 100/200, 80/200, and 20/200. The revised total maintenance costs allocated to the three operating departments would be $35,900, $28,720, and $7,180. Using step-down allocation, the total service department cost allocated to Department 1 would be $39,500 ($3,600 + $35,900); Departments 2 and 3 would be allocated $34,120 and $14,380, respectively.

In using the step-down procedure, management must specify which service cost is to be reallocated first. Often the service department with the highest cost is reallocated first. Next, the service department with second highest cost, including the first allocation of cost, is reallocated.

Other allocation procedures One additional allocation procedure less frequently found in practice is called *reciprocal* allocation. Under this procedure, costs from all service departments are simultaneously reallocated to each other, in addition to be allocated to the operating departments. Reciprocal allocation requires the solution of simultaneous equations, detailed descriptions of which are beyond the scope of this book. Reciprocal allocation is much more complicated than direct or step-down allocation. It may be appropriate, however, where every service department provides services to all other departments, including other service departments. For example, if the maintenance department of the Evans Manufacturing Company also maintained the equipment in the cafeteria, reciprocal allocation might be appropriate. In every case, however, management must decide whether the benefits obtained from receiving more refined cost estimates outweigh the complications of deriving these figures. All allocations are somewhat arbitrary, and caution should be exercised in interpreting the numbers produced by any allocation process.

Contrasting allocation procedures Differences in the four methods for allocating service department costs to the final product are illustrated in Exhibit 7–2. Part A of Exhibit 7–2 reflects the basic accounts underlying a process cost-accounting system for a manufacturing concern with two service departments and two production departments. Although not illustrated in the exhibit, labor and material costs are directly assigned to each of the four departments as their source documents are created. Service department costs are separated from other types of overhead for planning, control, and decision-making purposes, but they are treated exactly like other actual overhead costs for product costing purposes. The one applied overhead rate used to assign overhead cost to the production departments is established as follows:

$$\frac{\text{Estimated Annual Overhead Cost (including Service Departments)}}{\text{Estimated Annual Volume of Process 1 and 2}} = \text{Rate}$$

Part of the applied overhead assigned to the production departments represents

**EXHIBIT 7–2   ALTERNATE METHODS FOR ALLOCATING SERVICE DEPARTMENT
COSTS TO OPERATING DEPARTMENTS**

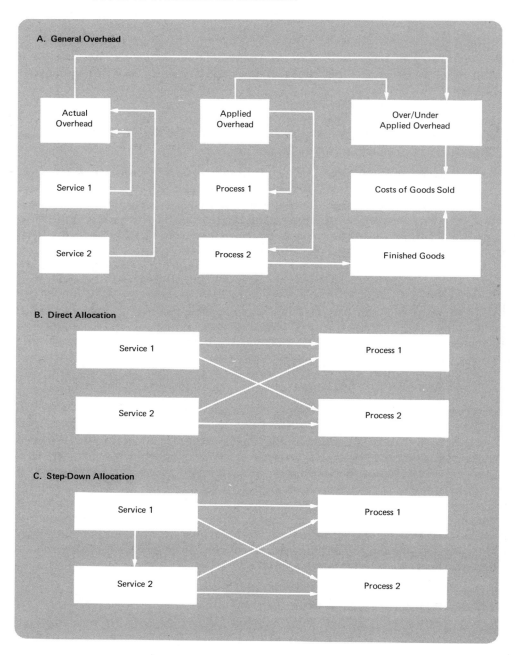

a charge for the benefits that they have received from the service departments. Costs from Process 1 flow to Process 2, and Process 2 costs flow through Finished Goods to Cost of Goods Sold. At the end of the accounting period, the Actual Overhead and Applied Overhead accounts are closed out, and the difference is assigned to Cost of Goods Sold. Under this system, the service department costs are assigned to the finished product in the same manner as all other overhead costs.

Part B of Exhibit 7–2 illustrates the direct allocation of service department costs to the production departments. Three overhead rates are used under a direct allocation system: a general overhead rate is calculated without consideration of service department costs to assign all other overhead costs to the production departments; a Service 1 overhead rate is used to assign Service 1 costs to the production departments; and a third overhead rate assigns Service 2 costs to the production departments. Except for the links between the service departments and the production departments, all other cost flows from Part A of Exhibit 7–2 are operable for the direct allocation case in Part B.

Step-down allocation differs only in that some Service 1 costs are assigned to Service 2. In calculation of an overhead rate for Service 1, the denominator would consist of estimated volume for the two production departments plus Service 2 volume. In calculation of the overhead rate for Service 2, the numerator would include additional costs expected from Service 1. The three rates used for a step-down allocation are determined as follows:

$$\frac{\text{Estimated Annual Overhead Cost (excluding Service Depts.)}}{\text{Estimated Annual Volume of Process 1 and 2}} = \text{General Rate}$$

$$\frac{\text{Estimated Service 1 Cost}}{\text{Estimated Annual Volume of Process 1, 2 and Service 2}} = \text{Service 1 Rate}$$

$$\frac{\text{Estimated Service 2 Cost (including some Service 1 Cost)}}{\text{Estimated Annual Volume of Process 1 and 2}} = \text{Service 2 Rate}$$

Part C of Exhibit 7–2 shows how the cost flows are modified to reflect the assignment of Service 1 costs to Service 2. Here again, the Actual Overhead, Applied Overhead, and Over/Under Applied Overhead accounting flows would also occur.

TRANSFERS BETWEEN DEPARTMENTS

The amounts charged to a department for goods or services supplied by another department within the same organization are called **transfer prices**. Transfer prices can be charged to an operating department for services received from a service department. In addition, the term transfer price is used to describe the amounts charged when output from one operating department is transferred to another operating department.

Transfer prices serve two distinct functions. First, they provide a basis for allocating scarce resources or services among departments within the organization. Second, use of transfer prices will produce an internal performance measure or "profit" that can complement other motivational and control procedures. Various proposals for establishing transfer prices that fulfill one or both of these functions have been developed. Transfer prices are generally cost-based or market-based prices.

Cost-based transfers   Cost-based transfer prices are constructed by using the actual product costs of each producing department. Full actual costs are very commonly used as the transfer price. Under full actual-cost transfer pricing, the acquiring department is charged the entire cost of production incurred up to the point of internal transfer. Full actual-cost transfer is the oldest method of internal transfer pricing (as described in Chapter 6).

Allocations of service department costs closely approximate cost-based transfer prices. Because most organizations make contemporaneous cost transfers during the year rather than determining actual costs at the end of the period, most service department allocations are based upon estimated costs. Because service cost allocation has been described earlier in this chapter, the remainder of the chapter will be concerned with transfers between operating departments, as in process cost-accounting systems.

Full actual-cost transfer pricing provides some assurance that all departmental expenditures will be recovered as long as the final product is sold at a profit. For example, consider the following case:

Acme Corporation has two manufacturing divisions[2] and a sales unit. Acme produces one product in a continuous processing operation. In 19X2, $300,000 of material, labor, and overhead was incurred by Division 1 and transferred to Division 2. Division 2 incurred an additional cost of $200,000 and transferred the finished product to the selling unit's warehouse. The sales unit incurs $5,000 costs for salaries and other departmental expenses. All of the finished product was sold in 19X2 for $600,000.

If Acme transfers production from one division to another at cost (as described in Chapter 6), Divisions 1 and 2 "earn" zero profit, while the selling unit "earns" $95,000, as shown below:

	Division 1	Division 2	Sales Unit	Total Firm
Revenue or Transfer (out) price	$300,000	$500,000	$600,000	$600,000
Cost:				
Direct, by Division	$300,000	$200,000	$ 5,000	$505,000
Transferred in	-0-	300,000	500,000	
Total Cost	$300,000	$500,000	$505,000	$505,000
Profit	-$0-	-$0-	$ 95,000	$ 95,000

[2] A *division* is an organizational unit composed of several related departments.

No "transfer-in" costs are recognized by Division 1, because it is the first in the production system. All of the costs transferred out of Division 1 are transferred into Division 2. This $300,000 transfer-out cost is very similar to revenue for Division 1: if the transfer-out amount is stated as on a per-unit basis, it would resemble a "price." In determining data for the total firm, the transfer-out amounts are offset by the transfer-in amounts, that is, the total firm only recognizes the sum of direct costs incurred by each division and the revenue from sales to third parties.

The Acme Corporation case was simplified to help explain a cost-based transfer price mechanism. More realistic cases would include beginning and ending inventories, which in turn require specification of cost-flow assumptions (e.g., LIFO or FIFO) to accommodate changes in prices or changes in productive efficiency. Determination of equivalent units of production would also be required. Nonetheless, cost-based transfers from one division or department to another are accounted for substantially as shown above.

Cost-plus-profit transfers Internal transfer prices also may be based upon cost plus a predetermined rate or amount. The added amount provides the transferring (out) division with an internal "profit." Although this internal "profit" has no effect on the profits of the total firm, it may motivate the transferring division manager to perform his tasks efficiently. For example, assume that Acme Corporation allows its two operating divisions to "recognize" a profit of 10% of costs, i.e., the transfer price is established at 110% of cost. Financial results would be as follows:

	Division 1	Division 2	Sales Unit	Total Firm
Revenue (or transfer-out price)	$330,000	$583,000	$600,000	$600,000
Costs:				
Direct, by Division	$300,000	$200,000	$ 5,000	$505,000
Transferred in	-0-	330,000	583,000	
Total Cost	$300,000	$530,000	$588,000	$505,000
Profit	$ 30,000	$ 53,000	$ 12,000	$ 95,000

Costs incurred directly in Divisions 1 and 2 and in Sales are $300,000, $200,000, and $5,000, respectively. The Sales Unit sells the product to third parties for $600,000. No beginning or ending inventories remain: all costs enter cost of goods sold during the period. These events were determined by visual inspection of physical flows, and they are evidenced by supporting source documents. The $30,000 and $53,000 "profits" for Divisions 1 and 2 represent 10% of their respective costs, and the $12,000 "profit" for the Sales Unit represents a residual; that is, the Sales Unit's revenue is determined by its market price transactions with third parties. The sum of the individual "profits" for the three divisions equals the profit for the total firm. Thus, transfer pricing is a means for allocating total firm profit to the individual divisions.

Note that the $95,000 total profit for the firm is unaffected as a result of internal transfer prices. Separate costs for each division are accumulated to produce total firm cost, and revenue is determined by transactions with external third parties. When the amounts in the total column are being determined, the "revenue" of one division is offset by the "transfer-in costs" of another division.

If Acme instituted a transfer price equal to 120% of cost, Division 1 would transfer units at $360,000, and Division 2 would transfer units at $672,000 (i.e., $360,000 = 120% × $300,000 and $672,000 = 120% × [$200,000 + $360,000]). The Sales Unit would accumulate $677,000 divisional cost and would experience a $77,000 internal "loss." Still, the profits for the whole organization would remain at $95,000 (i.e., $60,000 + $112,000 − $77,000 = $95,000). To reiterate, a transfer price scheme merely allocates profit for the whole organization to the individual divisions: the sum of divisional "profits and losses" equals the total for the firm.

The transfer price illustrated in the Acme example was based upon total costs (direct costs incurred by the division plus costs transferred in from other divisions). In some situations, the transferred-in costs would be excluded from the base used to determine "divisional profit." Including this cost in the base would cause a compounding problem. For example, Division 2 is allowed to recognize a 10% profit on the $30,000 profit of Division 1 included in its $330,000 transfer-in cost. A company using transfer pricing should establish a definite policy that specifies which costs are to be considered as part of the base.

Another common type of cost-plus-percentage-markup transfer price is based solely upon divisional variable costs. Fixed costs are considered to represent capacity charges. Variable costs approximate actual out-of-pocket costs incurred in production more closely than do total production costs: Some managers believe that better decisions can be made with a variable cost-based transfer price.

Market-price–based transfers   Market-price–based prices attempt to foster open market competition within the firm. In theory, each buying and selling division is free to deal internally or externally in price competition. In practice, the rule is generally established that sales and purchases should be made internally if price and quality are compatible. Under this approach, the prevailing market quotations are the basis for an intracompany transfer price. This amount may be reduced under certain situations by a "sales commission" to compensate for the absence of marketing expenditures. Internal sales require only a nominal amount of marketing cost. Direct advertising and other promotional costs are eliminated. Large organizations may require a token internal sales force, but smaller organizations should be able to process intracompany sales without one.

A market-based transfer price forces both the producing and the acquiring divisions to adhere to the price constraints established by external competitors. The main support for this method is that it simulates the pressures and activities of actual competitive pricing and represents an opportunity cost for the intermediate units of output.

An example   Assume that external markets exist for the intermediate product produced by Division 1 and that a wholesale market exists for the output of Division 2. Market prices for outputs of Divisions 1 and 2 are, respectively, $550,000 and $300,000. Financial results for Acme Corporation are as follows:

	Division 1	Division 2	Sales Unit	Total Firm
Revenue (or transfer-out price)	$550,000	$300,000	$600,000	$600,000
Costs:				
Direct, by Division	$300,000	$200,000	$ 5,000	$505,000
Transferred in		550,000	300,000	
Total Cost	$300,000	$750,000	$305,000	$505,000
Profit (Loss)	$250,000	($450,000)	$295,000	$ 95,000

Here again, note that the sum of profits and losses for the three divisions equals the profit for the whole firm, i.e., figures for the whole firm do not reflect the internal transfer prices, that is, transfer pricing results in an internal reallocation of total firm profit to the separate divisions.

When no external market for intermediate products exists, management may resort to *negotiated transfer prices*. Negotiated transfer prices result from bargaining and agreement among the division managers. Ideally, the buying and selling division managers should have equal power and authority to negotiate, so that the negotiated price approximates that which would have resulted in a free market situation.

SUBOPTIMIZATION

Transfer pricing is also a device that may promote motivation and control within decentralized firms. In such firms, it is important to promote decisions at the divisional level that are in the best interest of the company as a whole. **Suboptimization** occurs when one division "optimizes" its "profit" in a way that lowers the entire firm's total profit. Remember, divisional "profit" is a direct result of the transfer price allowed by top management. A transfer price policy is good only if it leads divisions to take actions in the best interest of the company. Occasionally, this becomes difficult. For example, consider the following case.

A large company has ten plants, each of which operates as a profit center. All plants make a standardized product for distribution to different sales territories. As a service to these plants, the company operates a box factory that makes a standard package for the product. The boxes are sold to the plants for $.05 each.

Recently, Plant No. 2 petitioned the main office for permission to acquire its boxes from an outside supplier, who quoted a price of $.04 for a similar box. Plant No. 2 uses 100,000 boxes annually. The box factory manager estimates that if Plant No. 2 buys its boxes outside the company, its box volume will drop from 1,000,000 units to 900,000. Current production costs are $.03 per box for materials and labor and $20,000 in annual machine rental costs. Should the sales division buy outside?

Initially, the answer seems to be "yes," since the market price of $.04 per box is less than the internal transfer price of $.05. But what about the company in total? Consider the total cost associated with each alternative.

	Buy Inside*	Buy Outside**
Paid to Supplier	-0-	$ 4,000
Machine Rental	$20,000	20,000
Material and Labor	30,000	27,000
Total Cost	$50,000	$51,000

*Volume is 1,000,000 boxes inside and 0 boxes outside.
**Volume is 900,000 boxes inside and 100,000 boxes outside.

The company would be $1,000 better off if the sales division bought the boxes internally (i.e., $51,000 − $50,000 = $1,000). Conflicts between divisions caused by transfer prices can be resolved in different ways, but all of them involve some trade-off between profit and motivation. The sales division might be required to purchase at $.05 per box; the box division might be required to sell for $.04 per box; a negotiated compromise price might be determined, or central administration might award a $1,000 subsidy to the complaining division in compensation for the lost opportunity.

Other forms of suboptimization occur. One purpose of transfer pricing is to motivate divisional managers. But in cost-based transfer pricing schemes, each manager may be motivated to maximize cost, in an effort to maximize divisional profits, even though profits for the residual division and for the whole firm will suffer. Sometimes divisional managers alter the transfer price base by selecting different sources of market information. Real market value transfer prices, for example, which relay comparative performance information from external sources throughout the firm, may enhance both motivation and control. Market-based techniques can be dysfunctional, however, if the adopted market is not representative of the actual situation. A market price relates to the sale of a specific quantity of certain goods, at a given location, at a particular time. Changes in any of these conditions will affect the price. Internal transfers may not have parallels to each of these external factors.

Negotiation may be a costly pricing technique for the total enterprise. Managers of divisions engaged in internal competition may bargain so forcefully that animosity is aroused and future cooperation is jeopardized. If large numbers of independent items are to be priced (say 1,000), time pressures may preclude negotiation. The executive's time is too costly for the enterprise to spare.

Transfer-price induced profits should motivate managers to modify their behavior in ways that will help the firm achieve its organizational objectives. Yet goals will be reached only if transfer prices are used with caution.

SUMMARY

Service department costs are collected for exactly the same reasons that operating department costs are: these data provide the basis for planning, information processing, control, and decision making. Source documents similar to those used in operating departments are generated as costs are incurred. Service department costs are summarized on departmental cost sheets. Periodically, service department costs are allocated to the departments that benefit from those services. Service department costs can be treated as part of general overhead, or they may be treated as special overhead and allocated directly to operating departments or allocated step-wise through other service departments to the operating departments.

Interdepartmental or divisional transfers can occur at amounts other than cost. The amounts charged to a department for goods or services supplied by other departments within the same organization are called transfer prices. Transfer prices are generally established with reference to historical costs or to competitive market prices. Variations include variable cost-based prices, cost-plus-profit prices, and market-less-discount prices. Transfer prices are used to induce motivation and facilitate control, but they also may create conditions that foster suboptimization. All methods of allocation and most transfer price schemes are somewhat arbitrary, and caution should be exercised in interpreting the numbers derived from these processes. Chapter 14 describes procedures for making decisions in situations where cost allocations have occurred.

APPENDIX: RECORDING TRANSFERS BETWEEN DEPARTMENTS

Internal divisions frequently are treated as independent companies. Each division maintains a set of accounting records describing all transactions (both internal and external) in which they are involved. For each division, internal sales reduce inventory, increase receivables, increase cost of goods sold, and increase revenue. Maintaining divisional records enables each division to calculate profits. These internal transactions may have no influence on the results of operations or the financial position of the company as a whole. The total firm must combine (or consolidate) the records of its component divisions by eliminating internal transactions. Outside readers of financial statements need not be concerned with internal transfers, and these data do not appear in financial statements.

An example The Hawke Company is a small manufacturing firm using two service departments and two operating departments in a process costing system. Production is initiated in response to market demand. On the basis of prior

EXHIBIT 7–3   SEQUENTIAL PROCESSING OF DATA TO THE ACCOUNTS

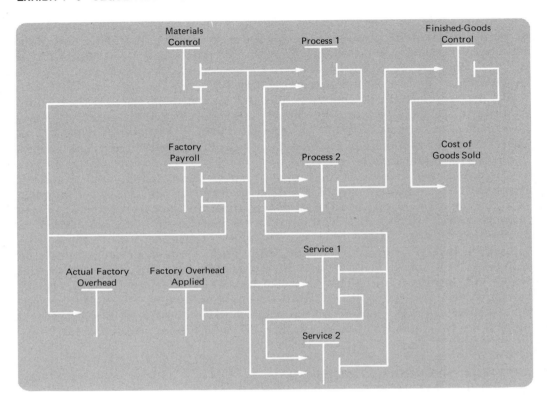

experience, management estimates overhead costs to be 30% of the total charge for direct labor. Exhibits 7–3 and 7–4 illustrate entries in general journal of the firm, reflecting the relevant account transfers, which are keyed to the letters of each transaction. Step-down allocation distributes costs of Service Department 1 to the other three departments. Service Department 2 cost is then reallocated to the production departments.

ACQUISITION OF MATERIALS

Materials Control	19,200	
Accounts Payable		16,000
Cash		3,200

A. (To record the purchase of raw materials for processing.

The firm has added raw materials to its inventory. The general account, "Materials Control," is supported by subsidiary accounts that specify which items are in inventory.

USE OF RAW MATERIALS IN PRODUCTION

Process 1	8,000	
Process 2	4,000	
Service 1	2,000	
Service 2	3,000	
Actual overhead	1,500	
Materials Control		18,500

B. (To record the transfer of raw materials to the production and service depts.)

The four accounts receiving material are work-in-process control accounts that summarize production activity. Each account has a zero beginning balance, and the transfers to each are supported by stores requisitions. Material or supplies that cannot be traced to process or service departments are changed to Actual Overhead. For example, the cost of paper supplies for the restrooms would be charged to Actual Overhead.

ACQUISITION OF LABOR

Factory Payroll	14,270	
Cash		14,270

C. (To record the payment, in cash, of the weekly payroll.)

Labor is also charged to each department. Labor costs for some employees who work in several departments in a facilitating capacity may be assigned to Actual Overhead. For example, costs of safety inspectors might be considered as an overhead item.

USE OF LABOR

Process 1	3,000	
Process 2	7,000	
Service 1	1,000	
Service 2	2,000	
Actual Overhead	1,270	
Factory Payroll		14,270

D. (To record the use of labor in the production processes.)

The clock cards used by employees paid an hourly wage can document the weekly payroll. The accountant uses information from the clock cards (or from a summary memorandum prepared by the payroll department) to charge the cost of labor to each department.

ASSIGNMENT OF OVERHEAD

Process 1	900	
Process 2	2,100	
Service 1	300	
Service 2	600	
Factory Overhead Applied		3,900

E. (To record the application of factory overhead at the predetermined rate.)

The overhead voucher is a document which supports the application of factory overhead at 30% of labor costs traceable to each department. In contrast to this example, some organizations would not assign overhead to the service departments: instead all general overhead would be assigned to the operating departments.

INCURRENCE OF ACTUAL OVERHEAD		
Actual Overhead	1,300	
Taxes Payable		400
Accumulated Depreciation		600
Prepaid Insurance		300
F. (To record the incurrence of actual overhead.)		

A control account, Actual Factory Overhead, is used to record actual overhead charges for the period. Another $1,300 has been incurred for taxes, insurance, and depreciation. At the end of the period, any differences between the applied and the actual control account balances will be transferred to either Cost of Goods Sold or to Inventory and Cost of Goods Sold.

TRANSFER FROM SERVICE DEPT. 1 TO OTHER DEPARTMENTS		
Process 1	1,500	
Process 2	1,400	
Service 2	400	
Service 1		3,300
G. (Step-down allocation of Service 1.)		

Service Department 1 costs are redistributed to the other departments on the basis of relative number of requests for services. In total, 1,100 requests were received, and these requests were charged out to the requesting departments at $3 per order.

TRANSFER FROM SERVICE DEPT. 2 TO OTHER DEPARTMENTS		
Process 1	2,800	
Process 2	3,200	
Service 2		6,000
H. (Step-down allocation of Service 2.)		

Service Department 2 costs are redistributed to the other departments on the basis of the relative number of personnel in each department.

TRANSFERS FROM PROCESS 1 TO PROCESS 2

Process 2	20,250	
Process 1		16,200
Transfer profit,		
Process 1		4,050

I. (Interdepartmental transfer at 125% of cost.)

All of the product from Process 1 is transferred to Process 2 using a 125% (of cost) transfer price, that is, 100% of the cost in Process 1 is transferred out. Process 2 records the receipt of 125% of these costs. The remaining 25% represents the "profit" recognized by Process Department 1. Since this is a simple case with few interdepartmental transfers and no beginning or ending inventories, this "profit" can be directly credited to Cost of Goods Sold, to produce a year-end cost basis. In more complicated situations, the "profit" from Process 1 would be allocated as an end-of-year adjustment to the balances in Process 2, Finished Goods, and Cost of Goods Sold.

TRANSFERS FROM PROCESS TO FINISHED GOODS

Finished-goods Inventory	41,745	
Process 2		37,950
Transfer profit,		
Process 2		3,795

J. (Interdepartmental transfer at 110% of cost.)

All of the product from Process 2 is completed and transferred to the Finished-Goods Inventory at 110% of cost. As before, the 10% profit in this simple case is immediately assigned to Cost of Goods Sold as an anticipated adjustment that will reduce Cost of Sales to a cost basis.

COST OF GOODS SOLD TRANSFER

Cost of Goods Sold	41,745	
Finished Goods		41,745

K. (Cost transfer that accompanies a sale in perpetual inventory systems.)

Whenever goods are sold, perpetual inventory systems record an accompanying reclassification from Finished Goods to Cost of Goods Sold.

ADJUSTING ENTRIES

Applied Overhead	3,900	
Cost of Goods Sold	170	
Actual Overhead		4,070

L. (To close overhead accounts.)

At the end of the year, the actual and applied overhead accounts are closed, and any remaining balance is used to adjust Cost of Goods Sold. Exhibit 7–4 presents the ledger accounts and entries used to reflect the cost flows illustrated in Exhibit 7–3.

EXHIBIT 7–4   LEDGER ACCOUNTS

Materials Control			Process 1		
A. 19,200	18,500	B.	B. 8,000		
			D. 3,000		
			E. 900		
			G. 1,500		
			H. 2,800	16,200	I.

Factory Payroll			Process 2		
C. 14,270	14,270	D.	B. 4,000		
			D. 7,000		
			E. 2,100		
			G. 1,400		
			H. 3,200		
			I. 20,250	37,950	J.

Applied Factory Overhead			Service 1		
L. 3,900	3,900	E.	B. 2,000		
			D. 1,000		
			E. 300	3,300	G.

Actual Factory Overhead			Service 2		
B. 1,500			B. 3,000		
D. 1,270			D. 2,000		
F. 1,300	4,070	L.	E. 600		
			G. 400	6,000	H.

Finished Goods			Cost of Goods Sold		
J. 41,745	41,745	K.	K. 41,745	4,050	I.
			L. 170	3,795	J.

SUGGESTED READINGS

Baumler, J. V., and D. Watson. "Transfer Pricing, A Behavioral Context." *The Accounting Review*, April 1975.

Cushing, Barry. "Pricing Internal Computer Services: The Basic Issues." *Management Accounting*, April 1976.

Thomas, Arthur. "The FASB and the Allocation Fallacy." *Journal Of Accountancy*, November 1975.

QUESTIONS

7–1   Identify the purposes for collecting service department costs. Contrast the source documents that reflect the acquisition or use of productive inputs for service departments with those used in operating departments.

7–2   Describe alternate ways to assign service department costs to operating departments.

7–3   Relate the general concepts of "direct variability," "usage," and "ability to pay" to service department cost allocation procedures.

7–4   List some common bases for reallocating service department costs to other service departments or to operating departments.

7–5   "The simplest method for assigning all service department costs to the producing departments is to consider them part of general overhead." What are the disadvantages of treating service department costs as part of general overhead?

7–6   Explain how step-down allocation of service department costs differs from reciprocal allocation.

7–7   "All transfer price schemes merely allocate total profit for the whole company among the operating divisions." Contrast the results obtained from cost-based and market-based transfer prices.

7–8   Explain what is meant by the term *suboptimization* and describe how it is related to the selection of a transfer price.

7–9   What are intracompany transfer prices? Why are they generally different from the normal external selling prices of the firm?

7–10 Briefly describe how an intracompany transfer price would be calculated using each of the following techniques:

(A) Cost-based

(B) Market-based

(C) Negotiated

7–11   Since a transfer price is only an artificial value assigned to exchanges within a firm, why is it any better than just valuing the exchanges at their accumulated cost up to the point of transfer?

EXERCISES

7–12   The Wesson Company has several plants that operate independently. As a service to these plants, Wesson operates a box factory that produces a standard package for the firm's total output. These boxes are sold to the individual plants for $.06 each. Recently, Plant A petitioned the main office for permission to purchase its boxes from an outside supplier, who quoted a price of $.04 for a similar box. Plant A uses 200,000 boxes per year. The box factory manager estimates that its volume will drop from 1,500,000 units to 1,300,000 units if Plant A is allowed to buy externally. Box factory costs are $.01 per box for labor, variable overhead and materials, and $45,000 for fixed overhead costs.

> (A) What will be the financial consequences for Wesson if Plant A purchases its 200,000 boxes from the external supplier?
>
> (B) How low must the external price fall before Wesson will benefit from the external purchase of boxes?

7–13   The Sanders Manufacturing Company has two operating departments and two service departments. Materials Handling Department costs are allocated on the basis of the dollar value of items requisitioned by the other departments. The Cafeteria costs are allocated to other departments on the basis of the relative number of employees in the departments. Total Materials Handling costs are $50,000 and Cafeteria costs are $20,000. Other data on the departments of Sanders are as follows:

	Department 1	Department 2	Materials Handling	Cafeteria
No. of Employees	50	30	15	5
Cost of items Requisitioned	$300,000	$200,000		$100,000

> (A) Using direct allocation, determine the service department costs allocated to Departments 1 and 2.
>
> (B) Determine the service department costs allocated to Departments 1 and 2, using step-down allocation. (Allocate the high cost service department, Materials Handling, first.)

7–14   The continuous production line of Kane Producers, Inc., runs through three operating departments. Costs directly incurred by each of these departments are $50,000, $200,000, and $300,000. The Sales Department incurred $10,000 in cost while selling all of Kane's production for $900,000.

    (A) Determine the "profit" recognized by the three operating departments and the sales departments, assuming that the operating departments transfer units at 110% of cost.

    (B) Determine the "profit" recognized by the four departments, assuming that the operating departments transfer units at 150% of cost.

7–15   Service department costs for Jones Construction Company are assigned to the three operating departments on the basis of estimated man hours of direct labor. The budget for 19X1 called for the following results:

| Service Department cost $600,000 | | | |
Operating Departments	1	2	3
Labor hours worked	10,000	20,000	30,000
Allocated costs	$100,000	$200,000	$300,000

At the end of the year, the following data became available: actual service department costs were $800,000, and actual hours worked in Departments 1, 2, and 3 were 5,000, 20,000 and 45,000.

    (A) What dollar amounts were allocated to each department in 19X1?

    (B) What purposes were served by allocating service department costs to the operating departments?

    (C) Was useful information provided by the allocation process?

    (D) What happened to the over- or underapplied service department cost?

7–16   The Ajax division of Gunnco, operating at capacity, has been asked by the Defco division of Gunnco to supply it with Electrical Fitting No. 1726. Ajax sells this part to its regular customers for $7.50 each. Defco, which is operating at 50% capacity, is willing to pay $5.00 each for the fittings. Defco will put the fitting into a brake unit that it manufactures on essentially a cost-plus basis for a commercial airplane manufacturer.

    Ajax has a variable cost of producing Fitting No. 1726 of $4.25. The cost of the brake unit, as built by Defco, is as follows:

Purchased Parts—Outside Vendors	$22.50
Ajax Fitting No. 1726	5.00
Other Variable Costs	14.00
Fixed Overhead and Administration	8.00
	$49.50

Defco believes the price concession is necessary to get the job.

The company uses dollar profits in measuring a divisional manager's performance.

(A) If you were the divisional controller of Ajax, would you recommend that Ajax supply Fitting No. 1726 to Defco? (Ignore any income tax issues.) Why or why not?

(B) Would it be to the short-run economic advantage of the Gunnco Corporation for the Ajax division to supply Defco division with Fitting No. 1726 at $5.00 each? (Ignore any income tax issues.) Explain your answer.

(C) Discuss the organizational and managerial behavior difficulties, if any, inherent in this situation. As the Gunnco controller, what would you advise the Gunnco Corporation's president to do in this situation?

(CMA adapted)

7-17 The Malcom Company is a decentralized continuous-process manufacturer with two production departments and a selling department. Separable costs for June are as follows:

	A	B	C	Total
Individual Variable Cost	$100,000	$200,000	$150,000	$450,000
Individual Fixed Cost	$100,000	$100,000	$100,000	$300,000

Malcom converted both cost centers into profit centers by instituting transfer prices equal to 200% of individual departmental costs, excluding transfers, even though there is no market for the intermediate product.

(A) How much "profit" is recognized by each department if production for June is sold for $2,000,000?

(B) If the sales department can buy the products normally supplied by Department No. 2 on the open market, what is the highest price it can pay without decreasing the profitability of the total firm?

7-18 The Holdings Corporation uses a market-based price to establish interdivisional transfer prices. A glass insert for their largest product has always been a purchasing problem. The insert is produced by only one company, and they are not reliable. After one bad experience with the glass insert, the Holdings Corporation built their own glass plant to make the insert.

(A) If the cost from the glass plant owned by Holdings is higher than that charged by the outside supplier, should the assembly plant buy from the outside supplier or from the plant inside? Explain why.

(B) If the assembly plant buys from the corporate glass plant and the external supplier stops production, what transfer price will they use next year for the insert?

(C) If the assembly plant buys from the outside supplier, what will happen to the corporate glass plant? Will this have any influence on the company?

(D) If transfer prices are all internal prices, why worry about setting a price at which to transfer a product from one division to another?

7-19 The Swartz Company, a large lamp manufacturer, uses a cost plus 10% profit method to establish the transfer prices between divisions of the company. Last year, every division in the Swartz Company made money except the assembly division. When the assembly division compared total costs with the revenue generated by sales, losses amounted to $30,000. The assembly division manager claimed that this loss was not all his fault.

(A) Is the assembly division manager right? Explain why or why not.

(B) What are the disadvantages of using cost-based techniques for transfer pricing?

(C) What are the advantages of using cost-based techniques for transfer pricing?

*(D) Why use a cost-plus transfer price instead of the price that the product could sell for on the outside market?

*(E) If no profit figure had been added to the divisional transfer price, could the problem that was illustrated above occur? Explain why or why not.

7-20 Sam Harvey, the manager of the stamping plant, is very anxious about yearly financial reviews. His plant has been in the red for the past two years. As Harvey explains, the plant would make a profit if only a portion of the corporate costs were not added to his plant costs. Harvey once said: "It's a vicious circle; I'm in the red because of the corporate salaries, and the corporation hires more people to figure out why I'm in the red." Jim Jones's plant is always in the black, and it is seldom visited by anyone from corporate headquarters. Yet Jim's plant is assigned a share of the corporate salaries used to evaluate the Harvey plant.

(A) Is the method of allocating corporate salaries to both plants the best system? Explain your answer.

(B) Sam Harvey wants the cost to be allocated to the plants that can pay it. What is wrong with this method, if anything?

(C) Jim Jones wants the cost allocated on the basis of use. What is wrong with this method, if anything?

(D) Do you think either plant manager will ever be satisified? Explain why or why not.

7-21 The Fair Play Corporation has called two of its divisional managers and asked them to meet in private and negotiate a fair price for internal transfers between their two divisions. The company management believes that negotiation will approximate an "arm's-length transaction" and thus will provide a useful complement to the performance measurement system. In each of the following cases, describe what, if anything, seems to indicate that the negotiated price will not be appropriate.

(A) Attila Hunler, a 320-pound ex-professional boxer, is noted for his violent temper. He and Marvin Meek, a 140-pound domino champion, arrived at a transfer price quickly. Marvin left work early for the day.

(B) John Play is the grandson of the company's president and major stockholder. After he spent three weeks with the firm, his grandfather promoted him to divisional manager. William Wilted, who has six more months to work before he is eligible for a company pension, did not stand up to John, who proved to be a hard bargainer and got a favorable price.

(C) Buddy Pal and Fred End have known each other since high school. Buddy once saved Fred's life, and Fred has helped Buddy out financially many times. Outside of work, Fred and Buddy are real friends. They arrived at a transfer price in five minutes.

(D) Sam Sneak and Larry Louse have never agreed on anything during the six years that they have been with the company. Sam and Larry have been negotiating for three weeks. Top management is considering giving them some more time to "iron out their differences."

*7–22 In recent years, distribution expenses of the Avey Company have increased more than other expenditures. For more effective control, the Company plans to provide each local manager with an income statement for his territory showing monthly and year-to-date amounts for the current and the previous year. Each sales office is supervised by a local manager; sales orders are forwarded to the main office and filled from a central warehouse; billing and collections are also centrally processed. Expenses are first classified by function and then allocated to each territory in the following ways:

Function	Basis
Sales Salaries	Actual
Other Selling Expenses	Relative Sales Dollars
Warehousing	Relative Sales Dollars
Packing and Shipping	Weight of Package
Billing and Collections	Number of Billings
General Administration	Equally

(A) 1. Explain responsibility accounting and the classification of revenues and expenses under this concept.

2. What are the objectives of profit analysis by sales territories in income statements?

(B) 1. Discuss the effectiveness of Avey Company's comparative income statements by sales territories as a tool for planning and control. Include in your answer additional factors that should be considered and changes that might facilitate effective planning by management and evaluation of the local sales managers.

2. Compare the degree of control that can be achieved over production costs and distribution costs and explain why the degree of control differs.

3. Criticize Avey Company's allocation and/or inclusion of (1) other selling expenses, (2) warehousing expense, and (3) general administration expense.

(AICPA adapted)

PROBLEMS

7-23 The Parker Manufacturing Company has two operating departments (fabrication and assembly) and three service departments (general factory administration, factory maintenance, and factory cafeteria). A summary of the costs and other data for each department prior to allocation of service department costs for the year ended June 30 appears below:

	Fabrication	Assembly	General Factory Administration	Factory Maintenance	Factory Cafeteria
Direct labor costs	$1,950,000	$2,050,000	$ 90,000	$ 82,100	$ 87,000
Direct material costs	$3,130,000	$ 950,000	—	$ 65,000	$ 91,000
Manufacturing overhead costs	$1,650,000	$1,850,000	$ 70,000	$ 56,100	$ 62,000
Total Costs	$6,730,000	$4,850,000	$160,000	$203,200	$240,000
Direct labor hours	562,500	437,500	31,000	27,000	42,000
Number of employees	280	200	12	8	20
Square footage occupied	88,000	72,000	1,750	2,000	4,800

The costs of the general factory administration department, factory maintenance department, and factory cafeteria are allocated to the operating departments on the basis of direct labor hours, square footage occupied, and number of employees, respectively.

(A) Assuming that Parker elects to distribute service department costs directly to operating departments without interservice department cost allocation, determine the total costs after allocation for the two operating departments.

(B) Assuming that Parker elects to distribute service department costs to the other service departments (starting with the service department with the greatest total costs), as well as the operating departments, determine the total costs after allocation for the two operating departments.

(AICPA adapted)

7–24   The costs of operating the maintenance department of Jemco Company are reallocated to three operating departments on the basis of total labor hours. Operating data for 19X3 were:

		Dept. 1	Dept. 2	Dept. 3
Maintenance department costs	$300,000			
Total labor hours		100,000	200,000	300,000
Allocated maintenance costs		$50,000	$100,000	$150,000

In 19X4, the activity of Department 1 increased greatly because a sudden temporary surge in demand for its output. The maintenance department established and maintained a second production line from surplus equipment. Operations of Department 1 returned to normal by the end of the year, and the second production line was discontinued. Costs of the maintenance department in 19X4 were $300,000. The total labor hours worked in the operating departments were 300,000, 200,000, and 300,000, respectively.

(A) Allocate the 19X4 maintenance costs to the operating departments using 19X3 data to determine the overhead rate.

(B) As the manager of Department 1, comment about the year-to-year changes in maintenance costs that are allocated to your department in relation to the year-to-year maintenance costs that are allocated to Department 2.

(C) As the manager of Department 2, how would you respond to the comments in Part B, above?

(D) As the manager of Department 2, would you change your position about the allocation of maintenance costs if Department 1 experienced decreased labor activity rather than the increase actually experienced?

7–25   The Tranz Fur Company produces a line of inexpensive fur coats for sale in retail outlets. The Company is decentralized into two main operating divisions—fur preparation and coat manufacture. The Company wants to establish these divisions as profit centers and, consequently, must arrive at a transfer price for the pelts "sold" by the fur preparation division to the coat manufacture division. The following historical and projected cost data were provided by the Company's managerial accountant.

Actual Cost per Pelt (last period):		
Direct Labor	$2.00	
Direct Material	4.00	
Overhead (variable)	.40	
Overhead (fixed)	.30	
Total Actual Cost per Pelt (last period)		$6.70
Standard Cost per Pelt:		
Direct Labor	$1.80	
Direct Material	3.90	
Overhead (variable)	.60	
Overhead (fixed)	.60	
Total Standard Cost per Pelt		$6.90
Current Market Price per Pelt		8.00
External Sales and Promotional Expense per Pelt		.20
Per-Pelt Profit Subsidy for Cost-Plus Techniques		.40
Per-Unit Overhead Subsidy for Cost-Plus Techniques		1.00

Using this information, determine the total value that will be assigned to a transfer of 1,200 pelts under each of the following transfer pricing methods:

(A) Full actual cost
(B) Standard cost
(C) Marginal cost
(D) Variable cost
(E) Base period cost plus profit
(F) Variable cost plus a subsidy
(G) Market price
(H) Market price minus
(I) Negotiated price
(J) Assignment

7–26 The Zeus Company has two operating departments (fabricating and finishing) and a service department. The service department provides services to both operating departments.

Service department expenses are allocated to operating departments as follows:

Expense	Allocation Base
Building maintenance	Space occupied
Timekeeping and personnel	Number of employees
Other	½ to fabricating, ½ to finishing

Service department expenses for December (not included in departmental overhead above) were:

Building maintenance	$ 45,000
Timekeeping and personnel	27,500
Other	39,000
	$111,500

Other information for December 19X1 is presented below:

	Square Feet of Space Occupied	Number of Employees
Fabricating	75,000	180
Finishing	37,500	120
	112,500	300

(A) Allocate service department costs to the two operating departments.

(B) Discuss alternate bases for allocating service department costs to the operating departments.

(AICPA adapted)

7-27   A manufacturer's plant with two service departments (S_1 and S_2) and three operating departments (P_1, P_2, and P_3) wishes to allocate all factory overhead to operating departments. A primary distribution of overhead to all departments has already been made, as indicated below. The company makes the secondary distribution of overhead from service departments to operating departments. Cost data are presented below:

		Primary Overhead to be Allocated		
S_1	S_2	P_1	P_2	P_3
$98,000	$117,600	$1,400,000	$2,100,000	$640,000

(A) Distribute service department costs directly to operating departments without interservice department cost allocation, assuming that P_1, P_2, and P_3 have allocation percentages of 60%, 30%, and 10%, respectively.

(B) Distribute service department costs to the other departments, starting with S_1, assuming that the allocation percentages for S_1 are 10%, 50%, 20%, and 20% assigned to S_2, P_1, P_2, and P_3, respectively, and S_2 are 60%, 30%, and 10% assigned to P_1, P_2, and P_3.

(AICPA adapted)

7-28   ToolCo is a decentralized continuous-process manufacturer that has two production departments and a selling department. All units are completed and transferred (sold) during June. Separable costs incurred by each department during June are shown below, exclusive of transfer-in costs.

Separable Costs	#1	#2	Sales	Total
Variable Cost	$100,000	$200,000	$50,000	$350,000
Allocated Fixed Cost	150,000	100,000	50,000	300,000

ToolCo converted both cost centers into profit centers by instituting transfer prices based upon separable departmental costs, exclusive of transfer costs. Production departments are allowed "profits" equal to 50% of separable costs.

(A) Determine divisional profits, assuming that all units sold for $900,000.

(B) Department No. 2 solicits bids for the material it usually acquires from Department No. 1. What is the highest price it can accept without causing suboptimization?

7–29 Costs within the Cooley Company's process cost-accounting system are transferred from one department to the next. Cooley has three departments; directly traceable costs for each have been accumulated, and ending inventories for each have been determined by the FIFO method.

(A) None of the departments has beginning inventories. Fill in the missing data for each department.

	Dept. 1	Dept. 2	Dept. 3
Directly traceable cost	$100,000	$200,000	$150,000
Ending work in process	$ 10,000	$ 45,000	C
Transfer-in cost	-0-	B	$245,000
Transfer-out cost	A	$245,000	$345,000

(B) Applied overhead in Cooley Co. is assigned at the rate of 50% of direct labor cost. *Directly* traceable cost in Part A is composed of three lements: labor, material, and overhead. Fill in the missing data:

	Dept. 1	Dept. 2	Dept. 3
Direct labor	$30,000	E	$60,000
Direct materials	$55,000	$50,000	G
Applied overhead	D	F	H

(C) Cooley actually incurred $103,000 of overhead costs during the full year. How large an adjustment for over/underapplied overhead must be made to cost of goods sold at the end of the year?

CHAPTER 8

Joint and By-Product Costing

Objectives

After studying this chapter, you should be able to do the following:

Describe the attributes of joint products *and define the term* joint costs.

Employ the several methods of allocating *common costs to joint products.*

Compare the accounting for joint products with the accounting for by-products. Determine the dollar differences in inventory values and cost of goods sold that result from using joint product or by-product accounting.

Describe the information that managers need to make informed pricing or production decisions about joint products. In particular, relate the usefulness of joint costs to managerial decisions.

The previous chapters of this section focused on manufacturing costs directly associated with and traceable to a specific production department or product. This chapter examines procedures to account for input costs that relate simultaneously to two or more products. Such costs are called *joint costs*. Two distinct problems are associated with joint costs: assigning costs to products and developing data relevant to decision-making.

JOINT PRODUCTS

In most manufacturing activities, raw materials and labor inputs could be used to produce more than one type of output. In cases in which *two or more outputs result from processing a single input*, the outputs are generally referred to as **joint products**. Joint products result when: (1) a single input unit yields a *cluster* of product outputs, or (2) the input has the *potential* to yield different outputs, depending on the amount and kind of processing chosen.

Often a cluster of inputs will be purchased as a single unit. For example, a beef processor will acquire an entire steer as an input unit. Obviously, this unit includes several distinct components, including meats, hide, and fertilizer. No processor would acquire just part of the animal and ignore the rest. The total steer represents a purchasable unit, or an input cluster.

Beef processors must also decide *how much processing activity* to undertake. For example, assuming that meats will be processed, should the hide be processed also, or should it be sold separately? To support such decisions, the processor needs information about the marginal benefits and costs of possible alternative actions. After making a decision and producing outputs, the processor must also determine the cost of each joint product for inventory valuation purposes. In turn, inventory values determine the cost of goods sold, and hence, the profitability of each product.

Other inputs are not clusters, but have the *potential* to yield different outputs. For example, in an oil refinery, the crude oil input can be transformed through different methods of processing into a variety of outputs, such as refined oil, gasoline, or fuel oil. To make optimal decisions, management must evaluate the cost and benefits associated with each successive step in refining. Accurate cost information is also essential for inventory valuation purposes.

Terminology   Producing multiple, or joint, products involves two types of costs, common and separable. **Separable costs** relate to items that are identified solely with a particular product and are directly *traceable* to a single output of the firm. Most products contain some elements of separable costs. In the case of the meat processor, tanning costs for steer hides would be separable because they are not connected with the meat or fertilizer operations.

Common costs cannot be associated directly with a single type of product output. These costs are *joint* because they relate to inputs used in manufacturing two or more distinct products; they are *nontraceable* and consequently *non-separable*. Thus, the cost of an entire steer is a joint cost for the meat processor.

Joint products may be differentiated to indicate their importance to the firm. Products of major importance are called *major products* or *co-products*. Products of minor importance are termed **by-products**.

Inevitably, some by-products result while major products are being produced. At an extreme, scrap such as sawdust or metal filings may be classified as a by-product. Usually the term scrap is reserved for by-products that are salable without additional processing but have little economic value.

If importance to the firm is used to distinguish major products from by-products, some criterion for judging importance must be established. The common basis for such a criterion is economic value. This criterion results from the traditional bias of profit-oriented firms — the more profitable product is considered the more important. Some accountants classify any joint product that produces less than 10% of the value of the total products as by-products.

The relationships between joint products and by-products are illustrated in Exhibit 8–1. The point at which the interrelationship among products ceases is termed the **split-off point**. From this point on, each product can be treated as an independent output. Identifying the split-off point is important in accounting for joint products.

ACCOUNTING FOR JOINT PRODUCTS

Accountants face a twofold task in accumulating information about joint products. First, some portion of the total cost must be assigned to each product in order to value the firm's inventories. This function may be termed *information preparation*. Second, accountants must provide relevant information about joint products to the firm's decision makers. This function is called *decision-making support*. The accountants' two tasks are not necessarily in agreement.

Information needs Accountants who prepare financial statements must assign the joint production costs to the firm's major and minor products. Techniques of **allocation**, or indirect cost assignment, are frequently used. Some specific allocation procedures will be explored later in this chapter.

Supporting decisions requires a different approach and different information from that used for financial-statement purposes. Decision-makers require information about the profitability of feasible alternatives. Cost allocations among products for such decisions are unnecessary and may prove misleading.

As an example, consider the following:

A company operates a commercial dairy. It processes and distributes whole milk, cream, and skim milk to its wholesale customers on a daily basis. Because of the quantities and relative sales prices, these three joint products are considered co-products.

EXHIBIT 8–1   INTERRELATIONSHIPS AMONG JOINT PRODUCTS

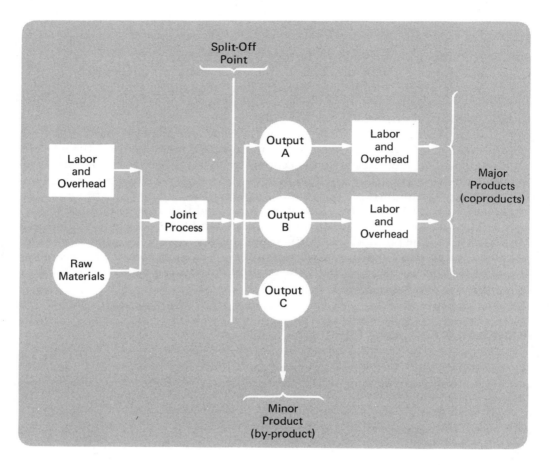

The company pays its supplying farmers $.30 per gallon for raw milk. This raw milk is processed and separated into whole milk, cream, and skim milk at an additional cost of $.10 per gallon. This is the split-off point and the joint, or common, cost incurred is $.40 per gallon of input.

At the split-off point, the raw milk is divided by weight and volume as follows: 60% whole milk, 30% skim milk, and 10% cream. Final processing, packaging, and distribution costs are $.40 per gallon for whole milk, $.60 per gallon for skim milk, and $.70 per gallon for cream. The normal volume of the dairy is 10,000 gallons of raw milk a day.

Management is currently reviewing the profitability of selling skim milk and cream. The sales prices per gallon on these products have recently dropped to $.50 and $1.40, respectively, although whole milk prices have remained constant at $1.10.

To evaluate the situation adequately, management must look at the costs and benefits from each of these operations. For the sake of simplicity, assume that the relationships are fixed and that the quantities derived from the raw milk cannot be altered.

EXHIBIT 8-2 PROFITABILITY OF ALTERNATE SALES OPPORTUNITIES

	Milk	Sell Milk and Cream	Sell Milk and Skim Milk	Sell Milk, Cream, and Skim Milk
Revenue Milk (6,000 @ $1.10)	$6,600	$6,600	$6,600	$6,600
Revenue Cream (1,000 @ $1.40)		1,400		1,400
Revenue Skim Milk (3,000 @ $ .50)			1,500	1,500
Total Revenue	$6,600	$8,000	$8,100	$9,500
Joint Cost (10,000 @ $ .40)	4,000	4,000	4,000	4,000
Separable Cost Milk (6,000 @ $ .40)	2,400	2,400	2,400	2,400
Separable Cost Cream (1,000 @ $ .70)		700		700
Separable Cost Skim Milk (3,000 @ $ .60)			1,800	1,800
Total Cost	$6,400	$7,100	$8,200	$8,900
Total Profit (Loss)	$ 200	$ 900	$ (100)	$ 600

How should an evaluation proceed? The most direct approach is to avoid allocation and evaluate each major alternative. In this example, the company has four major options, including: (1) sell only whole milk, (2) sell whole milk and cream, (3) sell whole milk and skim milk, and (4) sell whole milk, cream, and skim milk. Options to sell only cream or only skim milk are improbable.

The total profitability for each possibility may be calculated and compared. The respective profit results, computed in Exhibit 8-2, are: (1) $200, (2) $900, (3) $100 loss, and (4) $600. Obviously, management's choice should be alternative (2), sell whole milk and cream. The allocation of joint costs is unnecessary in this analysis and would add nothing to the solution.

Cost information is of basic importance to many decisions; its analysis, however, can vary. For example:

. . . Cost analyses which may be useful for one purpose (e.g., inventory evaluation for financial statements or tax purposes) often do not produce the information necessary for another purpose (e.g., product line decisions). Therefore, the cost analyses which are most appropriate in a given set of circumstances are determined primarily by the use to which the information will be put.[1]

Information sources Regardless of the analysis to be performed, managers need basic cost information. Data about particular products or processes must be collected on a timely basis. Information sources have been described in previous chapters of this book. Basic cost data may come from a variety of source documents: time cards, stores requisitions, and job-order or departmental cost

[1]*Management Services Technical Study No. 1* (New York: American Institute of Certified Public Accountants, 1958), p. 2.

sheets. Further summaries and classifications are available in the general accounting records, journals, and ledgers, both subsidiary and general. In performance of their information-preparation function, accountants frequently analyze the data and associate the common costs with the firm's joint products.

ALLOCATION PROBLEMS

Costs incurred after the split-off point are directly traceable to individual products and pose no fundamental accounting problem. Costs incurred prior to the split-off point, however, are joint, or common, and must be allocated to individual products. All bases for allocation contain an arbitrary element, because all allocations depend ultimately on some subjective judgment by an accountant. Equally competent accountants may make equally reasonable but differing assumptions, and they may arrive at quite different costs for the same product. Furthermore, there is no basis for judging whether one cost is more correct than another. The allocation itself cannot be proved correct. The accountant, however, should use a technique that seems appropriate for a particular cost situation. He must be prepared to justify a technique rather than a result. Allocations are important for inventory valuations.[2] Specifically, inventory values based on allocated costs are required by law or custom in reports submitted to stockholders, the Securities and Exchange Commission, the New York and American Stock Exchanges, and the Internal Revenue Service. *Although allocations support the reporting function, internal decisions should not be based on such information.*

APPROACHES TO ALLOCATION

Many allocation techniques are commonly practiced, essentially, they may be classified as variations of two basic approaches: **physical measures** and **ultimate market values**. In the absence of a directly traceable cost, both approaches identify a unit of measure that is traceable to the co-products. Common costs are divided among the products on the basis of this secondary, or supporting, measure. *The implicit assumption is that costs before split-off bear the same relationship to the products as to the secondary measures.*

Physical measures One method of allocating common costs relies on the physical relationships among the co-products. If weight is selected as the physical basis, and one product weighs twice as much as another product, the former will be assigned ⅔ of the common costs and the latter ⅓ of these costs. For example,

---

[2]In situations in which all jointly produced products are sold during a period, the entire joint cost is assigned to cost of goods sold. In this case, it is not necessary to segment these costs into particular products. Whenever inventory balances remain at the end of the period, cost allocation is required for conventional financial-statement presentations.

three joint products, A, B and C, are separated at the split-off point, with A weighing 1,000 pounds, B, 2,000 pounds, and C, 3,000 pounds. A joint cost of $30,000 would be allocated as follows:

Product	Product Weight	Allocation Basis	Assigned Cost
A	1,000 lbs.	1,000/6,000 × $30,000	$ 5,000
B	2,000 lbs.	2,000/6,000 × $30,000	10,000
C	3,000 lbs.	3,000/6,000 × $30,000	15,000
	6,000 lbs.		$30,000

This approach can be used with any physical measure of a product, including weight, size, and volume.

Using physical measures to allocate joint costs is justified by homogeneity, or similarity, among the products at the split-off point. In the oil refining industry, for example, crude oil undergoes processing into various products—gasoline, fuel oil, and motor oil. Since the products are fairly homogeneous at the split-off point, both in physical terms and in market potential, it may be reasonable to allocate these initial costs on the basis of volume.

In the meat-packing industry, however, dissimilar products, ranging from prime steak to cowhide, result at the split-off point. Physical measures may not be as appropriate in this case. The products are basically heterogeneous and do not seem to share a common market potential. Some accountants suggest that this inequity in market potential can be overcome by applying the ultimate market values to allocate costs among the products.

Ultimate market values Common costs can be allocated to co-products in proportion to the relative market value of the products. Ultimate market value is determined by multiplying the *expected* market price by the physical quantity of each product: this calculation is made before the co-products are actually sold. When ultimate market values of joint products are used to allocate common costs, more common costs are assigned to products with high market potential than to those with lower market potential. This approach focuses on "the ability to pay" of the joint products.

For example, if three joint products, A, B, and C, have potential market prices of $25,000, $15,000, and $20,000, a joint cost of $30,000 would be allocated as follows:

Product	Market Value	Allocation Basis	Assigned Cost
A	$25,000	25,000/60,000 × $30,000	$12,500
B	15,000	15,000/60,000 × $30,000	7,500
C	20,000	20,000/60,000 × $30,000	10,000
	$60,000		$30,000

The ultimate market value approach appeals to some practitioners because it relates the product outputs' market value to input values.

Strikingly dissimilar results may occur when different allocation techniques are used. For example, if three joint products, A, B, and C, receive no additional processing beyond the split-off point, product profitability is markedly different for each alternate allocation method (see Exhibit 8–3). Note, however, that the combined product income for A, B, and C equals $30,000 under both methods.

EXHIBIT 8–3   EFFECTS OF ALTERNATE ALLOCATIONS OF $30,000 JOINT COSTS

	Physical Measures			Ultimate Market Values		
	A	B	C	A	B	C
Traceable Revenues	$25,000	$15,000	$20,000	$25,000	$15,000	$20,000
Allocated Joint Costs	5,000	10,000	15,000	12,500	7,500	10,000
Product Income	$20,000	$ 5,000	$ 5,000	$12,500	$ 7,500	$10,000

A complication   The ultimate market value can best be applied when a market for the co-products exists at the split-off point. In such a case, market value, as a secondary measure, is not influenced by additional factors. A complication arises if no such intermediate market exists, or if the co-products are unsalable at the split-off point. In this case, the final market values must reflect different amounts of other inputs added to some of the co-products after the split-off point. Adjustments must be made if the market value technique is to work. One approach to this adjustment identifies the separable processing costs beyond the split-off point, subtracts them from the final market price, and arrives at an adjusted allocation.

An example   For an overview of the entire allocation process, assume that product cost information is requested by a firm that produces two co-products, Flash and Flop. The relevant data are summarized as follows:

	Flash	Flop
Co-products	20,000 lbs.	30,000 lbs.
Separable Costs	$10,000	$20,000
Product Revenue	$70,000	$50,000
Joint Cost = $60,000		

On the basis of physical measures, the joint cost of $60,000 would be allocated as follows:

Product	Product Weight (lbs.)	Allocation Basis	Assigned Cost
Flash	20,000	20,000/50,000 × $60,000	$24,000
Flop	30,000	30,000/50,000 × $60,000	36,000
	50,000		$60,000

At most, physical allocation should be restricted to information reporting:

		Flash		Flop
Revenue		$70,000		$50,000
Joint Cost	$24,000		$36,000	
Separable Cost	10,000	34,000	20,000	56,000
Product Income (Loss)		$36,000		$ (6,000)

These results seem to indicate that Flop should not be produced. The report implies that if production of Flop ceased, joint costs would be reduced by $36,000. This is not true. *Decisions should not be made using allocated costs.* Analyzing the total effect provides a clearer picture for decision-making.

There are three possible manufacturing alternatives in this example: (1) produce just Flash, (2) produce just Flop, and (3) produce Flash and Flop. Total profits for each of these alternatives are (1) $0.00, (2) $30,000 loss, and (3) $30,000 gain, as shown in Exhibit 8–4. The most profitable decision is to produce both products, although physically based cost allocation may point toward other conclusions.

EXHIBIT 8–4 PROFIT CALCULATIONS OF ALTERNATE SALES OPPORTUNITIES

	Flash	Flop	Flash and Flop
Revenue Flash	$70,000		$ 70,000
Revenue Flop		$ 50,000	50,000
Total Revenue	$70,000	$ 50,000	$120,000
Joint Cost	$60,000	$ 60,000	$ 60,000
Separable Cost Flash	10,000		10,000
Separable Cost Flop		20,000	20,000
Total Cost	$70,000	$ 80,000	$ 90,000
Total Profit (Loss)	$ —0—	$(30,000)	$ 30,000

Joint cost could have been allocated on the basis of ultimate market value, although the process becomes more complex, since the available sales prices reflect market values. Therefore, the separable costs must be deducted before determining the allocation.

Product	Expected Sales Revenue	Separable Costs	Adjusted Market Value
Flash	$70,000	$10,000	$60,000
Flop	$50,000	$20,000	$30,000

Then the allocation proceeds:

Product	Adjusted Market Value	Allocation Basis	Assigned Cost
Flash	$60,000	60,000/90,000 × $60,000	$40,000
Flop	30,000	30,000/90,000 × $60,000	20,000
	$90,000		$60,000

The cost assignment on this basis would significantly recast the profit calculations.

		Flash		Flop
Revenue		$70,000		$50,000
Joint Cost	$40,000		$20,000	
Separable Cost	10,000	50,000	20,000	40,000
Product Income		$20,000		$10,000

Allocated costs should be used only for information relating to inventory valuations required by law or custom, not for making decisions. For example, if the separable cost of producing Flop were $35,000 rather than $20,000, Flop would report a $5,000 loss, even though the firm as a whole is $15,000 more profitable with the continued sale of Flop than without it.

BY-PRODUCTS

By definition, a *by-product* is an offshooot of production that is of minor importance to the firm. Revenue generated from selling by-products can be accounted for in various ways. Because by-products are of slight consequence, however, the accounting practice that is used has only marginal significance.

Several situations affect the by-product valuation and accounting methods employed:

1. Value of by-product is uncertain at time of production.
2. Established market is available at split-off for by-products.
3. By-products are usable as substitutes for other materials.
4. By-products are alternatives to main products.
5. A separate profit and loss for by-products is needed for sales incentive or for control.[3]

In general, the cost-recovery methods treat the by-product revenue (or net realizable value) as a reduction in the cost of the main product. Perhaps the most popular technique is to subtract the by-product's **net realizable value** from the main product's total manufacturing cost. Market value of the by-product, less the separable costs needed to complete the by-product, is called the *net realizable value* of the by-product. This amount is used to reduce or offset the cost of manufacturing the main product.

Other cost-recovery methods treat the income from the by-product as additional revenue, other income, or a direct reduction to the cost of sales. In all cases, none of the joint cost is charged to the by-product. For inventory purposes, by-products are frequently valued at the separable costs associated with their completion, or are assigned a value of zero.

An example A company incurs $60,000 joint cost for an input that will produce 500 units of Product A, 2,500 units of Product B, and 3,000 units of Product C. Joint costs are allocated on the basis of proportionate output units. The per-unit sales prices at the split-off point are $2, $10, and $21, respectively, and all units are sold. If Products A, B, and C are accounted for as joint products, the cost allocation is determined as follows:

Product	Number of Units	Allocation Basis	Assigned Cost
A	500	500/6,000 × $60,000	$ 5,000
B	2,500	2,500/6,000 × $60,000	$25,000
C	3,000	3,000/6,000 × $60,000	$30,000
	6,000		$60,000

On the other hand, if Product A is considered to be a by-product, no joint cost will be allocated to it. Rather, the revenue from selling Product A, 500 units at $2 or $1,000, is treated as a cost recovery which reduces the remaining joint cost to $59,000. Alternately, the $1,000 cost recovery could be credited directly to

---

[3]*Research Series No. 31, Costing Joint Products* (New York: National Association of Accountants, 1957), pp. 13–24.

Cost of Goods Sold. This second alternative reduces computational complexity and, accordingly, is found more frequently in practice. Under this popular method, the joint costs (rounded) allocated to Products B and C can be calculated as follows:

Product	Number of Units	Allocation Basis	Assigned Cost
B	2,500	2,500/5,500 × $60,000	$27,273
C	3,000	3,000/5,500 × $60,000	$32,727
	5,500		$60,000

Exhibit 8–5 presents two different income statements which illustrate the joint product and by-product assumptions. The dollar amounts of both Revenue and Cost of Goods Sold reflect the different accounting methods used to allocate costs. Total gross profit is the same under each alternative solely because all units were sold, that is, none remained in inventory. Note that the individual gross profit numbers for Products B and C under the by-product method do not equal the total gross profit: the total reflects the cost recovered from Product A, but the individual gross profit figures do not. Furthermore, neither report in Exhibit 8–5 is especially useful for making decisions, e.g., the change in profitability of Product B from zero to a loss of $2,273 merely reflects differences in accounting procedures—nothing real is different. Decisions should be made without regard to allocated joint costs. Ordinarily, top-level management specifies whether a co-product is to be considered as a joint product or a by-product, and the managerial accountant implements the appropriate accounting procedures.

Inventory complications Sampson Company incurs a joint input cost of $36,000 in order to produce 2,000 units of Product X and 5,000 units of Product Y. Product X sells for $5 per unit, and Product Y sells for $10 per unit. During the year, 1,000 X and 4,000 Y were sold, and the remaining units are stored in inventory.

Under a joint-product assumption, joint costs could be allocated on the basis of relative market value (expected revenue), as follows:

Product	Expected Revenue	Allocation Basis	Assigned Cost	Units Produced	Cost per Unit
X	$10,000	10,000/60,000 × $36,000	$ 6,000	2,000	$3.00
Y	$50,000	50,000/60,000 × $36,000	$30,000	5,000	$6.00
	$60,000		$36,000		

The cost-per-unit numbers are used to assign production costs to Cost of Goods Sold and to Inventory.

EXHIBIT 8–5   INCOME STATEMENTS UNDER JOINT-PRODUCT AND BY-PRODUCT ASSUMPTIONS

Joint-Product Income Statement

REVENUE	A	B	C	Total
Product A, 500 @ $2	$1,000			
Product B, 2,500 @ $10		$25,000		
Product C, 3,000 @ $21			$63,000	$89,000
COST OF GOODS SOLD				
Joint Cost A	$5,000			
Joint Cost B		$25,000		
Joint Cost C			$30,000	
Separable Cost	—0—	—0—	—0—	
Total Cost				$60,000
GROSS PROFIT (LOSS)	($4,000)	—0—	$33,000	$29,000

By-Product Income Statement

REVENUE	B	C	Total
Product B, 2,500 @ $10	$25,000		
Product C, 3,000 @ $21		$63,000	$88,000
COST OF GOODS SOLD			
Joint Cost	$27,273		
Joint Cost		$32,727	$60,000
Less Cost Recovery A	—0—	—0—	1,000
Separable Cost	—0—	—0—	—0—
Total Cost	$27,273	$32,727	$59,000
GROSS PROFIT (LOSS)	($2,273)	$30,273	$29,000

	X	Y
Assigned Joint Cost	$6,000	$30,000
Inventory Cost		
1,000 @ $3	$3,000	
1,000 @ $6		$ 6,000
Cost of Goods Sold	$3,000	$24,000

A joint-product income statement could be prepared as follows:

	X	Y	Total
Revenue			
Product X (1,000 @ $5)	$5,000		
Product Y (4,000 @ $10)		$40,000	$45,000
Cost of Goods Sold			
Joint Cost X (1,000 @ $3)	$3,000		
Joint Cost Y (4,000 @ $6)		$24,000	
Separable Cost	-0-	-0-	
Total Cost			$27,000
Gross Profit	$2,000	$16,000	$18,000

In contrast, a by-product treatment of Product X would produce substantially different Inventory and Gross Profit figures.[4] None of the joint cost would be allocated to X: all of the joint cost would be assigned to Y, as follows:

Total Joint Cost	$36,000.00
÷Units of Y	5,000.00
Cost per unit of Y	$ 7.20

The 1,000 units of Y in ending inventory are valued at $7,200, while cost of Goods Sold (4,000 units) receives an initial assignment of $28,800. However, the net realizable value from the sale of Product X reduces the Cost of Goods Sold. A by-product income statement for the Sampson Company would appear as follows:

Revenue		
Product Y (4,000 @ $10)		$40,000
Cost of Goods Sold (4,000 @ $7.20)	$28,800	
− Cost recovery (1,000 @ $5)	5,000	23,800
Gross Profit		$16,200

The differences between joint and by-product accounting for the Sampson Company example can be summarized as follows: joint costing produced Gross Profit of $18,000 and total Inventory value for X and Y of $9,000, whereas by-product costing produced $16,200 Gross Profit and a $7,200 Inventory balance. The by-product method, in effect, reclassified $1,800 from Inventory to Cost of Goods Sold, thus reducing both inventory and profit values.

---

[4]The numbers used in this example are exaggerated to demonstrate the effect of alternative accounting treatments. Product X probably would never be treated as a by-product since its relative contribution to expected revenue is so large, i.e., 16.7%.

SUMMARY

Most manufacturing enterprises produce multiple outputs for a single input. The accountant must identify the joint costs associated with these inputs. Information releated to inventory valuation, product pricing, and income determination may require that joint costs be allocated. Allocation is fundamentally a subjective approach to distributing costs. The accountant identifies a secondary measure, such as relative weight, size, or value, and divides the joint cost in proportion to this secondary measure. Although allocated costs can provide useful information about a product or a department, they should not be made the basis for decisions. Chapter 14 describes procedures for making decisions on the basis of cost-benefit data.

APPENDIX: RECORDING JOINT-COST DATA

Manufacturing firms that produce joint products can use alternative methods to value their salable inventory. Inventory valuations should be entered into the accounting records to facilitate additional information-processing and financial-reporting activities.

Generally, the Inventory accounts will be affected by the valuation method used in the calculations. The following example illustrates the recording of joint and by-product costs.

An example   The George A. Pacific Company operates a tree farm and a sawmill. The cost of felling, transporting, and initially processing a section of trees is $6,000. Normally, a section of trees will yield the following:

- 20,000 pounds of bark, which is treated as a by-product and sold to another processor for $.15 a pound.[5]
- 35,000 board feet of plywood grade board, treated as a co-product.
- Additional processing costs for labor and applied overhead are $.05 per foot. Overhead is applied at the rate of 25% of labor cost. Plywood board may be sold for $.20 per board foot.
- 70,000 board feet of No. 1 grade planking, also treated as a co-product. The additional processing costs for labor and applied overhead are $.04 per foot. Planking may be sold for $.16 per board foot.

The Company uses a cost-recovery method in accounting for the by-product (bark) and a physical measure to allocate joint costs between the co-products

---

[5]The numbers used in this example are exaggerated to demonstrate the effect of alternative accounting treatments. The assumed prices in the example allow bark to be more profitable than planking, so bark would not be treated as a by-product.

(plywood and planking). Process 1 separates the joint input into the three products. Plywood board is then shipped to Process 2, while planking goes to Process 3.

The Company uses a process cost-accounting system because the production is continuous and all units of each output are similar. The total cost of production—$10,550 ($6,000 joint cost and $4,550 of separable cost related to the co-products)—would flow through the finished-goods inventory.

A Work-in-Process Inventory account accumulates cost information for all products. The following entry reflects the incurrence of joint production costs.

Process 1	6,000	
Payroll		4,800
Overhead Applied		1,200

A. (To record the joint cost of harvesting a section of trees.)

Accounting for the co-products   Before the separable costs relating to each of the co-products are accumulated, joint cost will be assigned to each of them. The George A. Pacific Company allocates joint cost on the basis of board foot composition of the co-products:

Product	Board Feet	Allocation Basis	Assigned Cost
Plywood	35,000	35,000/105,000 × $6,000	$2,000
Planking	70,000	70,000/105,000 × $6,000	4,000
	105,000		$6,000

The following entry transfers the joint cost of Process 1 to Processes 2 and 3 respectively:

Process 2—Plywood	2,000	
Process 3—Planking	4,000	
Process 1		6,000

B. (To allocate the joint cost between the co-products.)

Separable processing costs may then be accumulated in the respective accounts:

Process 2—Plywood	1,750	
Payroll		1,400
Overhead Applied		350

C. (To record the separable costs of producing plywood.)

Process 3—Planking	2,800	
Payroll		2,240
Overhead Applied		560

D. (To record the separable costs of producing planking.)

The labor cost amounts would be supported by time cards or other objective evidence. Overhead has been applied at the predetermined rate of 25% of the direct labor cost.

After both wood products have been processed, they will be transferred to finished-goods inventory at the total cost accumulated in the respective accounts.

Finished-Goods Inventory	10,550	
Process 2—Plywood		3,750
Process 3—Planking		6,800

E. (To record the transfer of completed products to the finished-goods inventory.)

Note that the charge to the Finished-Goods Inventory account does not reflect the allocation calculation; the total production cost is included in this account. Subsidiary records would be maintained for each product so that cost of sales could be determined as goods are sold.

Accounting for the by-product   There are alternative ways to account for by-products. One method assigns some cost to the by-product in a manner similar to that employed for the co-products. This example, however, illustrates a popular cost-recovery method. In essence, this method treats the revenue derived from by-product sales as a reduction in the costs associated with other joint products. Depending upon a managerial decision, this reduction could be made against manufacturing costs (Process 1 in this example) or against Cost of Goods Sold. Since the original joint costs usually have been transferred to other accounts by the time a by-product is sold, most often cost-recovery methods adjust the Cost of Goods Sold account.

If the latter approach were used, the following entry would be made when the by-product is sold:

| Cash | 3,000 | |
| Cost of Goods Sold | | 3,000 |

F. (To record the sale of the by-product, as a cost recovery, 20,000 @ $.15 = $3,000.)

Crediting Cost of Goods Sold reduces the balance of the account, which in turn, will increase the profitability of the co-products. When the plywood and planking are sold, the accounting records will recognize revenue of $18,200 ($7,000 for plywood and $11,200 for planking) to be matched against the accumulated cost. The two related entries follow:

Cash	18,200	
Sales Revenue		18,200
G. (To record the revenue associated with the sale of plywood and planking.)		

Cost of Goods Sold	10,550	
Finished-Goods Inventory		10,550
H. (To recognize the cost of the plywood and the planking involved in the sale.)		

Profitability may be determined by matching the sales revenue and the cost of goods sold. Recognize that the balance in the Cost of Goods Sold account is $7,550—the difference between the co-product cost and the cost recovered from the sale of the by-product.

Sales Revenue	18,200	
Cost of Goods Sold		7,550
Profit on Sale		10,650
I. (To record profit on the sale of the co-products.)		

The basic flow of joint-cost information through the accounts is illustrated in Exhibit 8-6. The flow parallels the sequence of journal entries made in the example.

SUGGESTED READINGS

Harris, Jr., William T., and Wayne R. Chapin. "Joint Product Costing." *Management Accounting*, April 1973.

Hartley, Ronald V. "Decision Making When Joint Products Are Involved." *The Accounting Review*, October 1971.

Moriarity, Shane. "Another Approach to Allocating Joint Costs." *The Accounting Review*, October 1975.

QUESTIONS

8-1   Define the following terms:

EXHIBIT 8–6   ACCOUNTING SEQUENCE FOR JOINT COSTS

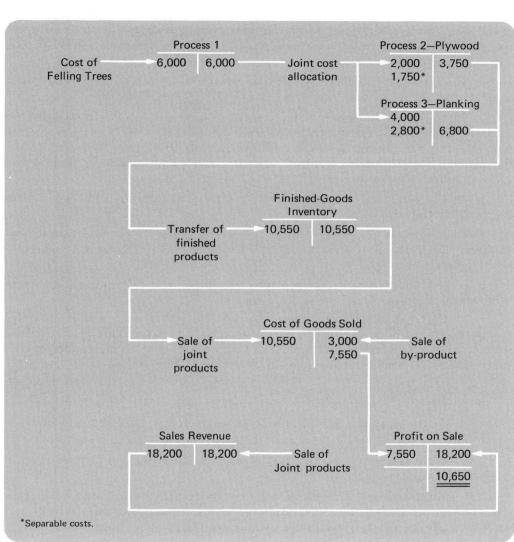

*Separable costs.

(A) Joint cost
(B) Joint product
(C) By-product
(D) Major product
(E) Co-product

8–2   Discuss the concept of the common cost and explain its relationship to joint products.

8–3   Which basic types of managerial decisions must be made in joint-product situations? Explain how these are related to characteristics of the inputs into manufacturing.

8–4   Joint costs are also classified as nontraceable and nonseparable costs. Why?

8–5   Suppose that a firm produces two co-products and wants to use the ultimate market value technique for allocating common costs. If an intermediate market exists for one of the products and not for the other, how should the managerial accountant determine the allocation basis? Briefly defend the reasonableness of your answer.

8–6   List four factors that influence by-product valuation and the accounting methods that will be used.

8–7   Identify and briefly discuss the methods used in accounting for by-products. Since alternative methods produce different costs, why is a particular method used?

8–8   (A) Differentiate between joint products and by-products. List one criterion for making such a differentiation.

(B) By-products that require no additional processing after the point of separation are often accounted for by assigning them a value of zero at the product separation and reducing cost of production as sales are made. Justify the treatment. Discuss the possible shortcomings of the treatment.

(AICPA adapted)

8–9   Discuss two approaches to product cost accounting for by-products.

8–10   In the case of joint products, all costs before the split-off point are (common/separate) while all costs after this point are (common/separate).

8–11   What is *allocation*? In what situations can allocation techniques provide cost information for joint products?

8–12   Although cost allocations are used frequently to provide information about joint products, is this information useful for decision-making? Why or why not? What are the limitations on the usefulness of cost allocations?

8–13   From what sources do the managerial accountant collect basic cost information about joint products?

8–14   How can the managerial accountant defend common-cost allocations? Are such defenses necessary?

8–15   What are the two basic approaches to cost allocation? Briefly explain each and list their similarities and differences.

EXERCISES

8–16 A firm produces two products, Product 1 and Product 2, through a joint process. The cost of the joint processing is $100,000. At the split-off point, the products have the following characteristics:

	Units Produced	Product Weight (lbs.)	Product Volume (gals.)	Market Value
Product 1	10,000	20,000	20,000	$250,000
Product 2	20,000	20,000	60,000	$150,000

From this information, allocate the common cost between these products, using the following techniques:

  (A) Units produced
  (B) Relative weights
  (C) Relative volumes
  (D) Market values

Which technique best allocates the common cost? Why?

8–17 A joint process yields two products, named Won and Tu, which can be sold at the split-off point for $2 a unit and $5 a unit, respectively. If these products are processed further, they can be sold for $7 and $8 a unit, respectively. The variable costs of processing Won and Tu through the additional departments are estimated at $4 per unit. Which product or combination of products should the company produce? Support your answer with appropriate calculations.

8–18 Cal Will, a gunsmith in northern Michigan, must decide whether to diversify his operations and, if so, how to diversify them. He can just repair guns, or he can repair and sell guns, or he can repair and sell guns and sell other sporting supplies as well. The revenue for repairing guns is $10,000 a year. Selling guns would add another $5,000, and selling sporting equipment could add a further $15,000. The added expense for a stock of guns would be $4,000 over the $2,000 cost incurred for providing the repair service. Adding sporting goods would necessitate an additional annual expenditure of $16,000. Existing overhead costs amount to $8,000.

  (A) Evaluate the three situations: repair only, repair and sell guns, or repair and sell guns and other sporting supplies. Which alternative is relatively most profitable?

  (B) Joint-cost information is most useful for which of the following functions of managerial accounting: planning, information-processing, control, or decision-making?

8–19 Joint products result (1) when an input unit represents a cluster of product potential, or (2) when it has the potential to yield different outputs, according to the method of processing. In each of the following cases, use the terms "cluster" or "potential" to identify the characteristics of the input:

(A) Raw milk delivered to a dairy
(B) Iron ore at a steel mill
(C) Trees harvested by a saw mill
(D) Animal pelts acquired by a furrier
(E) Wool yarn delivered to a carpet mill

8–20 The product costing procedures used in accounting for joint products seem to be different from those used in single-product situations. In many respects, however, they are similar. For each of the activities listed below, indicate whether or not the accounting procedures are different in the joint-product and individual-product situations. If they are different, briefly explain the differences.

(A) Sources of cost information
(B) Recording cost information
(C) Determining product costs
(D) Determining the cost of a manufacturing process
(E) Decision-makers' uses of the product cost information

*8–21 The Harbison Company manufactures two sizes of plate glass, which are produced simultaneously in the manufacturing process. Since the small sheets of plate glass are cut from large sheets that have flaws in them, the joint costs are allocated equally to each good sheet, large and small, produced. The difference in after-split-off costs for large and small sheets is substantial.

In 19X6, the Company decided to increase its efforts to sell the large sheets, because they produced a larger gross margin than did the small sheets. Accordingly, the amount of the fixed advertising budget devoted to large sheets was increased, and the amount devoted to small sheets was decreased. No changes were made in sales prices.

By midyear, the production scheduling department had increased the monthly production of large sheets in order to stay above the minimum inventory level. However, it also had cut back the monthly production of small sheets because the inventory ceiling had been reached.

At the end of 19X6, the net result of the change in product mix was a decrease of $112,000 in gross margin. Although sales of large sheets had increased 34,500 units, sales of small sheets had decreased 40,200 units.

(A) Distinguish between joint costs and after-split-off costs.

(B) In developing weights for allocating joint costs to joint products, why is the relative sales value of each joint product usually reduced by its after-split-off-costs?

(C) Identify the mistake that the Harbison Company made in deciding to change its product mix and explain why it caused a smaller gross margin for 19X6.

(AICPA adapted)

8-22 The Zeta Corporation produces three different products: A, B, and C. Zeta uses market valuation allocation, which requires that separable costs after the split-off point be subtracted from the final market price. In 19X4, the Corporation expects A to earn $150,000, B to earn $100,000, and C to earn $70,000 in gross revenues. The separable costs associated with these products are: $50,000 for A, $40,000 for B, and $40,000 for C. Joint costs amount to $100,000.

(A) Using Zeta Corporation's method, compute the allocation of joint costs. Compute the product income for the three products.

(B) Would this analysis be sufficient to make a decision on whether to drop one of the three products? Explain why or why not.

†(C) Prepare journal entries to record the cost allocation.

8-23 The Mix-Well Corporation is a large chemical company that treats some of its products as by-products. The net realizable value of the by-product is used to offset the production cost of the main product. Thus, no profit or loss is attributable to sales of the by-product. One by-product, an oil additive, produces revenue of $61,000. The expected revenue of the main product is $1,500,000. Common input cost is $1,300,000. The separable cost for the by-product is $40,000.

(A) What is the net realizable value of the by-product?

(B) What is the inventory value for the main product before any sales but after all costs have been considered?

(C) How much of the joint costs are assigned to the by-product?

(D) Why is cost allocation considered fundamentally a subjective approach to dividing costs?

†(E) Prepare journal entries to record the cost allocation.

8-24 A company has four joint products: Keena, Zeena, Deena, and Meena. The total product weight at the split-off point is 10,000 lbs., with Keena weighing 4,000 lbs.; Deena, 3,000 lbs.; Zeena, 2,000 lbs.; and Meena, 1,000 lbs. After further processing, Keena weighs 3,000 lbs.; Deena, 2,000 lbs.; Zeena, 1,500 lbs.; and Meena, 500 lbs. The joint costs to be allocated total $140,000.

(A) How would the costs be allocated using a physical measure?

(B) Assuming an ultimate market value of $50,000 for Keena, $30,000 for Deena, $60,000 each for both Zeena and Meena, how would costs be allocated under the market value approach?

(C) What assumptions must be made when selecting a physical measure for cost allocation?

(D) What assumptions are needed when selecting a market value method for cost allocation?

8–25 The diagram below relates to the manufacturing operations of the Bent Joint Company. Use this diagram to answer the following questions about the Bent Joint Company:

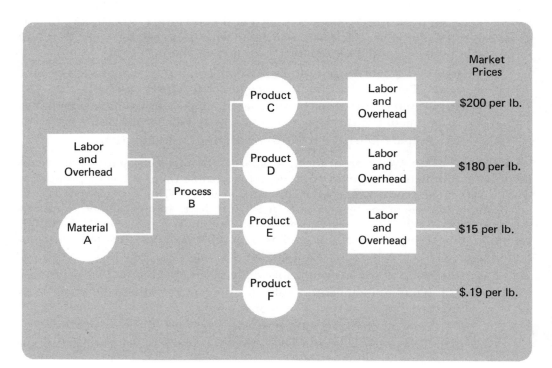

(A) What type of process is Process B?

(B) What is Product C?

(C) What can Product C and D be called? Why?

(D) What can Product E be called? Is it different from Products C and D? Why or why not?

(E) What is Product F?

(F) Indicate the split-off point in this operation.

8–26 Cope Co. buys 8,000 lbs. of input for $40,000. Cope plans to use 6,000 lbs. of this input to make 1,000 units of Product Y; the remaining 2,000 lbs. will be used to make 4,000 units of Product Z. Product Y will sell for $30 per unit and Z for $5 per unit. If $5,000 of additional processing is done to Y, it can be sold for $32 per unit. If $15,000 of additional processing is done to Z, it can be sold for $10 per unit.

(A) By what dollar amount will profits change if additional processing is done to Product Y or Z?

(B) For income determination purposes, joint costs are allocated to both products. Determine the profits for Products Y and Z, assuming that Cope Co. will elect to do additional processing only if profits will be increased, and that joint costs will be allocated on the basis of input weight.

(C) What are the profits on Products Y and Z, assuming that additional processing will be done only if profits will be increased, and that joint costs will be allocated on the basis of relative revenue dollars at the split-off point?

PROBLEMS

8–27   A process used by Ajak Corp. takes a common material input and produces four joint products: A, B, C, and D. 20,000 lbs. of raw material are sufficient to produce 10,000 lbs. of A, 5,000 lbs. of B, 2,000 lbs. of C, and 3,000 lbs. of D. Each output has a per-pound market value of $1, $2, $3, and $4, respectively, and raw material costs $1.50 per pound. Use the form illustrated in Exhibit 8–2 for analysis.

(A) Using the ultimate market value method of allocating joint costs to co-products, determine the gross profit for each product.

(B) Should Ajak Corp. discontinue production of Product A, since its market value is only $1 per pound and the raw material costs $1.50 per pound? Explain.

(C) What is the maximum separable cost Ajak should incur to produce and sell Product B, above and beyond its share of the joint cost? Does your answer depend upon the particular joint-cost allocation method used by Ajak?

(D) What is the joint cost per pound of Product D, assuming that joint costs are allocated according to the relative weight of each co-product? Should this value be given any consideration when determining a sales price for Product D?

†(E) Prepare journal entries to record the acquisition of 20,000 pounds of raw material, the production of all outputs, and the transfer of costs to Cost of Goods Sold, assuming that joint costs are allocated according to the relative weight of each co-product.

8–28   The Alphabet Company produces two joint products and one by-product through a single manufacturing division. The cost associated with operations in this division, Division A, is $30,500. The by-product, Product X, sells on the market for $2 a unit without additional processing. During the current period, 1,000 units of Product X were produced and 500 units were sold; the rest of the units will be sold in the near future. Selling expenses for Product X, consisting mainly of commissions, were $500. The co-products, Product Y and Product Z, are independently processed through separate divisions beyond the split-off point. The relevant information about these products is summarized below (the Alphabet Company has a policy of recognizing neither a profit nor a loss on sales of Product X):

	Cost of Additional Processing	Quantity Produced (units)	Quantity Sold (units)	Selling Costs	Selling Price (per unit)
Product Y	$10,000	25,000	12,500	$ 5,000	$40
Product Z	$20,000	50,000	25,000	$10,000	$20

Using this information, answer the following questions. Show calculations.

(A) How much cost will be assigned to Product X?

(B) Compute the cost to be assigned to Products Y and Z, using the ultimate market value method.

(C) Determine the profitability of Products Y and Z, given your answers to parts (A) and (B), above.

(D) Compute the cost that will be assigned to Products Y and Z if a physical measure method is used. Assume that Product Y weighs 2 lbs. per unit and Product Z weighs 4 lbs. per unit.

8–29 The LaBreck Company's joint cost of producing 1,000 units of Product A, 500 units of Product B, and 500 units of Product C is $100,000. The per-unit sales values of the three products at the split-off point are Product A—$20; Product B—$200; Product C—$160. Ending inventories include 100 units of Product A, 300 units of Product B, and 200 units of Product C.

(A) Compute the amount of joint cost that would be included in the ending inventory valuation of the three products, (a) on the basis of their relative sales value, and (b) on the basis of physical units.

(B) Discuss the relative merits of each of these two bases of joint-cost allocation, (a) for financial-statement purposes, and (b) for decisions about the desirability of selling joint products at the split-off point or processing them further.

(C) Assume that Product A is treated as a by-product and joint cost is allocated on the basis of physical units. Determine the following dollar amounts: Sales Revenue, Cost of Goods Sold, and Ending Inventory Valuation of Products A, B, and C.

(AICPA adapted)

8–30   Miller Manufacturing Company buys zeon for $.80 a gallon. At the end of processing in Department 1, zeon splits off into products A, B, and C. Product A is sold at the split-off point without further processing. Products B and C require further processing before they can be sold; Product B is processed in Department 2, and Product C is processed in Department 3. Following is a summary of costs and other related data for the year ended June 30, 19X3.

| | Department | | |
	1	2	3
Cost of zeon	$96,000	—	—
Direct labor	$14,000	$15,000	$65,000
Manufacturing overhead	$10,000	$21,000	$25,000

| | Products | | |
	A	B	C
Gallons sold	20,000	30,000	45,000
Gallons on hand at June 30, 1973	10,000	—	15,000
Sales in dollars	$30,000	$75,000	$135,000

There were no inventories on hand at July 1, 19X2, and there was no zeon on hand at June 30, 19X3. All gallons on hand at June 30, 19X3, were complete as to processing. Miller uses the relative sales-value method of allocating joint costs.

(A) Assuming that Product A is a joint product, allocate Department 1 costs to Products A, B, and C.

(B) Given your answer to part A above, determine the gross profit and inventory balances for the year ended June 30.

(C) Recalculate A and B above, assuming that Product A is a by-product rather than a joint product.

(AICPA adapted)

8–31   The MCB Corportation produces one principal product—"Main-Line." Incidental to this production are two additional products—"Co-Line" and "By-Line." Material is started in Process No. 1; the three products come out of this process. "Main-Line" is processed further through Process No. 2; "Co-Line" is processed further through Process No. 3; while "By-Line" is sold without further processing. The following data for February are available:

1. Material put in Process No. 1, $12,000.
2. Conversion costs: Process No. 1, $8,000; Process No. 2, $4,000; Process No. 3, $300.
3. There were no beginning or ending in-process inventories.
4. Production and sales data:

	Quantity Produced	Quantity Sold	February Average Sales Price	Market Price End of February
Main-Line	5,000	4,000	$6.00	$6.00
Co-Line	3,000	2,000	1.00	.90
By-Line	1,000	900	.50	.55

5. Selling and administrative expenses are related to the quantity sold. Selling and administrative expenses for the next period are estimated to be the same as actual expenses for February.

Main-Line	$2,000
Co-Line	800
By-Line	36

6. Standard net profit on Co-Line is 10% of sales.

7. No profit or loss is realized on By-Line sales.

(A) Compute the value of the By-Line inventory and the costs transferred from Process No. 1 to By-Line units during the period.

(B) Compute the value of the Co-Line inventory and the costs transferred from Process No. 1 to Co-Line units during the period.

(C) Copy and complete the following income statement:

	Main-Line	Co-Line	By-Line	Total
Sales				
Cost of Goods Sold				
Gross Profit				
Selling & Administrative Expenses				
Net Profit				

(AICPA adapted)

8-32   The Phast Buck Sales Company sells pretzels and potato chips in 5-lb. cans to regular customers on established routes. Sales and deliveries are handled by drivers of Phast Buck's two trucks. Pretzels and chips are purchased by the Company from a local supplier for $3 a can; in turn, pretzels are sold for $5 a can and potato chips for $4 a can by the driver-salesmen. Until recently, the Phast Buck Company sold a total of 100 cans of pretzels and 100 cans of chips per week. Expenses for operating the trucks amount to $300 a week.

Recently, the owner of the company, Mr. Rob Spindle, asked his bookkeeper, Miss Girtie Track, to allocate the operating expenses among the products sold. Her analysis is presented below.

	Product Weight	Allocation Basis	Assigned Cost	Adjusted Market Value	Allocation Basis	Assigned Cost
Pretzels	500	500/1,000	$150	$200	200/300	$200
Potato Chips	500	500/1,000	$150	$100	100/300	$100
	1,000			$300		

PRODUCT PROFITABILITY

	Physical Measure		Profitability Measure	
	Pretzels	Chips	Pretzels	Chips
Sales Revenue	$500	$400	$500	$400
Product Cost	300	300	300	300
Gross Margin	$200	$100	$200	$100
Allocated Cost	150	150	200	100
Net Profit (loss)	$ 50	$ (50)	-0-	-0-

Potato chips were clearly a loss for the company, so Mr. Spindle discontinued deliveries of them in an effort to increase profits. Sales of pretzels stayed the same, but during the first week of the new policy, instead of making money, the Company lost $100.

(A) Did Miss Track make an error in allocating the operating cost?
(B) What is the problem with Mr. Spindle's decision?
(C) Were the operating costs a joint cost? Why or why not?
(D) How should the costs have been allocated?
(E) What should Mr. Spindle do now?

8–33 The Town Company manufactures two principal products, X and M, and a by-product known as Bypo. The Company has three producing departments, Departments 101, 201, and 301. Raw materials A and B are started in process in Department 101. Upon completion of processing in that department, one-fifth of the material is by-product and is transferred directly to stock. One-third of the remaining output of Department 101 goes to Department 201, where it is made into X, and the other two-thirds goes to Department 301, where it becomes M. The processing of X in Department 201 results in a 50% gain in weight of material transferred into the department owing to the addition of water at the start of the processing. There is no gain or loss of weight in the other processes.

The Company considers the income from Bypo, after allowing five cents per pound for estimated selling and delivery costs, to be a reduction of the cost of the two principal products. The Company assigns Department 101 costs to the two principal products in proportion to their net sales value at point of separation, computed by deducting costs to be incurred in subsequent processes from the sales value of the products.

The following information concerns the operations during April 19X1:

INVENTORIES

	March 31		April 30
	Quantity (Pounds)	Value	Quantity (Pounds)
Department 101	None		None
Department 201	800	$17,160	1,000
Department 301	200	2,340	360
Finished stock—X	300	7,260	800
Finished stock—M	1,200	18,550	700
Finished stock—Bypo	None		None

Inventories in process are estimated to be one-half complete in Departments 201 and 301, both at the first and last of the month.

COSTS

	Material Used	Labor and Overhead
Department 101	$134,090	$87,442
Department 201	—	31,950
Department 301	—	61,880

The material used in department 101 weighed 18,000 pounds.

SALES PRICES

X	$29.50 per pound
M	17.50 per pound
Bypo	.50 per pound

Prices as of April 30 are unchanged from those in effect during the month.

You are to prepare the following statements covering the operations of the Town Company. Present all supporting computations in good form.

(A) Statement showing costs and production by departments for the month of April. The company uses first-in, first-out to cost out production.

(B) A schedule of inventory values for work in process and finished goods as of April 30.

(AICPA adapted)

CHAPTER 9

Direct Costing Reports for Decision Analysis

Objectives

*After studying this
chapter, you should be
able to do the following:*

Identify the information needs of internal decision makers.

*Distinguish between problem-oriented and person-oriented reporting
procedures.*

Relate the format of a report to its intended effect.

Describe the contribution-margin report form.

*Extend the contribution-margin approach to direct costing and contrast it to
conventional absorption costing.*

In the normal course of business, managerial accountants observe and process specific information about the organization and report their observations to the firm's decision-makers. The preceding chapters of this section dealt primarily with the accountant's processing activities — collecting, recording, and summarizing data. These data must be presented to management in a useful form.

For example, consider the case of a divisional manager who requests sales information so that he may evaluate a pricing policy. The accountant could present a report to him documenting each sales transaction of each division for the last five years. Obviously, such a report would be useless; the sheer volume of data would exceed the manager's comprehension. However, the same information, summarized and condensed, could be very useful to the manager. The *form* of the report can be just as important as its *content*.

This chapter focuses on some problems of reporting, describing methods of reporting that highlight information relevant to decision-making.

REQUIREMENTS OF THE DECISION-MAKER

Decision-making can be viewed as a threefold activity involving: (1) identifying a problem, (2) selecting an appropriate **decision rule**, and (3) processing available information. Basic problems are often obvious to a decision-maker: at other times, a problem may not become apparent until information has been processed. For example, production delays might become obvious immediately, but declining profits might not be noticed until an income statement has been prepared and reviewed.

Once a problem has been identified, the decision-maker must take remedial action. In some cases, company policy might specify a predetermined decision rule for solving particular problems. A decision rule provides a means of selecting an alternative (or making a decision) on the basis of the available information. A decision rule might take the following form: "Always select the alternative with the least cost (or fastest payback or least risk)."

After selecting an appropriate decision rule, the decision-maker must obtain information about the problem. Information can aid in selecting an alternative only if it is: (1) available when it is needed (*timely*), (2) related clearly to the immediate problem (*relevant*), and (3) in a form complementary to the decision rule (*useful*).

Lacking appropriate information at the time decisions are made can be a serious hindrance to managers. Thus, managerial accountants frequently organize a set of internal procedures to ensure timely processing of data. Some data, such as product costs, may be collected on a routine basis, whereas other information, such as capital budgets, is derived from special analysis.

The information supplied to the decision-maker must be *relevant to the problem*; irrelevant information could actually lead a manager to make an incorrect decision. For example, assume that a manager makes production decisions based on the expected break-even point of one product manufactured in his plant. If the accountant reports fixed costs for other products, this *spurious* or *irrelevant information* could cause the manager to arrive at an incorrect decision.

The form in which information is reported can be as important as the content of the report. Reports that fail to emphasize clearly the key variables relating to a decision may prove to be of marginal value to the decision-maker. A good report presents relevant information in a usable form.

Cost and revenue data often must be assigned to individual divisions of the firm. Decisions related to the object of such assignments can concern products, departments, or processes. *Assignment promotes reporting that will be relevant to the decision*; it supports reporting based on segments of the firm. The physical arrangements of such reports can vary. How the information is arranged influences the report's usefulness. Thus, the *form of presentation* can be designed to make the information *relevant to the user*.

REPORT FORMAT

Report format refers to the physical arrangement and the means of presenting the data. The arrangement can affect the way a reader will behave or react to the reported information. There are many possible formats for constructing a report. One common form of reporting is the *quantitative presentation.* A quantitative presentation is generally used to portray accounting data that can be expressed as numbers. Quantitative data can be arranged in many ways. The particular format emphasizes some aspect of the data and draws the user's attention to particular items or to an item's particular characteristics.

Accounting reports commonly group costs by some classification, such as cost behavior, control responsibility, time span, relation to product, and so on. Many possible classifications have been discussed in this text (see Exhibit 9–1). Each classification basis was designed to serve a different purpose and thus can have a different influence on the reader of the report. If costs on an income statement are classified as fixed or variable, the reader can use the data for planning purposes, but they are not especially useful for product costing or control.

Control responsibility, used as a basis of classification, emphasizes the degree of control that the user exerts over a particular cost. Classifying costs on this basis directs a user's attention primarily to the controllable items in the report. Control concepts are discussed in more detail in Section Four of this book.

EXHIBIT 9–1   ALTERNATE MEANS OF CLASSIFYING COSTS

Basis of Classification	Classes	Primary Purpose
Cost Behavior	Fixed cost, Variable cost, Mixed cost	Planning
Control Responsibility	Controllable cost, Noncontrollable cost	Control
Time Span of Control	Committed cost, Discretionary cost	Decision Making
Objectivity of Assignment	Traceable cost, Nontraceable cost	Product Costing
Relation to Product	Direct cost, Prime cost, Indirect cost	Product Costing
Activity Relationship	Manufacturing cost, Selling cost, Administrative cost	Income Determination

Classifying costs according to the *time span of control* generally serves a useful function: Decisions focus on the discretionary costs (changeable in the short run) rather than on the committed costs (unchangeable in the short run, but reflecting past decisions). In each case, the basis of classification should be apparent in the report format. The format influences the user's perception of the data. The data contained in a report could be disclosed in many forms, each having a different potential impact. The managerial accountant must recognize the importance to the entire reporting process of the report's structure. Variations in form can either reveal or obscure information for decision-makers. One format, the contribution approach, combines allocation and format considerations to support the tactical decision-making process within the firm.

THE CONTRIBUTION APPROACH

The basis of the **contribution approach** is the contribution margin (discussed in Chapter 4). The contribution margin is the difference between product revenues and variable costs, and represents the amount available for meeting fixed costs and profit expectations. The contribution approach emphasizes cost-volume-profit relationships, which are critical to many decisions within an organization. These decisions must necessarily focus on costs and revenues that can be altered in the short run. Except for certain contractual situations, per-unit revenue can be changed by adjusting the selling price. On the other hand, fixed costs reflect resource commitments over an extended time. For the most part, changes in fixed costs cannot be made in the short run. Variable costs, directly associated with output, generally are subject to immediate change by the organization's management—input quantities, acquisitions of both labor and material, and the types of material and labor acquired all can be altered.

Most short-run operating decisions have an immediate influence on the firm's revenues and/or variable costs. Therefore, the relationships among these elements are (or should be) important inputs into the decision-making process. The contribution approach to reporting can help managerial accountants present cost-volume-profit information in a form relevant to the decision-maker, without obscuring other classes of information.

Report structure   The contribution report identifies the relationships between product revenues and variable costs for segments of an enterprise. This approach can be contrasted to the traditional format of an income statement. Both forms are illustrated in the diagram below.

TRADITIONAL STATEMENT		CONTRIBUTION STATEMENT	
Sales Revenue	$XXX	Sales Revenue	$XXX
Cost of Goods Sold	XX	Variable Costs	XX
Gross Margin	$ XX	Contribution Margin	$ XX
Selling and Administrative		Fixed Costs	X
Costs	X	Net Income	$ X
Net Income	$ X		

Although each form could be expanded by including additional sub-classes of data, basic distinctions are evident in the illustration. The traditional income statement emphasizes the firm's fundamental activities, for example, producing, selling, and administering. Costs are classified by their relationship to these activities. Groupings relate costs to the manufacturing processes (cost of goods sold) and to the selling and administrative functions (selling and administrative expenses). In contrast, the contribution approach emphasizes cost behavior in relation to volume—variable costs and fixed costs are the main classifications. The contribution approach serves two purposes. First, variable costs are subject to short-run alteration and control. The format clearly identifies these costs. Second, fixed costs, which are necessary to support short-run activities, provide information to the decision-maker about organizational capacity; these costs are clearly shown also.

The contribution statement   The contribution approach gives the managerial accountant many opportunities to enhance the effectiveness of a report. As an example, consider the divisional income statement presented in Exhibit 9–2. This income statement displays a typical contribution format, which has many advantages for the user. Actual performance results are reported in total and also on a divisional basis. The assigned data enable a decision-maker to evaluate activities of individual divisions in context with similar activities. Such information can be extremely useful in determining the importance of a particular product or in judging the efficiency of a divisional manager.

The contribution format uses cost classifications to present the information to the user of the report. In Exhibit 9–2, several means have been used to classify and sub-classify the data. These include the following:

1. *Cost behavior.* This main classification basis identifies the costs as fixed or variable. This distinction is used to calculate a **contribution margin** and highlights cost-volume-profit relationships for planning purposes.

EXHIBIT 9–2   THE CONTRIBUTION APPROACH

	Total	Division 1	Division 2
Net Sales	$30,000	$10,000	$20,000
Variable Cost:			
Manufacturing	15,000	5,000	10,000
Transportation	1,500	500	1,000
Administrative	2,250	750	1,500
Contribution Margin	$11,250	$ 3,750	$ 7,500
Controllable Fixed Costs (discretionary):			
Marketing	1,000	500	500
Research	1,250	250	1,000
Short-Run Performance Margin	$ 9,000	$ 3,000	$ 6,000
Traceable Fixed Costs (committed):			
Depreciation	900	500	400
Insurance	1,200	200	1,000
Segment Margin	$ 6,900	$ 2,300	$ 4,600
Assigned Costs:			
Maintenance	600	200	400
Executive Salaries	1,500	500	1,000
Net Income before Taxes	$ 4,800	$ 1,600	$ 3,200
Income Tax	2,400		
Net Income after Taxes	$ 2,400		

2. *Control responsibility.* Fixed costs are identified as controllable or, by implication, noncontrollable by the management of the divisions. This distinction emphasizes responsibility and helps to measure the efficiency or effectiveness of managerial activities.

3. *Time span of control.* The fixed costs are further classified as either programmed or committed. This identifies for the decision maker cost data that are subject to periodic change (discretionary costs) and cost data that reflect long-term organizational commitments (committed costs).

4. *Objectivity of assignment.* Since the basic data have been assigned among segments of the firm, the traceability of the cost items to these segments is indicated. A distinction is made between traceable fixed costs and non-traceable fixed costs that have been allocated to the segments.

The various margins, or subtotals, presented in the statement can be used for evaluation.

The contribution margin   Chapter 4 emphasized the importance of the contribution margin to cost-volume-profit analysis concerning a product. The same analysis can be extended to encompass divisions, entire product lines, and other larger segments of the firm. The contribution margin represents an amount available to cover the fixed costs and profits of the firm. Obviously, a segment that does not have a positive contribution margin should be discontinued unless it is vital to other parts of the organization that are profitable.

Short-run decisions generally consider revenues and variable costs. Since the contribution margin emphasizes this relationship, the information is extremely useful for decisions concerning segments of the organization. The effect of previous decisions is also readily apparent in the contribution margin. Control can be made more efficient if managers review the comparative results of various segments of the firm.

Short-run performance margin   The **short-run performance margin** helps evaluate divisional management. Included in the computation are revenues, variable costs, and discretionary fixed costs that are traceable to some individual's responsibility.

The report in Exhibit 9–2 identifies costs that are subject to short-run change by decision-makers, and thus, subject to short-run decisions. Also, past performance can be readily evaluated on the basis of the information. Separating traceable items that can be altered by operating decisions highlights these costs for the user.

Segment margin   The **segment margin** expands the divisional cost analysis to include elements of traceable fixed costs that reflect long-term commitments.

Normally, committed fixed costs arise from decisions relating to capacity that are made at higher organizational levels. The purpose of presenting this information is twofold. First, employees at the operating level are made aware of the organization's long-term commitments. The data clearly reflect the amount and cost of support that the organization gives to the division. Thus, operating managers are shown how important the total organization is to the division. Second, the segment margin can be used by higher-level management to review previous decisions concerning committed cost levels in relation to current divisional performance. This method emphasizes the success or failure of these decisions and supplies a basis for future decisions.

Net income   Many contribution statements stop with the segment margin; that is, they do not assign nontraceable costs to divisions. This suggests that individual managers are not responsible for reported performance that includes subjective cost assignments. Some decisions concerning long-run strategies can benefit from total information inputs, however. For example, allocated costs can be used effectively if the decision-maker is aware of the nature of the cost and the basis for the assignment.

Income taxes and **net income** after taxes complete the statement. The contribution report presents complete information for decision-making and control. The emphasis on segment contributions makes the report well suited for short-run, or tactical, decision-making.

Types of reports   The contribution format just described segments operations by divisions. Many other types of segmentation can be made. For example, tabulations by product line, sales territory, or salesman also could provide useful information for a firm's marketing department. These reports may provide insights for decisions about advertising emphasis, selling effort, compensation plans, and so on. Similarly, a segmentation by production facility, type of operation, or production managers could be used readily by the production departments. These reports could assist in scheduling production, determining process efficiency, or evaluating personnel.

At higher levels, information could be summarized and reported by major types of activities: marketing, production, administration, and research and development. In each case, the contribution report can present information in a relevant context to the appropriate decision-makers.

INVENTORY VALUATION

A logical extension of the contribution approach to reporting is the practice of valuing the inventory of a firm. An inventory valuation is used to determine the cost of goods sold and is related directly to the income statement. Under a traditional approach, as described in Chapters 5 and 6, the full costs of production are absorbed by, or associated with, the units produced during a period. The traditional full-cost approach requires that all direct labor, direct material, variable and fixed overhead be combined to form the cost of units produced: this approach to costing is called **absorption costing.** For example, assume that a firm has $10,000 of committed fixed costs and variable costs of $1 per unit during a period in which 10,000 units were produced. The cost assignment in this case, $2 per unit, is derived as follows:

Fixed Costs	$10,000
Variable Costs ($1 × 10,000)	10,000
Total Costs	$20,000
Units Produced	÷ 10,000
Cost per Unit	$ 2

If the units are priced at $3 each and all are sold, no real problem arises. The resulting income calculation is:

Revenue ($3 × 10,000)	$30,000
Cost of Goods Sold ($2 × 10,000)	20,000
Net Income	$10,000

However, assume that only 4,000 units were sold during the period. The traditional income calculation would be:

Revenue ($3 × 4,000)	$12,000
Cost of Goods Sold ($2 × 4,000)	8,000
Net Income	$ 4,000

The ending inventory of 6,000 units would be valued at $2 × 6,000 or $12,000.

Although this calculation seems reasonable, compare it with another measure of activity—the breakeven point.

$$\text{Breakeven Point} = \frac{\text{Fixed Costs}}{\text{Selling Price} - \text{Variable Costs}}$$
$$= \frac{\$10,000}{\$3 - \$1}$$
$$= 5,000 \text{ units}$$

An inconsistency is immediately apparent. The breakeven point of 5,000 units supposedly represents a sales volume resulting in zero profits. Yet, at a sales volume of 4,000 units, the traditional income statement discloses a profit of $4,000. The reason for the apparent difference lies in the treatment of the fixed overhead expenses. The breakeven point established a level of volume necessary to cover all of these (fixed) costs. The traditional income statement, however, included only part of the overhead, specifically, that part assigned to units sold during the period, or $4,000 ($1 × 4,000 units). The remaining $6,000 of overhead expense was taken to the inventory account and shown on the balance sheet.

The problem   As with other reporting situations, the main problem with inventory valuation is in selecting the alternative that is most useful to decision-makers. Absorption costing is required for external financial reporting and is, therefore, available in the firm's financial records. Opponents of this approach contend that full-cost inventory and cost of sales information can be misleading and subject to manipulation. Under absorption costing, altering the production volume (regardless of sales) can drastically affect the reported income. Exhibit 9–3 uses the same basic cost data presented in the previous example and shows the resulting income figures for three levels of production volume.

In Exhibit 9–3, the income figures range from a $4,000 profit to zero profit to a $2,000 loss. Each depends solely on the production volume. These

EXHIBIT 9–3   ABSORPTION COSTING ALTERNATIVES

Basic Data:	Fixed Costs	= $10,000
	Variable Costs	= $1 per unit
	Selling Price	= $3 per unit
	Sales Volume	= 4,000 units

Production Volume	10,000 Units	5,000 Units	4,000 Units
Unit-Cost Calculation			
Fixed Costs	$10,000	$10,000	$10,000
Variable Costs	10,000	5,000	4,000
Total Costs	$20,000	$15,000	$14,000
Units Produced	10,000	5,000	4,000
Cost per Unit	$ 2	$ 3	$ 3.50
Sales Volume	4,000 Units	4,000 Units	4,000 Units
Income Calculation			
Revenue	$12,000	$12,000	$12,000
Cost of Goods Sold	8,000	12,000	14,000
Net Income (Loss)	$ 4,000	$ –0–	$ (2,000)

results are directly related to the number of output units over which the fixed costs are spread. Many accountants advocate using a **direct costing**[1] approach to inventory valuation so that profits will become a function solely of sales volume.

Direct costing   Direct costing uses cost behavior as a basis for valuations and statement construction. Costs are classified as product-related or period-related, depending on their observed characteristics. **Product costs** include those elements of material, labor, and variable overhead that are directly combined with the productive output. *These costs vary directly with production.* By contrast, **period costs** include those elements that do not combine directly with the product (such as depreciation and taxes on property). These costs are unresponsive to changes in volume and are incurred as the *result of a passage of time.*

Under the direct costing approach, only product costs are used in inventory valuation. These costs are assigned to the units produced and consequently are used in the income calculation in proportion to the number of units sold during the period. Period costs are taken directly to the income statement during the period in which they were incurred. No attempt is made to relate these costs to either production or sales volumes. Since they are considered to be related to time, they are reported as time passes, regardless of production volumes.

Under a direct costing approach, the different income figures presented in the preceding example would not occur. For all three production volumes, a direct costing income statement would be the same:

Revenue ($3 × 4,000)	$12,000
Product Costs ($1 × 4,000)	4,000
Contribution Margin	$ 8,000
Period Costs	10,000
Net Income (Loss)	$ (2,000)

The direct costing statement approximates the structure of a contribution approach statement and reveals the same information found in the cost-volume-profit analysis.

A distinction   The main difference between direct costing and absorption costing is timing. The direct costing approach takes all fixed costs (period charges) to the income statement immediately. Absorption costing assigns the fixed costs to units produced during the period. The amount of fixed costs reported on the balance sheet is in proportion to the number of units still in inventory.

The two costing methods can yield different periodic income figures, depending on the relationship between production and sales. For example, consider the two years of activity presented in Exhibit 9–4. Production in Year 1

[1]A more appropriate term for this approach is *variable costing*, although *direct costing* is more traditional.

EXHIBIT 9-4 INVENTORY VALUATION—TWO PERIODS

Basic Data: Fixed Costs = $10,000
Variable Costs = $1 per unit
Selling Price = $3 per unit

	Year 1		Year 2		Two-Year Total	
	Direct Costing	Absorption Costing	Direct Costing	Absorption Costing	Direct Costing	Absorption Costing
Volume Data						
Units Produced	6,000		4,000		10,000	
Units Sold	5,000		5,000		10,000	
Unit-Cost Calculation						
Fixed Costs	–0–	$10,000	–0–	$10,000	——	——
Variable Costs	$ 6,000	6,000	$ 4,000	4,000	——	——
Total Costs	$ 6,000	$16,000	$ 4,000	$14,000	——	——
Units Produced	6,000	6,000	4,000	4,000	——	——
Cost per Unit	$ 1	$ 2.67	$ 1	$ 3.50	——	——
Income Calculation						
Revenue	$15,000	$15,000	$15,000	$15,000	$30,000	$30,000
Cost of Goods Sold (product cost)	5,000	13,333	5,000	16,667	10,000	30,000
Period Cost	10,000	–0–	10,000	–0–	20,000	–0–
Net Income (Loss)	$ –0–	$ 1,667	$ –0–	$ (1,667)	$ –0–	$ –0–
Inventory Value	$ 1,000	$ 2,667	$ –0–	$ –0–	$ –0–	$ –0–

exceeded sales by 1,000 units (6,000 units produced and 5,000 units sold). In Year 2, however, sales were 1,000 units more than the amount produced (4,000 units produced and 5,000 units sold); some sales orders were filled with the inventory established in Year 1.

When annual sales and production volumes differ, direct-costing and absorption-costing net income amounts will be different also. Under the absorption costing approach, the fixed costs are assigned to the units produced. Thus, in Year 1, $1,667 of fixed costs (($10,000/6,000) × 1,000 unsold units) are placed in the ending inventory and not reported on the income statement. In Year 2, the annual fixed costs plus the $1,667 of inventoried charges are all taken to the income statement. By contrast, the direct costing approach treated all fixed costs as a period charge and assigned them directly to the income statement. The 1,000 unsold units in Year 1 are placed in the inventory at a value of $1 per unit, or the variable cost per unit.

Over the two-year period, production and sales are equal (10,000 units produced and sold). The total income for this two-year period under direct and absorption costing is the same, since all of the costs, both fixed and variable, have been reported on the income statement. When sales and production are equal, both methods will give the same amounts of income; when production and sales are different, the income amounts will differ also. Inventory values under absorption costing will always be larger than under direct costing, if any fixed overhead is incurred. These differences are presented in Exhibit 9–5.

Use of direct costing Direct costing has many advantages for internal report-

EXHIBIT 9–5 RELATIONSHIPS BETWEEN DIRECT AND ABSORPTION COSTING

Sales and Production	Inventory Levels	Direct-and Absorption-Costing Profits*
Sales equal to production	Unchanged	Same profits
Sales less than production	Increase	Absorption-costing profit higher than direct-costing profit
Sales greater than production	Decrease	Direct-costing profit higher than absorption-costing profit
Sales volume constant, production volume varies	Variable	Direct-costing profit is constant, absorption-costing profit varies

*Profitability is based on an assumption of constant production costs for the periods involved.

ing. First, variable cost data are readily available to support contribution reporting. Second, profitability does not fluctuate in response to adjustments in
production volume. Thus, profits may be used as a basis for divisional evaluations. Current costs are clearly evident to the user of a direct costing statement,
whereas, under absorption costing, the effect of the fixed costs is evident only
after all production is sold. Thus, direct costing emphasizes the current effect of
the fixed costs on divisional performance. In this sense, direct costing is closely
aligned with the contribution approach to reporting, to various planning activities, and to control within the firm.

Among the disadvantages of direct costing are the difficulty and expense
of recasting the existing data into a direct costing form. Also, mixed costs may
pose a classification problem for the managerial accountant. Overall, however,
direct costing can often be used effectively for internal reporting.

SUMMARY

This chapter described the contribution approach as a vehicle for reporting relevant information to management. A fundamental distinction between
this approach and the traditional form is that the contribution approach clearly
isolates a segment contribution margin as a major part of the report. This
margin measures the segment's contribution to covering the firm's fixed costs
and profits.

The contribution approach brings many subclasses of cost structure into
focus. These classifications emphasize planning and control concepts and make
the report relevant to the user. Similarly, assignments may subdivide information into meaningful components, making the reported information relevant to
many of the firm's problems.

The contribution approach can be extended to inventory valuation.
Under traditional methods of valuing the inventory, reported net income is a
function of both production and sales volume. Variations in production volume,
without any change in sales volume, can alter the reported income of a firm or of
a segment of a firm. Direct costing removes this inconsistency from the reports.
Under direct costing, manufacturing costs are classified as either product costs
or period costs. Product costs relate directly to the production volume and vary as
the production volume varies. Period costs are indirectly related to production
and tend to vary as a function of the passage of time. Under direct costing, only
product costs are used in the inventory valuation process. Period costs are taken
directly to the income statement during the period in which they are incurred,
regardless of volume for that period. Product costs are taken to the income
statement in proportion to the number of units sold during the period.

Advocates of direct costing contend that this method more closely approximates economic reality than does any other method, which makes it extremely

useful for managerial decision-making. Opponents argue that direct costing opposes generally accepted financial (external) reporting procedures and is more costly to operate. Direct costing is not acceptable for external reporting, but it is used widely for internal reporting.

SUGGESTED READINGS

Grinnell, D. J. "Product Mix Decisions: Direct Costing vs. Absorption Costing." *Management Accounting*, August 1976.

Largay, James. "Microeconomic Foundations of Variable Costing." *The Accounting Review*, January 1973.

Smith, A. W., and K. R. Smith. "Effects of Variable Costing in Breakeven Analysis." *National Public Accountant*, July 1976.

Williams, B. R. "Measuring Costs: Full Absorption Cost or Direct Cost?" *Management Accounting*, January 1976.

QUESTIONS

9–1   List three advantages to managers of using reports based on direct costing.

9–2   Explain the relationship, if any, that exists between the contribution approach to reporting and direct costing.

9–3   The value of a firm's inventory is reported as an asset on the balance sheet. How, then, can inventory values affect the income statement?

9–4   How can a firm sell fewer units than required by the break-even point calculation and still report a profit? Is this a long-run or a short-run phenomenon?

9–5   Contrast the absorption costing and the direct costing approaches to inventory valuation.

9–6   Mark the following statements "true" or "false."
   (A) Absorption costing is a full-cost technique for valuing inventory.
   (B) Product costs are variable costs.
   (C) Period costs are the total production costs for a given reporting period.
   (D) Product costs are related to production volume, whereas period costs are related to sales volume.
   (E) Fixed costs are assigned to units of output under absorption costing.

9-7 During its first year of operations, a company produced 10,000 units of a product and sold 8,000 units. Variable costs for the year were $25,000 and fixed costs were $10,000. The product was sold for $8 a unit. Using this information, construct two income statements for the firm, one using absorption costing and the other using direct costing.

9-8 Fill in the missing parts of titles from the following contribution statement:

> Net sales
> − _____ costs
> = _____ margin
> − Controllable fixed costs
> = _____ margin
> − Traceable fixed costs
> = _____ margin
> − _____
> = Net income before taxes

9-9 During periods when production does not equal sales, direct costing and absorption costing can lead to different valuations of a firm's ending inventory. Since the goal of reporting is to provide management with useful information for making decisions, these methods must be suited for different situations.

(A) List two types of decisions that require direct costing information.

(B) List two types of decisions that require absorption costing information.

EXERCISES

9-10 Product costs for the ABC Company include the following elements:

Direct labor	$400,000
Direct material	$300,000
Variable overhead	$200,000
Fixed overhead	$600,000

During the year, 10,000 units were produced and 7,000 were sold. Ending inventory consists of 3,000 units, since no inventory was on hand at the beginning of the year.

(A) Calculate the cost of ending inventory under absorption costing.

(B) Calculate the cost of ending inventory under direct costing.

9–11   The ABC Company (described above, 9–10) sells products at an established price of $200 per unit. Selling and administrative costs amount to $100,000.

    (A) Calculate net income under absorption costing.

    (B) Calculate net income under direct costing.

9–12   What reactions can be expected from reports that use the cost classifications listed below? In your answer, relate each classification to the area or areas to which the user's attention will be directed.

    (A) Fixed/variable

    (B) Direct/indirect

    (C) Controllable/noncontrollable

    (D) Manufacturing/selling and administrative

    (E) Traceable/nontraceable

    (F) Committed/discretionary

9–13   The contribution approach to reporting emphasizes _____ relationships that exist within the firm.

9–14   Contrast the format of a traditional income statement with that used in formulating a contribution approach statement.

9–15   A firm reported the following information about its operations last period: sales—$100,000, discretionary fixed costs—$20,000, variable costs—$40,000, committed fixed costs—$10,000, and joint (unassigned) costs—$5,000. If the firm uses a contribution approach to reporting, what are the following values?

    (A) Contribution margin

    (B) Short-run performance margin

    (C) Segment margin

    (D) Net income before taxes

9–16   Under what circumstances will the net income of a firm using a traditional approach to reporting be different from that of a firm using a contribution approach? Explain briefly.

9–17   The following information is available for Keller Corporation's new product line:

Selling price per unit	$ 15
Variable manufacturing costs per unit of production	8
Total annual fixed manufacturing costs	25,000
Variable administrative costs per unit of production	3
Total annual fixed selling and administrative expenses	15,000

There was no inventory at the beginning of the year. During the year, 12,500 units were produced and 10,000 units were sold.

 (A) Determine the ending inventory balance under direct costing.

 (B) Determine the ending inventory balance under absorption costing.

 (C) Determine the total variable costs charged to expense for the year, assuming that Keller uses direct costing.

 (D) Determine the total fixed costs charged to the current year's operations, assuming that Keller uses absorption costing.

(AICPA adapted)

 9-18 A visitor to the regular monthly executive meeting of the Williamson Manufacturing Company found the corporate executives in a heated discussion. The chief accountant, Mr. Johnson, was visibly upset. "For years, I've been trying to please you people," he shouted to the other managers present, "but now I'm ready to give up." The executive vice-president, Junior Williamson, called for order and asked Mr. Johnson to explain. Johnson proceeded with his story.

 "Three years ago, I prepared all of our internal reports in a manner consistent with what our auditors required for external reporting, and everyone seemed happy. Then, the marketing manager asked if we could break the information down by product line. I did this, and there was some grumbling, but marketing seemed happy. Then, two sales managers asked if we could report by sales territory. So we did that, and then marketing was unhappy. Next, the production vice-president asked for breakdowns by plant. When we switched to this, both sales and marketing were unhappy. Finally, some plant managers asked us to report by production function. When we did this, there were still many complaints. Our new report breaks the information into sales territories, within product lines, classified by production functions within plants. Now everyone is complaining about the reports and I don't know what to do about it."

 When the corporate executives adjourned to the water cooler to console Mr. Johnson, you were asked to study the situation and to come up with a solution. Specifically, you were asked to consider the following questions.

 (A) Why is everyone apparently unhappy with the new report? Is it Mr. Johnson's fault or are the other managers being unreasonable?

 (B) Would there be any advantage in preparing several different forms of the report, since all of the forms would be based on the same information?

 (C) Should Mr. Johnson consider going back to the original form of the report, which matched the one prepared for the auditors? Why or why not?

 (D) Was the information requested of Mr. Johnson reasonable or not?

 9-19 The Burner Company has two operating divisions that conduct their manufacturing activities in the same building. General maintenance for these two divisions is provided by the Company's maintenance department. Last year, the cost of operating the maintenance department was $68,000. This cost cannot be directly traced to either operating division, so the Company wants to allocate it. The following information is available.

	Division A	Division B
Labor Hours Worked	78,000	32,000
Machine Hours Used	115,000	230,000
Labor Cost	$234,000	$128,000

(A) Allocate the maintenance department cost to the operating divisions on the basis of: labor hours, machine hours, and labor cost.

(B) Suppose that the $68,000 cost included $5,000 in overtime premiums paid to maintenance workers while they were working in Division B. As the manager of Division A, comment on the cost allocations. Would the manager of Division B disagree with the manager of Division A? Why or why not?

9–20 The Brown Motor Company makes tank engines for large military tanks. Demand for tank engines has declined considerably since the war in Viet Nam ended, but the only change in the union labor contract calls for increases in the pay scale. One rule is particularly restrictive to management: any man who punches in to work for the 8:00 A.M. shift must be paid for eight hours of work.

(A) Is direct labor truly controllable by a foreman on the job? Explain why or why not?

(B) For budgeting purposes, direct labor is usually considered a variable cost. Is direct labor a variable cost in this case?

(C) Is direct labor cost traceable to the production foreman of the Brown Motor Company? If it is, explain why; if it is not, explain to what or to whom it is traceable.

9–21 An accountant wants to allocate a particular cost among the operating divisions of a firm. Since the cost is not directly traceable to any particular division, he decided to assign it on the basis of a secondary measure. To select the most reasonable basis, he observed the cost and some selected activity levels for a six-month period. The results are presented below:

	Cost	Labor Hours Worked	Machine Hours Used	Units Produced	Materials Used (in lbs.)
January	$10,000	5,000	1,190	8,020	23,700
February	12,000	9,280	1,576	9,624	25,100
March	14,400	6,172	1,962	11,549	27,300
April	17,280	7,596	2,348	13,859	18,600
May	20,736	10,200	2,734	16,631	14,200
June	24,883	14,720	3,120	19,957	20,200

Which secondary measure should the accountant use to allocate the cost? Would your answer be different if the cost to be allocated were identified as supervisory salaries? Why or why not?

9–22   The Walters Ice Cream Company has two production departments, chocolate and vanilla, that share a refrigeration facility in the factory. The Company allocates the cost of operating and maintaining the refrigeration facility between these two departments. Since every gallon of ice cream must pass through the refrigerators, the basis for allocation is usage, measured in gallons.

During the month of June, 80,000 gallons of chocolate and 40,000 gallons of vanilla were produced and sold. Total costs of the refrigeration facility were $60,000. In July, the refrigeration costs were the same; 80,000 gallons of chocolate and only 20,000 gallons of vanilla were produced.

(A) How much refrigeration cost would be allocated to the chocolate and vanilla departments for June?

(B) Would the cost allocations change in July? If so, how much would be allocated to each department?

(C) How would the manager of the chocolate department react to the cost allocations?

(D) Considering your answer to part (C), should the allocation basis be changed? If so, what should it be changed to?

PROBLEMS

9–23   Mr. Stan Lee is employed as an accountant at the Kahn Fuse Company. For the past several years, Mr. Lee has attended a local night school to study accounting. Recently, the class discussed various ways of classifying costs. As a result of his newfound knowledge, Mr. Lee reported for work one morning and promptly changed the format of all internal accounting reports to reflect the various classifications he had just studied. A sample of the new report is reproduced below.

Kahn Fuse Company
Divisional Income Statement

Net Sales—Element Division	$193,000
Net Sales—Casing Division	212,000
Total Net Sales	$405,000
Traceable Costs:	
Prime Costs:	
Material—Element Division	$ 42,000
Labor—Element Division	87,000
Material—Casing Division	35,000
Labor—Casing Division	47,000
Total Prime Cost	$211,000

Committed Fixed Costs:	
Depreciation—Element Division	$ 23,000
Depreciation—Casing Division	51,000
Total Committed Costs	$ 74,000
Element Division:	
Discretionary Costs:	
Advertising	$ 5,000
Supervisory	4,000
Selling Cost	3,000
Total of Element Division	$ 12,000
Casing Division:	
Discretionary Costs:	
Supervisory	$ 5,000
Selling Cost	2,000
Total of Casing Division	$ 7,000
Mixed Costs:	
Maintenance—Element Division	$ 2,000
Maintenance—Casing Division	2,000
Total Mixed Costs	$ 4,000
Net Income Before Taxes	$ 97,000

After looking at the new report, management unanimously agreed that they couldn't understand it. They sent Mr. Lee back to night school for advanced training and they ask you to reconstruct the statement in a meaningful form. The firm is interested in receiving a report that will reflect divisional performance.

9–24 The following information pertains to the operations of Ace Company:

	Division	
	A	B
Units Sold	50,000	50,000
Price per Unit	$10	$10
Variable Costs:		
Material	$80,000	$70,000
Labor	40,000	70,000
Factory Overhead	20,000	10,000
Sales Commissions	60,000	50,000
Fixed Costs:		
Advertising	$40,000	$30,000
Engineering	50,000	40,000
Depreciation	30,000	20,000
Joint Costs	20,000	10,000

The joint cost was subjectively allocated between the two divisions.
Using this information, calculate the following:

(A) What is the contribution margin for Division A? Division B?

(B) What is the short-run performance margin for Divisions A and B?

(C) What is the segment margin for Division A? Division B?

(D) What is the net income before taxes of Divisions A and B?

9–25 The Tiani Company markets a single product in four geographic regions of the country. Each region is headed by a product manager who makes production and marketing decisions for his region. Annually, the performance of each region is reviewed by the corporate president. The president receives an annual sales and production report from the firm's accounting department. Last year's report is reproduced below.

The Tiani Company
Comprehensive Regional Report

REGIONAL SALES SUMMARY

	Region			
	Northeast	Southeast	Northwest	Southwest
Units Sold	12,200	7,680	6,890	11,650
Sales Revenue	$488,000	$291,840	$261,820	$466,000
Price per Unit	$40	$38	$38	$40

REGIONAL MARKETING EXPENSE SUMMARY

	Region			
	Northeast	Southeast	Northwest	Southwest
Advertising	$50,000	$50,000	$70,000	$40,000
Sales Commissions	$36,600	$23,040	$20,670	$34,950
Sales Commission per unit	$3	$3	$3	$3

REGIONAL PRODUCTION EXPENSE SUMMARY

	Region			
	Northeast	Southeast	Northwest	Southwest
Production Cost	$305,000	$192,000	$172,250	$291,250
Production Cost per unit	$25	$25	$25	$25
Transportation Cost	$ 48,800	$ 46,080	$ 41,340	$ 46,600
Transportation Cost per Unit	$4	$6	$6	$4

SUMMARY INCOME STATEMENT

Sales Revenue		$1,507,660
Cost of Goods Sold		960,500
Gross Margin		$ 547,160
Selling and Administrative Costs:		
Transportation	$182,820	
Advertising	210,000	
Sales Commissions	115,260	508,080
Net Income before Taxes		$ 39,080

(A) On the basis of this report, the president concluded that operations in each region for next year should continue as they had in the past. Do you agree with his decision? Why or why not?

(B) Using the reported information, construct a contribution statement disclosing divisional performance for the president.

(C) Would your answer to part (A) change as a result of the report prepared in part (B)? Why or why not?

(D) What type of report should the president request in the future?

9-26 Berg and Sons build custom-made pleasure boats which range in price from $10,000 to $250,000. For the past 30 years, Mr. Berg, Sr. has determined the selling price of each boat by estimating the costs of material, labor, a prorated portion of overhead, and adding 20% to these estimated costs.

For example, a recent price quotation was determined as follows:

Direct Materials	$ 5,000
Direct Labor	8,000
Overhead	2,000
	$15,000
Plus 20%	3,000
Selling price	$18,000

The overhead figure was determined by estimating total overhead costs for the year and allocating them at 25% of direct labor.

If a customer rejected the price, and business was slack, Mr. Berg, Sr. would often be willing to reduce his markup to as little as 5% over estimated costs. Thus, average markup for the year is estimated at 15%.

Mr. Berg, Jr. has just completed a course on pricing and believes the firm could use some of the techniques discussed in the course. The course emphasized the contribution margin approach to pricing and Mr. Berg, Jr. feels such an approach would be helpful in determining the selling prices of their custom-made pleasure boats.

Total overhead, which includes selling and administrative expenses for the year, has been estimated at $150,000, of which $90,000 is fixed and the remainder is variable in direct proportion to direct labor.

(A) Assume that the customer in the example rejected the $18,000 quotation and also rejected a $15,750 quotation (5% markup) during a slack period. The customer countered with a $15,000 offer.

1. What is the difference in net income for the year between accepting or rejecting the customer's offer?

2. What is the minimum selling price Mr. Berg, Jr. could have quoted without reducing or increasing net income?

(B) What advantages does the contribution margin approach to pricing have over the approach used by Mr. Berg, Sr.?

(C) What pitfalls are there, if any, to contribution margin pricing?

(CMA adapted)

9-27   Flear Company has a maximum productive capacity of 210,000 units per year. Variable manufacturing costs are $11 per unit. Fixed factory overhead is $360,000 per year. Variable selling expenses are $5 per unit and fixed selling expenses are $252,000 per year. The unit sales price is $20.

The operating results for 19X1 are: sales, 150,000 units; production, 180,000 units; Flear had no beginning inventory.

(A) What is the breakeven point expressed in dollar sales?

(B) How many units must be sold to earn a net income of $60,000 per year?

(C) How many units must be sold to earn a net income of 10% on sales?

(D) Prepare formal income statements for 19X1 under:
1. Conventional costing.
2. Direct costing.

(E) Briefly account for the difference in net income between the two income statements.

9—28   The officers of Bradshaw Company are reviewing the profitability of the Company's four products and the potential effect of several proposals for varying the product mix. An excerpt from the income statement and other data follow:

	Totals	Product P	Product Q	Product R	Product S
Sales	$62,600	$10,000	$18,000	$12,600	$22,000
Cost of goods sold	44,274	4,750	7,056	13,968	18,500
Gross profit	18,326	5,250	10,944	(1,368)	3,500
Operating expenses	13,012	1,990	2,976	2,826	5,220
Income before income taxes	$ 5,314	$ 3,260	$ 7,968	$ (4,194)	$ (1,720)
Units sold		1,000	1,200	1,800	2,000
Sales price per unit		$ 10.00	$ 15.00	$ 7.00	$ 11.00
Variable cost of goods sold per unit		$ 2.50	$ 3.00	$ 6.50	$ 9.00
Variable operating expenses per unit		$ 1.17	$ 1.25	$ 1.00	$ 1.20

Each of the following proposals is to be considered independently of the other proposals. Consider only the product changes stated in each proposal; the activity of other products remains stable. Ignore income taxes.

(A) Determine the total effect on income, assuming that Product R is discontinued.

(B) Determine the total effect on income, assuming that Product R is discontinued and a consequent loss of customers causes a decrease of 200 units in sales of Q.

(C) Determine the effect on income, assuming that the sales price of R is increased to $8 and the number of units sold decreased to 1,500.

(D) Determine the effect on income, assuming that the plant in which R is produced can be utilized to produce a new product, T. The total variable costs and expenses per unit of T are $8.05, and 1,600 units can be sold at $9.50 each.

(E) Determine the effect on income, assuming that part of the plant in which P is produced can easily be adapted to the production of S, but changes in quantities may make changes in sales prices advisable. Production of P is reduced to 500 units (to be sold at $12 each) and production of S is increased to 2,500 units (to be sold at $10.50 each).

(F) Determine the effect on income, assuming that production of P can be doubled by adding a second shift, but higher wages must be paid, increasing variable cost of goods sold to $3.50 for each of the additional units. The 1,000 additional units of P can be sold at $10 each.

(AICPA adapted)

9-29 The Justa Corporation produces and sells three products. The three products, A, B, and C, are sold in a local market and in a regional market. At the end of the first quarter of the current year, the following income statement has been prepared:

	Total	Local	Regional
Sales	$1,300,000	$1,000,000	$300,000
Cost of Goods Sold	1,010,000	775,000	235,000
Gross Margin	$ 290,000	$ 225,000	$ 65,000
Selling Expense	$ 105,000	$ 60,000	$ 45,000
Administrative Expenses	52,000	40,000	12,000
	$ 157,000	$ 100,000	$ 57,000
Net Income	$ 133,000	$ 125,000	$ 8,000

Management has expressed special concern with regard to the regional market because of the extremely poor return on sales. This market was entered a year ago because of excess capacity. It was originally believed that the return on sales would improve with time, but after a year no noticeable improvement can be seen, as reported in the quarterly statement above.

In an attempt to decide whether to eliminate the regional market, the following information has been gathered:

	Products		
	A	B	C
Sales	$500,000	$400,000	$400,000
Variable Manufacturing Expenses as a Percentage of Sales	60%	70%	60%
Variable Selling Expenses as a Percentage of Sales	3%	2%	2%

Sales by Markets

Product	Local	Regional
A	$400,000	$100,000
B	300,000	100,000
C	300,000	100,000

All administrative expenses and fixed manufacturing expenses are common to the three products, and the two markets are fixed for the period. Remaining selling expenses are fixed for the period and separable by market. All fixed expenses are based upon a pro-rated yearly amount.

(A) Prepare the quarterly income statement showing contribution margins by markets.

(B) Assuming that there are no alternative uses for the Justa Corporation's present capacity, would you recommend dropping the regional market? Why or why not?

(C) Prepare the quarterly income statement showing contribution margins by products.

(D) It is believed that a new product can be ready for sale next year if the Justa Corporation decides to go ahead with continued research. The new product can be produced simply by converting equipment currently used in producing Product C. This conversion will increase fixed costs by $10,000 per quarter. What must be the minimum contribution margin per quarter for the new product to make the changeover financially feasible?

(CMA adapted)

9-30 For each of the following statements, select the *best* answer.

(A) The effect on a company's income before taxes of discontinuing a department that has a contribution to overhead of $16,000 and allocated overhead of $32,000, of which $14,000 cannot be eliminated, would be to:

1. Decrease income before taxes by $2,000
2. Decrease income before taxes by $18,000
3. Increase income before taxes by $2,000
4. Increase income before taxes by $16,000

(B) Profit-volume analysis is most important for determining the:
 1. Volume of operation necessary to break even
 2. Relation between revenues and costs at various levels of operations
 3. Variable revenues necessary to equal fixed costs
 4. Sales revenue necessary to equal variable costs

(C) Under direct costing, reporting is accomplished by:
 1. Including only direct costs in the income statement
 2. Matching variable costs against revenues and treating fixed costs as period costs
 3. Treating all costs as period costs
 4. Eliminating the work-in-progress inventory account

(AICPA adapted)

9-31 The Wilson Supply Company began its manufacturing operations on January 1, 19X4. At the end of the first year of production and sales activity, the following information was available:

Units Produced	25,000 units
Cost of Direct Material	$56,250
Cost of Direct Labor	$77,500
Variable Factory Overhead	$37,500
Fixed Factory Overhead	$75,000
Units Sold	15,000 units
Ending Inventory	10,000 units
Sales Revenue	$270,000
Selling Expense*	$17,000
Administrative Expense*	$13,000

*These expenses represent fixed costs.

Using this information, prepare the following statements for the Wilson Supply Company.

(A) Prepare an income statement for 19X4 using an absorption costing or traditional full-cost approach.

(B) Assuming that the firm uses an absorption costing approach, what value will be assigned to the ending inventory?

(C) Construct an income statement that uses the direct costing approach.

(D) If direct costing is used by the firm, what value will be assigned to the ending inventory?

9-32 The S. T. Shire Company uses direct costing for internal management and absorption costing for external reporting. Thus, at the end of each year, financial information must be converted from direct costing to absorption costing to satisfy external requirements.

At the end of 19X1, sales were anticipated to rise 20% for the next year. Therefore, production was increased from 20,000 units to 24,000 units to meet this expected demand. However, economic conditions kept the sales level at 20,000 units for both years.

The following data pertain to 19X1 and 19X2:

	19X1	19X2
Selling Price per Unit	$ 30	$ 30
Sales (unit)	20,000	20,000
Beginning Inventory (units)	2,000	2,000
Production (units)	20,000	24,000
Ending Inventory (units)	2,000	6,000
Under-absorbed Overhead	$ 5,000	$ 4,000

Variable Costs per Units for 19X1 and 19X2:

Labor	$ 7.50
Materials	4.50
Variable Overhead	3.00
	$15.000

Annual Fixed Costs for 19X1 and 19X2 (budgeted and actual):

Production	$ 90,000
Selling and Administrative	100,000
	$190,000

The overhead rate under absorption costing is based on practical plant capacity, which is 30,000 units per year. All accompanying under- or overabsorbed overhead is taken to cost of goods sold. All taxes should be ignored.

(A) Present the income statement based on direct costing for 19X2.

(B) Present the income statement based on absorption costing for 19X2.

(CMA adapted)

9–33   A firm began its manufacturing operations in 19X4. Its production process is characterized by large annual amounts of fixed cost. Over the years, the following amounts were produced and sold:

Year	Units Produced	Units Sold
19X4	10,000	8,000
19X5	5,000	7,000
19X6	5,000	5,000
19X7	10,000	4,000
19X8	10,000	4,000
19X9	0	12,000

Throughout the years, the productions costs were stable, although in 19X6, the sales price per unit increased from $10 to $15, where it stayed until 19X9. Using this information, complete the following table concerning characteristics of the firm.

Ending Inventory Level
(as compared to the beginning inventory)

Year	Number of Units	Dollar Value	Profits (as compared to absorption costing)
19X4	increased	?	?
19X5	?	decreased	?
19X6	same	?	?
19X7	?	?	lower
19X8	?	increased	?
19X9	?	?	higher

9–34   The New Process Company was formed in 19X4 with an original capital investment of $100,000 by its owner, Roger Buck. To house the manufacturing operation, a building with an expected useful life of 10 years was purchased for $50,000. Equipment was leased under a five-year agreement for $10,000 a year. Mr. Buck hired Rod Ram as manager of manufacturing. To attract Mr. Ram from his former employer, Mr. Buck gave him a three-year contract calling for a salary of $15,000 per year. During 19X4, the Company produced 14,500 units. Production costs included $33,350 of materials and $73,950 for labor (paid on a piece-work basis). Mr. Buck managed to sell 10,000 units in 19X4 at $12 each. In 19X5, the company produced 10,000 units using $20,000 of material and $28,000 of direct labor. Mr. Buck lowered the price per unit to $11 and was able to sell 12,000 units. The company uses a FIFO (first-in, first-out) method of inventory valuation.

Prepare comparative income statements for the New Process Company for the years 19X4 and 19X5, one using an absorption costing approach and one using a direct costing approach. Also, calculate the value of the ending inventory for both years, using both valuation approaches.

*9–35   Norwood Corporation is considering changing its method of inventory valuation from absorption costing to direct costing, and it has engaged you to determine the effect of the proposed change on the 19X8 financial statements. Norwood manufactures Gink, which is sold for $20 per unit. Marsh is added before processing starts, and labor and overhead are added evenly during the manufacturing process. Production capacity is budgeted at 110,000 units of Gink annually. The standard costs per unit of Gink are:

Marsh, 2 lbs.	$3.00
Labor	6.00
Variable Manufacturing Overhead	1.00
Fixed Manufacturing Overhead	1.10

A process cost system employing standard costs is used. Variances from standard costs are now charged or credited to cost of goods sold. If direct costing were adopted, variances resulting from only variable costs would be charged or credited to cost of goods sold. Inventory data for 19X8 follow:

	Units	
	January 1	December 31
Marsh (lbs.)	50,000	40,000
Work in Process		
2/5 Processed	10,000	15,000
1/3 Processed		
Finished Goods	20,000	12,000

During 19X8, 220,000 lbs. of Marsh were purchased, and 230,000 pounds were transferred to work in process. Also, 110,000 units of Gink were transferred to finished goods. Actual fixed manufacturing overhead during the year was $121,000. There were no variances between standard variable costs and actual costs during the year.

(A) Prepare schedules that compute:
    a. Equivalent units of production for material, labor, and overhead
    b. Number of units sold
    c. Standard unit costs under direct costing and absorption costing
    d. Amount of over- or underapplied fixed manufacturing overhead

(B) Prepare a comparative statement of cost of goods sold, using standard direct costing and standard absorption costing.

(AICPA adapted)

9–36 The Jack Palmer Company produces Better Flite golf balls which are sold in pro shops throughout the country. The Company uses an absorption costing approach to valuing its inventory. At the beginning of the current year, the inventory was 2,000 boxes of golf balls (each box contains 3 balls). The inventory was valued at $3 a box, or $6,000 in total. This valuation included a proportionate share of the fixed manufacturing costs, which are $18,000 per year. During the year, 10,000 boxes of golf balls were produced. Direct material, direct labor, and fixed costs were the same as they were the previous.

The owner of the Jack Palmer Company, Mr. Arnold Nicklaus, is considering changing from absorption costing to direct costing for income reporting and inventory valuation. He wants to know which method will produce the higher inventory valuation for each of the possible sales situations listed below. Use the terms "absorption costing higher," "direct costing higher," or "no difference" as your answer. Also, briefly explain the reasons for your answers.

(A) Sales for the period were 8,000 units.

(B) Sales for the period were 10,000 units.

(C) Sales for the period were 11,000 units.

(D) Sales for the period were 12,000 units.

(E) There were no sales during the period.

9–37 The following information is made available by the Conversion Corporation, which produces a single product. The data relate to the last two years of the firm's operations.

	Year 1	Year 2
Sales Revenue	$76,500	$153,000
Cost of Goods Sold	49,500	95,000
Gross Margin	27,000	58,000
Selling Expenses	9,200	14,800
Administrative Expenses	13,400	15,200
Net Income Before Taxes	$ 4,400	$ 28,000
Selling Price per Unit	$8.50	$9.00
Units Produced	12,000	14,000
Variable Costs per Unit	$4.50	$4.75
Units Sold	9,000	17,000
Units Produced	12,000	14,000
Beginning Inventory	-0-	3,000
Variable Costs per unit	$4.50	$4.75
Fixed Costs	$12,000	$12,000

The firm uses a FIFO (first-in, first-out) method for determining cost flows.

(A) Does the Conversion Company use direct costing or absorption costing in preparing an income statement? Briefly explain how you know.

(B) What was the value of the firm's inventory at the end of Year 1?

(C) Recast the income statements for Years 1 and 2, using the direct costing approach.

(D) What is the value of the firm's inventory at the end of Years 1 and 2 under a direct costing approach?

FOUR

*Control of
the Firm—
Responsibility
Accounting*

*Extensions of
Control in
Decentralized
Organizations*

*Standard Costs
and Measures
of Variance*

*Management
Control in
Nonprofit
Organizations*

*All organizations must exercise control if they are
to succeed. Control procedures are intended to
ensure conformance to plans; they include:
specifying individual expectations, coordinating
activities, motivating organizational members,
identifying deviations from plans, and instituting
corrective actions. The next four chapters will
discuss the control aspects of managerial
accounting in greater detail.*

CHAPTER 10

Control of the Firm— Responsibility Accounting

Objectives

After studying this chapter, you should be able to do the following:

Define responsibility accounting.

Identify three criteria by which managers can assign specific costs to specific managers.

Define control *and describe three elements of all control systems.*

Specify the appropriate frames of reference within which to analyze accounting data.

Calculate and interpret ratios for control evaluations.

CONTROL

In addition to planning and product costing, the third major function of managerial accounting is control. *Control is the process of trying to achieve conformity between goals and actions.* Managers attempt to make actions comply with plans. Simply stated, control encompasses all methods and procedures that direct employees toward achieving managerial objectives. Managerial accountants facilitate the control process by reporting control information to responsible line executives: these line managers then implement the control process.

Control has at least three major effects on the managerial accounting communications network. First, most people tend to act differently when they know in advance that their performance will be evaluated than they would act if no judgments were being made on their behavior. Second, analyzing past performance may indicate ways of obtaining superior performance in the future; that is, a historical analysis may turn up clues that suggest changes in actual production processes. Finally, explaining deviations from expected behavior might clarify the need to modify future planning procedures to represent better the relationships among production variables.

Control systems A **control system** is composed of people, resources, and procedures combined in such a way as to promote the attainment of organizational goals. In this sense, a control system may be viewed as a communications network that monitors activities within the organization and provides the basis for corrective actions in the future. On many occasions, the classical control model has been equated with a thermostat, in that: (1) existing conditions are continually monitored (the room's temperature), (2) deviations from a predetermined plan are identified (temperature variations), and (3) corrective actions are initiated (the heater is started).

In virtually all organizations, it is impossible for one individual to monitor all operational activities. Levels of managerial authority are often created to provide for specialization by decentralizing decision-making power and responsibility. Routine decisions can be delegated to individuals at lower organizational levels, leaving top management free to deal with unique situations and long-range planning for the enterprise. In such a setting, an effective control system must permeate all levels of the managerial hierarchy.

The basis of control is the overall organizational plan, which provides a benchmark for measurement. Obviously, the success of the total plan and the direction of future planning activities depend on the performance of all organizational levels. Deviations from the original plan require corrective actions, modifications of planned expectations, or replanning for the future. It is important, therefore, for managers to be able to identify these deviations. Just as the thermostat compared actual and desired temperatures, the control system must compare actual and planned performance in order to isolate deviations.

Within an organization, control activities are part of the management process. Control is essential to assure that activities conform to plans and goals of the firm. In most situations, a control system is *based upon exceptions* (i.e., "management by exception") and identifies deviations from the planned course of action. The observed deviations provide a basis for future managerial actions.

The managerial accountant plays a key role in the control process, primarily because of his direct involvement in the information flows of the firm. For example, historical data and future projections may be used in establishing goals. Normally, the accountant is a central figure in collecting and analyzing these data. Once plans are established, the managerial accountant monitors actual performance and records the results. Differences, or deviations, are logically a part of the accounting records. Remember, however, that although an accountant measures deviations from a plan (a staff function), managerial personnel are responsible for control.

RESPONSIBILITY ACCOUNTING

Under ideal conditions, **responsibility accounting** systems charge individual executives with only those costs subject to their control. Every manager has a role to perform in the organization. This role is shaped by the overall goals or objectives of the firm, the subobjectives over which the individual executive is delegated authority, and the financial, personnel, and physical constraints imposed by each situation. In well-run organizations, each manager knows exactly whom he must answer to and who answers to him, that is, there is an explicit understanding of superior-subordinate relationships. These relationships can be depicted in a typical organizational chart, as illustrated in Exhibit 10–1. In this instance, the production control supervisor knows that the receiving department foreman reports to him and that he reports to the vice-president for manufacturing. There are clear-cut lines of authority, and cost responsibility follows those same lines.

The concept of **responsibility-center** management stresses accountability for managerial actions. Responsibility centers decentralize authority so that divisional managers can make semi-independent decisions. Superiors generally believe that there is a hierarchy of tasks to be performed in an organization, and that if subordinates are given authority over certain activities, superiors will be able to devote more effort to problems of more general importance to the whole organization. A typical assignment of tasks to individual responsibility centers is illustrated in Exhibit 10–1.

Decentralized operations result in greater communication and cooperation among the operating units. Managers of responsibility centers can react and adapt more quickly than can centralized managers to changing conditions and thus, they can give greater attention to problems that develop. Localized man-

EXHIBIT 10–1   ORGANIZATION CHART

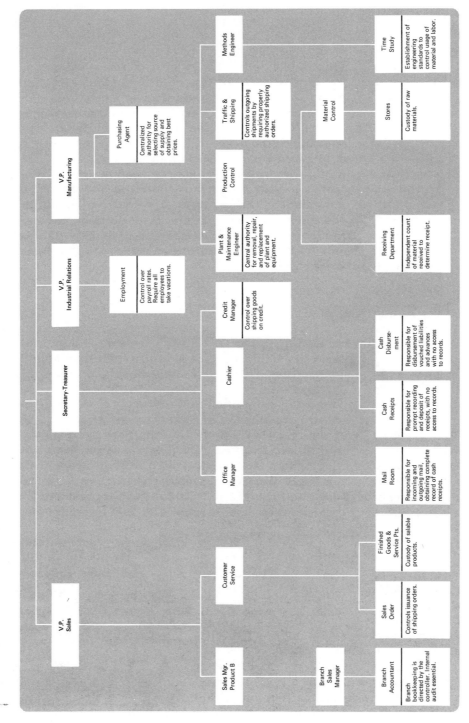

agement permits employees to see the results of their operations and motivates them to achieve their stated objectives. Under responsibility-center management, control is clear-cut, at least conceptually.

CHARGING COSTS TO RESPONSIBILITY CENTERS

The heart of responsibility accounting is assigning costs to individual managers. But how is this done? Some years ago, a committee of the American Accounting Association formulated guidelines for deciding which costs should be charged to individual responsibility centers. These guidelines are still relevant to current responsibility accounting.

1. If the person has authority over both the acquisition and the use of the services, he should be charged with the cost of such services.
2. If the person can significantly influence the amount of cost through his own action, he may be charged with such costs.
3. Even if the person cannot significantly influence the amount of cost through his own action, he may be charged with those elements with which the management desires him to be concerned, so that he will help to influence those who are responsible.[1]

Often, the executive who comes closest to meeting these criteria is the one who supervises the day-to-day activity around which costs are incurred. Supervising executives normally have a good idea of which costs they control, and their superiors also regard these costs as being under their subordinate's control.

CONTROLLABLE (ASSIGNABLE) COSTS

Controllable costs are those costs whose incurrence may be directly influenced by an identifiable manager, within a given time period. The three attributes of "controllability" are: (1) the cost can be made to vary in size, at management's discretion, (2) the manager responsible for the cost is identifiable, and (3) the time period is appropriate for the type of cost and the type of decision being made. The distinction between controllability and uncontrollability considers all three dimensions. If costs cannot be made to vary in size despite actions management may take, they are clearly not controllable. Although top-level managers assume ultimate responsibility for all of the firm's operations, in large organizations they often delegate some of their authority to lower echelons, and those to whom authority is delegated are usually held responsible for their actions.

[1] Report of the Committee on Cost Concepts and Standards,"*Accounting Review* (April 1956), p. 189.

Furthermore, all costs may be made to vary in period long enough to allow the firm to grow or shrink.

Although the conceptual distinction between controllable and uncontrollable costs is clear, real costs in any situation may not be so easily classified. Costs usually bear labels associated with the type of input to which they are related, for example, labor, materials, or overhead. These natural labels sometimes are subclassified as "direct" or "indirect," according to their functional relationship to a department or product. In some instances, the natural labels are subclassified as "fixed" or "variable," according to their relationship to levels of volume. Unfortunately, there is no clear-cut relationship among those costs labeled "controllable" for control purposes, those labeled "variable" for planning purposes, and those labeled "direct" for product costing purposes. Similarly, there need not be a relationship among the "uncontrollable," "fixed," and "indirect" classes of costs.

Although a great overlap exists among these costs, there are many differences. For example, consider some of the costs incurred in a machining department of a manufacturing plant that uses a process cost-accounting system. Individual costs can be classified as being controllable (by the department foreman), direct to the department for product costing purposes, and variable for planning purposes, as illustrated in Exhibit 10–2. Note that some cost classifications overlap, and some do not. Direct material cost is controllable by the foreman, is assigned to his department, and varies proportionally with output. While the foreman's salary can be directly assigned to the machining department, it cannot be considered either controllable or variable by that department. Allocated power costs need not be controllable or direct to the machining department even though they may vary with volume. Costs for other inputs can assume other relationships.

EXHIBIT 10–2   MACHINING DEPARTMENT COST CLASSIFICATION

Cost	Controllable	Direct	Variable
Direct Material	Yes	Yes	Yes
Foreman's Salary	No	Yes	No
Power (allocated)	No	No	Yes
Repairs (called in by foreman)	Yes	No	No
Assembly Department Labor	No	No	No

ELEMENTS OF THE CONTROL PROCESS

Generally, the **control process** consists of three interrelated functions: an explicit statement of plans or objectives; a measurement of actual compliance, behavior, or activity; and the feedback of information to the appropriate managers. A well-developed system of control includes such elements as budgeting, the use of a standard cost system, issuance of periodic reports of responsibility or performance, statistical analyses of reported data, and programs for training personnel. Section Two of this book discussed organizational goals and the planning process. Section Three discussed procedures for measuring actual activity performed within the firm. This chapter establishes the mechanics of control, and following chapters consider designing standards for judging and interpreting accounting clues.

What are controls? The AICPA defines controls as either accounting or administrative, as follows:[2]

Accounting controls comprise the plan of organization and all methods and procedures that are concerned mainly with, and relate directly to, safeguarding of assets and the reliability of the financial records. They generally include such controls as the systems of authorization and approval, separation of duties concerned with record keeping and accounting reports from those concerned with operations or asset custody, physical controls over assets, and internal auditing.

Administrative controls comprise the plan of organization and all methods and procedures that are concerned mainly with operational efficiency and adherence to managerial policies and usually relate only indirectly to the financial records. They generally include such controls as statistical analyses, time and motion studies, performance reports, employee training programs, and quality controls.

Plan of organization Every organization should establish clear lines of authority and responsibility. The formal network of such relationships is called the *plan of organization*. Although the appropriate plan of organization varies with the nature of the enterprise, each plan should stress the independence of four functions: operating, custodial, accounting, and internal auditing. Independence provides for a separation of duties so that the activities within a department are monitored by records external to each department. Thus, the authorization for all departmental activities or functions is separate from the accounting for them. Similarly, the accounting function is separated from the custody of assets in such a way as to prevent the same person from controlling both functions. The plan of organization also dictates the flow of information contained in managerial accounting reports.

---

[2]*Statement of Auditing Procedure No. 33* (New York: AICPA, 1963), p. 28. A revised definition of both accounting and administrative control was issued in *Statement on Auditing Standards No. 1* (New York: AICPA, 1973), par. 320.26, but the earlier definitions are more descriptive of applications to managerial accounting practices.

For example, consider the following situations in which a poor plan of organization results in poor control:

1. The foreman of a machining department hires the men in his own department, collects their time cards each day for submission to the payroll department, and picks up their payroll checks each week to be delivered within the department. There are no organizational controls to prevent this foreman from "creating" a fictitious time card and pocketing the paychecks as they are issued. If employees submitted their own cards and picked up their own checks, this type of fraud could not occur.

2. All tools in a machine shop are kept in a central toolroom. Whenever an employee needs (or wants) a tool, he goes and takes it from the toolroom. Each employee is supposed to return the tools when he finishes with them, but tools keep disappearing. Two alternate changes in organization might reduce tool disappearances: (1) create a new position of toolroom stock clerk, who has the responsibility of ensuring that employees who take tools also return them, or (2) decentralize the tool operation so that each employee is assigned a set of tools and is made responsible for keeping it intact.

3. The Chair Manufacturing Company originally constructed chairs on custom order, but one of their models, a captain's chair, was so popular (and profitable) that Chair dropped production of other models. Chair used a job-order cost-accounting system, with each batch of 20 chairs constituting a "job." Although this method was the one the Company had always used and was relatively simple to implement, unaccountable cost differences appeared from job to job (batch to batch). Assigning responsibility for these variances was most difficult since no one person guided a batch completely through production. A modification of the accounting method to a process system with clearly delineated departments headed by foremen who had designated responsibilities made it possible to identify factors that caused cost variations and to correct the underlying problems.

Standard methods and procedures   The methods and procedures used in a system of control must revolve around the formal chart of accounts, which provides a frame of reference within which all data may be collected. A chart of accounts lists every account (unit of information) on which the company will ever collect data. A satisfactory system of control would ensure that data on all operations and transactions are recorded in the appropriate accounts. To do this, a clear definition of what data are to be collected, how they are to be manipulated, and to whom they flow is essential. An accounting manual usually provides such a clear statement of procedures, examples of forms to be used, diagrams or directions on the flow of source documents and/or reports, procedures for approving and/or authorizing a given transaction, and instructions for the method, style, and content of the record-keeping function.

In the following situations, poor methods or procedures result in poor control.

1. The Ajax Co. mass-produces its products along a production line, and, accordingly, uses a process accounting system. Its chart of accounts for each department includes separate accounts for each input and an account for the output. One department located early in the production line was involved in a task that produced much breakage, but since Ajax did not have a "breakage" account in its chart of accounts, no information was collected about the extent of breakage. The cost of breakage was simply averaged into the cost of good units produced by that department. By adding an account, breakage, Ajax could collect a desirable unit of information, and, at the same time, not burden the departments farther down the production line with the excess transfer-in material costs.

2. The Acme Co. produces custom machines on demand, and, accordingly, uses a job-order costs system. When a specific order is received, the foreman in charge of production estimates what materials will be needed and draws them from the storeroom. He fills out a requisition, one copy of which is recorded on the job-order cost sheet. After the job is completed, excess material is returned to the storeroom, and the storekeeper simply increases the amount of the specific items on his inventory cards; he does not fill out a "material return" slip. Thus, individual jobs are charged with the material cost originally drawn from the storeroom, not with the cost of materials used. Creating a material return slip (which indicates the job number from which material returns originate) would correct the weakness in control and produce product costs that are not overstated.

3. Some customers of the Custom Printing Card Co. complained that they never received their orders, and Custom Printing could not even find the original customer orders. By consecutively numbering all order blanks, giving the customer a copy of his numbered order blank, and ensuring that all job sheets carried the same number as the order, Custom Printing would be able to account for all jobs. That is, as jobs were completed, one copy of the job cost sheet would be filed alphabetically (as was done previously), but another copy would be filed by job number. Missing numbers would indicate that the job was still in process (which could be verified by an inventory count) or else lost. Once a customer complained or a missing number was found, steps could be taken to find the missing job cost sheet.

4. The storeroom clerk in a process manufacturing shop was responsible for segregating material requisitions by department so that each department could be charged for the costs of materials drawn during the day. Because some of the requisitions were illegible, owing to carelessness, damage in passage, or other reasons, material costs frequently were charged to the wrong department. If the blank requisition pads for each department were printed on paper of a different color (as well as consecutively numbered), no mistake could occur in charging requisitions to departments.

Authorizations and other practices   In addition to identifying persons holding responsibility and implementing procedures to insure an adequate flow of information, a good system of control also requires proper authorization for any activity that is to take place. Control consists of obtaining conformity between goals and actions, and one element in this process may require that authorization from the person responsible be obtained *before* any action is taken.

The physical protection of assets also is part of any system of effective control. This protection would call for valuable assets to be kept under lock and key, to be physically retained on the premises, and to be moved only after proper authorization had been presented. Fenced-in work space, gate guards, restricted areas, badges or access passes are a few practices that can help control assets.

Adherence to managerial policies can be achieved, or at least encouraged, through sampling and statistical analysis to check actual performance against a predetermined standard. Time and motion studies can help managers make more intelligent or realistic plans, improve or standardize production processes, and provide a sound basis for judging actual performance. Employee training programs can help to ensure that each worker knows exactly what is expected of him and how he is to do his task.

Consider the following situations involving authorization or other methods of achieving conformance to objectives:

1. Can you think of a situation in which the failure to have a policy of obtaining prior authorization resulted in the theft of cash? Of inventories? Of tools, supplies, or equipment? Of excess expense allowances or travel reimbursements? In each of these cases, the undesirable action might have been prevented or at least restrained had a policy of prior authorization by the immediate supervisor been in effect.

2. The manager of a division that produces parts used later in production modified the design of his part to facilitate his production operation, without first obtaining proper authorization from his superior. The modified parts were later found to be unusable as components of the ultimate product. If authorization had been sought in this case,

the modification would have been vetoed, and the whole production line would not have shut down.

3. Why have the "fast foods" franchises, such as McDonald's, Burger King, Howard Johnson's, Baskin-Robbins, succeeded while hundreds of "mom and pop" eating establishments have failed? Part of the answer lies in standardization, time and motion studies, and proper employee training. In each of these operations, top management has determined the best way to produce and deliver the product, has ensured by routine inspection that all franchisees follow the prescribed operating practices, and has allowed a franchisee to operate only after he has undergone the central training program.

ACCOUNTING AND THE CONTROL PROCESS

Accounting provides an organization with a formalized system of information processing that involves control in three areas: (1) the budgeting process sets the basis for judging whether actual performance has conformed to plan; (2) the information-processing function formally collects data on actual performance; and (2) the control function is frequently initiated by accountants, who compare actual results with preconceived targets and report deviations to the appropriate managers. In other words, managerial accountants would probably have made projections, collected data, and prepared performance reports for each of the situations described above as examples in which control could be improved.

For control purposes, information from accounting reports is *compared* with other data to determine whether the observations are "reasonable," "acceptable," or "desirable." In other words, the accounting system produces data that are usually evaluated within a particular frame of reference. Three common frames of reference used by management are the *historical comparison*, the *similar activity comparison*, and the *expected results comparison*.

Historical comparisons A common method for analyzing data about an object, action, or function is to compare the data to similar information generated in a previous period. For example, the cost of manufacturing a product or the cost of labor for his period may be compared with the cost incurred last period. Patterns and trends become obvious under this historical comparison, as illustrated in Exhibit 10–3. Historical evaluation of the June 19X8 costs indicates that direct labor costs are increasing, while direct materials costs are decreasing. The cost of supplies has remained constant over the years. Departmental managers would pay particular attention to three items—repairs, supervision, and spoilage—since they evidence such a sharp decrease in costs. In addition, they

EXHIBIT 10–3   HISTORICAL ANALYSIS

	19X5	19X6	19X7	19X8
Direct Labor	$ 850	$ 910	$ 910	$ 940
Direct Materials	900	900	880	860
Indirect Labor	210	210	230	230
Supplies	350	350	350	350
Heat	90	93	96	100
Power, Light	160	167	173	180
Repairs	100	20	70	50
Supervision	800	700	600	400
Spoilage	400	200	100	50
Total	$3,860	$3,550	$3,409	$3,160
% of 19X5 (rounded)	100	92	88	82

would consider the last line of the report, which indicates the result of combining different inputs, measured in terms of total costs.

Two problems are associated with historical comparisons. First, underlying circumstances may change over time, so that the accounting reports from two periods might correspond to different circumstances, thus invalidating the comparison. For example, the top executive of Department A might want to know if the same output was produced in each of the four periods reported in Exhibit 10–3. If fewer units were produced, one could reasonably expect that lower costs should be incurred. In addition, the original 19X5 data might concern poor or inefficient operations, so that any comparison is only relative. By themselves, trends cannot be used for such absolute evaluations as "excellent" or "poor," but they may be used for such relative evaluations as "better" or "worse." For example, if the labor cost per unit of output last period was $9 (but this was excessive in relation to the amount of labor which *should have been* incurred), and in this period, labor cost amounted to $8.90, the manager can state only that the labor cost situation is improving, that is, costs are being reduced, but he cannot state whether the new costs were excessive (unless he knew the "right" cost). An executive evaluating Exhibit 10–3 would have little to say about the absolute efficiency of Department A.

Similar activity comparisons   A second common basis for comparing and analyzing data about one object, function, or department is to match it against data about another similar object, function, or department. For example, the material cost per unit of output incurred in Department A may be compared with the per-unit cost incurred in Department B. This method, too, yields relative evaluations; in addition, like historical assumptions, it suffers from two deficiencies: underlying circumstances may not be identical, and the size of a base number may reflect gross inefficiencies in the process that generated the number.

For example, examine the costs reported in the following excerpt from a comparative production report.

	Department 1	Department 2	Department 3
Direct labor	$8,000	$9,100	$8,600
Direct material	6,800	5,200	7,300
Indirect labor	4,700	4,900	4,800
Supplies	2,600	1,200	2,700

A supervisor might question why Department 2 incurred the highest labor costs and the lowest supplies costs. He might wish to determine why Department 3 consistently incurred more cost for each line item than did Department 1. Certainly, the supervisor would determine the total costs for each department and he might even calculate a cost per unit for each department. While other differences in costs between departments could be questioned, the supervisor could not reach an absolute judgment on the basis of this report that Department 1 evidenced "good" performance, while Department 3 evidenced "poor" performance. Such judgments require the supervisor to know the level costs should have been. If each department was authorized to incur up to $8,600 for direct labor, performance in Departments 1, 2, and 3 would be judged "good," "poor," and "satisfactory," respectively.

Expected results comparisons   Managers normally are familiar with the activities they control and frequently have expectations about future operating results within their departments. Most production lines are designed to standardize the technical combination of labor, material, and facilities employed in a given department. To organize a manufacturing process, managers must have an extremely good idea of the technical specifications of the production process: they must know how much and what types of materials are needed, what types of labor skills are required, and how long each process should take, using various facilities. These technical specifications of the *amount* and *cost* of each input required at each production stage are called **standards**. *Standards are predetermined targets of the technically feasible or expected input quantities and input prices.*

In addition to specifying technical standards for quantity and price of each major input, most firms prepare an explicit *operating budget*. Ordinarily, operating budgets specify what work is to be done during a given time period. In other words, the budget states a set of expectations that serves as a basis for evaluating actual results. Performance reports compare actual performance and budgeted performance, as illustrated in Exhibit 10–4. Thus, if actual costs are

EXHIBIT 10-4   PERFORMANCE REPORT

Type of Input	Actual Cost	Budgeted Cost	Variance
Direct Labor	$ 940	$1,000	$60*
Direct Materials	860	850	10
Indirect Labor	230	225	5
Supplies	350	300	50
Heat	100	100	–0–
Power, Light	180	180	–0–
Repairs	50	20	30
Supervision	400	400	–0–
Spoilage	50	90	40*
Total	$3,160	$3,165	$ 5*

*Favored Variance

greater than budgeted costs, the *variance* is often described as being "unfavorable." (Detailed analysis of performance reports occurs in a later chapter.) Favorable and unfavorable variances frequently are displayed in a separate column of the performance report. This enables managers to practice "management by exception," a method in which managers need pay attention to only those items that deviate from expectations. For example, the performance report shown in Exhibit 10-4 emphasizes that significant variances occurred in Department A during June, even though the total variance of dollars is not significant. If management can identify why labor and spoilage costs were lower than expected during this period, they might be able to produce lower costs in the future. If the reasons for using excess supplies or repairs were known, management would be able to take corrective action in the future. A variance or deviation from budget should lead the manager to ask the following questions:

1.   Which elements under my control deserve attention?

2.   What was the cause of variance in these elements?

3.   What corrective action can be taken to prevent this from recurring in the future?

4.   Should the budget or expectation for this item be modified for future control purposes?

DATA TRANSFORMATIONS—RATIOS

Ratio analysis facilitates evaluations of accounting information by reducing much data into a smaller set. As quantitative indicators, ratios are not influenced by the relative size of the activities or departments being compared. Ratios thus allow comparison between large and small departments or between large and small production runs.

Accounting reports for control purposes focus upon the accomplishments of a particular manager during a stated period of time. Ordinarily, the individual data elements relate to specific dollar balances and to physical quantitative measures, such as the number of units or the pounds of material. All of these data can be classified into one of two groups: static balances existing at one moment of time, or dynamic activity occurring over a period of time, e.g., ending inventory balances or quantities transferred to the next department. Three types of ratios can be constructed from these two classes of data: activity-to-activity ratios, activity-to-balance ratios, and balance-to-balance ratios. Ratios composed by dividing one activity into another activity indicate *rates of relative activity*. For example, the contribution margin ratio indicates the rate at which new sales revenue will contribute to meeting fixed costs or the desired profit target. Dividing an activity by a balance produces a measure of the *rate of utilization*. For example, dividing cost of goods sold by the average inventory balance produces an inventory turnover; inventory turnovers indicate the rate at which inventory is being sold. Dividing a balance by another balance indicates the *relative composition* of items. Dividing the balance of supplies by that of total inventories signifies the relative size of supplies.

In every case, evaluating ratios for control purposes is accomplished by the process of comparison. The desired ratios are calculated for the department, responsibility center, or manager being evaluated, and then compared with ratios for previous periods, ratios for other departments (centers or managers), or with predetermined target values (budgeted ratios).

An example—the credit department Many commercial ventures provide credit to their customers, and most large organizations that provide credit terms have credit departments to determine the financial soundness of potential customers. Credit department operations influence both the sales function and the finance function, so top organizational management wishes to control the credit department managers. Ratio analysis can provide measures useful for the control process.

For example, Exhibit 10–5 presents a list of information items that would be available for almost any credit department. Hypothetical data are presented for two divisions of a large diversified manufacturing company. Division 1, the largest one, produces and sells the major product for the company. Division 2 produces a minor product for sale in an entirely different market.

EXHIBIT 10-5   CONTROL DATA FOR TWO CREDIT DEPARTMENTS

Activities	Division 1	Division 2
A. Number of applications received this period.	10,000	1,000
B. Number of applications approved this period.	9,000	600
C. Dollar amount of credit granted this period, i.e., credit sales.	$965,000	$300,000
D. Dollar amount of accounts going into default this period.	$ 19,500	$ 3,000
E. Dollar amount of previously uncollectible accounts recovered this period.	$ 1,000	$ 700
F. Costs incurred by the credit department this period.	$ 66,000	$ 10,000
Static Balances		
G. Average age of the accounts receivable (days)	40	48
H. Beginning (or ending) balance of accounts receivable	$ 80,500	$ 36,500
I. Beginning (or ending) balance of allowance for bad debts	$ 4,000	$ 1,500
J. Total assets of the division	$420,000	$365,000
K. Number of employees in the credit department	7	1
L. Total number of active accounts	100,000	4,000

Of all the information presented in the exhibit, only Item G, the average age of accounts receivable, provides a direct clue for measuring the relative performance of each credit department: on the average, Division 1 collects its accounts eight days faster than does Division 2. Meaning of the remaining data is obscured by the great difference in the relative size of the two departments. Since Division 1 is known to be larger than Division 2, an analyst learns little when he sees larger numbers for Division 1 data.

Direct comparison between departments is possible when all data are expressed in ratio form. Since the size of each department can be measured in terms of the total number of active accounts, all of the data for each department can be deflated for size simply by dividing each by the number of active accounts. Thus, the ratio of applications received this period to total number of active accounts can be calculated for Divisions 1 and 2 as follows:

$$\frac{\text{Current applications}}{\text{Total active accounts}} \qquad \frac{10{,}000}{100{,}000} = 10\% \qquad \frac{1{,}000}{4{,}000} = 25\%$$

EXHIBIT 10-6 CONTROL DATA FOR TWO CREDIT DEPARTMENTS, DEFLATED FOR SIZE DIFFERENCES

	Division 1	Division 2
A. Applications received this period	10%	25%
B. Applications approved this period	9%	15%
C. Credit sales, per active account	$9.65	$75.00
D. Dollar default, per active account	$ .19	$ .75
E. Dollar recovery, per active account	$ .10	$ .175
F. Credit department costs, per active account	$ .66	$ 2.50
G. Nondeflated average age of accounts (days)	40	48
H. Average balance of accounts receivable	$ .805	$ 9.125
I. Allowance for bad debts, per active account	$ .04	$ .375
J. Divisional assets, per active account	$4.20	$91.25
K. Accounts per employee	14,286	4,000

SOURCE: Data from Exhibit 10-5, all divided by Line-item L (100,000 for Division 1, 4,000 for Division 2).

The ratio of applications approved this period to total active accounts is calculated in a similar fashion: the ratios for each division are 9% and 15%. Deflated data for both departments (excluding average age of accounts receivable) are illustrated in Exhibit 10–6. Deflated dollar amounts per active account result whenever the original data are stated in dollar amounts. The accounts per employee ratio is determined differently from the other ratios: the total number of active accounts becomes the numerator rather than the denominator. For Division 1, the accounts per employee ratio is calculated as follows: 100,000/7 = 14,286 (rounded).

These deflated data indicate that the credit department of Division 2 is growing at a faster rate (15% versus 9%) than that of Division 1, even though it is rejecting a larger proportion of applications received. The credit sales per active account is much larger in Division 2, as are the default and recovery figures. Credit department costs per account are also higher for Department 2 ($2.50 vs. $.66), partly because Department 1 has many more accounts per employee (14,286 vs. 4,000).

Ratio analysis also allows the direct comparison of related information within each division. Rates of activity can be developed by dividing one activity measure by another. Such rates would include the percentage of applications approved, the cost per approved application, and defaults as a percent of sales.

EXHIBIT 10–7   RATIOS ON PERFORMANCE OF TWO CREDIT DEPARTMENTS

	Division 1	Division 2
A. Rates of Activity		
1. Percent of applications approved (B/A = 9,000/10,000)	90%	60%
2. Cost per approved application (F/B = $66,000/9,000)	$7.33	$16.67
3. Defaults as percent of sales (D/C = $19,500/$965,000)	2%	1%
B. Rate of Utilization		
4. Cost per employee (F/K = $66,000/7)	$9,429	$10,000
5. Sale per account (C/L = $965,000/100,000)	$9.65	$75.00
6. Recovery effort (E/I = $1,000/$4,000)	25%	47%
C. Relative Composition		
7. Receivables as percent of assets (H/J = $80,500/$420,000)	19%	10%
8. Average age of receivables (G)	40	48

SOURCE: Data from Exhibit 10-5.

These measures are developed in the first section of Exhibit 10–7. Immediately following the name of each ratio are letters that identify the source line item of data from Exhibit 10–5, as well as the actual calculation of each ratio for Division 1. For example, the percent of applications approved is calculated by dividing line B by line A, i.e., applications approved by applications received: 9,000/10,000 = 90%. Section B of Exhibit 10–7 presents three measures of rates of utilization, and Section C has two measures of relative composition.

Although Division 1 collects its receivables faster than Division 2 does (line 8), it has a larger investment in receivables (line 7). Division 2 has a more stringent credit policy: it is rejecting more applications (line 1), incurring lower defaults (line 3), and achieving greater success in its recovery of defaulted receivables (line 6). Division 1 incurs less cost per approved application (line 2), but its sale per account is much smaller (line 5): on the whole, Division 1 cost per employee is not significantly lower (line 4).

A complete control evaluation would require an examination of additional ratios, as well as an analysis of historical changes in selected ratios and comparisons of current-period ratios with budget expectations.

SUMMARY

Responsibility accounting assigns costs to those managers responsible for the control of the process that generated the costs. A complete responsibility system involves establishing goals or objectives for individual managers, collecting data that document the accomplishment of the assigned tasks, and comparing actual performance with prespecified goals in a concerted effort to bring actions into conformity with goals. Actual costs may be assigned in accordance with the three guidelines for charging costs to responsibility centers or on some more arbitrary basis. In a broad sense, control is the process of obtaining conformity of actions to goals and involves all organizational relationships, methods, and practices instrumental in achieving this conformity. Efficiency and effectiveness are two criteria by which control may be evaluated: ratio analysis provides clues useful in controlling managers of responsibility centers. Like other control data, ratios should be viewed within the perspective of historical comparisons, similar activity comparisons, and expected-results comparisons.

SUGGESTED READINGS

Benke, Ralph. "Utilizing Operating Budgets for Maximum Effectiveness." *Managerial Planning*, September/October, 1976, pp. 33–40.

Judelson, D. N. "Financial Controls That Work." *Financial Executive*, January 1977.

Lindsey, B. A. "Forecasting for Control." *Management Accounting*, September 1976.

Stephens, H. V. "Efficiency and Effectiveness." *Management Accounting*, January 1976.

QUESTIONS

10–1 Define the term *control*. What is normally included in a control process? What is the goal, or purpose, of control in a firm?

10–2 What role does a managerial accountant play in the control process of a firm?

10–3 List and briefly describe three major purposes of the control function in the typical managerial accounting communications network.

10–4 Responsibility accounting systems charge individual executives with only those costs that they _____.

10–5   Costs can be classified many different ways. For example, manufacturing costs can be classified as direct or indirect, depending on their relationship to the product. What types, or classes, of costs would be used to evaluate a manufacturing division as opposed to evaluating the division manager? Briefly explain why different classifications would be used in each case.

10–6   The data supplied by managerial accountants can often be used only by comparing the numbers with some frame of reference. List three common frames of reference within which accounting numbers may be analyzed. List the weaknesses, if any, of each frame of reference.

10–7   In evaluating a control report, should the manager ever question the appropriateness of the budgeted or expected figure? Why?

10–8   What types of questions can an examination of variances or deviations from budget lead a manager to ask?

10–9   List and explain three guidelines for deciding which costs should be charged to a responsibility center.

10–10   William Omar is a production supervisor for a large manufacturing firm that uses responsibility accounting as the basis for internal reports. Regularly, William is charged a portion of the cost of the firm's maintenance department. "This is just plain ridiculous," he commented recently, "I have no supervisory authority over the maintenance department, yet, I'm regularly charged for some of their costs."

   (A) Is William's complaint valid?

   (B) Why does the management of the company authorize charging maintenance costs to a production supervisor?

   (C) Given William's feelings, draft a brief reply explaining the situation to him.

10–11   Identify three attributes that a cost must possess before it is deemed to be controllable.

10–12   Each of the costs listed below are traceable to a manufacturing division of a large company. In each case, state whether or not the cost is controllable by the division manager. Use the terms "controllable" or "uncontrollable" as your answer.

   (A) Direct labor costs
   (B) Depreciation on the factory building
   (C) Advertising costs for the division's products
   (D) Overtime premiums paid to the hourly employees
   (E) Electric power costs for the factory
   (F) Insurance premiums for the factory building
   (G) Insurance premiums for worker's compensation

10–13   Generally, the control process can be defined as consisting of three interrelated functions. Identify and briefly describe these functions.

10–14   Differentiate between accounting and administrative controls. Briefly describe each control and identify the areas of concern for each type.

10–15   Why is the plan of organization essential to good control? What is the inevitable result of a poor plan of organization?

10–16   In evaluating the control process, managers must look at efficiency and effectiveness. Define the terms *efficiency* and *effectiveness* and explain why each must be considered as part of the total evaluation.

EXERCISES

10–17   Harvey Cook, the president of Cook Enterprises, hired his brother-in-law, Boomer. Boomer was assigned to a foreman on the day shift, who was told to treat Boomer like any other new employee. The foreman claims that having Boomer on his crew completely eliminates the usefulness of responsibility accounting for his area of the firm.

> (A) Can personal relationships or other nonorganizational ties subvert formal control relationships?
>
> (B) In well-run responsibility centers, does a foreman normally have authority commensurate with his stated responsibility?
>
> (C) Is the position, "I will take no responsibility if I do not have equivalent authority," a reasonable one for a young foreman to take?
>
> (D) Are "responsibility centers" and "profit centers" identical in manufacturing organizations? Explain why or why not.

10–18   The Casting Company makes cast-iron motor blocks for truck engines. For the past 20 years, Casting has had a security force at the gates of the plant. There are four gates and three shifts, so a security force consists of a minimum of 20 men. At one executive meeting, Jack Johnson, from the personnel department, said, "Look, if an employee can lift one of those motor blocks and carry it out, no security man will be strong enough to stop him. Why not save all that money by letting the security force go?"

> (A) Does Johnson have a valid point? Explain why or why not.
>
> (B) What function does a security force accomplish in the Casting Company?
>
> (C) Can proper accounting procedures accomplish some of the functions performed by a security force? Cite an example to support your answer.

10–19   The Moon Motor Company hired new managers as top executives.

They decided to implement new techniques to analyze the production processes in the firm's manufacturing plants. The new controller noted that no report of scrap was being compiled by the accounting office, so he instituted a system of scrap control that not only reported the total scrap accumulated each day, but also separated contributions to scrap by department and by foreman. The subsequent reports indicated that Monday and Tuesday were heavy scrap days, and foremen were sent a memo urging them to seek a solution to the scrap problem. After the memo was sent, no scrap was reported on the next Monday or Tuesday.

(A) Should the production departments be congratulated on their solution to the scrap problem? Does it seem reasonable that no scrap was generated by production on those days? Explain why or why not.

(B) Was this system for analyzing scrap an efficient system? How might it be improved?

(C) If scrapped parts cannot be reconstructed, why should the firm spend time analyzing scrap amounts?

(D) How might the production foremen be encouraged to report all the scrap produced each day?

10-20   "Management by exception may sound like a tremendous time-saving procedure, but it requires that performance be compared against preestablished criteria. The success of meeting these criteria may be more an evaluation of the budget department's effectiveness than a measure of production efficiency."

(A) Is this a fair evaluation of management by exception?

(B) What role does past performance play in establishing the budgeted figures?

(C) What purpose does responsibility accounting serve in the organization? Is this purpose equally applicable to nonprofit organizations?

(D) If the corporation's production fluctuates greatly from year to year, should the company use budgetary controls? Discuss.

10-21   The managers of Harris Tool Company strongly believe in responsibility accounting. Each foreman is responsible for the actions of the men under his control. The amount of labor scheduled by each foreman each day is based on the number of units to be produced. When the union refused to agree to short-run layoffs in one department if additional hiring were taking place anywhere in the plant, management was forced to maintain employment of skilled labor at peak levels, even when there was no skilled work to be done. The excess skilled labor provides a pool available for any nonskilled production job. The production foremen claim that skilled labor cannot be made to produce efficiently, because they know that assignments from the pool are temporary and they cannot be fired by the production foreman.

(A) If a production foreman cannot fire skilled workers, should he be held responsible for their output?

(B) What morale problem might occur with skilled laborers moving into production jobs?

(C) If the production foreman is not held responsible for the skilled labor working for him, who is? If no one is held responsible, what will be the consequences to production?

(D) Since skilled workers will be paid a higher rate than unskilled workers, what should be done with the wage differential when a skilled worker is performing an unskilled task on a temporary assignment?

10–22 The administrator of the Parkville Community Hospital was concerned about a recent action taken by the hospital's board of trustees. Relying on the advice of a professional consulting firm, the board decided that responsibility accounting techniques should be used in the hospital to control expenditures.

"The situation is absurd," complained the administrator. "Theoretically, I have responsibility for all expenditures, but I have no control over them. When a patient is admitted, a staff physician provides the necessary care and treatment. We cannot look at costs when matters of life and death are at stake. I see no benefit from responsibility accounting in this situation."

(A) Is the administrator's point valid? Comment and explain why or why not.

(B) Can responsibility accounting techniques be used in any non-profit organization, such as a hospital? Would there be any benefit to the organization in using them?

(C) What advantages could the Parkville Community Hospital derive from using responsibility accounting; what disadvantages would also be present?

10–23 Responsibility accounting techniques trace costs to the individual responsible for the costs, or to whoever exercises control over them. What happens in situations in which one cost is controllable by two or more managers at the same time? Which type of accounting procedure should be used in these situations?

10–24 According to the formal organizational chart of the East Coast Sand Company, all advertising expenditures are made by the marketing manager, Mr. Phelan Poorly. Mr. Poorly suffered an illness about two years ago and has never completely recovered. He hired a new assistant to help him out. Mr. Poorly has become so dependent on his assistant that he makes no decisions himself. Instead, he just endorses any recommendations made by his assistant.

(A) Is responsibility accounting a reasonable approach for the East Coast Sand Company to use in controlling marketing costs?

(B) Will responsibility accounting work effectively in this environment? Why or why not?

(C) What suggestions could you make to the management of the company if they wanted to use responsibility accounting? Is the existing situation in the marketing department likely to be detected?

10–25   The president of a large manufacturing company became quite upset with the accounting department when they suggested that the firm use responsibility accounting as a control technique. At a recent meeting, the president made the following remarks.

"Responsibility accounting is just a fancy name for what we are currently doing. If I get concerned about manufacturing cost, I surely don't talk to the sales department about it. I know who is responsible for which costs, and so does everyone else in the company. We don't need to change our accounting system just to recognize the obvious."

As the controller of the company, respond to the president's comments. Outline the arguments that you could make to support a change in the accounting system.

10–26   Each of the following cases describes an independent situation. For each case, determine whether or not the manager should be held responsible for the cost. Use the terms "responsible" or "not responsible" as your answers. If the manager should not be held responsible for the cost, explain why.

(A) A production foreman is responsible for scheduling production workers on an assembly line. The wage rate is fixed by a contract negotiated between the company and the union.

(B) A maintenance foreman hires and assigns workers in response to requests from the production foremen.

(C) Production foremen are assigned a portion of the company's research and development costs.

(D) A personnel manager hires production employees and sets their wage rates in accordance with her perceptions of the existing job market.

(E) An advertising manager is given a fixed budget at the beginning of the year. She makes all decisions about how the budgeted funds will be spent.

10–27   Are the fixed costs of a firm controllable at any level? For example, if a firm constructed a new plant, should the cost of this plant be charged to a specific individual in the firm? Assume that the plant has an estimated useful life of 40 years. For how long should this cost be charged to the responsible individual?

10–28   Controls can be classified either as accounting controls or as administrative controls. Indicate the type of control described in each of the following cases. Use the terms "accounting" or "administrative" as your answers.

(A) Requiring signatures on all purchase orders
(B) Employee training programs
(C) A statistical analysis of spoilage patterns
(D) A company safe
(E) An internal auditing staff
(F) Quality-control inspections
(G) Periodic performance reviews
(H) A time clock

10–29   A small company is totally owned by the members of one family. Consequently, all of the executives, managers, and officers in the firm are related. Does this plan of organization have any major problems from a control viewpoint? Is it feasible for the company to fire the relatives and hire outsiders to run the firm? What other alternatives are available to the company in this situation?

10–30   "Our business is dynamic and therefore is constantly changing. The accounting system must be prepared to change also. If we were to make a manual of procedures for our system it would, or should, be out of date the next day. Therefore, it really doesn't make much sense for us to formalize our procedures." Comment on this statement.

10–31   Comment on control in each of the following statements.

(A) "All of our employees are honest. If they're not, the personnel department should have detected this. Therefore, we don't need a plant security force."

(B) "Since we use a periodic inventory system, we don't need any formal system of authorizations. After all, nobody could steal anything that we produce."

(C) "To institute any kind of security system right now would show our employees that we don't trust them. I'm sure that this would cause thefts to begin."

10–32   Mark the following statements either "true" or "false."

(A) The main responsibility for control rests with the corporate management, not with the managerial accountant.

(B) Managers must be able to make semi-independent decisions if responsibility accounting is to work.

(C) Frequently, in practice, the conditions necessary for responsibility accounting do not exist, although responsibility accounting is used.

(D) All variable costs are also controllable, whereas most direct costs are not.

(E) Effectiveness relates to the existing relationships between costs and benefits.

(F) Efficiency concerns the degree to which a given goal is accomplished, irrespective of costs.

(G) A good corporate control system should be effective and efficient.

(H) Nonprofit organizations require control systems that are effective only.

*10–33   An important concept in managerial accounting is that of responsibility accounting.

(A) Define the term *responsibility accounting*.

(B) What are the conditions that must exist for there to be effective responsibility accounting?

(C) What benefits are said to result from responsibility accounting?

(D) Listed below are three charges found on the monthly report of a division that manufactures and sells products primarily to outside companies. Divisional performance is evaluated by the use of "return on investment." You are to state which, if any, of the following charges are consistent with the responsibility accounting concept. Support each answer with a brief explanation.

a. A charge for general corporation administration at 10% of division sales.

b. A charge for the use of the corporate computer facility. The charge is determined by taking actual annual computer department costs and allocating an amount to each user in the ratio of its use to total corporation use.

c. A charge for goods purchased from another division. The charge is based on the competitive market price for the goods.

(CMA adapted)

*10–34   (A) Cite an example of a cost that is variable but not direct or controllable. Cite an example of a cost that is fixed and indirect but is controllable. Is it likely that any company's accounting system would be set up to classify each cost in terms of the three characteristics—variability, directness, controllability? If not, how are the purposes for each classification fulfilled?

(B) The control process consists of three broad, interrelated functions—explicit formal planning, measuring actual activity, and feeding back information on deviations. How are these functions related?

(C) "Plan of organization" is part of accounting control. Cite an example of inventory control through "plan of organization." Discuss ways to separate the functions of the operator, custodian, accountant, and internal auditor.

*10-35   Horngren prepared a checklist of ten characteristics that provide a starting point in evaluating the effectiveness of internal control.[3]

 1. Reliable personnel
 2. Separation of powers
 3. Supervision
 4. Responsibility
 5. Routine and automatic checks
 6. Document and control
 7. Bonding, vacations, rotation of duties
 8. Independent check
 9. Physical safeguards
 10. Costs and feasibility

How might each of these items relate to the general control process?

PROBLEMS

10-36   Foremen of each production department of Toolco receive comparative production reports at the end of each month. These reports contain data on the number of units produced, the total cost incurred, and the cost per unit of production for the current month and two preceding months. John Jackson, foreman of Department 1, received the following report at the end of June 19X7, and he requests that you assist him in interpreting the statement.

Comparative Production Report/Department 1
Month of June 19X7

	4/X7	5/X7	6/X7
Number of Units	10,000	9,000	8,000
Total Cost	$20,000	$18,900	$17,600
Cost per Unit	$ 2.00	$ 2.10	$ 2.20

(A)   From a historical perspective, is Jackson's performance improving or deteriorating? Was his performance for June satisfactory?

(B)   The per-unit cost for Department 1 is increasing at about a 5% per month rate. Assume that all departments of Toolco experienced increased costs per unit of 5% during these three months. In the context of cost increased for the whole company, would you evaluate Jackson's performance as improving, deteriorating, or remaining consistent?

(C)   Assume that the budgeted production for Department 1 for June called for the assembly of 7,900 units at a total cost of $17,700. Was

[3]Charles T. Horngren, *Cost Accounting: A Managerial Emphasis* (Englewood Cliffs, N.J.: Prentice-Hall, 1967).

Jackson's performance for June satisfactory in relation to managerial expectations?

(D) Can the decrease in units produced each month be used as a measure of effectiveness, even when costs are disregarded? If so, in what context? Disregarding the number of units produced, can the total cost per month be used as a measure of effectiveness? Will managers who use units of production as measures of effectiveness generally reach the same conclusions or make the same decisions as other managers who use total cost as a measure of effectiveness?

(E) Can either number of units produced or total cost be used alone as a measure of efficiency?

10–37 Each production foreman at Amco receives a comparative production report at the end of each week. These reports contain data on the number of units produced, the total cost incurred, and the cost per unit of production for each of the three production departments. All departments produce the same type of units. Norman Ives, foreman of Department 1, received the following report covering production activity for the last week in July, and he requests that you assist him in interpreting the statement.

Comparative Production Report/Amco
Last Week of July

	Dept. 1	Dept. 2	Dept. 3
Number of Units	1,000	1,200	1,300
Total Cost	$ 500	$ 612	$ 637
Cost per Unit	$ .50	$ .51	$ .49

(A) How does the performance of Department 1 compare with that of the other two departments? Should performance be measured in terms of number of units, total cost, or cost per unit?

(B) Assume that Department 1 had the oldest machines and the least experienced workers and that it was budgeted to produce 900 units at a total cost of $459 (whereas Department 2 was budgeted for 1,300 units @ $650, and Department 3 was budgeted for 1,400 @ $686). How would you evaluate Ives' performance?

(C) Assume that all three departments have met their production quotas for each of the past four weeks and that the per-unit costs for the first, second, and third weeks of July for each department were as follows:

Department 1:	$.54	$.52	$.51
Department 2:	.48	.49	.50
Department 3:	.45	.52	.50

Should Ives be congratulated or reprimanded for the relative performance of his department?

(D) Assume that the performance of each department relative to budget was as described in (B) above, but the historical trend was as in (C) above. Evaluations based on historical trends may conflict with those based on expectations. How are such conflicts to be resolved?

10-38 Eastco has four operating departments that produce identical units of output, although each has slightly different production facilities. Foremen of each department receive comparative production reports at the end of each month. These reports contain data on the number of units produced, the total actual costs, and the actual cost per unit, in addition to the amounts budgeted for these items for the current period. Bill Novak, foreman of Department 1, received the following report on the activity for September 19X4, and he requests that you assist him in interpreting the statement.

Comparative Production Report/Eastco
September 30, 19X4

	Actual	Budgeted	Variance
Number of Units	1,000	900	100
Total Cost	$5,500	$4,800	$700
Cost per Unit	$ 5.50	$ 5.33	$ .17

(A) Is it better to produce more or fewer units than called for by the budget? Is it better to incur more or less cost than called for by the budget? Which of the three numbers—number of units, total cost, or cost per unit—is a more meaningful guide in evaluating whether Novak has been relatively effective in complying with expectations?

(B) Assume that the variance column of the reports for Departments 2, 3, and 4 were as follows (parentheses and asterisk indicate that "actual" is smaller than "budget"):

	Dept. 2	Dept. 3	Dept. 4
Number of Units	200	(100)*	150
Total Cost	$900	$(150)*	$(100)*
Cost per Unit	$ .12	$(.05)*	$(.10)*

How effective was Novak's performance in relation to that of the other foremen?

(C) Assume that the cost per unit in Department 1 was $6.00, $5.25, $5.75, and $5.50 for the months May, June, July, and August, respectively. How could this information be used to help evaluate Novak's September performance?

10-39 Three elements of the control process include (A) plan of organization, (B) standard methods and procedures, and (C) authorizations and other practices. Using the letters A, B, and C, to designate each element, identify which element is central in each of the five cases presented below:

1. Whenever an employee needs materials for the job on which he is working, he goes to the storeroom and gets them. The plant is incurring an excess amount of wasted material. Interposing a third person between employees and the materials might reduce wastage, as would happen, for example, if the foreman were the only employee on a crew who could draw materials from the storeroom.

2. The sales manager of a manufacturing firm complained that his men lost potential sales because of production delays after orders were received, and the production manager complained that orders requiring excess setup and breakdown times cut into his production time. This problem might be solved by greater cooperation through a participatory comprehensive budgeting process, part of which might call for maintaining inventories on specific items, batch-processing some items of production, reducing sales effort on other areas, and specifying lead times on orders.

3. Many situations exist in which the construction of fences, the installation of gate guards, and the restriction of free access to certain areas have furthered adherence to managerial policy, whether that policy was concerned with physical safekeeping of assets, the protection of information, or simply freeing the employees of interference from those who have no business on the premises.

4. A company that experienced continued liquidity problems (lack of cash) required that the credit manager personally call each creditor who had accounts outstanding for more than 30 days to ascertain the reason for nonpayment or at least to expedite earlier payment. The manager frequently found customers saying that they (1) returned the goods, (2) sent in payment earlier that week, or (3) never received the order, and he had no way to verify these claims. If the credit manager received a daily report listing (for each customer) the date specific orders were delivered, the date of payments received on specific orders, and the dates returned materials were received, he would be in a position to answer any queries, clear up any misunderstandings, and contradict any falsehoods.

5. Productivity is low in a plant in which the supervisor has an office that is physically isolated from his workers. Simply moving his office to the workroom, having windows installed, or leaving the door open might be sufficient to increase productivity.

10–40   Credit department operations influence both the sales function and the finance function. Accordingly, top-level management attempts to control the credit department managers. Ratio analysis provides measures useful in the control process. Below is a list of measures for the credit departments of two divisions of a large diversified manufacturing company. Division 1, the largest one, produces and sells the major product for the company. Division 2 produces a minor product for sale in an entirely different market. Given their different sizes, evaluation of the relative performance of the two credit departments would be difficult without ratio analysis. Calculate relevant ratios and evaluate the relative efficiency of the two credit departments.

Activities	Division 1	Division 2
A. Number of applications received this period.	10,000	2,000
B. Number of applications approved this period.	7,000	1,600
C. Dollar amount of credit granted this period, i.e., credit sales.	$7,965,000	$6,600,000
D. Dollar amount of accounts going into default this period.	$39,500	$13,000
E. Dollar amount of previously uncollectible accounts recovered this period.	$21,000	$40,700
F. Cost incurred by the credit department this period.	$60,000	$22,000
G. Beginning balance of accounts receivable.	$680,500	$536,500
H. Beginning balance of allowance for bad debts.	$64,000	$81,500
I. Number of employees in the credit department.	7	2
J. Total number of active accounts.	100,000	84,000

CHAPTER 11

Extensions of Control in Decentralized Organizations

Objectives

After studying this chapter, you should be able to do the following:

Contrast a profit center with a cost center and describe how the accounting system for a profit center better facilitates the control function.

Calculate a return on investment (ROI) performance measure. Describe the relationships between and among the asset turnover, margin on sales, and return on investment.

Identify the elements needed to calculate a residual income, and specify how the implicit investment cost element differs from other costs.

Contrast residual income with ROI as alternate performance measures, and describe how to resolve any conflict that might arise in interpreting the implications of each measure.

Authority and responsibility in large organizations are distributed to managers at many functional and hierarchical levels. The functions of sales, finance, manufacturing, personnel, advertising, and others are all performed by different people. Top-level, middle-level and lower-level managers are responsible for different aspects of the planning, organizing, and supervising tasks that must be performed in any business. Control problems in large organizations stem from the sheer number of decisions and interactions that occur during a normal work day. While only one-to-one relationships occur in a two-person organization, four unique relationships are possible in three-person organizations. Eleven different relationships exist in four-person organizations, and twenty-six occur in five-person organizations. Some vast organizations, such as American Telephone and Telegraph Company and General Motors Corporation, employ hundreds of thousands of people, and the number of potential interrelationships among these people is astronomical.

Managers of large firms can maintain their effectiveness by restructuring their organizations to reduce the allowable interactions. *Decentralization* subdivides the total organization into manageable, semi-autonomous parts in order to diffuse authority throughout the organization. The managerial accountant's information-reporting function in decentralized firms must be adjusted to the demands of the organizational framework. This chapter analyzes the **profit center** as a means of fulfilling the accountant's role in extending control in decentralized firms. In particular, two measures of divisional performance are highlighted, rate of **return on investment** and **residual income**.

INFORMATION NEEDS IN DECENTRALIZED ORGANIZATIONS

Routine decisions in expanded organizations are too numerous for top executives to administer. Both the managerial hierarchy and the number of resources that must be controlled mushroom in size. Top managers in centralized organizations lose the ability to respond quickly if they are inundated with problems requiring decisions. Decentralization alleviates this problem by forcing the information flow and data-collection procedures to adjust to the needs of the new organizational structure. Exhibit 11–1 illustrates some of these changes. Divisional managers must have access to data used to support decisions, and higher-level management must be furnished summarized reports on performance. Divisional managers must receive detailed records of transactions among divisions, which are treated as independent entities. Furthermore, all levels of the firm should have access to planning information. Exhibit 11–1 contrasts the reporting activities in centralized and decentralized organizations.

Providing information for planning, control, and supporting decisions is the managerial accountant's prime task. Decentralization requires an expansion

EXHIBIT 11-1 ACCOUNTING CHANGES ASSOCIATED WITH ORGANIZATIONAL CHANGES

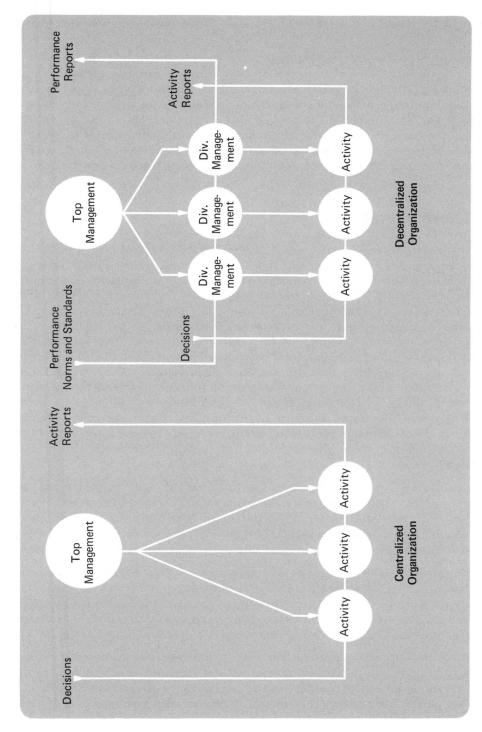

of this basic function—the control system and performance measures must be adjusted to reflect different hierarchies of authority. For example, individual divisional managers must be evaluated for salary and promotions; scarce resources, such as money, must be allocated among divisions; and operating procedures for each division must be examined for uniformity, or at least interdivisional consistency. Performance measures provide top management with information useful in evaluating divisional managers engaged in diverse activities.

THE PROFIT CENTER CONCEPT

Profit centers are decentralized subunits of an organization to which revenues, expenses, and, possibly, investment capital are assigned. Basically, the profit center concept implements responsibility accounting by identifying measurable results with the persons responsible for those results. In practice, two basic types of profit measures may be established. First, the performance of the division management can be evaluated according to profitability. This approach focuses on *measuring performance of a person*. Second, information about organizational segments can be concerned with *measuring an activity or product*. A managerial or cost accountant's basic task is to identify and measure costs, revenues, and invested capital items that are controllable by the respective divisional managers. Divisional profitability can be calculated and used to gauge performance. When some elements of profitability are not directly traceable to a particular division, cost allocations often are made. These approaches follow a hierarchy, depending on the amount of traceability. There are three major responsibility centers.

Cost centers   **Cost centers** are divisions for which the divisional manager is responsible for minimizing costs. Revenues and invested capital are not traced directly to the division. A service department that supports production operations is an example of a cost center. The general reports issued by the managerial accountant on cost center managers consist of budgets and variance analyses.

Profit centers   Profit centers exist where both costs and revenues can be traced to a division. Measuring profitability may motivate management. Invested capital is rarely traced to profit center divisions. An example of a profit center is a production division that shares capital resources with another division. Although costs and revenues are directly traceable, invested capital is not.

Investment centers   A refinement of the profit center is an **investment center**. As implied by the name, costs, revenues, and invested capital are traced to the internal divisions, thus increasing the potential for evaluation. Tracing all elements of corporate performance to the divisional level promotes full responsibility at lower levels.

REPORTING NEEDS

A decentralized firm consists of a set of semi-independent divisions. Each division, like the company as a whole, requires a complete set of relevant economic information for decision-making. Thus, the total accounting function must be segmented along parallel lines to support these needs for information. In addition, top corporate management shifts its informational needs from actual decision-making data to control data. Control over decentralized activities is extremely important because of the separation of top management from routine decision-making activities. To compensate for this separation, top management depends heavily on the internal accounting system for corporate control. The decisions made at all levels in the firm result in some quantifiable outcome. These outcomes pass through the accounting system, which places the managerial accountant in a good position to monitor performance and report on any observed exceptions to predefined expectations. The accountant's two main functions in a decentralized environment, therefore, are record-keeping and information-reporting.

Record-keeping Detailed data about divisional operations must be preserved internally. In many firms, production, cost, and profit information are collected at the division level and then combined into reports for the whole firm. Thus, the record-keeping function is segmented by division.

Some of the influences on the record keeping task were reported in a study by the National Association of Accountants:

> The decentralization of operations in an integrated company requires physical movement of materials, partly finished, and finished goods from one location to another as successive manufacturing and marketing steps are performed. Working inventories must also be maintained at each location. This raises the problem of accounting for inventory transfers between divisions, plants, and other units within the company. In some instances decentralization leads to establishment of subsidiary corporations which operate on a profit making basis with intercompany transfers accounted for as sales and purchases.[1]

The information recorded in a company's standard accounts provides the basis for the internal reports.

Information-reporting On a smaller scale, the managerial accountant assigned to a division must provide and maintain the traditional flow of accounting information within that division. For the company in total, however, internal accounting reports form an integral part of managerial control. Control reports flow two ways in an organization: one set of reports is generated about divisional operations and submitted to divisional management; a summary of these per-

[1]*Research Series No. 30, Accounting for Intracompany Transfers* (New York: National Association of Accountants), p. 4.

formance data is transmitted to higher-level executives as a means of monitoring the performance of the decentralized divisions. Exhibit 11–2 illustrates this flow of control reports.

Performance reporting has motivational implications for the operating management of a firm. The performance report indicates to operating managers performance expectations held at the corporate level, and these expectations are transmitted from top management down through the organization. Supplemental schedules detailing the components of the summary report give operating management indicators for decision-making. For example, a single monthly report that summarizes divisional sales volumes presents a clear performance indicator—top management is obviously focusing on sales volume. Supplemental divisional reports show sales volume by product, territory, salesman, and so on. The system of performance measurement must be supported through the internal accounting system.

MEASURING PERFORMANCE

Measuring performance is a necessary part of the corporate control system. It facilitates the two-way flow of information just described. Several "messages" and "measures" must be transmitted at once to ensure that divisional decisions promote the goals of the entire company. Performance measurement can become quite complicated in large organizations having multiple goals.

Typically, performance measures are tied to the reward system of the firm. Thus, managers are motivated to perform in accordance with the measurement system. For example, if a division is identified as a cost center, and the accountant issues performance reports on incurred costs, the cost center manager may attempt to minimize costs. Here, incurred costs provide a *direct measure of performance*. Alternatively, some factors can act as *complementary measures of performance*.

Direct measures   Direct measures highlight the influence of changes on the activity or outcome covered in the report. Profit center reports disclose revenues and costs as elements of profitability. Changes in cost or revenue directly alter the division's profitability and can influence managerial decisions. Managerial accountants must supply supporting information for the direct measure. Variance analysis, discussed in Chapter 12, may indicate ways to improve reported cost performance. Other factors indirectly influence the performance measure. These are complementary measures.

Flow of direct measurement documents   Each hierarchical level in a decentralized organization prepares periodic performance reports that compare budgeted data with actual data, as was discussed in Chapter 10. Four levels of responsibility are depicted in the responsibility accounting system illustrated in

EXHIBIT 11-2 FLOW OF CONTROL REPORTS

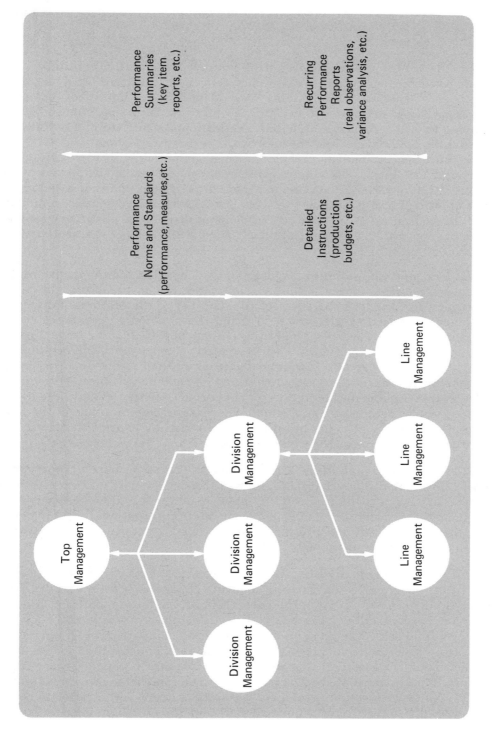

Exhibit 11–3. Although some organizations may have a unique number of reporting levels in their accounting systems, certain observations are applicable to all responsibility accounting systems. First, data from the bottom of the organization is accumulated upward. Second, the data substance may change between reporting levels. For example, the bottom two reports in Exhibit 11–3 are concerned with cost data, while the top two reports discuss income data. Third, performance reports usually provide multiple comparisons upon which to base judgments. Exhibit 11–3 facilitates comparisons of actual data with expectations (budget data), of variances for one material, department, plant, or division with those of others, and of variance for this period with the variance accumulated since the beginning of the year. The following discussion of the flow of documents in a decentralized organization will start at the lowest organizational level and proceed upwards.

Lowest level of responsibility A foreman usually holds administrative responsibility at the lowest link in the chain of command. The cost report for the cutting department foreman of the Denver plant is similar to the responsibility reports previously discussed in Chapter 10. During this reporting period, the cutting department incurred less cost than expected, as indicated by the $600 favorable variance. Prior to this period, the accumulated variance since the beginning of the year must have been $1,000 unfavorable, since the balance at this reporting date has been reduced to $400, including the current variance. This balance indicates better performance in the current period than in previous periods. The foreman would also be able to evaluate the relative consumption of the labor, material and overhead items in an attempt to identify possible tradeoffs, e.g., faster labor operations at the expense of greater material wastage.

Third level of responsibility The first line of the performance report for the whole Denver plant lists the data obtained from the report on the cutting department. Using this information, the plant manager would be able to evaluate the cutting department foreman's behavior relative to that of other foremen. In total, the Denver plant had an unfavorable variance, in contrast to the favorable one incurred by the cutting department.

Second level of responsibility Cost data from the third level report are incorporated in the second level income statement. Progression from cost centers to responsibility centers up to profit centers follows the normal path for large, decentralized organizations. Managers of profit centers are responsible for both revenues and costs. The division manager would compare data for the Denver plant against the performance of other plants. Denver accounted for $8,000 of the variance while the other four departments combined only incurred $10,000 variance. Furthermore, Denver's current variance represents one third ($8,000/$24,000) of its year-to-date variance, while the current variance for the whole electronics division represents one half ($18,000/$36,000) of its year-to-date var-

EXHIBIT 11–3   FLOW OF DOCUMENTS IN DECENTRALIZED ORGANIZATION

Profit Report to the President, Giant Corp.

	Budget	Actual	Variance	Variance, Year to Date
Division 1, Chemicals	x	x	x	x
Division 2, Electronics	$ 93,000	$ 85,000	$18,000	$36,000
Division 3, Airframe	x	x	x	x
Division 4, Softgoods	x	x	x	x
Total	$235,000	$232,000	$13,000	$74,000

Income Statement, Electronics Division

	Budget	Actual	Variance	Variance Year to Date
Revenues	x	x	x	x
Costs:				
Plant 1, Atlanta	x	x	x	x
Plant 2, Boston	x	x	x	x
Plant 3, Denver	$ 30,000	$ 38,000	$ 8,000	$24,000
Plant 4, San Diego	x	x	x	x
Selling and Administrative	x	x	x	x
Total Costs	x	x	x	x
Net Income	$ 93,000	$ 85,000	$18,000	$36,000

Performance Report, Denver Plant

	Budget	Actual	Variance	Variance Year to Date
Cutting Department	$ 6,700	$ 6,100	($ 600)	$ 400
Stamping Department	x	x	x	x
Wiring Department	x	x	x	x
Testing Department	x	x	x	x
Packing Department	x	x	x	x
Total	$ 30,000	$ 38,000	$ 8,000	$24,000

Cutting Department Cost Report

	Budget	Actual	Variance	Variance Year to Date
Machine operators	x	x	x	x
End twisters	x	x	x	x
Material handlers	x	x	x	x
A47 cable	x	x	x	x
Bx46 material	x	x	x	x
Department overhead	x	x	x	x
Total	$ 6,700	$ 6,100	($ 600)	$ 400

iance: this indicates that Denver has incurred greater variances in the past than has the total division.

Top level responsibility   The top level management of all decentralized organizations periodically reviews the performance of all major divisions. Top level executives have the prime responsibility for strategic planning; and long-run profitability is of major concern for most businesses. While the president exercises ultimate authority and bears ultimate responsibility within the organization, decentralization usually focuses control responsibility at the divisional level.

Complementary measures   Certain factors influence the direct measures of performance but are not disclosed in the performance report. Their effect, however, may be pronounced, and their importance should be recognized. For instance, the method used to trace or assign costs to a profit center has a significant influence on the reported results. Methods or bases of reporting represent managerial decisions on structuring and the performance-measurement and data-collection systems. Because methods do have an effect on measurement and, hence, behavior, they should be reviewed carefully prior to adoption.

The problem of simultaneously directing managerial attention to several corporate goals is partially solved by the use of *composite* measures, which combine several direct measures related to multigoal activity. Return on investment is one such composite measure.

RETURN ON INVESTMENT

Return on investment (ROI) is used widely to evaluate the performance of operating divisions within a firm. Quite simply, ROI measures the profitability of a division in relation to its investment base; it is analogous to the similar concept used in project planning. The formula for calculating the return on investment is:

$$\text{ROI} = \frac{\text{Net Income}}{\text{Investment}}$$

A division having net income of $250,000 and an investment of $5,000,000 has a return on investment of 5%.

In this sense, the ROI calculation measures the earnings achieved on an investment, making possible comparisons between divisions or alternative investments. For example, if a division has a ROI of 4% on an investment of $1,000,000, the 4% is analogous to an interest rate. ROI facilitates the evaluation of different-sized investments that yield different-sized returns. The structure of the ROI calculation provides more insights into its appropriateness.

Composition   The return on investment formula is composed of two supplemental measures of divisional activity, **asset turnover** (sales divided by investment) and **margin on sales** (net income divided by sales). The formula is derived as follows:

$$\text{ROI} = \text{Asset Turnover} \times \text{Margin on Sales}$$
$$= \frac{\text{Sales}}{\text{Investment}} \times \frac{\text{Net Income}}{\text{Sales}}$$
$$= \frac{\text{Net Income}}{\text{Investment}}$$

The margin on sales measures the percentage of profit included in each sales dollar. A high markup alone will not ensure a division's success. Profit must be considered in the context of the quantity of resources required to generate it, that is, the investment base. The asset turnover measures the velocity of utilization or turnover of investment. Other things equal, the fewer assets required to support divisional activity, the more assets available for other activities of the firm. Thus, the sales volume relative to the invested resources provides another measure of performance. Combined, these two measures produce a third, ROI.

Significance   Neither the margin on sales nor the asset turnover alone provides a complete picture of performance. But, combined, they bring together relevant variables and make possible comparisons of diverse operations. For example, consider the following situation:

A small firm was decentralized into two operating divisions — a jewelry store and a grocery store. Annually, a conflict arose over which was the more successful operation. The jewelry store manager supported his position by showing that, because of high markups, his profit on sales was 30%, in contrast to the grocery store's 4% profit.

However, the grocery store produced an asset turnover of 3 in comparison with the .4 achieved by the jewelry operation. The jewelry store divisional manager said that this comparison was unfair since, "Diamonds keep much better than vegetables, so a high turnover is not necessary in our operation." Thus, the argument continued.

On the surface, the operations seem too diverse for comparison. Each measure favors a particular type of operation — profit on sales for high markup and asset turnover for high volume.

The key to the problem, of course, is to use the return on investment, which considers both markups and volume, and enables management to focus on the profits generated on its required investment in the operation. In the case of the grocery and jewelry stores, their ROIs are the same, 12%; that is, each earned 12% profit on the investment associated with it.

The presence of idle resources in operations has a pronounced influence on the performance of the firm. Idle assets have a cost, in that these resources could be converted into some profit-generating use. The presence of excess cash or inventory is a problem many firms face. Certainly, some of the cash could be diverted to other opportunities that would generate revenue for the firm. Return on investment focuses attention on this often neglected phase of divisional management.

An example   Return on investment is a performance measure that considers all options open to divisional managers. Frequently, top management may establish a target rate as a performance standard. Operating managers then exercise discretion over how to reach the specified target. The following case is an example.

The Able Bakery Company is decentralized into several baking divisions at different locations. One division has an investment of $1,200,000 in ovens and other preparatory equipment. Last year, the division had sales of $3,200,000 and net income of $60,000. Its ROI was 5%.

Because of changes in the industry and expected shifts in demand, top management of the Able Bakery Company has set 6% as a target ROI for the coming year. Faced with this situation, the divisional manager investigated alternatives.

First, he looked at profit. Assuming that sales remained constant, an increase in net income of $12,000 would provide the desired return. This was calculated as follows:

$$\frac{\text{Net Income}}{\$1,200,000\ (\text{Investment})} = .06\ (\text{Desired Return})$$
$$\text{Net Income} = \$1,200,000 \times .06$$
$$= \$72,000$$
$$\text{Desired Income} - \text{Current Income} = \text{Change in Income}$$
$$\$72,000 - \$60,000 \qquad = \$12,000$$

To achieve this result, either annual costs would have to be reduced drastically or prices would have to be raised.

Next, the divisional manager looked at the second part of ROI—investment. In this case, the 6% return could be attained if the investment base were reduced to $1,000,000. This was calculated as follows:

$$\frac{\$60,000\ (\text{Net Income})}{\text{Investment}} = .06\ (\text{Desired Return})$$
$$\$60,000 = .06 \times \text{Investment}$$
$$\frac{\$60,000}{.06} = \text{Investment}$$
$$= \$1,000,000$$

A second means of attaining the desired result would involve releasing some assets from production. The $200,000 reduction in assets was thought to be too high at the present, so he decided to compromise.

Initially, $100,000 of assets was released and attention was again focused on cost reduction. Now, profits had to increase to $66,000 to reach the target.

$$\frac{\text{Net Income}}{\$1,100,000\ (\text{Adjusted Investment})} = .06\ (\text{Desired Return})$$
$$\text{Net Income} = \$1,100,000 \times .06$$
$$= \$66,000$$

In this case, several options were open to the divisional manager. Also, attention was directed to matters other than pure profitability as indicators of performance.

SOME PROBLEMS WITH ROI

Conceptually, the return on investment technique is appealing as a performance measure; however, it has limitations. Problems center on determining the investment base, calculating net income, and allocating costs to the divisions.

Measuring a divisional investment base requires a precise definition of all elements that should be included, and the value that should be assigned to them. The assets traceable to a division might not include those resources shared by several divisions. Frequently, nontraceable assets are allocated to divisions by some secondary measure of "benefit," but such arbitrary assignments are questionable. Traceability alone does not solve the valuation problem. There is no substantial agreement on what value should be assigned to the assets of a division. Some managers advocate using historical cost, whereas others use current replacement value. Managers must choose also between using gross cost or net book value (cost less depreciation).

Each method will influence the reported ROI, and each may suggest different directions for managerial actions. Under a gross cost method, the age of the plant or equipment is not considered, so early replacements of capital goods can be expected. The benefits of improved technology can outweigh the marginal increase in investment. Net book value, however, promotes the continued use of obsolete resources because their low value (investment base) will inflate ROI.

Proponents of replacement cost hold that it provides the best measure of current performance, because replacement cost measures assets at current values. Yet, replacement cost is difficult to determine and may require subjective estimates. For example, suppose that one division is currently earning $20,000 per year with $400,000 of assets. Assuming straight-line depreciation and a ten-year life, the net book value can be expected to decrease by $40,000 per year. Assume also that a 2% economic inflation is reflected in the replacement cost of the assets.

If earnings remain constant, the following patterns will pertain to the alternative ROI calculations.

Year	Gross Cost		Net Book Value		Replacement Cost	
1	$\dfrac{20,000}{400,000}$	= 5%	$\dfrac{20,000}{400,000}$	= 5%	$\dfrac{20,000}{400,000}$	= 5%
2	$\dfrac{20,000}{400,000}$	= 5%	$\dfrac{20,000}{360,000^*}$	= 5.5%	$\dfrac{20,000}{367,200^{**}}$	= 5.4%
3	$\dfrac{20,000}{400,000}$	= 5%	$\dfrac{20,000}{320,000}$	= 6.3%	$\dfrac{20,000}{326,400}$	= 6.1%
4	$\dfrac{20,000}{400,000}$	= 5%	$\dfrac{20,000}{280,000}$	= 7.1%	$\dfrac{20,000}{285,600}$	= 7%

*Calculated as: 400,000 − (400,000/10) = 360,000.
**Calculated as: 400,000 − (400,000/10) × 1.02 = 367,200. This assumes that replacement cost correlates with the net book value.

Net income   Net income must be considered in relation to the asset base. When current operating performance is evaluated, nonrecurring items, such as extraordinary gains and losses, should be excluded. Areas of responsibility must also be considered. The corporate tax rate is normally a function of activities outside the control of divisional management. Interest expense, incurred as a result of corporate borrowing, is uncontrollable by the division. For these reasons, net income is sometimes defined as net income before interest and taxes. Net income emphasizes areas controllable by divisional management. When large joint and common costs occur, ROI calculations frequently rely on divisional contribution margins rather than on net profit figures.

Allocations   In calculating divisional ROI, traceability must be considered. Many elements of cost and investment are directly traceable. Certain exceptions, such as the expense of central offices, are not generally directly traceable to a particular division. These costs and resources can be allocated by use of a variety of techniques (such as usage rates or ability to pay). When making allocations, however, extreme care must be exercised in order to avoid destroying the significance of the resulting ROI calculation.

ROI can be a valuable motivational tool and control device within the firm. Logically or not, many managers reason as follows: "If each subcomponent (division) of the firm maximizes its ROI, then ROI for the firm will be maximized." Remember, however, that this or any other motivational technique is good only to the extent that it fosters decisions in conformance with corporate goals.

RESIDUAL INCOME

Residual income is the amount that remains after deducting an implied interest charge from operating income. Implied interest reflects an opportunity cost rather than a real cost, that is, no real borrower and lender relationship exists, so no legal interest can be incurred. Rather, the interest charge resembles a separate application of central administrative overhead allocated to the decentralized divisions by top-level management. The base for determining the size of the interest charge is the dollar amount of assets invested in each profit center. The rate of interest charged to each separate profit center equals the overall minimum return on investment specified as part of the corporate strategic plan. In effect, then, central administration specifies a minimum desired return on investment, provides a stock of assets to each decentralized profit center, and imposes an interest charge on the centers as compensation for providing the original investment.

Residual income is a key index to be used in evaluating the performance of decentralized management. All profit centers are expected to achieve the minimum desired return on investment implicit in the interest charge: the quality of divisional performance is judged after this point has been achieved. For example, the Multi Corporation has three decentralized operating divisions. Operating decisions are made by the manager of each division. These decisions include a selection of investment projects that are financed out of internally generated funds. Top management at Multi allows divisional managers much latitude, as long as each generates a 15% minimum desired return on investment. This goal is imposed on the divisions by charging them an implicit interest equal to 15% of their net book values. Exhibit 11–4 presents the residual income statements for the three divisions. Note that the 15% interest charge has been deducted from operating income to produce a divisional residual income.

Division 1 has a greater amount of assets than the other divisions, and therefore, may generate greater amounts of income. Evaluations of division managers at the segment margin level will produce ambiguous results, because Division 1 has potential earnings advantage over the other two divisions. A comparative evaluation at the segment margin level would rank-order the divisions from best to worst as Divisions 1, 3, and 2 (given that more contribution is better than less). A comparative evaluation at the residual income level, however, would rank-order the divisions as 3, 2, and 1. The investment charge compensates for the potential earning advantage granted Division 1: divisions with greater amounts of assets receive proportionately greater amounts of investment charges. Also note that the investment charges are not accumulated and subtracted in computing total corporate income, since no real investment charge has been incurred.

The residual income approach to measuring divisional performance may actually encourage divisional managers to make decisions that are consistent with overall corporate strategy. For example, divisional performance in the ROI Company is evaluated on the basis of return on investment, while divisional performance in the Resid Corporation is evaluated on the basis of residual income. Division 1 in each company has $1,000,000 in operating assets. The segment margin contribution to income of each division is $250,000. Corporate strategy for both firms specifies a minimum desired return on investment of 20%, and Division 1 of both companies has an opportunity to invest $100,000 in projects that will generate profits of $23,000 per year.

Division 1 managers in both companies probably would make an analysis similar to that illustrated in Exhibit 11–5. The manager in ROI Company would calculate the return on investment expected under two conditions: do not invest and do invest. Since his return on investment would drop if he invested the $100,000, he probably would reject the opportunity to invest in a project yielding $23,000. Yet note that the project has a return on investment equal to 23%, which is higher than the strategic goal; that is, ROI's Division 1 manager would reject an opportunity to further company strategy simply because his personal evaluation criterion would decrease slightly. The manager in Resid Corporation would calculate his residual income under the two alternatives, and he would decide to invest, since his residual income would increase. Thus, the residual

EXHIBIT 11-4 RESIDUAL INCOME STATEMENTS FOR DIVISIONS OF MULTI CORPORATION

	Division 1	Division 2	Division 3	Total Firm
Revenue	$5,960,000	$1,345,000	$9,087,000	$16,392,000
Variable Costs	2,500,000	635,000	6,957,000	10,092,000
Contribution Margin	$3,460,000	$ 710,000	$2,130,000	$ 6,300,000
Discretionary Fixed Costs	1,500,000	100,000	530,000	2,130,000
Short-run Performance Margin	$1,960,000	$ 610,000	$1,600,000	$ 4,170,000
Traceable Committed Fixed Costs	960,000	210,000	800,000	1,970,000
Segment Margin	$1,000,000	$ 400,000	$ 800,000	$ 2,200,000
Assignable Central Administration	100,000	40,000	80,000	220,000
*Investment Charges	750,000	60,000	150,000	–0–
Residual Income	$ 150,000	$ 300,000	$ 570,000	$ 1,980,000
Nonassignable Costs				694,000
Net Income				$ 1,286,000

*Minimum desired 15% return based upon asset book values as follows: $5,000,000, $400,000, $1,000,000.

EXHIBIT 11–5 CONTRASTING RESULTS OF DECISIONS MADE UNDER RETURN ON INVESTMENT AND RESIDUAL INCOME EVALUATION CRITERIA

Part 1 Division 1, ROI Company

	Do Not Invest $100,000	Do Invest $100,000
Segment Margin	$ 250,000	$ 273,000
Investment	$1,000,000	$1,100,000
Return on Investment	25%	24.8%

Part 2 Division 1, Resid Corporation

	Do Not Invest $100,000	Do Invest $100,000
Segment Margin	$ 250,000	$ 273,000
Investment Charge (20%)	200,000	220,000
Residual Income	$ 50,000	$ 53,000

income approach created an incentive for the divisional managers to make a decision that was consistent with overall corporate strategy.

SUMMARY

As a business increases in size, modifications may become necessary in its organizational structure. Decentralization is one common modification. Decentralized firms operate divisions as independent units. This frees top management for creative planning and dealing with exceptions.

The profit center concept is intended to promote motivation and control within the decentralized firm. Divisional managers are given profit responsibility over their divisions. Managerial accountants face diverse information needs and reporting demands in decentralized organizations.

Return on investment can be an effective means for evaluating the relative performance of investment centers. The ROI calculation provides a common basis for evaluating divisional performance when each division has unique profits and assets: profits are deflated by the investment base to produce a compound index of performance that is comparable among divisions. Residual income is another means for evaluating relative performance of investment center management. Use of the residual income performance criterion may actually promote behavior that conforms to organizational goals better than does use of ROI.

SUGGESTED READINGS

Buzby, Stephen. "Profit Contribution by Market." *Management Accounting*, November 1976.

Clayden, Roger. "A New Way to Measure and Control Divisional Performance." *Management Services*, September/October, 1970.

Gordon, L. A. "The Return on Investment and the Cost of Capital." *Management Accounting*, February 1976.

Stallman, James C. "A Framework for Evaluating Cost Control Procedures for a Process." *The Accounting Review*, October 1972.

Walker, Charles W. "Profitability and Responsibility Accounting." *Management Accounting*, December 1971.

QUESTIONS

11-1   What is decentralization? Give an example of decentralization in your school. Give an example of decentralization in a business firm.

11-2   How can managerial effectiveness be enhanced by limiting interactions?

11-3   What differences in reporting activity exist in centralized and decentralized organizations?

11-4   Define the term *profit center*. What are the two basic types of profit centers? Present the main characteristic of each type.

11-5   Briefly differentiate cost centers, profit centers, and investment centers. Identify the basic characteristics of each.

11-6   In each of the following cases, match the terms *cost center*, *profit center*, or *investment center* with the appropriate characteristics:

    (A) A refinement of the profit center.
    (B) Managers are responsible for minimizing costs.
    (C) Promotes full responsibility at lower organizational levels.

(D) Costs and revenues are directly traceable.

(E) A service department that supports production operations is an example.

11-7   Why is return on investment classified as a composite performance measure? Present the formula for calculating ROI and explain its significance.

11-8   Define the terms *margin on sales* and *asset turnover*. What do these measures mean in relation to the performance of a division?

11-9   When Sam Sharpe, a managerial accountant, suggested to his boss, Mr. Hiram Firam, that using return on investment as a divisional performance measure would reduce investments in idle resources, Mr. Firam became upset.

"Sam, when you learn something about people instead of accounting, you'll learn that the only way to get rid of idle resources is to go out into the factory and find them. I make it a practice to visit each operating division once a year. If I find any unused equipment, I fire the manager on the spot. It must work; during the last four years I've found no unused resources."

(A) Do you suppose that Mr. Firam's method really works? Why or why not?

(B) What type of action does Mr. Firam's method probably lead his managers to use?

(C) As Sam Sharpe, how could you justify using return on investment in this situation?

11-10   Identify three basic problems associated with using the return on investment technique.

EXERCISES

*11-11   A common measure of a management's performance is "return on net worth." This is a particularly important measure from the shareholder's point of view. This ratio can be expressed as the product of three other ratios as shown below:

$$\underset{\text{Net Worth}}{\text{Return on}} \quad \frac{\text{Net Income}}{\text{Net Worth}} = \overset{\text{I}}{\frac{\text{Net Income}}{\text{Sales}}} \times \overset{\text{II}}{\frac{\text{Sales}}{\text{Assets}}} \times \overset{\text{III}}{\frac{\text{Assets}}{\text{Net Worth}}}$$

Required:

(A) Discuss the "return on net worth" as a management goal and as a measurement of management performance.

(B) What management activities are measured by each of the ratios I, II, III?

(C) Would separation of the "return on net worth" into the three ratios and use of these ratios for planning targets and performance measures result in goal congruence (or improvement toward goal congruence) among the responsible managers? Explain your answer.

(CMA adapted)

11–12 Below are three independent cases (with missing data) that concern performance measures to evaluate decentralized organizational efficiency. Determine the value associated with each letter.

	Case 1	Case 2	Case 3
Assets	$ A	$200,000	$ G
Return on Investment	20%	D%	H%
Sales	$ B	$600,000	$900,000
Asset Turnover	8	E	3
Net Profit	$40,000	$ F	$ I
Margin on Sales	C %	5%	3.3%

11–13 Selected data for three divisions of a decentralized company are presented below:

	Division 1	Division 2	Division 3
Assets	$1,000,000	$2,000,000	$3,000,000
Segment Margin	550,000	660,000	770,000

(A) Rank the divisions from "best" to "worst" in terms of their return on investment.

(B) Rank the divisions from "best" to "worst" in terms of their residual income, assuming that the strategic plan requires a 10% return on investment.

(C) Rank the divisions from "best" to "worst" in terms of their residual income, assuming that the strategic plan requires a 20% return on investment.

11–14 Below are presented the balances for the major classifications needed to construct a residual income statement. Data are presented in alphabetical order. Construct a residual income statement in good form.

Assignable Central Administrative Cost	$ 100,000
Discretionary Fixed Costs	450,000
Investment Charges	150,000
Revenue	1,800,000
Traceable Committed Fixed Cost	200,000
Variable Cost	630,000

11-15   Below are three independent cases that explore the relationship be-tween elements associated with the computation of residual income. In each case, two elements are missing. Determine the number that corresponds to each missing element, A through F.

	Case 1	Case 2	Case 3
Segment margin	$200,000	C	$ 500,000
Investment charge	$ 50,000	D	E
Residual Income	A	$100,000	$ 300,000
Divisional Assets	$250,000	$800,000	$1,000,000
Minimum Desired ROI	B	10%	F

11-16   The Washington Company reported sales of $1,000,000, an asset turnover of 4, and a return on investment of 30%. Strategic policy of Washington calls for a minimum desired return on investment for all assets of 10%. Deter-mine the residual income for Washington Company.

11-17   Although he was the youngest accountant in the central controller's office of Ace Corporation, John Bright wanted to be more than just another ac-countant. He stated publicly that he could greatly improve the return on invest-ment if he were promoted to plant manager at one of Ace's several plants. One day, the president of Ace Corporation overheard John, was impressed with this boast, and gave him a chance with a small plant outside Chicago. In the first year, John sold most of the facilities to the First National Bank of Chicago for $3,000,000 and then leased them all back for 99 years, on terms calling for pay-ment of $100,000 per year.

>   (A) Would this transaction improve John's return on investment figure for the plant?

>   (B) If it would improve the return on investment, why doesn't Ace do this for all its plants?

>   (C) If John leases his plant and another plant manager doesn't, can the returns on investment of the two managers be compared fairly?

>   (D) What other methods would improve return on investment? Explain.

>   (E) Do you think the company was happy with John's technique?

11-18   The Red Bird Corporation builds one product on a high-speed assem-bly line. The product, a connector for a light fixture, has ten separate parts that are manufactured in plants around Pittsburgh and assembled in one main plant. The market for these fixtures is highly competitive, but Red Bird has been able to beat the competition consistently in the past few years by fast, integrated pro-duction techniques and consistent high-quality service. Continued success is essential to Red Bird, for there are only ten large manufacturers using this type of fixture and there are many diversified competitors. The fixture is Red Bird's only product. To keep the cost edge, the controller has recommended decentralization, with each of the parts plants and the assembly plant operating as separate entities. The manager of a plant operating as a separate entity would be in a position to make modifications in the product or in the production techniques to meet the demands of a specialized segment of the total market.

(A) What should the Red Bird Corporation consider before making a decision for decentralization?

(B) In your opinion, should they decentralize? Explain why or why not.

(C) What are the behavioral implications of decentralization?

(D) What do you see as the major factors for and against decentralization in Red Bird?

11–19 A decentralized management organization functions well for production management — foremen report to superintendents, superintendents to production managers, and production managers to the plant manager. Each of their individual goals is basically consistent with that of the plant manager. This is not necessarily true for the controller. Top management evaluates the plants on information received from the plant controllers. At times the controller comes into conflict with the plant manager, much like the scorekeeper/referee and the team captain in a football game. One solution is to have the controller report directly to top management and not to the plant manager.

(A) What problem results when the plant controller reports directly to top management?

(B) How would the plant controller be evaluated if his direct superior were in the central office building miles away from the plant? How would he be evaluated if his direct superior were the plant manager?

(C) How does the communication down from top management function under the two methods of control in part (B)? Is this a problem?

(D) How would budget planning proceed if the controller reported directly to top management? Would this be different if he reported to the plant manager?

11–20 The Richards Manufacturing Company has a decentralized organization. The production superintendents are separated into individual cost centers, the plants function as profit centers, and the divisions as investment centers. The heat-treatment foreman understands the cost center concept but thinks top management at his plant is foolish. "If they want to increase production, all they have to do is give me better machines. It's the old machinery that keeps my production down."

(A) What isn't the heat-treatment foreman considering? Do you think his statement is unusual?

(B) What additional considerations differentiate a cost center from a profit center? A profit center from an investment center?

(C) Why does Richards Manufacturing wish to set up all this separate bookkeeping? Isn't it going to be more costly in the long run?

(D) Is the transfer price of an item between one profit center and another profit center important if the transfers are all within one single firm?

11–21 The Love Company was formed by three young sociologists to make some money, provide work for the unemployed, and spread love. The Love Company's product is footpads cut in the shape of a heart. Their production foreman was evaluated on worker-evaluation forms passed out to his employees in the plant. He received a predominance of "very goods" and, on this basis, was given a raise. Sales of the footpads had been good, but production was slow and of poor quality.

(A) What could the company do to improve production?

(B) Would the recommendation you made in part (A) conflict with the stated goals outlined by the company?

(C) Are the goals of spreading love and increasing production, contradictory? Explain why or why not.

11–22 The production foreman of Pressure Valve Company was in a reflective mood when he came home from work. He began to philosophize. "Return on investment! All this company thinks of is return on investment. What about return on the labor employed, or return on the natural resources expanded! By centering the evaluation on return on investment, all emphasis is placed on the investment base, ignoring all other factors necessary for good evaluation."

(A) Is this man's complaint valid? Explain why or why not.

(B) Is investment the only consideration when looking at return on investment? What else might be a consideration?

(C) What are the drawbacks in the exclusive use of return on investment?

(D) What other items may be used to evaluate a corporation? Is it important to know for what purpose the corporation is being evaluated?

11–23 The Howard Corporation is considering using return on investment as a method for evaluating its plants. Since corporate management knows that any method of evaluation will influence the performance of its plant managers, they wish to select the investment base very carefully. The three alternatives they are considering are gross cost, net book value, and replacement cost.

(A) If gross cost is chosen as the investment base, what inconsistency in goals could evolve between the plant manager and the corporate officers?

(B) If net book value is chosen as the investment base, what inconsistency in goals could evolve between the plant manager and the corporate officers?

(C) If replacement cost is chosen as the investment base, what inconsistency in goals could evolve between the plant manager and the corporate officers?

(D) Pick the investment base you think best and explain how you would resolve any inconsistencies in your choice.

11-24 A company is decentralized into two divisions, Division A and Division B. At the end of the year, Division A had a return on investment of 12%, and Division B had a return on investment of 10%.

(A) On the basis of this performance measure, is Division A superior to Division B?

(B) What does return on investment mean in this case?

(C) Should the company consider closing Division B because of its performance? List reasons both for and against this action.

(D) Would your answer to part (A) be different if it were known that Division A was a grocery store and Division B a jewelry store? Explain why or why not.

PROBLEMS

11-25 The Multiple Parts Corporation makes components and also assembles electronic calculators in its several operating divisions. One of these divisions, the Dot Company, makes the component that controls the positioning of decimal points in the calculators. The manager of Dot Company, Mr. Pres Key, has tentatively placed a selling price of $5 a unit on his product for both internal transfers and external sales. His division's asset and cost structure is as follows:

Total Assets	$500,000
Annual Fixed Overhead Cost	280,000
Variable Cost per Unit	$2.50

The Corporation treats each of its divisions as an investment center and uses return on investment as a performance measure. The Corporation has set 15% as the desired rate of return on investment for the Dot Company.

(A) How many units must Key sell to reach the desired return on investment?

(B) If sales do reach the level required in part (A), what would be the asset turnover?

(C) If sales reach the desired level, what would be the margin on sales?

(D) The Dot Company has an average annual sales volume of 180,000 units. Of these, 50,000 are transferred within the Corporation to the assembly division. Recently, the manager of the assembly division asked that the price per unit be lowered to $4.50 because of market conditions. Key estimates that he can reduce his assets by $30,000 and lower his annual fixed overhead cost by $80,000 if he does not lower the transfer price, and if the assembly division buys from an outside supplier. Should he lower the price for internal transfers to $4.50? Show any necessary calculations.

11–26 Bill Smith, the new president of Sanders Corporation, was recently promoted from his old position as vice-president for Sales. One of Bill's first acts was to evaluate his divisional managers. Examining the residual income statements, he extracted the following information:

	Division 1	Division 2	Division 3
Segment margin	$ 600,000	$ 400,000	$ 300,000
Investment charge	500,000	200,000	200,000
Residual Income	$ 100,000	$ 200,000	$ 100,000
Book Value of Assets	$1,000,000	$1,000,000	$ 600,000

Bill then divided the residual income by the book value of assets to determine a return on investment. ROI figures produced by Bill are 10%, 20%, and 16%, for Divisions 1, 2, and 3, respectively. When he saw that the manager for Division 1 had a ROI much smaller than those produced by other managers, Bill decided to fire him. But first he consults with you, the corporate controller.

(A) Do you agree with Mr. Smith's calculations of ROI? If not, recompute a more appropriate set.

(B) Should terminal action, such as firing a divisional manager, be based solely upon examination of ROI data for one period? If not, how should ROI figures be used?

(C) If the evaluation criterion was residual income instead of ROI, which manager would be evaluated as "best?" Can ROI and residual income measures rank-order divisional managers in different order for comparative evaluation purposes? Explain the causes of such differences.

11–27 Four levels of performance reports for the Midget Corporation are presented in Exhibit 11–6. These documents reflect information for the first three months of the current year on operations of the Cable Department in the Austin Plant of the Motor Division, as well as information pertaining to operations at higher organizational levels. Evaluate operating performance for the Cable Department.

EXHIBIT 11–6   FLOW OF DOCUMENTS IN MIDGET CORPORATION

Profit Report to the President, Midget Corporation

	Budget	Actual	Variance	Variance, Year to Date
Division 1, Chemicals	x	x	x	x
Division 2, Motor	$ 67,000	$ 85,000	$18,000	$36,000
Division 3, Airframe	x	x	x	x
Division 4, Softgoods	x	x	x	x
Total	$209,000	$232,000	$23,000	$54,000

Income Statement, Motor Division

	Budget	Actual	Variance	Variance, Year to Date
Revenues	x	x	x	x
Costs:				
Plant 1, Atlanta	x	x	x	x
Plant 2, Boston	x	x	x	x
Plant 3, Austin	$ 30,000	$ 28,000	($ 2,000)	($ 6,000)
Plant 4, Portland	x	x	x	x
Selling & Administrative	x	x	x	x
Total Costs	x	x	x	x
Net Income	$ 67,000	$ 85,000	$18,000	$36,000

Performance Report, Austin Plant

	Budget	Actual	Variance	Variance, Year to Date
Cable Department	$ 6,700	$ 7,100	$ 400	($ 1,600)
Stamping Department	x	x	x	x
Wiring Department	x	x	x	x
Testing Department	x	x	x	x
Packing Department	x	x	x	x
Total	$ 30,000	$ 28,000	($ 2,000)	($ 6,000)

Cable Department Cost Report

	Budget	Actual	Variance	Variance, Year to Date
Machine Operators	x	x	x	x
End Twisters	x	x	x	x
Material Handlers	x	x	x	x
A47 Cable	x	x	x	x
Bx46 Material	x	x	x	x
Departmental Overhead	x	x	x	x
Total	$ 6,700	$ 7,100	$ 400	($ 1,600)

11–28   The TRIAD Corporation has three decentralized operating divisions. Operating decisions made by the manager of each division include the selection of investment projects that are financed out of internally generated funds. Top management at TRIAD allows divisional managers much latitude, as long as each generates a 20% minimum desired return on investment. This goal is imposed on the divisions by charging them an implicit interest equal to 20% of their net book values. Exhibit 11–7 presents the residual income statements for the three divisions. Note that the 20% interest charge has been deducted from operating income to produce a divisional residual income.

> (A) Why aren't the investment charges for the three divisions totaled and subtracted from the segment margin in the "Total Firm" column?
>
> (B) Did Division 1 really have a loss? If not, explain the meaning of "Residual Loss."
>
> (C) Rank-order the performance of the three divisions from best to worst.
>
> (D) Assume that performance of the manager in Division 3 was evaluated in terms of his relative return on investment. Would he be elated with an opportunity to invest $100,000 in a project yielding profits of $30,000 per year? Explain your answer.

11–29   The divisions of Conglomerate Company are all independent subsidiaries that operate in separate markets. Central management plans to establish a single performance criterion for its divisions, and is currently considering either return on investment or residual income. Management wishes to select the criterion that promotes goal congruity; that is, management wants the goals of the subsidiaries to be in conformity with the goals of central management.

To help demonstrate the relationship between goal congruity and performance criteria, the controller of Conglomerate asked you to prepare a demonstration, based upon the assumed information:

> Corporate goal: maximize income, given a 20% minimum required return on investment
> Proposed Project A: $12,000 income on $50,000 investment
> Proposed Project B: $15,000 income on $80,000 investment
> Existing divisional income: $120,000
> Existing divisional investment: $400,000

> (A) Will Project A be accepted or rejected if residual income is the performance criterion? Explain.
>
> (B) Will Project B be accepted if residual income is the performance criterion? Explain.
>
> (C) Will Project A be accepted if ROI is the performance criterion? Explain.

EXHIBIT 11-7 RESIDUAL INCOME STATEMENTS FOR DIVISIONS OF TRIAD CORPORATION

	Division 1	Division 2	Division 3	Total Firm
Revenue	$5,960,000	$1,345,000	$9,087,000	$16,392,000
Variable Costs	2,500,000	635,000	6,957,000	10,092,000
Contribution Margin	$3,460,000	$ 710,000	$2,130,000	$ 6,300,000
Discretionary Fixed Costs	1,500,000	100,000	530,000	2,130,000
Short-run Performance Margin	$1,960,000	$ 610,000	$1,600,000	$ 4,170,000
Traceable Committed Fixed Costs	960,000	210,000	800,000	1,970,000
Segment Margin	$1,000,000	$ 400,000	$ 800,000	$ 2,200,000
Assignable Central Administration	100,000	40,000	80,000	220,000
*Investment Charges	1,000,000	80,000	200,000	–0–
Residual Income (loss)	($ 100,000)	$ 280,000	$ 520,000	$ 1,980,000
Nonassignable Costs				694,000
Net Income				$ 1,286,000

*Minimum desire 20% return based upon asset book values as follows: $5,000,000, $400,000, $1,000,000.

(D) Will Project B be accepted if ROI is the performance criterion? Explain.

11–30   Zoomber Company bought a machine for $100,000 four years ago. The useful life of the machine was estimated at 10 years, and the salvage value was expected to be zero. Yearly depreciation amounts to $10,000, so the current book value of the machine is $60,000. If the machine were sold tomorrow, however, it would bring in only $20,000. The annual out-of-pocket (expenditures) cost to produce 10,000 units of output is $95,000, not counting the $10,000 depreciation. A new machine can be purchased for $70,000 plus the old machine or for $100,000 cash. It will have a six-year life and zero scrap value, and will produce 10,000 units of output at an annual out-of-pocket cost of $75,000, not counting $15,000 depreciation ($90,000 ÷ 6).

(A) In calculating the return on the investment in new machine, what dollar amount belongs in the numerator (to represent annual income)?

(B) In calculating the return on the new machine, what dollar amount belongs in the denominator to represent the investment?

(C) List one objection to the use of ROI as a criterion for evaluating the new machine.

11–31   The Wilson Products Corporation is decentralized into several operating divisions. The company management is interested in evaluating the performance of the home-care products division. The following information about this division is made available. It is not arranged in any particular order.

Gross Sales	$4,700,000
Sales Returns and Allowances	200,000
Accounts and Notes Receivable	120,000
Accounts and Notes Payable	230,000
Inventory	470,000
Net Fixed Assets	910,000
Average Fixed Overhead Cost	50,000
Net Income before Interest and Taxes	189,000
Interest	9,000
Taxes	80,000
Contribution Margin per Unit	4.00

(A) What is the asset turnover for this division? What does this mean about the division's performance?

(B) What is the margin on sales for this division? What does this mean about the division's performance?

(C) What is the return on investment for this division? What does this mean about the division's performance?

(D) How many units must the division sell in order to have a return on investment of 10%, if all factors remain at the present levels?

(E) If sales of 40,000 units are expected, and all factors remain at their present levels, what must the sales price per unit be in order to have an asset turnover of 4?

CHAPTER 12

Standard Costs and Measures of Variance

Objectives

After studying this chapter, you should be able to do the following:

Define performance standards *and standard costs, and relate them to organizational control systems.*

Differentiate between standards and budgets.

Specify methods for establishing cost standards.

Calculate variable cost variances *and identify potential causes or other controllable factors.*

Extend variance analysis *to the overall operations of a firm by isolating general operational variances.*

Record variance data.

Control is the process of ensuring conformity of actions to plans. Once a course of action has been selected, management attempts to ensure that operational decisions and activities coincide with these plans. One approach to control reviews recently completed activities within the firm. Deviations from plans might suggest underlying problems and prompt corrective actions in the future.

Two logical questions can introduce this approach to control: "What *should* we have done last period?" and, "What *did* we do last period?" The first relates to knowledge of the organization's goals and strategies, and the second focuses on actual performance in relation to these goals. Both are important considerations for effective control. This chapter discusses major control concepts: **performance standards** and **variance analysis**.

STANDARDS

Standards are *performance expectations* for the activities of the firm. Standards usually are specified for each major productive input. For example, more than one thousand individual labor standards are specified for the assembly of an automobile, and several thousand material standards apply to the same car. Each standard usually is stated in terms of the quantity and cost of the input needed to complete one output, i.e., one battery at X dollars, six spark plugs at Y dollars each, and three fan belts at Z dollars each. Thus, standards provide predetermined targets for input quantities and costs for an ordinary unit of output. In this sense, standards reduce the planned expectations to a level compatible with the basic activities of the firm. Thus, they provide operating management with a clear picture of the corporate plan relating to their areas of responsibility. In this sense, a standard describes an approach to implementing and achieving the corporate goals.

Budgets, which also express corporate plans, are different from standards in their scope of activity. Whereas a budget relates to *an entire activity or operation*, a standard presents the same information on a *per-unit* basis. Thus, a *standard provides cost expectations per unit of activity and a budget provides the cost expectation for the total activity*. If the budget calls for material costs of $10,000, the standard would express this as $2 per unit.

There are other important differences between standards and budgets. Normally, the responsibility for setting standards rests with different people from those formally involved in budgeting. Budgets are ordinarily established by the budget committee; however, the sole authority for establishing standards may rest with the managerial accountant. The accountant, however, often consults engineers, managers, and others who could contribute to the process. Frequently, labor contracts provide for union consultation and/or participation in establishing standards.

Whereas budgets are a necessary part of *planning for coordination pur-*

poses, standards are used primarily for *control purposes*. In this sense, the standard determines performance expectations for the production activities. The budget combines and integrates these expectations for the anticipated volume or activity level. Thus, whereas budgets are flexible and can change with volume expectations, standards, which reflect underlying conditions, are less flexible. In other words, budgets reflect expected total levels of activity or costs, whereas standards reflect subtotal input/output activity or cost — that is, what you think will happen as a whole versus what you expect on a unit-by-unit basis. Budgets are modified each period, or continually, in some cases, whereas standards are modified less frequently, as, for example, whenever labor contracts are renegotiated.

ESTABLISHING COST STANDARDS

There are several ways to derive standards, including engineering estimates, observed behavior, predicted behavior, and desired behavior. A given standard is often based on two or more of these techniques.

Engineering estimates Standards may reflect engineering specifications for a product or process. A material standard could be set by determining the input quantity necessary for each output unit and the normal waste incurred in processing. For example, an investigation could disclose that a machine is capable of producing one unit of output from ten pounds of materials, with one unit in ten (10%) spoiled. The engineering standard for materials in this case would be eleven pounds per completed unit (ten pounds per unit plus one pound allocated for spoilage). In this case, the engineering staff would conduct a technical review and an activity measurement. The results would be used to establish standards.

Observed behavior Whereas engineering estimates measure "what *can* be accomplished," standards may be based on "what *was* accomplished." Under this technique, the past is used as a standard for the future. To continue the previous example, if observations of past performance indicated that twelve pounds of material were used per completed unit, the observed behavior standard would set twelve pounds per unit as the goal. Assuming that processes and procedures have not changed, observed behavior may provide the best guide for future performance.

Predicted behavior Many times, however, the production processes change over time. Logically, then, expectations for the future should change also. The anticipated effect of new equipment or techniques can be incorporated into standards that are based on predicted behavior. In the previous example, if a new machine were purchased in an effort to eliminate all spoilage, the predicted behavior standard would be ten pounds of material per completed unit. Such standards can combine past observed behavior with engineering estimates to derive the base. Therefore, the historical standard can be adjusted to present a "most likely" prediction, taking into account technological changes.

Desired behavior   Standards can also reflect management's desires. Performance standards may represent neither a most likely expectation nor an engineering estimate; instead, management may desire a higher level of performance established through other techniques. Management might desire to bring their material usage in line with industry averages. If the average is eight pounds of material per completed unit, the desired behavior standard in this case would be eight pounds per unit.

Setting standards on the basis of desired behavior may use other estimating techniques. For example, if performance has been fairly low in the past, expectations for the future might result in low standards. If, however, management decided to base their standards on industry averages calling for a higher performance level, the standards would reflect a level of desired behavior.

Determining the overhead standard   The procedures involved in determining the materials and direct labor standards are obvious. Both of these factors generally vary directly and completely with output units. Standards for factory overhead are more difficult to develop.

By definition, some portion of factory overhead varies with activity. For example, compensation insurance premiums (an overhead item) vary with the size of the labor force. The key to determining the standard for variable overhead is to isolate a relevant activity that can be controlled and that determines the relationship between cost and volume. Thus, several different bases of assigning variable factory overhead to the product are possible. For example:

1. *Direct labor hours.* Probably the most popular base, this assignment assumes a relationship between direct labor hours worked and variable overhead costs incurred. Such overhead items as overtime premiums and vacation pay can be related to this measure.

2. *Direct labor dollars.* This measure is indirectly related to the physical measure of hours worked, and is also susceptible to variations in labor rates paid. Social security taxes, for example, would relate to this measure.

3. *Direct material dollars.* This measure associates variable overhead with material costs, so that quantities used, as well as the value of material inputs, determine overhead assignments. Storage costs or inventory (property) taxes can be related to this measure.

4. *Other physical volume measures.* Other physical volume measures may be used to determine overhead standards. One common measure is machine hours.

Many other bases in use depend on the observed relationships of variable overhead cost behavior to other factors that vary with production activity. Several bases might also be combined.

Standards, then, become a formal part of the control system of the organization. By monitoring the results of actual performance, the system can identify situations in which performance deviated from expectations. The control process is based on comparison—comparing actual and standard performance isolates deviations. These performance deviations, or *variances*, are an important part of the information base of an effective control system.

VARIANCE ANALYSIS

Variance analysis provides information about the sources and responsibilities for deviations from planned activities by focusing on the three main inputs to production—materials, labor, and variable overhead.[1] Within each of these factors, two areas of responsibility can be identified: the *acquirer of the resource* and the *user of the resource*.

For example, the planned and actual expenditures for raw materials could vary. This variance could result from any of three possible situations. First, the acquirer of the materials (a purchasing agent) could have paid more or less than the standard price. Second, the user of the materials (possibly a production foreman) could have used more or less than the standard amount during production. Third, both the acquirer and the user could have varied from the standards. Therefore, responsibility can be determined by dividing a *total variance* for the input factor into price and usage components, since different people may be responsible for each component. The dollar amount of the total variance will be divided into and reported by these price and usage components.

Calculating the variance   The amount of any variance is the cost difference between the standard and the actual performance. Usually, a notation, reported with the variance amount, indicates whether performance was "favorable" or "unfavorable." If the actual cost is greater than the standard cost, the resulting variance is generally labeled "unfavorable." Similarly, if the actual cost is less than the standard cost, the resulting variance is generally labeled "favorable." In

---

[1]Committed fixed overhead generally arises as the result of long-term commitments on the part of the firm (constructing a new plant or acquiring new equipment). These items tend to be outside the scope of immediate control within the firm. Thus, periodic analysis would not aid in controlling this type of cost. Discretionary fixed overhead is usually established by top management policy. These policies should be reviewed periodically, but such a review is outside the scope of conventional variance analysis. For further discussion of these points, refer to Chapter 3.

other words, the standard is a target: given the cost minimization criterion, it is "favorable" to spend less (lower price or quantity) than the target. This label might be misleading if, for example, quality were sacrificed for lower price.

The total amount of variance for any input factor is calculated as follows:

1.   Total Variance = Price Variance + Usage Variance

This total variance may be subdivided into the price and usage components as follows:

2.   Price Variance = (Standard Price × Actual Quantity Acquired)
                           − (Actual Price × Actual Quantity Acquired)

3.   Usage Variance = (Standard Price × Standard Quantity Used)
                           − (Standard Price × Actual Quantity Used)

The subdivision is performed in such a way that the sum of the price and usage variances equals the total variance for any input factor. Although the price variance can be subdivided further to isolate a "mixed" variance, generally it is not. Productive inputs, such as materials and supplies, must be physically acquired *before* they are used, and often no quantity standards are set at acquisition (rather, quantity standards are set at the time of usage). Therefore, price variances are calculated on the total acquisition amounts without regard to quantity standards.

Sometimes, the amount of materials purchased during a period differs from the amount used. Which quantity—purchased or used—is appropriate for variance analysis? Its usefulness to management should be the criterion. Identifying price variances at the time of purchase is desirable since this point is closer to the activity to be controlled (the acquisition of factors of production). Furthermore, the purchasing agent is responsible for price deviations over the whole amount purchased. Thus, more timely control activity can be fostered by using the purchased quantity as the basis for the variance calculations. On the other hand, the user of materials should be responsible for the actual amount used, so the usage variance is based on this quantity.

VARIANCES FOR THE FACTORS OF PRODUCTION

Consider the following standard and actual performance data for a company. (Remember that standards are predetermined targets set by management; the actual data are derived after the fact by the accountant.)

	Standard for 1,000 units	Actual for 1,000 units
Raw Materials:		
Price	$1 per lb.	$1.50 per lb.
Quantity	1 lb. per unit	1,100 lbs.
Direct Labor:		
Price	$4 per hour	$4.10 per hour
Quantity	3 hr. per unit	2,500 hours
Variable Overhead:		
Price	$2 per direct labor hour	$1.50 per direct labor hour
Quantity (assigned on the basis of direct labor hours)[2]	3 hr. per unit	2,500 hours

Materials The total variance for materials represents the sum of the price and usage variances. The price variance is calculated as follows:

$$\begin{aligned}
\text{Price Variance} &= (\text{Standard Price} \times \text{Actual Quantity Purchased}) \\
&\quad - (\text{Actual Price} \times \text{Actual Quantity Purchased}) \\
&= (\$1 \times 1,100) - (\$1.50 \times 1,100) \\
&= \$1,100 - \$1,650 \\
&= \underline{\underline{\$550}} \text{ Unfavorable}
\end{aligned}$$

$$\begin{aligned}
\text{Usage Variance} &= (\text{Standard Price} \times \text{Standard Quantity Used}) \\
&\quad - (\text{Standard Price} \times \text{Actual Quantity Used}) \\
&= (\$1 \times 1,000) - (\$1 \times 1,100) \\
&= \$1,000 - \$1,100 \\
&= \underline{\underline{\$100}} \text{ Unfavorable}
\end{aligned}$$

The standard quantity used is determined by multiplying the standard quantity per unit by the number of units produced, 1 lb. × 1,000 units = 1,000 lbs.

The sum of the price and usage variances ($550 unfavorable + $100 unfavorable) equals the total variance ($650 unfavorable) for this factor.

Direct labor Like the variance for raw materials, the total direct labor variance reflects managerial performance with respect to both the acquisition (price) and the use of productive inputs. In the case of direct labor, these components are generally referred to as the **rate variance** (price) and the **efficiency variance** (usage). The calculations, however, are the same. Here again, the standard quantity is determined by multiplying the standard quantity per unit by the number of units produced, 3 hr. × 1,000 units = 3,000 hrs.

---

[2]In many cases, variable overhead is assigned on the basis of direct labor hours. Use of this measure results from a managerial decision. Other measures can be used also.

$$\begin{aligned}
\text{Rate Variance} &= \text{(Standard Rate} \times \text{Actual Quantity)} \\
&\quad - \text{(Actual Rate} \times \text{Actual Quantity)} \\
&= (\$4 \times 2{,}500) - (\$4.10 \times 2{,}500) \\
&= \$10{,}000 - \$10{,}250 \\
&= \underline{\$250} \text{ Unfavorable}
\end{aligned}$$

$$\begin{aligned}
\text{Efficiency Variance} &= \text{(Standard Rate} \times \text{Standard Quantity)} \\
&\quad - \text{(Standard Rate} \times \text{Actual Quantity)} \\
&= (\$4 \times 3{,}000) - (\$4 \times 2{,}500) \\
&= \$12{,}000 - \$10{,}000 \\
&= \underline{\$2{,}000} \text{ Favorable}
\end{aligned}$$

$$\begin{aligned}
\text{Total Variance} &= \text{Rate Variance} + \text{Efficiency Variance} \\
&= -\$250 + \$2{,}000 \\
&= \underline{\$1{,}750} \text{ Favorable}
\end{aligned}$$

Additional information is provided by segmenting the total variance into components that reflect responsibility. In this example, all actions relating to direct labor did not yield favorable results. Specifically, the amount of the factor used was less than the standard amount. The price paid for the factor, however, was in excess of the standard rate for direct labor. The rate and efficiency variances disclose this information.

Variable factory overhead   Since the variable portion of factory overhead is assigned as a standard charge, it, too, is subject to variance analysis. The efficiency (usage) component of the total variance, however, will generally reflect the performance of the selected variable measure. In our example, variable overhead is assigned on the basis of direct labor hours. Since direct labor hour usage was favorable, variable factory overhead will reflect a similar variance.

The **spending** and efficiency components of the total variance for variable factory overhead may be calculated as follows:

$$\begin{aligned}
\text{Spending Variance} &= \text{(Standard Price} \times \text{Actual Quantity)} \\
&\quad - \text{(Actual Price} \times \text{Actual Quantity)} \\
&= (\$2 \times 2{,}500) - (\$1.50 \times 2{,}500) \\
&= \$5{,}000 - \$3{,}750 \\
&= \underline{\$1{,}250} \text{ Favorable}
\end{aligned}$$

$$\begin{aligned}
\text{Efficiency Variance} &= \text{(Standard Price} \times \text{Standard Quantity)} \\
&\quad - \text{(Standard Price} \times \text{Actual Quantity)} \\
&= (\$2 \times 3{,}000) - (\$2 \times 2{,}500) \\
&= \$6{,}000 - \$5{,}000 \\
&= \underline{\$1{,}000} \text{ Favorable}
\end{aligned}$$

$$\begin{aligned}
\text{Total Variance} &= \text{Spending Variance} + \text{Efficiency Variance} \\
&= \$1{,}250 + \$1{,}000 \\
&= \underline{\$2{,}250} \text{ Favorable}
\end{aligned}$$

Both the price paid for the factor and the amount used were favorable. The sum of the spending and efficiency variances equals and explains the total variance for variable factory overhead.

The variance calculations provide a set of quantitative data about deviations from predetermined standards. Additional steps must be taken to analyze the cause of the variances.

SOME COMPLICATING FACTORS

Both the price and usage variances for all inputs require the knowledge of "actual price" and "actual quantity." In some instances, these values must be determined from the facts made available to you. For example, a problem may be worded as follows: The Smithson Company acquired 4,000 pounds of material for $840. Its payroll amounted to $5,800 for the week, and the average pay rate was $5.00 per hour. The calculation of variances for Smithson requires knowledge of the cost per pound of material and the number of labor hours worked by employees.

To determine these values, simply remember that the total cost is determined by multiplying unit cost by the quantity, i.e.,

$$\text{Total Cost} = \text{Unit Cost} \times \text{Quantity}$$

But this relationship can be restated in two other forms, as follows:

$$\text{Unit Cost} = \text{Total Cost} \div \text{Quantity}$$
$$\text{Quantity} = \text{Total Cost} \div \text{Unit Cost}$$

The cost per pound of material for Smithson is $.21 ($840 ÷ 4,000 = $.21), and the employees worked 1,160 hours ($5,800 ÷ $5 = 1,160).

A second complication arises when the standard price is specified on a per-input unit basis (i.e., $1 per pound), and the standard quantity is specified on a per-output basis (i.e., 3 pounds per unit). Should the usage variance be calculated on a per-unit or on a per-pound basis? For example, consider the following case:

Material standards for the Whipple Company were $5 per pound of material and 4 pounds per finished unit. During the production period, 4,200 pounds of material were used to build 1,000 finished units. The usage variance can be calculated either in terms of pounds or in terms of units, using the standard format:

$$\text{Usage Variance} = (\text{Standard Price} \times \text{Standard Quantity})$$
$$- (\text{Standard Price} \times \text{Actual Quantity})$$

To use pounds as the quantity, first determine the standard quantity needed to produce 1,000 units: $1,000 \times 4 = 4,000$. The usage variance is calculated as follows:

$$\text{Usage Variance} = (\$5 \times 4,000) - (\$5 \times 4,200)$$
$$= \$5 \times 200$$
$$= \$1,000$$

To use units as the quantity, first determine the standard material cost per unit: $\$5 \times 4 = \$20$. Next, calculate the standard number of units that should have been produced from the actual amount of material used: $4,200 \div 4 = 1,050$. The usage variance is calculated as follows:

$$\text{Usage Variance} = (\$20 \times 1,000) - (\$20 \times 1,050)$$
$$= \$20 \times 50$$
$$= \$1,000$$

In this case, using pounds as the quantity facilitated the calculation of the usage variance; however, using units may be easier in some cases.

VARIANCE ANALYSIS— DETERMINING THE CAUSE

The main purpose for calculating performance variances is to identify their underlying causes. The importance of variance analysis is illustrated by the following statement.

While the primary aim of management should be to obtain compliance with standards, perfection cannot be obtained in either standards or practice and some variances will always arise. Past losses from failure to meet standards cannot be retrieved, but the study of variance is an important step toward improving performance in the future.

However, before management can take effective action to realize the opportunities for improving control over costs, it needs to know not only the amount of variance, but also where the variances originated, who is responsible for them, and what caused them to arise. In other words, analysis is necessary to bring out the significance of the variances in terms of sources, responsibility, and causes. When such analyses are combined with an appropriate plan of reporting, management can rely upon the principle of [management by] exceptions to disclose problems calling for attention without laborious study of many detailed facts and figures.[3]

The managerial accountant actively participates in and supports this process.

A variance between standard and actual performance can emerge from

[3]*Research Report No. 22, The Analysis of Manufacturing Cost Variances* (New York: National Association of Accountants), p. 2.

any one of several distinct causes, or a combination of them, including: (1) performance deviations by those responsible for the factor, (2) incorrect standards, and (3) uncontrollable influences from outside the responsibility area.

Obviously, a variance can arise from superior or inferior performance by the individual responsible for the input factor. The purchasing agent may acquire materials at prices lower or higher than expected. The production foreman may spur his workers on to faster production, or his poor supervision may lead to excess waste, idle time, or spoilage. Favorable and unfavorable variances give direct clues to such underlying events.

Less directly, variances may indicate the existence of potential tradeoffs: higher-quality inputs may cost more to acquire but may require a smaller quantity to produce the given output. Higher-quality (priced) material may reduce expected levels of scrap, whereas lower quality may increase scrap. Less experienced labor may cost less but produce at a slower rate. Therefore, seeking underlying causes for deviations from expected behavior should include the examination of interrelated items. Unfortunately, interrelationships may be widespread. For example, low-quality material might be responsible for favorable material price variances (low price), unfavorable material quantity variances (much scrap), and unfavorable labor quantity variances (much rework, idle time). Or, higher-priced labor (unfavorable price variance) may produce faster than expected (favorable labor quantity variance) and produce less scrap (favorable material quantity variance).

In still another application, the work in one department of the plant might affect the work in another—poor quality in production might lead to idle time in assembly or require rework in finishing. The production manager should be aware of these tradeoffs for much friction but little control can be created by censuring people for poor performance that was beyond their control. Production foremen should not be criticized if their poor performance was caused by actions of the personnel division (hiring untrained workers), the purchasing department (acquiring poor quality material), or the previous processing department. Analyzing variances provides clues to underlying behavior, suggests questions to be asked, and identifies whom to question. Control can be exercised only after managers have obtained answers to their questions. When this occurs, variance analysis completes a feedback loop to the source of the deviation, directing managerial attention to the factor and ultimately to the responsibility area.

Another possible source of variance, which is sometimes overlooked, is an incorrect standard. Standards, which represent estimations or expectations of performance, may be formulated incorrectly. An analysis of the variance could expose this situation and lead to corrections in the future. Since standards are used also for purposes other than control (such as pricing and costing), better standards will lead to better decisions.

Factors outside the responsibility area can also lead to a variance. For example, a new labor contract negotiated by top management could result in a labor rate variance. In such a case, the resulting variance should be identified with the individual (or group) responsible for its incurrence. In this instance, top management would be responsible.

An evaluation must consider the performance expectations implied by the standard. Standards might be constructed with the intent of being practically unattainable; others might set quite reasonable performance levels.

Standards and expectation levels   Although several methods can be used to develop standards for a firm, the results of alternate methods can vary in their level of expectations—that is, their "tightness," or degree of attainability. In some situations, the standard is virtually unattainable, whereas in others, it presents an average of uncontrolled past behavior. Neither extreme is desirable from a control standpoint. Several types of standards based on attainability can be distinguished in actual practice. A standard should create credibility, act as a motivator, or establish direction.

At one extreme is the **ideal standard**. Also called a *theoretical* or *perfection standard*, this measure represents the ultimate in performance. No allowances are made for waste, spoilage, equipment breakdowns, operator fatigue, or other common production inefficiencies. Thus, the ideal standard is, for all intents and purposes, unattainable. Ideal standards are said to provide the highest performance goal, so that efficiency will improve if efforts are directed toward this goal. The motivational effects of such an approach, however, are questionable.

At the other extreme from an ideal standard is the **average past performance standard**. As its name implies, this approach merely averages past performance to derive a standard requiring future performance to be at least no worse than the past. Thus, if past performance has been low, the standard will also be low. "Beating" (or performing better than) the standard automatically results in an upward change in the standard. Thus, employees may be motivated to maintain low performance. Although average past performance yields an attainable standard, practitioners generally concede that it does not support control in the firm effectively; there is no motivation to change performance from what it was in the past. However, in situations in which interactive elements do not change over time, this goal may suffice.

Perhaps the most reasonable and effective approach to setting standards is the **attainable performance standard**. This approach permits the inclusion of certain acceptable inefficiencies in the base. Thus, elements of spoilage, waste, and inefficiency deemed to be impractical or unfeasible to eliminate are reflected in the standard. An attainable good performance standard can be met, but only through efficient operations, which would provide obvious benefits to the firm.

Random and nonrandom causes   Before making a variance analysis, the accountant should consider the type of standard that was used. Variances from attainable standards suggest the need for an investigation. However, in most situations, it is not practical to study all of the resulting variances. The decision to investigate should be based on cost-benefit considerations. Given the great effort necessary to complete a thorough analysis, the cost of investigating a variance may exceed the benefit of determining the cause of the variance. Furthermore, some variances may arise from *random* causes or from uncontrollable conditions and events, such as fire, sickness, or flood. These random influences are beyond the control of the firm's decision-makers. Investigations undertaken when these conditions prevailed generally would yield no valuable information.

EXTENSIONS OF VARIANCE CONTROL

Calculating variable cost variances provides a basic measure of the *efficiency*, or productivity, of past operations by focusing attention on manufacturing activities and the manner in which materials, labor, and overhead were combined into finished output. However, activities other than production are of interest to managers. Virtually all manufacturing firms have significant long-term investments in productive capacity, including production facilities, equipment, and trained personnel. Operational *effectiveness*, or conformity to goals, requires the utilization of these resources. Measuring effectiveness is an important part of the control process.

For example, if actual production is significantly less than the planned level, unused capacity is present. A portion of the firm's investment base is not producing profits because it is not in use. Also, desired profits cannot be attained because anticipated levels of sales will not be reached, which can have a significant effect on the firm.

Factors that can influence production volume include: the capacity of the manufacturing facility, the sales made or orders received, and the actual production scheduled and completed. Each of these generally relates to a different area of responsibility. Manufacturing capacity results from top management's decisions concerning acquisitions of plant and equipment. Sales performance concerns the sales manager, and production activities result from actions in the production department. Comparisons of output or output potential in these areas can yield **volume variances** that affect the firm. These variances, like other control techniques, direct managerial efforts toward areas in need of attention.

OVERALL OPERATIONAL VARIANCES

Four basic measures of overall operations are used in variance calculations: (1) the practical production capacity, (2) the budgeted sales volume, (3) the scheduled production volume, and (4) the actual production volume. The variances are calculated at top levels of management. They aid in setting goals and establishing means for attaining goals. In many cases, these calculations are not part of the regular control evaluations directed at lower-echelon managers.

Practical, or attainable, production capacity is the maximum level of activity realistically attainable from a manufacturing facility. Thus, the total capacity of the plant would be adjusted to reflect certain levels of inefficiencies that are likely to occur. Worker fatigue, machine repairs and breakdowns, and spoiled units would be used to adjust the total capacity to a *practical capacity* level.

The *budgeted sales volume* reflects the anticipated sales level at the time the master budget was prepared. The expected sales volume was used as a basis for many of the other planned activities of the firm. Material purchase requirements, for example, would be set as a function of the expected sales volume and existing inventories.

Since master budgets are prepared well in advance of the budget period, adjustments are necessary to reflect current conditions. *Scheduled production volume* represents the level of output actually scheduled to be processed through the production facility. In most cases, scheduling is based on sales orders. Thus, scheduled production volume represents an actual level of sales orders.

Actual production is based on orders scheduled and completed. Therefore, in many cases, actual production coincides with the actual level of sales achieved during the current period, plus adjustments to inventory levels.

Volume variances are calculated on the basis of these four measures of activity. An example may clarify these variance calculations. The following volume data from a company are available:

	Units
Practical Production Capacity	100,000
Budgeted Sales Volume	80,000
Scheduled Production Volume	70,000
Actual Production Volume	65,000

Anticipated idle capacity variance   At the time the master budget is prepared, an anticipated **idle capacity variance** can be calculated. This variance measures unused plant capacity and represents the difference between the practical capacity and the master budget. It is calculated as follows:

$$\text{Anticipated Idle Capacity Variance} = \text{Practical Production Capacity} - \text{Budgeted Sales Volume}$$

In the example, the anticipated idle capacity variance is 20,000 units (100,000 − 80,000). Several explanations for this variance are possible, including: expansion in anticipation of future growth, declining sales expectations, or overinvestment in productive facilities. An idle capacity variance focuses attention on the reasonableness of anticipated sales levels and the capacity of the production facility. Both considerations are important to the firm.

Marketing variance The **marketing variance** represents the difference between the expected sales volume when the master budget was prepared and the actual sales orders received. The variance is calculated as follows:

Marketing Variance = Budgeted Sales Volume − Scheduled
Production Volume

In the example, the marketing variance is 10,000 units (80,000 − 70,000) unfavorable. Generally, orders exceeding the master budget are termed *favorable*, and, conversely, orders below the master budget are termed *unfavorable*. The marketing variance is primarily the responsibility of the sales department, and it emphasizes the importance of meeting the master budget.

Production variance A **production variance** is the difference between scheduled production volume and actual production volume. It is calculated as follows:

Production Variance = Scheduled Production Volume − Actual
Production Volume

The production variance in our example is 5,000 units (70,000 − 65,000) unfavorable. Analysis of this variance must focus on production management. An unfavorable production variance indicates that scheduled production levels were not attained. Again, the influence on the firm of unfilled sales orders can be severe.

Volume variance The difference between planned expectations presented in the master budget and actual results is generally termed the *volume variance*. It represents the sum of the marketing and production variances or the difference between budgeted sales volume and actual production volume. The volume variance may be calculated as follows:

Volume Variance = Budgeted Sales Volume − Actual Production
Volume

It provides an overview of planning in relation to output volumes. As a control device, the volume variance is useful for directing attention to the planning phase, if significant deviations result. In the foregoing example, the volume variance is 15,000 units (80,000 − 65,000) unfavorable.

Quantifying the variances Dollar measures can be used to heighten the effect of volume variances. Ideally, the basis for assigning a dollar cost should be the opportunity cost of the foregone production. In many cases, however, opportunity cost is difficult to determine accurately. Therefore, the unit *contribution margin* may be substituted for the opportunity cost. Using the contribution margin for an opportunity cost has an intuitive appeal: the contribution margin represents a per-unit contribution to fixed costs and profit. However, most fixed costs are associated with productive capacity, which tends to remain constant in spite of volume changes. Thus, the contribution margin represents foregone profit potential when actual production levels are lower than the plant's capacity. In this sense, the contribution margin acts as a reasonable substitute for opportunity cost. Volume variances may be reported either in units or in dollars, as management chooses.

SUMMARY

The formal plans of an organization may be stated as standards that reflect performance expectations. The success of the firm will depend to a great extent on the degree of conformity to these plans achieved by actual operations. Attaining such conformity is the goal of the organization's control system. Reporting standards to operating managers provides them with necessary information about performance expectations. Measuring actual performance is necessary for reporting, long-range decision-making, and control. Variance analysis formalizes a part of the control process by measuring and quantifying deviations from standards.

The variances are promptly reported to appropriate levels of management, who may use them as a basis for future corrective actions. By formalizing the control process, it is possible for an organization to monitor all operational activities effectively. Variance analysis may be extended to monitor long-range decision-making and planning within the firm. The volume variances measure performance deviations at higher management levels in the firm, focusing on capacity and volume of output.

Generally, the process of calculating and investigating variances is an important part of control. The results of such analyses can enhance operational efficiency and effectiveness significantly.

APPENDIX: RECORDING PERFORMANCE VARIANCES

Variances are recorded in an accounting system for two general reasons:

1. To determine variance causes by special studies which are made apart from the recurrent operations of accumulating and reporting costs.

2. To incorporate the analysis into the cost accounting system by providing individual variance accounts for each of the principal causes for which a variance can be isolated. Periodic reports classifying variances by cause are then prepared directly from the accounts.

Under the first approach, variances are accumulated in the accounts by responsibility and by cost element, but not by cause. The variances developed serve to raise questions which are then answered by additional investigation to determine causes of the variances which have arisen. Under the second approach, the system is designed to provide direct answers in terms of variance causes without further analysis.[4]

The first approach is more frequently used in industry.

Any firm using a standard cost system has two distinct alternatives for the cost base: standard costs or actual costs. Using standard costs has the advantage of supplying management with information for control purposes. It is also useful for making product-related decisions that are independent of performance. The implied assumption in a standard cost approach is that the firm's product output should not absorb any cost inefficiencies in the production process.

Actual costs are also important to the firm since the actual costs must be covered in the long run if the firm is to survive. In addition, actual costs are necessary for preparing financial statements and determining tax liabilities. For these reasons, actual costs must be recorded by managerial accountants, even if standard costs are used as the basis for product costing. If both standard and actual costs are recorded in the ledger accounts, the variances also must be recorded to reconcile the performance differences.

An example There are two approaches to recording performance and variances in the ledger accounts. The first uses summary entries to record data and can be used only on a periodic basis. The second approach records standard and actual performance daily and reconciles entries for the variances periodically. The former (summary) process will be used for illustration.

Relevant information from the previous example in this chaper is summarized below.

	Standard	Actual	Price/Rate/Spending Variance*	Usage/Efficiency Variance*
Raw Materials	$ 1,000	$ 1,650	$ (550)	($100)
Direct Labor	12,000	10,250	(250)	2,000
Variable Overhead	6,000	3,750	1,250	1,000

*( ) are used to denote unfavorable variances.

Using this information, summary entries for the various factors of production can be made. The component variances rather than the total variance are usually used to increase the information content of the internal accounting

[4]*Research Report No. 22, The Analysis of Manufacturing Cost Variances* (New York: National Association of Accountants), p. 11.

records. These variance accounts will eventually be closed, either directly to net income from operations or indirectly to the income account through inventories, and hence, cost of sales.

Raw materials   The two component variances—price and quantity—that relate to raw materials will arise at different times. The price variance is determined at the time of acquisition, and the usage variance is determined at the time of application to the product. Using the data in the example, the following journal entries would be made.

Materials Control	1,100	
Materials Price Variance	550	
Accounts Payable		1,650

(To record the acquisition of raw materials on account. The actual price was above standard.)

Work-in-Process Control	1,000	
Materials Usage Variance	100	
Materials Control		1,100

(To record the transfer of raw materials to the production department. Usage exceeded the standard.)

Unfavorable variances are recorded as debits in the variance accounts. The materials control account maintains the inventory balance at its standard cost, and the work-in-process control account reflects the standard prices and quantities of the factors added to production. Accounting for materials under actual and standard cost assumptions is illustrated in Exhibit 12–1.

EXHIBIT 12–1   CONTRASTING ACTUAL AND STANDARD ACCOUNTING BALANCES

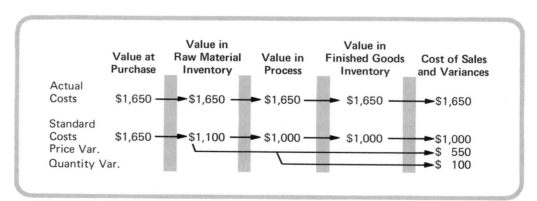

Direct labor   The two component labor variances, rate and efficiency, like the raw materials variances, are isolated and recorded for direct labor. Because labor is used as it is acquired, rate and efficiency variances are generally determinable at the same time.

Work-in-Process Control	12,000	
Labor Rate Variance	250	
Factory Payroll		10,250
Labor Efficiency Variance		2,000

(To record usage of direct labor in production. The rate exceeded the standard and usage was less than standard.)

The work-in-process control account was increased by the standard quantity of labor at the standard rate. The factory payroll account records the actual cost of labor. The unfavorable rate variance is shown as a debit and the favorable efficiency variance is recorded as a credit.

Factory overhead   The variances applicable to variable factory overhead, spending and efficiency, are generally recorded on an annual basis when the actual and applied overhead accounts are closed. Periodically throughout the year, standard amounts of variable overhead are added to the work-in-process inventory in the following manner:

Work-in-Process Control	6,000	
Factory Overhead Applied		6,000

(To record the application of overhead at the predetermined rate.)

At year's end, when the accounts are closed, the variable factory overhead variances are isolated and determined.

Factory Overhead Applied	6,000	
Factory Overhead Control		3,750
Factory Overhead Spending Variance		1,250
Factory Overhead Efficiency Variance		1,000

(To close the applied and control overhead accounts. Both prices and usage were less than the standard amounts.)

The favorable spending and efficiency variances are recorded as credits in the appropriate accounts, and the actual and applied overhead accounts are closed.

The closing process   Assuming that the foregoing activity reflects the performance for a year, the accounts have the following characteristics at closing time:

1. *Materials price variance.* A debit balance reflecting an unfavorable variance of $550.

2. *Materials usage variance.* A debit balance of $100 resulting from an unfavorable variance.

3. *Labor rate variance.* A debit balance of $250 reflecting actual rates greater than the standard—unfavorble.

4. *Labor efficiency variance.* A credit balance reflecting a favorable variance of $2,000.

5. *Factory overhead spending variance.* A credit balance of $1,250 resulting from actual rates lower than the standard—favorable.

6. *Factory overhead efficiency variance.* A $1,000 credit balance reflecting a favorable variance.

If management elects to close the accumulated variances directly to current income, the following compound entry can be made:

Labor Efficiency Variance	2,000	
Factory Overhead Spending Variance	1,250	
Factory Overhead Efficiency Variance	1,000	
Materials Price Variance		550
Materials Usage Variance		100
Labor Rate Variance		250
Income Summary[5]		3,350

(To close variance accounts to income of the period.)

Thus, the effects of the variances eventually become part of the reported income of the firm. The control process relies heavily on the accounting records of the organization. Data on expected performance are made available for short-run decision-making. Actual results, which reflect the operating performance, are disclosed. The variances are made available for managerial attention in a manner consistent with the concept of management by exception.

SUGGESTED READINGS

DeWelt, R. L. "Labor Measurement and Control." *Management Accounting*, October 1976.

Dobbie, John. "Planning Effectiveness." *Managerial Planning*, September/October, 1976.

---

[5]Some accountants suggest allocating the net variance balance pro rata to work-in-process inventory, finished-goods inventory, and cost of goods sold, rather than reflecting all of it as a period cost.

Magee, Robert. "A Simulation Analysis of Alternative Cost Variance Investigation Models." *The Accounting Review*, July 1976.

Piper, R. W. "Engineering Standards and Standard Costs." *Management Accounting*, September 1976.

QUESTIONS

12-1   Briefly describe in general terms the role played by the managerial accountant in the control process of a firm.

12-2   Contrast and compare budgets and standards. In which ways are they similar; how are they different?

12-3   There are several ways in which cost standards can be developed. Briefly describe each of the following techniques:

(A) Engineering estimates
(B) Observed behavior
(C) Predicted behavior
(D) Desired behavior

12-4   Igor Beaver was ecstatic about his new job as a variance analyst. "My job is to calculate variances and identify the party responsible for them," explained Igor. "It's like playing detective. Without me, the person or persons who caused the variance might go undetected."

Comment on Igor's impression of his new job. Do unfavorable variances mean that a "guilty" party exists within the firm? What is the purpose of variance analysis?

12-5   How can the total variance for any input into production be subdivided? What is the purpose of subdividing the total variance?

12-6   Does an unfavorable component variance for a factor of input necessarily mean that something went wrong during the period? Explain why or why not.

12-7   List possible sources of variance for variable input factors. Can a department head trade off an unfavorable variance for a favorable one? Give some examples of how or why this would be done.

12-8   The degree of attainability can vary significantly among different users of standard costs. Identify three standards based on degree of attainability and briefly explain each.

12-9   For each of the following managerial philosophies, identify the type of standard that should be used. Briefly defend your answer in each case.

(A) "I want a realistic performance standard that will provide some motivation for my employees to be efficient."

(B) "My employees should know what the best performance is. This will give them a level to strive continually toward attaining."

(C) "Let's set a realistic goal for performance and try to attain it."

12–10   Should all variances be investigated by a firm? What role does the type of standard play in deciding whether or not a variance should be investigated?

EXERCISES

12–11   ElTronics Company purchased 100,000 pounds of material for $46,000 and used 90,000 pounds to produce 20,000 finished units. The standard price for material was $.45 per pound, and the standard quantity was 5 pounds per unit.

(A) Determine the material variances.

(B) Identify possible causes for material variances. Identify the job title of persons who might bear responsibility for these variances.

(C) Define the meaning of the words "favorable" and unfavorable."

12–12   During January, Megleno Tool Company completed 2,000 units by combining 2,010 pounds of raw material inputs with 5,980 hours of labor. To meet these production needs, Megleno acquired 4,000 pounds of material for $14,800 and incurred total payroll costs of $30,463. The following standards had been established for material and labor:

Material 1 pound at $4.00 per pound
Labor   3 hours at $5.00 per hour

Calculate material and labor variances and determine possible causes for them.

12–13   ToolCo purchased 800 lbs. of material for $1,600. Exactly 600 lbs. were placed into production, and from them 100 equivalent units were produced. The standard price paid for material is $2.05 per lb., and the standard quantity used is 6.5 lbs. per unit.

Labor standards were set at $3.75 per hour and 4 hours per unit. Actual labor costs were $3.50 per hour: 420 hours were required to produce the 100 equivalent units.

(A) Determine price and usage variances for labor and material.

(B) The foreman argues that his labor quantity variance was the direct result of poor-quality material. Do you accept his explanation?

(C) The foreman explains his material quantity variance as follows: "Untrained, inexperienced, low-priced, new employees wasted too much material by creating too much scrap." Would you accept or reject his explanation? Why?

12–14   The Jones Furniture Company uses a standard cost system in accounting for its production costs.

The standard cost of a unit of furniture follows:

Lumber, 100 feet @ $150 per 1,000 feet	$15.00
Direct labor, 4 hours @ $2.50 per hour	10.00

The actual unit costs for the month of December were as follows:

Lumber used (110 feet @ $120 per 1,000 feet)	$13.20
Direct labor 4¼ hours @ $2.60 per hour)	11.05

Prepare a schedule that shows an analysis of each element of the total variance from standard cost for the month of December.

(AICPA adapted)

12–15   The H. G. Company uses a standard cost system in accounting for the cost of one of its products. The standard is based on budgeted monthly production of 100 units per day for the usual 22 work days per month. Standard cost per unit for direct labor is 16 hours at $1.50 per hour. During the month of September, the plant operated only 20 days. Actual direct labor cost for the 2,080 units produced was:

$$32,860 \text{ hours @ } \$1.52 = \$49,947.20$$

Determine the direct labor variances and suggest factors that might explain the reasons for these variances.

(AICPA adapted)

12–16   A company established $4 an hour as the standard rate for factory craftsmen. Recently, the personnel manager hired several more experienced craftsmen at $6 an hour, and the experienced workers were able to produce twice as much as their $4-an-hour colleagues. Obviously, an unfavorable rate variance of $2 an hour will result. To whom should this unfavorable variance be charged? Does this seem to be a reasonable action? How will the person charged react to the variance?

12–17   The Cal Lender Company is a manufacturing firm that incurred a considerable amount of material costs during the month of June. The actual price paid for material was $4 a pound. The firm purchased 7,000 pounds of material during the month and actually used 5,000 pounds to produce 1,000 units. The standard price per pound is $4.50, and the usage standard is 4.7 pounds per unit.

(A) What is the material price variance for the month of June? Who, within the firm, is generally held responsible for this variance?

(B) What is the material usage variance for the month of June? Who would be held responsible for it?

(C) How much was the total variance for materials for the month of June? What does this variance mean? Who would be held responsible for it?

12–18 A production foreman was forced to use master craftsmen, who were paid $7 an hour, for a job normally performed by apprentices. The craftsmen were able to complete the job in 150 hours, which was 40 hours less than the standard time. Apprentices are normally paid $4 an hour.

(A) What was the direct labor rate variance for this job?

(B) How much was the direct labor efficiency variance for this job?

(C) What was the total direct labor variance for this job?

(D) Was the foreman's action a wise one or not? Who, within the firm, should be held responsible for these variances?

12–19 Variable factory overhead is assigned to the stamping department of a particular company on the basis of direct labor hours. During the month of December, 10,480 direct labor hours were actually worked to produce 5,000 units of product. The labor standard is set at two hours per unit. Variable overhead is applied in the stamping department at a rate of $1.20 per hour. Actual overhead costs for December were $11,528.

(A) What was the variable factory overhead spending variance for December?

(B) What was the variable factory overhead efficiency variance in the stamping department for December?

(C) How much was the total variable factory overhead variance?

(D) Generally, who within the firm would be held responsible for these variances?

12–20 Standard costing procedures are widely used in manufacturing operations and, more recently, have become common in many nonmanufacturing operations.

(A) Define standard costs. Distinguish between ideal and attainable standards.

(B) What are the advantages of a standard cost system?

(AICPA adapted)

12–21 The Dearborn Company manufactures Product X in standard batches of 100 units. A standard cost system is in use. The standard costs for a batch are as follows:

Raw materials	60 lbs. @ $ .45 per lb.	$ 27.00
Direct labor	36 hrs. @ $2.15 per hr.	77.40
Overhead	36 hrs. @ $2.75 per hr.	99.00
		$203.40

Production for April 19X0 amounted to 210 batches. The relevant statistics follow:

Standard output per month	24,000 units
Raw materials used	13,000 lbs.
Cost of raw materials used	$ 6,110.00
Direct labor cost	$16,790.40
Overhead cost	$20,592.00
Average overhead rate per hour	$2.60

Management has noted that actual costs per batch deviate somewhat from standard costs per batch.

Prepare a statement containing a detailed explanation of the difference between actual costs and standard costs (ignore overhead variances).

(AICPA adapted)

12–22   The Level Load Corporation built a new factory designed to have a practical capacity of 500,000 units per year. During the first year's operations, the master budget for the factory was based on 310,000 units. Actual sales lagged somewhat behind the budgeted expectations—orders for only 250,000 units were received and scheduled for production. Because of periodic production overruns, the year ended with all of the orders filled and 5,000 completed units in the factory's inventory. The units are sold for $10 each, and the contribution margin ratio is 30%.

Using this information, calculate the following variances. Indicate whether or not the variances are favorable by using the terms "favorable" or "unfavorable" in your answer.

(A) Idle capacity variance in units
(B) Marketing variance in dollars
(C) Production variance in dollars
(D) Volume variance in dollars

Comment briefly on the meaning of each of these variances.

†12–23   Wilsonian Supply Company uses a standard cost accounting system and records all variances from the standards in its accounting records. The following events occurred in Wilsonian Supply during the month of July.

1. 1,200 pounds of raw material, which cost $2,040, were used in producing 5,000 units of product. The standard price of raw material is $1.50 a pound and the standard quantity is $\frac{1}{4}$ pound of material per unit.

2. A total of 10,000 direct labor hours were worked during the month. The direct labor payroll was $42,000. The standard labor cost per unit is $9, based on a standard rate of $4 an hour.

3. Variable factory overhead is applied at the rate of $.20 per direct

labor hour. During the month of July, actual overhead costs were $2,500.

Using this information, make summary journal entries to record the basic information and the component variances for the Wilsonian Company for the month of July. Also, make summary closing entries regarding this information.

12–24   The A. C. Counting Company uses a standard cost accounting system as a basis for evaluating operational performance. The following information concerning operations during the month of March, when 200 units of product were produced, is made available.

	Standard	Actual
Material Cost	$2.00 per lb.	$2.20 per lb.
Material Used	1½ lbs. per unit	280 lbs.
Labor Cost	$5.00 per hour	$2400
Labor Used	2½ man hours per unit	600 hours
Variable Overhead	$1 per direct labor hour	$580

Calculate the following variances for the A. C. Counting Company. Also, indicate whether or not the variance is favorable by using the words "favorable" or "unfavorable."

(A) Material price and usage variances; total material variance.

(B) Direct labor rate and efficiency variances; total direct labor variance

(C) Variable factory overhead spending and efficiency variances; total variable factory overhead variance

12–25   Variances can sometimes indicate the existence of performance tradeoffs within the firm. For example, more expensive material (unfavorable price variance) may result in less scrap (favorable usage variance). For each of the variances described below, indicate what possible tradeoffs could have taken place:

(A) Unfavorable labor rate variance; favorable labor efficiency variance

(B) Unfavorable material price variance; favorable labor efficiency variance

(C) Favorable material usage variance; unfavorable labor efficiency variance

(D) Favorable labor rate variance; unfavorable labor efficiency variance

(E) Favorable material price variance; unfavorable material usage variance

12–26   The Acme Corporation prepares weekly performance reports for each of its operating divisions. Reproduced below is a performance report for the finishing department for the week ended 6/7-X6.

Performance Report/Acme Corporation
Finishing Department/Week ended 6/7/X6

ACTUAL COSTS		VARIANCES	
Materials	$10,000	Material Price Variance	$2,000
		Material Usage Variance	(3,000)*
Labor	20,000	Labor Rate Variance	4,000
		Labor Efficiency Variance	(2,000)*
Overhead	30,000	Overhead Spending Variance	(1,000)*
		Overhead Efficiency Variance	1,000
Total Cost	$60,000	Total Variance	$1,000

*( ) Denotes an unfavorable variance.

After examining this report, answer the following questions about it.

(A)   What is the purpose of this report? Who would receive a copy of it?

(B)   What was the standard cost of materials? What was the standard cost of labor?

(C)   What are some possible bases that Acme Corporation could have used to assign overhead to the finishing department?

(D)   Present a possible explanation for the labor efficiency variance; for the material usage variance.

(E)   Who, besides the finishing department, should receive a report of the material price variance; the labor efficiency variance?

(F)   What reaction to this report would probably come from the supervisor of the finishing department?

PROBLEMS

*12–27   The Arsco Co. makes three grades of indoor-outdoor carpeting. The sales volume for the annual budget is determined by estimating the total market volume for indoor-outdoor carpeting and then applying the Company's prior-year market share, adjusted for changes due to company programs planned for the coming year. The volume is apportioned between the three grades based upon the prior year's product mix, again adjusted for changes due to company programs planned for the coming year.

Below are the Company budget for 19X3 and the results of operations for 19X3.

Budget

	Grade 1	Grade 2	Grade 3	Total
Sales — Units	1,000 rolls	1,000 rolls	2,000 rolls	4,000 rolls
Sales Dollars				
(000 omitted)	$1,000	$2,000	$3,000	$6,000
Variable Expense	700	1,600	2,300	4,600
Contribution Margin	$ 300	$ 400	$ 700	$1,400
Traceable Fixed				
Expense	200	200	300	700
Traceable Margin	$ 100	$ 200	$ 400	$ 700
Selling and				
Administrative				
Expense				$ 250
Net Income				$ 450

Actual

	Grade 1	Grade 2	Grade 3	Total
Sales — Units	800 rolls	1,000 rolls	2,100 rolls	3,900 rolls
Sales Dollars				
(000 omitted)	$810	$2,000	$3,000	$5,810
Variable Expenses	560	1,610	2,320	4,490
Contribution Margin	$250	$ 390	$ 680	$1,320
Traceable Fixed				
Expense	210	220	315	745
Traceable Margin	$ 40	$ 170	$ 365	$ 575
Selling and				
Administrative				
Expense				$ 275
Net Income				$ 300

Industry volume was estimated at 40,000 rolls for budgeting purposes. Actual industry volume for 19X3 was 38,000 rolls.

(A) Using budgeted contribution margins, calculate the profit impact of the unit sales volume variance for 19X3.

(B) What portion of the variance, if any, can be attributed to the state of the carpeting market?

(C) What is the dollar impact on profits (using budgeted contribution margins) of the shift in product mix from the budgeted mix?

(CMA adapted)

12–28 Last year Crowley Corporation adopted a standard cost system. Labor standards were set on the basis of time studies and prevailing wage rates. Material standards were determined from material specifications and prices then in effect. In determining its standard for overhead, Crowley estimated that a total of 6,000,000 finished units would be produced during the next five years to satisfy demand for its product. The five-year period was selected to average out seasonal and cyclical fluctuations and allow for sales trends. By dividing the total annual budgeted overhead by the annual average of 1,200,000 units, a standard cost was developed for manufacturing overhead.

At June 30, 19X9, the end of the current fiscal year, analysis of accounting records determined the following variances:

Materials price variance	$(25,000) favorable
Materials quantity variance	9,000 unfavorable
Labor rate variance	30,000 unfavorable
Labor efficiency variance	7,500 unfavorable
Controllable overhead variance	2,000 unfavorable
Noncontrollable (capacity) overhead variance	75,000 unfavorable

Standards were set at the beginning of the year and have remained unchanged. All inventories are priced at standard cost.

(A) What conclusions can be drawn from each of the six variances shown in Crowley's trial balance?

(B) The amount of nonvariable manufacturing overhead cost to be included in product cost depends on whether or not the allocation is based on: (1) ideal (or theoretical) capacity, (2) practical capacity, (3) normal capacity, or (4) expected annual capacity. Describe each of these allocation bases and give a supporting argument for each.

(C) Justify each of the following methods of accounting for the net amount of all standard cost variances: (1) Presenting the net variance as an income or expense on the income statement; (2) Allocating the net variance among inventories and cost of goods sold; (3) Presenting the net variance as an adjustment to cost of goods sold.

(AICPA adapted)

12–29 The Groomer Company manufactures two products, Florimene and Glyoxide, both used in the plastics industry. The company uses a flexible budget in its standard cost system to develop variances. Selected data follow.

	Florimene	Glyoxide
Data on Standard Costs:		
Raw Material per Unit	3 lbs. at $1 per lb.	4 lbs. at $1.10 per lb.
Direct Labor per Unit	5 hours at $2 per hour	6 hours at $2.50 per hour
Variable Factory Overhead per Unit	$3.20 per direct labor hour	$3.50 per direct labor hour
Fixed Factory Overhead per Month	$20,700	$26,520
Normal Activity per Month	5,750 direct labor hours	7,800 direct labor hours
Units Produced in September	1,000	1,200
Costs Incurred for September:		
Raw Material	3,100 lbs. at $.90 per lb.	4,700 lbs. at $1.15 per lb.
Direct Labor	4,900 hours at $1.95 per hour	7,400 hours at $2.55 per hour
Variable Factory Overhead	$16,170	$25,234
Fixed Factory Overhead	$20,930	$26,400

Using this information, calculate the following variances. Indicate whether or not the variances were favorable by using the terms "favorable" and "unfavorable" in your answer.

(A) The total variance for both products for September

(B) The labor efficiency variance for both products for September

(C) The labor rate variances for both products for September

(D) The variable factory overhead spending variances for both products for September.

(AICPA adapted)

12–30   During January, the Copen Tool Company completed 1,000 units of Product X, which required as inputs 3,110 pounds of raw material and 5,840 hours of labor. To meet these needs, Copen acquired 4,000 pounds of material for $15,200 and incurred total payroll costs of $18,104. Copen has established the following standards for material and labor (per one standard output of Product X):

Material	3 lbs. @ $4.00/lb.
Labor	6 hours @ $3.00/hr.

(A) What were the material price and quantity variances for the Copen Tool Company?

(B) What were the labor rate and efficiency variances for the company?

(C) Does an unfavorable variance necessarily mean that performance was unfavorable? Explain why or why not.

*12–31   The Clark Company has a contract with a labor union that guarantees a minimum wage of $500 per month to each direct labor employee having at least 12 years of service. One hundred employees currently qualify for coverage. All direct labor employees are paid $5.00 per hour.

The direct labor budget for 19X0 was based on the annual usage of 400,000 hours of direct labor × $5, or a total of $2,000,000. Of this amount, $50,000 (100 employees × $500) per month (or $600,000 for the year) was regarded as fixed. Thus the budget for any given month was determined by the formula, $50,000 + $3.50 × direct labor hours worked.

Data on performance for the first three months of 19X0 follow:

	January	February	March
Direct labor hours worked	22,000	32,000	42,000
Direct labor costs budgeted	$127,000	$162,000	$197,000
Direct labor costs incurred	$110,000	$160,000	$210,000
Variance (U—unfavorable; F—favorable)	$ 17,000F	$ 2,000F	$ 13,000U

The factory manager was perplexed by the results, which showed favorable variances when production was low and unfavorable variances when production was high, because he believed his control over labor costs was consistently good.

(A) Why did the variances arise? Explain and illustrate, using amounts and diagrams as necessary.

(B) Does this direct labor budget provide a basis for controlling direct labor cost? Explain, indicating changes that might be made to improve control over direct labor cost and to facilitate performance evaluation of direct labor employees.

(C) For inventory valuation purposes, how should per unit standard costs for direct labor be determined in a situation such as this? Explain, assuming that in some months fewer than 10,000 hours are expected to be utilized.

(AICPA adapted)

12–32   Mr. Lew Jones is an accountant employed by the Die-Mark Company. Through some careless filing, Lew lost some important information concerning the Company's performance last year. After finding what he could, Lew makes the following information available to you.

1. The expected idle capacity variance was $225,000.
2. 287,000 units had been scheduled for production during the year.
3. The Company's factory has a practical capacity of 425,000 units.

4. Because of excessive machine downtime, the Company's actual production was 7,000 units fewer than sales orders.
5. The products of the firm sell for an average price of $10 per unit. Average variable costs were $7 per unit last year.

Using this information, calculate the following volume variances for Lew. Also, indicate whether each variance is "favorable" or "unfavorable."

(A) Marketing variance
(B) Production variance
(C) Volume variance

12–33   The Lee Roberts Manufacturing Company used a standard cost system in accounting for the cost of its single product. Their standard was set as follows:

Standard Output per Month—10,000 units
Standard Direct Labor per Unit—8 hours @ $1.30 per hour
Standard Direct Material per Unit:
Material P—10 lbs. @ $.275 per lb.
Material Q—5 units @ $.64 per unit
Total standard cost per unit, including overhead, on a direct labor hour basis— $23.55.

The following operating data were taken from the records for the month of March 19X7.

In process first of month—none
Completed during month—8,000 units
In process end of month—1,000 units, which are one-half complete as to labor and have had all of material P issued for them and sufficient material Q for one-half of them
Direct labor was $88,440, which was at a rate of $1.32 per hour.

Material used to production:

94,000 lbs. of P @ $.26 per lb.
42,600 units of Q @ $.65 per unit

Overhead for the month amounted to $61,640.

(A) Prepare a schedule showing all variable cost variances relative to direct labor and materials.

†(B) In summary fashion, make a set of journal entries to record the variances in the firm's accounting records.

†(C) Make the necessary entry(ies) to close the entries made in part (B) above, at the end of the year.

(AICPA adapted)

12–34   The Carberg Corporation manufactures and sells a single product. The cost system used by the company is a standard cost system. The standard cost per unit of product is shown below:

Material—1 lb. plastic @ $2.00	$ 2.00
Direct Labor—1.6 hours @ $4.00	6.40
Variable Overhead Cost	3.00
Fixed Overhead Cost	1.45
	$12.85

The overhead cost per unit was calculated from the following annual overhead cost budget for a 60,000 unit volume.

VARIABLE OVERHEAD COST	
Indirect Labor—30,000 hours @ $4.00	$120,000
Supplies—Oil 60,000 gallons @ $.50	30,000
Allocated Variable Service Department Costs	30,000
Total Variable Overhead Cost	$180,000

FIXED OVERHEAD COST	
Supervision	$ 27,000
Depreciation	45,000
Other Fixed Costs	15,000
Total Fixed Overhead Cost	$ 87,000
Total Budgeted Annual Overhead Cost at 60,000 Units	$267,000

The charges to the manufacturing department for November, when 5,000 units were produced, are given below:

Material—5,300 lbs. @ $2.00	$ 10,600
Direct Labor—8,200 hours @ $4.10	33,620
Indirect Labor—2,400 hours @ $4.10	9,840
Supplies—Oil 6,000 gallons @ $0.55	3,300
Allocated Variable Service Department Costs	3,200
Supervision	2,475
Depreciation	3,750
Other	1,250
Total	$ 68,035

The purchasing department normally buys about the same quantity as is used in production during a month. In November, 5,200 pounds were purchased at a price of $2.10 per pound.

(A)   Calculate the following variances from standard costs for the data given:

    a. Materials purchase price
    b. Materials quantity
    c. Direct labor wage rate
    d. Direct labor efficiency
    e. Overhead budget

(B) The company has divided its responsibilities so that the purchasing department is responsible for the price at which materials and supplies are purchased; the manufacturing department is responsible for the quantities of materials used. Does this division of responsibilities solve the conflict between price and quantity variances? Explain your answer.

(C) Prepare a report that details the overhead budget variance. The report, which will be given to the manufacturing departmental manager, should display only the part of the variance that is the responsibility of the manager and should highlight the information in ways that would be useful in evaluating departmental performance and considering corrective action.

*(D) Assume that the departmental manager performs the timekeeping function for this manufacturing department. From time to time, analysis of overhead and direct labor variances has shown that the departmental manager has deliberately misclassified labor hours (for example, listing direct labor hours as indirect labor hours and vice-versa) so that only one of the two labor variances is unfavorable. It is not feasible economically to hire a separate timekeeper. What should the company do, if anything, to resolve this problem?

(CMA adapted)

12–35 The Fillep Co. operates a standard cost system. The variances for each department are calculated and reported to the departmental manager. It is expected that the manager will use the information to improve his operations and will recognize that the data are used by his superiors when they are evaluating his performance.

    John Smith was recently appointed manager of the Company's assembly department. He has complained that the system as designed is disadvantageous to his department. Included among the variances charged to the departments is one for rejected units. The inspection occurs at the end of the assembly department. The inspectors attempt to identify the cause of the rejection so that the department in which the error occurred can be charged with it. Not all errors can be easily identified with a department; such errors are totaled and apportioned to the departments according to the number of identified errors. The variance for rejected units in each department is a combination of the errors caused by the department plus a portion of the unidentified causes of rejects.

(A) Is John Smith's claim valid? Explain the reason(s) for your answer.

(B) What would you recommend the Company do to solve its problem with John Smith and his complaint?

(CMA adapted)

12–36   The CoPen Company prepared the following performance report for its production operations during the month of November 19X4.

Performance Report/Production Department
November 19X4

	Budget	Actual	Variance
Direct Materials	$24,000	$25,000	$(1,000)
Direct Labor	45,000	42,000	3,000
Supplies	1,000	500	500
Power	700	500	200
Repairs and Maintenance	600	900	(300)
	$71,300	$68,900	$ 2,400

The production process at CoPen involves stamping several patterns from large sheets of metal. The pattern dies are fitted to the press, and then the sheet metal is inserted for stamping. The number of good, finished units produced from any one sheet depends on the care with which the employee fits the pattern die and positions the metal sheet. One of the presses was repaired during the month because it seemed to be running at too high a rate of speed.

(A) List possible reasons for the variances shown.

(B) Which variances might be related to the same underlying phenomenon?

(C) Would your answers to (A) or (B) change if you knew that 9,000 units of production were budgeted but only 8,000 were produced? Explain.

12–37   Harden Company has experienced increased production costs. The primary area of concern identified by management is direct labor. The Company is considering adopting a standard cost system to help control labor and other costs. Useful historical data are not available, because detailed production records have not been maintained.

Harden Company has retained Finch & Associates, an engineering consulting firm, to establish labor standards. After a complete study of the work process, the engineers recommended a labor standard of one unit of production every 30 minutes or 16 units per day for each worker. Finch further advised that Harden's wage rates were below the prevailing rate of $3 per hour.

Harden's production vice-president thought this labor standard was too tight and the employees would be unable to attain it. From his experience with the labor force, he believed a labor standard of 40 minutes per unit or 12 units per day for each worker would be more reasonable.

The president of Harden Company believed the standard should be set at a high level to motivate the workers, but he also recognized that it should be set at a level that would provide adequate information for control and reasonable cost comparisons. After much discussion, the management decided to use a dual standard. The labor standard recommended by the engineering firm of one unit every 30 minutes would be employed in the plant as a motivation device, and a cost standard of 40 minutes per unit would be used in reporting. Management also concluded that the workers would not be informed of the cost standard used for reporting purposes. The production vice-president conducted several sessions prior to implementation in the plant, informing the workers of the new standard cost system and answering questions. The new standards were not related to incentive pay but were introduced at the time wages were increased to $3 per hour.

The new standard cost system was implemented on January 1, 19X4. At the end of six months of operation, the following statistics on labor performance were presented to top management:

	Jan.	Feb.	Mar.	Apr.	May	June
Production (units)	5,100	5,000	4,700	4,500	4,300	4,400
Direct labor hours	3,000	2,900	2,900	3,000	3,000	3,100
Variance from Labor Standard	$1,350U	$1,200U	$1,650U	$2,250U	$2,550U	$2,700U
Variance from Cost Standard	$1,200F	$1,300F	$ 700F	$ -0-	$ 400U	$ 500U

Raw material quality, labor mix, and plant facilities and conditions have not changed to any great extent during the six-month period.

(A) Discuss the impact of different types of standards on motivation, including the effect on motivation in Harden Company's plant of adopting the labor standard recommended by the engineering firm.

(B) Evaluate Harden Company's decision to employ dual standards in their standard cost system.

(CMA adapted)

CHAPTER 13

Management Control in Nonprofit Organizations

Objectives

After studying this chapter, you should be able to do the following:

Define nonprofit organizations and identify their unique characteristics. Contrast profit-oriented and nonprofit organizations according to their objectives and the market control mechanism.

Specify some information needs of managers of nonprofit entities. List opportunities for managerial accounting to contribute to better planning and control decisions.

Describe characteristics of accounting, control, and budgeting systems in nonprofit organizations.

Identify alternate measures of nonprofit performance, including compliance of expenditures and authorizations, the efficiency of resource utilization, and the effectiveness of programs.

Managers of **nonprofit organizations** have as great a need for information to help them in planning, control, and decision-making as do managers of private, profit-seeking business enterprises. Although the goals of satisfactory or maximum profits are absent in nonprofit organizations, other traditional organizational goals, such as growth, survival, and social service apply equally to both profit and nonprofit organizations. The primary characteristics of nonprofit organizations are the absences of private ownership and the opportunity for private profits.

A not-for-profit organization is one in which:

1.   There is no deliberate or conscious profit motive;

2.   There are no personally or individually owned equity shares or interests;

3.   Equity interest may not be sold or exchanged; and

4.   There is no usual or required direct or proportionate financial benefit to contributors of capital or to the patrons.[1]

This definition is useful because it encompasses the more common types of nonprofit organizations, such as colleges, churches, hospitals, charitable organizations, and governmental units, all of which share many problems of accounting and control, but it excludes such organizations as cooperatives, trade unions, and private clubs, which operate for the personal and collective benefits of their members.

Nonprofit organizations are created to provide goods and services that are considered socially desirable, but which might not be provided at all, as efficiently, or in the quality or quantity deemed necessary if the decision to provide the goods or services were determined by supply and demand in a competitive market. Thus, the quality, quantity, and mix of goods and services provided by nonprofit organizations are determined without benefit of those competitive market factors that regulate the allocation of resources in private enterprises. A nonprofit organization's resources are commonly limited by its fund-raising ability: the amount of tax assessments for governmental units, contributions for charitable organizations, donors' support for churches, and the fee structures for hospitals.

FUND ACCOUNTING

The most common accounting control in nonprofit organizations is the division of accounting systems into funds. A *fund* is a separate unit of accountability and the fund accounts contain data solely concerned with that fund. **Fund**

---

[1]"Report of the Committee on Accounting for Not-for-Profit Organizations," *Supplement to Vol. XLVI of the Accounting Review* (American Accounting Association, 1971), p. 94.

accounting provides some control by establishing a basis for measuring fiscal responsibility for the diverse activities conducted within a single nonprofit organization. The accounts of each organization are subdivided into several independent funds. For example, the accounting systems of governmental units have *general funds* to account for receipts and expenditures of general purpose (not restricted) resources, *special funds* to account for receipts and disbursements of resources earmarked for particular purposes, such as education and libraries, *revolving or self-sustaining funds* to account for operations that are self-sustaining once they are established such as motor pools and centralized purchasing, and *trust funds* to account for resources held in trust for specified purposes in accordance wth donor or legal specifications. Hospitals have similar funds with titles such as: *operating fund, special purpose fund, plant fund, endowment fund* and *construction fund*. Colleges, churches, and charitable organizations use *general funds, trust funds,* and others as appropriate to their operations.

As an example of administrative control through fund accounting, assume that a municipality expects to receive and spend $110,000 from all sources during the coming fiscal year. Legal, legislative, and administrative restrictions prohibit the $110,000 from being spent for unauthorized purposes. Approved expenditures are called **authorizations**. In order to measure compliance with authorizations, the accounting system is normally divided into funds, each of which is a self-balancing, fiscal and accounting entity.

A combined Statement of Revenue and Expenditures for these entities is displayed in Exhibit 13–1. For each fund, separate accounts are maintained and actual data are accumulated. The actual accounts for each fund should follow the format established in the budget. Comparing actual results with budgeted authorizations by funds provides assurances such as the following: (1) trust fund income has not been used to finance police operations or local schools, (2) taxes levied for education have not been spent for capital improvements, (3) amounts appropriated for teachers' salaries have not been spent for sanitation. The operations of the motor pool are financed from charges made against other funds that use motor pool services, and therefore, $3,000 of the total amount shown involves double counting. For example, the $1,000 salaries expenditure in the motor pool is also counted as part of the $400 interfund charges assigned to the school fund and the $2,500 assigned to the general fund. A separate fund for the motor pool is created as an administrative control to improve services and provide an equitable means of allocating the cost of motor pool facilities to common users of those facilities.

Another control feature of fund accounting for nonprofit organizations is the integration of budgetary accounts into the formal accounting systems.[2] This

---

[2]Budgetary accounts are not integrated into the formal accounting systems of most profit-oriented organizations.

EXHIBIT 13–1   STATEMENT OF REVENUES AND EXPENDITURES

	Total	General Fund	School Fund	Motor Pool	Cemetery Trust Fund
Revenue:					
Taxes	$108,000	$50,000	$58,000	$–0–	$ –0–
Investment Income	2,000	–0–	–0–	–0–	2,000
Interfund Charges	3,000	–0–	–0–	3,000	–0–
	$113,000	$50,000	$58,000	$3,000	$2,000
Expenditures:					
Salaries	$ 61,200	$20,000	$40,000	$1,000	$ 200
Supplies and Materials	19,700	7,500	10,000	1,000	1,200
Contractual Services	18,100	10,000	7,600	–0–	500
Capital Outlays	11,000	10,000	–0–	1,000	–0–
Interfund Charges	3,000	2,500	400	–0–	100
	$113,000	$50,000	$58,000	$3,000	$2,000

integration creates accounts for budgeted revenues and expenditures as well as for actual revenues and expenditures and makes possible the comparison by funds of actual results with budgeted expectations. Although an automatic comparison does not assure that resources were used efficiently, it does indicate the effectiveness of the budgeting process, as well as giving some assurance that expenditures were properly authorized and that resources were used only for authorized purposes. Assurance that expenditures are authorized is particularly important in accounting for governmental units because budgeted expenditures, when approved by a legislative body, become legal authorizations to spend. An excess expenditure would therefore constitute a violation of a spending ordinance.

Although efficient fund accounting systems in nonprofit organizations use many *accrual accounting* concepts for measuring revenues and expenditures,[3] the usual system of fund accounting is concerned with the flow of resources into and through the fund entities used by nonprofit organizations. The result of emphasizing the "flow of funds" is that expenditures rather than expenses and cash receipts rather than accrued revenue are the usual dimensions of budgetary control. In general, capital expenditures receive the same accounting treatment as current expenditures, and depreciation is not recognized as a

---

[3]Accrual accounting shifts the reporting of revenue to periods when it is "earned" and cost to periods when it is "used." Cash-basis accounting recognizes revenue when it is collected and cost when it is paid. The two pairs of terms, earned-received and used-paid, may not occur during the same period.

cost of operations. There are exceptions to this generalization for particular types of nonprofit organizations. Hospitals, for example, use many accrual accounting procedures, as do particular funds within most nonprofit organizations, including governmental units.

Budgetary control through measuring compliance of expenditures with authorizations has limitations for managerial control purposes. Most important, this method provides no assurance that the resources were used wisely, efficiently, or effectively in financing the nonprofit organization's activities and functions. Thus, other control features are necessary to measure the effectiveness with which available resources have been used in meeting the objectives of the nonprofit organization.

EARMARKING REVENUE SOURCES

The process of **earmarking** particular cash inflows for particular purposes is another device used by nonprofit organizations to control resources. Earmarking revenue sources assures financing for programs and activities considered essential—at least, considered so at the time of the earmarking. Often, the earmarking decision remains effective year after year without further action, thus providing a steady source of revenue. State sales taxes earmarked for education, gasoline taxes for highways, and liquor taxes for public improvements are examples. In the absence of a logical relationship between earmarked revenue and the programs to be financed by them, the earmarking device is subject to criticism. Programs financed from earmarked resources do not compete with other programs for available resources. Consequently, some programs may be assured of continued support through earmarked revenues while other programs are being cut for lack of financing. For example, consider a situation in which a decision was once made to earmark the money collected from dog licenses for restocking wildlife for hunters. The restocking may continue with no further deliberation, even if animal shelters are overcrowded and the local dog warden's facilities are understaffed owing to lack of funds. In this situation, the earmarking technique, in conjuction with the lack of a competitive market system to control the allocation of resources, may have resulted in a misallocation of resources.

THE BUDGETING PROCESS

The budgeting process in profit-oriented organizations usually starts with an estimate of sales volume. In contrast, the budgeting process in nonprofit organizations commonly starts with estimated costs of programs to be financed and functions to be performed by the various subdivisions within the organization. Thus, the police department, fire department, recreation department, and other divisions of a city propose specific activities and related costs for the coming year. These costs are combined by a budgeting committee into an overall budget proposal. Resources for financing the proposed level of public services should equal the total costs of such services (taking into account resources left over or deficiencies to be made up from earlier periods). Similarly, churches, hospitals, aid societies, and other nonprofit organizations develop programs of public service first and then find means of financing these programs or reducing them to realistic levels that can be financed from available sources.

   Although the level of activity for nonprofit organizations is typically constrained by limited funds, occasionally an excess of financing is available and the budgeting process attempts to find programs on which to spend the excess resources. This happens, for example, when additional taxes levied to provide for capital outlays, interest, or principal repayments are continued after the programs have been completed. Excess financing happens also when hospital charges and donations are in excess of amounts necessary to provide the levels of services considered desirable. In such cases, there is no assurance that resource utilization will be responsive to the public needs or the donors' desire.

BUDGETING CONCEPTS

Line-item budgets   The traditional format for budgets of nonprofit organizations is referred to as a **line-item budget**. A line-item budget is one in which the expenditures are expressed in considerable detail but the activities being budgeted are given little or no explicit recognition. Salaries, supplies, utilities, gasoline, equipment, and other expenditures appear in the typical line-item budget illustrated in Exhibit 13–2. The amounts are frequently established by referring to historical costs adjusted for anticipated changes in costs and activity levels. When compared with actual expenditures, line-item budgets provide a basis for evaluating compliance with budgetary authorizations. On the other hand, they usually fail to identify the costs of activities and programs to be implemented by the nonprofit organization. For example, the expected total costs of public safety, recreation, sanitation, and other public service programs are not revealed in the typical line-item budget of a municipality, as seen in Exhibit 13–2.

   The report format demonstrates the need to accumulate information on actual line-item costs and to compare them with budgeted amounts. Budgetary formats frequently dictate the accounting report formats used by an organization. A line-item budget suggests an input-oriented (line-item classified by department and fund) accounting and reporting systm. On the other hand, managers desiring control information on efficiency or effectiveness would want the

EXHIBIT 13–2   PROPOSED POLICE DEPARTMENT LINE-ITEM BUDGET

Account Number	Account Title	Budgeted 19X2	Actual 19X2	Surplus or (Deficit)	Proposed Budget 19X3
2341	Administrative Salaries	$ 23,500	$ 23,500	–0–	$ 25,000
2343	Uniformed Police	254,624	261,823	$(7,199)	264,000
2345	Detectives' Salaries	15,200	14,100	1,100	15,080
2347	Crossing Guards	6,000	6,200	(200)	6,400
2349	Police Auxiliary	4,000	3,712	288	3,500
2351	Clerical Staff	9,000	9,083	(83)	9,200
2361	Telephone Expense	600	685	(85)	700
2371	Vehicle Operation	8,050	9,000	(950)	9,250
2373	Car Rental	1,500	1,381	119	1,400
2381	Training Expense	1,200	984	216	1,100
2383	Memberships	250	250	–0–	250
2391	Office Supplies	450	478	(28)	450
2393	Other Supplies	250	400	(150)	400
2395	Maintenance	1,200	1,082	118	1,200
2399	Other Expense	200	281	(81)	300
		$326,024	$332,959	$(6,935)	$338,230

system to assemble and report information on programs and performance, and this information cannot be determined from line-item budgets.

The current trend in budgeting is to place less emphasis on line-item budgets and to rely more on (1) output-oriented budgeting, (2) accounting and reporting systems that provide information on planned and actual accomplishments, (3) the efficiency with which activities and functions have been performed, and (4) the effectiveness with which goals have been achieved. Although the changing emphasis does not eliminate the need for detail as found in line-item budgets or the need to measure compliance with authorizations, it does change the focal point of control from one of compliance to one of evaluating the efficiency with which programs have achieved their objectives.

Program budgeting   **Program budgeting** applies the accounting system to the objectives of the nonprofit organization according to activities to be provided, functions to be performed, and programs to be undertaken. Program budgets would include estimates of total costs for particular programs and functions,

EXHIBIT 13-3   PROPOSED PUBLIC SAFETY PROGRAM BUDGET

Objective: Protection of people and property within the jurisdiction of Moderate City				
	Total	Salaries	Materials and Supplies	Contractual Services
Police Programs				
Supervision	$ 27,000	$ 20,000	$ 5,000	$ 2,000
Crime Control	398,000	300,000	30,000	68,000
Criminal Investigations	138,000	120,000	3,000	15,000
Traffic Control	105,000	60,000	25,000	20,000
Community Relations	50,000	35,000	15,000	—0—
Police Education	12,000	10,000	2,000	—0—
Special Services	18,000	15,000	—0—	3,000
	$748,000	$560,000	$ 80,000	$108,000
Fire Department Programs				
Supervision	$ 25,000	$ 15,000	$ 10,000	—0—
Fire Fighting	250,000	200,000	50,000	—0—
Fire Prevention	180,000	100,000	80,000	—0—
Fire Training	80,000	50,000	30,000	—0—
Fire Communications	40,000	15,000	15,000	10,000
	$575,000	$380,000	$185,000	$ 10,000
Other Public Safety Programs				
Total Public Safety	$1,560,000	$1,050,000	$360,000	$150,000

regardless of the organizational units (departments, offices, or funds) involved and frequently without reference to the time period covered by a program. In a municipal accounting system, for example, a program budget might emphasize public safety and the activities involved in implementing the public safety program (such as traffic control, squad car patrols, and fire prevention rather than salaries, supplies, uniforms, equipment rentals, and other objects of expenditure). Exhibit 13-3, which shows an abbreviated program budget for public safety, reveals the fundamental differences between program and line-item budgets.

A program budgeting system contributes to better control in nonprofit organizations for at least two reasons. First, it forces management to identify the activities, functions, or programs to be provided, thereby establishing a basis for evaluating the worthiness of the program. Consequently, police effort might be shifted out of traffic control and into criminal investigations. Second, program budgeting systems provide information by which management can assess the effectiveness of its plans: for example, is the traffic control in Moderate City as well developed as it should be for an expenditure of $105,000?

Zero-based budgeting   Zero-based budgeting is quite similar to program budgeting in that budget elements are aggregated by output objective (e.g., programs). These objectives are called *decision packages* by zero-based budgeters. The first step in zero-based budgeting involves analyzing and describing each discrete activity in one or more decision packages. Packages are developed for current as well as new activities, and different levels of volume for a particular activity are treated as individual packages. For example, 20,000 decision packages were developed for existing and prospective activities during the first year that zero-based budgeting was introduced in the state of Georgia, and these only described three levels of volume for each activity planned by the executive branch of government. The second step in zero-based budgeting involves ranking the packages in order of importance. The final determination of activities to be accomplished during the budget period is achieved by selecting a cut-off point along the ranked list of decision packages: all packages above the point are accepted and those below the list are rejected. The chief advantage of zero-based budgeting is that new programs or activities are given an opportunity to compete for funds against old programs.

Performance budgeting   Although the terms *program budgeting* and *performance budgeting* sometimes refer to the same concept, the following distinction can be made: program budgeting measures total costs of programs or activities; **performance budgeting** measures both costs and activities. Performance budgeting emphasizes nonfinancial measures of performance, which can be related to financial measures in explaining changes and deviations from planned performance. Historical comparisons of nonfinancial measurements of activity are particularly helpful in justifying budget proposals and in showing how the resources of nonprofit organizations are being used. Exhibit 13–4 shows how nonfinancial measurements can be presented within a performance budgeting format.

   Performance measurements are useful both for evaluating past performance and for planning future activities. For example, nonfinancial information involving drug abuse activities, such as arrests, convictions, and deaths, can be used to justify increased appropriations for future drug control programs, as well as to explain current cost variances in existing programs. Similarly, data relating to increased outpatient activity may be used to justify increased staff and facilities for outpatient services. A decision or an evaluation may often require a combination of several different performance measures as support. For example, a budgeted increase in college enrollment would not be sufficient justification by itself for increasing food service personnel or dining hall facilities, since dormi-

EXHIBIT 13-4   PROPOSED PERFORMANCE BUDGET FOR PUBLIC SAFETY

	19X2 Actual	19X3 Proposed (estimated)
All Public Safety Programs		
Total Public Safety	$1,400,000	$1,560,000
Population	140,500	144,000
Per Capita Cost	$9.96	$10.83
Manpower		
Employees	50	53
Man-Hours	102,000	108,000
Average Cost per Man-Hour	$13.72	$14.44
Crime Control		
Total Cost	$ 362,000	$ 398,000
Man-Hours Worked	24,000	26,000
Miles Driven	400,000	450,000
Prisoner-Care Days	3,600	3,900
Community Relations		
Total Cost	$ 45,000	$ 50,000
Man-Hours Worked	8,000	8,000
Miles Driven	20,000	22,000
School Lectures	280	300
Community Lectures	40	50
Other		

tory occupancy, meals served, and a host of other variables have a bearing on the adequacy of food services. The challenge of performance budgeting is to find sufficient performance measures to represent adequately all important variables in determining the cost of an activity, function, or program.

The accountant must exercise considerable care in designing perform-ance measures to assure that the measures are relevant and adequate to repre-sent the activity. He must also take care in using the measures to evaluate past activity and plan future activity. For example, if too much emphasis is placed on arrests made by policemen, then the number of arrests is likely to increase at the expense of crime prevention. Emphasis on quantity can undermine the quality of the service. In judging the police department's performance, arrests for minor traffic violations should not be given the same weight as arrests for major crimes. Also, some results and activities do not lend themselves to performance measurements. For example, the real test of performance for a police department may be the number of crimes prevented, something practically impossible to measure. The test of a university's educational program may be its students' increased potential for gainful employment and for enjoying a good life, but again, this measurement is difficult to determine.

COST ACCOUNTING

Recent emphasis on performance budgeting has accelerated the development of cost accounting in nonprofit organizations. Performance budgeting requires activity measurements of performance, as well as cost measurements of functions, programs, and activities. A logical extension of performance budgeting is to combine cost and activity measurements into unit cost calculations. In this area, cost accounting has made its greatest contribution to private accounting.

Unit-cost calculations are used in private enterprises for pricing goods and services as well as for controlling costs. Sometimes, unit costs are used in nonprofit organizations also for pricing such things as water and sewer services, college tuition, dormitory charges, or hospital room fees, when the recipients are charged directly for the services they receive. For the vast majority of services provided by nonprofit organizations, however, the service is rendered without specific charges for benefits received, and the cost-benefit measurement that exists in private enterprise is absent.

There are many opportunities for cost accounting to contribute to pricing and other decisions, but the greatest opportunities in the nonprofit sector seem to be in controlling costs. Cost accounting aids nonprofit managers in controlling costs by identifying inefficiency so that correct action may be taken. Unit-cost calculations are particularly helpful in formulating corrective actions, because they provide a common base for comparison. Comparing unit costs with historical trends or similar cost data for other activities, functions, or organizations, or with performance standards are common approaches for promoting efficiency in nonprofit organizations. For example, unit-cost measurements per mile of streets resurfaced, per ton-mile of garbage hauled, per student credit-hour of instruction and per patient-day—all can provide valuable information when compared over time (historically), with similar data for other organizations and activities, or with performance standards that indicate what such costs ought to be.

Cost consciousness is a related area in which cost accounting can contribute to efficiency in nonprofit organizations. When employees, managers, and the general public are aware of the cost of public services, they are more likely to expose inefficiency and to support corrective action. For cost-consciousness programs, unit-cost calculations are frequently more useful than total-cost calculations for encouraging efficiency.

Although well-developed cost accounting systems remain the exception rather than the rule, there is a movement toward more unit-cost calculations throughout nonprofit organizations. Certain unit-cost measurements have become commonplace in many hospitals, which need such information for meeting reporting standards under Medicare and Medicaid programs. Colleges, under pressure from state legislatures to justify their support, also are providing more unit-cost calculations. The major obstacle in developing good cost accounting systems in nonprofit organizations lies in the fact that such systems require accrual accounting for their implementation. Most nonprofit organizations continue to use cash-basis or mixed cash-accrual basis accounting.

PPBS (PLANNING PROGRAMMING BUDGETARY SYSTEMS)

The recent impetus for adopting goal-centered, output-oriented accounting systems in nonprofit organizations comes largely from experiences of the federal government. Its **Planning Programming Budgeting System** (**PPB** or **PPBS**) was developed in the mid-1960s to improve planning and control in government. Since then, the concept has spread to state and local governments, colleges, and hospitals.

Basically, PPBS is a comprehensive decision model, which requires that an organization's objectives and programs be enumerated and that its long-term goals be established. To perform effectively, a decision model needs reliable data—data for planning and data for control. The data must be structured to evaluate programs and measure progress toward the goals. Thus, adopting a PPBS concept requires the development of a compatible, comprehensive information system. Differences in the nature and complexity of models require compensatory differences in the information systems.

The emphasis on objectives and programs in PPBS requires that cost data, both budgeted and actual, be accumulated by program. The same data may also be accumulated by department, responsibility, and object of expenditure, for control and other uses. In addition, PPBS requires that nonfinancial data be accumulated to help measure progress toward goals and efficiency of programs.

Implementation of PPBS customarily follows the pattern of (1) identifying the organization's objectives, (2) developing alternative programs to fulfill the objectives, (3) choosing those programs that will accomplish the objectives, and (4) developing an information system to measure progress toward objectives and provide feedback.

The first step, identifying objectives, is crucial to the success of the entire PPBS program. One may appreciate the difficulty of identifying existing objectives or formulating new ones when one attempts to identify the actual objectives of his **college** or church. A few possible objectives for a church might include survival, attendance, membership growth, community service, fellowship, religious education, or salvation. Each objective suggests a different program and different activities for effective implementation. Identifying and evaluating alternate programs can help select only those programs that are potentially effective.

PPBS requires in addition that goals be placed in a time-sequence structure so that progress toward the goals can be measured. For example, a goal of maximizing membership is not sufficiently operational for a PPBS system. Instead, the goal must be expressed in quantitative terms at definite time intervals. Assume that a church has 1,000 members and facilities to accommodate 800. In planning the construction of new physical facilities, membership goals must be projected into the future. A goal of 2,000 members within fifteen years may be set, with subgoals of 1,400, 1,700, and 2,000 members at the end of five, ten, and fifteen years, respectively. A multiyear budget plan (say, five years) would then be designed to show progress toward the 1,400-membership goal. Various programs and costs of achieving the 1,400-member goal will be reflected in the first multiyear budget.

Developing an information system that will accumulate sufficient data for evaluating the progress programs are making toward their objectives is a worthy challenge for the best accounting and administrative talents. Five-year programs toward meeting specific goals are typical, and a multitude of financial and nonfinancial data is required to measure periodic progress toward the goals. Implementing PPBS information systems may require automatic data-processing equipment capable of handling complex program structures and sophisticated quantitative statistical techniques.

PPB techniques have particular merit in that they facilitate budgetary appropriations being made on traditional line-item cash disbursements, expenditures, or obligational authority bases, supported by cost-based data that relate to the longer time spans relating to the continuing organization. Although cost-based budgeting may well be the ultimate solution to current weaknesses in larger NFP entity budgeting, control, and evaluation, PPB-supported systems or similar approaches appear to be the most promising avenue for progress in the immediate future.[4]

COST-BENEFIT ANALYSIS

Benefits received from the services of nonprofit organizations should be at least as great as their cost. Also, the cost of the last unit of a service provided should be equal to the benefit received from supplying that last unit of service. These observations are based on the economic theory that production of goods and services should be pushed to the point where marginal revenue (benefit) is equal to marginal cost for optimum resource utilization. The absence of a rev-

---

[4]"Report of the Committee on Accounting for Not-For-Profit Organizations," *Supplement to Vol. XLVI of The Accounting Review* (American Accounting Association, 1971), p. 88.

enue test of benefits provided by nonprofit organizations complicates **cost-benefit analysis**, even though the theory remains valid and useful for nonprofit organizations.

In applying cost-benefit analysis to nonprofit organizations, the final assessment of whether benefits are as great as their cost is a subjective evaluation. Knowledge of cost is an important factor in making any cost-benefit decision: Managers cannot evaluate benefits without knowing the magnitude of costs. If the cost of police protection is $5 per year per citizen in a given city, rather than $500 per year, city officials may decide that the police force should be expanded. A report showing that total expenditures for police salaries, supplies, and equipment cost $867,546 last year is not nearly as informative as the $5-per-citizen figure.

MANAGEMENT AUDITS

Traditional audits are concerned with financial records. **Management audits** extend into the effectiveness and efficiency with which resources have been used in carrying out an organization's activities, functions, and programs. They provide another type of control in nonprofit organizations. Such management, or performance, audits are intended to help management do a better job by identifying waste and inefficiency and recommending corrective action. Although management audits are applicable to both profit and nonprofit-oriented organizations, their greatest development has been by the General Accounting Office (GAO) of the federal government. The need to extend audits beyond financial records is well recognized by the GAO in its audits of federal agencies. GAO audits of such major organizations as the Defense Department, the U.S. Postal Service, and the Veterans Administration have reportedly saved taxpayers millions of dollars. Management audits investigate the entire managerial control system, including such things as goals, policies, procedures, personnel organization and design, and property utilization.

The result of a management audit differs significantly from traditional audit reports, which express an opinion on the fair presentation of financial statements. A management audit report comments on the conditions found, conclusions drawn, and recommendations made for improving efficiency, cutting costs, and otherwise promoting the objectives of the organization.

Management audits can be performed by internal auditors as well as by independent outsiders. Some internal auditing staffs of profit and nonprofit organizations have performed management audits for many years, and some have developed sophisticated procedures for conducting the management audit. There are advantages to having outside or independent audit firms perform the management audit. Public accounting firms (CPAs) will probably extend their expertise into audits of management in the future. In time, concepts and standards for management audits will be developed. Currently, the management audit is a significant control device for nonprofit organizations, although its potential is not yet realized.

An extension of the management audit that has received considerable attention in the Defense Department is the **"should cost" review** technique. "Should cost" reviews are essentially management audits of contractors' engineering, manufacturing, accounting, purchasing, and organizational structures for the purpose of renegotiating initial contract prices on the basis of any inefficient and uneconomical practices identified during the investigation. "Should cost" reviews are performed by "should cost" teams, or teams of specialists who determine what costs should be if the most efficient and economical means of production are used. Theoretically, the contractor should be willing to reduce contract prices by the amount of cost savings identified by the "should cost" review. Some defense contractors have already submitted to such contract reductions.

Although the "should cost" technique is still in its infancy, the concept appears to be applicable to all organizations that enter into large construction contracts, including many large nonprofit organizations.

SUMMARY

This chapter has identified some of the more common methods and techniques of control that are used in nonprofit organizations. These include fund accounting practices, which divide the accounting system into separate funds or units of accountability, earmarking particular resources for designated purposes, budgetary control, cost accounting, management audits, and "should cost" techniques. Two broad types of control distinguished throughout the chapter are control in the sense of measuring compliance with authorizations, and control in the sense of measuring the efficiency of resource utilization and effectiveness of programs, functions, and activities.

The current trend in nonprofit organizations is to develop budgeting and information systems that emphasize the latter type of control. Program budgeting, performance budgeting, cost accounting, cost benefit analysis, PPBS, and management audits are all oriented toward improving the efficiency with which resources are used. As a result, they strive toward increasing the operational effectiveness of nonprofit organizations in providing services to society.

SUGGESTED READINGS

Castello, Albert P. "The Model Cities Program: An Application of PPBS." *Management Accounting,* January 1973, pp. 29–33.

Hensler, Emil J., Jr., "Accounting for Small Nonprofit Organizations." *Management Accounting*, January 1973, pp. 41–44.

"Report of the Committee on Nonprofit Organizations." *Supplement to Vol. XLX of The Accounting Review* (American Accounting Association, 1975).

Steinberg, Harold I. "Programming Your Budget." *Management Adviser*, November/December, 1972, pp. 25–35.

Terre, Norbert C., Dale W. Warnke, and Albert P. Ameiss. "Cost/Benefit Analysis of Public Projects." *Management Accounting*, January 1973, pp. 34–37.

QUESTIONS

13–1   What common goals do both profit and nonprofit organizations share?

13–2   List four characteristics of a nonprofit organization. Briefly explain how each characteristic can be contrasted with those of a profit-oriented organization.

13–3   Why are nonprofit organizations created? How can they benefit from the services of an accountant and from good managerial accounting techniques?

13–4   What are *funds* as applied to accounting for nonprofit organizations? If someone tells you that all cities have general funds, is that person likely referring to working capital? Discuss.

13–5   Briefly explain how fund accounting can provide some control in nonprofit organizations.

13–6   "Fund accounting is like taking a total organization and subdividing it into a collection of several smaller organizations, all working together." Comment on this opinion of fund accounting. Is it reasonable? Is it accurate? Does it reflect the actual situation faced by accountants in dealing with funds?

13–7   What is meant by a "flow of funds" emphasis, rather than an accrual emphasis in fund accounting?

13–8   Total revenues for 19X4 of the First Christ Church were $186,000, and total expenditures for the same period were $156,000. Did First Christ Church have a profit for the period? Discuss.

13–9   Would you recommend that the city of New York begin the budgeting process by estimating revenue from property tax assessments? Discuss why or why not.

13–10   What can the board of regents (the governing body of a university) learn about financial control from a statement comparing actual revenues and expenditures with budgeted revenues and expenditures? Do you suppose that such a statement is prepared for your college? What evidence of this can you cite?

13-11   Budgetary control by measuring expenditures and authorizations has many limitations: it provides no assurance that resources were used wisely, efficiently, or effectively. Since these limitations seem significant, what good is this type of budgetary control for nonprofit organizations?

13-12   What are some advantages of earmarking revenue sources for particular purposes? List some disadvantages of earmarking. Will the decision to earmark revenue sources for particular programs add to the efficiency of these programs? Why or why not?

13-13   The Hays-Fells Community Hospital earmarks all donations to the hospital for capital improvement programs to the hospital buildings. Discuss the advantages and limitations of this practice.

13-14   Compare and contrast the budgeting procedures of a profit-oriented organization with those employed in a nonprofit organization.

13-15   Sometimes, when actual revenues and donations to a nonprofit organization exceed the budgeted expectations, control over resource utilization is lost. Why is this so? What can be done about it?

13-16   Identify and explain two broad concepts of control relating to nonprofit organizations. Compare these two concepts with similar control concepts in profit-oriented organizations.

13-17   Briefly describe what is meant by program budgeting. What are the major differences between a program budget and a line-item budget? What are line-item budgets? List some advantages and disadvantages of line-item budgets. How does a program budget contribute to control in nonprofit organizations?

13-18   The terms *program budgeting* and *performance budgeting* are sometimes used to refer to the same concept. What is the major distinction between them?

EXERCISES

13-19   In 19X3, Smallville had 12,000 residents and spent $14,400 for refuse collection. In 19X6, the population had grown to 15,200 residents and $17,600 was spent to collect refuse. In the current year, the population is estimated to be 18,000. What amount should reasonably be budgeted for refuse collection services?

13-20   The town of Pine Hills had a population of 10,000 people in 19X8 and spent $12,000 for snow removal services. In 19X9, the population declined to 9,000 people and only $11,000 was spent on snow removal. How much should the town budget for snow removal next year when the population is expected to be 8,500 people?

13–21   The directors of the Western Memorial Hospital are evaluating operating budget requests for next year. The Chief of the X-ray unit presented the following cost information for the directors' consideration:

	19X6	19X7	19X8
X-ray studies performed	10,750	12,125	14,650
Salary expense	$90,000	$90,000	$90,000
Supplies expense	$17,550	$19,475	$23,010
Depreciation expense	$12,900	$14,550	$17,580

The Hospital Administrator has suggested that managerial accounting techniques might be useful in predicting future costs.

Using this information, prepare the following budget estimations for the X-ray unit for 19X9.

(A) The Chief of the X-ray unit expects to perform 16,000 studies next year. What amounts should be budgeted for salaries, supplies, and depreciation?

(B) If the Administrator expects salaries to increase by 12% and supplies to increase by 10% over their expected levels, what amounts should be budgeted for these areas for next year?

13–22   The town of Middleburg uses fund accounting for control purposes. The town has created four fund accounts including: (1) General Fund; (2) School Fund; (3) Fire and Police Fund; and (4) Maintenance Fund. Beyond initial appropriations funded by property taxes, additional collections are added to related fund balances.

For each of the transactions listed below, indicate the fund that will be affected and whether the transaction will increase or decrease the fund balance.

(A) Payment of teacher salaries.
(B) Collection of parking ticket fines.
(C) Purchase of a new fire engine.
(D) Clearing snow from municipal properties.
(E) Payment of the Mayor's salary.
(F) Construction of a new municipal parking garage.
(G) Repaving a municipal parking lot.
(H) Purchase of school textbooks.
(I) Collection of property taxes.
(J) Cost of repainting the town hall.

*13–23   Frequently, in governmental circles, the end of the fiscal year marks the beginning of a spending spree for the various agencies. If appropriated funds are not spent, the agencies fear that subsequent appropriations will be reduced.

These spending sprees do not generally represent an efficient use of available financial resources. What managerial control programs could be implemented to prevent these situations from occurring? Why haven't they been implemented in the past?

13–24 The mayor of Taboria believes the performance of the Taboria Fire Department should be evaluated on the basis of its success in a fire-prevention crusade. Suggest some performance measurements that might help the mayor in his evaluation.

13–25 The average cost per pupil bussed to school was $.42 per day in Halley County during 19X4. How would you suggest that this information be used in determining the relative efficiency of Halley County's bussing program?

13–26 Cost accounting techniques can be used to derive unit-cost figures for nonprofit organizations. However, if an organization does not sell its services, of what use are unit-cost calculations? What difficulties do nonprofit organizations face in trying to derive unit costs for their products or services?

13–27 Describe an implementation pattern for a typical Planning Programming Budgetary System (PPBS). Briefly identify which types of information would be needed for each phase of implementation.

13–28 Costs and benefits are often considered by decision-makers in profit-oriented enterprises. Should cost and benefit also be a concern of decision-makers in nonprofit organizations? Why or why not?

13–29 "When revenues exceed expenses in a profit-oriented organization, it is called a profit; in a nonprofit organization, it is called a surplus. This is really the only difference between the two." Discuss this statement.

13–30 The Jones Company is concerned about its public image. For years, the Company has had a reputation for being ruthless in its dealings with people. Recently, the Company directors proposed a change in philosophy to help stimulate future consumer sales. They want to establish a nonprofit organization, the Jones Company Foundation, to support humanitarian projects and indirectly to help the Company's image.

> (A) Is the Jones Company Foundation a nonprofit organization? Briefly explain why or why not.
>
> (B) Will the accounting methods used for the Foundation reflect its goal of changing the corporate image?

13–31 State whether each of the following is or is not a nonprofit organization. In each case, justify your answer.

> (A) An Elks lodge
> (B) The University Alumni Association
> (C) Nassau County, New York
> (D) The American Red Cross

(E) University of South Carolina
(F) The Teamsters' Union
(G) Virginia Cooperative Savings and Loan Association

13–32 Suggest some performance measures that could be used to evaluate the following activities. Include sufficient performance measures in each case to ensure that all important aspects of the activity are represented.

(A) A city police department
(B) A county-run ambulance service
(C) A state-operated college or university
(D) A public library
(E) A hospital

13–33 Should the performance measures used for evaluation and planning activities by a nonprofit organization be any different from those used by a profit-oriented organization? Briefly explain why or why not.

13–34 In each of the following independent cases, identify any potential problems resulting from the performance measurement systems described.

(A) A resort city was concerned about traffic violations by visitors. The police force was evaluated on the number of violators apprehended. Traffic arrests increased significantly, but major crimes must have decreased because arrests in this area went down.

(B) A community hospital was evaluated on the amount of patient-day occupancy of its rooms. Admissions increased significantly.

(C) A city water department was evaluated on the cost of supplying fresh drinking water to the city. No appreciable change in cost was observed.

(D) A sanitation department was evaluated on the number of loads of refuse delivered to the city dump. The number of loads immediately doubled.

13–35 If Planning Programming Budgeting Systems can be an effective means of accounting for organizations in the nonprofit sector, why can't they be used also in the profit sector? Give some examples of activities conducted by profit-oriented enterprises that are similar to those performed by nonprofit organizations. Could PPBS be used in any of these activities? Explain why or why not.

13–36 Last year, the police force of Vela City operated on a total budget of $2,768,596. Vela City had a population of 102,000, according to the last census. During the year, the police force employed 150 officers and 25 support personnel. The force operated 50 squad cars, which were driven an average of 40,000 miles each, during routine patrols. Nine thousand arrests were made during the year, including 312 arrests for major crimes. Twenty-one thousand traffic violations were reported during the year, and the department responded to 54,000 citizen calls during the year.

The Vela City Council is considering an appropriation for the police force for next year. Using the information provided, prepare a cost report on the police force, which will supply meaningful information to the council members in their deliberations.

13–37 Mark each of the following statements "true" or "false." For each "false" statement, identify why it is incorrect.

(A) Management audits are traditional audits prepared for the management of an organization.

(B) "Should-cost" reviews are conducted for the purpose of identifying uneconomical practices and can provide the basis for renegotiating initial contract prices.

(C) When a nonprofit organization uses fund accounting techniques, the procedures will ensure operational efficiency for the organization.

(D) Both profit and nonprofit organizations begin their budgeting process with an estimation of sales or service volume.

(E) A major deficiency of line-item budgets could be overcome if separate budgets were prepared for each activity of the organization.

(F) If a nonprofit organization supports only one program, its operating budget is a program budget.

(G) A performance budget compares actual program performance levels with planned program performance.

13–38 The administrator of the Cureall Hospital was extremely happy. For the third straight year, actual expenditures in all departments were less than the amounts budgeted for these departments. "This proves that we are doing an efficient and effective job of running this hospital," he boasted. Evaluate the administrator's contention and also his idea of efficient and effective operations.

13–39 Earmarking revenue sources has certain advantages for nonprofit organizations; it can also prove to be restrictive if future changes are not instituted. In each of the following cases, comment on the appropriateness of earmarking revenue sources.

(A) The public library operates a copying center for the convenience of its users. All revenues are earmarked for defraying the cost of providing the service.

(B) The National Beriberi Society earmarks all donations for funding research to find a cure for beriberi.

(C) State University earmarks all contributions to the university for building a new field house for the basketball team.

(D) All contributions to the Flood Relief Fund are earmarked for aiding flood victims.

PROBLEMS

*13–40 The Municipal Hospital of Oakdale is a nonprofit organization with an objective of providing a complete health-care program for the citizens of Oakdale. The hospital is funded by governmental grants, donations, and patient revenues. Three main health-care programs are operated by the hospital, including: inpatient care in the hospital, an outpatient clinic, and a community health-education center.

Inpatient care is directed by the chief physician and a total professional staff of 73. The chief physician is paid $38,000 annually, and other professional salaries total $960,000 per year. Expected equipment purchases for next year will be $119,000, and hospital supplies, $165,000.

The outpatient clinic has a professional staff of ten, and an annual salary budget of $185,000. Supplies for the clinic will cost $73,000, and new equipment costing $58,000 will be purchased for the clinic.

The health-education center, which is new, has a staff of three and a salary budget of $52,000. Supplies costing $16,000 have been budgeted for next year.

Using this information, prepare a program budget for the Municipal Hospital of Oakdale. Segment the total cost by program and into categories representing salaries, supplies, and equipment.

13–41 After much public and private debate, the city of Beamsburg agreed on a budget for the recreation program for 19X5. The budget is as follows:

City of Beamsburg Recreation Department Budget
for the Year of 19X5

Director	$ 8,500
Secretary	2,000
Janitor	1,200
Wages	11,200
Telephone	240
Electricity	400
Membership and Subscriptions	75
Travel	500
Building Insurance	200
Repairs and Materials	500
Roof	300
Recreational Activities	400
Gas, Oil, and Auto Supplies	500
Janitorial Supplies	150
Fuel	1,100
Office Supplies	210
Park Improvements and Repairs	6,800
Park Equipment	1,000
Recreational Equipment	600
	$35,875

Also, the following additional information about the recreation department is available.

1. The recreation department operates the city youth center and a park.
2. The director administers the entire recreation program. The secretary works for him.
3. The janitor cleans up the city youth center.
4. The park and youth center both have some lighting equipment.
5. Recreational equipment is used in the park.

(A) Separate the budgeted items into the following categories: youth center, public park, joint or common.

(B) Assuming that 60% of all common or joint costs apply to the youth center and 40% to the public park program, prepare a program budget for the youth center using the classifications: (1) wages and salaries, (2) materials and supplies, (3) capital improvements, and (4) other costs.

(C) What performance measurements do you think could be developed to measure the effectiveness of the youth center?

13–42   The cost per mile of highway constructed by Hall County was $50,000 in 19X1 and $28,000 in 19X2. An analysis of construction data reveals that half of the highways constructed in 19X1 were four-lane highways, whereas all highway construction in 19X2 was two-lane. In addition, new equipment costing $2,500,000 was included in the total cost of $5 million for highway construction in 19X1. No new equipment was purchased in 19X2, when total costs were $2,800,000.

Do you agree that the highway department should be congratuled for its efficiency in cutting highway costs per mile by 40%? In answering the question, consider the questions of depreciation, cash-basis accounting, and the limitations of performance measurements. What adjustments in performance measurements do you propose? Prepare some new calculations per mile of highway constructed.

*13–43   A recent management audit of Big Town revealed idle cash balances of $3,000,000; uncollected taxes of $2,600,000 (some dating as far back as a decade); invoices for supplies and materials purchased of $2,000,000 in excess of average commercial costs for the same items; and a $20,000,000 contract in progress, which promises to yield the contractor a before-tax profit of 45%.

Draft a management audit report in which you (1) call attention to these matters, (2) identify the parties responsible for each of the situations, and (3) suggest action to correct the deficiencies.

*13–44   Mr. Ira Ate, a local businessman, was visibly upset when he addressed the town council of Muckville:

"Gentlemen, I've lived in this town for five years, and each year I'm more disgusted with its management. Taxes and other service costs consistently go up, and yet the services that we receive are constantly going down in quality. Why is this the case?

"To me, the answer is simple. The town is a nonprofit organization and we treat it like one. I've never seen a nonprofit organization yet that is efficient. Why not treat the town as a profit-making organization? Many profit-oriented corporations, like mine, can perform quite efficiently and effectively because we have a measurable goal-profitability. If our town were able to generate a profit through efficient operations, we could use the excess funds to improve the quality of services.

"In summary, I urge you to throw out those nonprofit accounting techniques, which foster inefficiency, and replace them with some proven techniques, which work in profit-oriented enterprises."

(A) Is there any validity in Mr. Ate's statement?

(B) Could profit-oriented accounting techniques work for a nonprofit organization such as the town of Muckville?

(C) As a member of the town council, write a brief, but complete, reply to Mr. Ate.

13-45 The Wilson County School Board, a nonprofit organization, uses fund accounting for administrative control. A combined statement of fund revenues and expenditures for the 19X4-19X5 school year is presented below.

Wilson County School System Statement of Revenue and Expenditures
for the Period 9/1/X4-8/31/X5

	Total	Building Fund	Operating Fund	Maintenance Division	General Fund
Revenue:					
Local Taxes	$2,870,000	$ 250,000	$2,620,000		
Interest Income	12,000				$ 12,000
State Subsidy	648,000		648,000		
Federal Grants	1,750,000	1,200,000			550,000
Interfund Charges	10,000			$10,000	
	$5,290,000	$1,450,000	$3,268,000	$10,000	$562,000
Expenditures:					
Salaries	$3,000,000		$2,866,000	$ 9,000	$125,000
Supplies	725,000		357,000	1,000	367,000
Services	55,000		20,000		35,000
Capital Additions	1,500,000	$1,450,000	20,000		30,000
Interfund Charges	10,000		5,000		5,000
	$5,290,000	$1,450,000	$3,268,000	$10,000	$562,000

Using this statement, answer the following questions.

(A) How many actual revenue dollars will the Wilson County School Board receive from all sources for the school year?

(B) How much will be spent for capital additions during the year? From what sources will this money be derived? If the building contractor misjudged the construction project, and the actual cost of capital additions was $1,500,000, will this amount be paid?

(C) How is the maintenance division funded for the year? Why was this item included in the statement?

(D) What type of control does fund accounting provide the Wilson County School Board? What are the advantages and disadvantages of this type of accounting for the school board?

13-46   The city of Strawser's Crossing has five funds included in its annual budget for 19X9. These funds and their appropriation amounts are as follows:

(1)	General Fund	$115,000
(2)	Capital Construction Fund	$420,000
(3)	Education Fund	$175,000
(4)	Civil Protection Fund	$150,000
(5)	Recreation Fund	$ 60,000

Initial appropriations are made on the basis of wage tax and property tax collection projections. All other receipts are added directly to the general fund balance.

During the first two months of the fiscal year, the following fund-related events occurred. Trace each transaction to the appropriate fund and determine its effect. Determine the amount in each fund after processing all information on the transactions.

(A) $120,000 was spent to add a wing to the city courthouse.

(B) Teacher and administrative salaries of $52,500 were paid.

(C) A new fire engine costing $37,000 was purchased.

(D) Maintenance expenditures for the city parks totaled $19,000.

(E) Traffic and court-related fines of $7,500 were collected.

(F) Administrative expenses and salaries relative to the city were paid. They totaled $58,250.

(G) An audio-visual system costing $9,750 was installed in the high school.

(H) New street-cleaning equipment was purchased for $10,950.

(I) The Director of Parks and Recreation was paid $6,500 in salary.

(J) The city received $20,000 as an out-of-court settlement from a contractor relating to the construction of the courthouse wing.

13-47   Rocky Marsh City has used budgeting and fund accounting to control expenditures for specific city activities. The budget and actual expenditures for 19X8 are reproduced below:

Rocky Marsh City
Budget for 19X8

	Budget	Actual
City Administration Fund:		
Supervision	$ 62,500	$ 62,500
Administrative	87,000	87,000
Clerical	126,000	110,250
Maintenance	21,250	20,500
Miscellaneous	42,000	48,000
Public Services Fund:		
Supervision	$ 52,000	$ 52,000
Salaries	211,500	210,000
Overtime	74,000	81,000
Vehicle Services	21,750	19,500
Vehicle Replacement	40,000	37,500
Supplies	9,800	10,100
Miscellaneous	37,900	36,850
Public Safety Fund:		
Supervision	$ 59,000	$ 59,000
Police Salaries	112,500	108,250
Fire Salaries	86,250	82,500
Vehicle Services	32,500	33,250
Vehicle Replacement	30,000	31,500
Support Services	62,250	67,500
Supplies	16,800	15,600
Miscellaneous	53,200	57,800
Totals:	$1,241,200	$1,230,600

In formulating a budget for 19X9, the City Council used the following guidelines:

(A) All overexpended items will be increased by the amount of the overexpenditure.

(B) All underexpended items will be decreased by the amount of the underexpenditure.

(C) Miscellaneous items will be cut by 25%.

(D) Supervision expenses will be increased by 30%.

(E) The Police Department will be allocated an additional $20,000 above their authorization for new vehicles.

(F) $10,000 will be taken from the authorization for vehicle replacement for public services.

(G) No overtime will be authorized.

Using this information, prepare a budget for Rocky Marsh City for 19X9.

FIVE

*Incremental
Analysis for Making
Short-term Decisions*

*Capital Budgeting:
Search for
Long-Run Alternatives*

*Additional
Complexities of
Project Planning*

*Accounting Data
for Inventory Management*

*Most managers in all organizations are called
upon to make decisions about the acquisition of
resources for the organizational unit under their
control. While judgment and experience play an
active role in this process, many business
decisions require an explicit statement of the
problem, identification of alternatives, and the
collection of all information pertinent to the
decision. In most organizations, the managerial
accountant is responsible for supplying financial
information about the consequences of
alternative decision choices. The next four
chapters relate accounting to the decision
making process.*

CHAPTER 14

Incremental Analysis for Making Short-term Decisions

Objectives

After studying this chapter, you should be able to do the following:

Define the word "decision," and identify attributes that make data relevant to a decision.

Describe how sunk costs are treated in an incremental analysis.

Determine the minimum acceptable price that will produce a positive contribution in regard to pricing decisions.

Select the best alternative regarding discontinuance of a product line and calculate the financial benefit of this alternative.

Specify the factors relevant to decisions to implement further processing and determine the financial consequences of the best alternative.

Determine the financial consequences of the best alternative for a make-or-buy decision.

All managers devote considerable amounts of time to the planning function. Top-level managers are primarily concerned with strategic elements of the long-range goals and policies for the whole organization. Managers at other organizational levels are concerned with tactical planning and scheduling. Organized planning for repetitive activities primarily involves the communication, coordination, and control functions of budgeting.

Planning often requires the evaluation of special nonrecurring decisions, such as the acquisition of plant or equipment, additions or deletions of a product line, and acceptance of special orders. Planning for special decisions such as these is the topic of this and the following three chapters. This type of planning or decision-making employs some concepts that were not highlighted in previous chapters on budgeting for recurring events. Like all budgeting, however, these decisions involve cost analysis that compels the managerial accountant to work right along with the engineer, the economist, the production manager, and all other employees directly associated with each decision. The accountant acts as a technical expert on cost analysis, and his responsibility is to summarize relevant data that can serve as a basis for making a decision.

DECISION-ORIENTED TERMINOLOGY

Problems requiring decisions are often described in technical terms that help convey meaning to business managers. Use of these decision-related terms reduces ambiguity, shortens the length of messages, and provides for greater emphasis than does use of nontechnical terms. The discussion below defines and amplifies common technical decision-oriented terms.

Decisions   A decision is the act of selecting a course of action from among alternatives. To *decide*, one must review alternatives, exercise judgment, reach conclusions, and finally settle upon a particular alternative. Decisions are action-oriented: the decision-maker is planning to buy, to make, to hire, to do, etc. One decision alternative always open to management, however, is to do nothing or to take no action; that is, all business decisions consider, at a minimum, two alternatives: to do or not to do the proposed activity. In most cases, however, the set of available alternatives is much larger: management can select activity A, B, C . . . , or none of the preceding.

Furthermore, decisions can be made only in the present or in the future: decisions imply future activities. For example, you cannot decide now whether or not to get up yesterday or what to eat for yesterday's breakfast: those choices have already been made. Choices among past alternatives are called evaluations, e.g., "I should never have gotten out of bed yesterday." Evaluations play an important role in the decision-making process, since they are basic elements in the judgment exercised in making a choice among alternative courses of action.

Relevant data   All information used to support a decision must be relevant: data must bear upon, influence, and be directly associated with actions that characterize the decision. Accounting information is relevant only if communicating it can influence the decision or the decision-making process. Relevance can be judged only by a report's effects on decisions or thought processes; it is a subjective concept, however, that may differ among persons using different decision-making processes.

Relevant information guides the decision-maker toward his objective. Ideally, relevant information should also be accurate and precise. However, some data may be relevant but imprecise, whereas others may be irrelevant but accurate. For example, although the expected benefits of an advertising campaign may be crucial data in deciding whether to introduce a new product, only crude estimations of them may be available. On the other hand, the advertising manager's salary may be known to the exact penny, yet have no bearing on a decision to market the new product.

In general, information that is relevant to choosing among alternatives must: (1) pertain to the future, and (2) indicate the differences among the alternatives. "Making decisions" means choosing among alternatives, which always relates to the future. The future may be a few seconds away, or it may be decades ahead. A decision's consequences must be estimated. Although relevant costs are expected future costs, they may be estimated from historical data. Historical cost is often the best basis available for estimating future costs.

In addition, relevant costs differ for each proposed alternative. If the economic consequences of all alternatives were identical, then the manager's decision would not be affected by economic factors. The decision would rest on factors not subject to accounting analysis. The key question in determining relevance is "what different consequences will occur in the future if I choose this alternative?"

Quantifiability   Quantifiability requires the association of a number with an activity where the numbers assigned obey prescribed arithmetic laws or procedures. Quantifiability provides a means for comparing alternative objectives, actions, or events. Furthermore, different types of objects or events can be combined according to their quantifiable attributes. For example, two different combinations of the labor, material, and overhead inputs needed to produce a given output can be evaluated in relation to the dollar value of the two pair of combined input costs.

Most business decisions have both quantitative and qualitative consequences. Quantitative consequences are those that can be reduced to a number, such as a dollar and cents figure. Consequences of a choice that are not subject to precise or direct measurement are said to be **qualitative**.

The attempt to quantify decision inputs may lead to discovery of inherent relationships among separate elements in the data. For example, weight of an input might be directly related to its size or volume. Furthermore, quantification forces specification of the attributes that are to be measured. Does the decision hinge upon the weight, height, volume, cost, or other element? In itself, identification of an important attribute is valuable for the decision-making process.

In many decisions, qualitative considerations carry greater weight than measurable dollar effects, as for example, when a food processor willingly incurs large inspection costs to ensure that his product contains no contaminants. In this case, the processor gives greater weight to the qualitative, unmeasurable, indirect "costs" of issuing contaminated products than to the quantitative, measurable costs of inspection. Qualitative factors may involve such socio-economic concerns as a loss of the consumer's goodwill, or potential legal and settlement costs resulting from lawsuits, or they may relate to general aesthetic values, such as the product's flavor. Although the accountant strives to simplify by reducing all factors to quantitative terms, qualitative factors are often incapable of being expressed in dollar terms.

Cost classifications and reclassifications   The term "cost" takes on several different meanings in managerial accounting. In general, the term is associated with any input to the productive process, such as labor, material, or facilities. Interchangeably, cost refers to the input item itself or to the dollar number associated with it, e.g., labor cost and $15 cost. Cost has been used as a noun, a verb, and an adjective, e.g., "The cost is high," "It cost much . . .," "The cost accountant did . . . ." Thus, the exact meaning of cost is determinable only by its modifying words and by the context in which the word appears.

Note that the modifying words and synonyms for cost also change names in different contexts. For example, a dollar value of material input is called "raw material" when it first arrives at the plant. Then it is relabeled "work in process," and again relabeled "finished goods" and "cost of goods sold." Similarly, the name of one input element might be modified by different adjectives, depending upon the purpose and context, e.g., direct(indirect), variable(fixed), or controllable(uncontrollable).

Discussion of other decision-related cost concepts appears below.

Opportunity costs   Opportunity costs represent the benefits forgone by rejecting the second best alternative in favor of the best one. For example, you own a building that could be rented to others or used by you: if you decide to use the building, your opportunity cost is the rent that will be forgone. If you can invest money in a machine or in a savings account but you buy the machine, the opportunity cost associated with acquiring the machine is the interest you have forgone by your decision. Virtually every alternative has an opportunity cost.

Opportunity costs are associated only with feasible alternatives: lost rent is an opportunity cost only if potential tenants are ready, willing, and able to rent your building at the determined value. Since opportunity costs are hypothetical values, they are never recorded in the accounting records. Although special study may be necessary to identify the second best alternatives and their accompanying opportunity cost, these values must be considered before making a decision.

Incremental analysis   Under conventional analysis, the consequences of each alternative are determined, and the alternative that produces the most favorable outcome is selected. In contrast, incremental analysis concentrates upon the differences between alternatives. Incremental analysis provides answers to different questions than those addressed by conventional analysis.

For example, examine the case illustrated in Exhibit 14–1. The Watson Manufacturing Company is considering two processes for producing output units. Process A can produce 9,000 units while incurring $15,000 cost, and Process B can produce 22,000 units for $33,000. Conventional analysis focuses on the two average cost-per-unit figures: Since Process B incurs the lowest cost per unit, it is the prime decision candidate. Furthermore, average cost savings per unit of $.17 would result from selecting Process B, rather than Process A ($1.67 − $1.50 = $.17).

Incremental analysis supplies an answer to the question: "Assuming that

EXHIBIT 14–1   CONVENTIONAL AND INCREMENTAL EFFICIENCY ANALYSIS

Conventional Analysis

	Alternative	
	A	B
Input Cost	$15,000	$33,000
Output units	9,000	22,000
Cost per unit*	$ 1.67	$ 1.50

Incremental Analysis

	A	B	Incremental Amount
Input Cost	$15,000	$33,000	$18,000
Output units	9,000	22,000	13,000
Incremental cost per unit*			$ 1.38

* Rounded

the first 9,000 units produced by Process A and Process B cost the same amount, what is the average cost per unit on the excess production that is available from Process B?" The additional 13,000 units available from Process B have an incremental cost per unit of $1.38. The $1.50 average cost and $1.38 incremental cost would be used to provide different types of insights. For example, if these data were relevant for pricing decisions, the $1.50 would set a floor on the average price for the whole 22,000 units, while the $1.38 would set a floor on the price for the last 13,000 units, assuming that a two-tier pricing schedule is implemented.

Incremental analysis becomes unwieldy when many alternatives are under consideration, since the number of unique alternative pairs exceeds the number of alternatives.

Sunk Costs   Sunk costs are historical costs that are found in the accounting records. Sunk costs are also called "book value" and "deferred charges." These original acquisition costs are rarely relevant for decision-making purposes, because they do not relate to present or future values. For example, a firm recently purchased a System 370 computer from IBM for $1,000,000. If IBM introduces a new system that makes the 370 obsolete, the original acquisition price is irrelevant to most future decisions. The relevant values for future decisions are the expected salvage value, resale price, or the value of equivalent processing capabilities.

An incremental analysis clearly indicates the irrelevance of sunk cost. The purchaser of the System 370 that becomes obsolete has two alternatives: dispose of the 370 or keep it over its mechanical life (say 3 years). Assume for simplicity's sake that the 370 has no salvage value now or three years in the future and that more efficient computing service is leased for $600,000. The analysis appears as follows:

	Keep the 370	Dispose of the 370	Incremental Costs
Lease cost for service	$ 600,000	$ 600,000	$ -0-
Depreciation, Year 1	$ 333,333	—	$ 333,333
Depreciation, Year 2	333,333	—	333,333
Depreciation, Year 3	333,334	—	333,334
Loss on disposal	-0-	$1,000,000	(1,000,000)
Total	$1,600,000	$1,6000,000	$ -0-

The effect of depreciation or loss on reported income over the three years for the two alternatives is equal, except for yearly timing differences.

Now, if additional lease cost for acquiring computer service can be reduced to $400,000 by retaining and using the obsolete 370 in some minor applications, the "lease cost" line of the analysis will change (and indicate a $200,000 cost savings for the "keep" alternative), but the depreciation and loss on disposal lines will not change—the original acquisition cost is the same for each alternative, irrespective of whether the $1,000,000 is recognized in the income statement in one year or over three years. In the same fashion, salvage value obtained from disposing of the obsolete 370 now or in the future would appear in the analysis as a separate line-item. (While salvage value technically would be offset against depreciation and loss on disposal, similar-sized salvage values would affect the alternatives identically). If immediate disposal of the 370 produced a higher cost recovery than a delayed disposal could produce, these cost recoveries would be reflected on the "salvage value" line, while the depreciation and loss lines would still reflect the aggregated $1,000,000 income effect. To reiterate, sunk costs are not relevant to most decisions.

Limiting factor of scarce resource Production requires the joint interaction of labor, materials and facilities, applied in concert in prescribed ratios. The absence of any one input may stop production, even though other inputs are abundant. For example, the absence of tires will halt automobile production (after inventories are depleted), as might happen during a prolonged strike by rubber workers. The one resource in shortest supply, hence the one most critical for continued production, is called the *limiting factor*.

Recognition must be given to the limiting factor when making decisions, since these critical factors may qualify the interpretation of traditional performance measures. For example, assume that a company produces two products, A and B. Operating information on these two products is as follows:

		A		B
Selling price		$25		$50
Variable costs				
Labor, 3 hrs. @ $4	$12			
7 hrs. @ $4			$28	
Material	5		3	
Variable overhead	3		8	
Total		20		39
Contribution Margin		$ 5		$11
Contribution Margin Ratio		20%		22%

Product B has the higher contribution margin and the higher contribution margin ratio: all other things equal, additional sales of Product B are more beneficial than proportionally equal sales of Product A. Therefore, all resources of the firm should be allocated for production of Product B (until its demand has been satisfied) before production is initiated on Product A.

A different analysis is required if labor is considered a limiting factor. A maximum amount of labor hours may be available for production, given a limited number of skilled workers, limited facilities, limited financial resources, or limited managerial capacities. For example, assume that only 21,000 labor hours can be placed into production during the current period. Given 21,000 hours,

7,000 units of Product A can be produced for a total contribution margin of $35,000. For the same 21,000 hours, 3,000 units of Product B will be produced for a total contribution margin of $33,000.

One way to take the limiting factor into consideration for decision-making purposes is to calculate a *contribution margin per limiting factor*. For this example, a contribution margin per labor hour for Product A is $1.67 ($5/3) and for Product B is $1.57 ($11/7). Given limiting factors, the best alternative is the one with the highest contribution margin per limiting factor. Another way to consider limiting factors is to perform an incremental analysis on the total volume and dollar data, rather than considering all data on the per-unit basis. An incremental analysis for this example follows:

	A	B	Increment
Revenue			
$25 × 7,000	$175,000		
50 × 3,000		$150,000	$25,000
Variable Costs			
$20 × 7,000	140,000		
39 × 3,000		117,000	23,000
Contribution Margin	$ 35,000	$ 33,000	$ 2,000

The incremental analysis clearly shows that Product A produces $2,000 greater contribution margin than Product B, given a limiting factor.

Decision terminology example Definitions of decision-related cost concepts can be clarified with references to an example. A customer places a special order for 10,000 units with the Curtus Manufacturing Company. Curtus currently is operating at full capacity, so existing business must be rejected if the special order is accepted. Existing production is sold for $26 per unit and has an $11 variable cost, thus providing a $15 contribution margin. Fixed costs on existing production amounts to $8 per unit. If the special order is accepted, Curtus would have to acquire a special device for $15,000, which will be discarded when the job is completed. Curtus could charge the customer $30 per unit on the special order, even though its variable production and distribution costs are only $16 per unit. For this example, decision-related cost concepts are as follows:

A. Full cost per unit on the special order amount to $25.50, and is composed of the labor, material, variable overhead ($16.00), existing fixed cost ($8.00), and new fixed cost ($15,000/10,000 units = $1.50).

B. Opportunity cost of accepting the new order (rejecting the old production) is equal to the old contribution margin per unit of $15.

C. The incremental price for the new order is the difference between the old price and the new price. Incremental costs per unit represents the difference between the existing full cost and the full cost of the special order, $25.50 − $19.00 = $6.50.[1]

D. The sunk cost in this situation is the $8 per unit fixed cost.

E. Capacity is a limiting factor, since Curtus is operating at 100% of capacity.

PRICING DECISIONS

Establishing sales prices for products and services represents a crucial decision that must be made in most business organizations. Pricing decisions have a direct impact on the inflow of funds and the profitability of the company. Once pricing policy has been established, it is often difficult and costly to change. Various aspects of the pricing decision are discussed in this chapter, and related topics appear in other chapters.

A pricing policy encompasses a philosophical goal as well as a package of specific tactical and implemental choices. The broad philosophical goal usually is specified by top-level management as part of its strategic planning function. For example, top-level management may specify that the prices for its top-quality product must always be larger than the price for its second-quality product. Alternately, a policy might require the bottom-line products to be priced lower than prices established by an industry price leader or equal to prices set by competing firms.

Once the philosophical issues have been resolved, they must be integrated into the company's overall goal. Pricing policy must reflect the various constraints established by governmental regulation, trade custom, and specific demands of the organization. Governmental regulations prohibit discriminatory pricing policies that constitute restraints of trade or that establish monopolistic business practices. Trade custom may be instituted to prevent such destructive practices as price wars or prohibitive advertising campaigns. The ultimate price should generate sufficient profits to justify the company's staying in business. Pricing policy is instrumental in affecting the growth rate of sales, market share, and public acceptance.

Accounting data traditionally have been used to help assess the viability of specific pricing policies, that is, costs often serve as a starting point from which management determines prices.

Target pricing Many firms establish prices at or above a particular target amount. Often this target is full cost; that is, the price for an item must be at least large enough to recover all costs, both fixed and variable, plus a normal

[1]Incremental revenue is $4 ($30 − $26). Since $4 is less than the incremental cost of $6.50, the special order should be rejected.

profit. For example, a product with costs composed of $2.00 per unit variable cost and $4.00 fixed cost might be priced at $7.20 to reflect full cost recovery plus a profit equal to 20% of cost. Full-cost pricing is widely used in practice.

Unfortunately, full-cost pricing techniques involve circular reasoning: fixed cost per unit is based upon total volume (fixed costs/number of units = fixed cost per unit), but volume in turn is determined by price. Solution of simultaneous equations that describe the fixed cost-volume-price relationship can produce an optimal price, assuming that the true underlying relationships are known. In general, these relationships are not known. Further discussion of simultaneous solution of complex cost-volume-price relationships is beyond the scope of this text.

Contribution margin approach to pricing   The contribution margin approach to pricing establishes a price that is at least high enough to recover all variable costs. Variants to this method add on to variable costs some targeted profit and fixed-cost contribution. The rationale behind this method is simple: price must at least cover all costs that would be incurred to replace the unit if it was sold. Any excess of price over variable cost helps recover fixed cost or achieve a normal profit.

For example, consider the following set of data: variable cost per unit, $55; fixed cost per unit (based upon expected volume of 10,000 units), $30; and normal profit per unit, $15. These data could be used to establish a price per unit, by working through an income statement relationship; that is, price less cost equals profit, so profit plus cost equals price. This relationship can be reflected in both traditional and contribution margin form, as shown below:

Traditional Form		Contribution Margin Form	
Price	$100	Price	$100
Variable Cost	$ 55	Variable Cost	55
Fixed Cost	30	Contribution Margin	$ 45
Total Cost	$ 85	Fixed Cost	30
Net Profit	$ 15	Normal Profit	$ 15
Price as a percent of total cost = 118%		Price as a percent of variable cost = 182%	

The contribution margin approach to pricing highlights variable costs as the primary element in short-run pricing decisions. Some contribution will be derived as long as price exceeds variable costs. In addition, the contribution margin format is entirely compatible with breakeven analysis and cost-volume-profit analysis, which were discussed in earlier chapters. Furthermore, fixed costs are fully recovered at volumes above 10,000 units. Thus, business managers using the contribution margin approach are more likely to accept orders for goods above 10,000 units at prices lower than $100. These excess units can be sold at $70 per unit while the normal $15 profit is maintained. Under the traditional form, information on potential price reductions is not readily apparent.

Elasticity of demand   Pricing policy should consider the interrelationships among prices, variable cost, and volume. The price-volume relationship is frequently described in the literature under the phrase "elasticity of demand." Elasticity of demand represents the relative change in quantity caused by a change in price. For example, a 10% price rise from $2 to $2.20 per unit may be accompanied by a decrease in volume of 5%, from 80,000 units to 76,000 units per year. Total revenues will increase from this change since the relative price increase is greater than the relative quantity decrease. On the other hand, if a 10% increase in price produces a 20% decrease in volume, total revenues will decrease.

Elasticity of demand is usually measured as the percentage change in volume divided by the percentage change in price. (Percentage change in volume is found by dividing the difference between the original and proposed volume by the original volume. Percentage change in price is determined in the same manner.) Demand is said to be *elastic* if a given change in price produces a larger percentage change in volume, i.e., the ratio of relative volume change over relative price change is larger than one. A price increase for products that have elastic demand will reduce total revenues while a price decrease will swell total revenues. Demand is said to be *inelastic* if a given change in price produces a smaller percentage change in volume, i.e., the ratio of relative volume change over relative price change is smaller than one. A price increase for products that have inelastic demand will result in larger total revenue while a price decrease will shrink total revenue.

Special orders   Decisions to accept or reject sales orders at special discounted prices involve much the same consideration as are applicable to pricing decisions. Here again, the contribution margin approach is especially helpful in evaluating the consequences of accepting a special order.

For example, suppose that management receives an offer from a customer to purchase 1,000 units of Product X at $12 per unit, even though the normal price of X is $19 per unit. Product X is usually sold in small quantities. Manufacturing and selling costs per unit are as follows, assuming normal volume of 10,000 units:

Manufacturing Costs		Selling Costs	
Direct labor	$ 4	Variable costs	$1
Direct material	3	Fixed Cost	2
Variable overhead	2		
Fixed overhead	5		
Total	$14	Total	$3

A manager applying a full-cost recovery criterion to this decision would reject the order, since total costs of $17 are above the $12 offering price. A contribution margin approach suggests that a $12 price, less a $10 variable manufacturing and selling cost, still yields a $2 per-unit contribution. The special order of 1,000 units would provide an incremental contribution of $2,000, which could be applied toward recovery of fixed costs or, if they have been completely recovered, toward an increase in profits.

Furthermore, some question might be raised about the relevance of the $1 variable selling cost, since Product X is usually sold in small lots, and this order amounts to 10% of normal volume. Additional consideration would be given the following questions:

1. What effect would this special price to one customer have on other existing customers when they learn of the offer?

2. What potential consequences will this current bargain sale have on future relationships with existing customers, potentially new customers, and the special customer?

3. What effect will this special order have on current and future capacity? Will this special order eventually lead to an expansion of plant, personnel, financial requirements, or other capacity constraints?

CONTINUATION OF A PRODUCT LINE

Decisions to discontinue a product line ordinarily are based upon data supplied by an incremental analysis. For example, consider the following information (in thousands of dollars) on three product lines distributed by the Mendon Corporation.

	Products			
	X	Y	Z	Total
Revenue	$200	$300	$400	$900
Variable cost	120	230	250	600
Contribution margin	$ 80	$ 70	$150	$300
Discretionary fixed cost	15	10	20	45
Committed fixed cost	55	65	85	205
Product line profit (loss)	$ 10	$(5)	$ 45	$ 50

At first glance, Product Y appears to be unprofitable. Management might reasonably wonder if this product line should be discontinued. Incremental analysis provides insights that can satisfy management's implied question, as can be seen below:

	Products		Incremental Loss From Dropping Y
	X, Y, Z	X, Z	
Revenue	$900	$600	$(300)
Variable cost	600	370	(230)
Contribution margin	$300	$230	$ (70)
Discretionary fixed cost	45	35	(10)
Committed fixed cost	205	205	-0-
Total profit (loss)	$ 50	$ (10)	$ (60)

The Mendon Corporation would be $60,000 worse off if Product line Y were discontinued. This $60,000 represents the lost contribution margin of Product Y, less the discretionary fixed costs that could be saved if Product Y were discontinued.

In general, fixed costs that cannot be reduced when a product line is discontinued are irrelevant for decision-making purposes. The cost of fixed plant, equipment, personnel, finances, and technology needed to provide the capacity for production and distribution probably does not readily adjust to changes in volume. Committed costs that cannot be reduced when a product line is discontinued are reallocated to continuing product lines. The economic effect of discontinuing one product line is an increase in the allocated costs to the remaining product lines. In the short term, the effect of discontinuing a product line must be considered in terms of its impact on total company profits. Incremental analysis provides this information.

If alternate uses are found for the capacity that becomes available when the product line is discontinued, then a new incremental analysis can be performed. If a new Product M is found that can employ the facilities currently devoted to Product Y, the appropriate incremental analysis would examine the differences between operating data for the alternatives (X, Y, Z) and (X, Z, M). That alternative that produces the greatest contribution would be judged superior.

ADDITIONAL PROCESSING

Production processes for some commodities involve numerous manufacturing steps. In some industries, external markets exist where semi-finished products can be sold at different stages of the production process. For example, markets exist for iron ore, pellet concentrates, pig iron, rolled steel, sheets, and other intermediate forms closer to the finished product. Whenever intermediate products can be sold, a producer must decide if more processing is warranted.

Decisions concerning further processing hinge upon the incremental contribution derived from selling products with greater refinement. Cost and revenue estimates at both states of completion are required. For example, assume that a given product can be sold at its present state of completion for $100,000. Costs incurred to date amount to $80,000, and so the contribution margin from this product amounts to $20,000. Management is given an opportunity to produce a refinement of this basic product simply by processing it in an additional manufacturing stage. After further processing, management estimates that the product will sell for $130,000. If further processing can be completed at a total cost of less than $30,000, management should be willing to consider the additional processing step. That is, additional processing should be contemplated if the additional costs are less than the additional revenues. For example, if the additional processing can be incurred at a cost of only $15,000, then the company should proceed with the additional processing.

Decisions to continue processing are frequently found whenever common inputs produce joint products or by-products, as was discussed in Chapter 8. Discussion of a decision about further processing in a joint product setting may best be illustrated by an example.

The Humbolt Company produces three products from a common input in a particular joint process. Each product may be sold at the split-off point or processed further. Additional processing requires no special facilities, and production costs of further processing are entirely variable and traceable to the products involved. During the current period, production of the three products consisted of 6,000 Product A, 8,000 Product B, and 4,000 Product C. Sales value at the split-off point was $24,000, $50,000, and $12,000, respectively. Additional cost associated with further processing would amount to $9,000, $5,000, and $3,000, respectively, after which the modified products could be sold for $31,000, $60,000, and $19,000. Which products should be processed further?

Incremental analysis provides a basis for a solution. The contribution resulting from further processing is determined by subtracting the additional processing costs from the sales value after processing. This contribution is then compared with the original sales value at the split-off point. Further processing should be done whenever the additional processing contribution exceeds the split-off sales revenue. For this case, incremental analysis appear below:

Product	Additional Processing Revenue	Additional Processing Cost	Additional Contribution of Processing	Sales at Split-off	Incremental Contribution of Processing
A	$31,000	$9,000	$22,000	$24,000	($2,000)
B	60,000	5,000	55,000	50,000	5,000
C	19,000	3,000	16,000	12,000	4,000

Further processing for Product A is not warranted. If A is sold at the split-off point, while B and C are sold after additional processing, Humbolt Company will maximize profits.

MAKE-OR-BUY DECISIONS

Many manufacturing firms have the technical capability to produce some of the component parts that they typically purchase from external suppliers. Whenever the current production volume falls below existing plant capacity, management has an opportunity to manufacture component parts rather than purchase them. The choice between internally produced parts and purchased parts is often referred to as a "make-or-buy decision."

Qualitative considerations Make-or-buy decisions often hinge upon qualitative considerations. The decision to *make* frees the manufacturer from its suppliers, reduces its dependence upon others and insures a smoother flow of parts for its production schedule. Furthermore, self-manufacture provides an opportunity to better control input quality. Frequently, the manufactured parts can be produced at incremental costs that are lower than the prices charged by external suppliers, which contain an element of profit for the supplier.

However, a firm that produces all of its own parts only when excess capacity becomes available runs the risk of destroying its working relationship with suppliers. Continued supplier reliability may be difficult to re-establish when purchase commitments have become sporadic. Since purchases from suppliers must be reinstituted whenever capacity is reallocated to the major product, continued amicable relationships with suppliers is vital. In some instances, external suppliers in competitive markets can supply components at lower prices and/or higher quality than may be obtained from a decision to *make*. Thus, many qualitative factors enter into the decision to make or buy.

Quantitative considerations   Incremental costs are relevant to make-or-buy decisions. The sum of purchase price plus transportation, insurance, and ordering costs represents the amount applicable to the "buy" alternative. Costs associated with the make alternative include the incremental variable elements for inputs needed to make component parts, such as labor, material, and variable overhead. Allocated fixed costs that remain unchanged in total when components are produced cannot be relevant to make-or-buy decisions.

The quantitative aspects of make-or-buy decisions may best be illustrated by an example. The Watson Company currently purchases a component part for its final product. During any one year, Watson will require 10,000 units that can be acquired for $260,000, or $26 per unit. Watson currently has under-utilized capacity that can be used to manufacture the component parts. Total manufacturing costs of $29 per unit include $10 direct labor, $7 direct material, $4 variable overhead, and $8 fixed overhead (allocated on the basis of capacity utilized).

Since variable costs can be avoided by buying component parts from external suppliers, the $21 variable cost is relevant to a make-or-buy decision. The $8 fixed cost is not relevant to the decision, since total fixed overhead will remain unchanged, irrespective of whether parts are produced or purchased. A make-or-buy analysis takes the following form:

	Per Unit		Total 10,000 Units	
	Make	Buy	Make	Buy
Purchase price	-0-	$26	-0-	$260,000
Direct labor	$10	-0-	$100,000	-0-
Direct material	7	-0-	70,000	-0-
Variable overhead	4	-0-	40,000	-0-
Total	$21	$26	$210,000	$260,000
Incremental benefit of making		$5		$50,000

According to these data, the Watson Company should make the components rather than purchasing them, as is currently being done. Obviously, qualitative factors must be considered before reaching a decision. In addition, consideration should be given to alternate uses of the idle capacity.

Alternate uses of idle capacity   Decisions to make or buy hinge upon the availability of idle capacity. If no idle capacity exists, the components must be purchased from external suppliers. If idle capacity exists, one use for this capacity is production of the components. But other uses for the idle capacity should be considered before reaching a final decision.

Once other uses for idle capacity are considered, the make-or-buy problem is transformed into an analysis of the best utilization of available facilities. Available alternate uses for idle capacity provide insights into the opportunity costs associated with using capacity for the "make" decision. New products may be manufactured, instead of the component parts, and the contribution margin from these products would be considered an opportunity cost of making components. Alternately, unused equipment or room may be leased or rented, and the net proceeds could be considered the opportunity cost of idle capacity.

For example, assume that the Watson Company can make its own component parts for $21 per unit relevant costs, or it could buy the parts for $26 per unit *and* rent the idle machinery and buildings for $60,000. A complete make-or-buy analysis takes the following form:

	Make	Buy	Buy and Rent
Cost of obtaining parts (from previous example)	$210,000	$260,000	$260,000
Rental income	-0-	-0-	(60,000)
Net relevant cost	$210,000	$260,000	$200,000

Explicit consideration of alternate uses of idle capacity indicates that costs can be minimized under the buy *and* rent alternative.

SUMMARY

Planning for nonroutine events requires the managerial accountant to act as a technical expert on cost analysis who summarizes data that serve as a basis for making a decision. Problems requiring decisions are often described in technical terms to reduce ambiguity, shorten the length of messages, and provide emphasis. A decision itself is the act of selecting one course of action from among all alternatives. Data that bear upon, influence, and are directly associated with a decision are termed relevant data. Opportunity costs and *incremental* analysis are two elements that highlight relevant data. Limiting factors must be properly evaluated if decisions are to produce optimal results.

Decisions concerning pricing problems, discontinuance of product lines, employment of additional processing, and make-or-buy alternatives have several elements in common. All decisions should ignore sunk costs. All decisions should consider the opportunity costs associated with rejecting the second best alternative. Future costs that differ between alternatives are relevant to making decisions. Incremental analysis can highlight the differences between alternatives for all decisions. Qualitative factors must be considered right along with the quantitative elements, even though they cannot be reduced to numbers and explicitly compared.

SUGGESTED READINGS

Blum, J. D. "Decision Tree Analysis For Accounting Decisions." *Management Accounting*, December 1976.

Brenner, Vincent. "An Evaluation of Product Pricing Models." *Managerial Planning*, July/August, 1971.

Heimann, S., and E. Lusk. "Decision Flexibility: An Alternative Evaluation Criterion." *The Accounting Review*, January 1976.

Leininger, Wayne. "Opportunity Costs: Some Definitions and Examples." *The Accounting Review*, January 1977.

QUESTIONS

14-1   Define the word decision and identify attributes necessary to make data relevant to a decision.

14-2   Identify the role of the accountant in the decision-making process.

14-3   Can decisions ever be associated with activity that has already occurred? Contrast the word evaluation with what this chapter defines as a decision.

14-4   Identify some qualitative factors that would be associated with a decision to discontinue a product line.

14-5   List some historical costs and some opportunity costs associated with a decision to make component parts rather than purchase them. In what ways do opportunity costs differ from historical costs?

14-6   Process A can produce 65,000 units for $32,500, while Process B can produce 100,000 units for $40,000. Determine the average cost per unit for A and B, as well as the incremental cost for the extra production available from B.

14-7   Why are sunk costs irrelevant to all decisions?

14-8   Product A has a total variable cost of $20 and sells for $30, while Product B has a total variable cost of $50 and sells for $80. For which of these two products should demand first be satisfied? Why? If Product A requires 2 hours of labor, and Product B requires 6 hours of labor, and only 10,000 hours of labor are available, which of these two products should be given first consideration? Why?

14-9   Product X is composed of $4 of variable cost and $6 of fixed cost. What price is required to recover full cost plus a profit equal to 20% of cost? What percent mark-up on variable-cost is required to produce the same price? What are the advantages of variable-cost pricing over full-cost pricing?

14-10   The Hardrock Salt Company currently sells 1,000,000 cases of salt per year for $2.40 per case. A 20% decrease in price is expected to boost volume to 1,100,000 cases per year. Should Hardrock decrease prices? Why? What one term technically describes the relationship between price and volume for Hardrock?

14-11   If the Hardrock Salt Company described above determined that a $.24 per unit increase in price would reduce volume by only 50,000 units, should it increase prices? Why?

EXERCISES

14-12   The Softwood Coffin Company has been unable to sell 8,000 coffins made of knotty pine. These coffins have an average cost of $69 each, and were priced at a mere $247. Management is considering the following alternatives:

1. Place legs on the coffins after removing lids and rails, and sell them as flower troughs. Cost of additional work and advertising will amount to $80,000, and the expected sales price is $100 per unit.
2. Continue selling coffins at a reduced price of $150, even though the opportunity costs associated with the space amounts to $50 per unit.
3. Sell them for firewood for an immediate return of $480,000.
4. Keep them and do nothing new.

Determine the financial consequences of the best alternative.

14-13   The Hubbard Corporation receives an order for 10,000 units, conditional upon receiving a 50% discount from the regular price. Hubbard normally sells its product at $40 per unit. Production and distribution costs normally amount to $10 variable cost and $25 fixed cost per unit, and normal volume is 30,000 units. Excess capacity for additional production is available. What are the financial consequences of accepting this order? What additional factors should be considered before a final decision is made?

14–14   The Trypod Company reported the following data for the most recent period:

	Products			
	A	B	C	Total
Revenue	$400,000	$300,000	$800,000	$1,500,000
Variable cost	$200,000	$100,000	$300,000	$ 600,000
Discretionary fixed cost	100,000	100,000	200,000	400,000
Commited fixed cost	150,000	110,000	100,000	360,000
Total cost	$450,000	$310,000	$600,000	$1,360,000
Profit (loss)	$ (50,000)	$ (10,000)	$200,000	$ 140,000
Profit				

(A) Determine the financial consequences of discontinuing Product A, Product B, and both Products A and B.

(B) The space currently occupied by Products A and B can be rented for $120,000 and $60,000, respectively. Should A, B, A and B, or neither A nor B be discontinued?

(C) List some qualitative factors that should be considered in the decision to discontinue a product line.

14–15   The Deep-pit Mining Company extracts and refines flumpaldump ore to three grades of fineness. One million ton of crude ore will convert into 10,000 gondolas of semi-refined pellets or 1,000 boxcars of superfine cubes. Prices at each stage of completion are $3 per ton, $500 per gondola, and $8,000 per boxcar. Extraction costs amount to $2.80 per ton. Variable refining costs amount to $1,500,000 for first-stage refining and $350 per gondola for second-stage refining. Depreciation, depletion, and other fixed costs amount to $2,000,000.

(A) Determine the profitability of Deep-pit, assuming that superfine cubes are produced.

(B) Should Deep-pit close down operations? If not, should it produce ore, pellets, or cubes? Support your answer with numbers.

14–16   The Ballbean Hammer Company has just received an offer from an external supplier to provide handles for some or all of its products at a price of $.15 per handle. Ballbean is currently operating at capacity, and so the offer is received with interest. If the offer is accepted for all its needs, Ballbean will experience a 20% reduction in variable costs. Under present conditions, Ballbean produces 10,000,000 units per year, which it sells for $1.50 per unit. Variable costs are $.60 per unit, and fixed costs amount to $5,000,000 annually.

(A) Should Ballbean accept the offer for the following year, assuming that volume is expected to rise to 11,000,000 units? How many units should be acquired?

(B) Should Ballbean accept the offer for all units, assuming that it could rent out the space currently occupied by the handle division for $1,400,000?

14–17   The Reduction Gear Company produces and sells its standard product to machinery manufacturers in the Southeastern United States. Each gear sells for $30, and total sales approximate 600,000 units each year. During the current budget year, variable production and distribution costs are expected to reach $18 per unit, while expected fixed production and distribution costs will amount to $6,000,000 (or $10 per unit for 600,000 units). Reduction received an offer from a foreign manufacturer to purchase 50,000 units. Domestic sales would not be affected by this transaction. If the offer is accepted, variable distribution costs will increase $2 per unit for insurance, shipping, and import duties. Fixed costs will be unaffected, since Reduction has excess capacity. If Reduction desires a minimum contribution of $3 per unit on foreign sales, what is the lowest price that it would consider for this special order?

14–18   Costs and other data for two component parts used by Griffon Electronics are presented below:

	Part A	Part B
Direct material	$ .40	$ 8.00
Direct labor	1.00	4.70
Factory overhead	4.00	2.00
Unit cost	$ 5.40	$14.70
Units needed per year	6,000	8,000
Machine hours per unit	4	2
Unit cost if purchased	$ 5.00	$15.00

In past years, Griffon has manufactured all of its required components; however, in 19X4 only 30,000 hours of otherwise idle machine time can be devoted to the production of components. Accordingly, some of the parts must be purchased from outside suppliers. In producing parts, factory overhead is applied at $1.00 per standard machine hour. Fixed capacity costs, which will not be affected by any make-buy decision, represent 60% of the applied overhead.

(A) The 30,000 hours of available machine time are to be scheduled in such a way that Griffon realizes maximum potential cost savings. What is the dollar amount of the relevant unit production costs which should be considered in the decision to schedule machine time?

(B) If the allocation of machine time is based upon potential cost savings per machine hour, then how many units of each part should Griffon produce?

(AICPA adapted)

14–19   Gyro Gear Company produces a special gear used in automatic transmissions. Each gear sells for $28, and the Company sells approximately 500,000 gears each year. Unit cost data for 19X3 are presented below:

Direct material	$6.00	
Direct labor	5.00	
	Variable	Fixed
Other costs:		
Manufacturing	$2.00	$7.00
Distribution	4.00	3.00

Gyro has received an offer from a foreign manufacturer to purchase 25,000 gears. Domestic sales would be unaffected by this transaction. If the offer is accepted, variable distribution costs will increase $1.50 per gear for insurance, shipping, and import duties. What is the dollar amount of the unit cost that is relevant to a pricing decision on this offer?

PROBLEMS

14–20 A valued custom parts customer has asked Mr. Jackson if he would manufacture 5,000 special units for him. Mr. Jackson is working at capacity and would have to give up some other business in order to take this business. He can't renege on custom orders already accepted, but he could reduce the output of his standard product by about one-half for one year while producing the specially requested custom part. The customer is willing to pay $7.00 for each part. The material cost will be about $2.00 per unit, and the labor will be $3.60 per unit. Mr. Jackson will have to spend $2,000 for a special device which will be discarded when the job is done. Variable production costs for existing customers is $4.00 per unit, and the current price is $6.50. Fixed cost per unit at capacity is $.42 per unit.

> (A) Calculate the following costs related to the 5,000-unit custom order:
> 1. The incremental cost of the order.
> 2. The full cost of the order.
> 3. The opportunity cost of rejecting the order.
> (B) Should Mr. Jackson take the order? Explain your answer.

14–21 From a particular joint process, Watkins Company produces three products, X, Y, and Z. Each product may be sold at the point of split-off or processed further. Additional processing requires no special facilities, and production costs of further processing are entirely variable and traceable to the products involved. In 19X3, all three products were processed beyond split-off.

Joint product costs for the year were $60,000. Sales values and costs needed to evaluate Watkins' 19X3 production policy follow:

Product	Units Produced	Sales Values at Split-Off	Additional Costs and Sales Values if Processed Further	
			Sales Values	Added Costs
X	6,000	$25,000	$42,000	$9,000
Y	4,000	41,000	45,000	7,000
Z	2,000	24,000	32,000	8,000

Joint costs are allocated to the products in proportion to the relative physical volume of output.

(A) For units of Z, what dollar amount of cost is most relevant to a sell-or-process-further decision?

(B) To maximize profits, Watkins should subject which products to additional processing? Determine the total profits from this product mix.

14–22 Southwest Company wonders if it should continue to manufacture or should purchase mansers, a component of their major product. The annual requirement for mansers is 10,000 units, and the part is available from an outside supplier in any quantity at $5 per unit.

The following information is available:

1. The Machining Department starts and substantially completes mansers, and minor finishing is completed by the use of direct labor in the Finishing Department. The Assembly Department places mansers in the finished product.

2. Machinery used to produce mansers could be sold for its book value of $15,000 and the proceeds invested at 6% per year if the mansers were purchased. Property taxes and insurance would decrease $300 per year if the machinery were sold. The machinery has a remaining life of 10 years with no estimated salvage value.

3. About 25% of the Machining capacity is used in the production of mansers, but labor and some other costs for mansers in this department could be reduced without affecting other operations. The Finishing Department's costs include direct labor totaling $800 devoted to mansers. If mansers were not manufactured, one-half of the resulting available direct labor would be used as indirect labor, and the remaining one-half would result in paid idle time of employees.

4. In 19X7, when 10,000 mansers were produced, pertinent Machining Department costs were:

	Total Costs	Costs Allocated to Mansers
Materials	$95,000	$24,200
Direct labor	39,400	12,200
Indirect labor	20,600	7,800
Heat and light	12,000	3,000
Depreciation	6,000	1,500
Property taxes and insurance	15,000	3,750
Production supplies	4,000	800

5. In addition, the machining Department total costs included $18,300 payroll taxes, $6,100 of which is related to mansers.
6. Overhead allocated on the basis of 200% of direct labor cost was $40,000 for the Finishing Department and $20,000 for the Assembly Department in 19X7. Overhead in these Departments is 25% fixed and 75% variable.
7. If mansers were purchased, Southwest will incur added costs of $.45 per unit for freight and $3,000 per year for receiving, handling, and inspection of the product.

(A) Prepare a schedule comparing Southwest's total annual cost of mansers if manufactured with their annual cost if purchased. (Ignore income taxes.)

(B) Without regard to your solution to Part "A," assume that the total annual costs of mansers if manufactured and if purchased were both $60,000. Compute the annual net cash outflow (1) if mansers are manufactured, and (2) if mansers are purchased. (Ignore income taxes.)

(AICPA adapted)

14–23   Berg and Sons build custom-made pleasure boats, which range in price from $10,000 to $250,000. For the past 30 years, Mr. Berg, Sr., has determined the selling price of each boat by estimating the costs of material, labor, and a prorated portion of overhead, and adding 20% to these estimated costs.
For example, a recent price quotation was determined as follows:

Direct Materials	$ 5,000
Direct Labor	8,000
Overhead	2,000
	$15,000
Plus 20%	3,000
Selling Price	$18,000

The overhead figure was determined by estimating total overhead costs for the year and allocating them at 25% of direct labor.
If a customer rejected the price and business was slack, Mr. Berg, Sr.,

would often be willing to reduce his markup to as little as 5% over estimated costs. Thus, average markup for the year is estimated at 15%.

Mr. Ed Berg, Jr., believes that the contribution margin approach to pricing would be helpful in determining the selling prices of their custom-made pleasure boats.

Total overhead, which includes selling and administrative expenses for the year, has been estimated at $150,000, of which $90,000 is fixed and the remainder is variable in direct proportion to direct labor.

(A) Assume that the customer in the example rejected the $18,000 quotation and also rejected a $15,750 quotation (5% markup) during a slack period. The customer countered with a $15,000 offer.
1. What is the difference in net income for the year between accepting or rejecting the customer's offer?
2. What is the minimum selling price Mr. Berg, Jr., could have quoted without reducing or increasing net income?

(B) What advantages does the contribution margin approach to pricing have over the approach used by Mr. Berg, Sr.?

(C) What pitfalls are there, if any, to contribution margin pricing?

14–24   The Vernom Corporation, which produces and sells to wholesalers a highly successful line of summer lotions and insect repellents, has decided to diversify in order to stabilize sales throughout the year. A natural area for the company to consider is the production of winter lotions and creams to prevent dry and chapped skin.

After considerable research, a winter products line has been developed. Because of the conservative nature of the company management, Vernom's president has decided to introduce only one of the new products for this coming winter. If the product is a success, the product line will be expanded in future years.

The product selected (called Chap-off) is a lip balm that will be sold in a lipstick-type tube. The product will be sold to wholesalers in boxes of 24 tubes for $8.00 per box. Because of available capacity, no additional fixed charges will be incurred to produce the product. However, a $100,000 fixed charge will be absorbed by the product to allocate a fair share of the company's present fixed costs to the new product.

Using the estimated sales and production of 100,000 boxes of Chap-off as the standard volume, the accounting department has developed the following costs:

Direct Labor	$2.00/box
Direct Materials	3.00/box
Total Overhead	1.50/box
Total	$6.50/box

Vernom has approached a cosmetics manufacturer to discuss the possibility of purchasing the tubes for Chap-off. The price of the empty tubes from the cosmetics manufacturer would be $.90 per 24 tubes. If the Vernom Corporation accepts the purchase proposal, it is estimated that direct labor and variable overhead costs would be reduced by 10% and direct material costs would be reduced by 20%.

(A) Should the Vernom Corporation make or buy the tubes? Show calculations to support your answer.

(B) What would be the maximum purchase price acceptable to the Vernom Corporation for the tubes? Support your answer.

(C) Instead of sales of 100,000 boxes, revised estimates show sales volume at 125,000 boxes. At this new volume, additional equipment, at an annual rental of $10,000, must be acquired to manufacture the tubes. This incremental cost would be the only additional fixed cost required, even if sales increased to 300,000 boxes. (The 300,000 level is the goal for the third year of production.) Under these circumstances, should the Vernom Corporation make or buy the tubes? Show calculations to support answer.

(D) The company has the option of making and buying at the same time. What would be your answer to Part (C) if this alternative was considered. Explain.

(CMA adapted)

14–25 The Largo Manufacturing Company makes and sells a single product, VOSTEX, through normal marketing channels. You have been asked by its president to assist in determining the proper bid to submit for a special manufacturing job for the Aztec Sales Company. Below is the information you have collected.

1. The special job is for MOFAC, a product unlike VOSTEX, even though the manufacturing processes are similar.
2. Additional sales of MOFAC to the Aztec Sales Company are not expected.
3. The bid is for 20,000 pounds of MOFAC. Each 1,000 pounds of MOFAC requires 500 pounds of Material A, 250 pounds of Material B, and 250 pounds of Material C.
4. Largo's materials inventory data follow:

Material	Pounds in inventory	Acquisition cost per lb.	Current replacement cost per lb.
A	24,000	$.40	$.48
B	4,000	.25	.27
C	17,500	.90	.97
X	7,000	.80	.85

Material X may be substituted for Material A in MOFAC. Material X, made especially for Largo under a patent owned by Largo, is left over from the manufacture of a discontinued product, is not usable in VOSTEX, and has a current salvage value of $180.00.

5. Each 1,000 pounds of MOFAC requires 180 direct labor hours at $3.00 per hour (overtime is charged at time and a half). Largo is working near its two-shift capacity and has only 1,600 hours of regular time available. The production manager indicates that he can keep the special job on regular time by shifting the production of VOSTEX to overtime if necessary.

6. Largo's cost clerk indicates that the hourly overhead rate at normal production is as follows:

Fixed element	$ .20 per DLH
Variable element	.80 per DLH
Total hourly overhead rate	$1.00 per DLH

7. The bid invitation states that a performance bond must be submitted with the bid. A local agent will bond Largo's performance for 1% of the total bid.

(A) Prepare a schedule to compute the minimum bid (i.e., the bid that would neither increase nor decrease total profits) that Largo Manufacturing Company may submit.

(B) Largo's president also wants to know what his new competitor, Melton Manufacturing Company, probably will bid. You assume that Melton's materials inventory has been acquired very recently and that Melton's cost behavior is similar to Largo's. You know that Melton has ample productive capacity to handle the special job on regular time. Prepare a schedule to compute the minimum bid (i.e., the bid that would neither increase nor decrease total profits) that Melton Manufacturing Company might submit.

(AICPA adapted)

14-26 The officers of Bradshaw Company are reviewing the profitability of the Company's four products and the potential effect of several proposals for varying the product mix. An excerpt from the income statement and other data follow:

	Totals	Product P	Product Q	Product R	Product S
Sales	$62,600	$10,000	$18,000	$12,000	$22,000
Cost of goods sold	44,274	4,750	7,056	13,968	18,500
Gross profit	$18,326	$ 5,250	$10,944	$ (1,368)	$ 3,500
Operating expenses	12,012	1,990	2,976	2,826	4,220
Income before income taxes	$ 6,314	$ 3,260	$ 7,968	$ (4,194)	$ (720)
Units sold		1,000	1,200	1,800	2,000
Sales price per unit		$ 10.00	$ 15.00	$ 7.00	$ 11.00
Variable cost of goods sold per unit		$ 2.50	$ 3.00	$ 6.50	$ 6.00
Variable operating expenses per unit		$ 1.17	$ 1.25	$ 1.00	$ 1.20

Each of the following proposals is to be considered independently of the other proposals. Consider only the product changes stated in each proposal; the activity of other products remain stable. (Ignore income taxes.)

(A) If Product R is discontinued, how will income be affected?

(B) If Product R is discontinued, and a consequent loss of customers causes a decrease of 200 units in sales of Q, what will be the total effect on income?

(C) If the sales price of R is increased to $8 and the number of units sold decreased to 1,500, what will be the total effect on income?

(D) The plant in which R is produced can be utilized to produce a new product T. The total variable costs and expenses per unit of T are $8.05, and 1,600 units can be sold at $9.50 each. If T is introduced and R is discontinued, what will be the total effect on income?

(E) Part of the plant in which P is produced can easily be adapted to the production of S, but changes in quantities may make changes in sales prices advisable. If production of P is reduced to 500 units (to be sold at $12 each), and production of S is increased to 2,500 units (to be sold at $10.50 each), what will be the amount of the total effect on income?

(F) Production of P can be doubled by adding a second shift, but higher wages must be paid, which would increase variable cost of goods sold to $3.50 for each of the additional units. If the 1,000 additional units of P can be sold at $10 each, what will be the total effect on income?

(AICPA adapted)

14–27 The president of Benjamin Industries requested your assistance in the evaluation of several financial management problems in his home appliances division, which he summarized for you as follows:

1. Management wants to determine the best sales price for a new appliance which has a variable cost of $4 per unit. The sales manager has estimated probabilities of achieving annual sales levels for various selling prices as shown in the following chart:

Sales Level (Units)	Selling Price			
	$4	$5	$6	$7
20,000	—	—	20%	80%
30,000	—	10%	40%	20%
40,000	50%	50%	20%—	
50,000	50%	40%	20%	—

2. The division's current profit rate is 5% on annual sales of $1,200,000; an investment of $400,000 is needed to finance these sales. The company's basis for measuring divisional success is return on investment.

3. Management is also considering the following two alternative plans submitted by employees for improving operations in the home appliances division:

Green believes that sales volume can be doubled by greater promotional effort, but his method would lower the profit rate to 4% of sales and require an additional investment of $100,000.

Gold favors eliminating some unprofitable appliances and improving efficiency by adding $200,000 in capital equipment. His methods would decrease sales volume by 10% but improve the profit rate to 7%.

(A) Prepare a schedule computing the expected incremental income for each of the sales prices proposed for the new product. The schedule should include the expected sales levels in units (weighted according to the sales manager's estimated probabilities), the expected total monetary sales, expected variable costs, and the expected incremental income.

(B) Prepare schedules computing (1) the company's current rate of return on investment in the home appliances division, and the anticipated rates of return under the alternative suggestions made by (2) Green and (3) Gold.

(AICPA adapted)

14–28   The management of the Southern Cottonseed Company has engaged you to assist in the development of information to be used for managerial decisions. The Company has the capacity to process 20,000 tons of cottonseed per year. The yield of a ton of cottonseed is shown below.

A special marketing study revealed that the Company can expect to sell its entire output for the coming year at the listed average selling prices.

Product	Average Yield Per Ton of Cottonseed	Average Selling Price Per Trade Unit
Oil	300 lbs.	$ .15 per lb.
Meal	600 lbs.	50.00 per ton
Hulls	800 lbs.	20.00 per ton
Lint	100 lbs.	.03 per lb.
Waste	200 lbs.	

You have determined the Company's costs to be as follows:

PROCESSING COSTS

Variable: $9 per ton of cottonseed put into process
Fixed: $108,000 per year

MARKETING COSTS

All Variable: $20 per ton sold

ADMINISTRATIVE COSTS

All Fixed: $90,000 per year

From the information above, you prepared and submitted to management a detailed report on the company's break-even point. In view of conditions in the cottonseed market, management told you that they would also like to know the average maximum amount that the company can afford to pay for a ton of cottonseed.

Management has defined the average maximum amount that the company can afford to pay for a ton of cottonseed as the amount that would result in the company's having losses no greater when operating than when closed down under the existing cost and revenue structure. Management states that you are to assume that the fixed costs shown in your breakeven point report will continue unchanged even when the operations are shut down.

(A) Compute the average maximum amount that the company can afford to pay for a ton of cottonseed.

(B) You also plan to mention to management the factors, other than the costs that entered into your computation, that they should consider in deciding whether to shut down the plant. Discuss these additional factors.

(C) The stockholders consider the minimum satisfactory return on their investment in the business to be 25% before corporate income taxes. The stockholders' equity in the company is $968,000. Compute the maximum average amount that the company can pay for a ton of cottonseed to realize the minimum satisfactory return on the stockholders' investment in the business.

(AICPA adapted)

14–29   The Rheta Rose Manufacturing Company produces an item which it sells directly to consumers under its own brand. The item sells at $12.50 per unit, which is a long-established price. Owing to a general decline in business activity, sales are currently being made at the rate of 5,000 units per month.

An analysis of the costs of the Company for a recent month, during which only 4,000 units were sold, is presented on page 476.

An offer has been received from a chain store by the treasurer of the Company to purchase 5,000 units a month of the products with only minor modifications, to be shipped and billed to the individual stores. The items would be sold under the store's label and would be packed and shipped as directed by the chain at their expense. They offer $7 per unit unpacked on the basis of a one-year contract. The management of the Rheta Rose Company does not expect that there will be an improvement in the business within the next year, and there is no fear that the sale of the items to the chain would reduce the present volume of sales to consumers. The Company does not believe it can afford to accept the offer since it is losing money on its present price of $12.50; therefore, it appears

MANUFACTURING COSTS

Direct Labor	$ 9,900.00
Superintendent's Salary	1,000.00
Assistant Superintendent's Salary	750.00
Power Purchased	560.00
Direct Materials	4,000.00
Purchased Parts	2,400.00
Depreciation of Building	1,420.00
Maintenance of Building	206.00
Heat and Light	348.00
Indirect Labor	2,240.00
Miscellaneous Supplies	800.00
Depreciation of Machinery	3,640.00
Repairs to Machinery	480.00
Property Taxes	600.00
Insurance (fire)	80.00
Social Security Taxes	456.00
Miscellaneous	1,120.00
	$30,000.00

SELLING COSTS

Manager's Salary	$ 833.33
Salesmen's Commissions	18,750.00
Travel	247.05
Advertising	500.00
Clerical Salaries	300.00
Packaging and Shipping	2,108.43
Miscellaneous	1,203.79
	$23,942.60

ADMINISTRATIVE AND GENERAL COSTS

Officers' Salaries	$ 1,525.00
Office Salaries	975.50
Telephone and Telegraph	217.73
Supplies	486.21
Bad Debts	625.00
Miscellaneous	392.86
	$ 4,222.30

that losses would be substantially increased by entering the sales contract with the chain.

The treasurer calls you in to prepare an analysis which will show the result of accepting the order in comparison with the result if the order is not accepted. In preparing your analysis, you are to assume that all items of cost are either completely fixed or completely variable, depending on the usual dominant characteristic of each item and the data given herein.

(AICPA adapted)

14–30   The Big Boyd Kyte Company can produce either of two models of luxurious kites. Selected information on each product is as follows:

	Model A	Model B
Sales price per dozen	$40	$30
Variable manufacturing and distributing costs	20	10
Contribution margin	$20	$20
Contribution margin ratio	50%	67%
Labor hours per dozen	1.5	2.5

(A) If prices for kites are "elastic," which model will be most financially renumerative, assuming that prices are lowered and that there are no production constraints?

(B) If only 30,000 hours are available for production, which model is preferable? Determine the incremental financial consequences of the best alternative.

14–31   The Hugger Belt Company has an old machine with a book value of $12,000 and a current salvage value of $5,000. This machine is expected to operate for an additional four years, at which time it will have a salvage value of $1,000. Hugger can now purchase a new machine for $20,000 which can reduce operating costs by $8,000 per year for the next four years.

Prepare an incremental analysis of the alternative to "buy new machine" and the alternative to "keep old machine." (Note: an extended analysis of this type of problem is contained in the following two chapters.)

14–32   The Split Tee Company acquires a common input and jointly produces two outputs, X and Y. During the forthcoming budget period, $240,000 will be expended on the common input. Units of X and Y produced from this input can be sold for $300,000 and $10,000, respectively. However, if product Y were refined (for an extra cost of $20,000), it could be sold for $40,000. Should Split Tee spend the extra money to refine product Y? Why?

14–33   Anders Manufacturing Company traditionally purchases its component part No. A-104, but the availability of excess capacity during the current period makes management wonder whether Anders should produce the part itself.

Total costs and costs per unit are presented for five different cost classes. Anders can acquire these same parts from an external vendor for $30 per unit. Should Anders' Company make or buy these parts?

	Cost per unit	Cost for 10,000 units
Raw Material	$16	$160,000
Direct Labor	6	60,000
Variable Overhead	3	30,000
Fixed Overhead, Discretionary	3	30,000
Fixed Overhead, Committed (Allocated)	4	40,000
	$32	$320,000

14–34   The Johnson Manufacturing Company receives an order for 10,000 units at $15 each from a new customer. The product will be slightly modified and will bear the trade name of the purchaser so as to differentiate it from the same products sold to regular customers. These modifications will not affect the direct production costs of the product. Management expects to incur its regular $12 unit variable cost for each unit produced under this special order. In addition, the customer demands that management absorb the $5,000 cost of freight to deliver the finished product. Since Johnson currently is working at 100% of capacity, regular production will be reduced by 10,000 units if the special order is accepted. The contribution margin on existing production is $3 per unit. Should Johnson accept the order? Why?

14–35   The Hermanson Company has three operating Divisions, X, Y, and Z. Monthly division income statements are prepared and serve as the basis for evaluating division performance. The current month's figures, shown below in thousands of dollars, continue to indicate a trend in operations. For the past several periods, Division Y has performed at a loss. Management is considering the discontinuance of Division Y. Determine the financial consequences of discontinuing operations of Division Y.

	Departments			Total
	X	Y	Z	
Revenue	$200	$300	$400	$900
Variable Costs	120	230	250	600
Contribution Margin	$ 80	$ 70	$150	$300
Fixed Costs:				
Separable	$ 30	$ 40	$ 60	$130
Allocated	40	40	40	120
Total Fixed Costs	$ 70	$ 80	$100	$250
Net Income	$ 10	$ (10)	$ 50	$ 50

14–36   Cope Company has a maximum production capacity of 20,000 units per year, but it has received orders for 25,000 units. Extra units acquired from outside suppliers cost $40 each, but all units (both purchased and produced) can be sold to the public for $50 each. Cope has fixed cost of $100,000.
        Consider each of the following independent questions.

(A) If Cope desires a profit of $26,000 and rejects the opportunity to subcontract some of its production, i.e., it sells only 20,000 units, its variable cost must equal how much per unit?

(B) If Cope accepts the opportunity to subcontract and sells the whole 25,000 units, how much profit will it make if its own production variable costs come to $38 per unit?

CHAPTER 15

Capital Budgeting: Search for Long-Run Alternatives

Objectives

*After studying this
chapter, you should be
able to do the following:*

Define investment decisions *and contrast* capital budgeting *with other forms of budgeting.*

Describe four steps in budgeting for or analyzing investment proposals.

Relate the time-value of money *preference to* compound interest, discounted present value, *and the* net present-value model.

Discuss the limitations of the net present-value model and the sensitivity of data inputs to decision outputs.

Employ the net present-value model and the internal (time-adjusted) rate-of-return model *in evaluating investment opportunities.*

Identify the assumptions and limitations of two capital-budgeting techniques that ignore the time-value of money concept: the average rate of return *and the* payback period.

Planning often requires the evaluation of special nonrecurring decisions, such as acquiring capital assets, adding or deleting a product line, choosing between production or purchasing, or accepting special orders. Nearly all these decisions involve cost analysis that requires the managerial accountant to work along with the engineer, the economist, the production manager, the sales manager, and all other line or staff employees directly associated with each decision.

PLANNING FOR INVESTMENT DECISIONS

This chapter is concerned with planning for **investment decisions**. An investment decision occurs when a decision-maker has an opportunity to incur current costs in expectation of deriving greater benefits in the future. Usually, investment decisions involve the acquisition of capital assets, such as plant, machinery, or equipment, in exchange for cash or some combination of cash and creditor claims. Investors normally obligate themselves to current cash payments only if they expect to receive greater returns in the future. The expectation that benefits may occur in the *future* implies uncertainty. Uncertainty is the condition of not knowing the exact outcomes of alternate courses of action at the time decisions are made. Although uncertainty presents the greatest practical problem facing decision-makers, first we will consider a model of investment decision-making that assumes certainty.

The word *decision* implies a choice: decision-making is essentially choosing among several courses of action. At a minimum, the alternative opportunities open in investment decisions are (a) to invest, or (b) not to invest. But in most cases, the number of alternatives is much greater, e.g., (c) to invest in Project A, B, C, or D.

Planning for investment decisions is commonly called **capital budgeting**. Capital budgeting differs from other forms of budgeting primarily in that investment opportunities occur randomly, that is, they are nonroutine, whereas the activity usually covered in operating or financial budgets is routine. Furthermore, capital budgeting projects may have extremely long lives, whereas other budgets have shorter time horizons. Finally, the primary purpose of capital budgeting is to help managers make decisions, whereas other budgets endeavor to help managers communicate, coordinate, and evaluate. However, all budgets deal with events that may occur in the future.

In this chapter, we shall present some simplified models of investment decision-making and discuss the kind of information a decision-maker needs to formulate appropriate plans. (Additional complexities of project planning are discussed in Chapter 16.) Planning for investment decisions demands data on the expected economic consequences of alternative investment decisions.

Specifically, the plan or analysis usually follows these steps:

1. Identifying the objectives that the investing company is trying to

achieve by making the proposed investment. Typical objectives include: speedy capital recovery, profit maximization, cost minimization, or risk minimization.

2. Selecting criteria by which to measure the consequences of alternative decisions. These criteria should be related to the investment objective and might include the number of years needed to recover the original investment, the dollar effect on reported profits or cost, or the effect on profits in relation to investment costs.

3. Proposing projects that appear to be feasible and projecting a set of data on each project to compare the relative values of each.

4. Employing the criteria from Step 2 to evaluate the data gathered in Step 3.

A simple decision-making situation Suppose a businessman noticed that his cash balance contained $1,000 more than the amount required for current operations. If he wished, he could leave the $1,000 in his checking account where it would be safe, but where it would not generate additional income. Suppose, therefore, that he found two possible investments—Investment A and Investment B—each requiring an initial outlay of $1,000 but promising different cash returns at the end of each of the next four years, as shown in Exhibit 15–1. Furthermore, assume that the cash flows will actually occur as planned (that is, they are known with certainty).

In which of the alternatives should the businessman choose to invest? One rule for reaching a decision is to compare the total returns from the two investments and choose the one having the higher return during the four-year period. Using this criterion, Investment A is selected, because it can return an extra $700 over four years, whereas Investment B promises to return only $500. This conclusion implies that the investor is interested only in the $200 greater payoff that Investment A provides over the total four-year period, but that he is unconcerned with the pattern of payoffs each year. That is, Investment A provides most of its payoff during its later life, whereas Investment B provides most of its payoff during its early life.

Would everyone accept the decision to select Project A? Probably not. One investor might prefer the higher (late) returns from Investment A over the earlier (small) returns of Investment B. On the other hand, another investment manager might wish to recapture his investment as soon as possible so that he might have the funds to meet other commitments or make other investments. Each businessman might have different criteria for evaluating investment opportunities.

The models of investment decision-making developed in this chapter allow each decision-maker to specify his decision goals. To build our models, however, three concepts used in the models must be understood. They are: (1)

EXHIBIT 15–1 CASH FLOWS

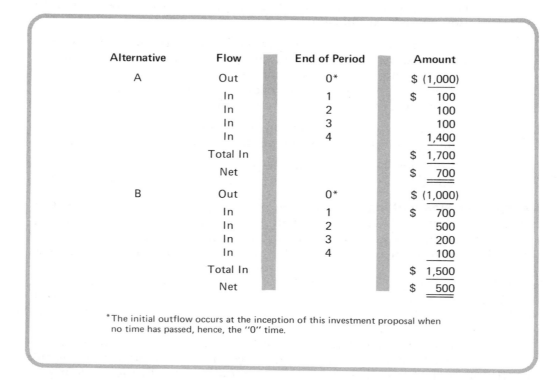

Alternative	Flow	End of Period	Amount
A	Out	0*	$ (1,000)
	In	1	$ 100
	In	2	100
	In	3	100
	In	4	1,400
	Total In		$ 1,700
	Net		$ 700
B	Out	0*	$ (1,000)
	In	1	$ 700
	In	2	500
	In	3	200
	In	4	100
	Total In		$ 1,500
	Net		$ 500

*The initial outflow occurs at the inception of this investment proposal when no time has passed, hence, the "0" time.

the time-value of money, (2) compound interest, and (3) discounted present value.

TIME-VALUE OF MONEY

If you were given an opportunity to receive $1,000 today or $1,000 a year from today, you would probably choose to receive the money now. Conversely, if you owed somebody $1,000 and were given the option of paying today or paying one year from today, you probably would elect to pay in one year. What rationale underlies such behavior? That is, why do most individuals prefer having cash in hand now rather than at some later time? The answer seems obvious. By having cash in hand, an individual has more options immediately open to him. For example, cash in hand might be used as a cushion against future unforeseen events that will require immediate cash. Or, the money could be used to satisfy existing pent-up desires—that is, it can be spent on consumer goods. Finally, cash in hand can be invested to produce an income as well as to maintain its original balance. Two other reasons relate to risk and inflation, but we shall not discuss these in detail in this chapter. Having cash in hand now reduces or shifts uncertainty about ultimate collection or payment from yourself to the other party. Furthermore, dollars in hand have greater purchasing power than dollars to be received in the future, given the accelerating inflation that has affected the United States for decades.

These examples illustrate a concept generally called the *time-value of money*, which represents a widely held preference to receive money earlier rather than later and to pay money later rather than earlier. Understanding the time-value of money is essentially a matter of understanding the concept of compound interest and the economic framework for determining the point at which investors cease to be indifferent to investment opportunities.

A person who has invested $100 and is indifferent to whether he receives $100 today or $100 next year does not place a value on the time differential. If this person remained indifferent when offered the choice of $100 now or $90 a year from now, he would not be acting "rationally," under the economic-man concept of economic analyses. If the choice was between current receipt of $100 and delayed receipt of $101, an individual still might be indifferent. But, as increases in the delayed payment continue—from $101 to $102 to $103, and so on—a point will be reached where the investor will cease to be indifferent; that is, he will state his preference.

Assume that the investor stops being indifferent when the delayed payment reaches $110. Suppose that another investor stops being indifferent when the delayed payment reaches $105. A mechanism for stating the relationship between the two individuals' investment preferences is readily available: the time-value of money can be characterized as an *interest rate*. The first investor dropped his indifference at a 10% rate of interest, and the second was satisfied with a 5% rate of interest. In these examples, interest is calculated as the percentage arrived at by dividing the investment *premium* by the investment.[1] Although the calculation of interest applies to every investment opportunity, each individual has a unique indifference-preference point. That is, each investor would cease to be indifferent at a different rate of interest.

COMPOUND INTEREST

Compound interest extends the concept of simple interest beyond one year. Using compound interest, investors can evaluate decisions that extend two, four, or more years into the future. Thus, once an investor has determined the rate of interest at which he will cease to be indifferent, he can determine the tradeoff amount on any given sum for any future period of time. For example, an

---

[1]A *premium* is measured as the difference between the current payment and the delayed payment.

individual with a 10% time-value of money and an opportunity to receive $100 now or some money in three years could calculate his indifference values as $100 now or $110 a year from now; $100 now or $121 two years from now, or $100 now and $133 three years from now. To deterine the second- and third-year amounts, consider each year as a separate proposition. For example, at the end of the first year, the payoff would have to be $110 to commit the investor. At the end of the second year, he would require 10% more than $110 or $121. At the end of the third year, he would require 10% more than $121 or $133 (rounded to the nearest whole dollar). The first year's interest would amount to $10, the second year's interest would amount to an additional $11, and the third year's interest would be an additional $12. In other words, each year's interest is calculated both on the interest from prior years and on the original $100.

Interest accumulated in the manner just described is called *compound interest*. A simple formula can be used to determine the indifference amount that an individual would demand after any number of future years in return for $1.00 given up initially at any rate of interest. Let r represent the decimal equivalent of the rate of interest, and let n represent the number of years before payoff. Then, the amount an individual would require in return for an initial $1.00 given up for n years at r rate of interest is equal to $1.00 multiplied by $(1.0 + r)^n$. Applying the formula to the previous example of a three-year indifference situation and a 10% rate of interest, the payoff at the end of three years equals $1.00 times $(1.00 + .10)^3$ or $1.33 (rounded). Since the initial investment was $100.00 rather than $1.00, the payoff is calculated by multiplying the $100 by the results determined from the formula, or $133. The initial investment is commonly called *principal*, and is abbreviated as the letter p. The compound interest formula for any amount, p, for n years at r rate of interest, is $P(1.0 + r)^n$.

For any given n, r, and P, the compound interest formula will produce only one answer, thus allowing a compound interest table to be drawn. Appendix A of this book contains a compound interest table. To use the appendix, select the desired interest rate in one of the columns. Next, select a row that corresponds to the number of periods during which the compounding is to occur. Then, find the intersection of the row and the column to find the compounded value of principal and interest for $1.00, for that rate and period of time. For example, the value of $1.00 to be invested for five years at 6% interest is 1.338; for six years at 8% interest it is 1.587. To simplify the following discussion, we shall label the number found at the intersection of a row and a column a *factor*. The factors contained in Appendix A can be used to find the future value of any principal amount: simply multiply the principal by the factor, i.e., principal × factor = future value. We shall label this form of the relationship between variables Format A. Algebraic substitution of the variables produces a Format B relationship: principal = (future value)/factor. A Format C expresses the relationship as: factor = (future value)/principal.

These formats for the relationships between variables allow a decision-maker to determine the value of any one of four variables (the principal, the rate, the number of years, or the future value), as long as he knows three of the variables. Consider the following examples:

1. Smith would like to know how much money will be available in eight years if he invests $4,000 at 6% interest. Solution: the factor at $n = 8$, $r = 6\%$ is 1.5938; consequently, $4,000 \times 1.5938 = 6,375$. Format A provided insight to the solution.

2. Smith would like to know how much money he will have to invest now at 5% interest so that he will have $10,000 in seven years. Solution: the factor at $n = 7$, $r = 5\%$ is 1.4071; $10,000 \div 1.4071 = 7,107$. Format B provided insight to the solution.

3. Smith would like to know how long he will have to wait before his investment of $1,000 grows into a balance of $2,000 at 8% interest. Solution: Format C solves for the factor associated with "years"; factor = future value divided by principal = $2,000/$1,000 = 2.000. Scanning down the 8% column, you will find that the factor 2.00 appears at slightly more than $n = 9$.

4. Smith would like to know at what rate he must invest his funds to turn $5,000 of principal into $12,000 in 15 years. Solution: $12,000/$5,000 = 2.40$; scanning along the $n = 15$ year row, the factor 2.3966 is found in the $r = 6\%$ column. Format C provided insight to the solution.

DISCOUNTED PRESENT VALUE

Discounted present value is the amount of current cash that is equivalent to some specified amount of cash to be received or given in some specified future period. Calculation of a discounted present value (DPV) requires data on the amount of the future flow, the date of the flow, and the interest rate. For example, we can readily calculate that $100.00 is the DPV of $106.00 one year from today, and $112.36 two years from today, assuming a 6% rate of interest compounded annually. Compound interest allows us to calculate the future unknown amount of some currently known DPV.

But this same problem can be reversed by asking, "How much would we be willing to pay now in order to receive $106.00 one year from today or $112.36 two years from today, assuming a 6% rate of interest?" On the basis of our prior calculation, we know that the amount would be $100.00. What we have done, however, is to discount some future amount back to its present value, hence the name of the technique—discounted present value.

A formula for DPV can be easily calculated, since it is nothing more than the reciprocal of the compound interest formula. That is, for compound interest we were willing to pay out $1.00 now in order to receive $1.00 multiplied by (1.0 + r)^n at some future date. Under the present-value assumption, we would be willing to receive $1.00 in the future only if the amount that we had to pay out now were $1.00 multiplied by $1/(1 + r)^n$. For example, consider the following case: How much would you be willing to pay now (discounted present value) in order to receive $100.00 (P) in three years (n = 3) if the rate of interest we require is 10% (r)? The terms in the square brackets equals 0.751. To find the discounted present value of $100.00, multiply $100.00 times 0.751, to produce the answer of $75.10.

$$\left[\frac{1}{(1 + .1)^3}\right] (\$100)$$

For any given n, r, and P, the DPV formula will produce only one answer, thus allowing a precalculation of present-value tables. Appendix B contains a present-value table. Each factor in Appendix B is the reciprocal of the corresponding factor in Appendix A. For example, look at the n = 15, r = 8% factors in both tables: 1/(3.1722) = 0.3152. To use Appendix B, select an interest rate corresponding to your time-value of money preference. Next, select a row corresponding to the number of future periods that will pass before the future flows will occur. Then, find the factor at the intersection of the row and the column and you have the discounted present value of $1.00 for that rate and period of time. For example, the DPV of $1.00 to be received in five years at 6% interest is $.747; in six years at 8% interest it is $.630. If the principal were some amount other than one dollar, simply multiply the principal by the factor found in the table. Appendix B can be used to determine the present value of a stream of cash flows simply by multiplying the appropriate factors from the table by the corresponding amount of cash flow for each year. However, if a future stream is composed of equal periodic amounts (called **an annuity**), an easier method exists, as discussed in Appendix C.

The factors contained in Appendix B can be used to find the present value of any future amount: simply multiply the future amount by the factor, i.e., future value × factor = present value. This format for determining present values allows a decision-maker to determine the value of any one of four variables (present value, rate, number of years, or future value), as long as he knows three of the variables. Consider the following examples:

1. Johnson would like to know how much money he will have to invest now at 9% interest in order to have $10,000 in twelve years. Solution: the factor at n = 12, r = 9% is 0.3555; $10,000 × 0.3555 = $3,555.

2. Johnson would like to know how much money will be available in eight years if he invests $6,000 at 6% interest. Solution: the factor at n = 8, r = 6% is 0.6274; $6,000 ÷ 0.6274 = $9,563.

3. Johnson would like to know how long he will have to wait before his

investment of $7,000 grows into a balance of $10,000 at 11% interest. Solution: an algebraic transformation of the present value format produces: factor = present value divided by future value. $7,000/$10,000 = 0.7000. Scanning down the 11% column, you will find the factor 0.7312 at $n = 3$ and the factor 0.6587 at $n = 4$, i.e., the answer is between 3 and 4 years.

4. Johnson would like to know at what rate he must invest his funds to turn $3,000 into $9,000 in nine years. Solution: $3,000/$9,000 = 0.3333; scanning along the $n = 9$ row, the factor 0.3329 is found in the $r = 13\%$ column.

A MODEL FOR INVESTMENT DECISIONS

An individual who can specify his time-value preference (interest rate) can determine the present-value equivalent of any future cash receipts, no matter what period of time these receipts are stretched over. For example, consider the situation presented in Exhibit 15–1, and assume that the decision-maker had a time-value preference of 10%. We can easily calculate the present values of both Investment A and Investment B, using the present-value factors from Appendix B.

The discounted present value of all of the flows during the four years is shown in Exhibit 15–2. When this time-value preference is introduced, Investment B produces the higher **net present value** of returns. Notice in Exhibit 15–2 that the initial cash outflow is netted out against the subsequent cash inflows. The output of the investment model is called the *net* present value for this reason. Note that Investment B is the more desirable project, i.e., B has the higher net present value once the time-value of money is considered, even though Investment A produces a total return that is $200 higher. An investor with a 10% time-value preference would choose Investment B rather than Investment A. That is, the $500 Net Amount illustrated on the bottom line of Investment B in Exhibit 15–2 represents the real *future* difference between inflows and outflows. But an investor who has a 10% time preference regards this as equivalent only to $267 *present* difference. The real future difference is relevant only to investors who have no time preference for money: A 10% time preference investor requires $233 (i.e., $500 − $267) to compensate for alternative earning opportunities, inflation, and risk, as well as other elements of his personal time preference for money.

To recapitulate, the steps followed in calculating a net present value for an investment decision are:

1. Specify the amount and timing of cash inflows and outflows.
2. Specify the interest rate equivalent for the time-value preference.

EXHIBIT 15–2   DISCOUNTED PRESENT VALUES

	Year	Amount	Discount Factor*	Present Value
Investment A	0	$(1,000)	1.000	$(1,000)
	1	$ 100	.909	$ 91
	2	100	.826	83
	3	100	.751	75
	4	1,400	.683	956
	Total In	$ 1,700		$ 1,205
	Net	$ 700		$ 205
Investment B	0	$(1,000)	1.000	$(1,000)
	1	$ 700	.909	$ 636
	2	500	.826	413
	3	200	.751	150
	4	100	.683	68
	Total In	$ 1,500		$ 1,267
	Net	$ 500		$ 267

*SOURCE: Appendix B (rounded)

3.   Calculate the present value of each cash inflow and outflow.

4.   Aggregate the present values of all positive and negative cash flows.

5.   Repeat the process for each investment opportunity.

6.   Choose that alternative having the highest positive net present value. A negative net present value implies that the investment will not return enough to compensate the investor for his time preference for money, and hence, he would decide not to invest at all.

SENSITIVITY OF THE NET PRESENT-VALUE MODEL

Use of the **net present-value model** requires knowledge of (1) the amount of cash inflows and outflows, (2) the timing of cash inflows and outflows, and (3) the individual decision-maker's unique time-value preference. Note that all of these data in the preceding examples were known with certainty. But in the real world, data on any investment decision must be projected into the future and these projections are rarely known with certainty. An obvious question, then,

EXHIBIT 15-3   PRESENT VALUE OF $1: $=1/(1+r)^n$

Period/Rate	5%	10%	20%	30%
1	.952	.909	.833	.769
2	.907	.826	.694	.592
3	.864	.751	.579	.455
4	.823	.683	.482	.350
5	.784	.621	.402	.269
≈				
10	.614	.386	.162	.073
≈				
15	.481	.239	.065	.020
≈				
25	.295	.092	.010	.001

SOURCE: Appendix B (Rounded)

is "How sensitive is the net present-value model to error in each of these assumptions?"

One way to evaluate the sensitivity of the net present-value model is to examine Appendix B, entitled "Present Value of $1.00," portions of which are reproduced in Exhibit 15-3. Remember that the columns of this table are associated with different interest rates that reflect the time-value preference, and the rows indicate when the cash flows will occur in the future. Take any column, say, the 10% column, and glance down the column. You will note that the discount factor rapidly decreases from 0.909 at period 1, to 0.621 at period 5, down to 0.386 at period 10, 0.239 at period 15, and 0.092 at period 25. The significance of this decline in discount value is that payments in the first period are almost ten times more important than payments to be received in the twenty-fifth period, or four times more important than payments to be received in the fifteenth period, or 50% more important than payments to be received in the fifth period, assuming a 10% time-value preference.

A scan of the 20% interest-rate column discloses that payments received in the first period are twice as important as payments in the fifth period, or five times as important as payments received in the tenth period, or more than ten times as important as payments received in the fifteenth period. Looking at the 30% interest-rate column, we can see an acceleration of the same phenomenon, namely, payments in the first period are three times as important as payments in the fifth period, and ten times as important as payments in the tenth period.

Payments in the twenty-fifth period are hardly important. In terms of sensitivity to time period then, *the discounted net present-value model weighs early receipts of cash much more heavily than late receipts of cash, and this phenomenon is accentuated at higher interest rates.*

For cash payments, the implications are similar. *Early cash payments involve a much greater sacrifice than later cash payments, and this phenomenon also is accentuated as the interest rate increases.* After a certain number of years, cash payments and cash receipts are reduced to insignificant amounts by the discounting process. The timing of cash inflows and outflows has a great effect on the result produced by the net present-value model. Since we cannot tell with certainty when future cash inflows or outflows will occur, we should at least recognize that a delay in cash receipt or an acceleration of cash payment by one or two years will affect the investment decision.

Furthermore, the effect of delaying or accelerating flows becomes more important as the time-value of money increases. At low interest rates, the discounted present-value method is relatively insensitive to a one-year delay in receipt or payment, but at high interest rates, such delay in receipt or payment becomes crucial.

Second, examine the first row in Exhibit 15–3, which indicates factors associated with first-period flows. The factors at 10%, 20%, and 30% are, respectively, 0.909, 0.833, and 0.769. In other words, the factor at the 30% interest rate is about 15% smaller than the factor at 10%. Now glance across the four-year row and you will see that the factor at 10% is 0.683 and at 30% it is 0.350 or, in other words, almost 50% less. The implication of this observation is that *the net present-value model is not especially sensitive to differences in interest rates when the cash inflow or outflow occurs during an early period, but the model is extremely sensitive to differences in interest rates whenever the cash flows occur in distant periods.*

Our third observation is derived from the first two and concerns the sensitivity of the net present-value model to errors in estimating the amount of future cash inflows or outflows. Here again, looking at the discount factor along row 1, which represents period 1 flows, we can see that *the model is much more sensitive to error for low discount rate than for high discount rates;* for example, compare the 10% rate with the 20% rate. If the first-year cash inflows were overestimated by $1,000, using the 10% rate of interest would include $909 of overestimation in the final calculation, whereas using a 20% rate of interest would include only $833 of the overestimation in the final determination. In later periods, say, the fifth period, another $1,000 overestimation of cash inflows will be counted as $621 at the 10% rate of interest and only $402 at the 20% rate of interest. This last example indicates also that over- or underestimating the amount of cash flows (to occur in the future) will affect the outcome of the model much less if the overestimation occurred in an early year rather than in a later year for any rate of interest —$76 ($909 less $833) versus $219 ($621 less $402).

REEXAMINING THE EXAMPLE

Returning to the example in Exhibit 15–1, what happens if the decision-maker had only a 5% time-value of moeny? Exhibit 15–4 repeats the original cash flow for Investments A and B, provides discount factors for 5%, and shows the discounted present value resulting when the cash flows are multiplied by the factors. The line titled "Net Present Value" gives the results of each alternative. Now, the decision-maker would choose Investment A rather than Investment B, which had previously appeared as the better investment. Thus, investment decisions can be reversed, solely on the basis of changes in the individual's time-value of money. Individual decision-makers who specify different time-values of money may logically and rationally choose different investment opportunities from the same set of possibilities.

Furthermore, sensitivity analysis indicates that a one-year delay in cash receipts would affect the decision-maker who had a 10% time-value of money to a greater extent than it would affect the decision-maker who had the 5% time-value of money. Also, a $100 error in the amount estimated to be received in the fifth year would affect the decision-maker having a 5% time-value of money much

EXHIBIT 15–4   DISCOUNTED PRESENT VALUES

Investment A	Year	Amount	Discount Factor*	Present Value
	0	$(1,000)	1.000	$(1,000)
	1	$ 100	.952	$ 95
	2	100	.907	91
	3	100	.864	86
	4	1,400	.823	1,152
	Total In	$ 1,700		$ 1,424
	Net	$ 700		$ 424
Investment B	0	$(1,000)	1.000	$(1,000)
	1	$ 700	.952	$ 666
	2	500	.907	453
	3	200	.864	173
	4	100	.823	82
	Total In	$ 1,500		$ 1,374
	Net	$ 500		$ 374

*SOURCE: Appendix B (rounded)

more than it would affect the decision-maker who had a 10% time-value of money.

LIMITATIONS OF THE
NET PRESENT-VALUE MODEL

Once again, there are limitations and unstated assumptions inherent in the net present-value model. At this point, it is useful to reiterate these assumptions and limitations. First, the model assumes that the cash inflows and outflows are known with certainty, that is, projections have not considered unforeseen flows or shifts in timing. Raising the time-value preference rate, shifting inflows to later periods, or shifting outflows to earlier periods, will produce a more conservative (smaller) DPV, compensating for the failure to consider uncertainty. Other sophisticated techniques for dealing with uncertainty are discussed in Chapter 16.

Second, there is an implicit assumption that the time-value preference rate used at the beginning of the analysis holds constant throughout the life of the project. Reflect a moment on real life to see if this assumption is sound. The fluctuations in interest rates during the 1970s, from about 6% at the beginning of the period, up above 10% and back down to 9% at the end of the period, indicate that the average investor would have faced significantly different opportunities for investing funds during that year. Similarly, opportunities differ over longer periods of time. If a decision-maker has excess funds and limited investment opportunities, he may well accept lower expected returns than he would when greater investment opportunities are available to him. In addition, a decision-maker who has limited funds and unlimited investment opportunities may well accept only higher expected returns than he would when he enjoys a greater surplus of available cash.

A third assumption of the net present-value model is that cash flows occur at equally spread intervals, usually at the end of the year. However, if expected cash flows were projected for six-month intervals in the future, the model could be adjusted by considering each row in Appendix B as a six-month period instead of a year and compensating by reducing the time-value of money rate to half the annual rate. For example, if cash flows would be $10,000 for each of the first two six-month periods and the applicable interest rate were 20% for the year, we could discount the $20,000 at the 20%, producing a rounded discounted present value of $16,666. More realistically, we could discount each of the $10,000 amounts at a 10% rate, producing a DPV of $17,355. The difference between the two DPVs is due to compounding earlier returns.

On the other hand, if monthly data were given, consider each row of Appendix B to represent one month and compensate by taking one-twelfth of the annual **stated** time-value of money. Compensation for cash flows that occur at other than annual periods can be made in this fashion. Alternately, a more sophisticated technique could apply mathematical analysis to calculate discount factors that represent unequal time periods during which cash flows would occur.

INTERNAL TIME-ADJUSTED RATE OF RETURN

The **internal time-adjusted rate of return** may be defined as "the maximum rate of interest that could be paid for the capital employed over the life of an investment without loss on the project."[2] The time-adjusted rate-of-return model selects a set of present-value discount factors that equate the present value of cash inflows to the present value of cash outflows. That is, this model seeks out an interest rate that will reduce the net present value of all flows for a project to zero.

Assume, for example, that a manager is considering purchasing a new machine for $3,993, payment on delivery. The machine promises to generate an additional income of $1,000 per year over its five-year life, after which it will be completely devoid of value. Exhibit 15-5 presents an analysis of this case using the internal time-adjusted rate-of-return model. Trial and error was used to find a

EXHIBIT 15-5 INTERNAL TIME-ADJUSTED RATE OF RETURN

Year	Amount	8% Discount Factor[*]	Present Value
0	$(3,993)	1.000	$(3,993)
1	1,000	.926	926
2	1,000	.857	857
3	1,000	.794	794
4	1,000	.735	735
5	1,000	.681	681
Total In	$5,000		$3,993
Net	$1,007		-0-

*The 8% factor was found by trial and error; that is, first a 5% factor was used but the project was found to have a positive net present value; then a 10% factor was used but the project was found to have a negative net present value; and so on. Chapter 16 discusses a method, the payback reciprocal, that can be used to approximate the internal time-adjusted rate of return in certain cases.

[2]Research Report 35, *Return on Capital as a Guide to Managerial Decisions*, National Association of Accountants (December 1959), p. 57.

set of discount factors (from Appendix B) that equates the cash inflows to the cash outflows. The rate of return corresponding to the set used in Exhibit 15–5 is 8%. The 8% discount factors equate the amount invested, $3,993, with the present value of cash inflows, $1,000 per year for five years. This implies that money could be borrowed at an 8% interest rate, that the money could be invested in this project, and that the flows from the project would be just sufficient to pay back the loan plus interest over the five years. If funds could be borrowed for less than 8%, the decision-maker stands to make a profit on this investment. On the other hand, if interest rates were higher than 8%, then the decision-maker would reject this investment, because there would be no possibility that he could earn more than the interest that he had to pay to use the funds.

The output of the time-adjusted rate-of-return model can always be compared to the minimum-desired rate of return.[3] Even when investment funds need not be borrowed, the minimum-desired rate of return must be more than zero. Investors should consider all alternative uses of funds whenever funds are available for a project. Under most circumstances, the investor can choose to lend the money to third parties. For example, he could invest in government bonds, which are relatively risk-free (and have correspondingly low rates of return). As a limit, then, the minimum-desired rate of return on any proposed investment ought to equal at least a lending rate of return on loans of equivalent risk.

To recapitulate, an internal time-adjusted rate of return is calculated by trial-and-error selection of the set of discount factors that will equate cash inflows and cash outflows. The interest rate associated with those factors is then compared to the minimum-desired rate of return. In contrast, the net present-value model uses the minimum-desired rate of return as the rate to discount expected cash inflows and cash outflows. If the net present value is zero or positive, the project is accepted. The net present-value model is easier to apply than is the time-adjusted rate-of-return model, since it does not involve searching for factors that will produce a "true" rate of return.

MINIMUM-DESIRED RATE OF RETURN

The outputs of both capital budgeting models are evaluated according to some minimum-desired rate of return. The net present-value model uses it to select the appropriate set of discount factors, and the internal time-adjusted rate-of-return model compares it to the calculated rate. Thus, the minimum-desired rate of return is an important variable to consider in evaluating capital-budgeting proposals.

The minimum-desired rate of return is frequently referred to as the **cost**

[3]If additional investments are required in periods subsequent to period 0, multiple internal rates of return can be calculated. Thus, the authors advocate use of the net present-value model to evaluate proposals that call for subsequent investments.

of capital. No uniform measure of cost of capital exists. Some business planners believe that cost of capital is limited to out-of-pocket interest and financing charges on any debt arising from an investment in capital assets. Another opinion of cost of capital measures it at an amount equivalent to long-run average costs of interest, dividends, and other equity charges, weighted by the relative importance of debt, preferred equity, and common equity in financing the operations of a firm. A third approach considers cost of capital a borrowing rate, that is, what a company must pay if it wishes to borrow money. Alternatively, cost of capital might be a lending rate—the amount that can be earned on an alternate investment having a like degree of risk.

Even though no single cost-of-capital concept is universally held by all authorities, most organizations engaged in capital budgeting select one definition and use it consistenlty as a measure for the minimum-desired rate of return. In practice, cost of capital rarely falls below the prevailing prime interest rate—between 6% and 10%. For very risky proposals, the minimum-desired rate of return may be set as high as 40%, as is common in the pharmaceutical drug industry.

TECHNIQUES THAT IGNORE
THE TIME-VALUE OF MONEY

Since acquiring and using capital projects extends over long periods of time, techniques for analyzing investments should consider the time-value of money. Two widely used methods, the **average rate of return** and the **payback period**, do not consider the time-value of money, however. Neither of these methods is recommended as an indicator of an investment's profit potential. Both are merely rule-of-thumb techniques for analyzing investments.

Average rate of return   The average rate of return (also called the "accounting" rate of return) is the ratio of the average annual profits after taxes to the book value of investment in the project. For example, assume that the average annual after-tax profit from a particular project with a five-year life is $3,000, and the original investment in the project is $18,000. Therefore, the average rate of return is calculated as follows:

$$\text{Average Rate of Return} = \text{Income/Investment}$$
$$= \$3,000/\$18,000 = 16.7\%$$

The words *profit* and *income* are technical accounting terms for the annual difference between the revenues and expenses incurred by an organization. Revenues are associated with increases in the assets of the firm, while expenses are associated with decreases in assets. A *matching* concept relates revenues to expenses in any one period: income results from the matching of expenses "caused by" the generation of revenue and revenues "induced by" the incurrence of expenses.

Yearly inflows to a particular project are analogous to revenues, and prorated outflows are analogous to expenses. For example, a project that costs $4,000 and generates inflows of $1,000 per year for five years produces an average annual income of $200. Prorated costs are $4,000/5, or $800 per year, and revenue less expense is $1,000 − $800 = $200. An alternative calculation of average annual income would divide the difference between the total inflows and outflows by the life of the project: ($5,000 − $4,000)/5 = $200. The average rate of return for this project is $200/$4,000 or 5%. (Contrast this 5% average rate of return with the 8% internal time-adjusted rate of return on a similar project, illustrated in Exhibit 15–5.)

The simplicity of calculating the average rate of return is its primary advantage, since it uses accounting information that is readily available. The average rate of return is used in the same fashion as the internal rate of return: After being calculated for all potential projects, it is compared with the required cost of capital (rate) to determine whether the particular projects should be accepted or rejected. Furthermore, projects can be ranked in declining order of "profitability," and only those with the higher rankings need be accepted.

The principal limitations of this method are its failure to account for the time-value of money and the fact that it is based on accounting income rather than on cash flows. We have seen previously that the timing of cash outflows and inflows can dramatically affect evaluations of a given project's worth. For example, consider four investment proposals, each costing $10,000 and each having an economic life of five years. Assume that these proposals are expected to provide identical total cash flows over the five years, as illustrated in Exhibit 15–6. Each of the proposals has the same average income: $10,000/5 = $2,000. Since the original investment in each project is $10,000, each has the same

EXHIBIT 15–6   INVESTMENT OPPORTUNITIES

Year	Flow	A	B	C	D
			Project		
0	Out	$(10,000)	$(10,000)	$(10,000)	$(10,000)
1	In	$ 6,000	$ 2,000	$ 4,000	$ 5,000
2	In	5,000	3,000	4,000	5,000
3	In	4,000	4,000	4,000	4,000
4	In	3,000	5,000	4,000	3,000
5	In	2,000	6,000	4,000	3,000
	Total In	$20,000	$20,000	$20.000	$20,000
	Net	$10,000	$10,000	$10,000	$10,000

average rate of return (based on original costs) $2,000/$10,000 or 20%. Few managers would be indifferent in their choice among these proposals. Most would prefer Project A, which provides a larger portion of the total cash benefits in the early years of the project. Thus, the average rate of return leaves much to be desired as a method of evaluating potential investment projects.

Payback period   The number of years required to recover the initial cash investment in any project is called the **payback period**. The payback period is calculated as the ratio of the initial investment divided by the average annual cash inflows over the life of the project. For example, consider Project C of Exhibit 15–6, in which the initial investment was $10,000, the life of the project was five years, and the total cash flows from the project were $20,000 (hence, average cash flows of $4,000). For this example, the payback period is 2½ years, calculated as follows:

$$\text{Payback Years} = \frac{\text{Original Investment}}{\text{Average Cash Flow}} = \frac{\$10,000}{\$4,000} = 2\frac{1}{2}$$

Obviously, the average annual cash inflows for the four projects listed in Exhibit 15–6 do not truly reflect the rate of capital recovery. *When annual cash inflows are not equal, the job of calculating a meaningful payback is more difficult.* Suppose we look at the annual cash inflows of Project A (Exhibit 15–6), which were $6,000, $5,000, $4,000, $3,000, and $2,000. The original investment of $10,000 will be recovered at the end of the project's second year. However, Project B, which had cash flows of $2,000, $3,000, $4,000, $5,000, and $6,000, will require 3.2 years before the original $10,000 investment is recaptured. Thus, a major limitation of the payback method is that it fails to consider the time-value of money, just as did the average rate of return. Furthermore, it does not measure a "rate of return" in any sense, but deals only with capital-recovery periods. However, it, too, shares the advantage of being easy to calculate.

The payback method is used to evaluate investments by comparing the payback period for any proposed project with some maximum acceptable capital-recovery period. If the payback period extends beyond the desired maximum, the project will be rejected. For example, if the calculated payback for a project is three years, but the required maximum is only two years, then the proposed project will be rejected. Since the payback method fails to consider cash flows after the payback period, it cannot measure profitability. For example, consider two proposals, each costing $10,000 and each having the same payback period of five years. If both projects are expected to produce equal *annual* cash flows of $2,000 but Project A has a seven-year life, whereas Project B has a ten-year life, Project B will obviously be more profitable than Project A. Since the payback method fails to recognize this difference, it is definitely not a yardstick of profitability.

Despite the fact that the payback method neither measures profitability nor considers the time-value of money, it continues to be used widely. Besides being easy to calculate, the payback period does provide limited insight into the risk and liquidity of a project. All other things being equal, the project having the shortest payback period is less risky than projects having more extended payback periods. In addition, this project also allows faster recovery of funds, which increases liquidity. For example, investors evaluating investments in East Asia certainly must consider risk and liquidity. Similarly, companies in poor cash positions must be concerned with early recovery of funds. Most sophisticated investors, however, use the payback method only to supplement other capital-budgeting techniques.

SUMMARY

Investment decisions involve current expenditures in expectation of deriving future benefits and usually include the acquisition of capital assets. Planning for investment decisions is called capital budgeting, which differs from other budgeting in the lack of routine scheduling, in the length of the period covered, and in its primary purpose. Capital budgeting identifies objectives, selects criteria, proposes projects, and evaluates alternatives.

Since capital projects have long lives, an evaluation of alternatives must consider the time-value of money, that widely held preference for accelerated cash inflows and delayed cash outflows. The time-value of money can be explained best through compound interest and discounted present value. Two capital-budgeting models that consider the time-value of money are the net present-value method and the time-adjusted rate-of-return method.

Two other techniques, the average rate of return and the payback period, are widely used in capital budgeting but both rely on so many assumptions that their value is limited. At best, these techniques should be used only to supplement other planning methods.

SUGGESTED READINGS

Jones, D. A. "Capital Budgeting: Mixing Up the Balance Sheet." *Financial Executive*, April 1976.

Junker, Joseph. "Capital Investment Analysis and Evaluation." *Managerial Planning*, March/April, 1976.

Liao, M. "Modified Payback Analysis." *Management Accounting*, September 1976.

Mehler, E. W. "Capital Budgeting: Theory and Practice." *Management Accounting*, September 1976.

QUESTIONS

15-1 How does capital budgeting differ from other forms of budgeting?

15-2 List four examples of nonrecurring investment decisions for which the executive should employ capital-budgeting techniques.

15-3 Capital-budgeting decisions involve comparing cash outflows with _____?

15-4 What common traits do all budgeting techniques share?

15-5 Various business entities analyze capital-budgeting decisions differently. One reason for the differing approaches may be that the firms have conflicting objectives. List three possible objectives of an investing firm.

15-6 Mr. Thompson, the controller of Shober Enterprises, must present an analysis of four capital investments to the next meeting of the board of directors. The president has specified the objective of the firm's investment policy to be profit maximization. What additional information does Mr. Thompson need to develop his analysis?

15-7 A capital-budgeting analysis that evaluates investments solely on the basis of total returns is ignoring what crucial factors?

15-8 Evaluate the following statement: "All firms of similar size will always have the same time-value preference rate (time-value of money)."

15-9 A firm may alter its time-value preference rate from year to year. What environmental factors could affect the firm's evaluation of the time-value of money?

15-10 "The discounted net present-value model weighs early receipts of cash much more heavily than late receipts of cash." Relate this timing sensitivity to the concept of compound interest.

15-11 What limitations are implicit in the net present-value model?

15-12 Compare and contrast the net present-value model with the time-adjusted rate-of-return method.

EXERCISES

15-13 How much is the future value of $5,000 that has been invested for 15 years at 5% interest? At 10% interest? At 10% interest for 30 years?

15-14 What is the present value of $10,000 to be received in 15 years, if your time preference is measured at 5%? At 10%? At 10% in 30 years?

15-15 Approximately how many years will it take to turn $3,000 into $9,000 at 6% interest? At 13% interest? At 17% interest?

15–16   Approximately what interest rate is needed to turn $2,000 into $8,000 in 18 years? In 12 years? In 6 years?

15–17   Should Smith invest $4,000 in a project that promises to return $6,000 in five years if his time-value of money is 10%? What is the internal time-adjusted rate of return on this project?

*15–18   Should Smith invest $10,000 in a project that promises to return $4,000 at the end of each year for four years if his time-value of money is 10%? What is the internal time-adjusted rate of return on this project?

15–19   Should Jones invest $5,000 in a project that promises to return $1,000 per year for 10 years if he expects a liquidity need for the $5,000 in four years? What is the minimum yearly inflow that will meet Jones' needs?

15–20   Copen Co. is considering the purchase of one out of two publicly held companies. Company A has assets of $1,000,000 and earns $150,000 per year. Company B has assets of $800,000, but earns only $130,000 per year. Which company has the higher accountants' rate of return? If Copen requires a minimum rate of return of 20%, what decision relative to A and B should be made?

15–21   Below are four independent cases that explore the relationship between present values, interest rates, length of the investment period, and future values. In each case, one element is missing. Determine the number that corresponds to each missing element, A through D.

	Case 1	Case 2	Case 3	Case 4
Present value	$5,000	$ 3,050	$2,000	D
Interest rate	12%	16%	C	11%
Number of years	8	B	10	15
Future value	A	$10,000	$4,318	$4,180

15–22   Joe Grogin has identified four projects as having investment potential. Expected cash flows on each project are described below:

Year	Flow	Project A	Project B	Project C	Project D
0	out	($4,000)	($3,500)	($4,500)	($3,000)
1	in	-0-	-0-	-0-	-0-
2	in	-0-	-0-	$1,000	$3,993
3	in	$6,100	$1,000	$2,000	-0-
4	in	-0-	$4,000	$4,000	-0-

(A) What is the net present value of each project at 10% time preference?

(B) Which should Joe accept, if he can invest in only one?

(C) What is the internal time-adjusted rate of return on Project D?

(D) If liquidity is a major consideration for Joe, which project seems most feasible? Why?

15–23   Toolco is considering the acquisition of a $60,000 machine that has a four-year life. The machine will do the work of four men, and the resulting cost savings (net of additional machine-related costs) are expected to amount to $20,000 per year. (Ignore tax considerations.)

   (A) What is the net present value of the proposed project, assuming that Toolco has a 15% time-value of money?

   (B) What is the internal time-adjusted rate of return on this project?

   (C) Is the proposed project better than an alternative that costs $80,000 but is expected to save $30,000 per year for four years?

15–24   Ajax Company has identified three investment opportunities that are summarized below:

Year	Flow	Project A	Project B	Project C
0	out	($20,000)	($20,000)	($20,000)
1	in	10,000	15,000	5,000
2	in	10,000	10,000	10,000
3	in	10,000	5,000	15,000
	Net	$10,000	$10,000	$10,000

   (A) Rank the projects in terms of desirability, assuming a 10% time-value of money.

   (B) Rank the projects in terms of desirability, assuming that liquidity is a major concern of Ajax.

   (C) What is the average annual profit of each project? Rank the projects in terms of desirability, using the average rate of return.

*15–25   Below are data relating to three possible investments.

	Project A	Project B	Project C
Original investment	$20,000	$30,000	$40,000
Annual cash inflows	$ 5,000	$10,000	$10,000
Life of project (years)	6	4	7

   Ignoring income tax considerations, rank the projects according to their desirability using the following criteria:

   (A) Net present value assuming a 10% time-value of money.

   (B) Internal time-adjusted rate of return.

   (C) Payback period.

   (D) Average accounting rate of return.

*15–26   Below are four independent cases that explore the relationship between present values of annuities, interest rates, length of the inflow series, and the annual inflow amount. In each case, one element is missing. Determine the number that corresponds to each missing element, A through D.

	Case #1	Case #2	Case #3	Case #4
Present value	$8,077	$9,976	$3,605	D
Interest rate	16%	20%	C%	8%
Years of inflow	7	B	5	4
Annual inflow	A	$3,000	$1,000	$2,000

15–27 A local delicatessen owner was considering purchasing a new meat case to replace the one he had used for 15 years. The cost of the new case was $2,400, payable in two equal annual payments. The store owner, Mr. Spendlow, felt that the new case would reduce refrigeration and spoilage costs by $800 per year and have a useful life of 5 years with no salvage value.

*(A) What is the internal rate of return for this investment?

(B) At an 8% rate of interest, what is the net present value of the investment?

(C) If Mr. Spendlow can borrw the required funds at 6%, should he make the investment?

(D) What is the net present value of the project, assuming that Mr. Spendlow has a 25% time-value preference?

15–28 The Hope Company operated for years without the aid of budgets. Two years ago, a budget department was organized and proved to be a great success. The department was small and consisted of selected individuals from other departments who, under one manager, formulated all the Company's budgets. Now the president has heard of capital budgeting and decides to place this function also under the direction of the budgeting manager.

(A) Is there any real difference between "normal" budgeting and capital budgeting? Define each.

(B) In the long run, does the Hope Company's approach to budgeting under a centralized budget management sound as if it will continue to be a success?

(C) What traits do "normal" budgeting and capital budgeting have in common? Is this sufficient to warrant both types being placed under the same manager?

(D) What is meant by the statement, "Uncertainty presents the greatest practical problem facing decision-makers"? How does this statement relate to "normal" budgets? To capital budgets?

15–29 To facilitate the computation of compound interest problems, tables for various compound interest rates are available. The tables take a standard form: Various interest rates head the columns of the table and periods are listed on the left-row margin. Tables speed computation and ensure accuracy. The use of tables is not essential, however, since the equation for compound interest is actually quite simple: Total return on $1 equals $(1 + r)^n$, where r represents the interest rate and n the periods.

(A) What would be the total return at the end of one year, 19X1, on $10,000 at an interest rate of 7%?

(B) If the total return in part (A) were reinvested at 7%, what would be the return at the end of the next year, 19X2?

(C) Write the formula that would produce the total return at the end of year 10. Is this the same as the reciprocal of the factor found at $n = 10, r = 7\%$ in Appendix B, times $10,000?

15-30 The Holt Company has two investment alternatives to choose between. The first alternative will necessitate a $10,000 investment in the first year and return $2,000 a year for the next ten years. The other project also necessitates a $10,000 investment but returns $25,000 at the end of ten years. The managers of Holt use an 8% discounted present-value rate for capital budgeting.

(A) Which alternative has the higher net present value?

(B) Should management invest in the second project or keep its funds in a bank account that earns 10%? Would it matter if the bank paid out interest each year instead of compounding it?

(C) Does the need for future cash flows play a part in determining investment decisions? Explain.

(D) What are the limitations to the type of analysis that you have just performed?

15-31 The Stevens Company, a processor of whole milk, uses the average rate-of-return method for computing rate of return. They have two alternatives to consider. The first requires an investment of $25,000 and earns an average after-tax profit of $5,000 for each of ten years. The second also necessitates an investment of $25,000, but produces an average after-tax profit of $4,000 for each of ten years.

(A) Compute the average rate of return for both projects.

(B) What essential considerations are not taken into account by the average rate-of-return method?

(C) In which of the two processes would you invest if you were using the average rate of return? Why?

(D) Using the internal time-adjusted rate-of-return method, calculate a discounted rate of earnings for the first project. Explain differences between this rate of return and the one you calculated in part (A) of this question.

15-32 The Rogers Corporation uses payback analysis to evaluate its investments. This year, three alternatives are considered, each requiring an outlay of $50,000. The first returns $10,000 for the first four years and $5,000 for five years following. The second returns $6,000 per year for ten years. The third returns $5,000 for the first eight years and $10,000 for the next seven years.

(A) Calculate the payback period for each of the three alternatives.

(B) What are the drawbacks of the payback method of capital-budgeting analysis?

(C) On the basis of simple payback, which of the three alternatives would be selected?

(D) Use the average rate-of-return method to analyze the three alternatives. Which alternative would this method favor?

(E) Use the net present-value method with a 20% discount rate to evaluate each alternative. Which would be selected?

15–33   The Curry Corporation, a small manufacturing company located in South Carolina, manufactures tire jacks. Curry's management asks all production superintendents to meet with the president once a year to allocate all available funds for the next year.

(A) Is this an acceptable method for allocating the capital-expenditure budget? Explain.

(B) If management does not understand or wish to become involved with the time-value of money computation, which methods can be used to evaluate alternative capital projects?

(C) What is lost when capital-expenditure evaluations are limited to those not involving the time-value of money?

15–34   The Harrison Gummed Label Company has no standard procedures for evaluating capital investments. Sometimes payback period is used, and sometimes average rate of return is used. The choice of method depends more on the analyst's preference than on an intelligent choice between methods. John Robinson, the superintendent of the gum department, needs a new machine that will cost $50,000 and increase yearly cash inflows by $10,000 over the next ten years. His brother, Bill Robinson, the superintendent of the label department, also needs a machine costing $50,000, but it will produce no inflows for the first three years, and then inflows of $20,000 each year for the next seven years.

(A) Which method, payback or average rate of return, would John prefer? Which method would Bill prefer?

(B) Compute the average rate of return and payback for both projects.

(C) Which is the better project? Explain.

PROBLEMS

15–35   Capital budgeting has received increased attention in recent years. The quantitative techniques employed for capital-budgeting decisions depend largely upon accounting data.

(A) Distinguish between capital budgeting and budgeting for operations.

(B) Three quantitative methods used in making capital-budgeting decisions are (1) payback period, (2) unadjusted accounting rate of return, and (3) discounted cash flow. Discuss the merits of each of these methods.

(C) Two variations of the discounted cash-flow method are (1) time adjusted rate of return and (2) net present value (sometimes referred to as excess present value). Explain and compare these two variations of the discounted cash-flow method.

(AICPA adapted)

*15–36   The M Co., manager of an office building, is considering putting in certain concessions in the main lobby. An accounting study produces the following estimates, on the average annual basis:

Salaries		$ 7,000
Licenses and Payroll Taxes		200
Cost of Merchandise Sold		
Beginnig Inventory	$ 2,000	
Purchases	40,000	
Available	42,000	
Ending Inventory	2,000	40,000
Share of Heat, Light, etc.		500
Pro Rata Building Depreciation		1,000
Concession Advertising		100
Share of Company Administrative Expense		400
Sales of Merchandise		49,000

The investment in equipment, which would last ten years, would be $2,000.

As an alternative, a catering company has offered to lease the space for $750 per year, for ten years, and to put in and operate the same concessions at no cost to the M Co. Heat and light are to be furnished by the office building at no additional charge.

What is your advice to the M Co.? Explain fully.

(AICPA adapted)

15–37   The capital-budgeting department of Acme Corporation is considering an investment in one of three projects. Characteristics of the projects are listed below.

Year	Flow	Project A	Project B	Project C
0	out	$(25,000)	$(25,000)	$(25,000)
1	in	15,000	5,000	10,000
2	in	12,000	5,000	10,000
3	in	10,000	5,000	10,000
4	in	8,000	5,000	10,000
5	in	3,000	5,000	10,000
6	in	2,000	5,000	-0-
Salvage	in	-0-	20,000	-0-

(A) Compute the average rate of return for each project, assuming "investment" is the original investment's cost. Rank projects from highest to lowest returns.

(B) Considering the flow associated with each project, what drawbacks do both of these methods have? Which project is considered superior under each method? Explain.

(C) Assuming a zero minimum rate for the time-value of money, which project is most desirable when evaluated by the net present-value method? Which project is most desirable if the time-value rate is 20%.

(D) Compute the payback period for the three projects.

(E) Discuss differences in rankings, as determined by the average rate of return and the payback methods.

(F) Compare advantages and disadvantages of the two methods. In what circumstances would payback be superior to average rate of return?

*15–38   The management of McAngus, Inc., has never used formal planning techniques in the operation of its business. The president of McAngus has expressed interest in the recommendation of its accountants that the company investigate various techniques it could use to manage the business more effectively.

McAngus, a medium-sized manufacturer, has grown steadily. It recently acquired another company located approximately 1,000 miles away. The new company manufactures a line of products that complements McAngus's present product line. Both manufacturing plants have significant investments in land, buildings, machinery, and equipment. Each plant is to be operated as a separate division headed by a division manager, who is to have virtually complete authority for the management of his division. Each manager will be responsible primarily for the profit contribution of his division. A complete set of financial statements is to be prepared for each division, as well as for the company.

The president and his immediate management team intend to concentrate their efforts on coordinating the activities of the two divisions and investigating and evaluating such things as new markets, new product lines, and new business acquisition possibilities. Because of the cash required for the recent acquisition and the cash needs for desired future expansion, the president is particularly concerned about cash flow and the effective management of cash.

Construct your answer to each of the following requirements to consider known facts about McAngus, Inc., as presented in the questions. Confine your answer to the accounting techniques and processes involved.

(A) Explain the objectives and describe the process which McAngus can use to plan for and evaluate the long-term commitment of its resources including cash.

(B) Describe three techniques, including one that considers the time-value of money that McAngus can use to help evaluate various alternatives in its long-range plan. Explain the advantages and disadvantages of each.

(AICPA adapted)

*15–39   The Gercken Corporation sells computer services to its clients. The company completed a feasibility study and decided to obtain an additional computer on January 1, 19X8. Information regarding the new computer follows:

1. The purchase price of the computer is $230,000. Maintenance, property taxes, and insurance will be $20,000 per year. If the computer is rented, the annual rent will be $85,000 plus 5% of annual billings. The rental price includes maintenance.
2. Owing to competitive conditions, the company feels it will be necessary to replace the computer at the end of 3 years with one that is larger and more advanced. It is estimated that the computer will have a resale value of $110,000 at the end of the 3 years. The comptuer will be depreciated on a straight-line basis for both financial-reporting and income tax purposes.
3. The income tax rate is 50%.
4. The estimated annual billing for the services of the new computer will be $220,000 during the first year and $260,000 during each of the second and third years. The estimated annual expense of operating the computer is $80,000 in addition to the expense mentioned above. An additional $10,000 of start-up expenses will be incurred during the first year.
5. If it decides to purchase the computer, the company will pay cash. If the computer is rented, the $230,000 can be otherwise invested at a 15% rate of return.
6. If the computer is purchased, the amount of the investment recovered during each of the 3 years can be reinvested immediately at a 15% rate of return. Each year's recovery of investment in the computer will have been reinvested for an average of 6 months by the end of the year.

(A) Prepare a schedule comparing the estimated annual income from the new computer under the purchase plan and under the rental plan. The comparison should include a provision for the opportunity cost of the average investment in the computer during each year.

(B) Prepare a schedule showing the annual cash flows under the purchase plan and under the rental plan.

(C) Prepare a schedule comparing the net present values of the cash flows under the purchase plan and under the rental plan.

(D) Comment on the results obtained in items (A) and (C). How should the computer be financed? Why?

(AICPA adapted)

*15-40 Niebuhr Corporation is beginning its first capital-budgeting program and has retained you to assist the budget committee in the evaluation of a project to expand operations designated as Proposed Expansion Project #12 (PEP #12).

1. The following capital expenditures are under consideration:

$ 300,000	Fire sprinkler system
100,000	Landscaping
600,000	Replacement of old machines
800,000	Projects to expand operations (including PEP #12)
$1,800,000	Total

2. The Corporation requires no minimum return on the sprinkler system or the landscaping, but it does expect a minimum return of 6% on all investments to replace old machinery. It also expects investments in expansion projects to yield a return that will exceed the average cost of the capital required to finance the sprinkler system and the landscaping in addition to the expansion projects.

3. Under Proposed Expansion Project #12 (PEP #12) a cash investment of $75,000 will be made one year before operations begin. The investment will be depreciated by the sum-of-the-year's-digits method over a three-year period and is expected to have a salvage value of $15,000. Additional financial data for PEP #12 follow:

Time Period	Revenue	Variable Costs	Maintenance, Property Taxes, and Insurance
0–1	$80,000	$35,000	$ 8,000
1–2	95,000	41,000	11,000
2–3	60,000	25,000	12,000

The amount of the investment recovered during each of the three years can be reinvested immediately at a rate of return approximating 15%. Each year's recovery of investment, then, will have been reinvested at 15% for an average of six months at the end of the year.

4. The capital structure of Niebuhr Corporation follows:

	Amount	Percentage
Short-Term Notes at 5% Interest	$ 3,500,000	10%
4% Cumulative Preferred stock, $100 par	1,750,000	5
Common Stock	12,250,000	35
Retained Earnings	17,500,000	50
	$35,000,000	100%

5. Additional data available to you are summarized below:

	Current Market Price	Expected Earnings per Share	Expected Dividends per Share
Preferred Stock, noncallable	$120	—	$4.00
Common Stock	50	$3.20	1.60

The average marginal tax rate for Niebuhr stockholders is 25%.

6. Assume that the corporate income tax rate is 50%.

(A) Assume that the cutoff rate for considering expansion projects is 15%. Prepare a schedule calculating (a) the annual cash flows from operations for PEP #12, (b) the present value of the net cash flows for PEP #12.

(B) Check the reasonableness of the cutoff rate. One of the factors to be considered is an estimate of the average cost of capital to this firm. Prepare a schedule to compute the average cost of capital weighted by the percentage of the capital structure which each element represents.

(C) a. Assume that the average cost of capital computed in item (B) is 9%. Prepare a schedule to compute the minimum return (in dollars) required on expansion projects to cover the average cost of capital for financing the sprinkler system and the landscaping in addition to expansion projects. Assume that it is necessary to replace the old machines.

b. Assume that the minimum return computed in item (C) is $150,000. Calculate the cutoff rate on expansion projects.

(AICPA adapted)

CHAPTER 16

Additional Complexities of Project Planning

Objectives

After studying this chapter, you should be able to do the following:

Define mutually exclusive *and* contingent projects *and discuss their effects on investment decisions.*

Describe the influence of capital rationing *on total investment strategy.*

Calculate the effects of different depreciation methods on investment decisons.

Discuss ways of modifying conventional capital budgeting to compensate for unequal project lives, risk and uncertainty, and income statement constraints.

Illustrate a network analysis *of a given project, describing the events and activities that lead to the* critical path *of the project's completion.*

TOTAL INVESTMENT STRATEGY

Chapter 15 implied that capital projects are evaluated independently of other projects. In most situations, investments reflect a global strategy. Thus, the range of alternatives considered feasible by management is limited to those expected to enhance managerial objectives or strategic plans. Furthermore, alternative proposals within the feasible set may be **mutually exclusive, contingent**, or constrained by a ceiling on available funds.

Mutually exclusive projects   In evaluating a group of investment proposals, it is important to determine whether the proposed projects are mutually exclusive. Two projects are said to be mutually exclusive if acceptance of one project will rule out acceptance of the other. For example, if a company is considering an investment in one of two computer systems, acceptance of one computer precludes the acceptance of the other. Two mutually exclusive proposals cannot be accepted.

Contingent projects   A contingent project is one that is inherently related to another project. Accepting one depends upon acceptance of the other. For example, a proposal to acquire a new computer also implies a proposal to acquire the software package of programs necessary to use the computer. Each depends on the other; both must be accepted. When an investment proposal is contingent on other proposals, the decision must explicitly recognize this relationship.

Capital rationing   **Capital rationing** implies that only a limited amount of funds is available for all investments during one time period. For most firms, potential capital investments are constrained by a yearly budget ceiling imposed by external financial considerations; therefore, firms facing capital rationing must attempt to select the combination of investment proposals that provides the greatest combined profitability.

For example, consider a firm that has the investment opportunities illustrated in Exhibit 16–1. These opportunities consist of seven projects costing $1,400,000 that are ranked in descending order of internal rate of return. If a budget ceiling limits the total dollar amount of outlays for the current budget period to $1,000,000, and the projects were neither exclusive nor contingent, a budget manager would select proposals in descending order of profitability, until the budget was exhausted. The first four proposals shown in Exhibit 16–1 total $1 million, and thus exhaust the limited capital budget. Therefore, the remaining proposals cannot be accepted, even though they may have internal rates of return that exceed the cost of capital. Capital rationing means that the proposed expenditures are limited by the budget ceiling regardless of the number of attractive investment opportunities available to the firm.

If any of these seven investment proposals are exclusive or contingent, the allocation of funds under capital rationing must be adjusted; that is, profitability alone is not a sufficient basis for allocating funds to individual projects. For

EXHIBIT 16–1 INVESTMENT OPPORTUNITIES

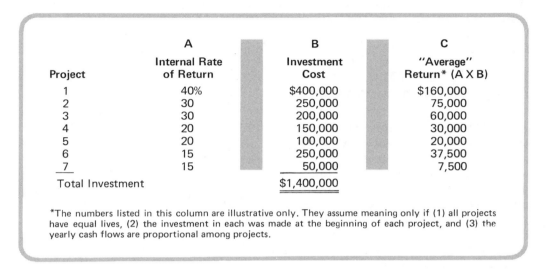

Project	A Internal Rate of Return	B Investment Cost	C "Average" Return* (A X B)
1	40%	$400,000	$160,000
2	30	250,000	75,000
3	30	200,000	60,000
4	20	150,000	30,000
5	20	100,000	20,000
6	15	250,000	37,500
7	15	50,000	7,500
Total Investment		$1,400,000	

*The numbers listed in this column are illustrative only. They assume meaning only if (1) all projects have equal lives, (2) the investment in each was made at the beginning of each project, and (3) the yearly cash flows are proportional among projects.

example, if Projects 2 and 3 are mutually exclusive, only one or the other would be chosen and that would probably be the one having the higher internal rate of return. By the same token, if Projects 3 and 4 were contingent on one another, excluding Project 3 because it was mutually exclusive to Project 2 automatically leads to rejecting Project 4. Contingent proposals should be grouped together under their common, average profitability and weighted by original cost outlays—instead of being listed as separate proposals. Only one listing should appear for contingent proposals.

Furthermore, capital budgeting of projects having discrete, fixed initial outlays under rationing may reorder desirability on a basis other than that of maximum project profit. For example, if the budget ceiling was fixed at $500,000, and the investment opportunities were those illustrated in Exhibit 16–1, the budget director would be able to invest the entire $500,000 in Projects 1 and 5; Projects 2, 3, and 7; or Projects 2, 4, and 5. Under this constraint, Projects 1 and 5 would yield a combined average return of $180,000, whereas Projects 2, 3, and 7 would yield a combined return of $142,500, and Projects 2, 4, and 5 would yield $125,000.

The combined profitability of Projects 1 and 5 is higher than that of any other set for which the total $500,000 budget could be allocated, even though Project 5 has a lower individual rate of return than Projects 2, 3, or 4. Under capital rationing, a profitability criterion implies a decision to select the combination of investment proposals that provides the highest combined profitability. This may entail accepting several smaller, less profitable, proposals to spend all budgeted funds rather than accepting more profitable proposals that leave part of the budgeted funds unallocated. Linear programming is a technique that allows a manager to consider the consequences of imposing constraints, such as limited capital, on total investment profitability. However, further discussion of linear programming is beyond the scope of this book.

CASH FLOW AND INCOME TAXES

The primary purpose of making an investment is to incrase or maintain the firm's level of profits. A firm's profitability does not increase by the full amount of additional income or cost savings resulting from an investment, since a substantial portion of this additional income must be paid to the government for additional income taxes. The net effect of any new investment can be seen only after additional taxes have been calculated.

A budgeting problem arises, however, because the "earnings" from an investment often are not identical to "additional profits subject to income taxes." Most firms take every advantage of tax options to minimize current tax payments by delaying or shifting as much taxable income as possible to future periods. Shifting taxable income implies accelerating tax-deductible expenses or delaying taxable revenues. Delaying taxable income delays tax payments, which will allow the taxpayer to reap the benefits associated with the time-value of money. A third tax-saving technique involves efforts to convert regular income into a form that is taxed at special rates, such as those applied to capital gains.[1]

The amount of taxes that must be paid in any period is dependent on (1) the timing of cash flows and (2) the amount of cash flows, as well as on the form of the business organization, the applicable tax rates, and the type of income being taxed. For the sake of simplicity, assume that the combined state and federal tax rates applicable to the problems discussed in this chapter are 55% of income.

Taxes and depreciation methods   Taxable income is the difference between revenues and expenses. Revenues are generally associated with the flow of funds (cash inflows or increases in accounts receivable); expenses can be subclassified into expenditures (cash outflows or increases in accounts payable) and amortized costs (depreciation). Both the fund and nonfund expenses decrease taxable profits, and hence, tax payments. That is, an allocated portion of original investment costs is a tax-deductible expense, even though no expenditure has occurred. Depreciation is often called a *tax shield* because it protects an equal amount of income from taxation.

[1]Probably the single most complicating factor in federal income taxation concerns "capital gains," which frequently result from the sale of assets acquired as feasible investment opportunities. Discussion of capital gains, however, is beyond the scope of this book.

To illustrate the tax-shield effect of depreciation, consider the following example:

The Cooper Printing Company is considering the purchase of a new press for $100,000. The press has an expected life of five years, after which it will have no measurable salvage value. Cooper's project engineer estimates that the press will generate additional cash savings of $60,000 per year. Cooper is in the 55% income tax bracket, when federal, state, and local taxes are considered.

Without considering depreciation, the expected yearly cash savings of $60,000 would be reduced by a $33,000 tax charge, leaving only $27,000 as the after-tax rewards for investing in the new press. But for every dollar of depreciation expense recognized in any year, the tax bill will be reduced by 55 cents. Cooper could shield the yearly tax payments by $11,000 if it recognized yearly depreciation of $20,000 under the straight-line method, which allocates the original cost evenly over the expected life. Thus, the annual tax bill would be $22,000 (.55 × $40,000), and the net after-tax cash flow would be $38,000 ($60,000 − $22,000). Other depreciation methods would produce after-tax cash flows of

EXHIBIT 16–2   FORMAT FOR DETERMINING AFTER-TAX FLOWS

Part I	Year 1	Year 2	Year 3	Year 4	Year 5
Expected cash revenues or yearly expenditure savings	$60,000	$60,000	$60,000	$60,000	$60,000
Minus Additional expenditures or revenues lost	—0—	—0—	—0—	—0—	—0—
Minus Additional depreciation or other noncash expense	20,000	20,000	20,000	20,000	20,000
Taxable Income	$40,000	$40,000	$40,000	$40,000	$40,000
Times Tax rate	.55	.55	.55	.55	.55
Tax expenditure	$22,000	$22,000	$22,000	$22,000	$22,000

Part II	Year 1	Year 2	Year 3	Year 4	Year 5
Net expected cash revenues or yearly expenditure savings	$60,000	$60,000	$60,000	$60,000	$60,000
Minus Tax expenditure	22,000	22,000	22,000	22,000	22,000
After-tax cash inflow	$38,000	$38,000	$38,000	$38,000	$38,000

EXHIBIT 16–3   NET PRESENT VALUE OF A PRINTING PRESS

Year	Amount	10% Discount Factor*	Present Value
0	($100,000)	1.0000	($100,000)
1	$ 38,000	.9091	34,546
2	38,000	.8264	31,403
3	38,000	.7513	28,549
4	38,000	.6830	25,954
5	38,000	.6209	23,594
Total In	$190,000		$144,046
Net In	$ 90,000		$ 44,046

*From Appendix B. All present values rounded. The present value of all inflows would equal $144,050 if calculated by using the factor found in the five-year, 10% column of the present-value-of-an-annuity table, Appendix C. The $4 difference represents accumulated rounding error.

different amounts, as discussed below under the heading "Tax shield and time-value of money."

Exhibit 16–2 depicts a format that can be used to determine the after-tax cash flows for any investment decision considered in this book. This format consists of two parts: (a) determining the yearly tax liability, and (b) determining the after-tax cash flows. This format can be modified to accommodate projects with long lives simply by increasing the number of columns. This format also can accommodate any depreciation method. (Alternate depreciation methods are discussed in the appendix to this chapter.)

Once the after-tax cash flows had been identified, a conventional net present value or internal rate-of-return analysis would be performed to evaluate the project. For example, assume that the Cooper Printing Company required a minimum of 10% time-adjusted rate of return on all projects selected for investment. The managerial accountant for Cooper would prepare an analysis similar to that appearing in Exhibit 16–3. Since this project has a positive net present value, Cooper Printing Company probably would invest in the new printing press.

EXHIBIT 16–4   INCREMENTAL TAX-SHIELD EFFECT OF DEPRECIATION

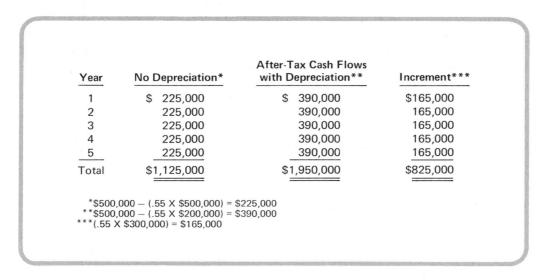

Year	No Depreciation*	After-Tax Cash Flows with Depreciation**	Increment***
1	$ 225,000	$ 390,000	$165,000
2	225,000	390,000	165,000
3	225,000	390,000	165,000
4	225,000	390,000	165,000
5	225,000	390,000	165,000
Total	$1,125,000	$1,950,000	$825,000

*$500,000 − (.55 X $500,000) = $225,000
**$500,000 − (.55 X $200,000) = $390,000
***(.55 X $300,000) = $165,000

Consider a second example: the Wilson Company is evaluating a project that costs $200,000, has a two-year life and no salvage value. The project generates cash inflows of $190,000 per year and will be depreciated at $100,000 per year. The tax rate is 55%. First, the tax payments would be determined by taking 55% of the difference between cash inflows and depreciation: .55 ($190,000 − $100,000) = $49,500. After-tax cash flows are determined by subtracting the taxes from the cash inflows: $190,000 − $49,500 = $140,500. Wilson would then calculate the net present value of the cash flows, and would use this information as a basis for making the investment decision.

Incremental effect of depreciation on cash flows   Depreciation is a tax-deductible expense solely because Internal Revenue regulations provide that depreciation may be deducted from revenue in the determination of taxable income. But tax regulations are subject to change: joint action by Congress and the president could eliminate or modify tax law regarding depreciation. While outright elimination of depreciation's tax-shield effect is extremely unlikely, other modifications are fairly common.

Depreciation is a very large element of business expense. In capital-intensive industries, depreciation may amount to 40% of all business expenses. Knowledge of the tax-shield effect of depreciation on cash flows provides business planners with useful insight. Incremental analysis highlights the tax consequences of depreciation. For example, consider the following case:

The Heavy Industry Company is considering the acquisition of a special-purpose machine that costs $1,500,000. The machine will have a five-year life and a zero salvage value. Net cash inflows (before taxes) of $500,000 will be generated by this machine each year. The Company is in the 55% tax bracket. What is the incremental benefit of the tax-shield effect of depreciation?

An answer to this question is reflected in Exhibit 16–4. If depreciation is ignored, net cash inflows would consist of the yearly $500,000, less the $275,000 yearly tax payments, yielding after-tax inflows of $225,000. If straight-line depreciation were deducted as a business expense, the $500,000 inflows would be reduced by $300,000 depreciation to produce a taxable income of $200,000. Taxes would amount to $110,000 at the 55% tax rate. Net after-tax cash flow amounts to $390,000 ($500,000 − $110,000). The incremental cash benefit resulting fom the tax-shield effect of depreciation is $165,000 per year, that is, *the incremental tax-shield effect of depreciation equals the yearly depreciation charge times the marginal tax rate.*

Tax shield and time-value of money　　Several depreciation methods can be used to calculate taxes. These include the *straight-line method*, the *sum-of-the-years'-digits method*, and the *double-declining balance method*. Each method produces a different pattern of yearly depreciation charges over the life of the asset. The straight-line method allocates the original cost of the asset evenly over its productive life, while the other two methods accelerate the depreciation charges by increasing the early amounts at the expense of latter charges. (See the appendix to this chapter for a more complete discussion of depreciation methods.)

The accelerated depreciation methods recognize more of the depreciation during the early life of the asset than does the straight-line method. For example, reconsider the Heavy Industry Company case, discussed above. Straight-line depreciation on the $1,500,000 press amounts to $300,000 per year. The sum-of-the-years'-digits method produces the following depreciation stream on the same asset: $500,000, $400,000, $300,000, $200,000, and $100,000. The total depreciation recognized over the life of the asset is identical for each method. Since the accelerated method front-loads the tax deductible expense, *the tax-shield effect of depreciation is recognized earlier and, hence, has a higher net present value.*

For example, assume that the Heavy Industry Company has a 20% cost of capital and is subject to a 55% tax rate. The net present value of the incremental tax benefit of accelerated depreciation is illustrated in Exhibit 16–5. Using sum-of-the-years'-digits depreciation (rather than straight-line depreciation) produces a $59,120 positive net present value, so the Company is substantially better off using the accelerated depreciation method. Using accelerated depreciation methods increases the available funds in the early years of the project's life at the expense of later flows. The flow of funds is constant under the straight-line method. Given a positive time-value of money, a project that is to be depreciated under an accelerated method would have a higher internal rate of return than the

EXHIBIT 16–5   PRESENT VALUE OF INCREMENTAL TAX SHIELDS, SYD VS. SL

Year	SYD* Depreciation	SL* Depreciation	Incremental Difference	Tax Shield	20% Factors	Present Value
1	$ 500,000	$ 300,000	$200,000	$110,000	.8333	$91,663
2	400,000	300,000	100,000	55,000	.6944	38,192
3	300,000	300,000	—0—	—0—	.5787	—0—
4	200,000	300,000	(100,000)	(55,000)	.4823	(26,526)
5	100,000	300,000	(200,000)	(110,000)	.4019	(44,209)
	$1,500,000	$1,500,000	—0—	—0—		$59,120

identical project depreciated under the straight-line method. Stated another way, use of accelerated depreciation increases the net present value of a project.

OTHER CONSIDERATIONS IN PROJECT PLANNING

A complete discussion of project planning requires much more space than is available in this volume. Three additional topics should be mentioned here, however, since they are relevant to current practice. These topics are: (1) the relationship between the **payback reciprocal** and the internal rate of return, (2) dealing with risk and uncertainty in project planning, and (3) the income-statement effects of capital projects.

Payback reciprocal   The payback reciprocal is calculated by dividing the average annual cash flows received from a project by the original investment cost. The payback reciprocal for a project having original costs of $20,000 and an average annual cash income of $4,000 is 20%. The payback period is five years and the payback reciprocal, 1 ÷ 5 years, equals 20%.

Whenever (1) the total cash outflow for the investment is made at the beginning of the life of the project, (2) all cash inflows from the project occur in equal amounts every year, and (3) the life of the project is at least twice as long as the payback period, the payback reciprocal closely approximates the internal rate of return. The internal rate of return is always some amount less than the reciprocal of the payback period, but under certain circumstances, it closely approximates this rate. Assuming a 10-year life on the project of our example, the internal rate of return would be 15%, which closely conforms to the 20% reciprocal of the payback. If the project has a twenty-year life, the internal rate of return increases to 19%, which is even closer to the payback reciprocal. On the other hand, if the project had only a seven-year life, then the internal rate of return falls to 9%, which poorly approximates the reciprocal.

Exhibit 16–6 presents a table showing the relationship between the payback reciprocal and the internal rate of return. If the initial investment were made at times other than at the inception of the project, or if subsequent investments have to be made, or if the cash returns are unequal each year, then the payback reciprocal cannot be used to approximate the internal rate of return.

The relationship between the payback period and the internal rate of return can best be explained in terms of the mechanics of solving a particular problem. The present value of an annuity table, Appendix C, contains lists of unique factors for each year (n) and each interest rate (r), predetermined according to a mathematically sound formula. These factors ordinarily are used to solve problems that require the determination of an unknown present value of a known future stream of cash flows for a known duration at a known interest rate. That is, the problem is stated:

$$\text{Present value} = \text{Future amount} \times \text{Factor}$$

Internal rate-of-return problems are solved by finding that unknown interest rate

EXHIBIT 16–6   PROJECT LIFE, PAYBACK RECIPROCAL, AND THE INTERNAL TIME-ADJUSTED RATE OF RETURN

PROJECT LIFE	Payback	3	4	5	6	7	8	9	10
	Reciprocal (%)	33	25	20	16	14	12	11	10
	Internal Rate of Return (%)								
4		13	0	0	0	0	0	0	0
5		20	8	0	0	0	0	0	0
6		24	13	5	0	0	0	0	0
7		27	18	9	4	0	0	0	0
8		29	19	12	7	3	0	0	0
9		30	20	14	9	5	2	0	0
10		31	21	15	11	7	4	2	0
15		33	24	18	14	12	9	7	6
20		33	25	19	16	13	11	9	8
25		33	25	20	16	14	12	10	9
30		33	25	20	16	14	12	11	9

which equates the present value of the known (annuity) inflows with the present value of the known original investment. That is, the amount of the factor is first determined by transposing the original problem into the form:

Factor = Present Value/Future Amount.

Note that the factor is exactly equal to the payback period, i.e., the original outflow divided by the yearly inflow. The internal rate of return is then found by entering the table in Appendix C along the row equal to the life of the project and searching for the table value that most closely approximates the payback factor. The internal rate of return is equal to the interest rate found at the head of the column containing the chosen factor. For example, consider a $20,000 investment that yields $5,000 per year for 30 years. The payback period is four years ($20,000/$5,000 = 4). Entering Appendix C along the 30-year (n) row, you will find the factors 4.1601 and 3.9950 in the 24% and 25% columns. The payback of four most closely approximate the amount found in the 25% column, i.e., the internal rate of return is 25%. This internal rate of return is also closely approximated by the payback reciprocal ($\frac{1}{4} = 25\%$).

Unequal project lives In the examples cited up to this point, we assumed that all investment proposals had equal project lives. Obviously, this assumption does not hold in most situations. To evaluate projects that have unequal lives, the analyst must artificially equate the projects by one of two methods: (1) consider only the cash flows for a period equal to the shorter life, or (2) consider a period equal to the longer life. Most analysts choose the latter alternative. In so doing, the analyst must assume that funds remaining after the life of the shorter project can be reinvested either at the rate the shorter project earned during its life, or at the rate of the company's minimum-desired rate of return.

These assumptions are implicit in the two techniques that consider the time-value of money. Implicit in the internal rate-of-return method is the assumption that funds reinvested from the shorter project (between its completion and the termination of the longer project) will earn the same rate that they earned while they were still invested in the shorter project. For example, if an analyst had the opportunity to invest $1,000 in a three-year project that yielded 20%, or in a six-year project that yielded 15%, and he used these internal rates of return as an index of profitability, he would choose the three-year project, as shown in Exhibit 16–7. But, inherent in his decision is the assumption that the funds recovered after the first three years could also be invested to yield 20%. Obviously, if the only investment opportunities open in the fourth year yielded 5%, the decision-maker would have violated the implicit assumption and would have invested in a combination of two short-term projects that have a smaller six-year yield than the six-year project. In other words, the internal rate-of-return method tends to overstate the true profitability of the shorter project whenever the reinvestment return is lower than the original return.

EXHIBIT 16–7   UNEQUAL PROJECT LIVES

Year	Project 1	Project 2
0	$(1,000)	$(1,000)
1	474	265
2	474	265
3	474	265
4		265
5		265
6		265
Unadjusted Net	$ 422	$ 590
Internal Rate of Return	20%	15%
Net Present Value (5%)	$ 289	$ 346

On the other hand, if the analyst used the net present value (at, say, a 5% time-value of money) of the two projects as an index of relative profitability, he would choose the six-year project because it appears to be more profitable. The net present-value method, however, tends to understate the true profitability of the shorter project whenever the time-value of money is lower than the reinvestment rate of return. If investment opportunities that yield a 20% return are available at the beginning of the fourth year, the decision-maker would have violated the implicit assumption of his analysis: the two three-year projects would, in fact, be more profitable than the six-year project. Obviously, the way to remedy the problem of implicit assumptions is to state explicity the reinvestment opportunities expected at the end of the shorter project. Once the reinvestment opportunities are specified, both the internal rate-of-return method and the net present-value method will yield similar indexes of profitability.

Risk and uncertainty   So far, we have treated both the dollar amounts and the dates of cash flows as if they were known with certainty. In most cases, neither the amount nor the timing of long-term future flows can be predicted confidently, although in some cases, either the amount or the timing is known. For example, the date of future payroll expenditures is usually known, since most companies establish fixed pay dates, although the exact amount of expenditures will be determined by the (unknown) amount of labor employed during the pay period. Or, the amount (price) of certain contracted purchase commitments may be known with certainty, although the timing may depend entirely on when the supplier delivers the materials.

As we have seen in Appendixes 3–B and 4–A, risk and uncertainty can be expressed as probabilities that an event will occur, and probabilities can be quantified on a 0.00 to 1.00 scale. The probability 0.00 indicates that the event will not occur, whereas a 1.00 probability indicates that the event will definitely occur. For example, consider the construction of a new smelter on a fixed-price contract basis in which the contractor indicates the probability of his completing the project within a certain amount of time.

Year of Completion	Probability of Completion	Expected (year) Value
3	.25	.75
4	.55	2.20
5	.15	.75
6	.05	.30
	1.00	4.00

The contractor implies that he really expects to complete the project in four years, but there is a 25% chance that it will be done in three years, and a very slight chance of 5% that the project may take six years. Since four years is the expected completion time, this value can be substituted in any capital-budgeting model for the previous "known" time.

Now, reconsider the example, but assume that the contract for the smelter was not on a fixed-fee basis. If the budgeted costs could be estimated as the following,

Dollar Costs	Probability of that Cost	Expected Value ($)
$1,000,000	.10	$ 100,000
1,200,000	.50	600,000
1,300,000	.30	390,000
1,400,000	.10	140,000
	1.00	$1,230,000

the expected cost of $1,230,000 could be substituted into any capital-budgeting model in place of the previous "certain" cost.

In other words, the risk and uncertainty inherent in predicting the amounts or the dates of long-run future flows can be explicitly recognized as long as the sum of the individual probability estimates adds up to 1.00 (certainty that the event will occur). If neither the dates *nor* the amounts are known with certainty, and the probability distributions are asymmetrical (as they were in our smelter example), then a more complicated procedure (not discussed here) should be used to consider the joint set of uncertainties.

Income statement constraints on project selection Capital-budgeting decisions must conform to the directions established by the strategic plans of the organization. Most business executives specify a profit objective as part of their strategic plans—they are concerned about the effects of a potential capital investment on their profit objective. But, the revenues and expenses of a capital investment may span many periods, and expenditures on the project usually occur well before any income can be derived. Thus, some executives impose an income statement constraint on investment decisions.

Most of the capital-budgeting techniques described so far do not consider the effect of a given proposal on the current earnings and future pattern of earnings that will be reported to stockholders. The importance of earnings, and especially earnings per share, to shareholders is well documented in the literature of financial accounting. Applying a single capital-budgeting model may produce a pattern of erratic earnings. If managers feel that stockholders prefer a stable pattern, or if they, themselves, prefer a stable pattern, then they may reject the ranking of proposals suggested by the capital-budgeting models.

For example, consider a case in which the project planner is extremely conscious of the current year's profits, and has $600,000 to invest, and the revenues, expenses, and so on for three proposals are as illustrated in Exhibit 16–8. Furthermore, suppose that any "uninvested" funds could be placed in insured savings accounts that yield 3% after taxes.

A summary of the investment opportunities faced by this project planner follows (x represents funds not allocated to Projects A, B, or C):

	Project			
	A	B	C	Bank
Initial Investment ($000)	100	300	200	x
First Year's Accounting Income	15	−20	30	.03x
First Year's Operating Cash Flow	40	40	130	.03x
Internal (time-adjusted) Rate of Return	30.4%	45.6%	13.5%	3%

Being sensitive to the first year's reported profits, the planner may reject Alternative B (which has a high total internal rate of return but a low first-year reported profit) in favor of investing in Projects A, C, and/or bank savings (which have a lower total internal rate of return but a higher first-year reported profit). Lerner and Rappaport hypothesize that many businessmen do make decisions in this manner.[2] They illustrate a linear-programming technique that explicitly considers profit constraints in investment strategies. Robichek and others expanded the model to include other constraints.[3] (Students interested in pursuing a linear-programming application beyond our discussion are referred to the latter source.)

[2]"Limit DCF in Capital Budgeting," *Harvard Business Review* (September/October, 1968), pp. 133–139.

[3]"Capital Budgeting: A Pragmatic Approach," *Financial Executive* (April 1969), pp. 26–38.

EXHIBIT 16-8 ALTERNATE INVESTMENT OPPORTUNITIES

Period 1	Investment 2	Revenues 3	Expenses 4	Depreciation 5	Operating Profit 6=(3-4-5)	Taxes-50% 7=.5(6)	Net Income 8=6-7	Operating Cash Flow 9=3-4-7
Project A*	100							
1		140	85	25	30	15	15	40
2		175	100	25	50	25	25	50
3		175	100	25	50	25	25	50
4		175	100	25	50	25	25	50
Project B**	300							
1		100	80	60	(40)	(20)	(20)	40
2		400	200	60	140	70	70	130
3		1100	600	60	440	220	220	280
4		900	400	60	440	220	220	280
5		1500	800	60	640	320	320	380
Project C***	200							
1		300	140	100	60	30	30	130
2		200	80	100	20	10	10	110

SOURCE: Adopted from Robichek, Ogilvie, Roach, *Financial Executive* (April 1969).

*Cost $100; first year's income $15; first year's cash flow $40; internal rate of return 30.4%.
**Cost $300; first year's income $20; first year's cash flow $40; internal rate of return 45.6%.
***Cost $200; first year's income $30; first year's cash flow $130; internal rate of return 13.5%.

TIMING OF CRITICAL EVENTS
IN PROJECT PLANNING

Network analysis is another budgeting technique useful in planning, scheduling, controlling, and analyzing projects. Two network approaches are commonly practiced, **PERT (Program Evaluation and Review Technique)** and **CPM (Critical Path Method)**. Both have common elements. Once a project is identified, a network analysis involves:

1. Dividing the project into discrete jobs, called *activities*.
2. Estimating the time required to complete each activity.
3. Developing explicit relationships among activities.
4. Analyzing the relationships to determine the effect on the total project's completion time of pursuing alternative paths among related activities.

Exhibit 16–9 illustrates a network consisting of four activities. Each activity starts and ends with an event (*node*, or a numbered circle) that represents a progress point. Activities link one event to another, occur within a certain amount of time, and require inputs of tangible or intangible resources. Each activity starts with one event and ends at another, and each event requires the completion of one or more activities. On typical network graphs, circles represent events, and arrows represent activities. The network illustrated in Exhibit 16–9 starts with the event shown as Node 1, and proceeds with a resource/time-consuming activity required to achieve the progress point (event) shown as Node 2. Node 3 indicates the initiation of an activity that helps achieve Event 4, when combined with the activity from Node 2. One final activity is required to achieve Event 5, which terminates the network. Note that the network illustrated could

EXHIBIT 16–9   A FIVE-EVENT, FOUR-ACTIVITY NETWORK

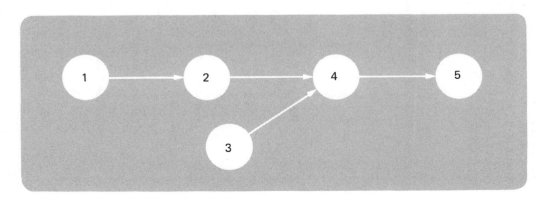

start with Event 1 or Event 3, but that Events 2, 4, and 5 cannot be achieved until some prior activity has been accomplished first.

PERT and CPM Two common network approaches are PERT (Program Evaluation and Review Technique) and CPM (Critical Path Method). Both techniques are concerned with the task's activities and the time required to accomplish each activity. Activities are measurable increments of work that can be related to physical production or some other indicator of progress. The total job is broken down into relatively short-term activities, rarely requiring more than a few months to complete. For PERT and CPM networks, the budgeting schedule shows: (1) estimates of the total time required to complete each activity, and (2) a description of the event, the physical output, or some other indication registering the successful completion of the activity. Both techniques were designed to plan and control the completion time of a project's specific activities.

A CPM (or PERT) network is best illustrated by an example. Consider a project to assemble a house. The CPM network would start with the first event, the blueprints, and work toward the completed project, the house. Required activities are added in sequence, event by event, until the house is completed. Assume that the activities required to build the house involve the physical and temporal inputs listed in Exhibit 16–10.

A CPM network of the activities required to build this house is illustrated in Exhibit 16–11. The time needed to accomplish each activity (arrow) is displayed above each activity. Note that certain events must be achieved before the next activity can be initiated. For example, the foundation must be poured before the carpenters start to assemble the wall frames; thus, the carpenters need not appear on the job site until (at least) the seventh day of construction. Similarly,

EXHIBIT 16–10 TIME INPUTS FOR ACTIVITIES

	Major Event		Major Activity	Time (man-days)
0.	Start (blueprints)	A.	Excavate basement	2
1.	Basement	B.	Lay foundation	5
2.	Foundation	C.	Assemble four walls	4
3.	Frame walls	D.	Assemble roof	3
4.	Roof	E.	Landscape grounds	2
5.	Grounds			

	Subevents		Subactivities	Time (man-days)
2a1.	Electrical units	a.	Install units	5
2a2.	Plumbing units	b.	Install units	3
3a1.	Interior siding	c.	Plaster	6
3a2.	Exterior siding	d.	Side	6

EXHIBIT 16–11   CPM NETWORK BUILDING A HOUSE

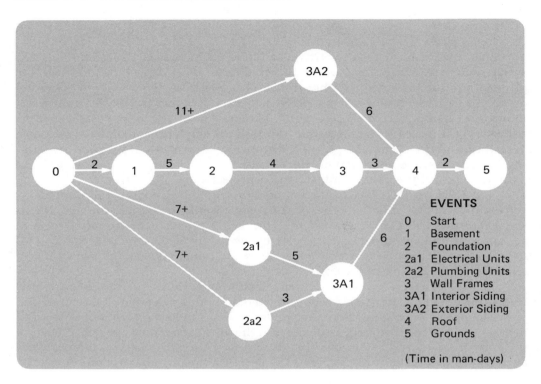

the plumbing units must be installed after the foundation is laid, but before the interior siding has been constructed. The *critical path* of any network displays the minimum completion time for the project: *the minimum completion time is the longest path through the network*. The trail of the critical path for this network requires about seven or more days before electrical units are installed, five days before interior siding is constructed, six days before the roofing is completed, and two more days for landscaping, or a minimum total of twenty days. This twenty-day schedule will be met only if the activities required to build the house are scheduled and performed as illustrated. If, for example, plumbers are scheduled to arrive at the site only after the electricians are completed with their tasks, the job will require an additional three days. The CPM network is useful because it is often easier to estimate the times required to do small tasks than to do larger projects, and the critical events or potential bottlenecks are highlighted.

PERT is a network technique similar to CPM, but it accounts for uncertainty explicitly. Three time estimates are made for each activity: optimistic, pessimistic, and most likely. Probabilities are attached to each estimate, so that the project planner can make probabilistic statements about the time required. Some PERT Networks incorporate input costs into their framework, and these are called *PERT Cost Networks*.

SUMMARY

This chapter discussed some additional constraints on project planning. Each project must be analyzed in relation to total investment strategy, and in relation to other projects (for example, are they mutually exclusive or contingent?) when the firm is faced with capital rationing. Further considerations include unequal project lives, risk and uncertainty, and the effects on income statements of individual projects. The cash-flow effect of alternate depreciation methods and the timing of critical events were discussed also.

APPENDIX: METHODS OF DEPRECIATION

Depreciation is the process of allocating the cost of a long-term productive asset over its economic life. As such, depreciation involves a reclassification of balances from assets to expenses, i.e., amounts that were previously included in the balance sheet asset classification subsequently appear in the income statement expense accounts. The depreciable amount of any fixed asset is limited to its book value. In no case can the sum of the yearly depreciation expense balances exceed the amount recognized as the cost of the asset. For example, the lifetime total for depreciation expense is limited to $1,500,000 for an asset that originally cost $1,000,000 but subsequently underwent an extensive $500,000 renovation. Ordinarily, this amount is reduced in recognition of salvage value expected upon disposal of the asset. That is, the depreciable amount for any fixed asset is limited to the cost minus the scrap value. If our $1,500,000 asset had an expected salvage value of $300,000, the depreciable portion would be limited to $1,200,000.

Straight-line (SL) depreciation   Straight-line depreciation allocates the depreciable costs of an asset equally over its economic life. The size of the yearly depreciation expense is determined by the following formula:

(Cost − Scrap Value)/Useful Life = Annual Depreciation Expense.

For example, an asset that cost $1,500,000, has a six-year life and a $300,000 salvage value will provide yearly depreciation of $200,000 ($1,200,000/6 = $200,000).

Sum-of-the-years'-digits (SYD) depreciation   The SYD method accelerates recognition of depreciation expense during the early life of the asset. That is, more expense is recorded in the first half of the asset's life than in the second half. To calculate SYD, the years of the asset's life are listed in consecutive order from 1 to n, and then totaled. The sum of the digits constituting the asset's life, S, can be quickly determined by the formula:

$$S = n(n + 1)/2$$

For example, an asset with a five-year life has an S (sum of digits) equal to $15 = 5 \times (5 + 1)/2$. The sum of digits is used as the denominator of a fraction which, when multiplied by the asset's depreciable cost, will determine the yearly depreciation expense. The numerator of the fraction is the digit for each year, taken in reverse order. The digits for a five-year life are 1,2,3,4, and 5. The numerator for the consecutive five years will be 5, 4, 3, 2, and 1. That is, the fraction of depreciable cost recognized as depreciation expense over a five-year period will be 5/15, 4/15, 3/15, 2/15, and 1/15. Thus, the stream of depreciation for a $1,500,000 asset with a $300,000 salvage value will be $400,000, $320,000, $240,000, $160,000, and $80,000.

Double-declining balance (DDB) depreciation   The double-declining balance method also accelerates the recognition of depreciation expense. *DDB does not consider salvage value* when determining depreciable cost. Of all methods, DDB depreciation produces the highest expense during the early life of the asset. To employ DDB, first calculate a fixed rate according to the formula:

$$\text{Rate} = 2/\text{useful life}$$

The rate for a five-year life is 40% ($2/5 = .4$). The yearly expense is found by multiplying the rate by the net book value of the asset (cost less accumulated depreciation). Net book value starts out equal to the original cost, but declines each year as the yearly depreciation accumulates. For a five-year, $1,500,000 asset, the first year's depreciation would amount to $600,000 ($1,500,000 × .4 = $600,000). The second year's depreciation is $360,000 ($900,000 × .4) and the remaining years' depreciation will be, respectively, $216,000, $129,600, and $77,760. Over the five-year period, $1,383,360 of the original $1,500,000 has been depreciated, a larger amount than would be depreciated under other methods that consider salvage. The remaining book value after five years is $116,640. This amount is lower than the book value remaining under methods that consider salvage value. Some users of DDB depreciation limit the depreciable amount so that book value does not dip below salvage value.

SUGGESTED READINGS

Hertz, D. "Risk Analysis in Capital Investment." *Harvard Business Review*, January/February, 1964.

Lerner, E., and A. Rappaport. "Limit DCF in Capital Budgeting." *Harvard Business Review*, September/October, 1968.

Robichek, A., D. Ogilvie, and J. Roach. "Capital Budgeting: A Pragmatic Approach." *Financial Executive*, April 1969.

Ross, W. "PERT/Cost Resource Allocation Procedure." *The Accounting Review*, July 1966.

Van Horne, J. *Financial Management and Policy.* 4th ed. Englewood Cliffs, N.J. Prentice-Hall, 1977.

QUESTIONS

16-1 What are *mutually exclusive projects*? Cite an example. How should mutually exclusive projects be dealt with when constructing the total investment strategy for a firm?

16-2 What are *contingent projects*? Cite an example. How should contingent projects be dealt with when setting the total investment strategy for a firm?

16-3 Do contingent projects raise any problems for the capital budgeter who has unlimited funds for investment purposes?

16-4 Critical operations of a system are often duplicated to provide backup support in emergencies. For example, aircraft usually have reserve oxygen systems, and hospitals have reserve electrical systems. Should these redundant or backup systems be treated as if they were mutually exclusive projects?

16-5 What events in the business world create the need for establishing a ceiling or maximum amount available for investments? Is it likely that investment possibilities may have a total expected cost greater than the budgeted ceiling? Under what conditions would the capital planning department recommend that the amount to invest should be lower than the budgeted ceiling?

16-6 "Investment planners should consider only relevant costs, that is, those future costs that will be different for each alternative. Since taxes must be paid in all cases, they are not relevant and should be ignored." Discuss this statement.

16-7 "In and of itself, depreciation is not a relevant consideration for capital budgeting. However, depreciation acts as a tax shield, and this is relevant for capital budgeting." Explain the "tax-shield" effect of depreciation. Do you agree with the statement?

16-8 Several depreciation methods are available for calculating income taxes. Each produces a different stream of after-tax cash flows. Which method should the capital budgeter use when evaluating investment proposals?

16-9   How does a budget committee determine the upper limit or ceiling for capital investments? What internal and external factors are most pertinent to this decision?

16-10   Assume that your company invested $150,000 for a machine that has a five-year life and no salvage value. The company has a 20% time-value preference for money. What is the net present value of tax savings, (assuming a 55% tax rate) resulting from using the sum-of-the-years'-digits method, rather than the straight-line method?

16-11   Sum-of-the-year'-digits and double-declining balance are two depreciation methods allowed for tax purposes. Calculate the yearly charges under each method that would result from acquiring a $300,000 machine that had a five-year life and a salvage value of $90,000. Which method provides the best tax shield? Why?

16-12   Your organization wishes to acquire an asset for $200,000 that is expected to produce cash savings of $50,000 each year for 16 years. The asset will have a zero salvage value at the end of its life. Your boss tells you to determine the time-adjusted internal rate of return on this project, and suggests that you start by calculating the payback reciprocal. Calculate the payback reciprocal and the internal rate of return.

16-13   What is the relationship between the payback reciprocal and the time-adjusted internal rate of return? Under what conditions will this relationship hold?

16-14   State the payback reciprocal and the internal rate of return for each of the following cases: (A) a project having a seven-year life and a three-year payback, (B) a project having a ten-year life and a four-year payback, (C) a project having a fifteen-year life and a six-year payback.

EXERCISES

16-15   An investor can acquire one of two machines, the first of which costs $10,000 and will produce cash savings of $2,000 each year for ten years, the second costs $15,000 and will save $4,500 for five years. Which project has the higher net present value, assuming a 10% time-value preference for money? Which project has the higher time-adjusted internal rate of return? What additional information does the investor need before he can make a choice?

16-16   Both the net present-value method and the time-adjusted internal rate-of-return method implicitly assume something about the reinvestment for earnings from projects that have unequal lives. What does each method assume?

16-17   An investor with a 10% time-preference for money is considering a project that costs $30,000 but has uncertain earnings. It has been estimated that the project has a five-year life and will yield yearly cash flows of $7,000 with a .10 probability, $8,000 with a .70 probability, and $9,000 with a .20 probability. What is the expected net present value of the project?

16–18 An investor with a 10% time-preference for money is considering a project that costs $7,000 but has an uncertain life. It has been estimated that the project will produce yearly cash savings of $2,000 and that it will last for five years with a .10 probability, six years with a .60 probability, and seven years with a .30 probability. Should the investment be made? If the investor's time preference were 20%, should the investment be undertaken?

16–19 "Since an income statement for financial-accounting purposes is constructed according to generally accepted accounting principles (which advocate allocating sunk costs or depreciation to each year's income), whereas capital budgeting considers only relevant costs, the two have nothing in common and ought not to influence each other." Discuss.

16–20 Can income statement constraints be used as criteria in evaluating investment proposals? If so, how?

16–21 What do the letters *PERT* and *CPM* stand for? What is a *node*? What are *events* and *activities*, and how do they relate to network analysis?

16–22 Consider a network for the assembly of a bicycle, given the following activities: (1) open box and read directions, (2) put on front wheel, (3) put on handlebars and seat, (4) put on back wheel, (5) put on chain, and (6) put on brake. Activities (1), (2), (3), and (4) can be done in any order, but (5) must follow (4), and (6) must follow (5).

    (A) Draw a graph of the network.

    (B) If each of the six activities takes five minutes to complete, and up to six people are available to work on the bicycle, what is the minimum time (critical path) required for assembly?

    (C) If there is a .20 probability that each event will require five minutes, a .60 probability that it will require eight minutes, and a .20 probability that it will require ten minutes, how long will it probably take two men to complete the critical assembly of the bicycle? Draw a PERT network of your solution.

16–23 Cope is considering an investment in a machine that has a four-year life and costs $100,000. Cope has a 60% tax rate, and wants to determine the present value of the incremental tax-shield effect from using the sum-of-the-years'-digits method of depreciation rather than the straight-line method.

    (A) Determine the incremental NPV of the tax shield, given that Cope has a 10% time-value of money.

    (B) If having the machine will increase Cope's after-tax cash inflow by $60,000, what is the project's internal time-adjusted rate of return? In one sentence, describe how you determined this estimate.

16-24   You are considering an investment of $100,000 in a project that has a 10-year life. Your time-value of money is 20%, and your income tax rate is 60%.

(A) If after-tax cash flows per year equal $33,000, how long will the payback period be? What percentage will the payback reciprocal be? Should you accept or reject the investment? In one sentence, state your reason for accepting or rejecting this project.

(B) How much is the present value at 20% (.8333 factor) of the extra (incremental) tax shield from using sum-of-the-years'-digits depreciation rather than straight-line depreciation for a $100,000 machine that has a 10-year life, for the first full year that you have the machine? (Assume a 60% tax rate.) Which depreciation method would you use? Why (in one sentence)?

16-25   Consider an investment in a machine that costs $100,000 and has a four-year life. The machine will produce before-tax cash savings of $55,797 per year, and the tax rate is 40%. Use of the straight-line method of depreciation for tax purposes will produce a stream of $25,000 depreciation expense each year. Determine the internal time-adjusted rate of return on this project, after taxes.

16-26   An investor with a 12% cost of capital is considering a project that costs $5,000 but has an uncertain life. This project will produce $1,000 per year, and has a 0.6 probability of lasting five years, and a 0.4 probability of lasting ten years. What is the net present value of this project?

16-27   You are to consider an investment in a machine that costs $200,000 and has a four-year life. The machine will produce before-tax cash inflows of $100,000 per year. Your tax rate is 60%. You can use the stragiht-line method of depreciation for tax purposes (which produces equal $50,000 amounts), or you can use the sum-of-year-digits' method (which produces a stream of $80,000; $60,000; $40,000 and $20,000). Your decision rule is as follows: If the net present value of tax savings resulting from use of SYD is at least $5,000, you will use this method; otherwise you will use SL. How much will you save by using SYD depreciation, assuming you have a 16% time-value of money?

16-28   An investor is considering a project that costs $24,000, but has uncertain annual returns (inflows). This project will produce $5,000 with a probability of 0.8 or $10,000 with a probability of 0.2. How long is the payback period on this project?

16-29   Copen Company has a machine that it purchased for $50,000 three years ago. The useful life of the machine was estimated at ten years, after which it would have a zero salvage value. Yearly depreciation amounts to $5,000, so the current book value of the machine is $35,000. However, if the machine were traded in, it would be granted an allowance for $20,000. The annual cost to produce 30,000 units of output is $95,000, *including $5,000 of depreciation*. A new machine can be purchased for $40,000 plus the old machine. It will have a life of seven years, have a zero salvage value, and produce 30,000 units of output at an annual cost of $89,500, *including $5,714 of depreciation* ($40,000 ÷ 7).

(A) In this case, what is the dollar amount of the *sunk cost*?

(B) If the new machine is acquired, will Copen be better or worse off? By what amount?

16-30 Ajax Inc., has decided to acquire a new piece of equipment, which can be purchased for an outright cash payment of $125,000. The full purchase price can be borrowed from a bank at 12% annual effective interest and could be repaid in one payment at the end of the fifth year. It is estimated that having this equipment will increase before-tax cash inflows by $50,000 per year. The estimated useful life of the equipment is five years, after which time it can be sold to salvage dealers for $25,000. Ajax uses the straight-line depreciation method for corporate reasons; and it is subject to a 60% annual income tax rate.

(A) The after-tax payback period is how many years?

(B) What is the estimated time-adjusted internal rate of return?

(C) Determine the net present-value of this project at 12%.

16-31 Below are four independent cases in which all cash inflows take the form of annuities. One lettered item of information is missing for each case. Determine the number associated with each letter.

	Case 1	Case 2	Case 3	Case 4
Yearly cash inflow	$ 2,000	$ 3,000	C	$4,000
Number of years	14	B	26	10
Interest rate	A	12%	16%	13%
Original investment cost	$10,016	$12,334	$61,182	D

16-32 James Hardy considered himself a very successful plant manager. His plant always produced more efficiently than any other in the company, although at a higher cost. Hardy's success stemmed directly from his phenomenal ability to secure capital improvements. His system was simple: if the desired improvement didn't generate an internal rate of return high enough to warrant its acquisition, the total improvement was divided into small pieces until one was found that did have an acceptable return. Then, once this item was purchased, the company was committed to purchasing all other parts.

(A) Is Jim's method good for the company? Is it good for Jim?

(B) What could a project approval (capital-budgeting) committee do to stop this practice?

(C) Should the other plant managers adopt Jim's "successful" method?

16-33 Individual businesses are free to choose any depreciation method they wish. Once a method has been selected, however, changing to another method of depreciation is considerably more difficult. Given that a new machine is to be purchased for $100,000, that it has a salvage value of $20,000, and a four-year life, respond to the following questions.

      (A) Compute straight-line, sum-of-the-years'-digits, and double-declining balance yearly depreciation charges for the machine.

      (B) What factors should be considered before deciding on a specific depreciation method?

      (C) The next two years should be banner years with high profits for this company. Should this additional information have any effect on the decision to choose a particular depreciation method?

16–34 Problem 16–33 took no explicit consideration of income taxes. Consider that the corporation is in the 60% tax bracket and that the machine is expected to produce cash savings of $50,000 each year for the next four years.

      (A) Compute the tax payments over a four-year period, assuming that each of the three depreciation methods is used.

      (B) Compute the after-tax cash flows over a four-year period for all three methods.

      (C) Calculate a discounted internal rate of return for this project under both the straight-line and sum-of-the-years'-digits methods. Is the difference between these rates solely attributable to depreciation methods?

16–35 The Collins Company is considering purchasing a new press, and management is interested in its net present value, assuming the press lasts five years. The press will cost $50,000 and is expected to have a salvage value of zero. The Collins Company is in the 40% tax bracket. The project engineer projected additional cash savings of $20,000 a year as a result of purchasing the press. Management uses a 16% time-value of money.

      (A) What is the net present value of the press under straight-line depreciation?

      (B) What is the net present value of the press under double-declining balance?

      (C) Why is there a difference in present values between the two methods?

      (D) What factors must be considered other than net present value in selecting a depreciation method?

16–36 The Cooper Company purchased a foot-forming machine for their boot factory. The foot-forming machine had an estimated useful life of 12 years. The original outlay for the machine was $40,000, and another $10,000 was expended on installation charges. The production engineer assures management that the machine will earn $10,000 per year for Cooper as long as it runs.

(A) What is the payback reciprocal for the foot-forming machine?

(B) What information does this figure supply the decision-maker?

(C) What assumptions underlie the use of the payback reciprocal?

(D) If the payback reciprocal simply approximates the discounted internal rate of return, why not compute this figure instead of the payback reciprocal? Calculate the internal rate of return on the machine.

16–37   The Keene Company uses the payback reciprocal as an approximation of the discounted internal rate of return. The projects evaluated have lump-sum initial costs but few continuing costs, and the return from the projects is an even flow throughout each project's life.

(A) Project Z, a machine that will last 15 years, will produce annual cash income of $2,000 on an original investment of $20,000. Is the payback reciprocal a good approximation of internal rate of return for this project? Why?

(B) Project X, a large press that should last 20 years, will produce $5,000 annually on an initial investment of $25,000. What can you say about the internal rate of return on this project?

(C) If Project X had a useful life of 10 years, would this alter your answer to part (B)? Explain.

16–38   The Cobb Corporation has two projects to evaluate. Both projects will cost $25,000. The first concerns a tire-forming machine that will return $10,000 for the three years of its useful life. The second project is for a zinc die-cast machine that will produce $7,000 over five years.

(A) Compute internal rate of return for both projects.

(B) What assumptions must be made to evaluate projects having unequal lives?

(C) Compute two alternate present values for each project, assuming a 10% time-value of money and that (1) reinvestments of returns from the tire machine will continue to return $10,000 each year for the fourth and fifth years, or (2) reinvestments will earn only 10% for the fourth and fifth years.

16–39   The Slayton Corporation needs a custom-made drill press, and only one company in the United States makes such a press. The president of the custom drill press firm has already made his fortune and pursues business as a hobby. He has just encountered some unexpected business problems and now refuses to give a firm date for completion of the drill press. He says, "There is a chance that it will be done next year. I think, though, that it will be done in two years, but it could take three, or at the outside, four." His son-in-law translated the old man's words by saying that "a chance" means 10%, "he thinks" means

70%, "could take" means 15%, and "at the outside" means about a 5% chance that it will take that long.

> (A) What year should the Slayton Corporation use for analysis? Show your computation.
>
> (B) As the analyst for Slayton, which would you prefer, the statement made by the president or a straight estimate of three years made by the son-in-law? Why?
>
> (C) Are all estimates really just probabilities? Discuss.

16–40 Planners for the Ajax Company prepared the following network. The network blueprints the six events after the start at Node 0 needed to complete Project X, and the number of man-days of labor needed to accomplish each event.

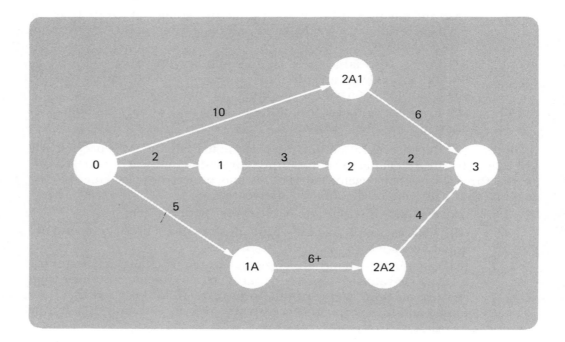

> (A) The network could be completed in how many days?
>
> (B) Which events must be completed before Event (2A2) can be started?
>
> (C) What does the + signify in the notation "6+" between (1A) and (2A2)?
>
> (D) What advantages does such an analysis have in project evaluations?

16–41 A construction company has contracted to complete a new building and has asked for assistance in analyzing the project. Using the Program Evaluation Review Technique (PERT), the following network has been developed.

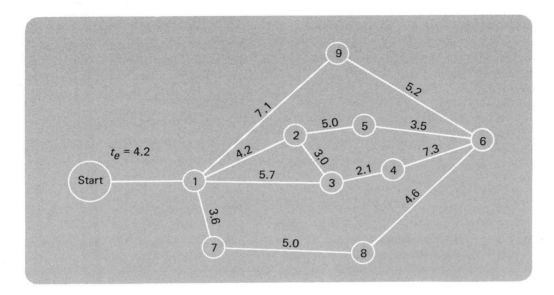

All paths from the start point to the finish point, Event 6, represent activities or processes that must be completed before the entire project, the building, will be completed. The numbers above the paths or line segments represent expected completion times for the activities or processes. The expected time is based upon three estimates. For example, the three estimates give an estimated time of 4.2 to complete Event 1.

(A) Identify the critical path (the path requiring the greatest amount of time) for this network.

(B) Slack time is the difference between one path and the critical path. Determine the slack time for Path 1-9-6.

(C) Determine the latest time for reaching Event 6 via Path 1-2-5-6.

(D) What is the earliest time for reaching Event 6 via Path 1-2-5-6?

(E) Redetermine the critical path, based upon a new time budget that projects an additional 1.9 time for Path segment 7-8.

(AICPA adapted)

PROBLEMS

16–42 The Beta Corporation manufactures office equipment and distributes its products through wholesale distributors.

Beta Corporation recently learned of a patent on the production of a semi-automatic paper collator that can be obtained at a cost of $60,000 cash. The semi-automatic model is vastly superior to the manual model that the Corporation now produces. At a cost of $40,000, present equipment could be modified to accommodate the production of the new semi-automatic model. Such modifications would not affect the remaining useful life of four years or the salvage value of $10,000 that the equipment now has. Variable costs, however, would increase by one dollar per unit. Fixed costs, other than relevant amortization charges, would not be affected. If the equpment is modified, the manual model cannot be produced.

The current income statement relative to the manual collator appears as follows:

Sales (100,000 units @ $4)		$400,000
Variable costs	$180,000	
Fixed Costs*	120,000	
Total Costs		$300,000
Net Income before income taxes		$100,000
Income taxes (40%)		40,000
Net income after income taxes		$ 60,000

*All fixed costs are directly allocable to the production of the manual collator and include depreciation on equipment of $20,000, calculated on the straight-line basis with a useful life of 10 years.

Market research has disclosed three important findings in relation to the new semi-automatic model. First, a particular competitor will certainly purchase the patent if Beta Corporation does not. If this were to happen, Beta Corporation's sales of the manual collator would fall to 70,000 units per year. Second, if no increase in the selling price is made, Beta Corporation could sell approximately 190,000 units per year of the semi-automatic model. Third, because of the advances being made in this area, the patent will be completely worthless at the end of four years.

(A) Prepare a schedule that shows the incremental after-tax cash flows for the comparison of the two alternatives. Assume that the corporation will use the sum-of-the-years'-digits method for depreciating the costs of modifying the equipment.

(B) If Beta Corporation, has a cost of capital of 18%, should it manufacture the semi-automatic collator? Use the net present-value decision rule and assume that all operating revenues and expenses occur at the end of the year.

(C) Calculate the accounting rate of return for each project. Using this method, would you recommend Beta manufacture the semi-automatic collator? Explain.

(D) What additional analytical techniques, if any, would you consider before presenting a recommendation to management? Why?

(E) What concerns would you have about using the information, as given in the problem, to reach a decision in this case?

(CMA adapted)

16–43   The Baxter Company manufactures toys and other short-lived fad-type items.

The research and development department came up with an item that would make a good promotional gift for office equipment dealers. Aggressive and effective effort by Baxter's sales personnel has resulted in almost firm commitments for this product for the next three years. It is expected that the product's value will be exhausted by that time.

In order to produce the quantity demanded, Baxter will need to buy additional machinery and rent some additional space. It appears that about 25,000 square feet will be needed; 12,500 square feet of currently unused, but leased, space is available now. (Baxter's present lease with 10 years to run costs $3.00 a foot.) There is another 12,500 square feet adjoining the Baxter facility which Baxter will rent for three years at $4.00 per square foot per year if it decides to make this product.

The equipment will be purchased for about $900,000. It will require $30,000 in modifications, $60,000 for installation, and $90,000 for testing; all of these activities will be done by a firm of engineers hired by Baxter. All of the expenditures will be paid for on January 1, 19X3.

The equipment should have a salvage value of about $180,000 at the end of the third year. No additional general overhead costs are expected to be incurred.

The following estimates of revenues and expenses for this product for the three years have been developed.

	19X3	19X4	19X5
Sales	$1,000,000	$1,600,000	$800,000
Material, labor and incurred overhead	400,000	750,000	350,000
Assigned general overhead	40,000	75,000	35,000
Rent	87,500	87,500	87,500
Depreciation	450,000	300,000	150,000
	$ 977,500	$1,212,500	$622,500
Income before tax	$ 22,500	$ 387,500	$177,500
Income tax (40%)	9,000	155,000	71,000
	$ 13,500	$ 232,500	$106,500

(A) Prepare a schedule that shows the incremental, after-tax, cash flows for this project.

(B) If the company requires a two-year payback period for its investment, would it undertake this project? Show your supporting calculations clearly.

(C) Calculate the after-tax accounting rate of return for the project.

(D) A newly hired business school graduate recommends that the company consider the use of the net present-value analysis to study this project. If the company sets a required rate of return of 20% after taxes, will this project be accepted? Show your supporting calculations clearly. (Assume that all operating revenues and expenses occur at the end of the year.)

(CMA adapted)

16–44   The Apex Company is evaluating a capital-budgeting proposal for the current year. The relevant data follow:

The initial investment would be $30,000. It would be depreciated on a straight-line basis over six years with no salvage. The before-tax annual cash inflow due to this investment is $10,000, and the income tax rate is 40% paid the same year it is incurred. The desired rate of return is 15%. All cash flows occur at year end.

(A) What is the after-tax accounting rate of return on Apex's capital-budgeting proposals?

(B) What is the after-tax payback reciprocal for Apex's capital-budgeting proposal?

(C) What is the net present-value of Apex's capital-budgeting proposal?

(D) How much would Apex have had to invest five years ago at 15% compounded annually to have $30,000 now?

(AICPA adapted)

16–45   Edwards Corporation is a manufacturing concern that produces and sells a wide range of products. The company not only mass-produces a number of products and equipment components but also is capable of producing special-purpose manufacturing equipment to customer specifications.

The firm is considering adding a new stapler to one of its product lines. More equipment will be required to produce the new stapler. There are three alternative ways to acquire the needed equipment: (1) purchase general-purpose equipment, (2) lease general-purpose equipment, (3) build special-purpose equipment. A fourth alternative, purchase of the special-purpose equipment, has been ruled out because it would be prohibitively expensive.

The general-purpose equipment can be purchased for $125,000. The equipment has an estimated salvage of $15,000 at the end of its useful life of 10 years. At the end of five years the equipment can be used elsewhere in the plant or be sold for $40,000.

Alternatively, the general-purpose equipment can be acquired by a five-year lease for $40,000 annual rent. The lessor will assume all responsibility for taxes, insurance, and maintenance.

Special-purpose equipment can be constructed by the contract equipment department of the Edwards Corporation. While the department is operating at a level that is normal for the time of year, it is below full capacity. The department could produce the equipment without interfering with its regular revenue-producing activities.

The estimated departmental costs for the construction of the special-purpose equipment are:

Materials and parts	$ 75,000
Direct labor	60,000
Variable overhead (50% of DL$)	30,000
Fixed overhead (25% of DL$)	15,000
Total	$180,000

Corporation general and administrative costs average 20% of labor dollar content of factory production.

Engineering and management studies provide the following revenue and cost estimates (excluding lease payments and depreciation) for producing the new stapler. The estimates depend upon the equipment used:

	General-Purpose Equipment		Self-Con-structed Equipment
	Leased	Purchased	
Unit selling price	$ 5.00	$ 5.00	$ 5.00
Unit production costs:			
Materials	$ 1.80	$ 1.80	$ 1.70
Conversion costs	1.65	1.65	1.40
Total unit production costs	$ 3.45	$ 3.45	$ 3.10
Unit contribution margin	$ 1.55	$ 1.55	$ 1.90
Estimated unit volume	40,000	40,000	40,000
Estimated total contribution margin	$62,000	$62,000	$76,000
Other costs:			
Supervision	$16,000	$16,000	$18,000
Taxes and insurance	—	3,000	5,000
Maintenance	—	3,000	2,000
Total	$16,000	$22,000	$25,000

The company will depreciate the general-purpose machine over 10 years on the sum-of-the-years'-digits (SYD) method. At the end of five years, the accumulated depreciation will total $80,000. (The present value of this amount for the first five years is $62,100.) The special-purpose machine will be depreciated over five years on the SYD method. Its salvage value at the end of that time is estimated to be $30,000.

The company uses an after-tax cost of capital of 10%. Its marginal tax rate is 40%.

(A) Calculate the net present-value for each of the three alternatives that Edwards Corporation has at its disposal.

(B) Should Edwards Corporation select any of the three options, and if so, which one? Explain your answer.

(CMA adapted)

16–46 Madisons, Inc., has decided to acquire a new piece of equipment. It may do so by an outright cash purchase at $25,000 or by a leasing alternative of $6,000 per year for the life of the machine. Other relevant information follows:

Purchase Price Due at Time of Purchase	$25,000
Estimated Useful Life	5 years
Estimated Salvage Value (if purchased)	$ 3,000
Annual Cost of Maintenance (contract to be acquired with either lease or purchase)	$ 500

The full purchase price of $25,000 could be borrowed from the bank at 10% annual interest and could be repaid in one payment at the end of the fifth year. Additional information:

1. Assume a 40% income tax rate and use of the straight-line method of depreciation.
2. The yearly lease rental and maintenance contract fees would be paid at the beginning of each year.
3. The minimum desired rate of return on investment is 10%.
4. All cash flows, unless otherwise stated, are assumed to occur at the end of the year.

Determine the following amounts:

(A) The present value of the purchase price of the machine.

(B) The present value of the estimated salvage value under the purchase alternative.

(C) The annual cash inflow (tax reduction) related to depreciation, under the purchase alternative.

(D) The annual after-tax cash outflow for interest and maintenance under the purchase alternative.

(E) The before-tax interest rate implicit in the lease contract, if salvage value is not ignored.

(AICPA adapted)

16-47 Amex Company is considering the introduction of a new product which will be manufactured in an existing plant; new equipment costing $150,000 with a useful life of five years (no salvage value) will be necessary. The space in the existing plant to be used for the new product is currently used for warehousing. When production of the new product takes over the warehouse space, on which the actual depreciation is $20,000, Amex Company will rent warehouse space at an annual cost of $25,000. An accounting study produces the following estimates of incremental revenue and expense on an average annual basis:

Sales	$500,000
Cost of Merchandise Sold (excluding depreciation)	385,000
Depreciation of Equipment (straight-line)	30,000
Marketing Expense	10,000

The Company requires an accounting rate of return of 11% (after income taxes) on average investment proposals. The effective income tax rate is 46%.

Determine the following amounts:

(A) The average annual incremental costs for the first five years (including income taxes), which must be considered in evaluating this decision.

(B) The minimum annual net income needed to meet the Company's requirement for this investment.

(C) The estimated annual residual income (after allowing for return on investment in new equipment) resulting from introduction of the new product.

(D) The estimated incremental cash flow during the third year.

(AICPA adapted)

16-48 Ben Johnson, head of the capital-budgeting department of BSO Manufacturing Company, identified seven projects with equal lives that seemed to be suitable candidates for investment. Each had a positive net present-value when discounted at BSO's minimum-required earnings rate. Ben ranked them in declining internal rate of return, as follows:

Project	Internal Rate of Return (%)	Investment Cost
1	45	$200,000
2	40	250,000
3	40	150,000
4	35	400,000
5	30	200,000
6	20	50,000
7	15	50,000

(A) If the budget ceiling were set at $800,000, which projects should be selected?

(B) If the ceiling were set at $700,000, which projects would be selected?

(C) If the budget ceiling were set at $750,000, and Projects 3 and 4 were mutually exclusive, which projects should be selected?

(D) If the budget ceiling were set at $750,000, Projects 4 and 5 were mutually exclusive, and Projects 3 and 7 were contingent, which projects should be selected?

16–49   Mr. A. B. Gale has an opportunity to undertake a five-year venture. At the beginning of the venture, Mr. Gale must invest $10,000 in current assets and $40,000 in fixed assets. At the end of the venture, the full $10,000 of current assets will be recoverable, however, the fixed assets have an expected cash value of only $5,000 at the end of the fifth year.

Revenues, expenses (excluding depreciation), and depreciation are expected to be as follows for each of the five years.

Year	Revenues	Expenses (excluding depreciation)	Depreciation
1	$100,000	$60,000	$7,000
2	$110,000	65,000	7,000
3	120,000	70,000	7,000
3	120,000	70,000	7,000
4	90,000	55,000	7,000
5	60,000	50,000	7,000

To take advantage of this venture, Mr. Gale will have to take a five-year leave of absence from his job, which pays him $10,000 per year. He will also have to liquidate certain investments that now yield a return of 10% after taxes. The federal income tax rate is 30%, and it is expected to remain 30% for the next five years.

Mr. Gale consulted an accountant about the feasibility of the project, and the accountant drew up the following schedules.

CALCULATION OF OPERATING CASH FLOWS

Year	1	2	3	4	5
Revenue	$100,000	$110,000	$120,000	$90,000	$60,000
Expenses (excluding depreciation)	60,000	65,000	70,000	55,000	50,000
Depreciation	7,000	7,000	7,000	7,000	7,000
Net Income Before Taxes	$ 33,000	$ 38,000	$ 43,000	$28,000	$ 3,000
Tax at 30%	9,900	11,400	12,900	8,400	900
Net Income After Taxes	$ 23,100	$ 26,600	$ 30,100	$19,600	$ 2,100
Add: Depreciation	7,000	7,000	7,000	7,000	7,000
Net Cash Flow after Taxes	$ 30,100	$ 33,600	$ 37,100	$26,600	$ 9,100

CALCULATION OF NET CASH FLOWS

	Outflows		Inflows		
Year	Investment	Lost Salary after tax	Operating	Recovery of Investment	Net
0	50,000		0		(50,000)
1		7,000	30,100		23,100
2		7,000	33,600		26,600
3		7,000	37,100		30,100
4		7,000	26,600		19,600
5		7,000	9,100	15,000	17,100

CALCULATION OF NET PRESENT VALUE

Year	Net Flow	PV Factors @ 10%	Present Value
0	(50,000)	1.000	$(50,000)
1	23,100	.909	20,997
2	26,600	.826	21,972
3	30,100	.751	22,605
4	19,600	.683	13,387
5	17,100	.621	10,619
	Net Present Value		$ 39,580

(A) Would you advise Mr. Gale to undertake the venture? State criteria by which you evaluated the decision.

(B) Are there any limitations on the analysis prepared by the accountant? Do techniques exist to overcome these limitations?

(C) Why wouldn't accrual accounting techniques be the best method of accumulating data for this decision?

(D) Assuming that you accept the idea that discounted cash flows are appropriate for investment decisions, how might the following items be relevant to an investment decision?

   a. Book value of present facilities
   b. Salvage value of present and proposed facilities
   c. Depreciation on present and proposed facilities
   d. Accelerated depreciation versus straight-line depreciation

CHAPTER 17

Accounting Data for Inventory Management

Objectives

After studying this chapter, you should be able to do the following:

Describe the interrelationships between sets of the following inventory management data: number of orders, order quantity, average balance in inventory, average usage per day, and number of days per order.

Identify the purposes for holding inventory balances. Contrast these purposes with those that relate to the maintenance of safety stocks.

Determine the reorder point and the economic order quantity from a given set of case data.

List the major assumptions embodied in an EOQ calculation and discuss the consequences of violating these assumptions.

Describe common accounting procedures used to monitor inventory balances and reorder points.

Inventories are an essential element in the production process for most manufacturing organizations. Manufacturers usually maintain three types of inventories: raw materials, work in process, and finished goods. Raw materials are the basic elements of production acquired from external suppliers. Work-in-process inventories represent the partially completed products found within the factory at any particular time. Finished goods are completed outputs awaiting sale and shipment to customers. Each type of inventory provides continuity to operations and reduces the risks associated with changes in production or sales activities: inventory balances can shrink or swell to accommodate many unforeseen contingencies, such as shipping delays by suppliers, raw material shortages, equipment malfunctions, strikes, or unanticipated accelerated sales.

INVENTORY MANAGEMENT

Inventories represent a major class of assets for most manufacturing companies. Large inventory balances require a significant investment of funds, so most companies establish policies for the management of inventories. On the basis of these policies, comprehensive budgets can be developed to specify the desired ending balance of raw materials, work in process, and finished goods for the budget period, as well as for the inflow and outflow activities associated with those inventories.

Some of the elements considered in establishing inventory management policies are discussed in this chapter. Inventory management policies usually include the following considerations:

1. Conflicting opinions about specific inventory policies may be advocated by management in the functional areas of finance, sales, production scheduling, and purchasing. Other conflicts can result from the relationships among inventory balances or activities, e.g., the number of orders for raw material placed per year is related to the yearly production demand for raw materials, the average balance of raw materials on hand, and the daily usage. Unresolved functional or operational conflict will hamper the attainment of inventory management goals.

2. The answer to the question, "When should a new order be placed?" is based upon many assumptions. These assumptions must be specified, and the interrelationships among them identified before establishing inventory management policy. Due concern must be given to the maintenance of adequate stocks.

3. Cost-accounting records and procedures should facilitate inventory management policy. Specific accounting issues of relevance to inventory management include the ABC classification method, the per-

petual inventory method, and methods for approximating periodic inventory balances.

4. The costs associated with managing inventories must be estimated. Any policy must be cost-justified, in the sense that the benefits from implementing the policy should be greater than the costs. Among inventory management policies that must be cost-justified is one concerned with the optimum-size inventory order, or the economic order quantity.

BASIC INVENTORY MANAGEMENT RELATIONSHIPS

This section first considers the diverse inventory needs and concerns of four managerial functions. Next, the relationships between inventory balances and related activities are described.

Functional inventory concerns   Sales managers typically are interested in customer service. This concern is expressed in a desire to have ample stocks of all products available to satisfy potential customer demand immediately. Large and balanced inventories of finished goods are desired by the sales department, to satisfy such demand and to enable them to accept special sales orders without qualm. In contrast, the production manager desires long production runs with few new set-ups, a policy that implies unbalanced finished-goods inventory, that is, large stocks of newly run products and depleted stocks of soon-to-be run products. This production policy builds unbalanced work-in-process and raw materials inventories. The production manager might demand expedited rush orders of raw material purchases to maintain inputs needed for production of special expedited sales orders. The purchasing department desires a flexible policy that allows it to take advantage of quantity discounts, favorable freight rates, and bargain purchases. Special rush purchase orders are not viewed as desirable by the purchasing department. The financial officer wishes to minimize the funds invested in finished goods, work-in-process, and raw materials inventory. His financial policy favors small balances of inventories.

Proper inventory management of any firm must balance the different needs of each functional area. The ultimate policy will first consider the total organizational goals with respect to profitability and service policy and then shape the desires of each functional area into conformance with these goals. If profit maximization is the organizational goal, the costs of alternative policies will be determined, and the policy with the lowest total cost will be adapted as the goal for each function.

Number of orders and order quantity   Inventory management is concerned with the size of inventories, the scheduling of orders, the order quantity, and the

EXHIBIT 17–1   YEARLY DEMAND, NUMBER OF ORDERS, AND ORDER QUANTITY

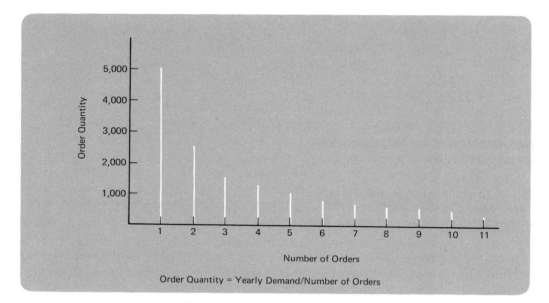

total inventory cost. The total scope of an inventory policy is influenced by the annual demand for the inventory items.[1] Together, the number of orders placed during the year and the annual demand determine the size of the average order, or the order quantity. For example, if the annual demand for raw material is 5,000 pounds, and if 10 orders are placed each year, then each order must equal 500 pounds. If the annual demand is 3,200 tons, and 5 orders are placed each year, then each order must equal 640 tons.

Exhibit 17–1 illustrates the relationship between the yearly demand, the number of orders, and the order quantity. The vertical axis measures the order quantity, while the horizontal axis measures the number of orders placed per year. If only one order is placed per year, then the order quantity must equal the yearly demand. If two orders are placed each year, the order quantity is one-half of the yearly demand. At four orders per year, the order quantity is one-fourth the yearly demand. The order quantity is determined by dividing the annual demand by the number of orders placed during the year.

Order quantity and the average balance in inventory   Stocks of inventory ordinarily are used up over time, e.g., raw materials are used for production and finished goods are delivered to customers. Assuming that inventory balances are

---

[1]Annual demand for raw materials is jointly determined by production and desired ending-inventory needs. Annual demand for finished goods is jointly determined by sales and desired ending-inventory needs. For further discussion, see Chapter 2.

EXHIBIT 17–2   ORDER QUANTITY, TIME, AND THE AVERAGE BALANCE IN INVENTORY

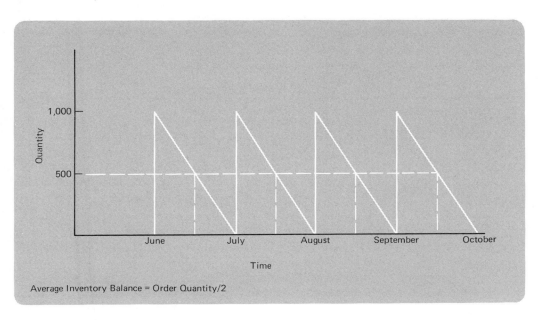

Average Inventory Balance = Order Quantity/2

fully depleted when a new order arrives, that inventories are used evenly over time, and that a second order will not be received until the first is depleted, then the relationship between order quantity and the average balance in inventory can be illustrated as in Exhibit 17–2.

The vertical axis of Exhibit 17–2 represents quantities of inventory, in units, while the horizontal axis represents time, in months. Assuming that annual demand is 12,000 units, and that 12 orders are placed each year, the order quantity will be 1,000 units. The average balance on hand during any one month can be determined by summing the beginning and ending balances and dividing the balance by 2:

$$\text{Average Balance} = (\text{Beginning} + \text{End})/2 = (1{,}000 + 0)/2 = 500.$$

Since the order quantity is 1,000, the *average balance is stated as one half of the order quantity*. An alternate view of the "average" balance examines the balance on hand at mid-month: the average balance in inventory still equals one-half of the order quantity. However, if six orders were placed during the year, the order quantity would be 2,000 (12,000/6 = 2,000), and the average inventory balance would be 1,000 (2,000/2). Exhibit 17–3 presents another illustration of the relationship between order quantity and the average balance in inventory. For any order quantity, the average balance is equal to one-half the order quantity.

EXHIBIT 17–3   ORDER QUANTITY AND THE AVERAGE BALANCE IN INVENTORY

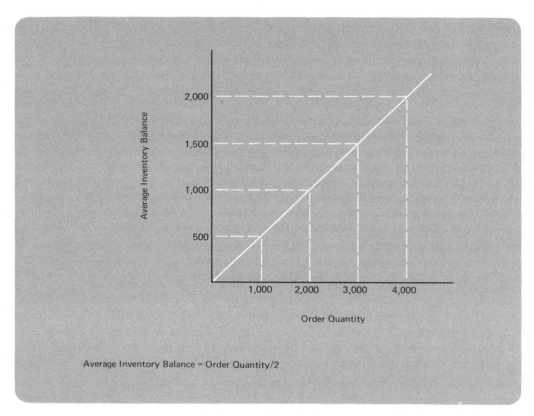

Average Inventory Balance = Order Quantity/2

Number of days per order   Knowledge of the basic relationship between order quantity, yearly demand, and the number of orders placed each year provides a basis for determining several other relationships. The number of days that an order will last can be determined by dividing the order quantity by the yearly demand and multiplying this product by the number of working days in a year. Since the order quantity divided by demand is nothing more than the reciprocal of the number of orders per year, the days per order can be determined by dividing the working days per year by the number of orders per year. For example, if 12 orders are to be placed every year, and there are 240 working days during the year, one order will last 20 days. If 12 orders are to be placed by a company that operates 360 days during the year, one order will last every 30 days.

Average usage per day   Another useful item of information is the *average usage per day*. Average usage per day can be determined by dividing the yearly demand by the number of working days per year. If a firm works 5 days a week for

50 weeks, and expects to use 5,000 pounds during the year, the average usage per day is 20 pounds. If the firm works 360 days and requires 320,000 pounds during the year, the average daily usage would be 889 pounds per day.

SAFETY STOCK

Safety stocks represent a balance of inventory above and beyond that intended for normal use. Safety stocks serve as a cushion or as insurance against unforeseen events. They are available for use whenever production demands exceed anticipated levels, or deliveries from suppliers extend beyond the expected arrival date.

The size of safety stocks reflects management's assessment of risks and costs associated with inventory deficiencies. Probabilities of delays (risk) often can be estimated from past experience. The consequences (cost) of using all inventory stocks include the costs of layoffs, plant shut-down costs, costs for expediting rush deliveries, costs for obtaining alternate sources of supply, or set-up costs to establish new production lines (runs). If delays affect potential customers, then the contribution margin from lost sales should also be considered a stock-out cost. On the other hand, excessive safety stocks create additional carrying costs for insurance, property taxes, handling costs, and obsolescence. The ultimate size of safety stocks must reflect managerial judgment about the trade-off between these competing elements.

DETERMINING THE REORDER POINT

The specific date or point of time in the inventory management schedule when an order must be placed so that it arrives on schedule is known as the *reorder point*. The reorder point is a function of three factors, including the size of the safety stock, the average usage per day, and the delivery time.[2] The first two of these factors have been discussed above. The delivery time represents management's best estimate of how long the shipments will be in transit between placing the order and receipt of the goods. Estimates of the delivery time may consider the supplier's normal or promised delivery schedule, or past experience with a particular shipper.

Determining the reorder point is a relatively simple task, once the three related parts are known. The reorder point is found by multiplying the average usage per day by the number of days delivery time required, and adding this product to the safety stock. The formula is:

Reorder Point = (Delivery Time × Average Usage Per Day) + Safety Stock

[2]Delivery time is also referred to as *lead time*.

EXHIBIT 17–4   DETERMINING THE REORDER POINT

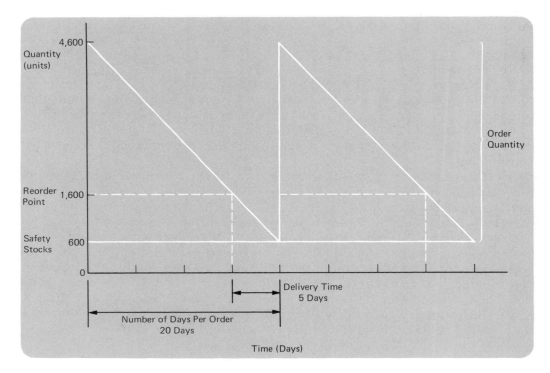

For example, consider a case where the safety stock is 600 units, the average usage per day is 200 units, delivery time is 5 days, and the order quantity is 4,000 units. The reorder point is 1,600 units, determined as follows: $(5 \times 200) + 600 = 1,600$ units.

The reorder point can be illustrated graphically, as in Exhibit 17–4. The vertical axis of Exhibit 17–4 represents quantities, in units, while the horizontal axis represents time, in days. Assuming that new orders arrive when the inventory level is down to the safety stock, the inventory balance will extend to 4,600 units after the new order arrives. This new balance shrinks at the rate of 200 units per day, given average usage. If an order is placed when the balance in inventory reaches 1,600 units, an additional 1,000 units will be consumed during the five days of delivery time. The inventory balance will be down to the safety stock when the new order arrives. Thus, the reorder point insures that desired inventory levels and safety stocks will be maintained.

In this example, if the delivery is delayed by one day, 200 units of safety stock will be consumed by production, i.e., the production process will not be interrupted. The new order will then increase the inventory balance to 4,400 units, which, in turn, will be consumed at the rate of 200 units per day. When the inventory balance reaches the 1,600 mark, a new order will be placed.

In some cases, it is best to view the delivery time as the quantity that will be consumed by production during delivery, rather than as a number of days. To derive this quantity, simply multiply the delivery time by the average daily usage. In the same fashion, the safety stock might be translated into a measure of days by dividing the safety stock by the average daily usage. For the example described above, the delivery time represents 1,000 units (5 × 200), and the safety stock represents 3 days (600/200).

ACCOUNTING PROCEDURES TO MONITOR INVENTORY BALANCES AND REORDER POINTS

Manufacturing inventories frequently list thousands of parts, pieces, and units in raw materials, work in process, and finished goods. Where the dollar value of these inventory items differ, management frequently employs different physical and accounting methods to monitor the inventory balances and reorder points. This section will describe the ABC method for segmenting inventories into three dollar classes and then discuss how perpetual and periodic inventory systems can be applied to the different classes.

The ABC method The ABC method classifies inventories into three groups, according to the relative magnitude of the dollar values of the annual amounts of inventory used by the organization. The ABC method requires that all inventory items be listed by identification number, cost per unit, average units used, and total cost, as shown in Exhibit 17–5, Part A. Next, the list is rearranged in rank order of total costs, with the highest total cost at the top of the list. Part B of Exhibit 17–5 presents the reordered list, ranked by total inventory costs, with two extra columns. Column 3 states the total cost of each inventory item as a percent of the total cost for all items, while Column 4 lists the ABC class. The ABC method requires that management specify boundaries for each of the three classes, A, B, and C. In the example, management specified that Class A should constitute 70% of total cost, Class B the next 20% of total cost, and Class C the remaining 10%. As can be seen in Exhibit 17–5, Class A represents only 4% of the number of units, even though it constitutes 77% of the total cost. Class B constitutes 23% of the total units, even though it represents 20% of the total cost. Class C, the largest class in terms of units, constitutes the smallest percent of total cost. Ordinarily, the ABC system assigns those items with a large dollar volume of usage to the A classification, and diminishing dollar volumes of usage to Classes B and C.

Each class of inventory organized under the ABC method is accorded different treatment by management. Since Class A represents the largest dollar

EXHIBIT 17–5   ABC INVENTORY LISTING

Part A

Item	Cost/Unit	Yearly Usage	Total Cost
XN120	$ 10.00	4,000	$ 40,000
XN121	.05	30,000	1,500
XN122	1.50	6,000	9,000
XN123	40.00	3,000	120,000
XN124	2.50	8,000	20,000
XN125	2.00	11,000	22,000
XN126	.15	36,000	5,400
XZ983	200.00	1,000	200,000
Totals	—	99,000	$417,900

Part B

Item	Costs	% of Total Costs*	ABC Class	% of Total Units
XZ983	$200,000	48	A	1
XN123	120,000	29	A	3
XN120	40,000	10	B	4
XN125	22,000	5	B	11
XN124	20,000	5	B	8
XN122	9,000	2	C	6
XN126	5,400	1	C	37
XN121	1,500	0	C	30
	$417,900	100%		100%

*Rounded

volume, as well as the smallest number of units, specific physical controls might be enforced to protect these assets. Managerial strategy might dictate that Class A inventories be maintained at minimum balances to conserve funds: this objective might be accomplished through frequent reorders of smaller quantities. In addition, bookkeeping controls such as the perpetual inventory system might be invoked to protect Class A assets. In the same fashion, the periodic inventory system, and other physical controls might be applied to Class B and Class C assets.

Perpetual inventory systems   Detailed inventory records for each item are maintained under perpetual inventory systems. The record for each inventory item usually shows the units and dollars of (a) each purchase, (b) each sale or transfer, and (c) the balance on hand. The perpetual inventory card uses the

EXHIBIT 17–6 PERPETUAL INVENTORY CARD

Part No.	A703						
Description	**Leg Assembly**		**Weight**	**Class**	**Reorder Point**	**Reorder Quantity**	
			2.5	A761	200	1,000	

Ordered		Received/Produced		Shipped		Balance	Unit
Date	**Quantity**	**Date**	**Quantity**	**Date**	**Quantity**	**Quantity**	**Price**
1-1	Balance					700	5.00
				1-6	200	500	5.00
1-10	1,000			1-10	300	200	5.00
				1-15	100	100	5.00
		1-17	1,000			100 1,000	5.00 5.50
				1-18	200	900	5.50

beginning balance as a base, adds the purchases and subtracts the sales to determine the ending balance. This continuous record is maintained for every transaction in the inventory item, thus providing an instant history of past activity, as well as highlighting the current balance. A perpetual inventory card is illustrated in Exhibit 17–6.

Perpetual inventory records may be maintained manually, mechanically, or by means of a computer. But whatever the means, preparing such records is relatively costly, so they are usually reserved for use with expensive, low-balance inventory items. Perpetual inventory records can be used to monitor inventory balances and trigger the reorder procedure. For example, the card illustrated in Exhibit 17–6 designates a reorder quantity; when the balance falls below this point, the inventory clerk initiates a reorder.

Periodic inventory systems   Periodic inventory systems do not require detailed records on specific inventory items. No count is kept of actual usage of these items. Rather, the periodic inventory system requires that physical counts of the goods on hand be taken at the end of each period. The number of units of each type of good on hand is then multiplied by the purchase cost per unit (determined from the accounting records) to compute the total dollar amount of inventory. Thus, the balance of goods on hand at any one moment is not known until the last day of the period. From an accounting point of view, the periodic inventory system can be conceived as:

$$
\begin{array}{l}
 \text{Beginning Inventory} \\
+\; \text{Purchases} \\
\hline
 \text{Available for Sale or Use} \\
-\; \text{Ending Inventory} \\
\hline
 \text{Units Sold or Used}
\end{array}
$$

The periodic inventory system measures both the cost of sales and the ending inventory by means of a physical count of the goods on hand, i.e., the goods transferred out or used in production are determined by deduction, rather than through direct observation.

Perpetual inventory systems usually require actions beyond the control of accountants to initiate a reorder. Two simple methods for controlling perpetual inventory balances include the *red-line method* and the *two-bin method*. Under the red-line method, a mark or "red line" is made on the container holding the inventory item at a distance from the bottom equal to the safety stock plus delivery quantity. A reorder is initiated when inventory items have been withdrawn down to the red line. The two-bin method is a simpler variation of the red-line method: inventory items are stored in two bins, but all withdrawals are made from one bin. When that bin is empty, a reorder is initiated, and the second bin is used to satisfy production demands while the first bin is refilled. The red-line and two-bin methods are especially well suited for large numbers of small items, such as nuts, bolts, nails, lubricants, or other items acquired in bulk.

Methods for approximating periodic inventory balances   Under the periodic inventory system, data are maintained about the beginning balance on hand, as well as the amounts purchased. No record is made of the amounts used, but estimates for the amounts used may be made with reference to budgeting techniques discussed in Chapters 2 and 3. Conventional cost/volume analysis can estimate the relationship between the (unmeasured) use of an inventory item and the (measured) volume activity. Once the unmeasured use of the inventory item has been estimated, then the inventory balance may be approximated by subtracting the estimated use from the amount available, as follows:

Estimated Balance = (Beginning Balance + Purchases − Estimated Usage)

For example, an examination of historical records indicates that 100 gallons of glue are used for every 10,000 units of production in the Stick E Manufacturing Company. Inventory records for the current period indicate that the beginning inventory of glue consisted of 300 gallons, that an additional 600 gallons were purchased, and that 75,000 units were produced. Estimated usage would be 750 gallons, i.e., $100/10,000 \times 75,000$, and 150 gallons are estimated to be on hand, i.e., $150 = (300 + 600 - 750)$.

COSTS FOR INVENTORY MANAGEMENT

Costs associated with inventories can be classified as *out-of-pocket costs* and *opportunity costs*. The first class represents those costs that are recorded in the accounting records as a normal function of the bookkeeping process. Costs such as clerical costs, transportation costs, storage space costs, handling costs, property taxes, and insurance all represent out-of-pocket costs. Opportunity costs represent a dollar value that has been forgone or preempted by the choice of a particular alternative; opportunity costs are those benefits that would have been obtained from an alternative if that alternative had been accepted. Opportunity costs associated with inventory management include an implicit interest on the funds invested in inventory, the dollar value of lost sales or customer ill-will resulting from carrying insufficient inventories, or quantity discounts lost by placing small orders.

The costs associated with inventory management can be subclassified into three groups. The first group represents the cost of ordering inventory. The second group represents the cost of storing inventory. The third group represents opportunity costs associated with the size of inventories. Examples of costs associated with each group are given below:

Costs of Ordering Inventory
Clerical costs
Communication costs
Transportation costs

Costs of Storing Inventory
Storage space costs

Insurance
Handling costs
Property taxes
Theft, deterioration, evaporation, and technological obsolescence

Opportunity Costs Associated with Size of Inventory or Order Quantity
Forgone quantity discounts associated with small order quantity
Set-up costs associated with short production runs
Lost sales and customer ill will associated with small finished-goods inventory balances
Special handling charges for transportation on rush purchase or sales shipments.

Costs associated with inventories are given serious consideration in determining inventory management policies. One goal of an inventory policy should be to minimize total annual inventory costs. However, minimizing inventory costs requires a direct trade-off between different classes of costs. For example, the interest on funds invested in inventory increases as the size of inventory increases, while the cost of lost sales or customer ill-will decreases as the size of inventory increases. Attempts to minimize these costs are also complicated by the fact that many of them are not easily determinable. In particular, opportunity costs associated with inventory management can be estimated only by special analysis. Since opportunities are not measured, these data are not available in the accounting records.

ECONOMIC ORDER QUANTITY

One of the major questions asked in inventory management concerns the size of orders to be placed: "How much should be ordered at any one time?" The amount to be ordered is commonly referred to as the "economic order quantity." The "economic order quantity" is that size of an order which will result in the lowest total annual cost for the inventory item.

All relevant costs, including the ordering, storing, and opportunity costs described above, must be considered in computing the economic order quantity. To simplify further discussion, however, only ordering and storing costs will be identified; opportunity costs have been included in these two classes. For example, the implicit interest on funds invested in inventory will be considered as a part of the total storing cost.

The trade-off between ordering and storing costs Since the number of orders placed each year varies inversely with the size of each order, a few large orders will produce lower ordering costs than many small orders. For example, a firm that uses 10,000 units of raw materials each year could place two orders of 5,000 units each, or it could place 5,000 orders of two units each. Obviously, the ordering costs per year will be lower for the two orders than for the 5,000 orders.

On the other hand, the number of orders per year is inversely related to the average balance in inventory. Thus, ordering costs are inversely related to storage costs; if orders of 5,000 units are placed, the average inventory balance will be 2,500, but it will be 1 if orders of 2 units are placed. Whenever the number of orders is reduced by increasing the order quantity, the average balance of inventory increases, and hence, inventory storage costs increase. Conversely, decreasing the average balance in inventories implies decreases in the order quantity, and hence, increasing the number of orders placed per year.

An example To illustrate the trade-off between ordering costs and carrying costs, consider the following case. The Ferrara Company estimates that its production needs for raw materials will be 4,000 tons during 19X6. The accountants for Ferrara Company estimate that the tasks associated with placing an order will cost $20 per order, while storing goods will cost $1 per ton per year for the average balance. Management wishes to determine the relationship between costs and order quantity. Alternatives considered include 800 tons per order placed five times a year, 400 tons placed ten times a year, or 200 tons placed twenty times a year. Exhibit 17–7 describes both storage costs and ordering costs, as well as the total costs for the three alternatives. As can be seen, total costs are minimized when 400 units are ordered 10 times a year. For any other inventory order quantity, a trade-off occurs between storage costs and order costs: for larger order quantities, storage costs increase, while ordering costs decrease; for smaller order quantities, order costs increase, while storage costs decrease.

The graphical approach Exhibit 17–8 illustrates the inventory cost consequences of every order quantity up to 800 units for the Ferrara Company, described above. The vertical axis relates to annual inventory costs. The first scale on the horizontal axis reflects order quantity, but immediately below that are two other scales for the average inventory balance and the number of orders placed during the year. The annual storing cost line on the graph is determined by multiplying one dollar per unit by the average balance in inventory, while the annual ordering costs are determined by multiplying the number of orders by the $20 per order charge. The total cost line represents the summation of both the storing and ordering costs.

Notice that the lowest total annual inventory cost occurs at the order quantity where the graphs of the storing and ordering costs intersect (at 400 units). That is, the economic order quantity (EOQ) is found at the point where the storing costs equal the ordering costs. The EOQ always will be found where these two costs meet, whenever ordering costs are a decreasing function of order quantity, and storing costs are an increasing function of order quantity. Furthermore, note that the annual total costs are not especially sensitive to changes in the order quantity: a 25% shift in the order quantity from 400 units to 500

EXHIBIT 17–7   ECONOMIC ORDER QUANTITY CALCULATION

	Alternatives		
	1	2	3
A. Storing Costs			
Order Quantity (Q)	800	400	200
Average Balance (Q/2)	400	200	100
Cost Per Unit	$1	$1	$1
Annual Storing Costs	$400	$200	$100
B. Ordering Costs			
Annual Demand (D)	4,000	4,000	4,000
Order Quantity (Q)	800	400	200
Number of Orders (D/Q)	5	10	20
Cost Per Order	$20	$20	$20
Annual Ordering Costs	$100	$200	$400
C. Total Annual Inventory Costs			
Annual Storing Costs	$400	$200	$100
Annual Ordering Costs	100	200	400
Total Annual Costs	$500	$400	$500

units raises total costs from the original $400 to $410, a mere 2.5% increase. A 25% decrease in order quantity from 400 units to 300 units will raise total costs to $410 or to $430, depending upon whether thirteen or fourteen orders are placed during the year to acquire the annual demand of 4,000 units.[3]

The formula approach   The economic order quantity can be found by means of a formula that incorporates the basic relationships between order quantity and costs. These relationships can be stated as follows: order costs equal a stated cost per order multiplied by the result of dividing total demand by the order quantity. In formula terms, $OC = O \times D/Q$, where OC is annual order costs, O is cost per order, D is annual demand, and Q is order quantity. Storage costs are equal to a stated amount per unit multiplied by one-half of the order quantity. In formula terms, $SC = S \times Q/2$, where SC is annual storage cost and S is storage cost per

---

[3]There is a slower increase in total costs as order quantity rises above the EOQ than there is as order quantity falls below the EOQ.

EXHIBIT 17-8   ECONOMIC ORDER QUANTITY CHART

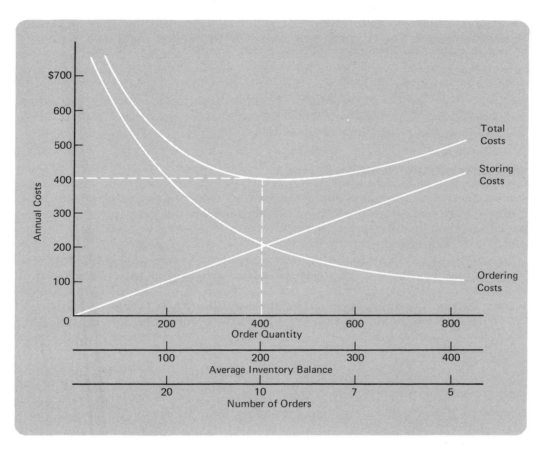

unit. Total costs for any order size can be found by summing order costs and storage costs. In formula terms, $TC = OC + SC = (O \times D/Q) + (S \times Q/2)$.

The economic order quantity is the order quantity that is associated with the lowest total cost. Whenever order costs are described as a decreasing hyperbolic function, and storage costs are described as an increasing linear function, the smallest total cost will always be found at that point where the order costs equal the storage costs. In mathematical terms, the order quantity with the lowest total cost is found at a point where the derivative of the total annual cost with respect to order size is zero, i.e., just before the total cost curve starts to increase.

The formula that describes these relationships can be used to compute the economic order quantity; it is usually expressed as follows: $Q =$

$\sqrt{(2 \times D \times O)/S}$, where Q is the order quantity in units, D is the annual demand in terms of units, O is the cost of placing one order, and S is the annual cost of storing one unit in inventory. This formula translates into the following words: The economic order quantity is determined as the square root of two multiplied by the annual quantity demanded times the cost per order, all divided by the annual cost of storing one unit. For example, consider the Ford Company, which estimates annual demand for raw materials at 1,800 tons during 19X6. Order costs are $5 per order, and storage costs are $20 per ton for the average balance on hand. The EOQ formula would take the square root of 2 times 1,800 times $5, all divided by $20, which equals 30 tons.

ASSUMPTIONS OF THE EOQ FORMULA

Several assumptions about cost/volume behavior are built into the EOQ formula, as described above. If these assumptions are not descriptive of underlying cost/volume relationships, then the output of the EOQ model must be interpreted with caution.

First, per-unit storage costs are described as a constant. While this relationship might properly characterize property taxes (a fixed rate times the value of property) or implicit interest on funds invested in inventory, it does not describe depreciation on buildings or salaries of inventory supervisors. Many storage costs are fixed (or at least nonvariable) with respect to order quantity.[4] Other costs, however, might reflect efficiencies of scale and drop on a per-unit basis as inventory size increases.

Second, total storage costs reflect the assumption that the average balance in inventory is equal to one-half of the order quantity. If safety stocks are maintained or if utilization of inventory is not constant per day, this assumption is violated. The size of safety stocks probably is not independent of order quantity: relatively larger safety stocks will be associated with smaller order quantities. Furthermore, seasonal and cyclical factors produce uneven usage over time.

Costs per order are also assumed to be stable for all orders. However, special rush orders associated with small order quantities may entail unusual expediting, tracing, or confirming. Furthermore, quantity discounts are not explicitly considered in the EOQ model described above. If quantity discounts are considered as a reduction in opportunity ordering costs, order costs become smaller as order quantity increases.

Finally, use of the EOQ model assumes that data on annual demand, ordering costs, and storing costs are available. In reality, these data can only be estimated.

---

[4]Fixed costs should be ignored in EOQ calculations, since the size of the cost is independent of the order quantity, i.e., changing order quantity will not change costs.

Consequences of violating assumptions   Estimates of the EOQ are useful, even though the data available are only rough approximations of actual costs and demand. Furthermore, some of the assumptions underlying the model may be violated without major distortions in the EOQ. These generalizations hold because the EOQ model is not very sensitive to errors in the specification of input variables.

Examining the EOQ model provides a clue to this lack of sensitivity:

$$EOQ = \sqrt{(2 \times Demand \times Ordering\ Cost)/Storing\ Cost}$$

Suppose that the estimate for cost per order was 20% too high, i.e., the real cost per order is 80% of the estimate. This "correction factor" can be introduced into the formula by multiplying the elements in brackets by .8. But since everything in brackets is under the radical sign, the EOQ will be modified by the square root of .8, which is approximately .9; that is, a 20% error under the radical sign produces a 10% change in the EOQ. If ordering costs are grossly estimated at four times the appropriate amount, then the EOQ will be modified by the square root of 4, or 2. For example, reconsider the case where annual demand is 4,000 units, order cost is $20 per order, storage cost is $1 per unit, and the EOQ is 400 units. If ordering costs were estimated at $80 per order, a fourfold restatement, the EOQ is merely doubled to 800 units.

The EOQ model can be modified to accommodate several of the limitations described above. Such discussion is beyond the scope of this chapter, however.

EXPANDING EOQ CONCEPTS BEYOND INVENTORIES

The economic order quantity concept can shed insight into other areas of managerial concern. One widely recognized application employs the EOQ formula to determine the length of a production run. To apply the EOQ formula to a production run problem, merely substitute *set-up costs* for the new production run in place of the purchase ordering costs. Set-up costs include labor, material, jigs, dyes, machine down-time, and other ancillary costs of getting facilities ready to produce. Carrying costs for production runs assume the same meaning as storing costs in the previous EOQ examples. All other factors parallel the EOQ application.

For example, consider the following assumed data: The Davison Company wishes to determine the most economical length of its production run. Annual production demand (D) is estimated at 200,000 units, set-up costs are expected to be $900 per set-up ($O$) to activate a production run, and costs to carry 1 unit in stock for one year (S) are $10. The optimum length of a production run can be determined with the formula:

$$Q = \sqrt{(2 \times D \times O)/S} = \sqrt{(2 \times 200,000 \times \$900)/\$10} = 6,000 \text{ units.}$$

Note that the relatively high set-up costs are effectively offset by the relatively high storage costs; 33 production runs of 6,000 units each are needed to meet production demands. However, if storage costs drop substantially, the high set-up costs will cause a lengthening of the production run. If storage costs are $1 per unit per year, the optimum production run is 18,974.

Other applications of the EOQ concept involve the determination of the optimum size of cash, receivables, or any other current asset. In each application, the costs of "having too much" or "having too little" of the asset must be determined, and the cost/volume relationship must be identified. Further discussion of additional applications is beyond the scope of this chapter.

SUMMARY

Inventories are an essential element of the production process in most manufacturing organizations. They provide continuity by bridging the gap between suppliers of raw materials and the production departments that consume these materials; they also facilitate the flow between the production departments and the customers who buy the finished products. Inventory management requires answers to several questions: (a) How large an order should be, (b) When an order should be placed, (c) What costs are associated with inventory management, (d) What factors determine the size of safety stocks, and (e) Which accounting procedures support inventory management policy. Suggested answers to these questions have been discussed in this chapter.

SUGGESTED READINGS

Brady, E., and J. C. Babbitt. "Inventory Control Systems." *Management Accounting*, December 1972.

Lambert, D. M., and B. J. LaLonde. "Inventory Carrying Costs." *Management Accounting*, August 1976.

Roemmich, R. A., and J. D. Edwards. "Scientific Inventory Management." *MSU Business Topics*, Autumn 1975.

QUESTIONS

17–1   Which factors should be considered in determining the optimal level of inventory?

17-2   Describe the relationship between the normal size of each order and the number of orders placed each year.

17-3   Describe how the size of each order relates to the number of orders that must be placed each year.

17-4   List at least three costs associated with inventory management. Identify at least one inventory cost that normally is not reflected in the accounting records.

17-5   Frequently, sales and finance executives have different attitudes about the size of finished-goods inventory. Discuss the general positions of each.

17-6   Frequently, the production and finance executives have different attitudes about the size of raw materials inventory. Discuss the general positions of each.

17-7   Why do manufacturing organizations maintain inventories of raw materials? Why do they maintain inventories of finished goods?

17-8   Describe the classes of information that might appear on a typical inventory control record.

17-9   Explain how a "red-line" or a "tag" system of inventory reorder control operates.

17-10   What are the chief advantages of the ABC inventory control system?

17-11   Define "economic order quantity." How is this amount determined?

17-12   How sensitive is the EOQ formula to minor misspecifications either in order costs or in carrying costs?

17-13   Define the terms "safety stock" and "lead time."

17-14   Do storage costs, carrying costs, and order costs actually behave (in relation to order quantity) as described in the conventional EOQ formula?

17-15   How are safety stock considered by the conventional EOQ formula?

EXERCISES

17-16   Cope Co. plans to purchase 1,800 lbs. of material during the year (which has 360 working days). Cope does not maintain safety stocks and uses materials evenly throughout the year. Storage costs (space, handling, clerical, damage, insurance) are $1 per lb. per year for the average balance on hand during the year. Ordering costs (letters, postage, phone) are $10 per order.

(A) Determine the EOQ for Cope Company.

(B) A standard order normally will last how many days?

(C) Cope suspects that its estimate of storage costs may be 100% in error. Redetermine the EOQ, assuming that storage costs are $2 per pound.

17–17   The EOQ formula assumes that storage costs are a monotonic (increasing straight-line) function of order quantity. Identify specific storage costs that may not relate to order quantity as assumed in the formula.

17–18   The EOQ formula assumes that order costs are a decreasing function of order quantity. Identify specific order costs that may not relate to order quantity as assumed in the model.

17–19   Many of these "costs" are not measured or recorded in the normal accounting process. Rather, special studies must be made to determine their magnitude. The measurement of forgone quantity discounts might be relatively simple, but the "costs" of running out of inventory require many estimations and assumptions. Describe how you would measure stock-out costs.

17–20   Ajax Co. expects production demand for raw materials to be 14,400 lbs. for 19X6. Ajax determines that: (a) normal orders will be placed every thirty days, (b) normal delivery time will be five days, (c) normal safety stock will be three days, (d) order costs are $15 per order, and (e) storage costs are $1 per lb. per year for the average balance.

(A) A new order will be placed when inventories reach what pound level, i.e., what is the reorder point?

(B) Just before a new order arrives, how many pounds will be on hand?

(C) Total inventory costs (storage and order costs) for 19X6 will be what dollar amount?

(D) Which variables in the EOQ formula would be affected by the presence of safety stocks?

17–21   The annual demand, order quantity, average inventory balance, and the daily usage of an inventory item are all related. Knowledge of two or more of these items will provide clues for determining other information. Substitute a number for every letter in each of the following independent cases. Assume a 360-day year.

	Case A	Case B	Case C
Annual Demand	15,000	e	i
Number of Orders	a	f	8
Daily Usage	b	5	j
Order Quantity	c	100	k
Average Inventory Balance	d	g	300
Number of Days per Order	60	h	l

17–22   The reorder point, safety stock, delivery time, and daily usage are all related. Knowledge of two or more of these items will provide clues for determining other information. Substitute a number for every letter in each of the following independent cases.

	Case A	Case B	Case C
Reorder Point, Quantity	a	3,000	1,200
Delivery Time, Days	b	10	g
Delivery Time, Quantity	1,500	d	h
Safety Stock, Quantity	c	e	500
Safety Stock, Days	4	5	i
Average Daily Usage, Quantity	300	f	100

17-23 The dollar value of total inventory is related to the dollar value found in each of the three classes determined under the ABC method. Substitute a number for every letter in each of the following independent cases.

	Case X	Case Y	Case Z
Dollar Value, Total Inventory	a	$100,000	$400,000
Class A% of Total Value	b	c	60%
Class A, Dollar Value	$140,000	$ 40,000	e
Class B% of Total Value	20%	d	20%
Class C% of Total Value	10%	10%	f

17-24 Cope Company plans to purchase 18,000 lbs. of claxon during the next year. Normal delivery time is three days, and Cope would like to maintain a safety stock equal to two days' needs.

(A) If standard lot size is 1,000 lbs. per order, the lead time can be considered as how many pounds?

(B) If standard lot size is 1,000 lbs. per order, the safety stock can be considered as how many pounds?

(C) If standard lot size is 1,000 lbs. per order, a new order must be placed when inventories reach the what lbs. level?

(D) Under ordinary circumstances, a new order will be placed every __?__ days.

(E) If inventories are down to 50 lbs. by the time a new order of 1,000 lbs. arrives, the next order will be placed in how many days?

17-25 Ajax Co. plans to purchase 36,000 lbs. of claxon during the year. Ajax does not maintain safety stocks, and uses materials evenly throughout the year. Storage costs (space, handling, clerical, insurance) are $.10 per lb. per year for the average balance on hand during the year. Ordering costs (letters, postage, phone) are $20 per order.

(A) If purchases are made in lot sizes of 1,000 per order, the yearly ordering costs are what amount?

(B) If purchases are made in lot sizes of 1,000 per order, the yearly storage costs are what amount?

(C) If purchases are made in lot sizes of 1,000 per order, the total yearly storage and order costs are what amount?

(D) Determine the EOQ for Ajax.

(E) If Ajax maintained a safety stock of 2,000 lbs. and ordered 4,000 units per order, the average inventory would be what amount?

17–26 The perpetual inventory method implies a specific relationship between the beginning inventory, amount purchased, amount sold or used in production, and the ending inventory balance. Substitute a number for every letter in each of the following independent cases.

	Case A	Case B	Case C
Beginning Inventory	600	800	c
Purchases	4,000	7,000	6,000
Sold or Used	3,200	b	6,600
Ending Inventory	a	1,000	800

17–27 An analysis similar to cost/volume analysis provides a basis for approximating periodic inventory balances. Such analysis provides an estimate of the quantity sold or transferred out of inventory. Substitute a number for every letter in each of the following independent cases.

	Case A	Case B	Case C
Volume Measure	400,000	600,000	c
Inventory Use/Volume	1/50	1/50	1/50
Purchases	7,000	8,000	10,000
Beginning Balance	3,000	b	2,000
Estimated Ending Balance	a	1,000	2,000

17–28 The EOQ formula manipulates estimates of the annual demand, per-order costs, and per unit storage costs to determine the order quantity with the lowest annual inventory costs. Data on each of these variables is provided for three independent cases. Substitute a number for a letter in each of the following independent cases.

	Case A	Case B	Case C
Annual Demand	36,000	9,000	500
Costs per Order	$13.33	$10.00	$5.00
Storage Costs per Unit	$6.00	$4.50	$2.00
EOQ	a	e	i
Number of Orders	b	f	j
Days per Order	c	g	k
Total Annual Inventory Cost	d	h	l

17–29 On top of page 573 is an unlabeled figure. First label the axes A and B, and then identify the lines C, D, E, and the point F.

17–30 The Dasher Company uses 9,000 lbs. of raw material each year. Management has determined that the costs of placing an order for raw materials is $45, and the cost of carrying inventory averages out to $.10 per pound. Calculate the economic order quantity for this raw material. How much will total annual inventory costs be if purchases are made at the EOQ? Without doing any written calculations, determine the magnitude of change in the EOQ caused by increasing the carrying costs fourfold, to $.40.

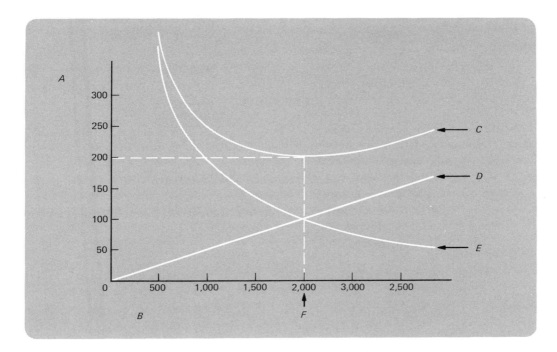

17-31   The Blitzen Company wishes to implement the ABC method of inventory control to facilitate its parts purchase policy. ABC categories are established as follows: A—top-ranked parts, accounting for approximately 65% of total cost, B—next-ranked parts, accounting for approximately 30% of the total cost, C—remaining parts that account for the remaining 5% of total cost.

   The raw material parts, along with estimated annual needs and per-unit costs, are listed below.

Part Stock Number	Estimated Annual Needs		Cost Per Unit	Total Cost	% of Total Cost
	(Units)	(%)			
KL 8	1,000	2	$ 15.00	$ 15,000	14
LZ 6	20,000	36	.05	1,000	1
PB 9	500	1	50.00	25,000	23
QM 3	4,000	7	1.50	6,000	6
LR 4	11,000	20	.50	5,500	5
KL 7	1,500	3	2.00	3,000	3
PB 8	800	1	30.00	24,000	22
RK 3	2,000	3	3.00	6,000	6
CO 2	15,000	27	.15	2,250	2
JM 5	100	0	200.00	20,000	18
	55,900	100%		$107,750	100%

Identify the parts that belong to the A, B, and C classes. What percentage of total units are associated with each class? For which class(es) is periodic inventory suitable?

17–32   The management of Sanders Machine Shop wanted to determine the economic order quantity for steel rods. A special accounting study indicated that order costs were $20 per order and that annual demand was 1,250 tons of steel. To estimate storing costs, the cost accountant examined historical records and determined that the warehouse costs (labor, supplies, and overhead) were $8,000 when the average inventory balance equaled 1,200 tons, and $8,500 when the average inventory balance equaled 1,300 tons.

(A) Should fixed inventory costs be considered in determining the EOQ? Why or why not?

(B) Will an examination of historical cost records identify all relevant storage costs? Explain.

(C) Determine the EOQ.

(D) If your estimate of the storage costs is inaccurate by a magnitude of 9 (900% off true costs), by what magnitude will the EOQ be misstated?

17–33   The Baker Manufacturing Company maintains its inventories of coolants under the periodic inventory system. Data about current inventory balances are not available under this system. However, other data are available, as follows:

Beginning coolant balance	1,000 gallons
Purchases	8,000 gallons
Amount used last month	9,000 gallons
Amount used two months ago	7,000 gallons
Volume last month, machine hours	45,000 hours
Volume two months ago, machine hours	35,000 hours
Volume, this month	42,000 hours

Using the data available, estimate the current balance in inventory and the quantity used during the current month.

PROBLEMS

17–34   The Robney Company is a restaurant supplier which sells a number of products to various restaurants in the area. One of their products is a special meat cutter with a disposable blade.

The blades are sold in packages of 12 blades for $20.00 per package. After a number of years, the demand for the replacement blades has been determined to be 2,000 packages per month. The packages cost the Robney Company $10.00

each from the manufacturer and require a three-day lead time from date of order to date of delivery. The ordering cost is $1.20 per order, and the carrying cost is 10% per annum.

Robney is going to use the economic order quantity formula

$$EOQ = \sqrt{\frac{2 \text{ (Annual Requirements) (Cost per order)}}{\text{(Price per unit) (Carrying Cost)}}}$$

(A) Calculate the following items:
    a. The economic order quantity,
    b. The number of orders needed per year,
    c. The total cost of buying and carrying blades for the year.

(B) Assuming that there is no reserve (e.g., safety stock) and that the present inventory level is 200 packages, when should the next order be placed? (Assume a 360-day year.)

(C) Discuss the problems that most firms would have in attempting to apply this formula to their inventory problems.

(CMA adapted)

17–35 Inventories constitute an important part of the financial position of many business enterprises. For such a firm, proper policies for inventory analysis and control are highly important in maintaining a sound financial condition.

(A) Why do manufacturing firms maintain merchandise and materials inventories? (Your answer should state the reasons for physical stocks of goods rather than the accounting and auditing significance of inventories.)

(B) Various types of inventory systems exist to control the ordering and amount of inventory on hand. For example, the ABC plan classifies high-carrying-cost and low-ordering-cost inventory as "A" items, low-carrying-cost and high-ordering-cost inventory as "C" items, and all other inventory as "B" items; the plan is appropriate for an inventory composed of a large number of items with a wide range of carrying and order costs. Explain the (1) order cycling and (2) min-max system inventory control plans and describe the conditions under which each is appropriate.

(C) What factors should be considered in computing:
    a. Optimum investment in inventory. Identify those costs which normally do and do not explicitly appear on formal accounting records.
    b. Economic order quantity.
    c. Minimum stock reorder point.

(D) Describe the advantages and disadvantages to a manufacturer obtained by stabilizing production of a durable seasonal product.

(AICPA adapted)

17–36   You have been engaged to install an accounting system for the Kaufman Corporation. Among the inventory control features Kaufman desires as a part of the system are indicators of "how much" to order "when." The following information is furnished for one item, called a komtronic, which is carried in inventory:

1. Komtronics are sold by the gross (twelve dozen) at a list price of $800 per gross F.O.B. shipper. Kaufman receives a 40% trade discount off list price on purchases in gross lots.
2. Freight cost is $20 per gross from the shipping point to Kaufman's plant.
3. Kaufman uses about 5,000 komtronics during a 259-day production year and must purchase a total of 36 gross per year to allow for normal breakage. Minimum and maximum usages are 12 and 28 komtronics per day, respectively.
4. Normal delivery time to receive an order is 20 working days from the date of purchase request is initiated. A rush order in full gross lots can be received by air freight in five working days at an extra cost of $52 per gross. A stock-out (complete exhaustion of the inventory) of komtronics would stop production, and Kaufman would purchase komtronics locally at list price rather than shut down.
5. The cost of placing an order is $10; the cost of receiving an order is $20.
6. Space storage cost is $12 per year per gross stored.
7. Insurance and taxes are approximately 12% of the net delivered cost of average inventory, and Kaufman expects a return of at least 8% on its average investment (ignore return on order and carrying cost for sake of simplicity).

(A) Prepare a schedule computing the total annual cost of komtronics based on uniform order lot sizes of one, two, three, four, five, and six gross of komtronics. (The schedule should show the total annual cost according to each lot size.) Indicate the economic order quantity (economic lot size to order).

(B) Prepare a schedule computing the minimum stock reorder point for komtronics. This is the point below which the komtronics inventory should not fall without reordering, so as to guard against a stock-out. Factors to be considered include average lead-period usage and safety stock requirements.

(C) Prepare a schedule computing the cost of a stock-out of kom-tronics. Factors to be considered include the excess costs for local purchases and for rush orders.

(AICPA adapted)

*17-37 Vendo, Inc., has been operating the concession stands at the university football stadium. The university has had successful football teams for many years; as a result, the stadium is always full. The university is located in an area in which it never rains during the football season. From time to time, Vendo has found itself very short of hot dogs; at other times, it has had many left over. A review of the records of sales of the past five seasons revealed the following frequency of hot dogs sold.

	Total Games
10,000 hot dogs	5 times
20,000 hot dogs	10 times
30,000 hot dogs	20 times
40,000 hot dogs	15 times
	50 total games

Hot dogs sell for 50 cents each and cost Vendo 30 cents each. Unsold hot dogs are given to a local orphanage without charge.

(A) Assuming that only the four quantities listed were ever sold, and that the occurrences were random events, prepare a payoff table (ignore income taxes) to represent the four possible strategies of ordering 10,000, 20,000, 30,000, or 40,000 hot dogs.

(B) Using the expected value decision rule, determine the best strategy.

(C) What is the dollar value of perfect information in this problem?

(CMA adapted)

*17-38 The Starr Company manufactures several products. One of its main products requires an electric motor. The management of Starr Company uses the economic order quantity formula (EOQ) to determine the optimum number of motors to order. Management now wants to determine how much safety stock to order. Starr Company uses 30,000 electric motors annually (300 working days). Using the EOQ formula, the Company orders 3,000 motors at a time. The lead time for an order is five days. The annual cost of carrying one motor in safety stock is $10. Management has also estimated that the cost of being out of stock is $20 for each motor they are short.

Starr Company has analyzed the usage during past reorder periods by examining the inventory records. The records indicate the following usage patterns during the past reorder periods:

Usage During Lead Time	Number of Times Quantity Was Used
440	6
460	12
480	16
500	130
520	20
540	10
560	6
	200

(A) Using an expected-value approach, determine the level of safety stock for electric motors that Starr Company should maintain in order to minimize costs.

(B) What would be Starr Company's new reorder point?

(C) What factors should Starr Company have considered to estimate the out-of-stock costs?

(CMA adapted)

SIX

The Behavioral Aspects of Accounting

Managerial accounting is often used as a motivational device in the control process of the firm. Accounting is heavily dependent on people—people perform accounting tasks; people receive and must react to the outputs of an accounting system. But, people are individuals; they often react in different and unique ways to the same situation. These reactions constitute an individual's behavior. The accountant must have a basic appreciation and understanding of human behavior if he is to operate effectively within the organization. The final chapter explores certain behavioral characteristics associated with the accounting process.

18-4 Briefly describe how managerial accounting can be considered a behavioral process.

18-5 Briefly define each of the following terms:
   (A) Motivation
   (B) Behavior
   (C) Goals
   (D) Needs

18-6 Maslow classified human needs in a hierarchy of five distinct levels. Describe the characteristics of each level. How, in general terms, do these classes relate to ongoing human needs?

18-7 In each of the independent cases listed below, an individual can identify several goals. According to the Maslow theory of motivation, which goals will lead to the *dominant need* in the individual?

   (A) John has always wanted to be an artist. Although he is a good painter, he is, as yet, unrecognized. Consequently, he has little money and has just been evicted from his apartment.

   (B) Wanda Jenkins is a successful businesswoman. She is in line for a promotion that will place her at the top of the organization, a goal she has had since childhood. Recently, there have been several muggings in the business district. Wanda is somewhat concerned for her safety.

   (C) Herbert Jones is president of an extremely large company. He earns a high annual salary, has a wonderful wife and family, and is openly admired and respected by his co-workers. Herbert has always wanted to be a truck driver.

   (D) The manager of a large company recently suffered severe losses in the stock market. As a result, he is facing possible bankruptcy.

18-8 What behavioral factors and conditions will lead an individual into action? Must an individual always take an action to pursue a goal? Why or why not?

18-9 What is the likely result when an individual fails to attain a goal?

18-10 In what sense are the formal plans of a business organization similar to human goals? Briefly discuss the similarities. Identify the dissimilarities.

18-11 What is meant by *goal congruence*? Does a lack of goal congruence necessarily mean that an organization is not effective or efficient?

18-12 In what manner can the business organization influence an individual's perception of a goal? Identify some methods that the organization can use to provide such an influence.

EXERCISES

18–13 A classic example of influences on perception concerns an honors student and a football player. During their college careers, the honors student had accumulated an almost perfect academic record, while the football player was barely able to graduate. In an experiment, both were given the same amount of time to read and study the sports page of a local paper. Both were tested on the contents. The football player amassed a very high score, while the honors student did poorly.

(A) How can the performance of both students be explained in this situation?

(B) What factors probably led the football player to do well and the honors student to do poorly on the test?

(C) Can a sports page be compared to a managerial accounting report? How are they similar?

(D) Briefly describe how the results of this experiment can be used by a managerial accountant to prepare more useful internal reports for management.

18–14 Differentiate between *actual* and *apparent* goal congruence. Should an organization strive to promote actual or apparent goal congruence among its members? Briefly explain and justify your answer.

18–15 Motivation can be classified as either positive or negative. Will positive motivation always lead employees into actions that will benefit the firm? In contrast, is negative employee motivation something that an organization should seek to avoid in its employees?

18–16 Comment on the following statement made by an executive in the Monrow Company: "We really need to take a hard look at behavior in this firm. Our employees are completely unmotivated. As a result, nothing gets done when it should or in the way that it should be done."

18–17 In seeking to motivate employees and promote efficiency and effectiveness in a firm, should management seek to identify the employees' actual attitudes or should they just consider results? Briefly explain your answer.

18–18 One reason that a company assigns parking spaces to its top executives is so that these valuable employees need not waste time looking for a place to park. Can you identify some other reasons for this practice?

18–19 How can the purposes of budgets come into conflict with each other? Do these conflicts negate the usefulness of budgeting within the firm?

18–20 How is "management by exception" practiced in relation to budgets? What implications does this have on the budgeting process?

18-21   What is meant by the term *slack*? Why is slack often built into the budget system? What can an organization do to remove slack from the system?

18-22   "Preparation of a master budget is the job of a managerial accountant. If slack is present in the budget, the accountant hasn't done his job correctly or is inefficient." Comment on this assertion. How can a budget be used as a pressure device? Is this the purpose for which budgets were intended? Can any budget be used effectively as a control device if pressure is not included in the budgetary system?

18-23   The Big Company is a large industrial firm which operates manufacturing facilities in 14 states and six foreign countries. To save on reporting costs, the accounting department normally prepares one report for each plant. This report is distributed to the production foremen, the plant manager, and to the Company president. A sample report from the DATACOUNT plant is reproduced below:

DATACOUNT PLANT
Weekly Performance Report

	Budget	Actual
Total labor cost	$100,000	$105,000
Hourly labor rate	$5.00	$5.00
Labor hours worked	20,000	21,000
Total material cost	$80,000	$78,000
Material cost per pound	$2.00	$1.50
Pounds of material used	40,000	52,000
Overhead assigned to production	$9,000	$8,000
Units produced	160,000	156,000
Units spoiled	1,000	2,000

(A) What problems might such a report cause within the firm? Is it useful in its present form?

(B) Prepare a report from this information which would be useful to the president of the Company. What constraints normally apply in reporting at this level?

(C) Prepare a report from this information which would be useful to the plant manager. Defend your use of specific data in this report.

(D) Prepare a report from this information which would be useful to the production foremen. What constraints normally apply in reporting at this level?

18-24   What problems can emerge in the budgetary system as a result of the differences in orientation of line managers and staff advisors? What can be done to overcome these problems?

18-25   Can job enlargement techniques be incorporated into the budgetary process? Why would such methods be used?

18–26   Describe three different situations that can occur when data are transmitted within a firm via an accounting report.

18–27   Define the following terms:

    (A) Interference
    (B) Noise
    (C) Information overload
    (D) Cognitive dissonance

18–28   In each of the following situations, describe the type of interference that could possibly hinder the flow of accounting information within the firm.

    (A) One monthly performance report is prepared for the entire company. A single copy of this report is routed to 67 key management and supervisory personnel.

    (B) Ray Tired is a fishing buff. He spends many hours during the day thinking about fishing trips he will take after his retirement.

    (C) Wilson Swift works hard every day. Because of the time he puts in, he believes that his division is the best in the company. He usually ignores performance reports. "I know that we're the best," he says.

    (D) A company prepares an information report for its divisional managers. The report contains between 60,000 and 80,000 "key items."

*18–29   How can a change in the accounting methods used to process information influence behavior in the firm? What is the probable result of a processing change that leads to no corresponding change in managerial behavior?

18–30   What is meant by the term *functional fixation*? What is the likely result of this situation in a firm? Identify the conditions that can lead to functional fixation.

18–31   The Separate Parts Company has decentralized its operations into several semi-independent divisions including Manufacturing, Assembly, Packing, Warehousing, and Marketing. The following information was available to the Accounting Department at the end of the last month:

	Direct Material	Direct Labor	Allocated Overhead
Manufacturing Division	$100,000	$ 75,000	$ 50,000
Assembly Division	10,000	60,000	40,000
Packing Division	15,000	20,000	15,000
Warehousing Division		10,000	8,000
Marketing Division		20,000	15,000
	$125,000	$185,000	$128,000

During the month, sales totaled $475,000, and the Company made a profit on its operations of $37,000. When preparing monthly performance reports, the accounting department attempted to incorporate profitability into the report base. Consequently, they prepared the following report for the Manufacturing Division:

MANUFACTURING DIVISION
Monthly Profit Report

Sales Revenue		$475,000
Costs of Manufacturing:		
Direct Materials	$100,000	
Direct Labor	75,000	
Allocated Overhead	50,000	225,000
Manufacturing Profit		$250,000

Upon receiving this report, the manager of the Manufacturing Division immediately asked for a $5,000 per month raise. When his raise was denied, the performance in the Manufacturing Division began to decline. "We are still the most profitable division in the Company," he frequently said. "Our rate of profit is about 800% greater than the Company in total, so we must be carrying the rest of the operation."

(A) Is the manufacturing manager correct in his interpretation of the report?

(B) Prepare another performance report for the Manufacturing Division which will emphasize profit, but will clarify the manager's thinking.

(C) Discuss some of the behavioral aspects of reporting which relate to this situation.

18-32 Helen Brimstone is the manager of a retail department store which is a part of a national chain. The company seeks participation of all management levels in the budgeting process. Consequently, Ms. Brimstone prepared the following budget for the forthcoming year:

BETTY'S BARGAIN BASEMENTS
Store Number 18 Annual Budget

Sales Revenue			$240,000
Cost of Goods Sold			100,000
Gross Margin			$140,000
Operating Expenses:			
Salaries	$50,000		
Commissions	5,000		
Advertising	5,000		
Rent	10,000		
Heat and light	2,000		
Miscellaneous	8,000		
Total		$80,000	
Administrative Expenses:			
Salaries	$15,000		
Personnel	5,000		
Supplies	10,000		
Miscellaneous	10,000		
Total		40,000	120,000
Net Income			$ 20,000

From past experience, it is obvious that Helen Brimstone behaves in several different ways when preparing a budget. She normally inflates her sales expectations by 20%, because she takes an over-optimistic view. However, in an effort to reduce pressure, she normally overstates all salaries by 15%. Commissions are normally 10% of operating salaries. All miscellaneous expenses are normally overstated by 50%, and supplies are overstated by 25%.

(A) Prepare a new budget which reflects what can reasonably be expected from Store Number 18 for next year.

(B) In response to Helen's past behavior, top management desires to place some pressure on her performance. Prepare a new budget that maintains Helen's sales projection, but cuts all expenditures by 20%.

(C) Which of the two budgets (A) or (B) would be most useful for planning purposes? Why?

(D) What motivational advantages and disadvantages might result from the budget prepared in (B) above?

18–33   The High Way Air Freight Company operates two terminals and sales offices in the cities of Here and There, which they serve. The terminal managers participate in annual budget meetings with the corporate accounting staff. Development of monthly sales estimations for each terminal is part of the budget process. Budgeted and actual sales data for each of the terminals for the first six months of this year are given below:

	Here City Terminal		There City Terminal	
	Budgeted Sales	Actual Sales	Budgeted Sales	Actual Sales
January	$ 50,000	$ 40,000	$ 50,000	$ 49,000
February	50,000	60,000	50,000	53,000
March	50,000	30,000	50,000	49,500
April	60,000	80,000	50,000	51,000
May	70,000	50,000	60,000	58,000
June	50,000	70,000	70,000	72,500
Total Sales	$330,000	$330,000	$330,000	$330,000

The Company has a very liberal salary and bonus plan, which it has been testing to evaluate its potential motivational advantages. For each of the following plans, evaluate the total cost to the firm and the total compensation accruing to each terminal manager. On the basis of this information, determine which terminal manager was probably assigned to the plan.

Plan A: A salary of $500 per month, plus a bonus of $2,000 any month that the budget is met, plus 10% of any sales over the budget.

Plan B: A salary of $800 per month regardless of sales.

(A) What would be the total cost to the firm if just Plan A were used?

(B) What would be the total cost to the firm if just Plan B were used?

(C) If both plans were being used, which terminal manager was probably assigned to which plan?

(D) Which plan should the firm adopt if it is interested in motivating the managers to increase sales? If neither plan is acceptable, what type of plan might work?

*18–34 How can an accounting report promote goal congruence in the firm?

18–35 Mr. Al Tadate has been a managerial accountant for many years. He is opposed to the recent interest in the behavioral sciences. "We're accountants, not psychologists. If a firm wants to study the behavioral sciences, let it find a behavioral science practitioner. I practice the science of accounting." Comment on the position taken by Mr. Tadate. What type of behavior is he exhibiting?

*18–36 Managerial accounting exists to supply the information needs of management. Yet, in filling this need, the accounting information, and thus the accountant, can influence managerial behavior. What ethical considerations must exist in such an environment?

18–37 It is difficult to "type" people purely on the basis of the job they hold. Yet, the managerial accountant must make such judgments when considering how to structure a report. Identify the factors you would consider in constructing a performance report for each of the following groups. Also, indicate what general characteristics the report would possess.

(A) A group of city sanitation workers

(B) Scientists in the research and development department of a large firm

(C) Faculty members of a university

(D) Production workers in a manufacturing firm

(E) Division managers in a large company

18–38 The Flectcher Fiber Company is having a problem in one of its manufacturing plants. Last year, the Company and a local union negotiated a new contract that provided for a substantial increase in wages. Instead of increasing productivity, the workers have begun to speak of the "dehumanizing effects of the production line" and "the insensitivity of the company." One main complaint centers on the accounting performance reports. The workers expressed the feeling that they resent being compared to a hypothetical standard—they want to be evaluated as individuals. Management contends that the workers are malcontents, since these conditions exist at many other plants where workers do not complain.

(A) Are the workers at this plant really different from those employed at other locations?

(B) What can explain the workers' change in behavior?

(C) Should the accounting performance reporting system be changed in response to these complaints? If so, what changes should be made? If not, what can be done about the complaints?

18–39 Labeling an accounting report as a performance report is one means of influencing an individual's perception of its contents: performance is normally related to the reward system, which, in turn, will influence an individual's wages, status, and position within the firm. List and explain some other means to influence readers' perceptions of an accounting report.

18–40 Harry Hardrock was always considered one of the brightest managers in the firm. Freewheeling and flamboyant, he reported for work when it pleased him, was always dynamic and outspoken, and would push for innovations. Lately, his behavior has changed. He reports for work early and stays late. Most of his day is spent in meticulously reviewing the details of reports that cross his desk. At meetings, he has become quiet and passive and rarely offers ideas and suggestions. Along with these changes and his new work patterns, the performance in his division has declined considerably.

Discuss Harry's change of behavior. Which general shifts in behavior does he seem to be exhibiting? Should the firm attempt to determine and resolve any problems that he is facing? Why or why not?

*18–41 The Glory Morning Cereal Company was concerned about motivation among its employees. They hired a psychological research firm to test all employees and to determine their attitudes toward the Company. The results were surprising: the firm found that most employees had favorable attitudes about the Company. The formal report submitted by the research firm concluded that a high degree of actual goal congruence was present. Yet, many employees' actions hindered production and seemed to conflict with Company policies and goals.

(A) What motivational problem does the Glory Morning Company seem to be facing?

(B) How could this problem be detected?

(C) What actions should the Company take to eliminate the apparent problem?

18–42 Identify and discuss any potential behavioral problems evident in the following attitudes and opinions about budgets in the Yogi Hoagie Company:

(A) "As an accountant, it's my job to trim the fat off the preliminary information supplied by managers. They don't want realistic budgets: they just want to take it easy and not work for their pay. Well, they won't get away with it."

(B) "Our budget is realistic. Therefore, if anyone beats the budget, they must have had help. Some people just get lucky and manage to turn in favorable performance."

(C) "Accountants are a real pain. They come around here once a year for a few days and then sit down and tell us how our operation should run. They really don't understand anything that we do or why we have to do it. I wish they would just leave us alone."

(D) "All that performance reports do is highlight things that are wrong. If something isn't going right, I don't need a report to tell me; I know it. If those budgeting people really want to help me, why don't they come up with constructive suggestions?"

18-43 The Kant Refuse Company has an interesting system of budgetary control. Performance standards are set at the beginning of the year. Anytime a favorable deviation from the standard occurs, the budget is adjusted by one and one-half times the variance ("to provide some motivation"). If an unfavorable variance occurs, the manager responsible is immediately fired and all workers' bonuses are eliminated in that division ("to provide some motivation"). For the past thirteen years, there have been no favorable or unfavorable variances reported in the Kant Refuse Company.

(A) Does the budgetary control system seem to be working? Why or why not?

(B) Do you suppose that the budgetary control system promotes effective and efficient operations? Explain your answer.

(C) What changes would you introduce into this system? How could you justify these changes to management, which is obviously pleased with the results attained over the last thirteen years?

18-44 The Quic Tick Clock Company is decentralized into several divisions according to product lines. Every day, certain key cost items are monitored in each of the operating divisions. This information is sent to the firm's accounting office, where it is compared with performance standards and budgeted expectations. A daily performance report is prepared for each division. This report includes the measured key cost items, the appropriate standard or budget data, and any deviations that were detected. There are about 30 key cost items reported for each division.

To promote quick feedback, each day the accounting office calls each division manager on the telephone and reads the performance report to him. The reports are accumulated in a file and given to the division managers once a month.

(A) Are there any inherent problems in the Quic Tick Clock Company's daily reporting system? What can be done to correct these problems?

(B) What problems can result from the practice of accumulating performance data and reporting it monthly? What can be done to correct these problems?

(C) What good features are present in the Quic Tick system?

18–45 Miss Carrie Meback has worked in the accounting department of Jones and Wilson Products Company for 32 years. She knows most of the employees in the Company. Lately, she has been modifying the daily reports to include a weather forecast and a description of upcoming company social events. Are any problems likely to result from introducing these changes into the report?

18–46 The Universal International Rocking Chair Company prides itself on its modern, firmwide information system. At the heart of the system is a large computer installation. Each executive in the firm has a desk equipped with a cathode ray tube (television screen) tied online to the computer. On a minute-by-minute basis, the display screens are altered to reflect the latest information concerning the worldwide operations of Universal International Rocking Chair Company. Are there any potential behavioral problems inherent in this system? What suggestions can you make to improve on this information system?

18–47 Igor Knorr has always disliked the accounting staff at the company for which he works. In the past, his production department has been racked with problems. As a result of these problems, his division has made a poor showing on the weekly performance reports issued by the accounting staff. Igor's immediate supervisor always used these reports as a basis for criticizing Igor's ability as a manager. You have recently joined the accounting staff of this firm and have been asked to meet with Igor and collect necessary information about his division for use in completing next year's budget.

   (A) Do you expect Igor to be a cooperative participant in the budgeting process? What type of behavior is he likely to display?

   (B) What conditions or situations probably led Igor to this type of behavior? Do you suppose that these can be corrected? Why or why not?

   (C) Briefly describe how you would approach your first meeting with Igor.

18–48 For each of the following situations, describe any problems that might be encountered as a result of making the indicated changes in reporting:

   (A) The inventory valuation method is changed from FIFO to LIFO.

   (B) Instead of issuing monthly and quarterly reports, the company changes to a 4-4-4 system, in which four weeks are equivalent to a month, and three, four-week periods are treated as a quarter.

   (C) The company changes from absorption costing to direct costing for internal reporting.

   (D) The unit sales price of a company's products is increased. This will affect reported revenues in the future.

18–49 Mr. I. M. Duped is the owner of a medium-sized manufacturing firm. After reading a chapter on the behavioral implications of accounting in a new managerial accounting book, he became convinced that there were problems in his firm's internal reporting system. The following day he called his chief accountant, Mr. Adam Kwick into his office. Mr. Duped instructed Mr. Kwick that all future accounting reports should be 100% objective. "We expect our employees to believe and use this information," he commented. "The least that you accountants can do is to make sure that it is completely unbiased and verifiable."

(A) Does Mr. Duped's request seem reasonable? Comment on it.

(B) What costs would be involved in preparing a completely objective report? If cost were no object, could such a report be prepared? Why or why not?

(C) As Mr. Kwick, respond to Mr. Duped's request in a brief, but complete, fashion.

18–50 Much of the discussion in this chapter seems to be related to profit-oriented business organizations, in which workers' motivation and efficiency contribute to the overall profitability of the enterprise. Do any of these behavioral observations apply to nonprofit organizations? If any are applicable, identify which ones and explain why. If none is applicable, explain why not.

18–51 Mark each of the following statements "true" or "false."

(A) Accountants have always been interested in behavioral sciences and their relationship to accounting.

(B) The main purpose of managerial accounting reports is to influence the behavior of decision-makers in the firm.

(C) An individual normally pursues one goal at a time; to pursue more than one will lead to confusion.

(D) According to Maslow, survival is the most basic human goal.

(E) To be efficient and effective, an organization must ensure that all members of the firm pursue the same goals as the firm.

(F) In practice, management by exception often is translated to mean that favorable variances were produced purely by luck.

(G) Participatory budgeting will cure many of the problems caused by budgetary pressure.

(H) Noise is a physical type of interference that inhibits the communication process.

*18–52 The operating budget is a common instrument used by many businesses. Although it is usually thought to be an important and necessary tool for management, it has been subject to some criticism from managers and researchers studying organizations and human behavior.

(A) From a behavioral standpoint, describe and discuss the benefits of budgeting.

(B) From a behavioral standpoint, describe and discuss criticisms leveled at the budgeting process.

(C) What solutions are recommended to overcome the criticism described in part (B).

(CMA adapted)

18–53   For each of the following sections, select the letter that corresponds to the "best" answer. Be prepared to explain or justify your choice.

(A) Which of the following statements is true with respect to upward communications?

a. Few barriers exist for communication from workers to management.
b. It tends to travel faster than downward communication.
c. It works well when handled officially but works rarely in social and casual contacts.
d. Minimal upward communication occurs unless management positively encourages it.

(B) Job enlargement:
a. Means a work layout providing more space
b. Reduces the need for training
c. Adds more functions to a job, increasing its scope and complexity
d. Does no work where there is procedural initiation of action

(C) Which of the following concepts is not related to communication theory?
a. Sequential search
b. Feedback
c. Noise
d. Perception

(D) The "needs hierarchy" theory is usually associated with the name of
a. Frederick Taylor
b. Douglas McGregor
c. A. H. Maslow
d. Max Weber

(E) According to the "needs hierarchy" theory:
a. Each of the needs is essentially infinite; that is, each is characterized by continuously rising aspiration levels.
b. There is a definite sequence of domination; that is, Need 2 does not dominate until Need 1 is reasonably satisfied.
c. Each individual tends to have a certain requirement for need

satisfaction which is relatively uniform across needs at any point in time.

d. Some individuals do not seem to require the fulfillment of lower-level needs.

(F) First-line supervisors would be most likely to describe their biggest problem as:

   a. Communication
   b. Working conditions
   c. Wages
   d. Security

(G) Which of the following statements is not generally accepted by modern organizational theory?

   a. Organizations do not have goals; only individuals have goals.
   b. Organizational behavior must be analyzed in terms of multiple goals.
   c. Organizations are the means by which individuals achieve their goals.
   d. In order for an organization to survive, it must pursue a single goal as efficiently as possible.

(H) Studies on the importance of allowing employees to participate in making decisions about plant policy reveal that:

   a. Such a procedure is the best way to achieve maximum production.
   b. Only small corporations can profit from such an approach.
   c. Success depends on the supervision.
   d. Results are conflicting; in some cases production is increased, and in others, it is decreased.

(I) An important prerequisite for effective participation is:

   a. The participant must be allowed to participate in all matters affecting him.
   b. Neither party should feel that his position is threatened by participation.
   c. The financial cost of participation should not be considered a limiting factor to its use.
   d. Participation for deciding a course of action should be both within and without the group's area of job freedom.

(J) Classical theories of organizational control stress the need for equivalence between which of the following?

   a. Power and authority
   b. Power and responsibility
   c. Responsibility and authority
   d. Leadership and responsibility

(CMA adapted)

18–54   The Alton Company is going to expand its punch press department. It is about to purchase three new punch presses from Equipment Manufacturers, Inc. Equipment Manufacturers' engineers report that their mechanical studies indicate that for Alton's intended use, the output rate for one press should be 1,000 pieces per hour. Alton has very similar presses now in operation. At the present time, production from these presses averages 600 pieces per hour.

A study of the Alton experience shows that the average is derived from the following individual outputs.

Worker		Daily Output
L. Jones		750
J. Green		750
R. Smith		600
H. Brown		500
R. Alters		550
G. Hoag		450
	Total	3600
Average		600

Alton management also plans to institute a standard cost accounting system in the very near future. The Company engineers are supporting a standard based upon 1,000 pieces per hour, the accounting department is arguing for 750 pieces per hour, and the department foreman is arguing for 600 pieces per hour.

(A) What arguments would each proponent be likely to use to support his case?

(B) Which alternative best reconciles the needs of cost control and the motivation of improved performance? Explain why you made that choice.

(CMA adapted)

Glossary

Absorption Costing   A traditional approach to valuing inventory and determining the cost of goods sold. The full costs of production, direct labor, direct material, and factory overhead, are all absorbed by, or associated with, the units produced during a period.

Accounting   A formal system for identifying, measuring, and communicating economic information about a particular entity to a particular group. Subclasses of accounting include: auditing, financial accounting, managerial accounting, and tax accounting.

Accounting Controls   The method and procedures used within an organization to safeguard the assets and ensure reliability of the financial records.

Administrative Controls   The methods and procedures employed within an organization to ensure operational efficiency and adherence to managerial policies. They are usually only indirectly related to the firm's financial records.

Administrative Costs   Costs that are not directly associated with production, selling, or distribution.

AICPA   The American Institute of Certified Public Accountants is a national organization of more than 70,000 professional, licensed accountants. Reports of the AICPA have codified generally accepted accounting principles (GAAP), as well as generally accepted auditing standards.

Allocation   A method of assigning common production costs indirectly to individual products. Allocation is necessary whenever costs cannot be traced directly to the products.

Annuity   A series of equal sums of money to be received or paid at regular intervals.

Asset Turnover   Asset turnover is the ratio of a segment's sales to its investment base. This measure focuses on the investment in productive resources and measures the velocity of resource utilization.

Assignment Techniques   A process of distributing costs and/or revenues among parts of the firm. Assignment techniques trace or assign costs and revenues as appropriate.

Attainable Performance Standard

A predetermined performance expectation that includes certain acceptable inefficiencies in the base, such as elements of spoilage or waste, which are impractical or unfeasible to eliminate.

Attestation

A communicated statement of opinion concerning the degree of correspondence between established criteria and accounting information issued by an entity. For external audits, attestation frequently is made by a CPA, an independent, authoritative, licensed professional, only after he has examined convincing evidence.

Auditing

A process of obtaining evidence regarding the assertions found in financial statements and evaluating it to determine the degree of correspondence between those assertions and established criteria.

Authorizations

Expenditures that have received prior approval. For governmental units, legal approval is required to create an authorization.

Average Past Performance Standard

A performance expectation derived by averaging past productive performances. This standard requires future performance to be at least no worse than the past.

Average Rate of Return

The ratio of average annual profits to book value of investment, often used as a criterion in evaluating capital-budgeting alternatives. (Also called "the accountant's rate of return.")

Balance Sheet

A report on the financial position of a company as of one particular moment, detailing adjusted historical costs of all resources available for future use. It lists also the creditor and owner claims against those resources.

Behavioral Science

Any scientific discipline relating to the actions, or behavior, of man, including: anthropology, economics, history, political science, psychology, and sociology.

Bias

An existing prejudice that may sway the mind. Freedom from bias is one criterion designed to make accounting data neutral, that is, not prejudicing interpretations.

Breakeven Point   The point on a cost-volume-profit chart where total costs exactly equal total revenue.

Budget   A formal plan of action, expressed in figures, that specifies an objective and the means for its attainment. Managerial accounting is frequently charged with the responsibility for budgeting.

Budget Committee   A group of top-level executives representing the major line functions, who serve as a consulting body in formalizing the budget. They gather expectations and forecasts about their areas of responsibility, establish relationships among data needs, prepare budgets, and see that the budgets are distributed to those concerned.

Budgeted Costs   Future estimated costs that are formally combined into a plan of action.

By-Product   An output of a joint production process that is considered to be of minor economic importance to the firm.

Capacity   The fixed amount of plant, equipment, or personnel committed to the operation of the organization. Capacity represents the ability to provide volume.

Capacity Costs   One type of fixed cost necessary to provide organization and operating facilities to produce and sell at the budgeted volume level.

Capital Budgeting   Planning for investment decisions, a form of long-run, nonroutine budgeting concerned with proposed capital projects and their financing.

Capital Rationing   A situation that arises when the amount of funds available for capital projects is smaller than the amount proposed for all projects and, therefore, must be allocated, or rationed, among the proposals.

Carrying Costs   Costs incurred in maintaining an inventory, including storage and warehousing, insurance, and cost of money invested in inventory.

Cash Budget   A formal plan of estimated future cash inflows, outflows, and balances.

Clock Card   An individual time record used in computing hourly payrolls and in accumulating labor cost information for product costing purposes.

Cognitive Dissonance A type of psychological noise that increases the likelihood of selective exposure, selective perception, and selective retention on the part of a report user.

Committed Fixed Costs Nonvariable costs associated with the firm's capacity to produce or provide output. These costs reflect the capability for sustaining a planned volume of activity, and generally arise from the acquisition of plant, equipment, or basic organization.

Common Cost Production costs that cannot be associated directly with a single product output; they are shared, or common, to all of the outputs.

Comparison Comparison is at the heart of financial-statement analysis. Accounting numbers are most meaningful when analyzed on a historical, similar activity, or expectational basis.

Complementary Measures of Performance Those factors that influence the direct measures of division performance but are not disclosed on the performance report.

Compound Interest Interest accumulated on both the original principal and all previously accumulated interest.

Constraints Restraining forces produced by the existence of limited resources, limited knowledge, or unfavorable legal climate.

Contingent Projects A set of projects that are inherently related, wherein acceptance of one will lead to acceptance of another.

Continuous Budget A technique of budget preparation that adds a new period (such as a month) in the future as the period just ended is completed.

Continuous Manufacturing A manufacturing process geared to producing many similar units in a series, each no different from the others, and all requiring the same amount of skill, attention, and effort.

Contribution Approach A form of internal reporting that emphasizes cost-volume-profit relationships. Variable costs and fixed costs are used as major bases of classification in a contribution statement.

Contribution Margin The arithmetic difference between revenue and variable costs, which represents the amount available first for meeting fixed costs and then for contributing toward profit. The unit contribution margin is the difference between the price and variable cost per unit.

Contribution-Margin Ratio

The ratio of the contribution margin divided by the revenue; alternately, the ratio of the unit contribution margin and the price. This ratio expresses the proportion of each sales dollar that first contributes toward meeting fixed costs and then toward profit.

Control

The process of obtaining conformity to plans through actions and evaluations. Managerial accounting is frequently responsible for accumulating data for the control process.

Control Process

The control process consists of three interrelated functions: (1) an explicit statement of plans, (2) the measurement of actual performance, and (3) the feedback of information to appropriate managers.

Control System

A control system includes people, resources, and procedures combined in such a way as to promote the attainment of organizational goals.

Controllable Costs

Costs whose incurrence may be directly influenced by an identifiable manager within a given time period. Controllable costs (1) vary in size, (2) are identifiable with a particular manager, and (3) relate to an appropriate time period.

Controller

The executive responsible for managing the accounting function (sometimes spelled "comptroller").

Conversion Costs

The sum of direct labor and manufacturing overhead costs.

Cost

The value of the resource obtained or the value forgone to achieve an economic benefit.

Cost Accounting Standards Board (CASB)

A federal agency established by Congress to assist governmental agencies as buyers of goods and services in understanding and negotiating cost-based prices.

Cost Accumulation

A data-gathering function assigned to managerial accountants to provide information for planning, information-processing, control, and decision-making purposes.

Cost-based Pricing   The process of determining a selling price by calculating the cost of a unit of product. An addition for profit may be made to some suitable cost base. Also called Cost-Plus Pricing and Average Cost Pricing.

Cost-benefit Analysis   A final, subjective assessment of a project's merits. The benefits received from the services associated with a project should be at least as great as their cost.

Cost Centers   Divisions of a decentralized firm in which the division manager is responsible for minimizing costs. Costs are traced directly to the cost center, although revenue and invested capital are not.

Cost of Capital   The minimum-desired rate of return used as a cutoff point in making investment decisions.

Cost-Volume-Profit Analysis (CVP)   A planning model that considers the inherent relationships among prices, cost structure, profit, and volume. The model is a mathematical expression of a generalized income statement, and is frequently referred to as a "break-even model."

CPM (Critical Path Method)   A form of network analysis that describes the temporal relationships among several activities. The "critical path" is the minimum completion time for the project, which is measured as the sum of time for each activity in the longest direct path through the network.

Decision-Making   Selecting a course of action from among all alternatives. Managerial accountants frequently gather and analyze information for decision-making purposes.

Decision Rule   A formal, prespecified, mode of action to select a particular alternative (or make a decision) on the basis of the information available.

Departmental Cost Sheet   A summary of the labor, material, and overhead costs assigned to a particular department or production process during a given period.

Differential Cost   The difference in total costs between two acceptable alternatives. Also called Incremental Cost.

Direct Costing   An approach to inventory valuation that assigns no fixed costs to inventories. Inventory costs under direct costing are generally lower than under absorption costing, since fixed costs are excluded.

Direct Costs   Costs that are capable of being traced and logically associated with a particular product, time period, or organizational unit.

Direct Labor   Labor that is expended directly on the final product and traced directly to the product by the accounting system.

Direct Materials   Materials used in the production of the final product and traced directly to the product by the accounting system.

Direct Measures of Performance   Items presented in a performance report that highlight the influence of changes on the reported activity or outcome.

Directly Traceable Cost   (See Direct Costs.)

Discounted Present Value (DPV)   The amount of current cash that is equivalent to some specified amount of cash to be received or paid after some specified number of future periods, adjusted to reflect a specified interest rate.

Discounting   The process of adjusting cash flows for the time value of money.

Discrete Manufacturing   A manufacturing process that treats each unit or customer order separately. Different orders require different amounts of skill, attention, and effort.

Discretionary Fixed Costs   Nonvariable costs created by managerial policy, which demand periodic appropriations. Although the magnitude of these costs can be changed from year to year, such changes need not bear any relationship to changes in volume. Also called "managed" or "programmed" costs.

Division   A responsibility center where the manager is held responsible for both production and marketing decisions.

Drive   An aroused state of the organism resulting from stimulation. The motive-directed drive leads to action.

Dysfunctional Consequences   Events that adversely affect the organization.

Earmarking   The process of restricting particular cash inflows for particular purposes. A device widely used by nonprofit organizations to control resources. Earmarked funds can be used only for the earmarked purpose.

Economic Order Quantity (EOQ)

The optimal size of purchase orders, determined according to the costs of ordering (which decrease with the size of orders) and the costs of storage (which increase with the size of orders).

Effectiveness

The accomplishment of a desired objective, goal, or action.

Efficiency

The accomplishment of a desired objective, goal, or action with the minimum resources necessary. Usually measured on a cost/benefit basis.

Efficiency Variance

A quantity or usage variance applied to direct labor or to variable factory overhead. It is the difference between the standard and actual quantities multiplied by the standard rate.

Elasticity of Demand

The responsiveness of consumers to price changes. If consumers are sensitive to price changes, demand is elastic. If consumers are unresponsive to price changes, demand is inelastic.

Equivalent Units

A concept used by accountants to provide a means of counting partially completed units in a beginning or ending inventory. Partially completed units are equated to a proportionate number of completed units.

Excess Material Requisition

A form used to request needed production materials in excess of the standard amount of materials allowed for the output.

Expectations

Anticipated but uncertain future outcomes.

Expected Volume

The anticipated level of activity for the coming year.

Favorable Variance

A variance where actual costs are less than budgeted or standard costs.

Feedback

Information about the consequences of past actions, which may be used for investigations, evaluations, and follow-up.

FIFO

The first-in, first-out method of accounting for production. The first units to enter a process are assumed to be the first units to leave a process.

Financial Accounting   That class of accounting primarily concerned with identifying and measuring data in accordance with generally accepted accounting principles and reporting its findings to parties external to the organization. The primary reports of financial accounting include the balance sheet, income statement, and statement of changes in financial position.

Financial Accounting Standards Board (F.A.S.B.)   An independent group of accountants concerned with establishing policy for external reporting practices.

Financial Budgets   Formal projections of expected cash receipts, disbursements, and budgeted financial statements.

Fixed Costs   Costs associated with inputs that do not fluctuate in response to changes in the firm's activity, as long as that activity is within a limited range. A more appropriate but less traditional name for such costs is "nonvariable."

Flexible Budget   A budget containing columns for costs at several levels of volume, or one that can be modified to compensate for changes in volume. These are especially useful for budgeting in uncertain environments.

Full Costing   (See Absorption Costing.)

Functional Fixation   A behavioral characteristic in which a person ascribes an unchanging meaning to a title of a report or to a situation and is unable to see alternative meanings, even if the content of the report changes.

Fund Accounting   A fund is a separate unit of accountability, and the fund accounts contain data solely concerned with that fund. The accounts of a nonprofit organization can be subdivided into several independent funds.

GAAP (Generally Accepted Accounting Principles)   A set of concepts, practices, and procedures uniformly applied to financial accounting practices in the United States. GAAP slowly evolved from fifteenth-century Italian bookkeeping practices and have been codified by the AICPA and F.A.S.B.

Generally Accepted Auditing Standards   A set of standards used by auditors to evaluate the quality of an audit. These have been codified by the AICPA.

Goal   Future objective associated with strategic policies or tactical means. Goals are usually directly related to

	the purposes that underlie an organization's existence.
Goal Congruence	That situation in which an individual's personal goals and the goals of an organization coincide. Actual goal congruence is a similarity of goals; apparent goal congruence is a similarity of goal-directed action.
Ideal Standard	Targets of ultimate performance. No allowances are made for any production flaws or human inefficiencies. These standards provide the highest performance goal.
Idle Capacity Variance	A variance calculated at the time the master budget is prepared. It measures unused plant capacity and represents the difference between the practical capacity and the master budget levels of output.
Idle Time	Labor time not involved in productive effort; usually treated as indirect labor.
Income Statement	A financial accounting report on the revenues and related input costs of an entity for the accounting period.
Incremental Analysis	The process of measuring the additional costs or benefits of one alternative chosen instead over another.
Incremental Cost	The total additional cost that will be incurred if a particular alternative is chosen. The difference in total costs between two alternatives.
Indirect Cost	Those cost elements that cannot be traced directly to the units of productive output of a firm. Overhead costs are classified as indirect costs.
Indirect Expenses	(See Overhead.)
Indirect Factory Costs	(See Overhead.)
Indirect Labor	Labor included in factory overhead because it cannot be traced directly to the units of output.
Indirect Manufacturing Costs	(See Overhead.)
Indirect Materials	Material costs that are not directly traceable to the finished products, and are included in factory overhead.

Information Overload   An amount of information that exceeds the processing capacity of the receiver. "Excess" information is lost, ignored, or produces interference that can distort decisions.

Input Cluster   A single unit of input that has the potential to yield several different outputs.

Interference   Factors, both physical and psychological, that can impair communications.

Internal Time-Adjusted Rate-of-Return Model   A procedure for making investment decisions by equating the present value of cash inflows from a project with the present value of cash outflows for that same project, at a calculated rate of return. Projects with rates of return exceeding a predetermined cost of capital are acceptable. Also called Discounted Rate of Return, True Rate of Return, and Time-Adjusted Rate of Return.

Investment Centers   A refinement of the profit center. As the name implies, costs, revenues, and invested capital are all traced to the internal divisions.

Investment Decision   A choice from among opportunities to incur current costs in exchange for expectations of receiving future benefits.

Invoice   A bill for materials purchased sent by a supplier; the invoice serves as a source document for the purchases entry.

Job Enlargement   Techniques that expand the duties of organizational personnel, in contrast to the trend toward restrictive specialization. The job-enlargement technique seeks to increase productivity by increasing the individual's interest in his work.

Job-Order Costing   A cost-accounting system that traces and assigns all the production costs incurred by a manufacturing firm to particular factory jobs or customer orders.

Job-Order Cost Sheet   In a job-order cost accounting system, a record of all costs assigned to a particular job is kept on a job-order cost sheet.

Joint Cost   The cost of a single input that must be associated with two or more products or departments.

Joint Process A production process in which a single input results in more than one output.

Joint Product One of two or more outputs that result from processing a single input.

Lead Time The interval between the time a purchase order is placed and the time materials are received and available for use.

Learning Curve A graphic representation of the effect of learning on the output per man hour or machine hour. With greater familiarity, the production time per unit should decrease from the initial value.

Least-Squares Method A form of regression in which a straight line is fitted to described costs (y) according to the formula $y = a + bx$, where a represents fixed costs, b is the rate of variability, and x is volume.

Line-item Budget A budget in which specific objects of expenditure are expressed in considerable detail but the activities being budgeted are given little or no explicit recognition. When compared with actual expenditures, line-item budgets provide a basis for evaluating compliance with authorizations.

Managed Costs Fixed costs whose amounts are determined by management, not by their direct relationship to production output. (See Discretionary Fixed Costs.)

Management Audits Audits that investigate the effectiveness and efficiency with which resources have been used in carrying out the activities, functions, and programs of an organization. Management audits are also intended to assist management by identifying inefficiencies.

Management by Exception The practice of focusing attention only on those activities where actual performance differs significantly from planned performance.

Managerial Accounting That class of accounting concerned with identifying, measuring, and communicating information to internal management for planning, information-processing, control, and decision-making purposes.

Manufacturing Process All those tasks necessary to combine a set of productive elements — materials, labor, and overhead — into some finished products.

Margin on Sales	The ratio of a division's net income, before interest and taxes, to its net sales. This ratio measures the percentage of profit included in each sales dollar reported by the division.
Marginal Costs	The cost of one additional unit of output.
Margin Revenue	The increment in total revenue obtained when output is increased by one additional unit.
Marketing Variance	Also called the "sales variance," this measure represents the difference between budgeted sales volume and actual sales orders. It is generally used to reflect the performance of the firm's sales department.
Maslow's Hierarchy	A classification, devised by Abraham Maslow, of human needs ranked by their importance to the individual. The hierarchy has five distinct levels: physiological, safety, belongingness and love, esteem, and self-actualization.
Master Budget	A comprehensive budgeting plan composed of all budgeting schedules, including financial budgets, operating budgets, and special-decision budgets.
Material Requisition	A source document that authorizes the release of material held in the storeroom to authorized personnel.
Material Transfer Sheet	(See Material Requisition.)
Mixed Costs	Costs composed of both fixed and variable elements.
Modified Flexible Budget	A flexible budget modified to consider additional attributes. These budgets may indicate expectations to a greater extent than do ordinary flexible budgets.
Motivation	The process by which a goal is perceived and sought by an organism. It represents the start of the process that induces the organism to take action.
Mutually Exclusive Projects	A set of projects wherein the acceptance of one will rule out the acceptance of another.
N.A.A.	The National Association of Accountants is a voluntary professional organization of managerial accountants.
Net Present Value	An analysis that determines whether the present value of future cash inflows at the desired rate of

	return is greater or less than the present value of the future cash outflows.
Net Present-Value Model	A procedure for making investment decisions that calculates the expected benefit of a given project by discounting all expected future cash flows to the present, using some predetermined minimum-desired rate of return. Projects having positive net present values are acceptable.
Net Realizable Value	The difference between price (or revenue) obtained from selling a finished product and separable costs of that product.
Network Analysis	A budgeting technique used in scheduling and controlling projects by dividing each into discrete activities, stating the relationships among activities, and estimating the time required to accomplish each.
Noise	Errors, distortions, and extraneous materials that confuse the content of a report. Noise can be physical or psychological.
Nonprofit Organization	An organization that has (1) no deliberate profit motive, (2) no personally owned equity interests, (3) an equity interest that cannot be sold or exchanged, and (4) no special benefits accruing to the contributors of capital. Nonprofit organizations are created to provide socially desirable goods and services outside a competitive market.
Objectivity	A characteristic of control report necessary to enhance its effectiveness. Objective reports are unbiased and verifiable. Objectivity need exist only to the extent needed to satisfy the parties involved.
Operating Budgets	Formal projections of expected primary activities, such as sales, production, purchasing, and labor scheduling.
Opportunity Cost	Benefit that would have been obtained from an alternative if that alternative had been accepted.
Out-of-Pocket Costs	Costs that will require an expenditure of cash as a result of an anticipated decision.
Overhead	All costs of operating the factory except those designated as direct labor and direct material costs. Also

called Factory Burden, Indirect Factory Costs, Manufacturing Overhead, Indirect Expense.

Overhead Rate

A method of allocating the indirect factory costs to the products, creating an average overhead cost per unit or production activity. (See Predetermined overhead rate.)

Overhead Voucher

A document assigning overhead to a particular factory job. The overhead voucher provides an amount for assignments of factory overhead at a predetermined rate.

Overabsorbed Overhead

The excess of overhead cost applied to the product over the actual costs incurred. Also called Overapplied Overhead.

Overapplied Overhead

(See Overabsorbed Overhead.)

Payback Period

The number of years required to recover the initial cash outlay invested in a project. Frequently used as a criterion for capital-budgeting decisions.

Payback Reciprocal

The result of dividing the average annual cash inflow from a project by the original investment cost. Whenever the investment is made in one lump sum, yearly inflows are of equal amounts, and the project's life is greater than twice the payback period, the payback reciprocal closely approximates the internal time-adjusted rate of return.

Perception

An individualized, or unique, psychological function that causes the individual to attach meaning to what is sensed.

Performance Budgeting

Budgeting that emphasizes nonfinancial measures of performance, which can explain changes and deviations from planned performance.

Performance Report

A report to a manager comparing actual results with planned results in his area of responsibility.

Performance Standards

Predetermined performance expectations of prices and quantities for most major productive inputs.

Period Costs

Under direct costing, period costs are charged directly against revenue in the period during which they are incurred, and are not directly combined with other product costs. These costs are unresponsive to changes in volume and are incurred as the result of the passage of time.

PERT (Program Evaluation and Review Technology)
A method of network analysis that explicitly recognizes probabilistic estimates of the temporal relationships among a series of activities.

Physical Measures Allocation
A method of allocating common production costs by using the physical relationships among the co-products as a basis for dividing the costs.

Planning
The selection of goals and the means for attaining those goals. Planning is formalized through the budgeting process.

PPBS
PPBS stands for Planning Programming Budgetary Systems. It is a comprehensive decision model that requires an organization's objectives to be enumerated and its long-term goals to be established.

Predetermined Overhead Rate
An overhead rate determined in advance of production by dividing estimated (budgeted) factory overhead costs by an estimated (budgeted) volume base.

Present Value of Money
The amount that must be invested now to reach a given amount at some future given point of time, assuming it is compounded annually at a given rate of interest.

Price Variance
That portion of the total materials variance that is attributable to the purchase price. It is calculated as the difference between the standard and actual prices multiplied by the actual quantity purchased.

Prime Cost
Those costs associated with materials and labor. These productive elements can be traced directly to the units of finished product; that is, these costs correspond directly to the productive outputs.

Probabilistic Budget
A modified flexible budget that explicitly recognizes uncertainty by stating each line-item as a range of values.

Probability
A measure of the likelihood that an event will occur, represented by a decimal ranging between 0 and 1.

Process costing
A cost-accounting technique that provides for the accumulation and control of product costs in a continuous manufacturing process. Production costs are accumulated and assigned on a pro rata basis to the units of output.

Producing Departments	Organizational units that contribute directly to the conversion of raw materials into finished products.
Product Costs	Product costs are associated with elements of material, labor, and overhead that combine to produce the output of a firm.
Production Budget	A budget schedule that establishes the level of production planned for some future period.
Production Variance	The difference between scheduled production volume and actual production volume. Analysis of this variance focuses on the performance of production management.
Profit Centers	Decentralized subunits of an organization, in which both costs and revenues are traced to a division. Division management is held responsible for the profit performance of the division.
Pro Forma Financial Statements	Estimated or budgeted financial statements.
Program Budgeting	Budgeting that relates the accounting system to the objectives of the nonprofit organization according to activities to be provided, functions to be performed, and programs to be undertaken. Program budgets include estimates of the total cost for particular programs without regard to time.
Programmed Costs	(See Discretionary Costs.)
Purchase Order	A form sent to a supplier by the purchasing department requesting the purchase of material.
Purchase Requisition	A form issued by the storeroom requesting the purchasing department to procure some specific material.
Purchasing Budget	A budget schedule showing planned purchases for some future period.
Qualitative	A nonnumerical description of an event or an object. Qualitative factors are rarely reflected in accounting reports.
Quantifiability	The capacity to be measured or described in numerical terms. One criterion useful for evaluating accounting reports.
Quantity Variance	A measure of how well actual quantities agreed with planned quantities; the difference between the actual

quantities used and the standard (budgeted) quantities for actual production, multiplied by the standard price.

Rate Variance
A price variance related to direct labor costs. It represents the difference between the standard and actual wage rates paid for direct labor multiplied by the actual quantity of direct labor acquired.

Raw Materials Inventories
Production materials on hand but not yet processed.

Regression Analysis
(See Least Squares Regression.)

Relevance
The major criterion for evaluating accounting numbers. To be relevant, the information or the communication thereof must influence designated actions.

Relevant Range
That band of activity over which budgeted fixed costs can be assumed to be fixed and variable costs will fluctuate in direct proportion to changes in volume.

Reorder Point
The inventory level at which an order must be placed to provide adequate lead time to ensure delivery when needed.

Report Format
The physical arrangement and means of presenting data. The arrangement may affect the way a reader will behave or react to the reported information.

Reporting Model
A set of rules representing a facsimile of the reporting process, specifying how an activity is observed (recorded, classified, interpreted), reported, analyzed, and used.

Residual Income
A measure of division performance calculated by deducting an implicit interest cost from division net income.

Responsibility Accounting
An accounting system that charges individual managers within the firm with only those costs subject to their control. The cost classification, controllable versus uncontrollable, is a significant part of responsibility accounting.

Responsibility Center
A decentralized unit of organization controlled by one manager who has been delegated authority commensurate with his responsibility.

Return on Investment (ROI)	A measure of the profitability of a division of a firm relative to its investment base. It is calculated as the ratio of the division's net income, before interest and taxes, to its investment base. This ratio represents the combination of two other measures of performance—asset turnover and margin on sales.
Risk	An exposure to loss because of inability to control conditions upon which the firm is dependent.
Safety Stock	The minimum inventory level that provides a cushion against running out of stock because of changes in demand or changes in lead time.
Satisficing	A goal that strives for a satisfactory level of performance rather than a maximum level.
SEC	The Securities and Exchange Commission is a federal regulatory body responsible for controlling the public securities market.
Segment Margin	The segment margin expands the division cost analysis of a contribution statement to include elements of traceable fixed costs.
Separable Cost	Elements of cost that are identified solely with a particular product. They are directly traceable to a single output of the firm.
Service Department	A department that supports the producing departments' activities but is not directly involved with converting the raw materials into finished products.
Short-run Performance Margin	Part of a contribution statement that helps readers evaluate operating management. Included in the computation are revenues, variable costs, and discretionary fixed costs that are traceable to an individual division.
Should-Cost Review	An extension of the management audit concept. Should-cost reviews are essentially management audits of supplying contractors' efficiency. The reviews are based on analysis of what products or services "should cost" if the most economical and efficient practices are used.
Special-decision Budgets	Formal projections of information used to support special decisions, such as those concerned with inventory levels, economic order quantities, capital

budgets, graphic presentations, or feasibility studies.

Spending Variance   A price variance representing the difference between the standard and actual prices paid for factors of variable factory overhead.

Split-off Point   The point in a joint production process at which the inter-relationship among the joint products ceases. It marks the end of the joint process.

Standards   Predetermined targets of expected input quantities and prices, often used as a basis for evaluation.

Statement of Changes in Financial Position   A report that lists the sources and applications of funds received or expended during the accounting period. Fund activities result from normal operations, purchase or sale of property, debtor-creditor transactions, issuing equity interests, or paying dividends.

Static Budget   A budget related to only one level of volume, frequently called a "fixed" budget.

Stores Requisition   A document authorizing the transfer of raw materials to the production process. Stores requisitions show precisely when materials were released from the raw materials inventory and for what department and job they were intended to be used.

Strategic Planning   Establishing long-run goals for the organization.

Suboptimization   Occurs in a decentralized firm when one division "optimizes" its internal "profit" in such a way that the total profit of the firm is lowered.

Sunk Costs   Original acquisition costs that are no longer relevant for planning purposes.

Tactical Planning   Establishing the means for accomplishing or implementing goals.

Tax Accounting   That class of accounting concerned with selecting data that already exist within the accounting system and reporting the data on forms provided by the Internal Revenue Service. The accountant strives to minimize the tax liability while conforming to all legal requirements.

Tax Shield   The tax savings resulting from applying a noncash expense against income for income tax purposes.

The most common tax-shield related expense is depreciation.

Time-value of Money

A widely held preference to receive money now rather than later and to pay money later rather than now. This behavior pattern may be attributable to inflation, risk avoidance, and/or earning capacity.

Transfer Prices

A means of pricing, or valuing, internal transactions between divisions of a decentralized firm. Transfer prices determine the "revenue" of the selling division and the "cost" of the buying division. There are many ways to construct the transfer price.

Ultimate Market Value Allocation

A method for allocating common costs that uses a product's market potential as a basis for proportionally dividing the common costs.

Underapplied Overhead

The amount by which overhead incurred exceeds overhead applied to the products.

Unfavorable Variance

A variance where the actual costs are greater than the budgeted or standard costs.

Unit Contribution Margin

The contribution margin for one unit of output, calculated as the difference between the price and the variable cost for that unit.

Usage Variance

The difference between standard and actual performance levels of materials used in production, multiplied by the standard price for materials.

Variable Cost

Costs that fluctuate in direct proportion to changes in volume.

Variable Costing

A system of measuring inventory costs that assigns variable production costs of material, labor, and variable factory overhead to the product unit cost. Fixed factory overhead costs and nonproduction costs are treated as period costs. Also called Marginal Costing and Direct Costing.

Variance

An observed performance deviation measured by comparing actual and standard performance. Variance analysis is an integral part of the control process of an organization.

Verifiability

A characteristic of accounting reports permitting qualified independent individuals to draw similar conclusions after examining the same evidence.

Volume
Volume measures the usage of capacity, such as units of output or quantity of input.

Volume Variance
The difference in productive output between planned expectations presented in the master budget and actual results. It is the sum of the marketing and production variances or the difference between budgeted sales volume and actual production volume.

Weighted Average Costing Method
A method for assigning processing costs to units produced. A cost per unit is calculated by dividing total processing costs by total equivalent units.

Work-in-Process Inventory
The cost of uncompleted products still in the factory.

Work Tickets
A record of the time worked by employees on particular jobs. Also called "labor summaries."

Zero-based Budget
An analytically developed budget that requires each budgeting unit to justify all costs each year rather than just justifying year-to-year cost changes, as is traditionally done.

APPENDIX A: Future Value Amount of \$1.00 Due in n Periods $V = (1 + r)^n$

n	Rate of Interest, % 1.0	2.0	3.0	4.0	5.0	6.0	8.0	10.0	15.0
1	1.0100	1.0200	1.0300	1.0400	1.0500	1.0600	1.0800	1.1000	1.1500
2	1.0201	1.0404	1.0609	1.0816	1.1025	1.1236	1.1664	1.2100	1.3225
3	1.0303	1.0612	1.0927	1.1249	1.1576	1.1910	1.2597	1.3310	1.5209
4	1.0406	1.0824	1.1255	1.1699	1.2155	1.2625	1.3605	1.4641	1.7490
5	1.0510	1.1041	1.1593	1.2167	1.2763	1.3382	1.4693	1.6105	2.0114
6	1.0615	1.1262	1.1941	1.2653	1.3401	1.4185	1.5869	1.7716	2.3131
7	1.0721	1.1487	1.2299	1.3159	1.4071	1.5036	1.7138	1.9487	2.6600
8	1.0829	1.1717	1.2668	1.3686	1.4775	1.5938	1.8509	2.1436	3.0590
9	1.0937	1.1951	1.3048	1.4233	1.5513	1.6895	1.9990	2.3579	3.5179
10	1.1046	1.2190	1.3439	1.4802	1.6289	1.7908	2.1589	2.5937	4.0555
11	1.1157	1.2434	1.3842	1.5395	1.7103	1.8983	2.3316	2.8531	4.6524
12	1.1268	1.2682	1.4258	1.6010	1.7959	2.0122	2.5182	3.1384	5.3502
13	1.1381	1.2936	1.4685	1.6651	1.8856	2.1329	2.7196	3.4523	6.1528
14	1.1495	1.3195	1.5126	1.7317	1.9799	2.2609	2.9372	3.7975	7.0757
15	1.1610	1.3459	1.5580	1.8009	2.0789	2.3966	3.1722	4.1772	8.1370
16	1.1726	1.3728	1.6047	1.8730	2.1829	2.5404	3.4259	4.5950	9.3576
17	1.1843	1.4002	1.6528	1.9479	2.2920	2.6928	3.7000	5.0545	10.761
18	1.1961	1.4282	1.7024	2.0258	2.4066	2.8543	3.9960	5.5599	12.375
19	1.2081	1.4568	1.7535	2.1068	2.5270	3.0256	4.3157	6.1159	14.232
20	1.2202	1.4859	1.8061	2.1911	2.6533	3.2071	4.6610	6.7275	16.366
21	1.2324	1.5157	1.8603	2.2788	2.7860	3.3996	5.0338	7.4002	18.821
22	1.2447	1.5460	1.9161	2.3699	2.9253	3.6035	5.4365	8.1403	21.645
23	1.2572	1.5769	1.9736	2.4647	3.0715	3.8197	5.8715	8.9543	24.891
24	1.2697	1.6084	2.0328	2.5633	3.2251	4.0489	6.3412	9.8497	28.625
25	1.2824	1.6406	2.0938	2.6658	3.3864	4.2919	6.8485	10.834	32.919
26	1.2953	1.6734	2.1566	2.7725	3.5557	4.5494	7.3964	11.918	37.856
27	1.3082	1.7069	2.2213	2.8834	3.7335	4.8223	7.9881	13.110	43.535
28	1.3213	1.7410	2.2879	2.9987	3.9201	5.1117	8.6271	14.421	50.065
29	1.3345	1.7758	2.3566	3.1187	4.1161	5.4184	9.3173	15.863	57.575
30	1.3478	1.8114	2.4273	3.2434	4.3219	5.7435	10.062	17.449	66.211
35	1.4166	1.9999	2.8139	3.9461	5.5160	7.6861	14.785	28.102	133.17
40	1.4889	2.2080	3.2620	4.8010	7.0400	10.285	21.724	45.259	267.86
45	1.5648	2.4379	3.7816	5.8412	8.9850	13.764	31.920	72.890	538.77
50	1.6446	2.6916	4.3839	7.1067	11.467	18.420	46.901	117.39	1083.7

APPENDIX B: Present Value of $1.00 $PV = (1 + r)^{-n} = \dfrac{1}{(1 + r)^n}$

n/r	1.0%	2.0%	3.0%	4.0%	5.0%
1	.990099	.980392	.970874	.961538	.952381
2	.980296	.961169	.942596	.924556	.907029
3	.970590	.942322	.915142	.888996	.863838
4	.960980	.923845	.888487	.854804	.822702
5	.951466	.905731	.862609	.821927	.783526
6	.942045	.887971	.837484	.790315	.746215
7	.932718	.870560	.813092	.759918	.710681
8	.923483	.853490	.789409	.730690	.676839
9	.914340	.836755	.766417	.702587	.644609
10	.905287	.820348	.744094	.675564	.613913
11	.896324	.804263	.722421	.649581	.584679
12	.887449	.788493	.701380	.624597	.556837
13	.878663	.773033	.680951	.600574	.530321
14	.869963	.757875	.661118	.577475	.505068
15	.861349	.743015	.641862	.555265	.481017
16	.852821	.728446	.623167	.533908	.458112
17	.844377	.714163	.605016	.513373	.436297
18	.836017	.700159	.587395	.493628	.415521
19	.827740	.686431	.570286	.474642	.395734
20	.819544	.672971	.553676	.456387	.376889
21	.811430	.659776	.537549	.438834	.358942
22	.803396	.646839	.521893	.421955	.341850
23	.795442	.634156	.506692	.405726	.325571
24	.787566	.621721	.491934	.390121	.310068
25	.779768	.609531	.477606	.375117	.295303
26	.772048	.597579	.463695	.360689	.281241
27	.764404	.585862	.450189	.346817	.267848
28	.756836	.574375	.437077	.333477	.255094
29	.749342	.563112	.424346	.320651	.242946
30	.741923	.552071	.411987	.308319	.231377
35	.705914	.500028	.355383	.253415	.181290
40	.671653	.452890	.306557	.208289	.142046
45	.639055	.410197	.264439	.171198	.111297
50	.608039	.371528	.228107	.140713	.087204

n/r	6%	7%	8%	9%	10%	11%
1	0.9434	0.9346	0.9259	0.9174	0.9091	0.9009
2	0.8900	0.8734	0.8573	0.8417	0.8264	0.8116
3	0.8396	0.8163	0.7938	0.7722	0.7513	0.7312
4	0.7921	0.7629	0.7350	0.7084	0.6830	0.6587
5	0.7473	0.7130	0.6806	0.6499	0.6209	0.5935
6	0.7050	0.6663	0.6302	0.5963	0.5645	0.5346
7	0.6651	0.6227	0.5835	0.5470	0.5132	0.4817
8	0.6274	0.5820	0.5403	0.5019	0.4665	0.4339
9	0.5919	0.5439	0.5002	0.4604	0.4241	0.3909
10	0.5584	0.5083	0.4632	0.4224	0.3855	0.3522
11	0.5268	0.4751	0.4289	0.3875	0.3505	0.3173
12	0.4970	0.4440	0.3971	0.3555	0.3186	0.2858
13	0.4688	0.4150	0.3677	0.3262	0.2897	0.2575
14	0.4423	0.3878	0.3405	0.2992	0.2633	0.2320
15	0.4173	0.3624	0.3152	0.2745	0.2394	0.2090
16	0.3936	0.3387	0.2919	0.2519	0.2176	0.1883
17	0.3714	0.3166	0.2703	0.2311	0.1978	0.1696
18	0.3503	0.2959	0.2502	0.2120	0.1799	0.1528
19	0.3305	0.2765	0.2317	0.1945	0.1635	0.1377
20	0.3118	0.2584	0.2145	0.1784	0.1486	0.1240
21	0.2942	0.2415	0.1987	0.1637	0.1351	0.1117
22	0.2775	0.2257	0.1839	0.1502	0.1228	0.1007
23	0.2618	0.2109	0.1703	0.1378	0.1117	0.0907
24	0.2470	0.1971	0.1577	0.1264	0.1015	0.0817
25	0.2330	0.1842	0.1460	0.1160	0.0923	0.0736
26	0.2198	0.1722	0.1352	0.1064	0.0839	0.0663
27	0.2074	0.1609	0.1252	0.0976	0.0763	0.0597
28	0.1956	0.1504	0.1159	0.0895	0.0693	0.0538
29	0.1846	0.1406	0.1073	0.0822	0.0630	0.0485
30	0.1741	0.1314	0.0994	0.0754	0.0573	0.0437
35	0.1301	0.0937	0.0676	0.0490	0.0356	0.0259
40	0.0972	0.0668	0.0460	0.0318	0.0221	0.0154
45	0.0727	0.0476	0.0313	0.0207	0.0137	0.0091
50	0.0543	0.0339	0.0213	0.0134	0.0085	0.0054

n/r	12%	13%	14%	15%	16%	17%
1	0.8929	0.8850	0.8772	0.8696	0.8621	0.8547
2	0.7972	0.7831	0.7695	0.7561	0.7432	0.7305
3	0.7118	0.6931	0.6750	0.6575	0.6407	0.6244
4	0.6355	0.6133	0.5921	0.5718	0.5523	0.5337
5	0.5674	0.5428	0.5194	0.4972	0.4761	0.4561
6	0.5066	0.4803	0.4556	0.4323	0.4104	0.3898
7	0.4523	0.4251	0.3996	0.3759	0.3538	0.3332
8	0.4039	0.3762	0.3506	0.3269	0.3050	0.2848
9	0.3606	0.3329	0.3075	0.2843	0.2630	0.2434
10	0.3220	0.2946	0.2697	0.2472	0.2267	0.2080
11	0.2875	0.2607	0.2366	0.2149	0.1954	0.1778
12	0.2567	0.2307	0.2076	0.1869	0.1685	0.1520
13	0.2292	0.2042	0.1821	0.1625	0.1452	0.1299
14	0.2046	0.1807	0.1597	0.1413	0.1252	0.1110
15	0.1827	0.1599	0.1401	0.1229	0.1079	0.0949
16	0.1631	0.1415	0.1229	0.1069	0.0930	0.0811
17	0.1456	0.1252	0.1078	0.0929	0.0802	0.0693
18	0.1300	0.1108	0.0946	0.0808	0.0691	0.0592
19	0.1161	0.0981	0.0829	0.0703	0.0596	0.0506
20	0.1037	0.0868	0.0728	0.0611	0.0514	0.0433
21	0.0926	0.0768	0.0638	0.0531	0.0443	0.0370
22	0.0826	0.0680	0.0560	0.0462	0.0382	0.0316
23	0.0738	0.0601	0.0491	0.0402	0.0329	0.0270
24	0.0659	0.0532	0.0431	0.0349	0.0284	0.0231
25	0.0588	0.0471	0.0378	0.0304	0.0245	0.0197
26	0.0525	0.0417	0.0331	0.0264	0.0211	0.0169
27	0.0469	0.0369	0.0291	0.0230	0.0182	0.0144
28	0.0419	0.0326	0.0255	0.0200	0.0157	0.0123
29	0.0374	0.0289	0.0224	0.0174	0.0135	0.0105
30	0.0334	0.0256	0.0196	0.0151	0.0116	0.0090
35	0.0189	0.0139	0.0102	0.0075	0.0055	0.0041
40	0.0107	0.0075	0.0053	0.0037	0.0026	0.0019
45	0.0061	0.0041	0.0027	0.0019	0.0013	0.0009
50	0.0035	0.0022	0.0014	0.0009	0.0006	0.0004

n/r	18%	19%	20%	21%	22%	23%
1	0.8475	0.8403	0.8333	0.8264	0.8197	0.8130
2	0.7182	0.7062	0.6944	0.6830	0.6719	0.6610
3	0.6086	0.5934	0.5787	0.5645	0.5507	0.5374
4	0.5158	0.4987	0.4823	0.4665	0.4514	0.4369
5	0.4371	0.4190	0.4019	0.3855	0.3700	0.3552
6	0.3704	0.3521	0.3349	0.3186	0.3033	0.2888
7	0.3139	0.2959	0.2791	0.2633	0.2486	0.2348
8	0.2660	0.2487	0.2326	0.2176	0.2038	0.1909
9	0.2255	0.2090	0.1938	0.1799	0.1670	0.1552
10	0.1911	0.1756	0.1615	0.1486	0.1369	0.1262
11	0.1619	0.1476	0.1346	0.1228	0.1122	0.1026
12	0.1372	0.1240	0.1122	0.1015	0.0920	0.0834
13	0.1163	0.1042	0.0935	0.0839	0.0754	0.0678
14	0.0985	0.0876	0.0779	0.0693	0.0618	0.0551
15	0.0835	0.0736	0.0649	0.0573	0.0507	0.0448
16	0.0708	0.0618	0.0541	0.0474	0.0415	0.0364
17	0.0600	0.0520	0.0451	0.0391	0.0340	0.0296
18	0.0508	0.0437	0.0376	0.0323	0.0279	0.0241
19	0.0431	0.0367	0.0313	0.0267	0.0229	0.0196
20	0.0365	0.0308	0.0261	0.0221	0.0187	0.0159
21	0.0309	0.0259	0.0217	0.0183	0.0154	0.0129
22	0.0262	0.0218	0.0181	0.0151	0.0126	0.0105
23	0.0222	0.0183	0.0151	0.0125	0.0103	0.0086
24	0.0188	0.0154	0.0126	0.0103	0.0085	0.0070
25	0.0160	0.0129	0.0105	0.0085	0.0069	0.0057
26	0.0135	0.0109	0.0087	0.0070	0.0057	0.0046
27	0.0115	0.0091	0.0073	0.0058	0.0047	0.0037
28	0.0097	0.0077	0.0061	0.0048	0.0038	0.0030
29	0.0082	0.0064	0.0051	0.0040	0.0031	0.0025
30	0.0070	0.0054	0.0042	0.0033	0.0026	0.0020
35	0.0030	0.0023	0.0017	0.0013	0.0009	0.0007
40	0.0013	0.0010	0.0007	0.0005	0.0004	0.0002
45	0.0006	0.0004	0.0003	0.0002	0.0001	0.0001
50	0.0003	0.0002	0.0001	0.0001	0.0000	0.0000

n/r	24%	25%	26%	27%	28%	29%
1	0.8065	0.8000	0.7937	0.7874	0.7813	0.7752
2	0.6504	0.6400	0.6299	0.6200	0.6104	0.6009
3	0.5245	0.5120	0.4999	0.4882	0.4768	0.4658
4	0.4230	0.4096	0.3968	0.3844	0.3725	0.3611
5	0.3411	0.3277	0.3149	0.3027	0.2910	0.2799
6	0.2751	0.2621	0.2499	0.2383	0.2274	0.2170
7	0.2218	0.2097	0.1983	0.1877	0.1776	0.1682
8	0.1789	0.1678	0.1574	0.1478	0.1388	0.1304
9	0.1443	0.1342	0.1249	0.1164	0.1084	0.1011
10	0.1164	0.1074	0.0992	0.0916	0.0847	0.0784
11	0.0938	0.0859	0.0787	0.0721	0.0662	0.0607
12	0.0757	0.0687	0.0625	0.0568	0.0517	0.0471
13	0.0610	0.0550	0.0496	0.0447	0.0404	0.0365
14	0.0492	0.0440	0.0393	0.0352	0.0316	0.0283
15	0.0397	0.0352	0.0312	0.0277	0.0247	0.0219
16	0.0320	0.0281	0.0248	0.0218	0.0193	0.0170
17	0.0258	0.0225	0.0197	0.0172	0.0150	0.0132
18	0.0208	0.0180	0.0156	0.0135	0.0118	0.0102
19	0.0168	0.0144	0.0124	0.0107	0.0092	0.0079
20	0.0135	0.0115	0.0098	0.0084	0.0072	0.0061
21	0.0109	0.0092	0.0078	0.0066	0.0056	0.0048
22	0.0088	0.0074	0.0062	0.0052	0.0044	0.0037
23	0.0071	0.0059	0.0049	0.0041	0.0034	0.0029
24	0.0057	0.0047	0.0039	0.0032	0.0027	0.0022
25	0.0046	0.0038	0.0031	0.0025	0.0021	0.0017
26	0.0037	0.0030	0.0025	0.0020	0.0016	0.0013
27	0.0030	0.0024	0.0019	0.0016	0.0013	0.0010
28	0.0024	0.0019	0.0015	0.0012	0.0010	0.0008
29	0.0020	0.0015	0.0012	0.0010	0.0008	0.0006
30	0.0016	0.0012	0.0010	0.0008	0.0006	0.0005
35	0.0005	0.0004	0.0003	0.0002	0.0002	0.0001
40	0.0002	0.0001	0.0001	0.0001	0.0001	0.0000
45	0.0001	0.0000	0.0000	0.0000	0.0000	
50	0.0000					

n/r	30%	31%	32%	33%	34%	35%
1	0.7692	0.7634	0.7576	0.7519	0.7463	0.7407
2	0.5917	0.5827	0.5739	0.5653	0.5569	0.5487
3	0.4552	0.4448	0.4348	0.4251	0.4156	0.4064
4	0.3501	0.3396	0.3294	0.3196	0.3102	0.3011
5	0.2693	0.2592	0.2495	0.2403	0.2315	0.2230
6	0.2072	0.1979	0.1890	0.1807	0.1727	0.1652
7	0.1594	0.1510	0.1432	0.1358	0.1289	0.1224
8	0.1226	0.1153	0.1085	0.1021	0.0962	0.0906
9	0.0943	0.0880	0.0822	0.0768	0.0718	0.0671
10	0.0725	0.0672	0.0623	0.0577	0.0536	0.0497
11	0.0558	0.0513	0.0472	0.0434	0.0400	0.0368
12	0.0429	0.0392	0.0357	0.0326	0.0298	0.0273
13	0.0330	0.0299	0.0271	0.0245	0.0223	0.0202
14	0.0253	0.0228	0.0205	0.0185	0.0166	0.0150
15	0.0195	0.0174	0.0155	0.0139	0.0124	0.0111
16	0.0150	0.0133	0.0118	0.0104	0.0093	0.0082
17	0.0116	0.0101	0.0089	0.0078	0.0069	0.0061
18	0.0089	0.0077	0.0068	0.0059	0.0052	0.0045
19	0.0068	0.0059	0.0051	0.0044	0.0038	0.0033
20	0.0053	0.0045	0.0039	0.0033	0.0029	0.0025
21	0.0040	0.0034	0.0029	0.0025	0.0021	0.0018
22	0.0031	0.0026	0.0022	0.0019	0.0016	0.0014
23	0.0024	0.0020	0.0017	0.0014	0.0012	0.0010
24	0.0018	0.0015	0.0013	0.0011	0.0009	0.0007
25	0.0014	0.0012	0.0010	0.0008	0.0007	0.0006
26	0.0011	0.0009	0.0007	0.0006	0.0005	0.0004
27	0.0008	0.0007	0.0006	0.0005	0.0004	0.0003
28	0.0006	0.0005	0.0004	0.0003	0.0003	0.0002
29	0.0005	0.0004	0.0003	0.0003	0.0002	0.0002
30	0.0004	0.0003	0.0002	0.0002	0.0002	0.0001
35	0.0001	0.0001	0.0001	0.0000	0.0000	0.0000
40	0.0000	0.0000	0.0000			
45						
50						

APPENDIX C: PRESENT VALUE OF AN ANNUITY OF $1.00

An annuity is a series of equal sums of money to be received or paid at regular intervals. Such a series of identical cash flows can be converted into present values in a straightforward fashion, using the factors available in Appendix B. For example, the present value of a series of $1,000 flows that occur at the end of each year for three years can be determined as follows, assuming a 10% time-value of money:

Year	Flow	Factor	PV
1	$1,000	0.9091	$ 909.10
2	1,000	0.8264	826.40
3	1,000	0.7513	751.30
		2.4868	$2,486.80

The mathematical process for converting this annuity into a present value required three multiplications of present-value factors by a constant amount, and then an addition of the products. But simple algebra allows us to "factor out" the constant, add the remaining elements, and then multiply the sum of the elements times the constant. For this example, we could reduce three multiplications and an addition to one addition and a multiplication, i.e., $(0.9091 + 0.8264 + 0.7513) = 2.4868 \times \$1,000 = \$2,486.80$.

Appendix C contains factors for the present value of an annuity of $1 per period. These factors represent the algebraic summation of the single period present-value factors shown in Appendix B. For example, compare the 10% columns of both tables: both have 0.9091 as the factor for $n = 1$. For $n = 2$, Appendix B has 0.8264 and Appendix C has 1.7355, which is the sum of 0.9091 and 0.8264. The third factor in the 10% column of Appendix C is 2.4869, which represents the sum of the first three factors from Appendix B (accumulated rounding error accounts for the 0.0001 difference).

The factors contained in Appendix C can be used to find the present value of an annuity for any amount: simply multiply the constant (i.e., one-year amount) of the future flow by the factor, i.e., constant future value × factor = present value of series. This format allows a decision-maker to determine the value of any one of four variables (present value, rate, number of years, or constant future amount), as long as he knows three of the variables. Consider the following examples:

1. Curry was offered an annuity that would pay him $1,000 per year for 10 years. What is the most Curry should pay for the annuity, assuming that he has a 12% time preference? *Solution:* the factor at $n = 10$, $r = 12\%$ is 5.6502; $1,000 × 5.6502 = $5,650.

2. Curry would like to know how much money he will receive each year

for eight years if he buys an annuity yielding 9% for $11,070. *Solution:* the factor at $n = 8$, $r = 9\%$ is 5.5348; $11,070 ÷ 5.5348 = $2,000 (rounded).

3. Curry would like to know the number of years he could reasonably expect to receive annuity of $3,000 if he originally invested $30,051 at 8% interest. *Solution:* an algebraic transformation of the format for Appendix C produces: factor = present value divided by constant yearly future value: $30,051 ÷ $3,000 = 10.017. By scanning down the 8% column, this approximate factor is found at $n = 21$.

4. Curry would like to know at what rate he must invest $25,100 so that he can draw an annuity of $5,000 per year for 10 years. *Solution:* the factor is $25,100 ÷ $5,000 = 5.02; by scanning along the $n = 10$ row, an approximation of this factor is found in the $r = 15\%$ column (5.0188).

Present Value of an Annuity of $1.00 Received per Period $PV = \dfrac{1 - (1 + r)^{-n}}{r}$

n/r	1.0%	2.0%	3.0%	4.0%	5.0%
1	.99010	.98039	.97087	.96154	.95238
2	1.97040	1.94156	1.91347	1.88609	1.85941
3	2.94099	2.88388	2.82861	2.77509	2.72325
4	3.90197	3.80773	3.71710	3.62990	3.54595
5	4.85343	4.71346	4.57971	4.45182	4.32948
6	5.79548	5.60143	5.41719	4.24214	5.07569
7	6.72819	6.47199	6.23028	6.00205	5.78637
8	7.65168	7.32548	7.01969	6.73274	6.46321
9	8.56602	8.16224	7.78611	7.43533	7.10782
10	9.47130	8.98259	8.53020	8.11090	7.72173
11	10.36763	9.78685	9.25262	8.76048	8.30641
12	11.25508	10.57534	9.95400	9.38507	8.86325
13	12.13374	11.34837	10.63496	9.98565	9.39357
14	13.00370	12.10625	11.29607	10.56312	9.89864
15	13.86505	12.84926	11.93794	11.11839	10.37966
16	14.71787	13.57771	12.56110	11.65230	10.83777
17	15.56225	14.29187	13.16612	12.16567	11.27407
18	16.39827	14.99203	13.75351	12.65930	11.68959
19	17.22601	15.67846	14.32380	13.13394	12.08532
20	18.04555	16.35143	14.87747	13.59033	12.46221
21	18.85698	17.01121	15.41505	14.02916	12.82115
22	19.66038	17.65805	15.93692	14.45112	13.16300
23	20.45582	18.29220	16.44361	14.85684	13.48857
24	21.24339	18.91393	16.93554	15.24696	13.79864
25	22.02316	19.52346	17.41315	15.62208	14.09394
26	22.79520	20.12104	17.87684	15.98277	14.37519
27	23.55961	20.70690	18.32703	16.32959	14.64303
28	24.31644	21.28127	18.76411	16.66306	14.89813
29	25.06579	21.84438	19.18845	16.98371	15.14107
30	25.80771	22.39646	19.60044	17.29203	15.37245
31	26.54229	22.93770	20.00043	17.58849	15.59281
32	27.26959	23.46833	20.38877	17.87355	15.80268
33	27.98969	23.98856	20.76579	18.14765	16.00255
34	28.70267	24.49859	21.13184	18.41120	16.19290
35	29.40858	24.99862	21.48722	18.66461	16.37419
40	32.83469	27.35548	23.11477	19.79277	17.15909
45	36.09451	29.49016	24.51871	20.72004	17.77407
50	39.19612	31.42361	25.72976	21.48218	18.25593

n/r	6%	7%	8%	9%	10%
1	0.9434	0.9346	0.9259	0.9174	0.9091
2	1.8334	1.8080	1.7833	1.7591	1.7355
3	2.6730	2.6243	2.5771	2.5313	2.4869
4	3.4651	3.3872	3.3121	3.2397	3.1699
5	4.2124	4.1002	3.9927	3.8897	3.7908
6	4.9173	4.7665	4.6229	4.4859	4.3553
7	5.5824	5.3893	5.2064	5.0330	4.8684
8	6.2098	5.9713	5.7466	5.5348	5.3349
9	6.8017	6.5152	6.2469	5.9952	5.7590
10	7.3601	7.0236	6.7101	6.4177	6.1446
11	7.8869	7.4987	7.1390	6.8051	6.4951
12	8.3838	7.9427	7.5361	7.1607	6.8137
13	8.8527	8.3577	7.9038	7.4869	7.1034
14	9.2950	8.7455	8.2442	7.7862	7.3667
15	9.7122	9.1079	8.5595	8.0607	7.6061
16	10.1059	9.4466	8.8514	8.3126	7.8237
17	10.4773	9.7632	9.1216	8.5436	8.0216
18	10.8276	10.0591	9.3719	8.7556	8.2014
19	11.1581	10.3356	9.6036	8.9501	8.3649
20	11.4699	10.5940	9.8181	9.1285	8.5136
21	11.7641	10.8355	10.0168	9.2922	8.6487
22	12.0416	11.0612	10.2007	9.4424	8.7715
23	12.3034	11.2722	10.3711	9.5802	8.8832
24	12.5504	11.4693	10.5288	9.7066	8.9847
25	12.7834	11.6536	10.6748	9.8226	9.0770
26	13.0032	11.8258	10.8100	9.9290	9.1609
27	13.2105	11.9867	10.9352	10.0266	9.2372
28	13.4062	12.1371	11.0511	10.1161	9.3066
29	13.5907	12.2777	11.1584	10.1983	9.3696
30	13.7648	12.4090	11.2578	10.2737	9.4269
31	13.9291	12.5318	11.3498	10.3428	9.4790
32	14.0840	12.6466	11.4350	10.4062	9.5264
33	14.2302	12.7538	11.5139	10.4644	9.5694
34	14.3681	12.8540	11.5869	10.5178	9.6086
35	14.4982	12.9477	11.6546	10.5668	9.6442
40	15.0463	13.3317	11.9246	10.7574	9.7791
45	15.4558	13.6055	12.1084	10.8812	9.8628
50	15.7619	13.8007	12.2335	10.9617	9.9148

n/r	11%	12%	13%	14%	15%
1	0.9009	0.8929	0.8850	0.8772	0.8696
2	1.7125	1.6901	1.6681	1.6467	1.6257
3	2.4437	2.4018	2.3612	2.3216	2.2832
4	3.1024	3.0373	2.9745	2.9137	2.8550
5	3.6959	3.6048	3.5172	3.4331	3.3522
6	4.2305	4.1114	3.9975	3.8887	3.7845
7	4.7122	4.5638	4.4226	4.2883	4.1604
8	5.1461	4.9676	4.7988	4.6389	4.4873
9	5.5370	5.3282	5.1317	4.9464	4.7716
10	5.8892	5.6502	5.4262	5.2161	5.0188
11	6.2065	5.9377	5.6869	5.4527	5.2337
12	6.4924	6.1944	5.9176	5.6603	5.4206
13	6.7499	6.4235	6.1218	5.8424	5.5831
14	6.9819	6.6282	6.3025	6.0021	5.7245
15	7.1909	6.8109	6.4624	6.1422	5.8474
16	7.3792	6.9740	6.6039	6.2651	5.9542
17	7.5488	7.1196	6.7291	6.3729	6.0472
18	7.7016	7.2497	6.8399	6.4674	6.1280
19	7.8393	7.3658	6.9380	6.5504	6.1982
20	7.9633	7.4694	7.0248	6.6231	6.2593
21	8.0751	7.5620	7.1015	6.6870	6.3125
22	8.1757	7.6446	7.1695	6.7429	6.3587
23	8.2664	7.7184	7.2297	6.7921	6.3988
24	8.3481	7.7843	7.2829	6.8351	6.4338
25	8.4217	7.8431	7.3300	6.8729	6.4641
26	8.4881	7.8957	7.3717	6.9061	6.4906
27	8.5478	7.9426	7.4086	6.9352	6.5135
28	8.6016	7.9844	7.4412	6.9607	6.5335
29	8.6501	8.0218	7.4701	6.9830	6.5509
30	8.6938	8.0552	7.4957	7.0027	6.5660
31	8.7331	8.0850	7.5183	7.0199	6.5791
32	8.7686	8.1116	7.5383	7.0350	6.5905
33	8.8005	8.1354	7.5560	7.0482	6.6005
34	8.8293	8.1566	7.5717	7.0599	6.6091
35	8.8552	8.1755	7.5856	7.0700	6.6166
40	8.9511	8.2438	7.6344	7.1050	6.6418
45	9.0079	8.2825	7.6609	7.1232	6.6543
50	9.0417	8.3045	7.6752	7.1327	6.6605

n/r	16%	17%	18%	19%	20%
1	0.8621	0.8547	0.8475	0.8403	0.8333
2	1.6052	1.5852	1.5656	1.5465	1.5278
3	2.2459	2.2096	2.1743	2.1399	2.1065
4	2.7982	2.7432	2.6901	2.6386	2.5887
5	3.2743	3.1993	3.1272	3.0576	2.9906
6	3.6847	3.5892	3.4976	3.4098	3.3255
7	4.0386	3.9224	3.8115	3.7057	3.6046
8	4.3436	4.2072	4.0776	3.9544	3.8372
9	4.6065	4.4506	4.3030	4.1633	4.0310
10	4.8332	4.6586	4.4941	4.3389	4.1925
11	5.0286	4.8364	4.6560	4.4865	4.3271
12	5.1971	4.9884	4.7932	4.6105	4.4392
13	5.3423	5.1183	4.9095	4.7147	4.5327
14	5.4675	5.2293	5.0081	4.8023	4.6106
15	5.5755	5.3242	5.0916	4.8759	4.6755
16	5.6685	5.4053	5.1624	4.9377	4.7296
17	5.7487	5.4746	5.2223	4.9879	4.7746
18	5.8178	5.5339	5.2732	5.0333	4.8122
19	5.8775	5.5845	5.3162	5.0700	4.8435
20	5.9288	5.6278	5.3527	5.1009	4.8696
21	5.9731	5.6648	5.3837	5.1268	4.8913
22	6.0113	5.6964	5.4099	5.1486	4.9094
23	6.0442	5.7234	5.4321	5.1668	4.9245
24	6.0726	5.7465	5.4509	5.1822	4.9371
25	6.0971	5.7662	5.4669	5.1951	4.9476
26	6.1182	5.7831	5.4804	5.2060	4.9563
27	6.1364	5.7975	5.4919	5.2151	4.9636
28	6.1520	5.8099	5.5016	5.2228	4.9697
29	6.1656	5.8204	5.5098	5.2292	4.9747
30	6.1772	5.8294	5.5168	5.2347	4.9789
31	6.1872	5.8371	5.5227	5.2393	4.9824
32	6.1959	5.8437	5.5277	5.2430	4.9854
33	6.2034	5.8493	5.5320	5.2462	4.9878
34	6.2098	5.8541	5.5356	5.2489	4.9898
35	6.2153	5.8582	5.5386	5.2512	4.9915
40	6.2335	5.8713	5.5482	5.2582	4.9966
45	6.2421	5.8773	5.5523	5.2611	4.9986
50	6.2463	5.8801	5.5541	5.2623	4.9995

n/r	21%	22%	23%	24%	25%
1	0.8264	0.8197	0.8130	0.8065	0.8000
2	1.5095	1.4915	1.4740	1.4568	1.4400
3	2.0739	2.0422	2.0114	1.9813	1.9520
4	2.5404	2.4936	2.4483	2.4043	2.3616
5	2.9260	2.8636	2.8035	2.7454	2.6893
6	3.2446	3.1669	3.0923	3.0205	2.9514
7	3.5079	3.4155	3.3270	3.2423	3.1611
8	3.7256	3.6193	3.5179	3.4212	3.3289
9	3.9054	3.7863	3.6731	3.5655	3.4631
10	4.0541	3.9232	3.7993	3.6819	3.5705
11	4.1769	4.0354	3.9018	3.7757	3.6564
12	4.2784	4.1274	3.9852	3.8514	3.7251
13	4.3624	4.2028	4.0530	3.9124	3.7801
14	4.4317	4.2646	4.1082	3.9616	3.8241
15	4.4890	4.3152	4.1530	4.0013	3.8593
16	4.5364	4.3567	4.1894	4.0333	3.8874
17	4.5755	4.3908	4.2190	4.0591	3.9099
18	4.6079	4.4187	4.2431	4.0799	3.9279
19	4.6346	4.4415	4.2627	4.0967	3.9424
20	4.6567	4.4603	4.2786	4.1103	3.9539
21	4.6750	4.4756	4.2916	4.1212	3.9631
22	4.6900	4.4882	4.3021	4.1300	3.9705
23	4.7025	4.4985	4.3106	4.1371	3.9764
24	4.7128	4.5070	4.3176	4.1428	3.9811
25	4.7213	4.5139	4.3232	4.1474	3.9849
26	4.7284	4.5196	4.3278	4.1511	3.9879
27	4.7342	4.5243	4.3316	4.1542	3.9903
28	4.7390	4.5281	4.3346	4.1566	3.9923
29	4.7430	4.5312	4.3371	4.1585	3.9938
30	4.7463	4.5338	4.3391	4.1601	3.9950
31	4.7490	4.5359	4.3407	4.1614	3.9960
32	4.7512	4.5376	4.3421	4.1624	3.9968
33	4.7531	4.5390	4.3431	4.1632	3.9975
34	4.7546	4.5402	4.3440	4.1639	3.9980
35	4.7559	4.5411	4.3447	4.1644	3.9984
40	4.7596	4.5439	4.3467	4.1659	3.9995
45	4.7610	4.5449	4.3474	4.1664	3.9998
50	4.7616	4.5452	4.3477	4.1666	3.9999

n/r	26%	27%	28%	29%	30%	31%
1	0.7937	0.7874	0.7813	0.7752	0.7692	0.7634
2	1.4235	1.4074	1.3916	1.3761	1.3609	1.3461
3	1.9234	1.8956	1.8684	1.8420	1.8161	1.7909
4	2.3202	2.2800	2.2410	2.2031	2.1662	2.1305
5	2.6351	2.5827	2.5320	2.4830	2.4356	2.3897
6	2.8850	2.8210	2.7594	2.7000	2.6427	2.5875
7	3.0833	3.0087	2.9370	2.8682	2.8021	2.7386
8	3.2407	3.1564	3.0758	2.9986	2.9247	2.8539
9	3.3657	3.2728	3.1842	3.0997	3.0190	2.9419
10	3.4648	3.3644	3.2689	3.1781	3.0915	3.0091
11	3.5435	3.4365	3.3351	3.2388	3.1473	3.0604
12	3.6059	3.4933	3.3868	3.2859	3.1903	3.0995
13	3.6555	3.5381	3.4272	3.3224	3.2233	3.1294
14	3.6949	3.5733	3.4587	3.3507	3.2487	3.1522
15	3.7261	3.6010	3.4834	3.3726	3.2682	3.1696
16	3.7509	3.6228	3.5026	3.3896	3.2832	3.1829
17	3.7705	3.6400	3.5177	3.4028	3.2948	3.1931
18	3.7861	3.6536	3.5294	3.4130	3.3037	3.2008
19	3.7985	3.6642	3.5386	3.4210	3.3105	3.2067
20	3.8083	3.6726	3.5458	3.4271	3.3158	3.2112
21	3.8161	3.6792	3.5514	3.4319	3.3198	3.2147
22	3.8223	3.6844	3.5558	3.4356	3.3230	3.2173
23	3.8273	3.6885	3.5592	3.4384	3.3253	3.2193
24	3.8312	3.6918	3.5619	3.4406	3.3272	3.2209
25	3.8342	3.6943	3.5640	3.4423	3.3286	3.2220
26	3.8367	3.6963	3.5656	3.4437	3.3297	3.2229
27	3.8387	3.6979	3.5669	3.4447	3.3305	3.2236
28	3.8402	3.6991	3.5679	3.4455	3.3312	3.2241
29	3.8414	3.7001	3.5687	3.4461	3.3316	3.2245
30	3.8424	3.7009	3.5693	3.4466	3.3321	3.2248
31	3.8432	3.7015	3.5697	3.4470	3.3324	3.2251
32	3.8438	3.7019	3.5701	3.4473	3.3326	3.2252
33	3.8443	3.7023	3.5704	3.4475	3.3328	3.2254
34	3.8447	3.7026	3.5706	3.4477	3.3329	3.2255
35	3.8450	3.7028	3.5708	3.4478	3.3330	3.2256
40	3.8458	3.7034	3.5712	3.4481	3.3332	3.2257
45	3.8460	3.7036	3.5714	3.4482	3.3333	3.2258
50	3.8461	3.7037	3.5714	3.4483	3.3333	3.2258

n/r	32%	33%	34%	35%	36%	37%
1	0.7576	0.7519	0.7463	0.7407	0.7353	0.7299
2	1.3315	1.3172	1.3032	1.2894	1.2760	1.2627
3	1.7663	1.7423	1.7188	1.6959	1.6735	1.6516
4	2.0957	2.0618	2.0290	1.9969	1.9658	1.9355
5	2.3452	2.3021	2.2604	2.2200	2.1807	2.1427
6	2.5342	2.4828	2.4331	2.3852	2.3388	2.2939
7	2.6775	2.6187	2.5620	2.5075	2.4550	2.4043
8	2.7860	2.7208	2.6582	2.5982	2.5404	2.4849
9	2.8681	2.7976	2.7300	2.6653	2.6033	2.5437
10	2.9304	2.8553	2.7836	2.7150	2.6495	2.5867
11	2.9776	2.8987	2.8236	2.7519	2.6834	2.6180
12	3.0133	2.9314	2.8534	2.7792	2.7084	2.6409
13	3.0404	2.9559	2.8757	2.7994	2.7268	2.6576
14	3.0609	2.9744	2.8923	2.8144	2.7403	2.6698
15	3.0764	2.9883	2.9047	2.8255	2.7502	2.6787
16	3.0882	2.9987	2.9140	2.8337	2.7575	2.6852
17	3.0971	3.0065	2.9209	2.8398	2.7629	2.6899
18	3.1039	3.0124	3.9260	2.8443	2.7668	2.6934
19	3.1090	3.0169	2.9299	2.8476	2.7697	2.6959
20	3.1129	3.0202	2.9327	2.8501	2.7718	2.6977
21	3.1158	3.0227	2.9349	2.8520	2.7734	2.6991
22	3.1180	3.0246	2.9365	2.8533	2.7746	2.7000
23	3.1197	3.0260	2.9377	2.8543	2.7754	2.7008
24	3.1210	3.0271	2.9386	2.8550	2.7760	2.7013
25	3.1220	3.0279	2.9392	2.8556	2.7765	2.7017
26	3.1227	3.0285	2.9397	2.8560	2.7768	2.7019
27	3.1233	3.0289	2.9401	2.8563	2.7771	2.7022
28	3.1237	3.0293	2.9404	2.8565	2.7773	2.7023
29	3.1240	3.0295	2.9406	2.8567	2.7774	2.7024
30	3.1242	3.0297	2.9407	2.8568	2.7775	2.7025
31	3.1244	3.0299	2.9408	2.8569	2.7776	2.7025
32	3.1246	3.0300	2.9409	2.8569	2.7776	2.7026
33	3.1247	3.0301	2.9410	2.8570	2.7777	2.7026
34	3.1248	3.0301	2.9410	2.8570	2.7777	2.7026
35	3.1248	3.0302	2.9411	2.8571	2.7777	2.7027
40	3.1250	3.0303	2.9412	2.8571	2.7778	2.7027
45	3.1250	3.0303	2.9412	2.8571	2.7778	2.7027
50	3.1250	3.0303	2.9412	2.8571	2.7778	2.7027

Index

and contribution
    margin, 120
definition of, 116
direct costing, 290
graphic approach to,
    117
multiproduct CVP, 124
probabilistic estimates
    for, 133–135
relevant range in, 127
reliability in, 130
Costing (see Absorption
    costing; Direct
    costing; Job order
    costing; Process
    costing; Product
    costing)
CPM (Critical Path
    Method), 526
CVP analysis (see
    Cost-volume-profit
    analysis)

Decentralization,
    and centralization, 353
    cost center in, 354
    information needs in,
        352
    investment center in,
        354
    performance
        measurement in,
        356
    profit center in, 354
    and rate of return, 360
    reporting needs in, 355
    and responsibility
        accounting, 323
    system design in, 353
    and transfer pricing,
        230
Decision making,
    models for,
        average rate-of-return,
            360, 495
        cost-volume-profit
            model, 117, 122,
            123

expected value (see
    Probabilities)
minimum-desired
    rate-of-return,
    494
net present-value, 487
payback period, 117
time adjusted rate-
    of-return, 493
reports for,
    contribution
        statement, 116,
        289
    format of, 287
    and uncertainty, 90,
        133
Decision rule, 286, 448,
    455, 458
Department cost sheet,
    195, 198
Depreciation, 529
Differential cost, (see
    Incremental cost)
Direct costing, 285ff
    and absorption costing,
        296
    definition of, 295
    income statement,
        illustrated, 289
    and inventory valuation,
        295
Direct labor (see Labor)
Direct material (see
    Material)
Discounted cash flow,
    depreciation in, 514,
    517, 529
Direct measures of
    performance, 356
Directly traceable cost,
    156
Discounted present value
    (DPV), 485
    table of, 635ff, 641ff
Discounting, 485
Discrete manufacturing,
    158

Discretionary fixed costs,
    76
Division, 232 fn
Drive, 588
Dysfunctional
    consequences, 51, 589

Earmarking, 421
Economic order quantity
    (EOQ), 562
Effectiveness, 393
Efficiency, 382
Efficiency variance, 387
Elasticity of demand, 457
Equivalent units, 199
Excess material
    requisition, 619
Expectations, 34, 331
Expected value, (see
    Probabilities)
Expected volume, 73

Factory ledgers, (see
    Journal entries)
Factory overhead (see
    Overhead)
Favorable variance, 385,
    619
Feedback, 6
Financial accounting, 12
Financial Accounting
    Standards Board, 12
Financial budgets, 40,
    48–50, 70
First-in, first-out (FIFO)
    method, 201
Fixed costs, 74
Fixed overhead (see
    Overhead)
Flexible budget (see
    Budget, flexible), 73
Functional fixation, 593
Full costing (see
    Absorption costing)
Fund accounting, 418
    authorizations in, 419
    revenue sources for, 421
Funds flow statement, 13